W9-AQG-445

265870

Foreign Relations of the United States, 1964–1968

Volume X

National Security Policy

General Editor   David S. Patterson

United States Government Printing Office
Washington
2002

DEPARTMENT OF STATE PUBLICATION 10921

OFFICE OF THE HISTORIAN

BUREAU OF PUBLIC AFFAIRS

For sale by the Superintendent of Documents, U.S. Government Printing Office
Internet: bookstore.gpo.gov   Phone: (202) 512-1800   Fax: 512-2250
Mail: Stop SSOP, Washington, DC 20402-0001
ISBN 0-16-051033-3

Preface

The *Foreign Relations of the United States* series presents the official documentary historical record of major foreign policy decisions and significant diplomatic activity of the United States Government. The Historian of the Department of State is charged with the responsibility for the preparation of the *Foreign Relations* series. The staff of the Office of the Historian, Bureau of Public Affairs, plans, researches, compiles, and edits the volumes in the series. Official regulations codifying specific standards for the selection and editing of documents for the series were first promulgated by Secretary of State Frank B. Kellogg on March 26, 1925. These regulations, with minor modifications, guided the series through 1991.

A new statutory charter for the preparation of the series was established by Public Law 102–138, the Foreign Relations Authorization Act, Fiscal Years 1992 and 1993, which was signed by President George Bush on October 28, 1991. Section 198 of P.L. 102–138 added a new Title IV to the Department of State's Basic Authorities Act of 1956 (22 USC 4351, *et seq.*).

The statute requires that the *Foreign Relations* series be a thorough, accurate, and reliable record of major United States foreign policy decisions and significant United States diplomatic activity. The volumes of the series should include all records needed to provide comprehensive documentation of major foreign policy decisions and actions of the United States Government. The statute also confirms the editing principles established by Secretary Kellogg: the *Foreign Relations* series is guided by the principles of historical objectivity and accuracy; records should not be altered or deletions made without indicating in the published text that a deletion has been made; the published record should omit no facts that were of major importance in reaching a decision; and nothing should be omitted for the purposes of concealing a defect in policy. The statute also requires that the *Foreign Relations* series be published not more than 30 years after the events recorded.

Structure and Scope of the Foreign Relations Series

This volume is part of a subseries of volumes of the *Foreign Relations* series that documents the most important issues in the foreign policy of the 5 years (1964–1968) of the administration of Lyndon B. Johnson. The subseries presents in 34 volumes a documentary record of major foreign policy decisions and actions of President Johnson's administration. This volume documents U.S. national security policy.

Documentation on arms control and disarmament issues is in volume XI, published in 1997. Documentation on the organization and management of the national security agencies, as well as the intelligence community, will be included in volume XXXIII, Organization of Foreign Policy; United Nations.

Focus of Research and Principles of Selection for Foreign Relations, 1964-1968, Volume X

The editor of the volume sought to present documentation illuminating responsibility for major foreign policy decisions in the U.S. Government, with emphasis on the President and his advisers. The documents include memoranda and records of discussions that set forth policy issues and options and show decisions or actions taken. The emphasis is on the development of U.S. policy and on major aspects and repercussions of its execution rather than on the details of policy execution.

The editor tried to document as much as possible the roles of President Lyndon Johnson and his key foreign policy advisers, particularly his White House assistants McGeorge Bundy and Walt W. Rostow, Secretary of Defense Robert S. McNamara, and Secretary of State Dean Rusk, in the administration's consideration of a wide range of national security issues. Major topics covered in the volume include: analyses of the Soviet military threat, the development of new U.S. weapons, the question of U.S. development and deployment of an anti-ballistic missile (ABM) system, chemical and biological weapons, tactical nuclear weapons, counter-insurgency policy, improvement of command and control systems, and military force structure.

The editor included a selection of intelligence estimates and analyses seen by high-level policymakers, especially those that were made available to President Johnson.

Editorial Methodology

The documents are presented chronologically according to Washington time or, in the case of conferences, in the order of individual meetings. Memoranda of conversation are placed according to the time and date of the conversation, rather than the date the memorandum was drafted.

Editorial treatment of the documents published in the *Foreign Relations* series follows Office style guidelines, supplemented by guidance from the General Editor and the chief technical editor. The source text is reproduced as exactly as possible, including marginalia or other notations, which are described in the footnotes. Texts are transcribed and printed according to accepted conventions for the publication of historical documents in the limitations of modern typography. A heading has been supplied by the editors for each document included in the volume. Spelling, capitalization, and punctuation are retained as found in the source text, except that obvious typographical errors are silently corrected. Other mistakes and omissions in the source text are corrected by bracketed insertions: a correction is set in italic type; an addition in roman type. Words or phrases underlined in the source text are printed in italics. Abbreviations and contractions are preserved as found in the source text, and a list of abbreviations is included in the front matter of each volume.

Bracketed insertions are also used to indicate omitted text that deals with an unrelated subject (in roman type) or that remains classified after declassification review (in italic type). The amount of material not declassified has been noted by indicating the number of lines or pages of source text that were omitted. Entire documents withheld for declassification purposes have been accounted for and are listed by headings, source notes, and number of pages not declassified in their chronological place. All brackets that appear in the source text are so identified by footnotes.

The first footnote to each document indicates the source of the document, original classification, distribution, and drafting information. This note also provides the background of important documents and policies and indicates whether the President or his major policy advisers read the document.

Editorial notes and additional annotation summarize pertinent material not printed in the volume, indicate the location of additional documentary sources, provide references to important related documents printed in other volumes, describe key events, and provide summaries of and citations to public statements that supplement and elucidate the printed documents. Information derived from memoirs and other first-hand accounts has been used when appropriate to supplement or explicate the official record.

The numbers in the index refer to document numbers rather than to page numbers.

Advisory Committee on Historical Diplomatic Documentation

The Advisory Committee on Historical Diplomatic Documentation, established under the Foreign Relations statute, reviews records, advises, and makes recommendations concerning the *Foreign Relations* series. The Advisory Committee monitors the overall compilation and editorial process of the series and advises on all aspects of the preparation and declassification of the series. The Advisory Committee does not attempt to review the contents of individual volumes in the series, but it makes recommendations on problems that come to its attention.

The Advisory Committee has not reviewed this volume.

Declassification Review

The Information Response Branch of the Office of IRM Programs and Services, Bureau of Administration, Department of State, conducted the declassification review of the documents published in this volume. The review was conducted in accordance with the standards set forth in Executive Order 12958 on Classified National Security Information and applicable laws.

The principle guiding declassification review is to release all information, subject only to the current requirements of national security as embodied in law and regulation. Declassification decisions entailed concurrence of the appropriate geographic and functional bureaus in the Department of State, other concerned agencies of the U.S. Government, and the appropriate foreign governments regarding specific documents of those governments.

The final declassification review of this volume, which began in 1996 and was completed in 2001, resulted in the decision to withhold about 3.5 percent of the documentation proposed for publication; 9 documents were withheld in full. The editor is confident, on the basis of the research conducted in preparing this volume, that the documentation and editorial notes presented here provide an accurate account of U.S. national security policy.

Acknowledgments

The editor wishes to acknowledge the assistance of officials at the Lyndon B. Johnson Library of the National Archives and Records Administration, especially Regina Greenwell and Charlaine Burgess, who provided key research assistance. The editor also wishes to acknowledge the assistance of historians at the Central Intelligence Agency, particularly Michael Warner.

David S. Patterson, General Editor of the *Foreign Relations* series, collected documentation for this volume and selected and edited it. Douglas R. Keene and Rachel Swartz assisted in the preparation of the lists of names, sources, and abbreviations. Rita M. Baker and Vicki E. Futscher did the copy and technical editing, and Susan C. Weetman coordinated the declassification review. Juniee Oneida prepared the index.

Marc J. Susser
The Historian
Bureau of Public Affairs

March 2002

Johnson Administration Volumes

Following is a list of the volumes in the *Foreign Relations* series for the administration of President Lyndon B. Johnson. The titles of individual volumes may change. The year of publication is in parentheses after the title.

Contents

Sources

Sources for the Foreign Relations Series

The *Foreign Relations* statute requires that the published record in the *Foreign Relations* series include all records needed to provide comprehensive documentation on major U.S. foreign policy decisions and significant U.S. diplomatic activity. It further requires that government agencies, departments, and other entities of the U.S. Government engaged in foreign policy formulation, execution, or support cooperate with the Department of State Historian by providing full and complete access to records pertinent to foreign policy decisions and actions and by providing copies of selected records. Many of the sources consulted in the preparation of this volume have been declassified and are available for review at the National Archives and Records Administration.

The editors of the *Foreign Relations* series have complete access to all the retired records and papers of the Department of State: the central files of the Department; the special decentralized files ("lot files") of the Department at the bureau, office, and division levels; the files of the Department's Executive Secretariat, which contain the records of international conferences and high-level official visits, correspondence with foreign leaders by the President and Secretary of State, and memoranda of conversations between the President and Secretary of State and foreign officials; and the files of overseas diplomatic posts. All the Department's indexed central files for these years have been permanently transferred to the National Archives and Records Administration at College Park, Maryland (Archives II). Many of the Department's decentralized office (or lot) files covering this period, those that the National Archives deems worthy of permanent retention, have been transferred or are in the process of being transferred from the Department's custody to Archives II.

The editors of the *Foreign Relations* series also have full access to the papers of President Johnson and other White House foreign policy records. Presidential papers maintained and preserved at the Presidential libraries include some of the most significant foreign affairs-related documentation from the Department of State and other Federal agencies including the National Security Council, the Central Intelligence Agency, the Department of Defense, and the Joint Chiefs of Staff.

Sources for Foreign Relations, 1964–1968, Volume X

In preparing this volume, the editor made extensive use of Presidential papers and other White House records at the Lyndon B. Johnson Library.

The bulk of the foreign policy records at the Johnson Library are in the relevant component parts of the National Security file. Within the National Security file, the NSC Meetings file, the Agency file, and the Subject file proved to be of particular value. The editor also made extensive use of the files of President Johnson's Special Assistant for National Security Affairs Walt W. Rostow and Charles E. Johnson, a member of the NSC staff with primary responsibility for national security issues. Transcripts of President Johnson's telephone conversations, especially with Secretary of Defense McNamara, added important depth to the record.

Second in importance to the White House records at the Johnson Library were the records of the Department of Defense, particularly the records of the Secretaries of Defense, the Assistant Secretaries of Defense for International Affairs, and other major assistants and the Joint Chiefs of Staff.

Some important documents are found only in the Department of State lot files. The conference files maintained by the Executive Secretariat contain briefing materials as well as records of conversations.

The Central Intelligence Agency provides the Department of State historians access to intelligence documents from records in its custody and at the Presidential libraries. This access is arranged and facilitated by the CIA's History Staff, part of the Center for the Study of Intelligence, pursuant to a May 1992 memorandum of understanding.

All of this documentation has been made available for use in the *Foreign Relations* series thanks to the consent of the agencies mentioned, the assistance of their staffs, and especially the cooperation and support of the National Archives and Records Administration.

The following list identifies the particular files and collections used in the preparation of this volume. The declassification and transfer to the National Archives of the Department of State records is in process, and many of those records are already available for public review at the National Archives.

Unpublished Sources

Department of State

Central Files and Lot Files. See under National Archives and Records Administration below

INR/IL Historical Files

National Archives and Records Administration

RG 59, Records of the Department of State

Subject-Numeric Indexed Central Files

DEF 1, Defense affairs, policy, plans, readiness
DEF 1 EUR, Defense affairs, policy, plans, readiness concerning Europe

DEF 1 EUR W, Defense affairs, policy, plans, readiness concerning Western Europe
DEF 1 US, U.S. defense affairs, U.S. policy, plans, readiness
DEF 1–1, Defense affairs, contingency planning
DEF 1–2 US, Defense affairs, U.S. stockpiling of strategic and critical materials
DEF 12, Defense affairs, armaments
DEF 12 US, Defense affairs, U.S. armaments
DEF 12–1 US, Defense affairs, armaments, U.S. research and development
DEF 15 US, Defense affairs, armaments, U.S. bases, installations
INT 6, Intelligence, collection of intelligence
ORG 7, Organization and administration, visits
POL 1 US, General policy, U.S. political affairs and relations
POL 1 US–USSR, General policy, U.S.–U.S.S.R. political affairs and relations
POL 15–1 USSR, Political affairs and relations between the heads of state of the U.S. and the U.S.S.R.

Lot Files

Ball Papers: Lot 74 D 272
   Files of Under Secretary of State George Ball, 1961–1966

Bohlen Papers: Lot 74 D 379
   Files of Ambassador Charles E. Bohlen, 1942–1970

Bruce Diaries: Lot 64 D 327
   Files of Ambassador David K.E. Bruce, 1948–1974

Presidential Correspondence: Lot 66 D 294
   Presidential exchanges of correspondence with heads of government for 1953–1965, maintained by the Executive Secretariat

S/MF Files: Lot 66 D 182
   Multilateral force documents, 1960–1965, maintained by the Executive Secretariat

S/P Files: Lot 74 D 344
   Senior Interdepartmental Group memos, agenda, and correspondence, January 1968–December 1969

S/PC Files: Lot 70 D 199
   Files of the Policy Planning Council, 1963–1964

S/S Files: Lot 67 D 272
   Presidential and Secretary of State's official exchanges of correspondence with various foreign statesmen for 1966

S/S Files: Lot 70 D 217
   White House and executive departments' memoranda and letters to the Secretary of State and Under Secretary of State for 1963–1966

S/S Files: Lot 71 D 228
   Transition Books for members of the Nixon administration, December 1968

S/S Files: Lot 71 D 460
   Files of Foy D. Kohler for 1962–1968, including memoranda of his discussions with Soviet Ambassador Dobrynin and Foreign Minister Gromyko

S/S Files: Lot 74 D 164
   Files on President's Evening Reading, 1964–1973, and Secretary-President Luncheon Meetings, 1964–1969

S/S–I Microfilm Files: Lot 79 D 246
   Microfilmed master files of international conferences attended by the President, the Secretary of State, and other U.S. officials for 1956–1966

S/S–NSC Files: Lot 70 D 265
   Master set of papers pertaining to National Security Council meetings, including policy papers, position papers, and administrative documents for 1961–1968

S/S–NSC Files: Lot 72 D 316
   Master file of National Security Action Memoranda (NSAMs) for 1961–1968

S/S–NSC Files: Lot 72 D 318
   Files on NSC meetings, 1966–1968, the Cabinet, 1967, and the NSC Special Committee, 1967

S/S–RD Files: Lot 71 D 171
   Restricted data files maintained by the Executive Secretariat for 1957–1967

S/S–SIG Files: Lot 70 D 263
   Senior Interdepartmental Group files for 1968–1969

RG 200, Records of Robert S. McNamara

Defense Programs and Operations

RG 218, Records of the U.S. Joint Chiefs of Staff

JCS Files

RG 263, Records of the Central Intelligence Agency

Washington National Records Center, Suitland, Maryland

Records of the Department of Defense

McNamara Files: FRC 330 71 A 3470
   Files of Secretary of Defense Robert S. McNamara, 1961–1968

OASD/ISA Files: FRC 330 68 A 4023
   Subject decimal files of the Office of the Assistant Secretary of Defense for International Security Affairs for 1964

OASD/ISA Files: FRC 70 A 6648 A, 70 A 6649
   Subject decimal files of the Office of the Assistant Secretary of Defense for International Security Affairs for 1966

OASD/ISA Files: FRC 330 71 A 4919
   Subject decimal files of the Office of the Assistant Secretary of Defense for International Security Affairs for 1967

OASD/ISA Files: FRC 330 72 A 1498
   Subject decimal files of the Office of the Assistant Secretary of Defense for International Security Affairs for 1968

OASD/ISA Files: FRC 330 72 A 1499
   Subject decimal files of the Office of the Assistant Secretary of Defense for International Security Affairs for 1967–1968

OSD Files: FRC 330 69 A 7425
   Subject decimal files of the Office of the Secretary of Defense for 1964

OSD Files: FRC 330 70 A 1265, 70 A 1266
Subject decimal files of the Office of the Secretary of Defense for 1965

OSD Files: FRC 330 70 A 4443, 70 A 4662
Subject decimal files of the Office of the Secretary of Defense for 1966

OSD Files: FRC 330 72 A 2467, FRC 330 72 A 2468
Subject decimal files of the Office of the Secretary of Defense for 1967

OSD/AE Files: FRC 330 69 A 2243
Records of the Assistant Secretary of Defense (Atomic Energy)

Records of the Arms Control and Disarmament Agency

Central Policy File: FRC 383 86 A 5
Top Secret numbered documents for 1961–1983

Central Intelligence Agency

DCI (McCone) Files

Executive Registry Subject Files, Job 0167R

Library of Congress, Manuscript Division

Paul H. Nitze Papers

Lyndon B. Johnson Presidential Library, Austin, Texas

Papers of Lyndon B. Johnson

National Security File
    Agency File
    Country File
    Foreign Intelligence Advisory Board
    Harold H. Saunders Files
    Intelligence File
    Charles E. Johnson Files
    Meetings and Memoranda Series
    Memos to the President
    Name File
    National Intelligence Estimates
    National Security Action Memoranda
    NSC Meetings
    Rostow Files
    Subject File

Special Files
    Clifford Papers
    President's Daily Diary
    Records and Transcripts of Telephone Conversations and Meetings
    Rusk Appointment Books
    Tom Johnson's Notes of Meetings

White House Confidential File
    Confidential File
    Subject File

Other Personal Papers

Clifton Papers
    Papers of Major General C.V. Clifton

John F. Kennedy Presidential Library, Boston, Massachusetts

National Security Files
    William H. Brubeck Series
    Departments and Agencies Series

Published Sources

Day, Dwayne A., "Rashomon in Space: A Short Review of Official Spy Satellite Histories," *Quest*, Volume 8, Issue 2, pages 45–53

Enthoven, Alain C. and K. Wayne Smith, *How Much Is Enough? Shaping the Defense Program, 1961–1969* (New York: Harper & Row, 1971)

Hall, R. Cargill, *A History of the Military Polar Orbiting Meteorological Satellite Program* (Washington, National Reconnaissance Office)

___, "Postwar Strategic Reconnaissance and the Genesis of Corona," in Dwayne A. Day, John M. Logsdon, and Brian Latell, eds., *Eye in the Sky: The Story of the Corona Spy Satellites* (Washington, Smithsonian Institution), pages 86–118

Halperin, Morton H., "The Decision To Deploy the ABM: Bureaucratic and Domestic Politics in the Johnson Administration," *World Politics*, XXV (October 1972), pages 62–95

Maechling, Charles, Jr., "Counterinsurgency: The First Ordeal by Fire," in Michael T. Klare and Peter Kornbluh, eds., *Low-Intensity Warfare: Counterinsurgency, Proinsurgency, and Antiterrorism in the Eighties* (New York: Pantheon Books, 1987), pages 21–48

Ruffner, Kevin, C., ed., *Corona: America's First Satellite Program* (Washington: Central Intelligence Agency, 1995)

Sagan, Scott D., "SIOP-62: The Nuclear War Plan Briefing to President Kennedy," *International Security*, XII (Summer 1987), pages 22–51

Seaborg, Glenn T., *Journal of Glenn T. Seaborg, Chairman, U.S. Atomic Energy Commission, 1961–1971* (Berkeley, CA: Lawrence Berkeley Laboratory, University of California, 1989–1992)

Statement of Secretary of Defense Robert S. McNamara Before the Senate Armed Services Committee on the Fiscal Year 1969–73 Defense Program and 1969 Defense Budget (Washington, 1969)

U.S. Department of State *Bulletin*, 1964–1969 (Washington)

U.S. National Archives and Records Administration, *Public Papers of the Presidents of the United States: Lyndon B. Johnson, 1964, 1965, 1966, 1967, 1968–69* (Washington)

U.S. National Reconnaissance Office, *The Corona Story* (Washington, November 1987)

___, Oral History Program, An Interview With William O. Baker by R. Cargill Hall, 7 May 1996, Murray Hill, New Jersey

___, Oral History Program, An Interview With Robert S. McNamara by R. Cargill Hall, 25 March 1999

Abbreviations

AAI, Authorized Active Inventory
ABM, anti-ballistic missile
ABMIS, Airborne Missile Intercept System
ABRES, Advanced Ballistic Reentry System
ACDA, Arms Control and Disarmament Agency
ACS, Assistant Chief of Staff
AD, assured destruction
AD, destroyer tender
AEC, Atomic Energy Commission
AEW&C, Airborne Early Warning and Control
AGC, amphibious flagship
AID, Agency for International Development
AJCC, Alternate Joint Communications Center
AMM, anti-missile missile
AMSA, Advanced Manned Strategic Aircraft
ANG, Air National Guard
ANMCC, Alternate National Military Command Center
AOR, fleet oilers
ARA, Bureau of Inter-American Affairs, Department of State
ARNG, Army National Guard
ASD, Assistant Secretary of Defense
ASM, air-to-surface missile
ASROC, anti-submarine surface launched rockets
ASW, anti-submarine warfare
ATS, salvage tug
AWACS, Airborne Warning and Control System

BMD, ballistic missile defense
BMEWS, Ballistic Missile Early Warning System
BMS, ballistic missile ship
BNSP, Basic National Security Policy
BOB, Bureau of the Budget
BUIC, back-up interceptor control
BW, biological warfare

C, Confidential
CASP, Country Analysis and Strategy Paper
CB, chemical and biological
CDP, Civil Defense Program
CENTO, Central Treaty Organization
CEP, circular error probable; circular error projection
ChiCom, Chinese Communist
CI, Counterinsurgency
CIA, Central Intelligence Agency

CINCARIB, Commander in Chief, Caribbean Command
CINCMEAFSA, Commander in Chief, Middle East, Southern Asia and Africa, South of the Sahara
CINCNORAD, Commander in Chief, North American Defense Command
CINCONAD, Commander in Chief, Continental Air Defense Command
CINCPAC, Commander in Chief, Pacific
CINCSO, Commander in Chief, United States Southern Command
CINCSTRIKE, Commander in Chief, STRIKE
CJCS, Chairman, Joint Chiefs of Staff
CNO, Chief of Naval Operations
COMINT, communications intelligence
CONUS, continental United States
CPR, Chinese People's Republic
CSAF, Chief of Staff, U.S. Air Force
CW, chemical warfare
CY, calendar year

DASH, drone anti-submarine helicopters
DCI, Director of Central Intelligence
DDG, guided missile destroyer
DDR&E, Director, Defense Research and Engineering
DE, destroyer escort
DEPEX, Nike-X Deployment Study
DEW, Defense Early Warning
DIA, Defense Intelligence Agency
DICBM, depressed trajectory delivery system,
DL, damage limiting
DLG, conventional frigate
DLGN, nuclear-powered guided missile frigate
DOD, Department of Defense
DOD/ISA, Office of the Assistant Secretary of Defense for International Security Affairs
DOD/SA, Office of the Assistant Secretary of Defense for Systems Analysis
DPM, Draft Presidential Memorandum
DUCC, Deep Underground Command Center
DXGN, nuclear guided missile destroyer

E.O., Executive Order
EUR, Bureau of European Affairs, Department of State
EUR/RPM, Office of Regional Political-Military Affairs, Bureau of European Affairs, Department of State

FBI, Federal Bureau of Investigation
FBM, fleet ballistic missile
FBO, Foreign Buildings Office, Department of State
FDL, Fast Deployment Logistics ships
FE, Bureau of Far Eastern Affairs, Department of State
FFD, Forward Floating Depot
FIAB, (President's) Foreign Intelligence Advisory Board
FIDP, Foreign Internal Defense Policy

FMP, force modernization program
FOBS, fractional orbit bombardment system
FOT, follow-on test
FRC, Federal Records Center
FRG, Federal Republic of Germany
FWMAF, Free World military assistance forces
FY, Fiscal Year

GCD, general and complete disarmament
G/PM, Office of Politico-Military Affairs, Department of State
GTE, greater than expected

HF, high frequency
HPD, hard point defenses
HUMINT, human resources intelligence

ICBM, inter-continental ballistic missiles
ICIS, Interdepartmental Committee on Internal Security
ICM, improved capability missile
IDP, internal defense plan
IIC, Interdepartmental Intelligence Conference
IMI, Improved Manned Interceptor
IOC, initial operating capability
IRG, Interdepartmental Regional Group
ISA, Assistant Secretary of Defense for International Security Affairs
IUS, International Union of Students

JAEIC, Joint Atomic Energy Intelligence Committee
JCS, Joint Chiefs of Staff
JCSM, Joint Chiefs of Staff Memorandum
JLRSS, Joint Long-Range Strategic Study
JSCP, Joint Strategic Capabilities Plan
JSOP, Joint Strategic Objectives Plan
JWGA, Joint War Games Agency

KP, kilopound

LF, low frequency
LFS, landing force support ship
LHA, amphibious assault ship
LOC, line of communication
LRA, long-range aviation
LST, tank landing ship

MAAG, Military Assistance Advisory Group
MAD, airborne magnetic anomaly detection
MAP, Military Assistance Program
MAR, multi-function array radar
MCS, mine countermeasures support ship
MIRV, multiple, independently-targeted re-entry vehicle
M/KP, million per kilo pound

MLF, Multilateral Force
MOBS, multiple orbit bombardment system
MOL, Manned Orbital Laboratory
MRBM, medium-range ballistic missile
MRV, multiple re-entry vehicle
MSO, minesweeper ship
MSR, Missile Site Radar
MSS, special minesweeper ship
MSTS, Military Sea Transportation Service
MT, megaton
MTR, missile tracking radar

NAC, North Atlantic Council
NASA, National Aeronautics and Space Administration
NATO, North Atlantic Treaty Organization
NAVCOSSAC, Naval Command System Support Center
NCA, National Command Authorities
NEA, Bureau of Near Eastern and South Asian Affairs, Department of State
NEACP, National Emergency Airborne Command Post
NECPA, National Emergency Command Post Afloat
NESC, Net Evaluation Subcommittee
NFZ, nuclear-free zone
NG, National Guard
NIE, National Intelligence Estimate
NIPP, National Intelligence Projections for Planning
n.m., nautical mile
NMCC, National Military Command Center (or Command and Control)
NMCS, National Military Command System
NMLCP, National Mobile Land Command Post
NOA, new obligational authority
NORAD, North American Air Defense
NSA, National Security Agency
NSA, National Student Association
NSAM, National Security Action Memorandum
NSC, National Security Council
NU-OPTS, nuclear options

OAD, operational availability date
OAS, Organization of American States
OCB, Operations Coordinating Board
OCD, Office of Civil Defense
ODR, Office of Defense Resources
OECD, Organization for Economic Cooperation and Development
OEEC, Organization for European Economic Cooperation
OEP, Office of Emergency Planning
ONE, Office of National Estimates, Central Intelligence Agency
OSD, Office of the Secretary of Defense
OT, operational flight tests
OTH, over the horizon (radar)

PAL, permissive action link
PAR, Perimeter Acquisition Radar
PC, patrol craft
PCP, Program Change Proposals
PDP, Project Definition Phase
PFIAB, President's Foreign Intelligence Advisory Board
PJDB, Permanent Joint Defense Board
P.L., Public Law
PMG, Political-Military Group
POLAD, Political Adviser
PONAST, Post-Nuclear Attack Study
PRC, People's Republic of China
PSAC, President's Science Advisory Committee

QRA, quantitative risk analysis

R&D, research and development
RD, Restricted Data
RDT&E, research, development, test, and evaluation
RG, Record Group
RISOP, Red Integrated Strategic Operational Plan
RV, re-entry vehicle

S, Secret
SABMIS, sea-based ABM system
SAC, Strategic Air Command
SACEUR, Supreme Allied Commander, Europe
SACLANT, Supreme Allied Commander, Atlantic
SACSA, Special Assistant to the Director, Joint Staff, for Counterinsurgency
   and Special Activities
SAGE, semi-automatic ground environment
SAM, surface-to-air missile
SCAD, Subsonic Cruise Armed Decoy
SCI, Sensitive Compartmented Information
SEATO, Southeast Asia Treaty Organization
SecDef, Secretary of Defense
SETD, systems-engineering-technical-direction
SF&ET, Strategic Force and Effectiveness Tables
SHAPE, Supreme Headquarters, Allied Powers, Europe
SIG, Senior Interdepartmental Group
SIGINT, signals intelligence
SIOP, single integrated operations plan
SLBM, surface-launched ballistic missile
SLCM, surface-launched cruise missiles
SNIE, Special National Intelligence Estimate
SOSUS, sound and surveillance underwater system
S/P, Policy Planning Council, Department of State
SPADATS, space detection and tracking system
S/PC, Policy Planning Council, Department of State

SRAM, short-range attack missile
SSBN, nuclear-powered ballistic missile submarines
SSDSG, Special State–Defense Study Group
SSG, Special Studies Group (JCS)
SSKN, nuclear-powered killer submarines
SSN, nuclear attack submarine
STANAVOR, standing naval force (NATO)
STRAF, U.S. Strategic Army Forces
SUBROC, submarine-launched rockets

TAC, Tactical Air Command
TAF, The Asia Foundation
TAPS, trajectory accuracy prediction system
TDI, Target Data Inventory
TERCOM, terrain matching guidance
TFG, Tentative Force Guidance
TOW, tube-launched optically-tracked wire-guided missile
TS, Top Secret

U, Unclassified
UE, Unit Equipment
UHF, ultra high frequency
UK, United Kingdom
ULMS, Undersea Long-range Missile System
UN, United Nations
USAF, United States Air Force
USAFE, United States Air Forces in Europe
USCINCEUR, United States Commander in Chief, European Command
US/FWMAF, U.S. Free World Military Assistance Forces
USIA, United States Information Agency
USIB, United States Intelligence Board
USN, United States Navy
USOIDP, United States Overseas Internal Defense Policy
USSR, Union of Soviet Socialist Republics

VDS, variable-depth sonar
VHF, very high frequency
VLF, very low frequency
VMO, velocity, maximum operating

WEU, Western European Union
WFDY, World Federation of Democratic Youth

Persons

Ball, George W., Under Secretary of State to September 30, 1966; Representative to the United Nations, June 26, 1968–September 25, 1968

Bohlen, Charles E., Ambassador to France until February 9, 1968; thereafter Deputy Under Secretary of State for Political Affairs

Bowman, R.C., Member, National Security Council Staff, 1964–1966

Brown, Harold, Director of Defense Research and Engineering, Department of Defense, until September 30, 1968; thereafter Secretary of the Air Force

Bryant, Farris, Director, White House Office of Emergency Planning

Bundy, McGeorge, Special Assistant to the President for National Security Affairs until February 28, 1966

Clifford, Clark, Chairman, President's Foreign Intelligence Advisory Board, April 1963–February 1968; Secretary of Defense from March 1, 1968

Clifton, Chester V., President's Military Aide

Dean, Patrick, British Ambassador to the United States from April 13, 1965

Dobrynin, Anatoly F., Soviet Ambassador to the United States

Eisenhower, Dwight D., President of the United States, 1953–1961

Ellington, Buford, Director, White House Office of Emergency Planning

Enthoven, Alain, Assistant Secretary of Defense for Systems Analysis from September 10, 1965

Fisher, Adrian, Deputy Director, Arms Control and Disarmament Agency

Foster, John S., Jr., Director of Defense Research and Engineering, Department of Defense

Foster, William C., Director, Arms Control and Disarmament Agency

Goldberg, Arthur J., Permanent Representative to the United Nations, July 28, 1965–June 24, 1967

Goodpaster, General Andrew J., Assistant to the Chairman of the Joint Chiefs of Staff to July 31, 1966; thereafter Director of the Joint Staff

Gordon, Kermit, Director, Bureau of the Budget, until 1965

Greene, General Wallace M., Jr., Commandant of the Marine Corps, January 1, 1964–December 31, 1967

Gromyko, Andrei A., Soviet Foreign Minister

Helms, Richard, Deputy Director of Central Intelligence, April 28, 1965–June 30, 1966; thereafter Director of Central Intelligence

Hornig, Donald F., President's Special Assistant for Science and Technology after January 1964

Horwitz, Solis, Assistant Secretary of Defense for Administration from July 1, 1964

Johnson, General Harold K., Chief of Staff, U.S. Army, July 3, 1964–July 2, 1968

Johnson, Lyndon B., President of the United States

Johnson, U. Alexis, Deputy Under Secretary of State for Political Affairs until July 12, 1964; Deputy Ambassador to Vietnam, July 1964–September 1965; Deputy Under Secretary of State for Political Affairs, November 1, 1965–October 9, 1966; Ambassador to Japan from November 8, 1966

Katzenbach, Nicholas DeB., Under Secretary of State from October 3, 1966

Keeny, Spurgeon, Member, National Security Council Staff

Kitchen, Jeffrey C., Deputy Assistant Secretary of State for Political-Military Affairs until February 1967

Komer, Robert W., Member, National Security Council Staff, until September 1965; Deputy Special Assistant to the President for National Security Affairs, October 19, 1965–March 1, 1966; Special Assistant to the President for National Security Affairs during March 1966; Special Assistant to the President, March 28, 1966–May 1967; after March 1966 Special Assistant to the President for Peaceful Reconstruction in Vietnam; Ambassador to Turkey after December 3, 1968

Kuznetsov, Vasili Vasilievich, First Deputy Soviet Minister

Leddy, John M., Assistant Secretary of State for European Affairs from June 1965

LeMay, General Curtis, Chief of Staff, U.S. Air Force, until January 31, 1965

McCone, John A., Director of Central Intelligence until April 28, 1965

McConnell, General John P., Chief of Staff, U.S. Air Force, from February 1, 1965

McDermott, Edward A., Director, White House Office of Emergency Planning

McDonald, Admiral David L., Chief of Naval Operations until August 1, 1967

McMillan, Brockway, Under Secretary of the Air Force

McNamara, Robert S., Secretary of Defense until February 29, 1968

McNaughton, John T., Assistant Secretary of Defense for International Security Affairs, July 1, 1964–July 19, 1967

Nitze, Paul H., Secretary of the Navy until June 20, 1967; thereafter Deputy Secretary of Defense

Rostow, Walt W., Counselor for the Department of State and Chairman of the Policy Planning Council until March 31, 1966; thereafter President's Special Assistant

Rusk, Dean, Secretary of State

Saunders, Harold K., Member, National Security Council Staff

Schultze, Charles L., Director, Bureau of the Budget, June 1, 1965–January 29, 1968

Seaborg, Glenn T., Chairman, Atomic Energy Commission

Smith, Bromley, Executive Secretary of the National Security Council

Stevenson, Adlai E., Representative to the United Nations until July 14, 1965

Taylor, General Maxwell D., Chairman of the Joint Chiefs of Staff until July 1, 1964; Ambassador to Vietnam, July 14, 1964–July 30, 1965; Chairman of the President's Foreign Intelligence Advisory Board from February 1968

Thompson, Llewellyn E., Ambassador at Large until December 26, 1966; also Acting Deputy Under Secretary of State for Political Affairs

Vance, Cyrus, Deputy Secretary of Defense until June 30, 1967

Warnke, Paul, Assistant Secretary of Defense for International Security Affairs from August 1, 1967

Wheeler, General Earle G., Chief of Staff, U.S. Army, until July 2, 1964; thereafter Chairman of the Joint Chiefs of Staff

Wilson, Harold, British Prime Minister

Yost, Charles W., Deputy Representative to the United Nations until August 6, 1964

National Security Policy

1.   **Memorandum From the Chief of Staff, U.S. Air Force (LeMay) to the Joint Chiefs of Staff**[1]

CSAFM 6–64   Washington, January 4, 1964.

IMPROVED MANNED STRATEGIC AIRCRAFT

1. At their meeting with the President on 30 December 1963, the Joint Chiefs of Staff were asked to review and provide their comments on certain recommendations by the Chief of Staff, U.S. Air Force, concerning a proposed follow-on manned strategic weapon system.[2] Accordingly, the basis for these recommendations is provided below for the consideration of the Joint Chiefs of Staff.

2. By the end of 1972, the B-52 will be twenty-one years beyond its design date and the last production B-52 and B-58 will be ten years old. With the passage of time, we have had to rely increasingly on tactics which these aircraft were not designed to employ. Even with the planned modifications to the B-52 fleet these aircraft will be subject to the combined effects of continued structural fatigue and a diminishing capability for effective mission performance in an environment of modern offensive and defensive Soviet weapon systems. If there is further delay in initiating action toward the provision of a suitable replacement capability, there will be no recourse for the nation but to place principal reliance for its security in the 1970s on ballistic missiles. In my judgment, such reliance is both dangerous and militarily unsound.

3. I am in complete agreement with the need for a modern effective ballistic missile force as an element of our deterrent posture. These weapons provide the quick time to target delivery capability which is essential to underwrite the time urgent nuclear threat targets. Additionally, a secure ballistic missile force, in concert with other survivable strategic forces, provides the strongest possible incentives to the USSR to abstain from attacks on the population centers of the United States, either in an initial attack or as a rational option during conflicts of lower intensity.

---

[1] Source: National Archives and Records Administration, RG 200, Defense Programs and Operations, LeMay's Memo to President and JCS Views, Box 83. Secret.
[2] See *Foreign Relations, 1961–1963*, vol. VIII, Document 154.

1

4. It is important to recognize, however, that ballistic missile forces represent both the U.S. and Soviet potential for strategic nuclear warfare at the highest, most indiscriminate level, and at a level least susceptible to control. The employment of these weapons in lower level conflict would be likely to escalate the situation, uncontrollably, to an intensity which could be vastly disproportionate to the original aggravation. The use of ICBMs and SLBMs is not, therefore, a rational or credible response to provocations which, although serious, are still less than an immediate threat to national survival. For this reason, among others, I consider that the national security will continue to require the flexibility, responsiveness, and discrimination of manned strategic weapon systems throughout the range of cold, limited, and general war. Specifically, there will be a continuing requirement for:

a. A system that can be used to provide visible evidence, through increased alert and dispersal and show of force flights, of national determination as an element of diplomatic maneuver and negotiating strength in times of international crisis. Regardless of the size of the force, ICBMs and Polaris missiles have no meaningful utility for this purpose.

b. A fully credible national response option to provocations below those which would warrant the employment of ICBMs. Manned strategic systems have a capability for selective and discriminate application of force which is not provided by ballistic missiles.

c. A capability to respond quickly under national direction to unforeseen and rapidly changing circumstances.

d. A system that can be tested again and again under conditions approximating actual combat as opposed to ballistic missiles which must function perfectly the only time they are ever called upon. In 1963, strategic bombers flew more than 80,000 missions involving 700,000 flying hours, and the crews performed nearly 150,000 scored bomb runs. With ICBMs a very small statistical sample will be fired annually from special test sites which do not correspond to the operational environment. Further compounding the risk of placing undue reliance on ballistic missiles is the ever-present possibility, based on several examples to date, that a single unanticipated failure may negate or drastically reduce the capability of the entire force. Last year, for example, all Wing I Minuteman missiles were determined to be unreliable for a period due to difficulties with the re-entry vehicle. Concurrently, all Wing II Minuteman missiles, comprising the remainder of the force, were considered unreliable by the Atomic Energy Commission as a result of warhead deficiencies. Finally, the reliability of the Polaris A-1 fleet, during a period in 1963, was suspect in its entirety due to bonding problems with the propellant. Although these difficulties all have been corrected, they are indicative of the vulnerability of the total capability to a single unforeseen system deficiency. Such far reaching effects have not been encountered with manned systems. Temporary difficulties may cause restrictions for peacetime flight safety purposes but they have no immediate repercussions upon our war fighting capability.

e. Timely information, as a basis for informed national decisions in times of conflict, which can be provided only by placing man over the enemy with a capability to look, act, and report.

f. A diversified threat to the enemy so that a single break-through on his part, such as an effective anti-ballistic missile defense will not neutralize our retaliatory power; additionally, to continue the requirement that the enemy dilute his already limited resources between anti-ballistic missile and air defenses.

g. A system that can be used to effect a favorable war termination, irrespective of the level of conflict, and which can be used to police a truce, once it has been achieved.

5. Throughout the period of the last year, various study groups within the Air Force have analyzed the requirement for a follow-on strategic aircraft. From these efforts, the prescribed characteristics of an improved manned strategic system have evolved. The aircraft would be designed primarily for low level penetration at subsonic speeds but also would be capable of dash speeds in excess of Mach 2.0 at high altitude. The basic armament would consist of internally carried, short range air to surface missiles with variable yield warheads. A reconnaissance subsystem consisting of side-looking radar, infra-red, and photographic sensors also would be integral to this system. This aircraft would have intercontinental range, unrefueled, and would be compatible with the KC-135 tanker for range extension through aerial refueling.

6. In my discussion of this subject with the President during the meeting on 30 December 1963, I stated my intentions to recommend the following:

a. The initiation of system definition effort on an improved manned strategic aircraft in FY 1964 with $5 million from funds already available to the Air Force.

b. A level of effort in FY 1965 adequate to complete the design studies and program definition and to provide the option for the earliest practicable system IOC by funding at a minimum level the long lead time items such as propulsion and avionics. Based on our studies to date, this effort would require approximately $50 million. In this case also, due to the importance which I place on this matter, I anticipate recommending certain adjustments within the Air Force budget to accommodate this effort without increased funds.

7. It is recommended that:

a. The memorandum at the Enclosure[3] be forwarded to the Secretary of Defense.

b. This paper NOT be forwarded to the commanders of unified or specified commands.

c. This paper NOT be forwarded to US officers assigned to NATO activities.

d. This paper NOT be forwarded to the Chairman, US Delegation, United Nations Military Staff Committee.

---

[3] Not printed.

---

2.   Memorandum for the Record by Director of Central Intelligence McCone[1]

Washington, January 8, 1964.

SUBJECT

Meeting with the President—5:30 on 8 January 1964

1. Reviewed Estimate 11–14[2] as outlined in attached memorandum dated 8 January.

2. Reviewed general reconnaissance satellite program, demonstrating two or three photos, particularly the one of Washington. Advised the President we had now identified 234 ICBM launch sites and about 700 IRBM launch sites, about 125 probably in operation. While this was a lesser number of ICBMs than we had, we must always bear in mind that they are very large and carry warheads in the several megaton range and this gives me concern.

3. Advised the President we were going to conduct the inspection of the Dimona reactor in Israel starting January 14th, a good team had been selected from the AEC and I knew they were good because of the background of my personal relationship with them.

4. Gave the President the memorandum on 20 Latin American countries which he retained to read.[2]

---

[1] Source: Central Intelligence Agency, DCI (McCone) Files, DCI Meetings with the President, 01 January–30 April 1964, Box 6. No classification marking. An undated outline of topics for this briefing of the President is attached but not printed.

[2] Not further identified.

5. Reviewed the status of Cuban economic developments, armed shipments and troop training as reported in [*less than 1 line of source text not declassified*] dated 8 January 1964, attached.

6. Discussed briefing of Congressional Committee Chairmen. President advised he planned a dinner for the Chairmen and the senior minority members of principal committees and their wives. After dinner—the wives upstairs—he would ask me to give a 10-minute review of the Soviet economics; McNamara 5 minutes on the military posture; and Rusk 5 minutes on the political problems.

7. Advised the President I had completed plans to brief the Heads of State, Europe, as follows:

President Segni and Saragat of Italy when they are here next week. Following week I would brief de Gaulle and others in Paris and Erhard and others in Bonn.

Then I would brief Lord Home and his party when they are here in February.

This was agreed.

8. Reviewed briefly President Kennedy's letter to me of January 16 and asked for reaffirmation of DCI responsibilities as outlined in the letter or any modifications which he desired.[3] The President kept the letter and advised he would communicate.

Attachment[4]

NOTES FOR BRIEFING OF PRESIDENT JOHNSON ON
SATELLITE RECONNAISSANCE

We now have [*less than 1 line of source text not declassified*] satellite photography for intelligence purposes.

[*less than 1 line of source text not declassified*] *Search* of very large areas for new installations. This coverage is supplied by the Corona satellite, which has been primarily a CIA development.
[*1 paragraph (5 lines of source text) not declassified*]

[*1-1/2 lines of source text not declassified*] pictures are taken from an altitude of about 100 miles over targets in the Soviet Union and elsewhere when required. The satellites stay in orbit [*less than 1 line of source text not declassified*] and the film is recovered in special reentry vehicles by aircraft near Hawaii.

---

[3] See *Foreign Relations*, 1961–1963, vol XXV, Document 99.
[4] Top Secret; [*codeword not declassified*].

The Corona/Search satellite first returned film from orbit in August 1960, and has performed successfully 29 times since then out of 46 attempts. It is launched from a Thor–Agena at a total cost of about [*less than 1 line of source text not declassified*] dollars per shot. The Corona can cover three million square miles per mission in stereo, mowing a two hundred mile wide strip below its trajectory.

We are able to blow these film strips up to 40–60 times their original size and produce photographs of ICBM sites and other critical targets which are truly remarkable. The quality of photographs that we get is especially highly classified.

This type of photography provides a major source of raw intelligence data and is one of the most important inputs for our national estimates of Soviet strategic capabilities. So far, we have covered over 100 million square miles of the earth's surface. 95% of the USSR has been filmed to date. In this year alone, we have covered 65% of the USSR and 45% of China. From all of this photographic coverage we have identified some 18 ICBM Complexes in the USSR containing more than 234[5] ICBM pads. Over 700 IRBM/MRBM positions and more than 1100 surface-to-air missile sites have also been located and reported.

We are now looking at ways to improve the present system further and to invent a successor with greatly improved capabilities. In the meantime, we have constructed the National Reconnaissance Plan so as to provide one Corona/Search flight each month indefinitely.

[*2 paragraphs (14 lines of source text) not declassified*]

[*1 line of source text not declassified*] will bring you especially important examples of this photography to discuss in conjunction with our regular intelligence meetings.

---

[5] The typed number "220" is crossed out, and "234" was inserted by hand.

3.   Memorandum From the Joint Chiefs of Staff to Secretary of
Defense McNamara[1]

JCSM–4–64   Washington, January 10, 1964.

SUBJECT

    Deep Underground Command Center (DUCC) (S)

1. Reference is made to:[2]

a. JCSM–405–63, dated 29 May 1963.
b. JCSM–484–63, dated 3 July 1963.
c. JCSM–753–63, dated 27 September 1963.
d. JCSM–914–63, dated 2 December 1963.
e. Secretary of Defense Decision/Guidance (Format B), dated 19
December 1963, subject: Deep Underground Command Center.

2. The Joint Chiefs of Staff have considered on a continuing basis
over the past several months the matter of the Deep Underground
Command Center (DUCC). On those occasions in which this subject has
been addressed directly (references 1a through 1d), the response has
dealt with separate but related aspects of the problem. In view of the
bearing of this matter on other programs under consideration, the Joint
Chiefs of Staff wish to state their views as to the justification for a
DUCC and as to the military requirement therefor.

3. It is the opinion of the Joint Chiefs of Staff that a DUCC as a military command center cannot be justified and it is not recommended for
inclusion in the National Military Command System (NMCS) program
for the following reasons:

a. It would not, in their opinion, permit top military leaders to operate as effectively as would be possible through use of other survival
means. Specifically, it would involve their operating without adequate
staff or support in a "buttoned-up" environment from which communications and egress would be uncertain following a nuclear attack.

b. The adverse effect of the DUCC on the NMCS program,
planned to establish an effective and survivable system of command
and control facilities, is exemplified best when viewed in relation to
the long-term aspects of the program. The proposed funding for the
Five-Year Program (FY 1965–69) indicates that approximately $860
million may be committed to the NMCS. The cost estimate for a 300-
man DUCC is approximately $310 million which represents over 36

---

[1] Source: Washington National Records Center, OSD Files: FRC 330 70 A 4662, 381
DUCC (10 Jan 64) 1963 and 64 Papers. Top Secret.

[2] The four JCS papers referenced are ibid. The last reference was not found.

per cent of the total budget proposed for the NMCS. The $310 million basically provides for only construction costs, and does not include in-house or entrance communications equipment or operational support systems essential to the realization of initial operational capability. If the DUCC were to be included in the NMCS program, there are indications that it would absorb in future years considerably more than 36 per cent of the total NMCS funds now programmed for the NMCS, and, unless additional funds were provided, would thereby force severe reductions in other NMCS programs, such as deferral of the First Generation National Military Command Center, limitations in number and degree of enhancement of the more desirable mobile alternate command centers, and curtailment of communications and other support systems.

 c. The weakest link in a hardened communications system is the antenna. In view of limited progress to date in the design of hardened antennas, the probability of survival of DUCC communications depends primarily on redundancy of antennas. Various means of communications have been considered as possible solutions to this problem. One such means particularly suited for use in a DUCC installation is the substrata earth transmission of electromagnetic waves. However, research on this project has not progressed to the point where operational feasibility can be determined nor can reliable operational use be predicted with any degree of confidence.

 d. An examination of the functions to be performed by the National Command Authorities, which include the Joint Chiefs of Staff, indicates that for this decision group to operate within the isolated environment of a DUCC, adequate space and facilities to house sufficient staff personnel and to provide appropriate supporting data would require that the facility be considerably larger in size and scope than the 300-man DUCC estimated to cost $310 million. To meet the demands of nuclear war, it will be of vital importance that a tremendous volume of actions be performed swiftly by trained and experienced people.

 e. An austere size (50-man) DUCC would be totally inadequate to accommodate the decision element of the National Command Authorities together with minimum essential staff support and housekeeping support. It is clearly evident that a 50-man DUCC is essentially a survival facility. As a follow-on step, it is highly probable that immediate expansion to a 300-man DUCC will be required to provide a minimum national command facility. However, such an expanded DUCC would be inadequate for military purposes.

 4. A deep underground facility could be useful as an emergency shelter to safeguard the President for continuity of government, provided escape and survivable communications can be assured. The following factors are considered germane to the issue:

a. It would be a facility affording improved protection to which the President and a minimum number of selected advisors could rapidly relocate in times of international tension.

b. The minimum amount of time would be lost during the relocation process, and confusion, disruption of operations, and adverse public impact would be minimized.

c. Studies indicate that a deep underground facility could be designed to permit relocation within the time period now described as "tactical warning" due to its ready accessibility to the President and selected advisors.

d. Escape and survivable communications from a DUCC would be problematical in case of a direct attack on Washington with large-yield nuclear weapons.

5. In summary, the Joint Chiefs of Staff consider that the DUCC would be too small, and its communications too uncertain, to serve as a military command center. They recommend against the allocation of resources to such a facility at the expense of existing and currently planned elements of the NMCS. They consider that it is a question for executive decision as to whether the DUCC would be worth its cost as a safe shelter for the President and a minimum number of selected advisors, from which he might or might not be able to communicate in case of attack.

For the Joint Chiefs of Staff:
Maxwell D. Taylor[3]
Chairman
Joint Chiefs of Staff

---

[3] Printed from a copy that indicates Taylor signed the original.

4.   Memorandum From the President's Deputy Special
       Assistant for National Security Affairs (Kaysen) to the
       President's Special Assistant for National Security Affairs
       (Bundy)[1]

Washington, January 16, 1964.

Harold Brown and I discussed the matter of the DUCC this morning. In view of the problems between the Secretary and the JCS,[2] we agreed that the best way to handle the matter was to create a limited interdepartmental committee to study the problem from the point of view of the civilian top level of Government; and at the same time suggest to the Secretary of Defense that he request the Joint Chiefs to give their views on the nature of their relations with both the President–Secretary of State–Secretary of Defense level and the CINCs in a crisis situation toward the end of the sixties. The target date for this is the 15th of March.

The purpose of this would be to get the Chiefs to deal explicitly with their view of the relations between the top civilian level and the operational commanders during the period of crisis, and make clear both their ideas of what kinds of crisis situations they are thinking of and the amount and character of communication they would expect in both directions from and on location.

The interdepartmental study group would try to answer four questions, against the background of some likely scenarios of crisis in which a thermo-nuclear war is either imminent or has actually begun.

A. What would the utility of the DUCC be in this situation in the late sixties?

B. How big would the facility have to be in terms of the number of people it could hold to provide this utility?

C. Are there any unresolved technical problems which would have to be dealt with to make the installation effective?

D. What would its relation be to the other elements of the National Military Command System (NMCS)?

Harold and I think the committee should be chaired formally by you, and that its members might be himself, Andy Goodpaster, Alex Johnson, Walt Rostow and Ray Cline. Spurgeon and I would join to represent you on the committee, and I could convene the meeting and act as Chairman in your absence. The main staff of the committee who

---

[1] Source: Johnson Library, National Security File, Subject File, Deep Underground Command Center, Box 8. Top Secret.

[2] For the views of the JCS, see Document 3.

would be available for full-time work would be furnished by Harold Brown's office. In addition, Jim Clark of BOB who is knowledgeable on these problems, might serve on its staff.

E. Secretary McNamara might prefer to deal with this purely as an internal problem within the Department of Defense. However, the arguments for the other arrangement are convincing to Harold Brown and me. First, if there is to be a fight with the Congress, the President himself must be convinced of the need for the proposed facility, and this can best be done through the participation of his own staff. Second, there is not within the Pentagon the kind of experience that the White House–State–CIA are likely to have that is requisite to a thorough examination of the issues. While nobody has the relevant experience, the suggested group would come closer to having a basis for speculation about it than any other we can think of.

CK

5.   **Memorandum From the Secretary of Defense's Assistant for Atomic Energy (Howard) to Charles E. Johnson of the National Security Council Staff**[1]

Washington, January 18, 1964.

SUBJECT

Status Report on Anti-satellite Capabilities

In accordance with your request for a status report on the anti-satellite capabilities, the following information is submitted:

Program 437

Program 437 involves the attainment of an anti-satellite capability based on the employment of [*2 lines of source text not declassified*]. SPADATS, the worldwide satellite tracking system, provides target satellite position data from which an intercept point is determined. [*2 lines of source text not declassified*] In general, the system will have at least two opportu-

---

[1] Source: Johnson Library, National Security File, Subject File, Nuclear Weapons, Vol. I, Box 32. Top Secret. According to a January 23 covering memorandum from Charles Johnson to McGeorge Bundy, Bundy had requested this status report so the President could "be brought up to date with this special capability."

nities each day to intercept from Johnston Island any satellite which passes over the United States. The response time of the system is determined by the ability of SPADATS to provide the necessary satellite position prediction data. Presently the system requires approximately 36 hours of tracking to provide sufficiently accurate data. Performance of the SPADATS system is being improved and further evaluated to determine feasible improvements in response time and accuracy.

Program 437 is a concurrent effort with the research and development and operational implementation actions occurring simultaneously.

The research and development phase, which was funded at $7.9 million in Fiscal Year 1963 and $16.0 million in Fiscal Year 1964, has reached the point of launch demonstration. [9 lines of source text not declassified] Other than the radio frequency interference problem, all elements of the system have demonstrated a capability to support a successful intercept up to the point of launch. SPADATS has completed five targeting exercises, each time providing sufficiently accurate satellite position predictions within the 36-hour system capability.

On June 27, 1963, the Secretary of Defense directed that Program 437 achieve a short reaction operational capability by June 1964. Subsequently, the 10th Aerospace Defense Squadron has been activated with duty station at Vandenberg Air Force Base. It is planned that launch teams from this squadron will rotate on temporary duty at Johnston Island, thereby providing a full standby alert capability. [1 line of source text not declassified]

Required training facilities have been completed at Vandenberg Air Force Base. Necessary technical data is in final stages of preparation. The first launch team has completed individual training and is in crew-training status as of January 13, 1964, with completion programmed for March 1, 1964. An actual launch by this crew is scheduled between completion of the research and development launches and the directed operational date.

On December 2, 1963, the Secretary of Defense approved investment expenditures of [less than 1 line of source text not declassified] for obtaining the Program 437 operational capability. This will provide a trained unit, on alert, [2 lines of source text not declassified]. Approximately $7 million per year will be required for operations and maintenance. At this point, all actions concerning the operational phase of Program 437 are on schedule, and no significant difficulties in meeting the directed June 1964 date are forecast.

Program 505

On May 23, 1963, [4 lines of source text not declassified]. The development program leading to this highly successful demonstration required one year and a funding of $15 million.

On May 28, 1963, the Secretary of Defense directed that the [2 *lines of source text not declassified*]. A total of $8 million has been provided for this purpose. [13 *lines of source text not declassified*]

[11 *lines of source text not declassified*] adaption kit. This round successfully met test objectives. Two additional successful test firings will be required to complete warhead certification program. These firings are currently planned for February and March 1964. Since the personnel required to perform the [2 *lines of source text not declassified*] operation and maintenance costs for this special capability are minimal.

W.J. Howard

---

6.   **Memorandum From the Deputy Under Secretary of State for Political Affairs (Johnson) to Secretary of State Rusk and Secretary of Defense McNamara**[1]

Washington, January 21, 1964.

MEMORANDUM FOR

State—Secretary Rusk
Defense—Secretary McNamara
CIA—Mr. McCone
ACDA—Mr. Fisher
White House—Mr. McGeorge Bundy
White House—Dr. Wiesner
White House—Dr. Welsh
White House—Mr. Johnson
NASA—Mr. Webb
USIA—Mr. Murrow

SUBJECT

Possible Disclosure of Satellite Reconnaissance

Conclusions:

Following discussions among your representatives, we have concluded that no additional action to disseminate more knowledge of our

---

[1] Source: Johnson Library, National Security File, Intelligence File, TKH Jan. 1964–Feb. 1965, Box 1. Top Secret; [*codeword not declassified*]. Copies were sent to William Bundy and Brockway McMillan (DOD); Wheelon and Cline (CIA); and Ambassador Thompson, Chayes, and Hughes (Department of State).

satellite reconnaissance capability is required at this time in support of our disarmament and other policies.

This memorandum summarizes our findings on the nature of present official and unofficial knowledge of U.S. satellite reconnaissance, and on ways in which wider knowledge might affect allied and Soviet acceptance of our disarmament proposals.

State of Allied Knowledge of U.S. Satellite Reconnaissance Program:

As a result of actions taken following the review of the political and public handling of the U.S. satellite reconnaissance program under NSAM 156[2] in the summer of 1962, all NATO heads of government, Foreign Ministers and NAC Permreps were told officially of our reconnaissance satellite program—the fact that we had it, that it was developing well and was directly benefiting the alliance, and finally, that the U.S. must maintain it at all costs. A somewhat similar briefing was given to several selected neutral officials. None of those briefed [2 *lines of source text not declassified*] were shown pictures, and no details of the quality or extent of coverage were given. Changes have occurred in four NATO Governments and in the NAC since these briefings, and we have made arrangements to brief the appropriate [3 *lines of source text not declassified*].

A list of foreign officials who have been briefed on the program is at Tab A.[3]

Much satellite-derived information is presently being incorporated into NATO planning documents, particularly the Target Data Inventory which provides exact locations on such military targets as Soviet SAM, MRBM and ICBM launch pads. This information is classified Secret and there is no attribution of source. The nature of the data is such, however, that we must assume that many of the more than 500 non-U.S. NATO officials who have access to the TDI deduce its overhead photographic origin.

We are aware of no basic disagreement within NATO on the accuracy of our intelligence, and thus find no present necessity for additional disclosures to our Allies, either in terms of briefing more people or of giving more details about the program.

Non-Bloc Attitudes:

We have examined NATO and other non-Bloc press coverage of reconnaissance satellites but, with the exception of the U.S. press, find

---

[2] NSAM No. 156, May 26, 1962, requested the Department of State to organize an interagency committee to review the negotiations on disarmament and international cooperation in outer space. For the workings of this committee, see *Foreign Relations, 1961–1963*, vol. VII, Document 226.

[3] This two-page list is not printed.

nothing of significance. We plan to query selected U.S. Embassies in an effort to determine more clearly the level of public and official awareness of the U.S. satellite program and attitudes toward it. If our experience with recent proceedings of the UN Outer Space Committee is a valid indicator, most non-Bloc states tend to accept space reconnaissance as a fact of life and to view attendant political considerations with indifference. This situation is satisfactory from our standpoint.

Soviet Statements on and Awareness of U.S. Satellite Reconnaissance Program:

Over the past 18 months we have noted a decline in Soviet press articles and statements on U.S. satellite reconnaissance. The Soviet press regularly reports "secret" launches of U.S. "spy" satellites, but these are only two or three sentence summaries of U.S. press agency stories, usually without Soviet comment. We have seen little else in the Soviet press since last summer on any aspect of reconnaissance satellites, and certainly nothing to compare either with earlier Soviet assaults on such activity or with recent U.S. articles on this subject. There has been no Soviet commentary yet on these U.S. articles adverting to extensive U.S. space reconnaissance operations.

In the UN Outer Space Committee negotiations, the Soviets have relaxed (but not abandoned) their position of long standing on banning reconnaissance satellites, at least to the extent of making agreement possible last fall on general principles of space law, without reference to reconnaissance. It is clear that the Soviets have taken this action without prejudice to future negotiations, but it does represent a significant shift in Soviet tactics.

The new Soviet attitude may result in part from experience they have acquired with reconnaissance satellites. In the last year the USSR has launched a large number of recoverable satellites, some of which carried low resolution cameras. We have intercepted Soviet video transmissions of pictures from these cameras. It is quite possible, given the 10,000 lb. weight of the Soviet Cosmos vehicles, that higher resolution cameras were aboard as well. Khrushchev hinted as much when he told Spaak last summer that the Soviets were photographing the U.S. and even offered to show Spaak some pictures. Adzhubey is reported to have made a similar statement in Finland in September 1963.

On the basis of the inconclusive evidence we have acquired in the last year or so, we believe that (a) the Soviets are certainly aware of the program, although probably still uncertain of its precise scope and quality; (b) they are prepared for the moment to live with it, in part because there is no feasible alternative open to them to stop it, and (c) they are probably engaged in a reconnaissance effort of their own. As they acquire first hand experience, their awareness of the strength and weaknesses of space reconnaissance may have some influence on their future proposals in space and disarmament matters.

Relationship of Satellite Reconnaissance to Current U.S. Disarmament Proposals:

At Tab B is a study, prepared by ACDA, attempting to gauge the impact of satellite photography on the principal current arms control proposals under consideration in ACDA, and on the contribution satellites can make in monitoring agreements already in effect, i.e., the test ban and the resolution against bombs in orbit.

A separable first stage proposal on strategic nuclear delivery vehicles and production cutoff would, of course, be heavily dependent on our unilateral reconnaissance capabilities. The degree of this dependency may well have to be revealed in part to make a separable first stage proposal acceptable to our Allies and domestically. Until a U.S. position on this matter is fully worked out, however, we cannot usefully anticipate possible solutions to this problem.

U. Alexis Johnson

Tab B

The Contribution of Satellite Photography to the Verification of Current Arms Control and Disarmament Proposals

Problem

The United States has developed an observation satellite system which is now able to furnish reasonable quality and reasonably timely photography of any area in the world which may be of interest. This unilateral capability effectively provides the "open skies" coverage of the USSR which was requested by President Eisenhower in 1955 as part of a disarmament agreement. It is clear that possession of this photography changes the requirements for ground or other types of inspection as part of the verification of a number of different proposed arms control agreements although it does not obviate the need for complementary means of data collection. This brief discussion has been prepared as an attempt to gauge the impact of satellite photography on the principal current arms control proposals under consideration in the U.S. Arms Control and Disarmament Agency.

Capabilities of Current Satellite Photography

Currently the most important single U.S. intelligence asset is satellite photography. Since the first successful recovery of a Keyhole vehicle in August 1960, there have been about 30 recovered missions, providing cloud-free, usable photography of approximately 90 percent of the USSR. The quality of the photography has now reached the level, in some instances, of early U-2 photography, and long focal-length camera systems, first successfully used in the summer of 1963, can now provide even better materials on selected targets. With photography from the normal search mode, using the KH-4 camera system, photo-interpreters can detect objects as small as 8 to 10 feet on a side. [*8 lines of source text not declassified*]

Satellite photography will be of particular value in the investigation of suspect locations. It is particularly well suited for the identification of new construction activity, for example, and existing photo interpretation procedures include, as a matter of course, the examination of comparative photographic coverage of a given area to detect changes. Tunneling and digging operations, requiring the dumping of spoil, would be readily apparent, for example.

The appearance of new transportation nets, even if only a few dirt roads into a relatively inaccessible area, is readily identifiable.

For nearly four years photography from earth satellites has been an important source of information on the ground force in the Soviet Union. The extensive high level photography from aircraft (Talent) of military installations and training areas acquired during the period from mid-1956 to mid-1960 is still useful to photo-interpreters for comparison with photography from satellites (Keyhole). Usable Keyhole photography acquired since mid-1960 covers virtually all of the USSR, East Germany, Poland, and Hungary. This photography is good enough to locate and describe military installations including such details as the dimensions, and probable functions of buildings. It can reveal whether installations are currently in use, although the extent of usage at any time cannot be determined. Military training areas, firing ranges, tank moving-target ranges, and vehicle driving courses are easily discerned, and the photography can reveal whether such facilities have been in recent active use. However, it cannot pick up major land combat equipment. Enhanced image resolution offers the hope for sufficient further improvement to eliminate this difficulty. However, there is no certainty that overhead photography can provide a complete and independent confirmation of the existence of a unit or of its strength in manpower and equipment.

Arms Control and Disarmament Proposals

1. *Comprehensive Nuclear Test Ban Including Underground Tests.*

The evidence of actual underground nuclear testing, both in the United States and the Soviet Union, has already been detected in photography. The major deterrent to effective use of satellite photography is likely to be lack of adequate coverage resulting from weather conditions or long time lapses between photography. Few areas in the USSR remain which have not yet been photographed, and none of these is readily accessible by existing transportation facilities. Certain portions of the USSR, however, provide more information than others. In far northern latitudes, light conditions generally preclude much usable photography during winter months. Meteorological conditions also hamper interpretation in places—the Kamchatka Peninsula and the Kuriles, for example, are nearly always cloud covered, as is the Baltic area. On the other hand, desert areas between the Caspian Sea and Lake Balkhash are nearly always cloud-free.

The time between photographic missions covering a given area varies considerably, depending on the location of the area under study. Although to date an average of at least one mission per month has been orbited, the areas covered by each mission vary, and few areas receive repeated coverage on consecutive missions. With the added factor of unfavorable cloud conditions, it is frequently possible that a specific target may not be covered more frequently than every six to eight months. On the other hand, some areas located near significant targets, such as ICBM sites or known R&D facilities, and in desert areas where cloud conditions are generally good, are covered nearly every time a satellite is programmed.

[*2 paragraphs (22 lines of source text) not declassified*]

2. *Strategic Nuclear Delivery Vehicles, Interim Reduction and Production Cut-off.*

The current proposal specifies armament reductions and curtailment of test and production for the following major strategic weapons categories: ICBMs and IRBM/MRBMs; heavy and medium bomber aircraft with air-to-surface missiles; submarines equipped to deliver weapons by ballistic or cruise missiles; and ABMs.

[*2 paragraphs (7 lines of source text) not declassified*]

a. *Land Based Missiles:*

Satellite photography has permitted the identification of all or nearly all the fixed launch facilities for strategic missile systems in the USSR and would provide an effective check on Soviet declarations of such bases as well as initiation of new launch site construction. [*2-1/2 lines of source text not declassified*]

b. *Submarine Launched Missiles:*

[*1 paragraph (6 lines of source text) not declassified*]

c. *Heavy and Medium Bomber Aircraft:*

[*1 paragraph (6 lines of source text) not declassified*]

d. *Production of Strategic Weapons:*

[*1 paragraph (18 lines of source text) not declassified*]

3. *Fissionable Material Production Cut-off*

Satellite photography is admirably suited to support any arms control agreement on the cut-off of production of fissionable material. Installations capable of contributing significantly to the fissionable material stockpile of any of the nuclear powers would, of necessity, be sufficiently large and characteristic to be detectable by all present reconnaissance systems. In fact it is believed that essentially all of the important elements of the Soviet AE production complex have been so photographed and identified. Thus Soviet declarations of production sites could be confidently checked by satellite photography and decisions made on the Soviet compliance. A solid basis would be provided for reaching a decision on inspection to locate an undeclared facility. Construction of a new AE production facility could also be detected and probably identified well in advance of actual operation.

[*2 paragraphs (13 lines of source text) not declassified*]

4. *Nuclear Free Zones*

The proposal provides for the prohibition of nuclear weapons from defined geographic regions, such as Latin America. Photographic satellites could provide broad-base coverage on which to establish a base or mosaic of large-scale military activities in a particular region. It would be a useful means of obtaining wide area coverage to be used for targeting more specific collection means such as low altitude or ground observation.

[*1 paragraph (8 lines of source text) not declassified*]

5. *Other Proposals*

Photographic satellites would have limited applications in providing background information pertinent to the enforcement of a number of other arms control measures.

a. *Observation Posts and Surprise Attack:*

Satellite photography would have only limited value in support of the observation post proposal. In general the time delay in obtaining reliable coverage of any area make this source unattractive as a unique source for detecting any surprise attack or clandestine maneuver. Furthermore, the quality of the [*12 lines of source text not declassified*].

b. [*less than 1 line of source text not declassified*]

[*1 paragraph (6-1/2 lines of source text) not declassified*]

c. *Bombs in Orbit:*

The US and the USSR have agreed to a UN resolution forbidding the orbiting of nuclear weapons. Verification is by unilateral means and, presumably, the orbiting of the number of large, low-orbit satellites sufficient to have real military significance would be noticed even though intentions were not known. [*6 lines of source text not declassified*]

d. *Conventional Armaments and Force Levels:*

[*1 paragraph (5 lines of source text) not declassified*]

---

7.   **Memorandum From the Executive Secretary of the President's Foreign Intelligence Advisory Board (Coyne) to the President's Special Assistant for National Security Affairs (Bundy)**

Washington, January 29, 1964.

[Source: Johnson Library, National Security File, Intelligence File, Foreign Intelligence Advisory Board, Vol. 1 [2 of 2], Box 5. Top Secret. 2 pages of source text not declassified.]

---

8.   **Editorial Note**

Following the discovery of audio surveillance devices or "bugs" in the Great Seal at the U.S. Embassy in Moscow, along with the microwave bombardment of that Embassy, the U.S. Government increasingly sought methods to counter this threat to sensitive information. While an NSC subcommittee (NSC Special Committee on Technical Surveillance Countermeasures) had been in existence for many years, during the Kennedy administration the issue engaged the President, the President's Special Assistant for National Security Affairs, the Director of Central Intelligence, and senior Department of State and Defense and FBI officials. A coordinated program was undertaken to install secure facilities in many overseas posts, and regular progress reports on the program were provided to the NSC. Details remain classified. Documents covering the issue are in the Johnson Library, National Security File, Intelligence File, Foreign Intelligence Advisory Board, Vol. 1, Box 5; ibid., Agency File, Central Intelligence Agency, Vol. II, Box 9; ibid., Subject File, President's Foreign Intelligence Advisory Board, Box 41; and ibid., Agency File, Central Intelligence Agency, Filed by LBJ Library, Box 10.

9.   **Final Report of the Central Intelligence Agency/Defense Intelligence Agency Scientific Guidance Panel**

Washington, February 3, 1964.

[Source: Johnson Library, National Security File, Intelligence File, Foreign Intelligence Advisory Board, Vol. 1 [2 of 2], Box 5. Secret. 7 pages of source text (including 5-page Appendix A) not declassified.]

10. Memorandum From Secretary of Defense McNamara to the Chairman of the Joint Chiefs of Staff (Taylor)[1]

Washington, February 6, 1964.

SUBJECT

Improved Manned Strategic Aircraft

REFERENCES

(a) JCSM–37–64, dated 20 January 1964[2]
(b) CM–1140–64, dated 20 January 1964[3]
(c) Memo for Sec AF, dated 23 January 1964[4]

Reference (a) recommends approval of an Air Force proposal to reprogram FY 1964 and apportion FY 1965 Air Force funds to initiate a program definition for a follow-on manned strategic aircraft system and to initiate advanced technology on "long-lead-time" development items, including avionics and propulsion, to reduce the time required to achieve an operational capability. This recommendation is derived from two basic considerations: (1) That strategic aircraft in general can be justified on the basis of diversity, flexibility, responsiveness, reliability and the need for timely reconnaissance; and (2) that the B-52/B-58 force will be reaching the end of its effective service life in the early 1970's. Specifically what is being proposed are budgetary actions, in

---

[1] Source: National Archives and Records Administration, RG 200, Defense Programs and Operations, LeMay's Memo to President and JCS Views, Box 83. Secret.

[2] Not found, but reference may be to a January 20 JCS memorandum on "Improved Manned Strategic Aircraft," at least part of which McNamara quoted in a January 21 memorandum to the Secretary of the Air Force, as follows: "This effort will require approximately $50 million in FY 65, which will be provided by certain adjustments within the current and proposed Air Force budgets if this proposal is approved." He asked the Joint Chiefs to propose their adjustments by January 25. (Ibid.)

[3] Not found, but reference may be to a January 20 memorandum by the Chairman of the Joint Chiefs of Staff on "Manned Strategic Aircraft," at least part of which McNamara quoted in a January 23 memorandum to Chairman Taylor, as follows: "The Joint Chiefs of Staff have requested the Chief of Staff, Air Force to provide them by February 15 a statement concerning the concept of employment of the proposed bomber and an analysis of the reasons of the Chief of Staff, Air Force for favoring a new bomber with the characteristics indicated." McNamara also asked for copies of this memorandum as well as General LeMay's January 4 memorandum. (Ibid.) For LeMay's January 4 memorandum, see Document 1.

[4] In this memorandum, which responded to the January 20 JCS memorandum on "Improved Manned Strategic Aircraft," McNamara asked for "the general specifications and characteristics which you have in mind for such a plane, including speed, range, bomb load, general design approach, engines to be used, defense suppression equipment to be carried, nature of offensive weapons systems, reconnaissance sensors, etc., etc., and the time schedule for the development plan." (National Archives and Records Administration, RG 200, Defense Programs and Operations, LeMay's Memo to President and JCS Views, Box 83)

advance of programmatic decisions, beyond the funds currently being applied to the over-all program concerning strategic aircraft.

The present program relating to strategic aircraft includes: (1) aircraft design studies to further delineate possible characteristics of a new strategic aircraft; and (2) a rather extensive advanced technology program including avionics, propulsion, and sensors.

The aircraft design studies will serve as the basis for a specific proposal (or proposals) by the Air Force. The Air Force proposal, when available, will provide something concrete on which to base a decision whether or not to proceed with a Project Definition Phase. It is to be noted that the basic objective of a Project Definition Phase is to provide detailed technical and management data upon which incentive or fixed price contracting can be based. It is not a substitute or supplement to the studies required to establish the basic design and utility of a proposed system.

With regard to the program on avionics and propulsion, I would welcome specific suggestions as to what are possible deficiencies and improvements. These suggestions must, of course, be judged on a case-by-case basis in comparison with other claims for resources.

In my view, the case has not yet been made that the additional capability that would be provided by an Improved Strategic Aircraft warrants a decision to proceed with the development program recommended by the Air Force. First, the detailed studies by the Air Force have not progressed to the point where detailed aircraft specifications are available. When they are, the potential superiority of the now proposed aircraft can be compared to the B-52. This superiority must be such as to warrant the large expense of replacing the B-52. It is to be noted that the investment in the B-52/B-58 fleet, along with the KC-135, is over $15 billion. Second, I have not been presented with convincing evidence that this fleet will, from the standpoint of air vehicle wear-out, be at the end of its useful service life in the early 1970's. This question is currently being studied by the Air Force and by my own staff. Third, the Air Force has not yet submitted the information requested in CM–1132–64 dated 16 January 1964, Subject: Requirement for Follow-on Manned Strategic Aircraft.[5] In that memorandum the Chiefs asked the Air Force to provide an analysis setting forth the reasons why a strategic bomber system is required as a follow-on of the B-52/B-58 systems and why such a bomber system should have the characteristics of the aircraft described in JCS 1478/104–1.[6] The Chiefs pointed out that: "Such an analysis should undertake to determine whether any follow-on manned bomber system of attainable characteristics is justified in view of the competing systems in the time period in question, and, if so,

---

[5] A copy is ibid.
[6] Not found.

whether the particular system proposed with its specific characteristics is the preferred follow-on system."

I can see no advantage to pre-judging proposals not yet received by now taking budgetary actions beyond those already in force. Certainly it is not necessary to make a decision now on FY 65 apportionment. As to reprogramming of current year funds, that is possible at any time.

I will want the views of the Chiefs on the specific proposals of the Air Force when they are available.

Robert S. McNamara[7]

---

[7] Printed from a copy that bears this typed signature.

---

11. Memorandum From Director of Central Intelligence McCone to the Deputy Director of Central Intelligence (Carter)[1]

Washington, February 10, 1964.

Two subjects on which we must reach an agreed policy decision are (a) the surfacing of the Ox and (b) the management of NRO.

With reference to the former, I reviewed the "visibility" of the Ox on Friday.[2] I find that Drs. Wheelon and Maxey[3] are agreed that the improved Soviet radar capability makes the Ox visible both to the long range search radar and the radars associated with the surface-to-air missile systems. Therefore it is impossible to fly the Ox over Soviet territory without detection. Originally it was thought—and as recently as 18 months ago—that the Soviet radar would not pick up the Ox. The findings of Dr. Wheelon disprove this and this fact bears heavily on the future use of the Ox.

If the decision is made by higher authority not to use the Ox for the purposes originally planned—i.e., clandestine surveillance of the Soviet Union—then it must be considered as a "quick reaction" surveillance

---

[1] Source: Central Intelligence Agency, DCI (McCone) Files, DCI McCone Memoranda, 01 March 1962–30 April 1965, Box 9. Secret.

[2] February 7.

[3] Albert D. (Bud) Wheelon, Deputy Director for Science and Technology, Central Intelligence Agency. Jackson Maxey, Chief of the Special Projects Staff, Central Intelligence Agency.

asset to be used in times of danger, under circumstances of heightened tension, with the full appreciation of the risks and the provocations.

This raises the question of whether in its reconnaissance configuration it should continue as a CIA asset or be turned over to the Air Force. This question must be examined carefully and, quite naturally, the use of the Oxcart over non-Soviet denied territory such as Communist China, Southeast Asia and even Cuba should be taken into consideration.

The above problem is one of the important questions associated with surfacing the Ox—probably[4] the most important long term question from the standpoint of CIA, our budget, etc.

I feel it must at some time be surfaced because of the military versions. Also we are sure to have an accident or forced landing at a public airport, or a "leak", which will have the effect of surfacing. Timing is of importance as well as method, and these should be studied and an in-house decision reached for guidance in talking with the Secretary of State, Secretary of Defense and Director, NRO and higher authority.

The second question is the management of NRO. My last discussion with a representative of DoD was with Fubini about three weeks ago at which time he drafted a memo which I felt outlined a very sensible plan.[5] I understand it has run into some difficulties with McMillan[6] and also I note Dr. Wheelon's alternate proposal.

I would like to reach an in-house agreement as to what part, if any, CIA must play in the operation of proven article, the technical improvements of such an article in order to produce better quality product and the development of a new generation search and spotting satellite to give the ultimate resolution.

Since both Fubini and McMillan want to see me early this week, the above should be discussed at this afternoon's meeting.

JAM[7]

---

[4] The word "probably" is inserted by hand, and the words "but is not" are crossed out.

[5] See *Foreign Relations, 1964–1968*, vol. XXXIII, Document 186.

[6] Brockway McMillan, Under Secretary of the Air Force.

[7] Printed from a copy that indicates McCone initialed the original.

12. Paper Prepared by the Joint Chiefs of Staff[1]

Washington, undated.

JOINT STRATEGIC OBJECTIVES PLAN FOR
FY 1969–1971 (JSOP) (U)

Part I—Purpose

1. The purpose of JSOP–69 is to:

a. Provide information to commanders of unified and specified commands and planning guidance to the military services for the mid-range period beginning 1 July 1968 (M-day) under conditions of cold, limited, and general war.

b. Translate national objectives and policies into military objectives, prescribe strategic concepts for the employment of forces, and define basic undertakings which support these objectives and concepts.

c. Provide the Services with program guidance derived from the basic undertakings in terms of objective force levels considered necessary to support the US military strategy delineated in the plan.

---

[1] Source: National Archives and Records Administration, RG 200, Defense Programs and Operations, JSOP—FY 1969–1971, Feb. 14, 1964, Box 41. Top Secret; Special Handling Required; Not Releasable to Foreign Nationals. Attached but not printed are a title page; a September 5, 1963, memorandum from Colonel R.C. Forbes (SM–1082–63); a table of contents; and a February 14 memorandum from General Taylor to McNamara (CM–1181–64), which noted that Parts I–V of the JSOP, approved by the Joint Chiefs of Staff, were being forwarded prior to final development of Part VI. Parts I–V, Taylor added, "constitute guidance to the commanders of unified and specified commands for their submission of force requirements and a basis for the Joint Chiefs of Staff to determine objective force levels." He described their contents as follows:

"I. Purpose—States the various purposes of the JSOP.

"II. Strategic Appraisal—Analyzes the world-wide threat through the mid-range period.

"III. Military Objectives—Describes military objectives to support national objectives.

"IV. Strategic Concept—Describes anticipated employment of forces on a functional and geographical basis.

"V. Basic Undertakings—Describes the basic undertakings of the unified and specified commands envisaged for this period."

Taylor continued that Part VI, "Force Tabs," of JSOP–69, which would be forwarded on March 16, "will contain views of the Joint Chiefs of Staff on major combatant forces required to carry out strategy presented in Parts I through V." He concluded that the entire JSOP–69 was designed to provide the Secretary of Defense with military advice for the development of the FY 1966 budget, justification for Defense Department FY 1966 program objectives as they pertained to major combatant forces, and a basis for reassessment of the previously approved Five-Year Force Structure and Financial Program. Part VI of JSOP–69 is in the National Archives and Records Administration, RG 218, JCS Files, 3130 (16 Sep 63) Sec 4A–6A.

d. Provide logistics planning guidance which will serve as a basis for development of Service logistic program objectives in support of the JSOP objective force levels for 1 July 1968, and as a basis for industrial mobilization planning.

e. Provide research and development planning guidance in support of military objectives and strategy delineated in the plan.

f. Provide chemical, biological and radiological warfare guidance in support of military objectives and strategy delineated in the plan.

g. Provide nuclear weapon and nuclear weapon delivery planning guidance in support of the objectives, strategy, and basic undertakings in the plan.

h. Provide guidance for the conduct of psychological and counter-insurgency operations, and unconventional warfare.

i. Provide nuclear weapons damage considerations.

j. Provide an estimate of desirable and reasonably attainable force objectives for countries, Allied or potentially Allied, in support of US military strategy.

k. Provide planning guidance for command and control systems in support of military objectives and strategy delineated in the plan.

l. Provide communications and electronics planning guidance in support of the military objectives and strategy delineated in the plan.

m. Provide the Secretary of Defense:

(1) Military advice for the development of the FY 1966 military budget;

(2) Justification for departmental FY 1966 program objectives as they pertain to major combatant forces; and

(3) A basis for reassessment of military aspects of the previously approved Department of Defense Five-Year Force Structure and Financial Program.

n. Provide military basis for the establishment of a US position with respect to:

(1) Military assistance to our Allies and other friendly countries under conditions of cold, limited, and general war.

(2) The development and review of NATO and other Allied mid-range plans.

Part II—Strategic Appraisal

2. *General.* This appraisal summarizes the probable changes in the world situation likely to affect warfare, military strategies and world balance of military power, from the present through the period of the plan. It contains a brief analysis of the communist threat to the security, objectives and stability of the United States and other Free World nations based on more detailed information contained in the

Intelligence Annex (Annex A).[2] Advances in technology will continue to affect the development of weapons and conduct of warfare during the period. The major powers and other technically advanced nations will continue efforts to reduce their vulnerability to attack, protect their military forces, and improve their relative technical, political, economic and military postures. For factors influencing specific technological developments during the period of the plan see appropriate annexes.

3. *Development of the World Situation Up to the Period Beginning 1 July 1968*

a. The world situation will continue to be influenced by (1) the struggle between communist nations on the one hand and the free societies and other nations who share similar interests on the other; (2) the struggle of newly emergent and/or underdeveloped nations for self determination and a greater share of the world's material wealth; (3) the struggles resulting from traditional rivalries between nations wherein their own interests are involved; (4) the internal struggles within Free World nations which tend to move them away from Free World orientation; and (5) the struggle within Bloc nations.

b. The Soviet Union will increase pressures on the Free World as opportunities present themselves, and will relax pressures when it is to her advantage to do so. Any US or Allied retreats in critical situations will intensify Soviet tactics aimed at achieving advantages, including their inclination to employ force or threats of force. The Chinese Communists will seize every opportunity to undermine US standing; when they judge that circumstances permit, they will supplement political warfare with guerrilla action by indigenous forces as well as by higher intensity military action if they consider that the attendant risks are not too great. Both the Soviet Union and Communist China individually and possibly in concert will continue to instigate and support what they term "wars of liberation" with the aim of weakening the position of the West and establishing communist-oriented governments. Means used to support dissidents will probably range from political and economic assistance to providing military equipment, military training, military advisors, and even cadres. Other communist nations and communist parties in the Free World nations, with the support and encouragement of the Soviet Union, and/or Communist China, will attempt increasingly to embarrass and harass the United States and nations of the Western Alliances. The Soviet and ChiCom estimates of relative US-Soviet-Communist Chinese strength will be no less important to their decision as to the courses of action to pursue than their evaluation of Western reactions to Sino or Soviet probes.

---

[2] Annexes A–L are not printed.

c. Disarmament, nuclear testing and international agreements for the exploitation of space are likely to remain active subjects of international importance. Efforts by the United States to negotiate with the Soviets on disarmament will be continued in an effort to effect some reduction in armaments without jeopardy to US security. Despite any future Soviet willingness to negotiate either an arms agreement or an unlimited nuclear test ban, her basic motive will remain one of subverting the world to international communism. There appears to be little reason to believe that any such agreement can be achieved which will not be predicated on the assumption by the Soviet Union that the Soviet Union and her allies will derive some advantage. Communist China's eagerness for a voice in world affairs and her unwillingness to abide by international agreements reached without her participation probably will continue to inhibit the effectiveness of any agreement on these subjects.

d. The inclination toward neutralism or relaxed military efforts in many nations may have these effects: (1) create therein a political climate susceptible to communist internal and external influence; (2) weaken Western Alliances; (3) restrain newly emerging nations from adopting pro-Western policies; and (4) discredit US leadership. Individual differences, divergent national objectives, nationalistic drives and personal ambitions of their leaders should prevent the neutralist nations from becoming a cohesive military and political entity.

e. Newly emergent nations will continue to be characterized by nationalism, internal dissension, instability in political and economic institutions, and a tendency to concentrate disproportionately on external affairs in order to assert their independence. Political, military, and economic weaknesses will offer the communists opportunities, at relatively minor risk, for supporting subversive insurgency, political, and economic exploitation, including restrictive trade agreements, and the supply of arms and technicians. It is expected that many new nations will identify themselves with "anti-imperialistic" causes. However, Free World assistance, disenchantment with Soviet forms of assistance, and the political, economic, military and cultural ties between former colonialist powers and their former colonies will tend to counter Bloc efforts. Success of Western efforts to maintain a non-communist alignment among these new nations will depend largely upon the methods and the initiative displayed by Free World nations in combating communist subversion and persuasion. Communist control of a nation, once established, is unlikely to end except through introduction of outside military force.

f. The communists will continue to employ threats, alternating belligerency and tractability in the attempt to erode normal diplomatic usage and the rule of law in international relations. They will continue attempts to discredit the United Nations Organization and impede peace-keeping arrangements, unless it serves their purposes to do otherwise.

g. Divisive forces probably will become more pronounced within the Sino-Soviet Bloc as a result of differences between Moscow and Peiping over doctrine and strategy, over ChiCom desires for a nuclear capability, and over the more fundamental questions of authority in the International Communist movement. It is anticipated that these differences will continue to be important considerations in Sino-Soviet Bloc courses of action and will offer some opportunities for exploitation by the Free World. In any event, the Sino-Soviet dispute will continue and will present the Soviet leaders with increasing difficulties in their management of the International Communist movement, resulting in a further diminution of their control over it.

h. Technological and scientific advancement is expected to continue at a rapid pace within the Soviet Union. Soviet propaganda will equate spectacular successes such as those in space to military, economic and social gains and will cite them as proof of the superiority of the communist system.

i. In economic strength, the United States is presently well ahead of other countries. The Common Market area and Japan will continue to show impressive economic gains. The quality, diversity and technological level of production in Communist China will remain considerably below that of Japan, the USSR and the industrial nations of the West. Soviet Bloc policy will continue to emphasize growth and expansion of the bases of national power. Bloc economic planning will include continued maintenance of great military strength, continued efforts to enlarge their penetration of world markets, and selective expansion of trade and aid programs to underdeveloped countries and prospective satellites.

j. The socio-politico-economic bases of the Soviets and Communist Chinese will continue to contain inherent though slow-acting weaknesses potentially vulnerable to exploitation by the United States and its Allies, particularly through political, psychological and unconventional warfare.

k. The process of closer economic union of West European nations under the Common Market concept will continue with some unevenness and will be accompanied by the development of closer political and military ties with the possibility of a growing independence within [11 lines of source text not declassified].

l. Regional Appraisal. It can be expected that communist policy will be marked by subversion and opportunism. Communist leaders undoubtedly will continue to seek new developments favorable to their interests in a number of areas, but more especially in Africa, Latin America, Southeast Asia and the Middle East. They probably intend to give particular attention to establishing a strong presence in Africa, to stimulating and exploiting leftist and revolutionary movements in Latin America, and to encouraging the growth of a radical anti-American mass movement in Japan and elsewhere as expediency dictates. The communists will use any form of enticement and pressure which they consider advantageous and appropriate to any particular time. These pressures will include political, diplomatic, cultural and economic, as well as propaganda and the threat of military action. The communists will continue to drive aggressively for the control of peoples and areas through subversion and inspiration or capture of insurgent movements. Although the Soviets for propaganda purposes, will label such activity as "wars of liberation," they will be attempting to bring the non-aligned nations into the communist camp. Above all, however, the Soviets intend to build up their national base of power in the belief that they can improve their over-all power position. They will continue to believe that, as they do so, more opportunities for readily exploitable communist expansion will open up for them.

(1) *European area.* The Soviet Bloc seeks to: (a) confirm the division of Germany; (b) develop the prestige of East Germany; (c) perpetuate the status quo of the European satellites; (d) prevent the resurgence of West Germany as a potent military power; (e) force the withdrawal of US forces from overseas bases; (f) discourage increases in Allied military capability; (g) prevent the proliferation of Allied nuclear capability; (h) reduce the credibility of the Allied response in critical situations; and (i) weaken and bring about the dissolution of NATO. They are expected to continue to take those actions designed to improve their general military posture, intimidate and divide the West and convince the world that they are determined to pursue their objectives in the face of high risks.

(2) *Middle East.* Bloc objectives in this area appear to be to achieve the dissolution of CENTO, use the Arab nationalist movement to their advantage, weaken the credibility of US response, deny the area and its resources to the West and expand Bloc influence. Major Bloc goals are to obtain a land bridge to Africa and control the Middle East.

(3) *Africa.* The Soviet Union and Communist China will continue to develop economic, cultural, and diplomatic relations with African nations, seeking to penetrate and subvert their political structure and influence their alignment with and dependence on the Sino-Soviet Bloc through external and internal pressures. Frustration of communist objectives, the stability and growth of sound, democratic political institutions and the development of a viable economy among the new nations of Africa will be dependent in a very large degree on the assistance rendered by the Western World.

(4) *Asia and the Far East*

(a) Despite Sino-Soviet differences, the Bloc is expected to continue its efforts to reduce Western influence in Asia and undermine the government and politico-economic institutions of selected non-communist or neutral Asian nations. Efforts of the communists to reduce the effectiveness and force dissolution of SEATO will continue. Communist China will continue efforts to achieve recognition as a major world power and the dominant power in Asia. Generally, Asians probably will become more reluctant to assume a strong stand in opposition to China in the absence of credible guarantees of Western protection.

(b) Indonesia probably will attempt to maintain a neutralist position and seek a balance in relations with major communist and non-communist nations. Indonesia probably will attempt to achieve hegemony over additional island territory in the area, particularly Portuguese Timor and the island portions of Malaysia, while simultaneously attempting to spread her influence in Southeast Asia. Indonesia will continue to rely on the USSR for substantial military assistance and aid and on any other opportune arrangements with Western or communist nations.

(c) The Soviets desire to build up good will and enhance Soviet prestige in India against the time when prospects for communist acquisition of power are considerably improved. India appears determined to check Chinese expansion in the Northern border areas.

(d) No settlement of the India/Pakistan Kashmir dispute is foreseen. A by-product of this dispute, however, could have far-reaching effects in spheres of immediate US interests. The prospect of continuing US/UK military aid to India has caused strong resentment in Pakistan and has increased her dissatisfaction with CENTO and SEATO. She has threatened to withdraw from the latter. To counter both the presumed threat from India and the perennial danger of pressure from the USSR, Pakistan may seek further rapprochement with Communist China.

(e) The USSR's political relations with Japan are likely to remain at an impasse. Moscow will continue to reject Japanese claims to the southern Kuriles and to insist upon abrogation of the defense treaty with the United States as a precondition for normalizing Soviet-Japanese relations with a peace treaty. The USSR would probably relax somewhat its present unyielding position, however, if it detected in Tokyo signs of a willingness to loosen ties with the United States.

(f) The communists desire to establish control in Laos and South Vietnam at an early date. The USSR is not disposed to make heavy sacrifices however, or to jeopardize other objectives vis-à-vis the West in order to make immediate advances in an area which is of more direct concern to Hanoi and Peiping. The USSR is likely, therefore, to urge a less precip-

National Security Policy 33

itous strategy and to accept some temporary setbacks in preference to the
risks of substantial involvement to sustain the Viet Cong. The threat of
large-scale intervention by ChiCom military forces will continue behind
the communist's activities in the area. Communist infiltration, subversion, and support of so-called "wars of national liberation" in Southeast
Asia will increase. The ChiComs are not likely, however, to resort to limited or general war as long as they calculate that their ends can be
achieved through means short of overt war. They will not hesitate, however, as illustrated by their actions in Tibet and on the China/Indian border, to resort to overt military action when they believe it is necessary and
when in their opinion the risk of military confrontation with the United
States is low. The development of effective measures to halt infiltration,
insurgency and subversion will continue to be an urgent requirement in
SEATO. While ChiCom concern over retaliation by the United States will
deter it from attempting a military conquest of Taiwan or the Offshore
Islands, they may undertake limited military action in the straits area to
test Nationalist Chinese defenses and to probe US determination.

(5) *Latin America.* Latin America will continue to be a primary target for Bloc penetration. The conflict will almost certainly intensify during the period. The Bloc will continue to push its campaign to:

(a) Isolate the United States from its traditional Allies;
(b) Nullify hemispheric unity;
(c) Infiltrate and subvert vulnerable countries; and
(d) Strengthen and exploit its present foothold in Latin America.

The Soviets and ChiComs will continue to use Cuba as a base from
which to expand communist influence further into the Western
Hemisphere and as a significant factor in world-wide negotiations.
Cuba will be closely watched by Latin American and other nations as a
measure of the relative strength and resolution of the US and the Soviet
Union. Periodic crises will almost certainly continue to occur in Latin
America throughout the period. In general, based on the assumption of
continued US support, the area will almost certainly remain US-oriented, although in the face of internal and external Bloc pressures, some
nations can be expected to adopt an increasingly independent position.
The Soviets will attempt to turn to their advantage such promising revolutionary developments as may occur.

4. *The Soviet Bloc Threat*

a. *General.*

(1) While striving to improve Soviet Bloc security, especially that of
the USSR, the Soviet rulers will attempt to advance toward their over-
all objective of achieving a communist world under Soviet leadership.
This basic Soviet Bloc objective remains constant and is supported by
every member of the Bloc.

(2) Soviet thinking about military policy is influenced by a general outlook which asserts that historical forces are moving inexorably in the direction of communism. In theory, this movement is carried forward by the struggle of the "masses," led by the communist parties, to overthrow the existing social-economic order during an indeterminate period of "peaceful coexistence" rather than by the direct use of the military power of the Soviet Bloc. Soviet leaders see military power as serving two basic purposes: defense of their system and support for its expansion. Thus, one of the most important objectives of Soviet military policy is to deter general war while the USSR prosecuted its foreign policies by means short of actual hostilities involving Soviet forces. Military power is constantly brought into play in direct support of these policies, through the threats which give force to Soviet political demands, through the stress on its growing power which is intended to gain respect for the Soviet state and its communist system, and through the military aid and support rendered to allies, friendly but neutral regimes, and anti-Western movements. Despite a strong Soviet military posture, the relative strategic balance of forces is in favor of the West and as long as this condition exists it is doubtful, except through miscalculation or misadventure, that the Soviets would initiate general war. There is, however, good evidence that the Soviets, in recognition of this imbalance, are striving for weapon systems which could, in the future, enhance their capabilities relative to the West.

b. *Attitude Toward War.*

(1) The Soviets wish to have the forces to fight wars effectively should they occur. One of the most important objectives of Soviet policy is to deter general war. Except for so-called wars of national liberation, their political outlook, their military programs of recent years, and intelligence on their current intentions all suggest that the Soviet leaders do not regard war as desirable. They realize their deterrent must be credible in the sense that it rests upon powerful military forces. Moreover, they recognize that deterrence may fail in some key confrontation in which, despite their best efforts to retain control over risks, either they or their opponents come to feel that vital interests are under challenge. Against this contingency they wish to have a combination of offensive and defensive capabilities which will enable them to seize the initiative if possible, to survive enemy nuclear attack, and to go on to prosecute the war successfully. Although logically they must think that a deliberate Western attack on them is improbable, they appear to have genuine apprehensions.

(2) Devoted as they are to the need for implacable struggle against the "capitalist" world until communist domination is assured, and to the view that power—in its broadest economic, military and political sense—is the key ingredient in this struggle, the Soviets see their prior-

ity objective as constantly trying to change the East-West balance of power and the world conception of that balance in their favor. To this end they persistently endeavor to enhance the components of their economic, military, and scientific strength and no less important, their political position in the world arena. Soviet boasts of military prowess and superiority over the West are designed to back up their political initiatives by exploiting present and future Soviet power potential. At the same time, the Soviets do what they can to undermine and denigrate the power of the West in these respects.

(3) Fundamental hostility toward the noncommunist world defines one limit of Soviet foreign policy; so long as it persists, the USSR will regard international issues as opportunities progressively to weaken and undermine its opponents, and not as occasions for conciliation which would protect the interests of all parties. The other limit, which puts a check upon this aggressiveness, is the Soviet leaders' awareness that their own nation and system would face destruction in a general nuclear war. Both their statements and their actions in recent years have demonstrated their unwillingness to run any considerable risks of this eventuality. This does not mean, however, that they would always estimate the risks correctly, nor does it mean that they would abandon interests they considered vital in order to avoid grave risk of nuclear war. Barring the development of a decisive weapon system, the Soviets almost certainly consider that neither side will deliberately initiate a general war or react to any crisis in a manner which would gravely risk such a war, unless vital interests were considered to be in jeopardy.

(4) It is believed that the Soviets are unlikely, as a matter of general policy, to assume the military and political risks involved in using their own forces in formal military operations to achieve local gains. They would probably employ Soviet forces, as necessary, if some Western military action in areas adjacent to a communist country threatened the integrity of the Bloc itself. Even in the latter case, however, they would attempt to use their forces in a way calculated to achieve their local objectives, to end hostilities rapidly and to control risks of escalation. At a much lower level, they will almost certainly encourage and support the use of force by pro-communist forces when they believe that a local situation is ripe for forceful exploitation and that the challenge to Western interests is not direct enough to involve uncontrollable risks of a direct encounter between United States and Soviet forces.

(5) This estimate of Soviet views on general and local war is generally consistent with the positions expressed by them on 6 January 1961, when they defined various types of wars and their attitude

toward them.[3] On that occasion, in addition to stating Soviet opposition on both world wars and local wars between states, they distinguished a category of "wars of national liberation, or popular uprisings." Such internal wars, ranging pro-Soviet or anti-Western forces against colonial or pro-Western regimes, were declared to be "just" and deserving of communist support. They were carefully vague, however, in discussing the forms which this support would take, and in particular, neither promised nor hinted that Soviet forces would join in the fighting. Subsequent Soviet actions, however, indicate that this was not a statement of intent to usher in a new phase of vigorous Soviet incitement of such conflicts everywhere or of maximum military assistance to "national liberation" forces.

(6) It seems likely that Soviet emphasis on "national liberation" warfare, was intended in part to meet Chinese criticisms then being made that the USSR, by its stress upon the need to avoid war, was in fact ruling out altogether the use of force in advancing the communist cause. This charge is a major component of the Chinese attack upon the correctness of Soviet policies and, therefore, upon the legitimacy of the USSR's traditional leadership of the communist movement. It is also designed to win for China the allegiance of communists and radicals in the less developed countries, who are less firmly tied to Soviet leadership than their European counterparts. Despite these Chinese pressures, the USSR has not given full political and material support nor committed its prestige to all armed anti-Western movements in the underdeveloped areas. It is believed that the Soviets will continue to follow an opportunistic policy in this regard.

c. *Military Balance of Power.*

(1) The Soviets maintain substantial forces-in-being and a large mobilization potential. As far as ground forces are concerned, they probably regard the balance of power in Eurasia as being in their favor. They also have a large short-, medium-, and intermediate-range missile arsenal with which they could attack targets anywhere in the European area. They have acquired an intercontinental missile capability in addition to their long-range bomber forces. Their force of missile-firing submarines continues to increase and forms an increasingly important part of their strategic capabilities. However, their capability for intercontinental attack remains decidedly inferior to that of the West.

(2) Bloc leaders probably continue to view their combined military power as adequate to meet military situations in Eurasia in which the nuclear capabilities of the Western Powers were not involved. They

---

[3] For extracts of Soviet Chairman Khrushchev's address before the Moscow Conference of Communist Parties, January 6, 1961, see *American Foreign Policy: Current Documents, 1961*, pp. 555–558; and *Documents on Disarmament, 1961*, pp. 1–15.

probably also conclude that they possess sufficient military power to deter the West from launching general war except under extreme threat to vital national or common interests. They almost certainly conclude that in the event of general war their military power would be unable to prevent unacceptable damage to the Soviet Union.

d. *Mutual Deterrence and the Deliberate Initiation of War.* The Soviet leaders evidently continue to base their military and foreign policy planning on the assumption that the present over-all military relationship, in which each side can exert a strong deterrent upon the other, will continue for some time to come. The Soviets do not view this situation as a stalemate, but rather as an opportunity to conduct aggressive maneuvers of many sorts and to undertake a comprehensive effort aimed at attaining a military technological breakthrough. They are clearly determined to maintain and improve their strong military posture. The Soviets are vigorously pursuing programs for research and development in advanced weapons, hoping if possible to create a strategic imbalance favorable to them. It is estimated that these research and development efforts include defense systems against ballistic missiles, the military application of space vehicles and very high yield warheads. It is possible that some future technological breakthrough could lead them to believe that they had acquired a decisive advantage and that they could, therefore, be far more aggressive toward the West. It is not beyond the realm of possibility that, under these circumstances, a decision to initiate a first strike might be made. It is not believed, however, that the Soviets base their policies upon the expectation that they will be able to achieve, within the foreseeable future, a military posture which would make the deliberate initiation of general war a rational decision; the Soviets realize that the West is determined to maintain second-strike capabilities which would inflict intolerable destruction upon them. In any case, their policies rest on the proposition that communist victory can be won without resort to general war.

e. *Miscalculation.* Soviet strategy recognizes that, while general war is unlikely, it cannot be excluded as the result of miscalculation by either side or as the outcome of a crisis in which both sides become progressively committed. The Soviets are unable to be certain in advance what the circumstances surrounding the beginning of a general war would be. A miscalculation could occur if the Soviets misjudged either the importance to the West of an issue and the actions which the West might take in support of its position, or even the consequences of the policies being pursued by a third party associated with the Soviet Union. On the other hand, such a crisis might arise should the West miscalculate in a similar way.

f. *Pre-emptive Attack.* If the Soviet leaders were ever convinced that the West was irrevocably committed to an imminent strategic nuclear attack against them, there is little question that they would themselves strike pre-emptively. Such conviction, however, on the part of any country about the intentions of another is extremely unlikely. The Soviet leaders have probably concluded that it would be impossible to count upon incontrovertible advance evidence that the enemy was irrevocably committed to an imminent attack. Moreover, the compulsion to strike first, if the threat of hostile attack is still ambiguous, declines as missile systems become more important and less vulnerable, and if the net military advantage to be derived from a first strike decreases. This trend of Soviet thinking is suggested by assertions that an aggressor cannot neutralize the retaliatory capability of a powerful opponent. Nevertheless, a surprise attack—that is to say, one delivered in a period of no particular tension and after entirely secret military preparations— is the only one which would give the Soviet Union a chance of destroying any significant part of the Western nuclear strike capability before it could be launched. Therefore, in spite of its unlikelihood, it remains a possible, though improbable, course of action for the Soviet Union.

g. *Escalation.* A number of Soviet statements in recent years have expressed the view that limited war involving the major nuclear powers would inevitably escalate into general war. While such statements are intended in part to deter the West from local use of force, this official view also reflects a genuine Soviet fear of the consequences of becoming directly engaged in limited war involving Soviet and US forces. This probably also extends to involvement of Soviet forces with certain Allied forces in highly critical areas, notably Western forces in the European area. Nevertheless, they might employ their own forces to achieve local gains in some area adjacent to Bloc territory if they judged that the West, either because it was deterred by Soviet nuclear power or for some other reason, would not make an effective military response. They would probably employ Soviet forces as necessary if some Western military action threatened the integrity of the Bloc itself. Should the USSR become directly involved in a limited war with the US or Allied forces, it is believed that the Soviets would not necessarily expand it immediately into general war, but that they would probably employ only that force which they thought necessary to achieve their local objectives. They would also seek to prevent escalation by political means.

5. *Chinese Communist Threat*

a. *General.* Communist China's foreign policy will probably continue generally along current lines. Peiping will remain strongly anti-American and will strive to weaken the US position, especially in East Asia, but is unlikely, knowingly, to assume great risks. China's military force will probably not be used overtly except in defense of its own or satellite borders or, in the absence of US/Allied military power, to assert territorial claims against India. Subversion and covert support of local revolutions will continue to be Peiping's primary mode of operation in Southeast Asia and, to a necessarily more limited degree, elsewhere in Asia, Africa, and Latin America.

b. *Modernization of Armed Forces.* The modernization of the armed forces, which was progressing steadily until about 1960, has practically ended, except for the continued introduction of radar and certain other electronic equipment. No advanced aircraft, submarine components, or other items of advanced equipment have been received from the USSR in the past two and one-half years, domestic production of fighter aircraft and submarines has ceased and inventories are being reduced by deterioration and cannibalization. In general, the Army has been less affected than the other Services. During the depths of the domestic decline, the military forces suffered shortages of even routine items of supply, but this condition has apparently been alleviated in the past year.

c. *Advanced Weapons.*

(1) The intelligence data available does not permit a high degree of confidence in estimating the future development of the Chinese nuclear program, and this appraisal is made in light of this general caution.

(2) The Chinese Communists have given high priority to the development of nuclear weapons and missiles. The earliest date a first plutonium device could be tested is believed to be early 1964, but if the normal number of difficulties are encountered this date would be postponed to late 1964 or 1965. Beginning the year after a first detonation, the single reactor thus far identified could produce enough material for only one or two crude weapons a year. The Chinese have a few bombers which could carry bulky weapons of early design.

(3) Communist China is probably concentrating on a medium-range ballistic missile (MRBM) system of basically Soviet design, such as either the 630 mile SS-3 or the 1,020 mile SS-4. The earliest date either missile would be ready for deployment is believed to be 1967. It is unlikely that a compatible nuclear warhead would be available by that date.

(4) The detonation of a nuclear device would boost domestic morale. Although it is possible that the ChiCom leaders would experience a dangerous degree of overconfidence, it is more likely that they will concentrate on furthering their established policies to:

(a) Force their way into world disarmament discussions and other world councils,

(b) Overawe their neighbors and soften them for Peiping-directed communist subversion, and

(c) Tout Chinese-style communism as the best route for an underdeveloped nation to achieve industrial and scientific modernity. In pursuing these policies, increased confidence of ChiCom leaders would doubtless be reflected in their approach to conflicts on the periphery of Communist China.

d. *Domestic Production.* Peiping almost certainly intends to achieve domestic production of all necessary weapons and matériel for its armed forces. It has a long way to go before reaching this goal, however. The Chinese at present are probably unable to produce even MIG-17's entirely by themselves, and it will be a number of years before they can design and produce more advanced types of military aircraft. Indeed they may have chosen instead to concentrate their limited resources on missiles. Their wholly domestic naval shipbuilding capacity is likely to be restricted to surface ships of the smaller types during the next few years.

e. *Military Policy.* Communist China's military policy has always been characterized by caution in undertaking initiatives in the face of superior power. Hence, the decline in the relative effectiveness of its military equipment and weapons is likely further to temper its policy, especially in circumstances where it might confront US armed power or US-equipped Asian air forces. However, the Chinese Communist Army will continue to be the strongest in Asia and will provide a powerful backing for Chinese Communist foreign policy. The Sino-Soviet dispute will probably place additional demands on Chinese military dispositions and capabilities, since one of the consequences of China's new "independence" from the USSR will be the need to keep a closer watch than previously on the long China-Russia border—which the Chinese still consider a "difficult" and "unsettled" question. Her slowly developing nuclear weapon and missile capability will increase an already considerable military advantage over Asian neighbors. However, for the foreseeable future she will not approach the advanced weapons might of the United States or USSR, particularly in the field of long-range striking power. For this reason, among others, Peiping would be unlikely to attribute a decisive importance to modern weaponry. They would probably continue to rely primarily on a huge ground force and, unless confident of Soviet support, would try to avoid hostilities which might escalate into nuclear war. Considering the chances of retaliation, it is difficult to conceive of any situation in which Peiping would be likely to initiate the use of nuclear weapons in the next decade or so.

f. *Foreign Policy.* Communist China's foreign policy objectives can be distinguished roughly by the amount of risk the regime is prepared to take. The obvious first rank objective is the preservation of the regime and the protection of its existing boundaries. For these purposes the ChiComs are willing to go to war, almost regardless of the odds. If US or SEATO troops approached its borders through Laos or North

Vietnam, they would almost certainly be ready to commit their forces openly, unless in the particular circumstances they saw greater advantage in more covert military operations. The acquisition of Taiwan falls in the second rank of objectives—those for which they are fully prepared to use overt military force, but only when the prospects of success are judged to be high. To achieve this goal, they are prepared to run fewer risks and are particularly anxious to avoid direct conflict with the United States. They almost certainly will not attempt to seize by military force either Taiwan or any of the major offshore islands which they believe the United States would help defend. It is not believed that the explosion of a nuclear device, or even the acquisition of a limited nuclear weapons capability, will produce major changes in her foreign policy in the sense that they will adopt a general policy of open military aggression, or even become willing to take significantly greater military risks. China's leaders recognize that their limited capabilities will not alter the real power balance among the major states and could not do so in the foreseeable future. In particular, they will recognize that they remain unable either to remove or neutralize the United States' presence in Asia. Nevertheless, the Chinese would feel very much stronger and this mood would doubtless be reflected in their approach to conflicts on their periphery. They would probably feel that the United States would be more reluctant to intervene on the Asian mainland and thus the tone of Chinese policy would probably become more assertive. Further, their possession of nuclear weapons would reinforce their efforts to achieve Asian hegemony through political pressures and the indirect support of local "wars of liberation."

g. *Spread of Communism.* For the broader and longer range goal of spreading communism throughout the under-developed world, Communist China is probably not prepared to accept any substantial risk, although it must be noted that it tends to estimate the risks involved in supporting "wars of national liberation" much lower than does Moscow. It apparently does not intend to undertake overt conquests of foreign lands in the name of communism, but intends to let indigenous revolutionaries do the fighting and the "liberating." The ChiComs are prepared to train foreign nationals in guerrilla and political warfare, and will back revolutionary movements to the extent of their limited capabilities with equipment, funds, propaganda, and support in international affairs.

[Here follow Part III. Military Objectives, Part IV. Strategic Concept, Part V. Basic Undertakings, and Annexes A–L.]

13. Memorandum for the Record by Director of Central Intelligence McCone[1]

Washington, February 26, 1964, 1 p.m.

SUBJECT

Discussion with the President at 1:00 o'clock, February 26th; No one was present

[Here follow items 1 and 2.]

3. I told the President we had completed an extended Corona coverage of the Soviet Union involving the photographing of about 54% of the Soviet landmass. I explained this was the first time in which we had returned two reels of film from one satellite. This gave me an opportunity to discuss the Corona J development. I said that the photography had not been completely studied but the evidences were that the Soviets were slowing up or stopping construction of soft ICBM sites and were emphasizing the construction of hard sites. I explained that after Penkovsky[2] was apprehended, Khrushchev had stated, and we had learned, that he had told the Presidium that Penkovsky had revealed the location of their missile sites, therefore he had to spend an enormous amount of money—50 billion rubles—to relocate the missiles because we now knew where they were. This was untrue because Penkovsky had not told us the location of a single missile site. However Khrushchev knew that through satellite photography we were learning the exact location of missile sites. He was not relocating them—what he was doing, he was hardening them, and this was costing them an enormous amount of money. The President expressed great interest in the subject of satellite photography and I asked for an hour's time to go over the program, the pictures and other details. He agreed. I suggested perhaps when he was flying some place I go with him and we could spend an hour or so together on this one subject. This he felt might be a good idea.

Action: Remind me to follow this up and to make arrangements on a Presidential trip in the near future.

4. I then discussed the surfacing of the Oxcart and advised him that Chairman Vinson and Senator Russell felt that their Committees should be fully informed by them and they wished to do this in advance of the

[1] Source: Central Intelligence Agency, DCI (McCone) Files, DCI Meetings with the President, 01 January–30 April 1964, Box 6. Secret. Drafted on February 27.

[2] Colonel Oleg Penkovsky was a KGB agent who provided U.S. and British intelligence sources with information on Soviet missile forces and technology, among other things, beginning in 1961 until 1963 when the Soviets arrested, tried, and executed him.

announcement and also stated that Mr. Cannon wished me to meet with his Subcommittee prior to the announcement and that George Mahon wished to inform his committee prior to the announcement. I recommended that this be done but it be timed so the Committees would be advised practically concurrently with the announcement so that the press would not get the news before the President announced it. I said that if, for instance, he was to make the announcement Saturday[3] morning (which he did not confirm at the time), then all of the Congressional actions should be taken Saturday morning. Thus the Congressmen would know in advance but not so much in advance that the press would get hold of the story. The President was very much against this. He felt that if the announcement was made on Saturday, we could inform the Committees on Monday. I stated that this would cause the Committee Chairmen and the Committees a great deal of trouble. With this Johnson picked up the phone to call Senator Russell; however the call was not returned and I did *not* get a final decision.

Action: Later I mentioned the question to Bundy and he said that he would have to get to the President and get a decision. Until this decision is forthcoming we should take absolutely no action with respect to the Hill. Bundy and I discussed the problem several times during the day, including a brief discussion at Mrs. J.F. Kennedy's residence when the President was there. However, Bundy did not think it appropriate to discuss it with the President on the particular occasion at Mrs. Kennedy's residence. This should be followed up with Bundy today.

[Here follow items 5–8.]

---

[3] February 29.

14. Memorandum From the President's Special Assistant for National Security Affairs (Bundy)[1]

[*document number not declassified*] Washington, February 27, 1964.

MEMORANDUM FOR

The Secretary of State
The Secretary of Defense
The Director of Central Intelligence
The Administrator, Federal Aviation Agency

The enclosed statement has been drafted for consideration at a meeting of the National Security Council on February 29.[2] After consideration in the NSC, the President may decide to make this statement public on Saturday at 11 A.M.

There is also attached a list of questions and answers[3] which have been reviewed on an interagency basis for the use of Mr. Salinger, whom the President expects to designate as the responsible background officer if he decides to make the public statement.

The probability that the President will decide this matter affirmatively is high, and the President authorizes entirely private disclosure of the statement to NATO allies, Japan and Australia, not more than twenty-four hours in advance of 11 A.M. Eastern Standard Time, Saturday, February 29. Those who are informed should be warned of the great importance of privacy with respect to this information until the President does make an announcement. In the case of European capitals, it is the President's desire that information not be revealed before Saturday morning, European time. In the case of the U.K., the disclosure will take the form of a private letter from the President to the Prime

---

[1] Source: National Archives and Records Administration, RG 59, S/S–NSC Files: Lot 70 D 265, NSC Meeting, February 29, 1964, 10:00 a.m. Top Secret. Attached are copies of transmittal notes, all dated March 5, from Read to Secretary Rusk, Under Secretary Ball, Under Secretary for Political Affairs Harriman, Deputy Under Secretary for Political Affairs U. Alexis Johnson, Llewellyn Thompson, and others.

[2] The draft statement is not attached. It may be the same as an undated typescript, "Statement by the President," which, with only a few minor changes in wording, was the statement the President made at his press conference on February 29. (Johnson Library, National Security File, Intelligence File, Aircraft Contingency, Box 9) See Document 15 and footnote 2 thereto.

[3] Not attached, but a list of questions and answers is in a draft telegram to all NATO capitals, Canberra, and Tokyo. (Johnson Library, National Security File, Intelligence File, Aircraft Contingency, Box 9) Attached to this cable is an undated, handwritten note from Spurgeon Keeny to Bundy opposing release of anything more than the President's statement, and arguing that the questions and answers should be cleared by McNamara and McCone. No final version of these questions and answers has been found, but following the President's February 29 statement, Salinger held a background briefing on the A-11 aircraft at 1 p.m. (Transcript ibid.)

Minister. Appropriate instructions should be sent to our Ambassador in Moscow.

The Secretary of Defense and the Director of Central Intelligence are authorized to take the necessary operational steps to position A-11 aircraft at Edwards Air Force Base.

The Secretary of Defense and the Director of Central Intelligence are requested to take appropriate steps to inform all those holding Oxcart clearances of the limits within which this disclosure is being held.[4] Those limits are defined by the enclosed statement and the enclosed questions and answers.

The Director of Central Intelligence is authorized to brief Congressional leaders holding Oxcart clearances so that they in turn may give the approved information to members of the appropriate committees not earlier than 11 A.M. on Saturday, February 29. Any additional briefing of any sort with respect to this project will require White House approval.

McGeorge Bundy

---

[4] In the margin next to this sentence is written: "after Sat."

---

15.   Memorandum for the Record by Director of Central Intelligence McCone[1]

Washington, February 29, 1964, 10:05 a.m.

SUBJECT

Discussion at the NSC meeting. Attended by the President, all members and the four members of the President's personal staff.

1. I opened the meeting by explaining briefly the background of the development of the Oxcart, the features which were applicable to military aircraft, contribution the plane would make to supersonic transport and the reasons why it was necessary to surface the development at this time. I explained there was a growing danger that it would surface itself through a leak, accident or forced landing and this would be more awk-

---

[1] Source: Central Intelligence Agency, DCI (McCone) Files, DCI Meetings with the President, 01 January–30 April 1964, Box 6. Secret. Drafted on March 2. The time of the meeting is taken from the President's Daily Diary. (Johnson Library)

ward than if we announced it in advance. I avoided any reference to the reconnaissance mission, however, Secretary McNamara added very considerable amount of information bearing on the reconnaissance development which brought out some discussion [*less than 1 line of source text not declassified*] the amount of flying, the number of planes, etc. McNamara made a point of the fact that a total of over 40 planes, together with the entire development cost of the plane and engine, had been accomplished in a remarkably short time, 4 or 5 years, and at a cost of about $1 and 1/2 billion. He compared this to the B-70 on which there has been about $2 billion spent and the plane is still not out of the hangar. Both during the meeting and afterwards he spoke with great enthusiasm on the performance of the Agency, Lockheed and other contractors in the development and he expressed a wish that the Department of Defense could perform in the same way. He attributed the performance to people who were doing the job and actually knowing what was going on in detail in the areas of their responsibility.

2. The President and Speaker McCormack were most praiseworthy of the secrecy, the President asking what the formula was as he would like to invoke it in departments and also in the White House itself. There was no dissension to the surfacing, although it was known that General LeMay had dissented at the Joint Chiefs on Friday afternoon. General Taylor did not reflect the dissension at this morning's meeting.

3. No other business was transacted at the meeting.[2]

---

[2] The Record of Actions noted that this NSC meeting "considered a draft Presidential statement containing certain information about the advanced experimental jet aircraft, the A-11," which the President decided to made public. (Johnson Library, National Security File, NSC Meetings, Vol. 1, Tab 3, Box 1) The President made the statement at his press conference on Saturday, February 29, beginning at 11 a.m. For text, see *Public Papers of the Presidents of the United States: Lyndon B. Johnson, 1963–64*, Book I, pp. 322–323. See also footnotes 2 and 3, Document 14.

16.   Paper Prepared by the Joint Chiefs of Staff[1]

Washington, undated.

EXPENDITURE OF NUCLEAR WEAPONS IN EMERGENCY CONDITIONS

1. The Joint Chiefs of Staff have simplified the format of the currently approved Instructions for the Expenditure of Nuclear Weapons in Emergency Conditions, and have updated the language to make the instructions editorially compatible with terminology employed in current plans.

2. Subject to presently approved restrictions, the instructions authorize [*1-1/2 lines of source text not declassified*].

[*4 paragraphs (32 lines of source text) not declassified*]

3. Also, in the period since the original instructions were approved, a new commander of major U.S. forces has been designated: CINC-STRIKE/USCINCMEAFSA   (Commander-in-Chief   STRIKE/U.S. Commander-in-Chief Middle East, Southern Asia and Africa, South of the Sahara). In addition, CINCARIB (Commander-in-Chief Caribbean Command) has been redesignated USCINCSO (Commander-in-Chief United States Southern Command), and the area in which he exercises command has assumed greater military significance. [*3 lines of source text not declassified*]

---

[1] Source: Johnson Library, Clifton Papers, Joint Chiefs of Staff Meetings with the President, Vol. I, Box 2. Top Secret. Drafted by Major General C.V. Clifton. This may be the paper the Joint Chiefs discussed with the President on March 4; see Document 17.

17.   Memorandum of Conference With President Johnson[1]

Washington, March 4, 1964, 6:10 p.m.

OTHERS PRESENT

General Taylor
General Wheeler
General McKee (for General LeMay)
Admiral McDonald
General Greene
General Clifton

General Taylor introduced the subjects to be discussed in the order in which they appear on the attached agenda from General Taylor (Tab A).[2]

On the Furtherance document,[3] General Taylor gave the President a summary memorandum. This memorandum reflects the Chiefs' recommendations and was approved by the President (Tab B).[4] (Note: a blue-covered document entitled "Furtherance" and classified Top Secret was given to the President and later taken to Mr. Bundy's office to be filed there.) The Furtherance document consists of currently approved instructions for the expenditure of nuclear weapons in emergency conditions as brought up to date and containing minor changes.

In the situation described in the document, the Chiefs described that [10-1/2 lines of source text not declassified].

General Taylor said there is a Furtherance document here at the White House and that he would like to have it back and the new one, which he gave to me, substituted for it. The President directed that this be where it can be available to all who should know about it.

(Mr. Bundy, the Military Aide, Bromley Smith, and whoever else Mr. Bundy directs should know about this.) The decision on it should be held very closely.

General Taylor also pointed out that they have modified the emergency action book called the "Gold Book" and that they would give this

---

[1] Source: Johnson Library, Clifton Papers, Joint Chiefs of Staff Meetings with the President, Vol. I, Box 2. Top Secret. Another record of this meeting prepared by Taylor is in the National Archives and Records Administration, RG 200, Defense Programs and Operations, Presidential Meetings, Box 142.

[2] Not attached, but reference may be to a memorandum from General Taylor to President Johnson (CM–1229–64), February 28, containing a list of topics the Joint Chiefs of Staff wanted to discuss with the President. (Johnson Library, Clifton Papers, Joint Chiefs of Staff Meetings with the President, Vol. I, Box 2)

[3] Not found.

[4] The "summary memorandum" is not attached, but may be Document 16.

new Gold Book to us.[5] They would like the superseded one returned to the Joint Chiefs.

[Here follows discussion of unrelated topics.]

C.V. Clifton
Major General, USA
Military Aide to the President

---

[5] Not found.

---

18.   **Memorandum From Acting Director of Central Intelligence Carter to the President's Special Assistant for National Security Affairs (Bundy)**

Washington, March 12, 1964.

[Source: Johnson Library, National Security File, Intelligence File, Foreign Intelligence Advisory Board, Vol. 1 [2 of 2], Box 5. Secret. 7 pages of source text not declassified.]

---

19.   **Memorandum From the Deputy Assistant Secretary of State for Politico-Military Affairs (Kitchen) to the Counselor and Chairman of the Policy Planning Council (Rostow)**[1]

Washington, March 12, 1964.

SUBJECT

BNSP Planning Task II (E)—"U.S. Government Organization for Internal Defense"

Attached is the paper "U.S. Government Organization for Internal Defense" developed in response to the BNSP Planning Task II (E) and in collaboration with other bureaus within the Department of State as

---

[1] Source: National Archives and Records Administration, RG 59, S/PC Files: Lot 70 D 199, Internal Security. Secret. Cleared by Eric E. Oulashin (AF), Ellwood M. Rabenold (ARA), Richard E. Usher (FE), and Donald W. Bunte (NEA).

well as other agencies with responsibilities in the field of overseas internal defense.

While this document was prepared in consultation with other interested agencies and in it we have payed attention to those internal defense organizational changes that have come about since the early days of the Kennedy Administration, it has not been subjected to formal interdepartmental clearance. I assume that, if formal interdepartmental clearance is desired, you will initiate this. Within the Department, however, the paper has been formally cleared with the appropriate bureaus and consequently officially represents the Department's organization for internal defense policy and related activities.

Unless notified to the contrary, I will assume that G/PM has now satisfied the requirements of BNSP Planning Task II (E).

Attachment

U.S. GOVERNMENT ORGANIZATION FOR INTERNAL DEFENSE
(BNSP PLANNING TASK II E)

A. Introductory

The purpose of this paper is to outline the organization of the U.S. Government for the task of detecting and either preventing or defeating subversive insurgency in friendly foreign countries. Its scope embraces both Washington and the field.

B. Background

The document entitled "United States Overseas Internal Defense Policy" (USOIDP) September 1962[2] sets forth the pattern, factors, and lessons of communist insurgency, and describes the scope and application of U.S. strategy to counter it. This document, promulgated as national policy by NSAM 182 on August 24, 1962[3] and distributed to all departments, agencies, and field posts in September, 1962, is currently under review by an interdepartmental panel under the chairmanship of the Department of State.

The thesis of the USOIDP document is that subversive insurgency represents primarily a Communist attempt to retard, exploit and/or gain control of the development process in underdeveloped countries, and that this threat requires an effective response by the threatened

---

[2] See *Foreign Relations, 1961–1963*, vol. VIII, Document 106.
[3] See ibid., Document 105.

government covering a wide spectrum of political, economic, military, psychological, and other measures. The U.S. role in countering this subversive threat is regarded as ancillary to the local government's. The way in which the U.S. Government organizes itself to assist in this task in any given situation will normally be a reflection of the degree of U.S. influence and freedom of action the U.S. may enjoy in the country threatened by subversive insurgency.

C. U.S. Internal Defense Role

The U.S. purpose in the field of internal defense is to encourage and assist vulnerable nations to develop balanced capabilities for the internal defense of their societies. The U.S. role is normally supplementary to the local effort and therefore designed:

1. To assist in the immunization of vulnerable societies not yet seriously threatened by Communist subversion or insurgency.
2. To assist countries where subversive insurgency is latent or incipient by removing the causes before the stage of insurgency is reached.
3. To assist in the establishment or strengthening of intelligence and internal security organizations.
4. To defeat subversive insurgency in countries actively threatened by assisting the government under attack with military and non-military means.
5. To build confidence in and loyalty to the host government.
6. To minimize the likelihood of direct U.S. military involvement in internal war by maximizing indigenous capabilities for identifying, preventing, and if necessary, defeating subversive insurgency, and by drawing on, as appropriate, the assistance of third countries and international organizations.

To play its role effectively, the United States must be in a position to mobilize, coordinate, and apply its own and other free world resources to strengthen the local internal defense capability in the following critical areas: (a) military, (b) police, (c) economic development, (d) youth, (e) labor, (f) education, (g) leader groups, (h) political institutions, (i) informational and psychological.

As a corollary, the U.S. Government must strengthen organization, and procedures to enable it to apply these resources in a unified, coordinated, and effective manner.

D. Current Washington Organization

1. *Special Group (CI)*

In recognition of the growing problem of subversion and insurgency, the Special Group (CI) was established in January 1962 by Presidential directive (NSAM 124)[4] to provide unity of effort and use of

---

[4] See ibid., Document 68.

all available resources to identify, prevent, or defeat subversive insurgency and related forms of indirect aggression in friendly countries.

The functions of the Special Group (CI) are to insure: proper recognition of the subversive insurgency threat; reflection of such recognition in training, equipment, and doctrine; marshaling of resources to deal with the threat, and development of programs aimed at defeating it. In addition, its purpose is to insure the development of adequate programs aimed at identifying, preventing, or defeating subversive insurgency and indirect aggression in countries and regions specifically assigned to it by the President, and to resolve any interdepartmental problems which might impede their implementation.

In performing the above functions, the members of the Special Group (CI) act on behalf of their respective departments and agencies, and depend for staff support upon their own staffs, and upon such country, regional, or functional interdepartmental committees (normally chaired by a State Department Assistant Secretary) as may be established. Consequently, the Special Group (CI) itself has no permanent organizational structure except for its Subcommittee on Training. This has the responsibility for keeping under review internal defense training conducted by all departments and agencies. Agency training requirements have been established by National Security Action Memorandum 131.[5]

2. *Departmental Organization*

It will be noted that the charter of the Special Group (CI) specifically provides that program implementation is the responsibility of the departments and agencies represented on the Group. Each department and agency represented on the Special Group (CI) has organized itself differently for its internal defense mission. By and large, they have relied on their various "roles and missions" as set forth in "United States Overseas Internal Defense Policy". Each department and agency (State, DOD, AID, USIA, and CIA) has therefore designated an element within its organization that is charged with the functional task of giving continued attention to overseas internal defense activities. The elements so designated are:

Department of State: Office of Politico-Military Affairs
Department of Defense: International Security Affairs: Special Assistant (to Assistant Secretary) for Special Operations; Joint Chiefs of Staff: Special Assistant to the Director, Joint Staff, for Counterinsurgency and Special Activities (SACSA)
AID: AID/PC—Special Assistant for Internal Defense
CIA: Deputy Director for Plans, Special Group Office
USIA: Office of Policy (IOP)

Program and policy responsibility for particular geographic areas rests in the regional organizations of the above departments and agen-

---

[5] See ibid., Document 128, footnote 3.

cies. Thus, the day-to-day coordination of the many programs and policy decisions involved in the U.S. internal defense effort is normally effected by the regional officers of the several departments and agencies making contact with each other and meeting as the occasion requires in coordination with the designated elements identified above. In addition, ad hoc groups under the chairmanship of State meet as required to develop and monitor country programs and to review country internal defense plans and progress reports prior to submission to interdepartmental regional policy committees and as required to the Special Group (CI).

a. *Department of State*

The Department of State, in accordance with its primary responsibility in the field of foreign affairs, provides policy guidance and coordination of overseas internal defense policy. Such guidance and coordination is normally effected through the Chiefs of Mission and principal officers overseas and the Department of State in Washington.

Within State, the focal point for the functional coordination of internal defense policy and activity is the responsibility of the Office of Politico-Military Affairs (G/PM—Internal Defense). Responsibility for internal security assessments, policy, and program implementation coordination for particular countries and areas rests in the regional bureaus in coordination with the appropriate regional politico-military affairs advisors and G/PM—Internal Defense.

b. *Department of Defense*

Within the Department of Defense, responsibility for the functional coordination of internal defense activities is divided between the civilian staff element (ISA) and military staff element (JCS).

International Security Affairs (ISA)

The civilian element responsible for direction, coordination and guidance for internal defense policy within the Department of Defense is the Assistant Secretary of Defense, ISA. To support the Assistant Secretary in this function, a Special Assistant for Special Operations has been designated whose responsibilities include providing policy guidance to the military assistance program—a vital and major element of US overseas internal defense programs.

Joint Chiefs of Staff

The Special Assistant to the Director, Joint Staff, for Counterinsurgency and Special Activities (SACSA) is charged with assisting the Director, Joint Staff, and the Joint Chiefs of Staff in all matters pertaining to insurgency and counterinsurgency. Accordingly, SACSA serves as the focal point for such matters for the Joint Chiefs of Staff. His duties include planning, programming, resource development and allocation, and doctrinal guidance. Additionally, he is responsible for discharging Department of Defense staff responsibilities pertaining to the planning and direction of those special cold war operations and special activities, not principally intelligence in character, in which the Department of Defense participates.

c. *Agency for International Development*

The Administrator of AID has appointed a Special Assistant for Internal Defense to coordinate the formulation of internal defense programming and programming guidance. The Special Assistant for Internal Defense serves as a focal point within AID on internal defense matters and establishes and maintains those interagency relationships necessary to ensure that AID activities are in consonance with U.S. overseas internal defense policy and integrated with the programs of the other U.S. agencies. It is his further responsibility to provide general direction to program planning and development in this field. Programming responsibility for internal defense activities, as in the case of all AID programs, rests with each regional assistant administrator and, for police assistance programs, with the Director of the Office of Public Safety.

d. *United States Information Agency*

Coordination and general direction of internal defense policy and activities in USIA is the responsibility of the Office of Policy (IOP). The several geographic area offices are responsible for participation in internal security assessments and Agency program implementation in particular countries.

e. *Central Intelligence Agency*

Responsibility for the staff coordination of overseas internal defense and counterinsurgency matters rests with the Special Group Officer of CIA's Deputy Director for Plans. He is assisted in this responsibility by a very small staff known as the Counterinsurgency Group. Intelligence support to the Special Group (CI) and its member agencies, both in Washington and to the Country Team abroad, is provided by the Deputy Director for Intelligence. Operational support to U.S. overseas internal defense programs in both the clandestine intelligence and covert action fields is exercised through the office of the Deputy Director for Plans and CIA's Chiefs of Station abroad.

E. Internal Defense Plan Program

Pursuant to the directive of the Special Group (CI), country internal defense plans (IDP) have been required for a wide range of underdeveloped countries, including, but not limited to, those countries under the immediate cognizance of the Group. Such plans are normally developed after detailed internal security assessments are made either on the initiative of the Chief of Mission or Washington. Each IDP is given a comprehensive screening and review by an interdepartmental working group assembled under the chairmanship of the State regional bureau. The results of this critique are incorporated in an explanatory memorandum from the regional Assistant Secretaries of State to the Special Group (CI) recommending approval or modification as required. After approval by the Group the IDP becomes the basis for a program of specific actions.

In general, the IDP is designed to serve the following purposes:

(1) To assure continuing attention by the Country Team to details of the local situation.

(2) To sharpen the Country Team's ability to forecast dangerous trends and suggest remedies.

(3) To provide a framework within which to assess programs suggested by the local government.

(4) To persuade the local government to adopt the most promising course of action.

(5) To facilitate planning and program coordination in Washington.

(6) To provide clearly defined U.S. courses of action and establish resource requirements (including funding) covering a one-year projection which, if approved by the Special Group (CI), is binding on all participating agencies.

F. Conclusions

Except for the creation of the Special Group (CI), the U.S. organization for the internal defense effort has been mounted and executed by and large within the framework of existing governmental organization. It is believed that by adhering to the traditional lines of organization and by its determination not to recreate an OCB-type structure, President Kennedy gave the Foreign Affairs agencies an opportunity to develop a more vigorous response to the problem of Communist subversion and insurgency. To insure this, the Administration created the Special Group (CI) and confined its role primarily to finding the weak spots in our internal defense effort and to spurring governmental action where necessary. On reflection, it appears from this vantage point in time, that the determination of the White House not to recreate an OCB and to thrust the primary responsibility for internal defense policy and programs on the appropriate departments and agencies has proven to be sound.

Accordingly, it is concluded that the official Washington community has effectively responded to the organizational requirements set forth under the basic National Security Policy Planning Tasks II (E). The present organization for internal defense provides the U.S. Government a far better ability to cope with the growing problem of subversive insurgency today as compared to the general situation prevailing in Washington in early 1961. Although the success or failure of a particular course of action can not be a valid test of whether the organization supporting it is adequate, the ability to develop, plan and initiate programs responding to newly developing problem situations is testimony to effective organization.

20.   **Memorandum From Secretary of Defense McNamara to President Johnson**[1]

Washington, March 14, 1964.

After a review of the currently approved Instructions for Expenditure of Nuclear Weapons in Emergency Conditions, the Joint Chiefs of Staff have recommended approval of redrafted instructions which are in simplified format and which have been updated to make them editorially compatible with the terminology employed in current plans. A copy of these updated instructions was delivered to you during your meeting with the Joint Chiefs of Staff on March 4, 1964.[2]

[1 paragraph (9 lines of source text) not declassified]

You will recall that the instructions currently in use were approved by President Eisenhower on December 3, 1959,[3] and were continued in effect by President Kennedy.

Your approval of the updated instructions is requested together with your authorization to place these instructions in effect.

Robert S. McNamara

---

[1] Source: Johnson Library, National Security File, Subject File, Nuclear Weapons, General, Vol. I, Box 32. Top Secret.

[2] See Documents 16 and 17.

[3] See *Foreign Relations*, 1958–1960, vol. III, p. 353. A copy of the mostly-declassified Eisenhower administration's "Instructions for the Expenditures of Nuclear Weapons in Accordance With the Presidential Authorization Dated May 22, 1957," which contains revisions dated January 28, 1959, November 2, 1959, and May 12, 1960, is available on the Internet, National Security Archive (www.gwu.edu/~nsarchiv), Electronic Briefing Book No. 45, "Eisenhower and Predelegation," Document 3.

21.   Memorandum From the Joint Chiefs of Staff to Secretary of Defense McNamara[1]

JCSM–219–64   Washington, March 16, 1964.

SUBJECT

   Joint Strategic Objectives Plan for FY 1969–1971 (JSOP–69), Part VI—Force Tabs and Analysis (U)

   1. On 14 February 1964, the Chairman, Joint Chiefs of Staff, forwarded Parts I through V of the Joint Strategic Objectives Plan for FY 1969–1971 (JSOP–69) (CM–1181–64). Attached is Part VI, Force Tabulations.[2]

   2. Section A of Part VI contains force objectives and associated rationale in the format of the Five-Year Force Structure and Financial Program, as requested in your memorandum of 21 December 1963 (subject: "Program and Budget Reviews Calendar Year 1964 Schedule").[3] Recommendations of the Joint Chiefs of Staff concerning reserve personnel are provided in Table 13; therefore, Table 12, Army Reserve Components Program, was not addressed. Section B contains force objectives, deployments, expansion, and selected reserve tables in the normal JSOP format. Section C consists of situational analyses which were designed to assist the Joint Chiefs of Staff in their determination of the objective force levels recommended in Sections A and B. Although logistic implications were considered in the situational analyses (see paragraph 5, Section C, Volume II of Part VI), specific logistic guidance will be recommended to you in the Logistic Annex to JSOP–69 on 1 April 1964. The Joint Chiefs of Staff will provide their views on personnel in conjunction with their comments on your tentative decisions on all programs by 15 June 1964, as required by your schedule for Calendar Year 1964. The individual views of the Chief of Staff, US Army, the Chief of Naval Operations, the Chief of Staff, US Air Force, and the Commandant of the Marine Corps are briefly and clearly summarized in the Tables of Section A and footnotes thereto. The rationale associated with these Tables provides additional explanation of these views.

   3. The objective force levels herein are considered essential for national security in support of the US military strategy delineated in Parts I through V, JSOP–69. In considering objective force requirements,

   [1] Source: National Archives and Records Administration, RG 200, Defense Programs and Operations, JSOP—FY 1969–1971, Feb. 14, 1964, Box 41. Top Secret.
   [2] Not attached. Regarding this paper, see Document 12 and footnote 1 thereto.
   [3] A copy is in the Washington National Records Center, OSD Files: FRC 330 69 A 7425, 110.01 FY 66 1964.

the Joint Chiefs of Staff were agreed in many areas as to the degree to which FY 1966 programmed forces meet our basic military objectives. In other areas, however, there exist major unresolved questions and divergencies regarding forces and weapon systems which are reflected in differences in individual and collective force recommendations. As concerns our general war posture, there is the problem of the optimum balance of offensive and defensive means. In connection with our limited war posture, issues exist concerning: force levels; mix of land, sea, and air capabilities; weaponry to be used; rates of modernization; and the use of tactical nuclear weapons and the degree of reliance to be placed on them.

a. *Strategic Retaliatory Forces.* There is agreement that the United States should maintain a clear margin of strategic superiority as a deterrent. A major issue is whether or not the Minuteman force should be increased above the programmed level. This issue stems from differing views concerning relative emphasis as between counterforce, damage-limiting operations, and assured destruction of the enemy as a modern industrial society. A related issue concerns planning factors and the application thereof to translate differing target lists into delivery system requirements. A second major issue is whether an advanced manned strategic aircraft should proceed beyond the program definition phase at this time.

b. *Continental Air and Missile Defense.* The Joint Chiefs of Staff are agreed that programmed force levels do not provide sufficient capability for CONUS defense in the mid-range period against the threat of manned bombers and missiles. They further agree that the defense should be composed of a balance between active and passive defense; a balanced air and missile defense, to include antisubmarine forces; and a proper mix of air defense weapons systems. There are significant differences with respect to the balance and mix and the selection of specific air defense weapons systems. The Joint Chiefs of Staff agree to continue with the development of the Nike X system, as a matter of priority. One issue, however, is whether a decision can be taken now for production and operational deployment, as justified by research and development progress, or whether final selection of a system for defense against ICBMs and SLBMs should be deferred pending evaluation of further research and development and completion of the study now underway regarding the integration of all components affecting the defense of CONUS. They agree that research to pursue other approaches for missile defense should also be emphasized and that development of increased capability against SLBMs must continue, both in antisubmarine and antimissile capabilities. A second issue relates to the IMI— whether to proceed with deployment beginning in FY 1968 with related phase-down of Century series aircraft and their transfer to the Air

National Guard, or to keep open an option to procure the IMI subject to a review of the above study.

c. *General Purpose Forces.* The specific major issues pertaining to General Purpose Forces center on the number of Army divisions, the numbers and concept of employment of attack carriers, concept of employment of Marine Corps forces, and Air Force tactical aircraft required to carry out the strategy in the mid-range period. The individual force level recommendations vary from proposals for significant increases above the program level to those for substantial reductions. Underlying these recommendations are the differing views regarding the levels and mix of forces required to provide, with an acceptable level of risk, the capability to meet the estimated requirements of a separate major contingency operation while maintaining the readiness to reinforce NATO. A matter which makes the problem more complex is the difficulty of forecasting accurately whether or not it would be advantageous for the United States to use tactical nuclear weapons and, if so, the relative effectiveness and timing of their use. The current intensive study being given these questions should assist in the continuing evaluation.

d. *Airlift and Sealift Forces.* The Joint Chiefs of Staff agree that there is a continuing need to improve our airlift and sealift capability in order to permit the rapid deployment of our combat forces. An issue in this regard is whether MSTS troopships should be in active status or are sufficiently responsive when retained in ready reserve. Fundamentally, the basic problem with respect to the levels of these forces is the appropriate balance and mix of sealift and airlift with due consideration being given to selective pre-positioning of supplies and equipment. Continuing studies will assist in better understanding of their relationship.

4. The scenarios used in the situational analyses are illustrative, designed to test alternative degrees and types of response with varying levels of combat and support forces. The conclusions derived are valid to the extent that they provide useful information to the decision-making process. Certain assumptions, which necessarily had to be made, and the concepts and factors used, are critical in the derivation of the forces employed in the postulated situations. Individual comments regarding the limitation and usefulness of the scenarios are included in the footnotes. There are differing views regarding the value of the scenarios for deriving forces. One view holds that the scenarios of Section C, prepared separately from Sections A and B, provided an insufficient and inappropriate basis from which to develop over-all objective force levels. The other view, while recognizing limitations, utilized the situational analyses insofar as practicable as a basis for developing and evaluating the force structures for each program and for quantifying support and logistics requirements.

5. Part VI of this year's JSOP has been prepared with a view to serving as a primary vehicle for providing military advice on force structures, particularly as it applies to the FY 1966 budget. The combatant force objectives contained herein have been derived from consideration of such factors as requirements to support the national objectives and strategy in Parts I–V, the recommendations of the commanders of the unified and specified commands, technical feasibility, levels of military capability established in current programs, and reasonable attainability. However, the Joint Chiefs of Staff desire to emphasize that the force levels recommended beyond the period requiring appropriations in FY 1966 are for planning purposes and require recurring evaluation.

6. The further views of the Chairman, Joint Chiefs of Staff, will be forwarded by separate memorandum.

For the Joint Chiefs of Staff:

Maxwell D. Taylor
Chairman
Joint Chiefs of Staff

---

22. Memorandum From the Chairman of the Joint Chiefs of Staff (Taylor) to Secretary of Defense McNamara[1]

CM–1272–64   Washington, March 20, 1964.

SUBJECT

Joint Strategic Objectives Plan for FY 1969–1971 (JSOP–69), Part VI—Force Tabs and Analysis (U)

1. I have forwarded, by JCSM–219–64, Part VI (Force Tabs and Analysis) to the Joint Strategic Objectives Plan covering the period 1969–971 (JSOP–69).[2] As indicated in Tables 4–13 and the footnotes thereto of Volume I, the Joint Chiefs of Staff did not reach agreement with respect to certain major programs, including Minuteman, the Advanced Manned Strategic Aircraft (AMSA), Nike X, the Improved Manned Interceptor (IMI), Army divisions, Navy aircraft carriers, and Air Force tactical fighter wings.

---

[1] Source: National Archives and Records Administration, RG 200, Defense Programs and Operations, JSOP—FY 1969–1971, Feb. 14, 1964, Box 41. Top Secret.

[2] See Document 21 and footnote 2 thereto.

2. The divergent views of the Joint Chiefs of Staff stem primarily from the same issues as those reviewed last year in JSOP–68,[3] i.e., the extent of counterforce targeting in the future, the optimum balance between strategic offensive and defensive systems, uncertainties as to the effect of tactical nuclear operations on the requirements for general purpose forces, and the rate and extent of modernization of all forces. During the past year, these problems were the subject of additional study, and they were given further consideration in the situational analyses, or scenarios, which comprise Volumes II–V of Part VI, JSOP–69.

3. The scenarios were designed to assist the Joint Chiefs of Staff in their determination of objective force levels. As indicated in the footnotes throughout the analyses, the Service Chiefs have many reservations concerning the assumptions, factors, concepts of employment and conclusions of these analyses. Nevertheless, in my opinion, they have been a valuable asset in bringing additional light to bear on these major issues which all Services are earnestly endeavoring to resolve.

4. After review of the scenario on strategic retaliatory forces, and other studies on this subject during the last year, I am impressed by the uncertainties regarding the value of a more extensive counterforce effort and hence am not convinced as to the need for additional strategic missiles over and above the present program of 1,200 Minutemen.

5. a. Although there are many reservations concerning the scenario on continental air and missile defense forces, I am convinced that the force levels now programmed will not provide adequate CONUS defense in the mid-range period. In looking forward to that period, we are presently faced with a choice, in my opinion, between (1) primary reliance on strategic offensive forces as a means for effecting deterrence or for limiting damage if deterrence fails (without major improvement of defensive means); and (2) a balance of offensive and improved defensive forces which, while also providing for deterrence, will afford the optimum practicable capability for limiting damage. In view of the greater loss of life and productive capacity shown in war games based upon the first choice, I am convinced that it is the second alternative which we should adopt.

b. In order to resolve this issue with understanding, there is an immediate requirement to determine the optimum balance between offensive and defensive systems. Hopefully, the studies now underway in both your office and the Joint Staff will be of assistance in this determination. In the interim, feeling that some requirement will be validated for such programs as Nike X, Phase II SOSUS, and the IMI, I recommend proceeding with these programs in such a way as not to delay

---

[3] Not found.

their time of availability, but without attempting to establish force objectives at this time. Finalization of the optimum total numbers of the various strategic offensive and defensive systems will require prior determination of the optimum balance among the systems involved.

6. a. With respect to the limited war operations considered in the scenarios, a point of particular interest is that upon the outbreak of major hostilities in Europe, we could not continue operations in Southeast Asia beyond a possible holding action employing about four divisions. If, on the other hand, a decision were made to continue the limited war operations with a force of eight divisions as planned in the Southeast Asia scenario, any buildup in Europe, over and above the five divisions now there, would be limited initially to no more than seven divisions for a total of twelve divisions in Western Europe, and this could only be done by transfer of the two divisions from Korea. Further expansion of the US ground force contribution in Europe would have to await the availability of the six Army ready reserve divisions which could not be made combat ready, deployed and committed to battle until sometime during the period M+120–M+180.

b. A second point of importance brought out in the examination of the scenarios is that an apparent imbalance exists between Army combat forces and the associated combat support and logistic support units. These Army support units appear to be the limiting factor in the ability of the United States to respond on the postulated scale and timing to major contingencies.

7. The limited war scenarios also indicate possible deficiencies in logistic support in the form of personnel, supplies and equipment for the operations considered. These deficiencies are being analyzed in greater detail and recommendations regarding additional logistic guidance will be covered in the Logistic Annex to JSOP–69.

8. I concur with the force levels in JSOP–69 which are supported unanimously by the Service Chiefs. With regard to those major programs about which there are divergent opinions, my personal views and recommendations are as follows:

a. Program I—Strategic Retaliatory Forces

(1) *AMSA.* I recommend that the decision with respect to R&D funding in FY 1966 be deferred pending review of the program definition phase.

(2) *Minuteman.* I do not foresee any requirement for increased funding in FY 1966 or increasing Minuteman force levels beyond those programmed for FY 1969, but recognize the requirement for orderly system modernization.

b. Program II—Continental Air and Missile Defense Forces

(1) *IMI.* In my opinion, the numbers and types of air defense environment systems and weapons systems are dependent on the determination of a basic concept for air defense in the mid-range period. I recommend that the decision on a procurement program for the IMI be deferred, but that the necessary funds for a first increment of approximately eighteen aircraft in 1968 be included in the FY 1966 budget pending review of the integrated studies of all components of continental air and missile defense now underway.

(2) *Nike X.* After review of numerous studies during the past year, I am convinced that the deployment of an effective anti-ballistic missile system is an urgent necessity. I recommend, pending completion and review of the integrated continental air and missile defense studies which should develop over-all deployment requirements, that the FY 1966 budget provide for the maximum practicable effort toward completion of development and, if justified by research and development progress in FY 1965, the initiation of production of long lead time items in order to permit initial deployment of approximately 200 missiles (the defense of one area) in FY 1970.

c. Program III—General Purpose Forces

(1) *Army Divisions.* Although an increase over the presently programmed sixteen divisions might be desirable, in my opinion the provision of adequate support in terms of logistic units and supplies for sixteen divisions is more important than the maintenance of more divisions with inadequate support. I recommend the continuation of a force level of sixteen appropriately supported divisions and seven brigades throughout the mid-range period.

(2) *Navy Carriers.* I continue to support the recommendation in your 18 December 1963 memorandum to the President to maintain the present force level of fifteen CVAs through FY 1969, to reduce the force to fourteen in FY 1970, and to thirteen in FY 1972.[4] The total number of carriers should remain at twenty-four with the CVSs increasing from nine to ten in FY 1970 and to eleven in FY 1972.

(3) *Air Force Tactical Fighter Wings.* I recommend continuing the present FY 1968 program of twenty-four wings (1,740 total tactical aircraft) throughout the period FY 1968–1973. I consider this number to

---

[4] Reference is to a draft memorandum from Secretary McNamara to President Johnson, entitled "Attack Carrier (CVA) Forces," December 18, 1963, included in "Department of Defense Draft Memoranda for the President: Recommended FY 1965–1969 Defense Programs," a December 19 compendium of 14 such draft memoranda. (National Archives and Records Administration, RG 218, JCS Files, JMF 7000 (3 Jan 64) Sec 1A)

be in balance with the requirements for the support of sixteen Army divisions and the accomplishment of related air tasks.

9. As reported by JCSM–146–64,[5] the Joint Chiefs of Staff had divergent views concerning the amount of detail which should have been included in the force tabs of JSOP–69. In order to insure the submission by the Joint Chiefs of Staff of the maximum useful advice concerning military forces in future JSOPs, I recommend that, prior to approval of the study being conducted by your staff on restructuring the tables of the Five Year Force Structure and Financial Program, it be forwarded to the Joint Chiefs of Staff for comment.

10. Subject to the comments in paragraph 8 above, I recommend approval of the major elements of the force composition indicated in the tables of Volume I, Part VI to the Joint Strategic Objectives Plan for FY 1969–1971 (JSOP–69). For those elements not covered in the preceding discussion, I will provide my views in the review of PCPs when they are submitted.

Maxwell D. Taylor

---

[5] Not found.

23.   Circular Airgram From the Department of State to All Posts[1]

CA–9837   Washington, March 26, 1964, 2:50 p.m.

SUBJECT

US Policy of Neither Confirming or Denying Presence of Nuclear Weapons on Board US Naval Ships or Aircraft Visiting Foreign Territory

Joint State–Defense Message.

Policy

It is firm US policy neither to confirm nor deny presence nuclear weapons on board any US warship or aircraft seeking entry foreign ports or airports. This policy, based on overriding operational and security considerations, has since 1958 been reaffirmed on several occasions, and remains basic US policy today.

Recent Ceylonese Requirement for Assurances on Nuclear Weapons

Recent action of Ceylonese Govt in issuing Circular Note of January 24, 1964, to diplomatic missions in Colombo,[2] denying entry to its ports or airports to any foreign ship or aircraft without prior assurance that it is not carrying nuclear weapons and is not "equipped for nuclear warfare", has again highlighted need for reaffirmation this policy and complete understanding of it. Stated reason for Ceylonese action is "to oppose further spread of nuclear weapons and to support creation of atom free zones."

Dangers Inherent in Ceylonese Requirement

Danger is that such requirement may offer superficial appeal to certain governments who may adopt it without examining its implications.

---

[1] Source: National Archives and Records Administration, RG 59, Central Files 1964–66, DEF 1 US. Secret. Drafted by Duncan A. D. Mackay (G/PM) on March 25, cleared by Captain Calvert (Navy), Reynolds (USAF/GC), William Lang (DOD/ISA), Captain Bennett (OSD/AE), O'Donnell (AEC), David H. Popper (EUR/RPM), M. Gordon Knox (EUR/BNA), Ellwood M. Rabenold (ARA), Robert B. Wood (FE), Eric E. Oulashin (AF), James P. Grant (NEA), Jeffrey C. Kitchen (G/PM), Jerry C. Trippe (L), Richard N. Gardner (IO), Jeanne Davis (S/S), and Charles Johnson (White House); and approved by U. Alexis Johnson. Also sent to the political advisers at major military commands: CINCEUR, CINCLANT, CINCPAC, CINCSAC, CINCSO, CINCSOUTH, CINCSTRIKE, COMATS, HICOM RYUKYUS, and SHAPE. In a March 25 memorandum to U. Alexis Johnson, Jeffrey Kitchen explained that once the airgram was sent, the Navy would send it "to the four CINC's involved, drawing their attention to it, and requesting their assessment of the countries in which this problem could become sufficiently serious to have our Ambassadors take it up with the Governments concerned." (Johnson Library, National Security File, Subject File, Nuclear Weapons, General, Vol. I, Box 32)

[2] Not found.

We are concerned over possibility that other governments, either as deliberate harassment effort, effort display "neutrality" or perhaps as misguided effort support establishment nuclear free areas, may be considering similar or related actions.

Such action, which the Communists are quick to encourage and take advantage of, would seek to have us divulge the deployment of our nuclear deterrent, divide air and naval forces into black and white (nuclear and non-nuclear) components and seek to embarrass some of our Allies who do not wish to draw attention of their publics to presence of nuclear weapons in their territories.

Possibility It May Become Adopted By Other Countries

Ceylonese requirement of assurances on nuclear weapons has already been strongly endorsed by TASS News Agency, and ChiCom PriMin Chou En Lai joined with Ceylonese Prime Minister in final communiqué February 29[3] at end of visit to Ceylon in exhorting other states take similar action.

There is distinct possibility that Ceylonese requirement may be placed on agenda for Second Non-Aligned Conference in Cairo next September by planning group for conference meeting in Colombo March 23. If expected support for requirement grows, Ceylonese may also later introduce resolution in UNGA calling for adoption by member states in interest halting "spread of nuclear weapons." However, the Dept has no evidence yet that the Ceylonese have this in mind.

Last summer Mexican President Lopez Mateos, in announcing Joint Declaration of five LA states on proposed formation of nuclear free zone, stated that it was Mexican policy to deny national territory for transportation of nuclear weapons (although declaration itself silent on transport of nuclear weapons). GOM, however, is not known to have formalized this policy.

Basis for US Policy

Our policy is based on overriding operational and security considerations. We consider armament of naval ship or aircraft to be an integral part of it and not being "transported" into national territory in sense which Mexico has in mind, or increasing "spread of nuclear weapons" in Ceylonese sense. We cannot accept any requirement that we identify or deny nuclear armament of naval ship or aircraft, for to do so would breach important information regarding extent of our deterrent, and seriously hamper the mobility of the US Forces by dividing them into nuclear and non-nuclear elements. We consider that any con-

---

[3] Not found.

ventional ship or aircraft can be fitted with nuclear weapons and given nuclear delivery capability; and, furthermore, that any ship or aircraft can be "equipped for nuclear warfare" if only to defend itself. We are not prepared give blanket assurance to any government, in order gain approval for port entry of naval ships or landings of military aircraft, that no nuclear weapons are carried or would be carried in the future. We consider that such self-imposed limitation on types of aircraft or ships for which we might wish request port entry or landing right neither realistic or in best interests of US.

If any such assurance or requirement is made a precondition of port entry, we would plan to hold the visit in abeyance, leaving original request outstanding until host government in prepared approve visit without reference to any such requirement.

In connection with any denuclearized zone which may be established, we would consider it important to reserve our right of transit for all naval ships or aircraft without having to identify those armed with nuclear weapons or having nuclear delivery capability.

Consultation with Allies on Problem

We have initiated preliminary informal exchange of views in Dept at staff level with Embassy representatives of UK, Canada, Australia and New Zealand on Ceylonese requirement. We are exploring whether it may be possible find some common approach to problem.

We have advised UK informally that we do not believe that their initial approach to problem is either realistic or helpful. British tactic thus far has been to have informal assurances given by Mountbatten to PriMin Bandaranaike that no British ship (he inadvertently omitted aircraft) carrying nuclear weapons would ever visit Ceylon. Although GOC has permitted one British military transport land without giving such assurances, GOC has categorically informed UK none will be permitted land in future in absence such assurance in each case. The British HiCom has informed GOC that Mountbatten's overall assurances were intended to apply to aircraft as well, and are awaiting clarification from GOC whether UK military aircraft will be able land in future based on Mountbatten's assurances to PriMin Bandaranaike.

Canadians have destroyer visiting Ceylon at end of March during planning meetings in Ceylon for Second Non-Aligned Conference. Since approval for Canadian ship visit given prior issuance Ceylonese requirement on nuclear weapons, Canadians have not had to give assurances and do not intend to do so. Neither Australia or New Zealand have any immediate requirement for visits to Ceylon by naval ships or military aircraft. While both governments fear that refusal furnish Ceylonese with information on nuclear weapons they request will damage their position with non-aligned states, they have indicated interest informally in finding some agreed formula which would be helpful to us.

Dept believes it would be unwise at present to initiate any discussions on this subject which would tend to give Ceylonese requirement undue importance. We do not intend to acknowledge circular note informing us of requirement or to seek "clarification" of it as France apparently has done with respect to the meaning of the phrase "equipped for nuclear warfare". We believe, however, it would be profitable for us to acquaint friendly governments selectively with our position in order to give them basis on which they can decide not adopt Ceylonese requirement. Dept will issue specific instructions in this regard to certain posts once we have received action called for below.

Action Required

Without initiating any discussions on this subject, addressees are requested report soonest (1) any indications that any other governments or local port officials may be considering possible adoption of Ceylonese requirement of assurances of nuclear weapons and (2) any official or press comment on Ceylonese action, particularly degree of support for it.

For USUN—Dept would appreciate report of any indication of intention Ceylonese or other delegation raise this in UN context.

For USRO—Your recommendation is requested on utility of US raising this question for discussion in POLAD meeting with view to obtaining common NATO front.

Rusk

24.   **Memorandum From President Johnson to Secretary of Defense McNamara**[1]

Washington, March 26, 1964.

I accept the recommendation made by you and the Joint Chiefs of Staff in your memorandum of March 14th[2] and hereby authorize you to put into effect the updated "Instructions for Expenditure of Nuclear Weapons in Emergency Conditions" which were brought to me by the Joint Chiefs on March 4, 1964.[3] It is my understanding that the redrafted instructions are basically the same as those approved by President Eisenhower and continued in effect by President Kennedy.

I would like to receive copies of all implementing directives which the Joint Chiefs issue on the basis of these instructions.

I have asked Mr. McGeorge Bundy to discuss with you and Secretary Rusk whether a substantive review of the instructions is needed to ensure that they reflect our coordinated views.[4]

Lyndon B. Johnson[5]

[1] Source: Johnson Library, National Security File, Subject File, Nuclear Weapons, General, Vol. I, Box 32. Top Secret.

[2] Document 20.

[3] See Documents 16 and 17.

[4] In a March 31 note to Secretary Rusk, attached to another copy of his memorandum of March 26, McGeorge Bundy wrote: "The action referred to in paragraph 3 of this memorandum will await the completion of the Joint Staff studies which Secretary McNamara mentioned at a recent luncheon meeting with the President." (National Archives and Records Administration, RG 59, Central Files 1964–66, DEF 12 US)

[5] Printed from a copy that indicates President Johnson signed the original.

25.   Memorandum From the Joint Chiefs of Staff to Secretary of
Defense McNamara[1]

JCSM–260–64   Washington, March 27, 1964.

SUBJECT

Development of Very High-Yield Nuclear Weapons (U)

1. By memorandum, dated 4 March 1964,[2] subject as above, the
Assistant to the Secretary of Defense (Atomic Energy) expressed your
desire for the views and comments, as appropriate, of the Joint Chiefs
of Staff on a draft of a proposed memorandum for the President on
the above subject. The Joint Chiefs of Staff note that while the proposed memorandum would no longer support the recommendation
made in JCSM–117–63, dated 11 February 1963,[3] that the development
of a very high-yield laydown bomb [less than 1 line of source text not
declassified] to be compatible with the B-52 aircraft be initiated immediately, it does not preclude reconsideration of this subject at a later
date.

2. In view of the Limited Nuclear Test Ban Treaty, the Joint Chiefs of
Staff consider the following factors to be pertinent to this decision at this
time:

a. The development, without atmospheric testing, of the proposed
[less than 1 line of source text not declassified] laydown bomb for B-52
delivery would not advance appreciably the nuclear state-of-the-art in
the yield-to-weight ratios.

b. It is too early to know, in detail, what can be accomplished
through the redirection of weapons development effort necessitated by
the restriction against testing in the prohibited environments.
Significant advancement in the development of very high-yield nuclear
weapons may be attainable without atmospheric testing.

c. The effort to be expanded in very high-yield weapons development could be directed toward advancing the state-of-the-art so that
knowledge and new weapon designs are available to permit rapid

---

[1] Source: Washington National Records Center, OSD Files: FRC 330 69 A 7425,
A–471.61 (25 Jan 64). Top Secret; Restricted Data.

[2] Not found.

[3] Not found, but this JCS paper led to a Department of Defense initiative in early
1963 to persuade the Atomic Energy Commission to sign a joint DOD–AEC letter to
President Kennedy proposing the development of a multi-megaton nuclear weapon. AEC
Chairman Glenn Seaborg had reservations about the proposal, however, and prevailed in
having the issue referred first to the White House for thorough study. For background, see
Journal of Glenn T. Seaborg, Chairman, U.S. Atomic Energy Commission, 1961–1971 (Lawrence
Berkeley Laboratory, University of California, 1989), vol. 5, pp. 258, 410, 436, 501, 525.

advancements should the decision be made to resume testing in the prohibited environments.

d. Future large boosters potentially available could provide a capability for delivery of very high-yield warheads. The facilities for missiles such as Atlas F and Titan II conceivably could be modified to accept such large boosters.

3. The Joint Chiefs of Staff conclude that:

a. A [less than 1 line of source text not declassified] weapon should not become for the indefinite future the largest yield weapon available for military application.

b. Although the [less than 1 line of source text not declassified] laydown bomb for the B-52 would have met the recommendations set forth in JCSM–117–63 referred to in paragraph 1, above, the effort and expenditure of resources for its development would be better oriented toward the advancement of the state-of-the-art directed toward the attainment of very high-yield weapons with advanced technology, i.e., [less than 1 line of source text not declassified] and higher yield of aircraft laydown delivery and/or missile delivery.

c. Because of the uncertainties in high-yield weapons effects and in requirements for nuclear weapons during the 1970s, research, experimentation, and testing in the area of very high yields should be conducted by the Atomic Energy Commission to the maximum extent possible within the constraints of the Limited Test Ban Treaty.

d. Development should not be undertaken at this time of a [less than 1 line of source text not declassified] high-yield warhead for present missile systems.

4. The Joint Chiefs of Staff recommend that the draft of the proposed memorandum for the President, as changed by the line-in, line-out rewrite in the Appendix hereto,[4] be submitted as the response to National Security Action Memorandum No. 245.[5]

For the Joint Chiefs of Staff:
Maxwell D. Taylor
Chairman
Joint Chiefs of Staff

---

[4] Not printed.

[5] The study Seaborg requested (see footnote 3 above) was authorized in NSAM No. 245, "High Yield Nuclear Weapons," May 21, 1963. (Johnson Library, National Security File, National Security Action Memoranda, Box 2)

26.   Circular Airgram From the Department of State to Certain Posts[1]

CA–9940   Washington, March 30, 1964, 10:50 a.m.

SUBJECT

    Survey of U.S. Overseas Bases

Joint State/Defense Message. The basic National Security Policy Planning Task Program calls for a re-examination of U.S. base and installation requirements,[2] both military and non-military, over the next five years on a world-wide basis with a view to:

    1. Restricting number and kind to those most urgently needed.
    2. Determining alternate ways of meeting future requirements through exploitation new technology (such as space-borne communications, use of U.S. or U.K-owned islands, establishment floating bases, etc.)
    3. Exploring various ways essential requirements can be met through cooperative arrangements, sharing of facilities, standby agreements, etc.

DOD has been given responsibility for directing re-examination and has established steering committee in Washington under Asst. Sec. Def. for Installations and Logistics.[3] Committee, composed of representatives from State, Joint Staff JCS and DOD (ISA), has developed guidelines and procedures for conduct of examination provided for under part 1, which are outlined in latter part of this message. Committee has also established liaison with other U.S. agencies having facilities abroad for purposes of securing accurate reflection of the interests of and appropriate participation by all such agencies. Parts 2 and 3 of task outlined above will be prosecuted separately, under guidance provided by steering committee.

---

    [1] Source: National Archives and Records Administration, RG 59, Central Files 1964–1966, DEF 15 US. Secret. Drafted by Richard G. Colbert (S/P) and George L. Warren (G/PM) on January 31; cleared by Henry D. Owen (S/P), Howard Meyers (G/PM), Arthur E. Pardee, Jr. (SCI), John J. Conroy and Charles R. Stout (EUR), Richard W. Barrett (O), Thomas P. Dillon (P), James R. Johnstone (FBO), Dillon (USIA), Heath (FAA), William P. Bundy (DOD/ISA), Thomas D. Morris (DOD/I&L), Arnold W. Frutkin and Packard (NASA), Joint Staff (JCS), Captain Muzzey (Coast Guard), David Rowe (S/S); and approved by U. Alexis Johnson. Sent to Ankara, Athens, Bonn, Brussels, London, Madrid, Paris, Rome, The Hague, and USCINCEUR.
    [2] This review, coordinated by the Policy Planning Council, covered 34 subjects. Documentation on the assignments, status, and terms of reference of these tasks is ibid., S/S–NSC Files: Lot 70 D 265, Basic National Security Policy.
    [3] Thomas D. Morris.

As the initial step to carry out part 1 above, a small interagency survey group will proceed to Europe on or about May 6.[4] This group and subsequent groups will conduct an on the ground country by country survey of existing facilities. Local participation in the survey group will be requested as appropriate from local commands and agencies. As shown in following guidelines, primary objective will be recommendations for collocation and consolidation of U.S. facilities where feasible with full consideration local and area political and economic factors.

Italy has been selected as the first country for examination. A timetable for other country surveys will be announced as experience factors are developed.

The survey group, under the general guidance of the Ambassador in each country, will work closely with appropriate military commanders, representatives of U.S. non-defense agencies with facilities in the country under study—i.e., NASA, USIA, FAA, Coast Guard and the diplomatic mission. A physical inspection of selected facilities is anticipated.

To facilitate work of survey group, certain basic data is to be prepared by overseas military commands and by non-military agencies in advance of group's arrival. Data prepared by non-defense agency activities in any country should be solicited and held by the Embassy concerned for the use of the survey group. All military data should be collected as directed by USCINCEUR and held by the senior U.S. commander in the country under survey. Details on the data required and the installations to be reviewed will follow immediately by separate instruction. All data should be completed so as to be available prior to the beginning of the work of the survey group in Rome, Italy on May 11.

To further assure that elements involved in supporting the work of the survey are fully informed of the objectives of this effort, a briefing by the chairman of the steering committee will be held at Camp Des Loges on April 20. USCINCEUR will designate required representation from subordinate commands and a separate message will outline the desired Embassy and non-defense agency representation. Additional briefings will be held in convenient locations as the survey group moves from country to country.

GUIDELINES

I. Objectives

A. To develop an inventory and description of current utilization for all U.S. bases and installations overseas including nature of real

---

[4] Documentation on the European visit of this survey group, as well as later visits by other groups to other regions, is in the National Archives and Records Administration, RG 59, Central Files 1964–66, DEF 15 US, and S/PC Files: Lot 70 D 199, Bases.

property interest, number, kind and cost of personnel, basic and collateral mission of activities, or other prime characteristics determining need for the property.

B. To exploit opportunities for collocating several of the U.S. military Services at the same base or installation (i.e., Army/Air Force or Army/Air Force/Navy, etc.).

C. To determine feasibility and economic desirability of collocation of non-military activities on military installations or military activities on non-military installations.

D. To determine which of the U.S. real property holdings overseas can be released, which can be reduced in size, and which are urgently needed to support current operations or are to be retained in standby.

E. To develop and recommend policy guidelines which contribute to the most efficient and economic utilization of U.S. Government overseas facilities.

F. To examine the local as well as area political and economic implications of any recommended adjustment in the present U.S. base structure in each country surveyed.

II. Policy Assumptions

A. Only those U.S. bases and installations overseas shall be retained that are most urgently needed to support U.S. Government or operations under joint agreements with other countries and all other property holdings shall be released or reduced in size to conform to need.

B. Collocations of activities both military and non-military shall be recommended where dollar savings can be realized and where such relocation does not significantly interfere with the performance of the assigned task or mission or other basic policy considerations.

C. In those cases where U.S. bases or installations are maintained in a standby status or operations are greatly reduced, the facilities shall be utilized on an interim basis where practical to house or otherwise support U.S. activities, both military and non-military. Where economically practical, relocations shall be planned to such installations although the duration may be indefinite.

D. Maximum joint use of facilities will be made with NATO, SEATO and similar alliances with proportionate sharing of construction and operational costs.

E. Maximum utilization shall be made of large multi-purpose bases and installations to obtain effective withdrawal of U.S. activities from urban centers.

F. Relocation of U.S. activities shall be recommended where present location interferes with local expansion or municipal growth.

III. Specific Guidance

A. Headquarters and Administrative Facilities

1. Inspection of headquarters and administrative facilities shall be undertaken with particular interest in vacating leased space involving significant rental payments by the U.S. Government.

2. Maximum utilization of administrative space in major U.S. bases and installations shall be a principal objective to be accomplished through consolidation of like activities or by collocation.

3. Particular care shall be taken to identify the space in facilities vacated as a result of the recently directed reduction in Armed Forces Headquarters operations.

B. Depots

1. Inspections of depot facilities shall include a review of inactive depots to determine their adaptability for other uses.

2. Alternate uses for standby facilities shall be developed for interim utilization.

3. Excess depots shall be noted and recommended for release and disposition.

C. Family Housing

1. Family housing shall be reviewed to determine degree of utilization (present and estimated future), condition, and cost of operation.

2. Leased housing shall receive particular attention with consideration given to rental savings possible from use of U.S.-owned facilities.

3. Family housing available on active and inactive bases and installations shall be noted for possible utilization by relocated activities.

D. Communications

1. Communication facilities shall be reviewed with consideration given to economic and/or technical advantages of relocation, consolidation, substitute facilities, etc.

2. Retention of major properties due entirely to the retention of communication facilities shall be the subject of specific review. Possible relocation to hard core installations shall be explored.

E. Air Bases

Air facilities retained for current or future requirements shall be utilized to the maximum extent possible and alternate uses developed for vacant facilities which may be utilized to satisfy requirements for all U.S. Government activities overseas.

F. Public Affairs Guidance

1. The survey groups from Washington will be limited in numbers and will maintain an inconspicuous presence. There will not be discussions with the host Government at this time. No announcement will be made by Washington or in the field on the mission of the survey groups.

2. In the event questions arise in the individual countries, the survey group should be described as a routine inspection and evaluation of the effectiveness of the U.S. utilization of facilities stating that similar inspections have been held in the past and more can be expected in the future.

G. Diplomatic and Consular Facilities

Insofar as diplomatic and consular facilities are concerned, the steering committee, in advance of the departure from CONUS of the survey group, will coordinate with the FBO to determine if current space utilization of such facilities in the country under survey permits incorporation of miscellaneous needs of other U.S. agencies. Conversely, any additional diplomatic or consular space requirements which might be located in facilities currently administered by other agencies will be made known. This data plus any other supplementary information provided by the Country Team will be made available to the survey group for consideration.

Rusk

27.   Memorandum From the Executive Secretary of the
       Department of State (Read) to the President's Special
       Assistant for National Security Affairs (Bundy)[1]

Washington, April 15, 1964.

SUBJECT

   Audio Surveillance and Countermeasures Problems Within the United States
   Intelligence Community

REFERENCE

   (a) March 20 memo from Mr. Bundy to the Secretary of Defense, Secretary of State,
   and the Attorney General[2]
   (b) March 12 memo on subject to Mr. Bundy by the Acting DCI[3]
   (c) August 14, 1963 report of the NSC Special Committee on Audio Surveillance
   Countermeasures[4]

   In reply to your memorandum of March 20, 1963, appropriate officers of the Department of State have reviewed the referenced Acting
DCI memorandum and the annual NSC Special Committee report.

   1. The Department would first like to comment on the DCI memorandum of March 12 which in part deals with audio countermeasure
activities. The Department's primary role in the field of audio countermeasures is based on the authority and responsibility of the
Department as the major foreign affairs agency of the United States
Government. We are strongly opposed to any change of leadership in
the audio countermeasure community and we object to relinquishing
our role as Chairman of the NSC Special Committee or of any resultant
new committee that may evolve. The Department of State has been the
leader in the U.S. audio countermeasures community since the late
1940's and continues to hold this position today. The Department's
position of leadership in the audio countermeasures field has been
established by the fact that the Office of Security of the Department of
State is responsible for the over-all security of approximately 300 U.S.
diplomatic and consular establishments. The Department of State cannot delegate the authority to guide and coordinate audio countermeasures activities to any other agency in view of the Department's responsibility for the security of the greatest bulk of penetration target areas.

---

   [1]   Source: Johnson Library, National Security File, Intelligence File, Foreign
Intelligence Advisory Board, Vol. 1 [1 of 2], Box 5. Secret.
   [2]   Dated March 20, 1963; not found.
   [3]   Document 18.
   [4]   Not found.

The Department's position is further supported by having in effect the largest number of trained engineers and technicians in the field supported by a major research and development effort under the guidance of experienced engineers. The present Department of State research and development efforts have been in effect since 1961 and these efforts have been successfully translated into operational countermeasure equipments and techniques. A few specific examples of Department of State accomplishments in this area are the acoustic conference room, the panoramic receiver, the signal recognizer system and standardization of a secure telephone system. Further evidence of the Department's leadership in the audio countermeasures field is witnessed by the fact that Department of State security engineers have been responsible for over 95 per cent of all U.S. Government "finds", including six additional microphones and one transmitter discovery since the NSC Special Committee report of August, 1963.

For the same reason [2 *lines of source text not declassified*] the Department of State feels that it must also chair *any* audio countermeasures body in view of the Department's primary role in this field.

Regarding Sections 7(c) and 7(d) of the DCI report, we wish to make the following comments:

(1) Technical Inspections

The question of coordination of "sweeps" or technical inspections as stated in the DCI memorandum does not exist. Clear-cut areas of responsibility for the security of our overseas military and diplomatic missions have been long established. The Office of Security of the Department of State is clearly responsible for the over-all security of all U.S. diplomatic representation and has provided security services to all tenant agencies operating within U.S. diplomatic missions abroad. Security within U.S. military installations is clearly a military responsibility and conflict between military and the Department of State interests does not exist. [4 *lines of source text not declassified*]

The Department of State feels that the coordination of countermeasures equipment requirements are best resolved directly in the committee responsible for the coordination of research and development efforts as provided for in the present NSC Special Committee. A division of the operational elements from the research and development elements of any countermeasures body can serve only to delay translation of these requirements into tangible results. This condition characterizes the confusion and lack of progress of the NSC Special Committee during the initial period of its formation.

It is the Department's opinion, therefore, that the proposal for a new technical subcommittee to coordinate inspection schedules and stimulate requirements has little foundation.

(2) Counter-audio Research and Development

The Department of State is in favor of coordinating countermeasure development, equipment and procedure requirements and believes the present NSC Special Committee on Technical Surveillance Countermeasures has made significant progress in this regard within the last three years. The impetus gained by this Committee in translating these requirements into realistic development objects is, in the opinion of the Department of State, a direct result of (a) the growing awareness of all member agencies of the need for close cooperation in establishing policy and program guidelines, and (b) technically competent and experienced leadership of the Special Committee by the Department of State.

The Department of State recognizes the need for expansion of basic and applied research within the countermeasures field and for greater coordination of this research among the member agencies. The inability of the present NSC Special Committee to achieve greater progress can be attributed to (1) its lack of member representation of a sufficiently high level of individual authority and technical competence and (2) the unavailability of information concerning current U.S. advances in positive audio surveillance equipment and techniques. The offer by the Acting DCI of cooperation in regard to this latter impeding factor is warmly accepted.

The Department of State can see no need for the proposed transfer of the present Special Committee from the NSC to the USIB. Analysis of the Special Committee's structure has not revealed any deficiencies in this body that can be attributed to its relationship with the NSC. However, if such a transfer is determined as being in the best interests of the United States, the Department of State feels that any audio countermeasures body established under the USIB should occupy full committee status. The importance of the efforts of any body concerned with the problem of audio surveillance countermeasures, in view of known existing threats, is of far too major a magnitude to be relegated to subcommittee status.

2. We concur with the recommendations contained in the NSC Special Committee report of August 14, 1963. These recommendations have in fact been enacted during the past three years by the Department of State.

The Department of State feels that the Special Committee's report is both timely and comprehensive in view of present day threats against the security of the U.S. Government. However, the Department considers the list of recommendations generated by the Special Committee lacking in one major respect. Specifically, there is needed a recognition of and an appropriate recommendation for action on the present lack of cooperation and exchange of information between the positive Intelligence and the Counter Surveillance Communities.

The alarm expressed by the Scientific Guidance Panel in Section II-4 of the Guidance Panel's interim report dated August 19, 1963[5] was, in the opinion of the Department of State, not well founded. The Scientific Guidance Panel has not reviewed the Department of State's present countermeasure program with the exception of having received a comprehensive briefing in February, 1964 by the Department of State on the present status of our efforts in resolving the Moscow Signal problem.

Summary

In reply to those recommendations in Sections 7(c) and 7(d) of the DCI memorandum, we submit the following recommendations:

(1) That the present Special Committee be retained under the NSC, or if deemed necessary be established as an independent committee under the USIB.

(2) That membership of a new audio countermeasure coordinating body be limited to technically-qualified representatives from the Department of Justice, the CIA, the Department of State and the DIA.

(3) That the present Technical Subcommittee of the NSC Special Committee be retained as a working technical group with representatives from all U.S. Government agencies having formal technical countermeasure programs in effect.

(4) That the Department of State retain chairmanship of any interagency audio countermeasures body.

John A. McKesson[6]

---

[5] Attached to Document 9.

[6] Printed from a copy that indicates McKesson signed for Read.

28.   Memorandum From the President's Special Assistant for National Security Affairs (Bundy) to President Johnson[1]

Washington, undated.

SUBJECT

High Yield Nuclear Weapons

A year ago President Kennedy requested the Department of Defense and Atomic Energy Commission to re-examine the need for the development of very high yield nuclear weapons—particularly a weapon in the [*less than 1 line of source text not declassified*] category. He also requested a review of the question of developing a high yield warhead to be delivered by presently programmed missile systems.[2]

AEC and DOD have now recommended that we should not proceed with the development of a high yield weapon [*less than 1 line of source text not declassified*] for delivery by a B-52 bomber. The B-52 can now carry two [*less than 1 line of source text not declassified*] bombs, which bombs are already in the stockpile and are compatible with dual carriage in the B-52. There is [*less than 1 line of source text not declassified*] difference in the effectiveness between [*less than 1 line of source text not declassified*] bombs and one [*less than 1 line of source text not declassified*] bomb, and the expense of developing the [*less than 1 line of source text not declassified*] option is not warranted. They have also recommended that we should not develop a high yield warhead for present missiles. The additional expense is not justified by the increase in the capability of these missiles.

The memorandum[3] also recommends that we should continue to conduct a vigorous program of research, experimentation, and underground testing directed toward the advancement of the state-of-the-art to the extent possible under the Limited Test Ban Treaty for the development of very high yield weapons of advanced design in the order of [*less than 1 line of source text not declassified*] or higher. The AEC is already pursuing this research objective without further authorization. The report also recommends that we improve our capability to test such large weapons in the

[1] Source: Johnson Library, National Security File, Memos to the President, McGeorge Bundy, Vol. 3. Top Secret; Restricted Data.

[2] Regarding this review, see footnotes 3 and 5, Document 25.

[3] Reference apparently is to an April 10 memorandum from Deputy Secretary of Defense Vance to President Johnson, which spelled out in some detail the reasons for opposing at that time development of high-yield nuclear weapons. (Washington National Records Center, OSD Files: FRC 330 69 A 7425, A–471.61 (25 Jan 64)) This memorandum incorporated almost all the proposed revisions suggested by the JCS in its Appendix to Document 25.

atmosphere if the Treaty is broken. I believe this recommendation is justified and is consistent with the "safeguards" assurances we have given to the Congress and the terms of the partial test ban treaty.

If you approve, I will send the attached memorandum to Mr. Vance.[4]

McGeorge Bundy[5]

---

[4] Not attached, but printed as Document 29.
[5] Printed from a copy that bears this typed signature.

---

29. Memorandum From the President's Special Assistant for National Security Affairs (Bundy) to the Deputy Secretary of Defense (Vance)[1]

Washington, April 23, 1964.

SUBJECT

High Yield Nuclear Weapons

The President has noted the memorandum[2] reporting the results of the Department of Defense and Atomic Energy Commission re-examination of the need for very high yield nuclear weapons, and concurs in the recommendation of the Department of Defense, in which the Atomic Energy Commission has concurred, that programs should not be initiated at this time for the development of a high yield warhead for our present missiles or high yield bomb for the B-52.

The President has also noted and concurred in the recommendation that the AEC be authorized to carry out certain ground and airborne operations to prepare itself to develop a three-month readiness posture to make tests in the atmosphere of high yield devices if such tests become necessary and are authorized. He has expressed his desire that such tests be conducted in so far as possible without any publicity.

McGeorge Bundy

---

[1] Source: Washington National Records Center, OSD Files: FRC 330 69 A 7425, A-471.61 (25 Jan 64). Top Secret; Restricted Data. Stamped notations indicate that Vance and Howard saw the memorandum. It is also reproduced in sanitized form in Seaborg, *Journal*, vol. 26, p. 245.
[2] See footnote 5, Document 28.

30. National Security Action Memorandum No. 299[1]

Washington, May 12, 1964.

TO

The Secretary of State
The Secretary of Defense
The Chairman, Joint Chiefs of Staff
The Director of Central Intelligence

SUBJECT

Evacuation and Protection of U.S. Citizens in Danger Areas Abroad

The President has rescinded NSC 6019/1 (Evacuation and Protection of U.S. Citizens in Danger Areas Abroad) dated January 2, 1961[2] and has directed that the Secretaries of State and Defense be responsible for carrying out this program.

McGeorge Bundy

---

[1] Source: National Archives and Records Administration, RG 59, S/PC Files: Lot 70 D 199, National Security Action Memos (NSAM). Confidential.

[2] Regarding NSC 6019/1, see *Foreign Relations*, 1958–1960, vol. III, p. 532.

31.   Memorandum From Secretary of Defense McNamara to the
       Secretary of the Navy (Nitze), the Secretary of the Air Force
       (Zuckert), and the Chairman of the Joint Chiefs of Staff
       (Taylor)[1]

                                              Washington, May 16, 1964.

SUBJECT

   Force Guidance for Submission of PCP's on Strategic Retaliatory Forces (U)

REFERENCE

   ASD(C) Memorandum of February 20, 1964[2]

I have completed my review of the Strategic Retaliatory Forces recommended in JSOP–69.[3] This memorandum summarizes my tentative
guidance for the preparation of Program Change Proposals for these
forces. In those cases in which my tentative guidance corresponds with
previously approved forces, my guidance is shown in the Previously
Approved and Tentative Force Guidance (PA&TFG) line; in other cases,
my guidance is shown in the Tentative Force Guidance (TFG) line. In
those cases in which Previously Approved and Tentative Force
Guidance differ, the Services will submit PCP's to implement the latter.

   As I indicated in my Draft Memorandum for the President on
Recommended FY 1965–FY 1969 Strategic Retaliatory Forces, December
6, 1963,[4] I believe that our Strategic Retaliatory Force requirements
should be based on two objectives:

       1. "Assured Destruction." An essential test of the adequacy of our
posture is the assured capability to destroy the Soviet [*1-1/2 lines of
source text not declassified*] after absorbing a well planned and executed
Soviet surprise attack. The purpose of such a capability is to give us a
high degree of confidence that, even under conditions extremely favorable to the Soviets, we can deter a calculated deliberate nuclear attack.
       2. "Damage Limiting." Beyond the force required to meet the test of
"Assured Destruction" additional forces may be justified for counterforce targeting if they could reduce the damage to the U.S. in the event
of a Soviet attack by an amount sufficient to justify their added costs.

   I do not believe that there can be any reasonable doubt about the adequacy of our forces to achieve the first objective. As I showed in last

---

[1] Source: National Archives and Records Administration, RG 200, Defense Programs
and Operations, 1966 Budget Guidance, May–June 1964, Box 41. Top Secret. Three pages
of tables are not printed.

[2] Not found.

[3] Document 12.

[4] For text, see *Foreign Relations*, 1961–1963, vol. VIII, Document 151.

December's Memorandum to the President, referred to above, the approved 1969 Strategic Retaliatory Forces including 1000 Minutemen could be expected to be able to destroy about [1 *line of source text not declassified*] in a second strike after a surprise attack. Even under extremely favorable assumptions from the Soviet viewpoint, which now seem even more unlikely than they did last December, these forces could destroy about [1 *line of source text not declassified*]. Therefore, I believe that the adequacy of our forces, with 1000 Minutemen rather than 1200 for "Assured Destruction" has been established beyond a reasonable doubt.

As for additional Strategic Retaliatory Forces for the "Damage Limiting" objective, it is clear that they must be considered in relation to our other programs intended for the same purpose, e.g., Continental Air and Missile Defenses and Civil Defense. Moreover, to the extent that we buy additional Strategic Retaliatory Forces for "Damage Limiting", they should be justified as part of a balanced program, that is, a program that maximizes the number of lives saved for the amount of money spent. There are several studies under way now in the Department that are examining this matter, including:

1. A Study of Alternative General Nuclear War Postures to be completed by the CJCS Special Studies Group no later than 1 September (SecDef memorandum to CJCS of 9 January 1964).[5]
2. A study plan on Strategic Offensive and Defensive Forces integrating study efforts of the Military Departments and other contributing agencies (DepSecDef multi-addressee memorandum March 12, 1964).[6]

As these studies are completed, I will consider recommendations from the Service Secretaries and the Joint Chiefs of Staff if they believe that revisions of any tentative force guidance are indicated. After I have had an opportunity to review such recommendations and studies themselves, I shall issue revised guidance if necessary.

Minuteman

I question whether it would be a wise use of our resources to include the funds for 100 additional Minutemen in the FY 1966 budget for deployment by end FY 1968, for the following reasons.

1. We are not ready to decide on the deployment of Nike-X and the character and scale of our damage limiting program at this time. There are a number of strategic and technical uncertainties yet to be resolved. Moreover, the timing and Congressional support for the necessary full fallout shelter program is still uncertain.

---

[5] See footnote 7, Document 61.

[6] Not printed. (Washington National Records Center, OSD Files: FRC 330 69 A 7425, 381 Strategic Retaliatory Forces (9 Jan 64) Jan–Jun 64)

2. Moreover, even if we were to go ahead with a full fallout shelter program and deployment of Nike-X beginning in FY 1966, it has not been established that additional Minuteman ICBM's would form a part of a balanced damage limiting program.

3. Furthermore, even if it were established that additional Minutemen were a part of a balanced program that included full fallout protection and a Nike-X deployment, these missiles must be time-phased to match the availability of other damage limiting forces.

4. Finally, because of the Minuteman II retrofit program, we will be continuing production of Minuteman missiles. Therefore, if a larger force is required at a later date, we retain the option to buy it with no loss in lead time or production re-start costs.

Therefore, I request that the Air Force submit a PCP which levels off the Minuteman force at 1000 missiles. I recognize that the previously approved retrofit schedule was designed on the basis of a 1200 rather than a 1000 missile force objective and that therefore, in all probability, it should be modified. I would like the Air Force to reconsider the deployment of Minuteman II in light of this change and to recommend one that is consistent with achieving the ultimate force objective economically.

The previously approved decisions on spare missiles, missile motor shelf life, extended survivability of Wings I and II are unaffected. In addition, missile-away indicator, radio-launch overlay, improved launch enable system, time-on-target and squadron status reporting subsystems approved for RDT&E, production, and retrofit into Wings I–V will be implemented. Initiation of the retrofit of the Minuteman II system could become necessary in the 1972–1973 period because of the shelf life of the system. Studies should continue determining the best follow-on system.

Last year the Air Force proposed the siting of a squadron in a location which would allow peacetime launches under conditions as near as possible to operational reality. A possible location was the Hunter Liggett reservation north of Vandenberg AF Base. The basis for the proposal was to provide actual operational tests of missile, launcher, control systems, human factors, and technical data. It also would provide a control sample from which to determine bias in test launches and control system, and anomalies introduced by and during shipment of missiles from operational sites to Vandenberg missile range. If the Air Force still recommends such a plan, I request that its Minuteman PCP include this siting as an alternative to the basic plan that would not include isolated siting, together with a cost comparison and an evaluation of its cost and effectiveness in relation to such alternatives as an additional flight at Vandenberg AF Base.

B-52

The Joint Chiefs of Staff recommend no change in the B-52 force structure through FY 1970. The phase-down of this force beyond FY

1970 was contingent upon the phase-in of an Advanced Manned Strategic Aircraft proposed by the Air Force.

The issue of the force level is related to the structural integrity of the B-52. Last year the Air Force proposed a comprehensive modification program to correct all known faults of the B-52. At that time, I approved the program for all B-52s except the "B" series. Recently my staff with the cooperation of the Air Force and other agencies has completed a review of the structural problems. It now appears that additional modifications will have to be undertaken to assure the integrity of this force into the '70's.

I have requested that the Secretary of the Air Force provide me with alternative bomber force levels, their effectiveness over the planning period, and the associated costs and schedules for the modification program necessary to sustain these alternatives. These studies will provide a basis for a decision at a later date.

B-58

The Joint Chiefs of Staff show in their proposed force a faster attrition in the B-58 force beginning in FY 1967. Unless there are compelling reasons to show that the quantities of command support aircraft available cannot support the recommended quantities, no change should be made. If a change is required, I request that the Air Force submit an appropriate PCP.

Matériel Acquisition Guidance for Programmed Strategic Bombers

The approved bomber force will carry with them those equipments necessary for redeployment in the event of hostilities. Therefore, prepositioning of stocks of spares, supplies or equipments is not required at other than existing approved squadron deployed locations. Procurement of chaff, tanks and pylons, engines, etc., are required only to support peacetime training and one wartime sortie per bomber.

Advanced Manned Strategic Aircraft (AMSA)

With respect to a follow-on aircraft, the Chiefs of Staff, less the Chief of Staff, Air Force, recommend that we defer a decision on development and procurement programs for AMSA pending review of the program definition phase. The Chief of Staff, Air Force, recommends for planning purposes a force level of 200 aircraft with operational availability of 105 aircraft by end FY 1973.

I support the view of the majority that the decision on the development and procurement be deferred. In addition to any PCP which the Air Force might wish to submit in support of a new strategic bomber development program, separate comprehensive R&D proposals concerning exploratory engine development (not limited to AMSA) and advanced avionics development should be submitted. However, I believe that a decision on deployment would be premature at this time.

Atlas D, E and Titan I

I understand that the Air Force has given serious consideration to the early phase-out of Atlas D and E, and Titan I. I agree that such a plan merits careful attention and request that the Air Force submit a PCP which phases out these missiles by end FY 1965 and Atlas F by end FY 1968.

The Atlas D is configured in a soft, three missile complex and has a slow reaction time. The first missile cannot be launched until fifteen minutes after an execution order; the second missile not before eight minutes later; and the third missile after still eight minutes later. The Atlas E, configured one missile per site, is hardened only to 25 psi and has a reaction time of fifteen minutes. The Titan I is configured three missiles per complex. Theoretically, it is hardened to between 150–200 psi, but the great complexity of the system makes its actual survival potential very uncertain and most probably lower. Moreover, the reaction time of Titan I is also slow—the first missile fifteen minutes after an execution order; the second missile eleven minutes later; and the third missile eleven minutes later, a full 37 minutes later, a full 37 minutes after the order to fire is given. The survival probability of these missiles has been estimated by the JCS to be very low. Since large quantities of Minuteman missiles will be in the inventory, it seems appropriate to phase out these complex and unsatisfactory first generation systems in order to realize cost savings that can be applied to more effective systems. Studies should be initiated which examine the possibility of using the fully hardened silos for other missile systems.

Atlas F procurement beyond FY 1964 is no longer required since Atlas E missiles can be converted into Atlas F missiles with very little modification. In addition, Atlas E assets could also be used for other space booster requirements. Atlas F and Titan II follow-on operational reliability tests are reduced to six firings each per year, as opposed to 12 firings previously approved, bringing the proportion of missiles expended into line with the Minuteman and Polaris test programs.

ICBM Reliability Program

Last year the Services proposed a reliability improvement program consistent with the Joint Chiefs of Staff guidance. We have allocated large numbers of missiles for the operational test firings. To assure continued reliability of our missile systems during their operational deployment lifetime, follow-on operational tests are also programmed. The following quantities of ICBMs are tentatively approved.

Missiles Reqd for Follow- on Reliability Test	End Fiscal Year				
	1966	1967	1968	1969	1970
Atlas F	6	6	3	0	0
Titan II[a]	6	6	6	6	6
Minuteman I	20	55	45	35	25
Minuteman II[a]		20	35	45	55

[a] Requiring continued procurement.

In addition, the previously proposed test program for sea-launched ballistic missiles will continue.

Robert S. McNamara[7]

[7] Printed from a copy that indicates McNamara signed the original.

---

32. Intelligence Note From the Director of the Bureau of Intelligence and Research (Hughes) to Acting Secretary of State Ball[1]

Washington, June 1, 1964.

SUBJECT

Khrushchev on Reconnaissance Satellites

Twice in two weeks Khrushchev has raised the subject of satellite reconnaissance in conversations with Americans—Drew Pearson and Senator Benton. The Soviet Premier probably has two things in mind. First and most immediate, to maximize pressure on the US to cease overflights of Cuba; second, over time to gain acceptance for the idea that satellite reconnaissance obviates the need for extensive disarmament controls.

Cuban Overflights. In both the Pearson and Benton conversations Khrushchev raised the subject of satellite reconnaissance in the context of threatening to shoot down a U-2. As Khrushchev described them, the flights were not only increasingly dangerous but unnecessary, a point similar to Castro's May Day argument that the U-2 flights were unnecessary because the US had reconnaissance satellites.

[1] Source: Johnson Library, National Security File, Charles E. Johnson Files, Reconnaissance Satellites. Secret.

Argument Against Disarmament Controls. Although the current emphasis is on Cuba, the idea that satellites obviate the need for disarmament controls appears to have been in Khrushchev's mind longer. On July 8, 1963 Khrushchev raised the subject in a conversation with Belgian Foreign Minister Spaak, arguing that satellites made aerial inspection unnecessary for a European arms control system. Since then the argument has been taken up by lower-ranking Soviet officials, for example by Viktor Karpov of the Soviet Embassy here.

Legitimacy of Satellite Reconnaissance. Like Khrushchev's May 1960 suggestion in Paris that he would not have objected to US use of a satellite instead of a U-2, Khrushchev's statements to Spaak, Pearson, and Benton all suggest that Moscow is seeking to legitimize satellite reconnaissance.

The degree of Soviet acceptance to date of satellite reconnaissance should not be overstressed, however. For example, in the UN Outer Space Committee the Soviets have been willing to forego discussion of the subject but they have not made explicit statements accepting the practice. Moreover, the Soviet media have not published Khrushchev's remarks, Adzhubei's boast in Helsinki last September about Soviet pictures of New York and Castro's May Day statement. Moscow is also apparently reluctant to suggest to the home audience that the Soviet Union is vulnerable to American surveillance.

Next Moves. Khrushchev's semi-public references to reconnaissance satellites could reflect his intention to pursue more formal discussions in this field. He could formally put to the US the proposition on Cuba he has put informally to Pearson and Benton. More broadly, he could seek to inject new momentum into old disarmament debates by formally proposing use of satellites instead of traditional forms of inspection.

For the moment, however, we would expect Khrushchev to continue his semi-public remarks to foreigners: they avoid formally accepting US satellite programs as legitimate while showing Khrushchev as seeking a way out of a crisis over Cuba. At the same time they permit him to make threats about the Cuban overflights without putting them formally on the record. He may be calculating that he can with his present tactics maneuver the US into a position where it must choose between three relatively awkward alternative responses: (1) it could remain silent and appear adamant in face of his "reasonable" suggestion; (2) it could agree with his arguments and stop the U-2s; or (3) it could counter his simple proposition with a complex technical, and possibly revealing, argument about the limitations of satellite photography.

If Khrushchev finds that his tactics backfire—i.e. that the US welcomes his acceptance of the legitimacy of satellite photography but continues flying the U-2s—it would become more likely that he would make a formal, high-level approach to us to get us to substitute satellites for U-2s.

33.   Letter From the Director of the White House Office of
        Emergency Planning (McDermott) to Secretary of State
        Rusk[1]

Washington, June 17, 1964.

Dear Mr. Secretary:

I recently submitted to The President a report about the progress
that has been made on the Supply-Requirements Study for Nuclear War
and Reconstruction that is currently being carried out by the Office of
Emergency Planning in cooperation with a number of Federal agencies,
including the Department of State.[2] On June 4, 1964, the Honorable
Walter Jenkins, Special Assistant to the President, wrote me that "The
President has asked to be kept advised periodically of your progress,"
and added that "Because of the obvious need for nuclear war objectives
to provide guidance for stockpile policy, the participating Federal agencies should give high priority to this work." A copy of Mr. Jenkins'
memorandum is enclosed.[3]

The Department of State, under guidance issued by the Office of
Emergency Planning, is contributing to this study through the development of estimates covering the supply of and requirements for various
major resources following a nuclear attack on the United States. The study
was explained at a special meeting of the Interdepartmental Emergency
Planning Committee on October 1, 1963.[4] Since that date, all departments
and agencies having either resource or claimant responsibilities for specific materials, products, or services during emergency periods have been
conducting detailed evaluations in their assigned areas.

The results of the study will be invaluable in our planning for the
postattack recovery of the nation, *and will provide the basis for setting
nuclear war stockpile objectives.* Our present stockpile objectives are based
on supply-requirements studies reflecting the needs of a conventional
war. We are currently being urged, both by members of the Congress
and representatives of industry, to develop stockpile objectives which
will meet the needs of nuclear war and reconstruction.

---

[1] Source: National Archives and Records Administration, RG 59, Central Files
1964–66, DEF 1–2 US. No classification marking. An attached June 26 note from Marion
A. Baldwin (S/S–S) to William E. Knepper (S) requested approval of an attached draft letter from G. Griffith Johnson to McDermott, as a reply to McDermott's letter to the
Secretary. A "yes" is handwritten in the margin of Baldwin's note.
[2] The progress report has not been found. Regarding what apparently is the final
report, see footnote 4, Document 44.
[3] Attached but not printed.
[4] Not further identified.

I would appreciate your informing the individuals in your agency that are engaged in this study of its importance and of the necessity for ensuring that no unjustifiable delays prevent its completion as soon as possible. In this connection, I would also appreciate having you bring a copy of Mr. Jenkins' memorandum to their attention.

Sincerely,

Ed

---

34.   Memorandum Prepared in the Central Intelligence Agency[1]

No. 1391/64   Washington, June 18, 1964.

SUBJECT

The Soviet Reconnaissance Satellite Program

A Soviet military reconnaissance satellite program appears to be well under way with possibly as many as 12 flights since 1962. The program uses recoverable vehicles launched from Tyuratam under the mantle of the Cosmos series. The camera system, providing an estimated resolution between 10 and 30 feet, probably is carried in the 10,400-pound Vostok vehicle. The program is expensive, possibly costing as much as 500 to 700 million dollars so far, and places added demands on resources available for Soviet space programs. A requirement for precise targeting information on US targets, not obtainable through other collection means, seems to be the primary reason for the program. Also, Soviet collection of other military intelligence on the US could be usefully supplemented by satellite photography. Khrushchev's open acknowledgments of the program have been aimed at stopping U-2 flights over Cuba, but also imply a desire for a tacit understanding on reconnaissance satellites. The existence of the Soviet program tends to reduce the likelihood of a Soviet attempt to attack a US satellite.

1. We have concluded that the Soviet military reconnaissance satellite program may have involved as many as 12 flights since 1962. The evidence is convincing that these were military reconnaissance satel-

---

[1] Source: Johnson Library, National Security File, Subject File, Space, Outer, Vol. II, 5/1– , Box 37. Secret. Prepared jointly in the Directorate of Science and Technology and the Directorate of Intelligence.

lites, although they may have had additional missions. Their launch times and orbits were ideally suited for reconnaissance coverage of the US during daylight hours, the payload was recovered, they were earth oriented and stabilized within the requirements of a sophisticated camera system, and telemetry from them reflected payload activity like that of a reconnaissance photographic payload.

2. A study of the 16 Cosmos satellites successfully launched from Tyuratam between 26 April 1962 and 10 June 1964 leads us to believe that four of them were military reconnaissance satellites, eight others probably were, and four probably were not.

3. We cannot make a firm judgment on the quality of the Soviet reconnaissance photography with the limited data now available. On the basis of what we know about Soviet optical competence and film technology and the operational characteristics of these satellites, we estimate that the camera system could provide resolution between 10 and 30 feet. Telemetry from some of the Cosmos satellites suggests that they employed three framing cameras plus an indexing camera.

4. Moscow has held that the purpose of the Cosmos series, which began in March 1962, was to collect scientific data. It became clear, however, that different types of vehicles were being launched from two different rangeheads, Kapustin Yar and Tyuratam, and the characteristics of the 14 satellites successfully orbited from Kapustin Yar rule out a reconnaissance mission.

5. The 16 successful Cosmos operations from Tyuratam which we have examined are believed to have used the basic 10,400-pound Vostok vehicle, with the possible exception of Cosmos 22 and 30. All were recovered in the Soviet Union three to ten days after launching. The most recent in the series, Cosmos 32, had an inclination of 51 degrees to the equator, while all previous Tyuratam Cosmos satellites had inclinations of 65 degrees. This change suggests that the Soviets are improving their reconnaissance program because the inclination of Cosmos 32 permitted greater coverage of the US each day.

6. The series launched from Tyuratam may have had other missions in addition to photographic reconnaissance. The presence of a small radiation package aboard most vehicles is one example of such a secondary mission. Four meteorological satellites in the series transmitted cloud pictures from orbit but this photography was not of military reconnaissance quality. Two of these could also have provided geodetic mapping data. Other research work probably is involved, such as development of lunar and planetary mapping.

7. We have identified most of the Tyuratam satellites as military reconnaissance vehicles on the basis of detailed examination of all their

known characteristics. Among the indicators of a reconnaissance mission, we note the following:

a. *Orbital elements:* With the exception of Cosmos 4 and 9, the apogees, perigees, and orbital periods of these satellites were ideally suited for reconnaissance and were not completely compatible with any other mission. (see Table 1 and Figure 1)[2]

b. *Launch times:* All Tyuratam Cosmos vehicles have been launched during a time which assured daylight conditions on the ground on all south to north passes over the Northern Hemisphere. (see Figures 2 and 3)

c. *Payload recovery and mission lifetime:* Each vehicle stays up at least until it begins to retrace the same ground area, and the payloads are recovered.

d. *Weather factors:* Preliminary analysis suggests that launch dates have coincided with generally clear weather over the United States.

e. *Orientation and stabilization:* The vehicles are earth oriented and stabilized about three axes with the rate of vehicle motion—.01 to .02 degrees per second—held within the requirements of a sophisticated camera system.

f. *Ground command activity:* The ground command system, which is capable of handling at least 240 different commands, is the kind which would be needed to support present and future reconnaissance satellite requirements. The Cosmos satellites so far are known to have employed at least twenty different commands involving three different ground stations in the USSR.

g. *Telemetry data recorded during payload activity:* Every one of these satellites stored data during certain times of interest when the vehicle was not over the Soviet Union, and subsequently played it back when over Soviet ground stations. We have determined after analyzing this activity that stabilization corrections were made during the early recording period, and that after the vehicle was stabilized, operation of payload mechanisms began. At no time during the payload operation was any attitude correction applied. The way in which the four mechanisms observed on Cosmos 20 functioned was consistent with the operation of a small indexing camera and three higher resolution cameras. (see Figure 3)

h. *Soviet statements:* Khrushchev himself has alluded to Soviet satellite reconnaissance on several occasions. In 1963, he told Belgian Foreign Minister Spaak that the Soviets were engaged in photographing the United States and that he could produce the photographs to prove

---

[2] Neither the table nor any of the figures is printed.

it. Former Senator Benton also quoted Khrushchev as saying, during their recent meeting in Moscow, that Soviet space cameras have filmed US military installations.[3]

8. If we are correct in concluding that most of the Cosmos satellites launched from Tyuratam have a reconnaissance mission, it would seem that Moscow is devoting a substantial share of its space effort to the collection of military intelligence. According to preliminary estimates based on the costs of US scientific satellites, the cost of Tyuratam Cosmos operations to date may have amounted to the equivalent of about 700 million to one billion dollars, roughly 20 percent of total expenditures estimated for all observed Soviet space programs. As a rough proportion of this estimate, the costs of a military reconnaissance program including the 12 satellites launched so far would be on the order of 500 to 700 million dollars.

9. Also important is the additional strain imposed on the human and material resources available for Soviet space programs by the demands of a reconnaissance program.

10. We believe that the USSR has made this large investment primarily for missile targeting purposes. Strategic missile systems require precise information on the geodetic relationship of the target to the launch point, particularly in the case of hardened targets. The precise targeting information needed on the hundreds of targets in the US is only obtainable by satellite photography. The resolution we estimate the Soviets can achieve—10 to 30 feet—would be sufficient to obtain such targeting information when combined with other geodetic mapping data.

11. Despite the USSR's comparatively easy access to much information on military weapons and installations in the US it has requirements for military reconnaissance satellites beyond those for targeting data.

a. Supplementary intelligence on trends in the organization, deployment, and strengths of US strategic missile, long-range bomber, and naval carrier forces could be gained through satellite photography.

b. The USSR also has a requirement for high resolution photography—five feet or better—for technical analysis of classified US installations only accessible to overhead reconnaissance.

c. The Soviets probably have a requirement for a reconnaissance system capable of transmitting photos while in flight. Such a system could provide intelligence on movements of US strategic forces during crisis and wartime situations, and on results of wartime strikes.

12. In view of Soviet activity in the reconnaissance satellite field, Moscow may be more tolerant of similar US programs than it has been

---

[3] See Document 32.

in the past. Khrushchev's recent open acknowledgment of both US and Soviet efforts tends to bear this out. Although his immediate objective in these remarks has been to secure a cessation of U-2 flights over Cuba, they suggest a desire on his part for a tacit understanding with the US on reconnaissance satellites.

13. We believe that the Soviets intend to develop an antisatellite capability. We have no evidence of such a development, but they may develop a limited capability at an early date so as to be able to retaliate if the US should interfere with a Soviet satellite. In our view, however, the existence of a Soviet reconnaissance satellite program tends to reduce the likelihood of a Soviet attempt to destroy or neutralize a US satellite.

---

35. Memorandum From President Johnson to Secretary of Defense McNamara[1]

Washington, June 18, 1964.

SUBJECT

FY 1966 Nuclear Weapons Production and Stockpile

I approve the proposed Nuclear Weapons Stockpile for the end of FY 1966 submitted to me by the Department of Defense and Atomic Energy Commission on December 19, 1963 (as subsequently amended by the joint memorandum by the Department of Defense and Bureau of the Budget on May 29, 1964).[2]

Accordingly, I approve a total of [*number not declassified*] complete nuclear weapons ([*number not declassified*] nuclear warhead elements) as the stockpile composition for the end of FY 1966. I also approve a total of [*number not declassified*] complete nuclear weapons ([*number not declassified*] nuclear warhead elements) as the adjusted stockpile composition for the end of FY 1965. This will mean a planned production by the Atomic Energy Commission of [*number not declassified*] complete weapons and a planned retirement of [*number not declassified*] complete weapons during FY 1966.

---

[1] Source: Washington National Records Center, OSD Files: FRC 330 69 A 7425, A–400.23 (6 Mar 64). Top Secret; Restricted Data. A stamped notation, dated July 13, indicates that McNamara saw the memorandum.

[2] Neither found.

I authorize you, in coordination with the Atomic Energy Commission, to make such minor changes (±10%) within the production total of [number not declassified] complete weapons for FY 1965 as may be necessary to adjust production schedules to meet AEC material availabilities. I further authorize you to make minor changes (±10%) in any line item or collective total that may be required because of adjusted delivery system assets or changes in strategic, tactical, air defense, or antisubmarine warfare concepts. Any changes indicative of a major shift in defense policy or AEC production capability will be submitted for my approval.

Lyndon B. Johnson

36.　　**Letter From the Chairman of the Joint Chiefs of Staff (Taylor) to Secretary of Defense McNamara**[1]

Washington, July 1, 1964.

Dear Mr. Secretary:

With more warning of my departure from the arena of the Joint Chiefs of Staff,[2] I would probably be leaving with fewer regrets over the unfinished business which I must leave behind. Given the circumstances of my reassignment, I have been unable to complete or even expedite work in many of the important areas where I had hoped to make a contribution during my terminal years of military service. The purpose of this letter is to note and comment upon some (but clearly not all) of the important issues which are still unresolved.

a. The effectiveness of the Joint Staff.

In spite of the many able and dedicated officers who serve on the Joint Staff, I leave it with a feeling that it is still marginally effective. It continues to be hampered by an uneven and sometimes excessively heavy workload, by cramped working conditions, and by inadequate

---

[1] Source: Washington National Records Center, McNamara Files: FRC 330 71 A 3470, Joint Chiefs of Staff, Folder 17. Secret; Personal & Confidential. "Sec Def has seen" is stamped on the letter.

[2] General Taylor was appointed Ambassador to Vietnam on July 1.

recognition of its members by their Service of origin. While some progress has been made in giving greater incisiveness to Joint Staff papers and in preserving the integrity of the Joint Staff input from distortion by Service views, there is still an inherent slowness in the Joint Staff operations which often affects adversely the timeliness of the views of the Joint Chiefs of Staff and thus dulls their impact. An excessive concern over Service representation among the incumbents of the various key posts is another factor which works against continuity of assignment and flexibility in the use of Joint Staff personnel. Finally, the Services are still not putting their best people on the Joint Staff—not always. These factors in combination work against its effectiveness and require correction. J-1 has this whole field presently under study and will, I hope, come forward soon with constructive suggestions.

b. *Proportionate distribution of assignments by Service.*

I mentioned the disadvantage of the current practice of distributing important jobs in the Joint Staff rigidly by service. I am opposed to this practice in principle in filling any and all important posts within the Department of Defense. While we should follow the general policy of roughly proportionate Service sharing of participation in the important functions of the Department, we should not accept a strait-jacket policy which prevents choosing the best man for the job regardless of Service. I would favor calling for nominations from all Services to fill all important positions and then endeavor to pick the best qualified man from among the nominees. In the long run, I do not believe this practice would work against an adequate and fair representation of all the Services in the key billets within the Department of Defense.

c. *The readiness of contingency plans.*

In working on the Cuba and Southeast Asia plans, I have been impressed by the incompleteness of our past contingency planning. With the exception of these two plans which have lately received a great deal of special attention, our other contingency plans are little more than outlines which could not be expanded for implementation other than on a "crash" basis without months of additional staff work both in the field and in the Joint Chiefs of Staff. As I leave the Joint Staff, it is not yet clear whether CINCPAC's 32 series can be supported without considerable mobilization and within an acceptable time frame. Once these CINCPAC plans are put in order, the same kind of treatment should be accorded all of the contingency plans which have a reasonable possibility of implementation.

d. *Inadequacy of Army support units.*

From this examination of contingency plans, it is becoming quite clear that the force structure of the Army is out of balance. There are insufficient support type units to permit the deployment of the combat forces as they become ready for commitment to action. The implementation of virtually any contingency plan will require some mobilization, if not to meet the needs of the immediate contingency then to replace units deployed from CONUS reserves. There are three alternatives open to us; either (a) to increase the size of the regular Army to permit the formation of the missing support units, or (b) to reduce the combat structure to a proper balance with the existing support structure, or (c) to accept the fact that partial mobilization will be indispensable in any contingency situation.

e. Need for rational logistic guidance.

A further byproduct of the study of contingency plans is a growing recognition of the need for rational logistic guidance to assure the combat readiness of the forces required to execute the approved strategy. We should re-read paragraph 40, Part IV, JSOP–69,[3] and decide whether or not we really mean the language contained therein. If we do, we should then formulate the logistic guidance which will permit the creation, maintenance, and combat support of the general purpose forces described therein. General Meyer has considerable work in progress directed toward this end. He needs full support to carry it forward to completion.

f. New SIOP guidance.

[1 paragraph (10-1/2 lines of source text) not declassified]

g. Army–Air Force relations.

I regret to report that the relations between the Army and Air Force in Washington have not improved—indeed, I believe that they are worse than when I arrived on my present tour of duty. We are paying the price today of unsound and incomplete decisions and uncoordinated doctrine developed over past years. The immediate need is for the approval of a statement differentiating between organic Army aviation and that Air Force aviation provided in support of the Army. I have made a recommendation to you on this subject with which you are familiar. The second requirement is to make clear that sustained land combat is the primary function of the Army to which the Air Force is in a supporting relationship. The Army commanders responsible for conducting sustained land combat must always have available under their operational control that indispensable element of air power necessary for the success of the land battle. If necessary, the attachment of Air

---

[3] See Document 12. Part IV is not printed.

Force units should be made without hesitation. If such procedures are not adopted, I would consider an overhaul of the statement of roles and missions to be indispensable.

h. Review of roles and missions.

With regard to the possible requirement for a review of roles and missions, I would point out that the last statement of roles and missions was effected in 1947 and was based largely upon the capabilities of the Services at that time. Since then, there have been many changes in weapons, in warfare, and in the capabilities of the Services so that a review would appear to be timely. When it takes place, specific consideration should be given to the desirability and feasibility of the following adjustments of roles and missions:

(1) Assumption by the Air Force of the provision of all air vehicles for the Army in accordance with CSAFM–408–64 dated 12 May 1964,[4] provided to you on that date.
(2) Assumption by the Army of the close air support responsibilities now assigned to the Air Force.
(3) The assignment of the Army role in continental air defense to the Air Force.
(4) Restatement of the mission of the Marine Corps in consistence with present capabilities and probable employment in contingencies.
(5) Placing of all or part of Marine aircraft aboard Navy carriers.
(6) Elimination of equipment now organic within various units of the Services which is subject to intermittent rather than habitual use and the pooling thereof at another echelon.

To resolve such questions as the foregoing in a temperate atmosphere will be difficult. However, until it is accomplished there will be a continuing struggle among the Services over missions and parts of missions which presently overlap agreed frontiers.

i. Civilian-military relationships in the Pentagon.

During my service as Chairman, I have worked to the best of my ability to attenuate or, if possible, to eliminate the differences—sometimes real, sometimes imaginary—between the civilian and military authorities in the Department of Defense. I hope that our own personal relationship of which I have been very proud has set an example for those around us and has contributed to proper team play. Inevitably, however, there are areas of potential friction where there is an overlap or gray zone of common interest between subordinate elements of DOD. Insofar as the business of the JCS is concerned, it is the Comptroller's office and ISA which by the nature of their duties are

---

[4] Not found.

most likely to impinge upon the responsibilities of the Joint Chiefs of Staff. While informal discussions have tended in the past to remove most of the abrasive corners, there are still potential difficulties arising from the fatal attraction which some of our civilians find in military planning. To cite a recent example, I suggest a look at DEF 975264 to Vientiane.[5] I feel that it is very important for ISA and the Systems Analysis area of the Comptroller's office to understand that they are not in the business of military planning and are not a rival source of military advice in competition with the Joint Chiefs of Staff.

In closing, let me say what a pleasure it has been to have been associated with you in the last year and nine months. In my former unhappy days as Chief of Staff of the Army, I cried out for a decisive Secretary of Defense to end the unending conflicts. I got one and am now content. If you will only stay with your present job and not allow yourself to be diverted to other tasks, I have no concern over the soundness of the future policies and programs of the Department of Defense.

Sincerely yours,

Maxwell D. Taylor

---

[5] Not found.

---

37.   **Memorandum From the Deputy Secretary of Defense (Vance) to the Chairman of the Joint Chiefs of Staff (Wheeler)[1]**

Washington, July 10, 1964.

SUBJECT

FY 1966 Nuclear Weapons Stockpile (U)

On 18 June 1964 the President approved the Proposed FY 1966 Nuclear Weapons Stockpile submitted jointly by the Department of Defense and Atomic Energy Commission on 19 December 1963[2] (as later amended to show the retirement in FY 1966 of all Atlas D warheads remaining in inventory).

---

[1] Source: Washington National Records Center, OSD Files: FRC 330 69 A 7425, A–400.23 (6 Mar 64). Top Secret; Restricted Data; Special Clearance Required.

[2] See Document 35.

Accordingly, the President approved a total of [*number not declassified*] nuclear weapons ([*number not declassified*] nuclear warhead elements) as the stockpile composition for the end of FY 1966. The President also approved a total of [*number not declassified*] complete nuclear weapons ([*number not declassified*] nuclear warhead elements) as the adjusted stockpile composition for the end of FY 1965. This will mean a planned production by the Atomic Energy Commission of [*number not declassified*] complete weapons ([*number not declassified*] warhead elements) and a planned retirement of [*number not declassified*] complete weapons ([*number not declassified*] warhead elements) during FY 1966.

The President has authorized the Department of Defense, in coordination with the Atomic Energy Commission, to make such minor changes (±10%) within the production total of [*number not declassified*] complete weapons for FY 1966 as may be necessary to adjust production schedules to meet AEC material availabilities. The President further authorized the Department of Defense to make minor changes (±10%) in any line item or collective total that may be required because of adjusted delivery system assets or changes in strategic, tactical, air defense or anti-submarine warfare concepts. The President directed that any changes indicative of a major shift in defense policy or AEC production capability will be submitted to him for his approval.

Subsequent to the submission of the Proposed FY 1966 Nuclear Weapon Stockpile decisions were made within the DoD which would affect some of the pegpoints set forth therein. These decisions should now be confirmed and appropriate adjustments made to the pegpoints under the authority granted by the President. The adjusted pegpoints are identified in the inclosure[3] and are hereby approved, together with minor adjustments to inventory objectives for AEC weapons overbuild and non-nuclear components for FY 1965 and FY 1966.

Cyrus Vance[4]

---

[3] Entitled "Adjusted Weapons Overbuild for Quality Assurance Program;" not printed.

[4] Printed from a copy that indicates Vance signed the orginal.

38.   Memorandum From Secretary of Defense McNamara to
       President Johnson[1]

Washington, July 18, 1964.

SUBJECT

Release of Nuclear Weapons to National Guard Air Defense Units

The Joint Chiefs of Staff have recommended that authority be dele-
gated to the Commander in Chief, Continental Air Defense Command
(CINCONAD) and the Commander in Chief, Pacific (CINCPAC) to
release nuclear air defense weapons to National Guard air defense units
under their operational control prior to their federalization in surprise
attack situations or upon the declaration of Defense Condition 1 or Air
Defense Emergency. Further, the JCS have recommended that CIN-
CONAD and CINCPAC be authorized to redelegate this authority to
their designated representatives. The foregoing release of nuclear
weapons from federal custody would be effected only in accordance
with approved emergency action procedures, rules of engagement, and
applicable safety rules.

National Guard units constitute a significant proportion of the
forces available in the Continental United States (CONUS) and Hawaii
for the air defense mission. The National Guard forces available to the
Commander in Chief, North American Air Defense Command are
shown on a comparative basis as follows:

a. Of the total of 130 Nike Hercules batteries within the Continental
United States, 28 are now Army National Guard (ARNG) and an additional 20 are to be transferred from the U.S. Army to the ARNG by 1 July
1965. None of the ARNG Nike Hercules batteries (in being or programmed) is located in Alaska.

b. Of the total of 61 fighter-interceptor squadrons within the
Continental United States, 24 are Air National Guard (ANG) squadrons.
Seventeen (17) of the 24 ANG squadrons are, or are programmed to be,
nuclear capable. None of the ANG squadrons is located in Alaska.

c. Air defense forces in the State of Hawaii consist of one ANG
F-102 squadron, which is programmed for a nuclear capability in late
1964, and six ARNG batteries of Nike Hercules. All of the air defense
capability in Hawaii, with the exception of Naval air defense on ships
at Pearl Harbor, are National Guard units.

---

[1] Source: Johnson Library, National Security File, Agency File, Department of
Defense, Vol. II, 12/64, Box 12. Top Secret.

Under existing authority, [3 *lines of source text not declassified*]. In such circumstances there would be no opportunity for the immediate federalization of NG air defense units. The full realization of the air defense potential of NG units, under operational control of JCS Commanders, is precluded at present unless arrangements are made whereby nuclear air defense weapons can be released to these forces under emergency conditions for use prior to their call to federal active duty.

Appropriate arrangements have been made between Continental Air Defense, Pacific Command component Commanders and the appropriate state authorities to place the majority of national guard air defense units under the operational control of CINCONAD/CINCNORAD and CINCPAC. These units are to be made available for participation in active air defense missions prior to federalization. Similar arrangements are contemplated for all National Guard air defense units.

The advantages of nuclear weapons over conventional weapons are:

a. The kill probabilities for single aircraft are considerably higher with nuclear weapons.

b. Nuclear weapons provide an effective deterrent against mass bomber attack.

c. Weapon kill of enemy nuclear weapons in bomber aircraft is significantly enhanced by the use of nuclear air defense weapons.

In an examination of this proposal to release nuclear air defense weapons to National Guard air defense units, the following considerations are relevant:

a. *Present Alert Status of Army and National Guard Units*

(1) Periodically (now about one-third of the time) the Army National Guard Nike Hercules units, manned by National Guardsmen employed by the State on a full time basis and paid from federal funds, maintain the same alert status (15 minutes) as maintained by active Army Nike Hercules units. With the exception that nuclear warheads cannot be released to them until they are federalized, the National Guard units are capable of responding in an emergency on a basis similar to that of the active Army.

(2) The time for National Guard Nike Hercules units to achieve readiness to launch is 15 minutes (for those units in the 15 minute alert status). However, this time is contingent upon weapon release authority being granted within the first five minutes. The readiness preparation would be suspended at that point (ten minutes prior to achieving a readiness to fire) because the warhead cannot be placed in the proper configuration until it is released from custody.

(3) The Air Force maintains nine aircrews on federal active duty in each Air National Guard air defense squadron. Two of these crews are on five minute alert and two are on one hour alert. The other five aircrews on federal active duty are in a crew rest status. The aircrews of the squadron which are not on federal active duty cannot participate in nuclear air defense operations under present arrangements until they have been federalized and the squadron has been notified of the federalization.

b. *Time Required for Federalization*

The time required for federalization of National Guard air defense units has not been specifically war gamed or tested. The Joint Staff has estimated that it could be accomplished quickly, within six to ten minutes after receipt of BMEWS warning. However, there is no assurance that federalization will be accomplished on this time schedule or even within the estimated 15 minute period of time between receipt of warning and missile impact. If federalization were not accomplished prior to arrival of weapons on CONUS targets, conditions subsequent to the attack might preclude federalization for a matter of hours or days.

c. *Time Lapse Between USSR Aircraft Detection to Penetration Over the Location Indicated*

Alaska (Northern Border)—about 30 minutes

Alaska (Anchorage area)—about 1-1/3 hours

U.S.-Canadian border—about 3 hours

(Times are based on Bison/Badger speed of .8 mach at 40,000 feet)

d. *Time Lapse Between USSR Aircraft Detection and Launch of Defensive Aircraft*

This would depend upon an evaluation of the specific tactical situation and instructions issued at the time. It could be as soon as possible (about 5–10 minutes) for the purpose of deploying aircraft forward from CONUS and establishing combat air patrols at designated locations over Canadian air space.

e. *Commanders [less than 1 line of source text not declassified]*

CINCONAD	1
CONAD REGION CMDRS	6
CINCPAC	1
CINCPACAF	1
CMDR HAWAIIAN AIR DEF DIVISION	1
	10

f. *The Sequential Steps that an Air Defense Commander Takes in Going to a Nuclear Defense Mission*

CINCONAD

[3 paragraphs (8 lines of source text) not declassified][2]

CONAD Region Commanders

[1 paragraph (8 lines of source text) not declassified]

(1) Establish Air Defense Warning [less than 1 line of source text not declassified]

[1 paragraph (3 lines of source text) not declassified]

(3) Immediately advise CINCONAD of action taken.

[1 paragraph (1-1/2 lines of source text) not declassified]

g. *Variations in Attack Strategy/Loss of Communications*

[12 paragraphs (48 lines of source text) not declassified]

Robert S. McNamara

---

[2] In the event of surprise attack with no time for consultation as contemplated in 2 above, CINCONAD can [3 lines of source text not declassified]. Region Commanders would conduct air defense missions as directed by CINCONAD/CINCNORAD. [Footnote in the source text.]

---

39. Memorandum for the Record by Director of Central Intelligence McCone[1]

Washington, July 24, 1964.

SUBJECT

Meeting with the President—11:15 a.m., 24 July 1964

[Here follows discussion of item 1.]

2. I then reviewed orally the results of recent satellite reconnaissance photography and advised the President that what we were seeing was a dynamic developmental program in ICBMs, which had brought three new missiles into being in the last two years. We did not know what the three missiles were for but we believed that they could deliv-

---

[1] Source: Central Intelligence Agency, DCI (McCone) Files, Memo for the Record, 7/9/64–10/10/64, Box 2. Top Secret. Attached but not printed are McCone's briefing notes prepared for this meeting.

er [*less than 1 line of source text not declassified*] warheads. This did not seem to explain this very expensive program satisfactorily to me. They might be experimenting with multiple warheads, each of which would have its own guidance. If they were successful with such a development it might possibly redress the present balance of numbers. I said we saw continued expansion of nuclear materials production and no cutbacks. Some of the expansion did not seem to be associated with earlier policy decisions and hence I questioned the veracity of Khrushchev's statements concerning the cutback. I said he may shut down two reactors, but they would be obsolete designs and new reactors were under construction.

[Here follows discussion of items 3 and 4.]

5. I asked the President if he was receiving satisfactory intelligence reports and he said, yes he was very satisfied. I said I would like the opportunity to sit down with him occasionally to exchange views on matters of importance to him, that he had in the CIA the most competent group of intelligence experts and analysts that existed anywhere in the world and that he was not getting the full benefit of their views and judgments through the written word. I said that any time that his calendar would permit and he was so disposed, I would like to discuss personally with him any problems of interest to him which were within our competence. I took this occasion to tell the President that in my experience in many departments in government and in industry I had never encountered as high level of competence or intellectual capability as I found in the CIA.

Note: I left a copy of OCI's memorandum on de Gaulle's speech[2] with Mr. Valenti for guidance for the President's press conference.[3]

---

[2] On July 23 de Gaulle said, among other things, that "the powers which directly or indirectly bear a responsibility in what was or is the fate of Indochina and which are France, China, the Soviet Union and America, be effectively resolved to be involved there no longer." For extracts, see *American Foreign Policy: Current Documents, 1964,* pp. 977–978. The OCI memorandum has not been found.

[3] At his press conference on the afternoon of July 24, President Johnson made only perfunctory remarks in response to a question about de Gaulle's July 23 statement. For text, see *Public Papers of the Presidents of the United States: Lyndon B. Johnson, 1963–64,* p. 889.

40.   Memorandum for the Record[1]

Washington, July 31, 1964.

SUBJECT

Meeting of the President and the Joint Chiefs of Staff, 31 July 1964

The following were present at the meeting:

President Johnson
General Wheeler
General Johnson
Admiral McDonald
General LeMay
General Greene
Major General Clifton

1. Prior to the meeting, the Chiefs went out with the President and were photographed together in a formal picture on the steps and later on the grass with the White House as background.

2. General Wheeler opened the meeting with a briefing on High Heels III, which will take place Sept. 7–28, the preliminary phase of it taking place Sept. 7–20, in which the situation is developed. This exercise, which is a command post exercise involving senior government officials, somewhat coincides with a NATO exercise called Fallex 64 and a NATO naval exercise called Teamwork. In High Heels on September 21, certain Soviet moves are made which precipitate action and consultation on our part; and finally on Sept. 24 the Joint Chiefs of Staff and the Secretary of Defense and the Secretary of State displace to the National Military Command Post afloat which will be just off Annapolis.

The Joint Chiefs of Staff requested that the President participate with them, leaving the White House by helicopter about 8 a.m. and arriving at Annapolis at 8:20, returning to the White House no later than noon. They want his participation because it will give him a chance to supervise the command and control functions that would be used in an emergency.

The President said he would like to do anything the Joint Chiefs of Staff wanted him to do but that they must think about this in the atmosphere of the campaign, that there are aspects of this, in spite of the public relations preparation for it, that could be misinterpreted.

On the international scene, he also pointed out that it could precipitate a certain amount of uneasiness and even drastic action unless it were very carefully explained that this is a normal exercise which is held regularly

---

[1] Source: Johnson Library, National Security File, Agency File, JCS, Filed by the LBJ Library, Box 29. No classification marking. Drafted by Clifton.

and that other Presidents have participated in similar ones. The President made it clear that even in spite of their best public relations efforts, certain people would draw certain conclusions that would not be beneficial.

The President directed the Joint Chiefs of Staff to give this careful consideration, outline the public relations approach they would choose and consult with Secretary McNamara, then come back to him with a further recommendation.

General Wheeler pointed out that there could be some positive results from this participation in that people would know that in spite of the preoccupation with the campaign, the President was still vitally concerned with his obligations as President and Commander-in-Chief.

The President directed General Clifton to mention this to Mr. Valenti and if possible to make sure that this was programmed into the President's schedule on that date so that if he finally decided to do it we will be available.

[Here follows discussion of unrelated topics.]

C.V.C.

---

41.   Memorandum From Charles E. Johnson of the National Security Council Staff to the President's Special Assistant for National Security Affairs (Bundy)[1]

Washington, July 31, 1964.

SUBJECT

Satellite Reconnaissance

On the initiative of the State Department, the "Alex Johnson Working Group" since early June has been developing recommendations for future courses of action in light of probable Soviet knowledge of and attitude toward photographic satellite reconnaissance and our long-range policy objectives relating to the best exploitation of our satellite reconnaissance capabilities.[2]

---

[1] Source: Johnson Library, National Security File, Charles E. Johnson Files, Reconnaissance Satellites, Box 11. Top Secret.

[2] Two memoranda from U. Alexis Johnson to members of this interagency committee, June 2 and undated, describe some of the workings of the committee. (Ibid.)

Among various courses of action discussed was the early briefing of the North Atlantic Council on the U.S. and Soviet satellite reconnaissance programs. It is fair to say that most of the working group favored this course of action and the result was a draft briefing document that appeared to satisfy all the members of the group (although the CIA representatives made it clear that they could not guarantee a favorable response from the Director).

Subsequent to the last meeting of the group Mr. McCone informed Ambassador Thompson that he could not, for security reasons, agree to a briefing of the North Atlantic Council and indicated his intention of personally briefing the heads of State in October as an alternative to the NAC briefing. His proposed briefing reportedly is much less complete than the proposed draft for NAC and contains little that has not appeared in the press.

Ambassador Thompson informed Secretary Rusk of Mr. McCone's position and found that the Secretary agreed with Mr. McCone reportedly for "political reasons" that the NAC should not be briefed at this time.

The specific reasons behind Mr. McCone's and the Secretary's position are not clear and Spurg Keeny and I are of the opinion that the decision on this matter should be reviewed by the President because of its extremely important foreign policy and domestic political implications.

For your background, here are some of the pertinent considerations that prompted Alex Johnson to initiate this exercise in the first place:

(1) The public knowledge of our reconnaissance satellite capability has been steadily increasing. Last December Howard Simons printed a feature article in the *Post* that compromised the general capability although, of course, the extent to which we use the capability and how refined it is is still highly secret and closely protected by CIA. Other publications have carried pieces similar to Simon's.

(2) Khrushchev's remarks to William Benton and Drew Pearson indicated an awareness and knowledge of our capability.[3] Although this has done a great deal to legitimize satellite reconnaissance, Soviet intentions here are not yet clear. The State Department is concerned with the possibility that the Soviets may be pushing the question to attack the need for aerial reconnaissance of Cuba.

(3) The principal objective of the Alex Johnson group (and of U.S. policy), which was to work toward achieving legality and international support for the use of satellites for space observation and photography, has largely been achieved and the principal remaining task for U.S. pol-

---

[3] See Document 32.

icy is a tactical one of exploiting the capability to our national advantage without jeopardizing essential security aspects of the program.

(4) Our intelligence community agrees that we can no longer assume that the top Soviet policy makers are ignorant of the U.S. capability or that Soviet technicians cannot soon, if they have not already, achieve a close estimate of the true U.S. observation capability.

(5) The U.S. capability has been basic in the thinking underlying our principal arms control and disarmament proposals. Certain of these proposals would not be advanced or negotiated unless we could depend on the continued existence of satellite reconnaissance. If our disarmament policies become subject to partisan political attack, it might be difficult to defend them without revealing the assurances we gain from satellite reconnaissance in the absence of other satisfactory inspection arrangements. Similarly, satellite reconnaissance underlies much of our military planning for the defense of Europe and the deployment of U.S. forces in connection therewith. This also might enter into the political debates over the next few months.

(6) The NAC has already, through our bilateral arrangements, largely obtained the end results of our reconnaissance program. The only thing they have not received has been an integrated presentation concerning our reconnaissance program, indicating how extensive it is, something of its technique, a comparison with the Soviet observation program, specific analysis of satellites in relation to Cuba, and the relationship of reconnaissance satellites to military defense and arms control and disarmament programs. The working group felt that such an integrated briefing was needed to bring our Allies up to date and to provide them with an organized body of information instead of the bits and pieces they now have. It would also be an interim step in the ultimate releasing of increasing amounts of knowledge concerning the U.S. program—since many on the working group feel that disclosure will be inevitable in any case and therefore it should be planned rather than capricious or accidental.

Charles E. Johnson[4]

---

[4] Printed from a copy that bears this typed signature.

42.   Memorandum From Director of Central Intelligence
McCone to the President's Special Assistant for National
Security Affairs (Bundy)

Washington, August 5, 1964.

[Source: Johnson Library, National Security File, Intelligence File, Foreign Intelligence Advisory Board, Vol. 2 [3 of 4], Box 6. Secret. 3 pages of source text not declassified.]

43.   Paper Prepared by the Joint Chiefs of Staff[1]

Washington, undated.

JOINT STRATEGIC OBJECTIVES PLAN FOR
FY 1970–1974 (JSOP–70) (U)

Part I—Purpose

1. *Time Period.* This Plan covers the mid-range period beginning on 1 July 1969 (M-Day) and extends for five years thereafter.

2. *Purpose.* The purpose of the Joint Strategic Objectives Plan for FY 1970–1974 (JSOP–70) is to translate national objectives and policies into military objectives, to prescribe strategic concepts for the employment of forces, to define basic undertakings to achieve these objectives and concepts, and to provide:

a. Information to commanders of unified and specified commands, and planning and program guidance to the military services, for the mid-range period under conditions of cold, limited, and general war.

b. The Secretary of Defense with military advice for the development of the FY 1967 budget, justification for departmental FY 1967 pro-

---

[1] Source: National Archives and Records Administration, RG 218, JCS Files, 3130 (15 July 64) Sec 1. Top Secret. Although the paper is undated, the bottoms of several pages are marked "Revised" followed by one of the following dates: July 21, July 22, and August 5, 1964. The paper is attached to a covering report by the J-5 to the Joint Chiefs of Staff. This report is dated July 15, but contains revised and corrected pages, dated August 5 and 11, that reflect the decisions of the JCS at their August 5 meeting. Also attached are a distribution list and table of contents.

gram objectives as they pertain to major combatant forces, and a reassessment of military aspects of the previously approved annual increment of the Department of Defense Five-Year Force Structure and Financial Program.

c. Intelligence estimates of potential enemy capabilities, including capabilities of communist satellite countries, and estimates of future force levels of selected Free World countries, for use in the development of military strategy for the attainment of national objectives during the mid-range period; and planning guidance which will provide a basis for the development and accomplishment of intelligence support commensurate with planning, operational, and strategic concepts.

d. Logistic planning guidance as a basis for the development of Service logistic plans and programs to support JSOP objective force levels.

e. General nuclear weapon planning guidance and nuclear weapons damage considerations.

f. Planning guidance for the conduct of counter-insurgency, unconventional, and psychological warfare.

g. Planning guidance for the development, control, and use of chemical, biological, and radiological materials.

h. Planning guidance for the development of requirements for appropriate maps, charts, and geodetic analyses.

i. Communications and electronics planning guidance to support the strategy and basic undertakings of the plan.

j. An estimate of strategically desirable and reasonably attainable force objectives for Free World allied countries as the military basis for the establishment of a US position with respect to military assistance, and for the development and review of NATO and other allied mid-range plans; and a military estimate of the minimum country forces (Force Guidelines) to achieve US objectives in nonaligned Free World countries.

k. Advice and assistance on research and development matters by preparing statements of:

(1) Broad strategic guidance to be used in the preparation of an integrated Department of Defense program;
(2) Broad military capabilities desired; and
(3) The military importance of these development activities which are essential to support the strategic concept, the military objectives, and the needs of the commanders of unified and specified commands.

l. Planning guidance for command and control systems in support of military operations and administration.

m. Planning guidance for development and employment of space systems in support of military objectives, strategy, and basic undertakings.

Part II—Strategic Appraisal

1. *General.* This appraisal summarizes the world situation likely to affect warfare, military strategies, and the global balance of military power from the present through FY 1974. It contains a brief analysis of the communist threat and probable trends in the world situation which affect the security, objectives, and stability of the United States and other Free World nations. More detailed information is contained in the Intelligence Annex (Annex A).[2] While advances in science and technology will continue to affect the development of weapons and conduct of warfare during the period, the major powers and other technologically advanced nations will continue efforts to reduce their vulnerability to attack, to protect and improve their military forces, and to improve their relative technological, political, and economic postures. For factors influencing specific technological developments during the period of the plan, see appropriate annexes.

2. *Development of the World Situation.*

a. The world situation will continue to be influenced by (1) the struggle between communist nations on the one hand and the free societies and other nations who share similar interests on the other; (2) the struggle of newly emergent and underdeveloped nations for self-determination, increased international status and influence, and a greater share of the world's material wealth; (3) the conflicts of interests and traditional rivalries between nations and ethnic groups; (4) the internal struggles within Free World nations which tend to move them away from Free World orientation; and (5) varying degrees of discord.

b. The Soviet Bloc will increase pressures on the Free World as opportunities present themselves, and will relax pressures when it is to its advantage to do so. Any signs of US or Allied weakness in critical situations will intensify Soviet tactics aimed at achieving advantages; the employment of communist military power will remain a constant threat. The Asian communists will seize every opportunity to undermine US standing; when they judge that circumstances permit, and attendant risks are acceptable, they will supplement political warfare with organized and externally directed and supported guerrilla action by indigenous forces, as well as by higher intensity military action. Communist China and the Soviet Union, individually and possibly in

---

[2] A footnote to a list of Annexes A–N in the table of contents indicates that the annexes would be published and forwarded separately. They have not been found.

concert, will continue to instigate and support what they term "wars of liberation," with the aim of weakening the position of the West and establishing communist-oriented governments. Means used to support dissidents will probably range from political and economic assistance to providing military equipment, training, and advisors. Other communist nations and communist parties in the Free World nations, with the support and encouragement of the Soviet Union and/or Communist China, will attempt increasingly to embarrass and harass the United States and nations of the Western Alliance. The Soviet and ChiCom estimates of relative US-Soviet-Communist Chinese strength and their evaluation of Western reactions to Sino or Soviet probes will be equally important to their decision as to the courses of action to pursue.

c. Both the Soviet Union and the United States can be expected to continue their advocacy of general and complete disarmament, but basic differences continue to block any substantive agreement. Disarmament conferences, along the lines of the current Eighteen Nation Disarmament Conference, will in all probability continue. Recognizing that agreement on a comprehensive general and complete disarmament treaty cannot be achieved in the foreseeable future, both East and West are expected to continue to seek agreement on separable, more limited measures following the precedent established by the Limited Test Ban Treaty, the "Hot Line" Agreement, and the UN resolution prohibiting the orbiting of weapons of mass destruction in space. A major bar to the adoption of substantive proposals has been the unwillingness of the USSR to agree to adequate verification measures necessitating inspection on or over Soviet territory. There is little possibility that the USSR's position on verification will make possible major disarmament agreements during the period of this plan. A basic objective of Soviet disarmament policy has been, and is expected to continue to be, elimination of the nuclear threat at the outset of disarmament without materially reducing the preponderant conventional capability of the USSR. As long as the Soviets hold to this position, any substantive disarmament agreement would be possible only at the expense of United States nuclear superiority. Unilateral measures coincident with fulfillment of military requirements or budgetary considerations are expected to be announced by both sides from time to time for their political impact as steps toward peace, and in the hope that the announcement will stimulate a similar response by the other side. Such measures might include shut-down of fissionable material production, destruction of obsolescent equipment, and total or selected cessation of weapon system production. Each side may seek propaganda advantages by selecting measures which the other side will find politically difficult or undesirable to implement. The pace, nature, and scope of arms control and disarmament measures during the period will be dependent largely upon the economic burden of armaments, concern over stability of the world balance of power, emergence of nuclear capable third powers, and the mutual desire to reduce the risk of nuclear war by accident, miscalculation, or surprise attack. In any case, it is possible that—in order both to achieve stabilization and to meet world pressures for reducing the danger of war—the two sides will undertake tacit agreements resulting in some degree of arms limitation.

d. During the period of this plan the neutralists will fall into different degrees of neutrality and on many issues will tend to have conflicting positions among themselves. Nevertheless, the aggregate effect of neutralism favors the communists because the latent fear of the aggressive policies of the communist nations leads neutralists to condone communist actions which they would condemn in the West. It is probable that the period will be marked by an intense East-West struggle to attain degrees of influence over the neutralists. Thus neutralism frequently will prolong existing tensions or create new ones. If the present trend toward neutralism of some nations which are currently Western oriented is not reversed, it will become so strong that during the period of this plan it may draw nations away from the West. This development might come about through revolutions in countries such as Iran or South Vietnam with seizure of power by neutralist forces, through decisions by existing regimes in quest of the supposed benefits of neutralism, or through loss of confidence in the ability and/or willingness of the United States to support them and safeguard their sovereignties. The neutralist posture of some of these countries may produce serious security problems for the United States. Aside from the possibility of their withdrawing from Western alliances and of their efforts to balance Western with Soviet or Chinese influence, there will be continual pressures imposed on the United States for economic aid and political support; denunciations of colonialism; concessions on disarmament; and withdrawal from positions of predominance or influence. Pure neutralism, as a principle, is fundamentally incompatible with the Soviet objective of complete world domination. Nevertheless, neutralism will provide the communists with greater opportunities for penetration and subversion. Particularly in the new states, the communists will energetically foster neutralist leanings and seize upon rivalries among nations and tribes, upon the need for economic and technical aid, and upon the naivete and weaknesses of inexperienced leaders. They will thus increasingly attempt to capitalize on the fact that when a previously pro-West nation becomes neutralist, it symbolizes a defeat for the West. This provides the communists with more direct opportunities to subject these neutralist nations to new pressures and inducements.

e. Khrushchev, Mao Tse-Tung, de Gaulle, Chiang-kai-Shek, Ho Chi Minh, Franco, Salazar, and Tito are all in their 70's. The personality of each one plays an exceedingly important role in the policy formulation of the government which he leads. It can be conservatively assumed that by 1976 at least half of these leaders will have disappeared from the world scene, and others may no longer be involved in the effective control of the government in their nation. In each country there are elements desirous of changing the patterns of governmental authority. Thus, the departure or fall from power of these leaders may be marked by internal struggles for power, adjustments in national objectives and tactics, and changes in international relations.

f. Newly emergent nations will continue to be characterized by extreme nationalism, internal dissension, instability in political and economic institutions, and a tendency to concentrate disproportionately on external affairs to assert their independence and bid for world status. Political, military, social, and economic vulnerabilities will offer the communists opportunities, at relatively minor risk, for supporting subversive insurgency, for political, psychological and economic exploitation, including restrictive trade agreements, and for the supply of arms and technicians. It is expected that many new nations will identify themselves with revolutionary and "anti-imperialistic" causes. However, Free World assistance, disenchantment with Soviet and ChiCom forms of assistance, and the political, economic, military and cultural ties between former colonial powers and their former colonies will tend to counter communist efforts. Success of Western efforts to prevent a communist alignment among these new nations will depend largely upon the methods, resoluteness, and initiative displayed by Free World nations in combating communist subversion and persuasion. Full communist control of a nation, once established, is unlikely to end except through introduction of outside military assistance or forces. The communists will continue to employ threats and alternating belligerency and tractability in the attempt to gain advantage. They will continue to use to their advantage the United Nations Organization and impede peacekeeping arrangements, unless it serves their purposes to do otherwise.

g. The Sino-Soviet dispute will probably continue to have its ups and downs, and in certain circumstances relations between the two states might improve considerably. However, the rift is so deep and the national interest of each party so heavily engaged that there is now virtually no chance of reconciliation under the present leaders. The international movement may now be on the eve of a formal split, but whether or not this step is taken, the bitter struggle for control and influence over the Communist parties will continue. Further tension in state relations between China and the USSR also seems likely, especially on the common frontier. The demise of either or both of the present leaders would offer some prospect of temporary amelioration of the dispute, but it is believed that the fundamental differences between the two powers would remain.

h. The international communist movement as a whole is likely to be characterized by increased dispersion of authority and by more independent conduct by various parties. Although Soviet power remains a major factor in Eastern Europe, further manifestations of autonomous and nationalist behavior will probably occur. Among world-wide communist parties a trend toward regionalism is foreseen in the Far East, and perhaps in Western Europe and Latin America. The Sino-Soviet competition for influence will in some cases lead to further splits within individual parties. At the same time the USSR and Communist China will remain powerful sources of material support for their respective followers, and will retain considerable operational influence. For the noncommunist world this situation offers important advantages and some dangers. The assertion of divergent national interests by communist powers offers an opportunity for the West to deal profitably with some of them individually. The Sino-Soviet conflict increasingly is absorbing the energies of the USSR and Communist China and diverting them from sharp contentions with the major Western powers. Among the non-governing communist parties, a few have already suffered severe setbacks as a result of the conflict. On the other hand, some communist parties will become more effective and will gain greater freedom of action and respectability because of their more independent status. While in some countries the parties will tend to lose their rationale and elan, in others they will probably emerge as more formidable revolutionary organizations, though more national than international in character. Regardless of internal quarrels, Communists will retain an underlying enmity toward the West if only because their convictions are in so many respects incompatible with traditional Western concepts of political and economic life.

i. Technological and scientific advancement is expected to continue at a rapid pace within the Soviet Union. Soviet propaganda will capitalize on any success such as those in space and will cite any significant advance as proof of the superiority of the communist system.

j. In economic strength, the United States is presently well ahead of other countries. The Common Market area and Japan will continue to show impressive economic gains although some slowing of the rate of economic growth is expected. The quality, diversity and technological level of production in Communist China, although improving, will remain considerably below that of Japan, the USSR and the industrial nations of the West. Soviet Bloc policy will continue to emphasize growth and expansion of the bases of national power. Bloc economic planning will include continued maintenance of great military strength, continued efforts to enlarge its penetration of world markets, and expansion of trade and aid programs to selected underdeveloped countries and prospective satellites.

k. The socio-politico-economic bases of the USSR and Communist China will continue to contain inherent though slow-acting weaknesses potentially vulnerable to exploitation by the United States and its allies.

l. The period under review may witness various changes directly influencing the future of NATO. Critics of NATO will be increasingly active, seeking and examining alternatives to the present concepts, organization, and power relationships in the Alliance. New national leaders will undoubtedly emerge, perhaps bringing new policies and proposals. Future developments within the Common Market (EEC) will have implications for NATO. Such questions as independent nuclear capability and nuclear sharing are issues which will present complex problems within the Alliance. France can be expected to continue to press forward her concepts of regional groupings of "independent national forces," while nevertheless continuing assurances of wartime support of the Alliance. West Germany is likely to continue her efforts to establish bilateral, logistical and other arrangements with various nations, and may seek to reduce remaining treaty restrictions on armaments imposed by the Western European Union (WEU). Problems of defense arising out of member-nations' military commitments outside of the NATO area may place a strain on NATO's force levels. Individual nations will no doubt exercise an increased freedom of action and there may be changes in the present NATO Treaty arrangements. Within the NATO area, current trends suggest the development of European policies less responsive to US leadership. Similarly, there may be criticisms or agitation for changes in other Alliances of which the United States is a member. The continuing strength and cohesion of US military alliances will depend to a large degree upon the ability of the United States to recognize and cope with the divisive forces threatening our mutual security arrangements.

m. Yugoslavia will continue to take positions on many matters which coincide with those of the USSR and which give considerable support to the Bloc; it will not abandon its basic policy of nonalignment. Yugoslavia is unlikely to become a member of the Warsaw Pact and would probably seek to remain nonbelligerent in any East-West confrontation.

n. Sweden and Finland are expected to maintain their present nonalignment. Spain, while continuing to desire closer ties with NATO, will be preoccupied with internal problems, particularly with regard to raising the level of its economy.

o. *Trends.* There are certain discernible world trends affecting the development of strategy. Although the evolution of these trends cannot be predicted with precision, the United States must be aware of them and give them appropriate consideration. Among these trends are the following:

(1) Many independent actions by current allies and newly emerging nations may induce modifications to policies and posture. Changes in the communist policies and power alignments may have equal and probably greater impact on the world situation. The Soviet and Chinese Communist split will probably continue, and the European satellites will continue to have a greater measure of latitude in their own management. The Mao Tse-Tung–Ho Chi Minh–Che Guevara concepts of the "wars of national liberation" will continue to be exploited in rural peasant societies all over the world. In Cuba, in North Vietnam, in Algeria, this concept has been successful. In many countries in Latin America, Africa, and in Southeast Asia, the communists can be expected to continue their efforts.

(2) There will be continuing pressure towards neutralization in Southeast Asia, which, should it occur, would present an inevitable opportunity for communist acquisition of power in that part of the world.

(3) Control of world events probably will become more diffused with a proliferation of centers of influence, with possible unexpected turns. Cuba will continue to be a Latin American political influence, even though militarily confined and economically weak. France, Communist China, and Egypt will continue to exert influence in their respective spheres. Africans are groping toward some kind of cohesiveness, and, if successful, may exert some common influence on world issues.

(4) The rate of development during the period of this plan of the latent power potential of India and Communist China and their relationships with Japan will be critical factors in the future of Asia. If these states grow in influence in relation to their potential, and, although unlikely, if either or both achieve an economic and political accommodation with Japan, Asia may develop an international political system that is less dependent on the West. The relative influence of the United States and the USSR may thus decrease correspondingly.

(5) The shift to polycentrism will be at the tolerance of the United States and the USSR. The world power structure may contain several centers of political power, but at the same time will remain largely bipolar in terms of military power. Many of these new, and militarily weak, centers of influence will be vulnerable to internal communist subversion or internal instability.

(6) The nature of the communist threat has altered; it is now becoming more diffused and world-wide. Continued failure of some Allies to

meet force goals, the inability to reach agreement on new strategic concepts, and the trend toward national control of forces, are significant indications that the current NATO military concept will continue to have diminished acceptability. US military concepts should take into account:

(a) the increased European potential to defend itself conventionally and to support European interests world-wide when these are threatened;

(b) the continued European reliance on the US nuclear arsenal along with the lesser capabilities of Great Britain and France; and

(c) the continued reliance on the cohesive common link of maritime communications.

(7) The emergence of new nations and the rehabilitation of old ones, all with a high emotional content of nationalism, probably will mean a continuation rather than a diminishment of US overseas base problems. Exceptions to this would include such places where the continued presence of US forces is needed to serve the national interests of the countries concerned or of the governments now in power in those countries. An overseas base will be tolerable to the host country only to the extent that the interests of the host and tenant coincide.

(8) As the power structure of the world moves from bipolarity to polycentrism, the interests of the many nations around the world may diverge. The basic problems will be political and ideological and often overlain with national ego and emotion. In this environment, it would appear that the US military apparatus should be able to meet the full spectrum of possibilities with a strategy of flexible response.

3. *Regional Appraisal.*

a. *General.* It can be expected that communist policies and actions will be marked by subversion and opportunism. Soviet and Chinese Communist leaders undoubtedly will continue to seek, instigate and support new developments favorable to their interests, particularly in Africa, Latin America, SE Asia, and the Middle East. Both Communist China and the Soviet Union will continue to compete in establishing a strong influence in Africa, in stimulating and exploiting leftist and revolutionary movements in Latin America, and in encouraging the growth of a radical anti-American mass movement in Japan and elsewhere as expediency dictates. The USSR and Communist China will use forms of enticement and pressure which they consider advantageous and appropriate to a particular time and circumstance. These pressures will include political, diplomatic, cultural and economic initiatives as well as propaganda and the threat of military action. Both the Soviets and the Chinese Communists will continue to drive aggressively for the control of peoples and areas through subversion and infiltration to capture and exploit local movements and issues. Above all, the Soviets intend to build up their national base of power and their "great nation" image in the belief that they can improve their over-all position.

b. *European Area.* The Soviet Bloc is expected to continue to take actions designed to improve their over-all military posture, intimidate and divide the West. They will seek to:

(1) confirm the division of Germany;
(2) consolidate communist rule in Eastern Europe;
(3) gain Western acceptance of the permanence and legitimacy of communist regimes;
(4) limit the resurgence of West Germany as a potent military power;
(5) bring about the withdrawal of US military power;
(6) discourage increases in Allied military capability;
(7) frustrate NATO nuclear arrangements and prevent the further proliferation of Allied nuclear capability;
(8) reduce the credibility of the Allied response in critical situations;
(9) weaken and bring about the dissolution of NATO; and
(10) increase the political participation of communist parties in the national political life of some Western European countries.

c. *Middle East.* The prime objective of the USSR is to expand Soviet Bloc influence in the Middle East in order to exercise control of the area. To achieve this objective attempts will be made to:

(1) Eliminate important Western positions and influence in the area; and, deny the Middle East and its resources to the West;
(2) Dissolve CENTO;
(3) Exploit the Arab nationalist movement to their advantage;
(4) Obtain access to Africa through the Middle East; and
(5) Control strategically important communications routes in the area.

The Soviet Union will continue to face setbacks in attempting to achieve their objectives in the area and will remain alert for diplomatic moves or local communist action arising from the intricate political rivalries in the area. The Soviets will be willing to assist the UAR to achieve those objectives common to both countries including resistance to presence of US and UK in the Middle East. The UAR can be expected to continue its drive for Arab unity under its leadership. It is believed that Communist China will not achieve a significant position in the area within the mid-range period.

d. *Africa.* The Soviet Union and Communist China will continue to develop economic, cultural, and diplomatic relations with African nations, seeking to penetrate and subvert their political structure and influence their alignment.

(1) Frustration of the communist objectives of developing socialist states aligned with the Soviet Union or Communist China, and the creation of democratic political institutions supported by a viable, free

enterprise economy will be a most difficult struggle. If this goal is to be attained, it will be due to a program of helpful guidance and material support from various Western powers extending some of the traditional influence of the former colonial regimes which have engendered a loyalty to the West and an aversion to communist dictatorial schemes.

(2) Most of the independent states of Africa have to a degree been penetrated by communist movements or agents. In those countries disrupted by internal strife such as the two Congos and Sudan, and in those states disrupted by hostilities with their neighbors such as Somalia and Algeria, communist inroads have been substantial. In newly emerging states and those dominated by over-eager dictators such as those in Guinea and Ghana, communists have been invited into positions of authority or influence.

(3) The blandishments of the Soviets and Chinese Communists will undoubtedly be effective in many African states in the future, particularly as independence is observed to carry more responsibilities and fewer benefits than anticipated. Communist cadres and agents now exist in North, West, Central and East Africa and their influence and success in individual countries will continue during the mid-range period. Communist penetration within the area will be enhanced through the training of revolutionary leaders in Communist China and the Soviet Union.

e. *Asia and the Far East*

(1) Despite Sino-Soviet rivalry, the USSR and Communist China are expected to continue their efforts to supplant Western influence in Asia and undermine the governments and politico-economic institutions of non-communist or neutral Asian nations. Efforts of the communists to denigrate the effectiveness and to bring about the dissolution of SEATO will continue. Communist China will continue efforts to achieve recognition as a major world power and the dominant power in Asia. In contrast, Asian national leaders probably will be more reluctant to assume a strong stand in opposition to Communist China unless they have guarantees of swift, successful and unequivocal Western protection. Even with such guarantees, however, the countries of SE Asia will be strongly influenced by their appraisal of the actual circumstances in which the loss of any territory in SE Asia to the communists might occur, particularly with respect to the attitude and actions of the United States.

(2) Indonesia probably will attempt to maintain a neutralist position and seek a balance in relations with major communist and non-communist nations. Indonesia will continue to use available means to achieve hegemony over additional island territory in the area, particularly Portuguese Timor and Malaysian Borneo, while simultaneously

attempting to spread her influence in SE Asia. Indonesia will continue to rely on the USSR for substantial military assistance and aid and on opportune arrangements with Western or with other communist nations. In view of growing Indonesian economic difficulties, it cannot be ruled out that Sukarno may elect to precipitate an external involvement to avoid internal crises which might topple his regime and upset the Indonesian communist and non-communist political groupings.

(3) The Soviets desire to build up good will and enhance Soviet prestige in India against the time when prospects for communist acquisition of power are considerably improved. While India appears determined to check Chinese expansion in the Northern border areas, she remains more preoccupied with Pakistan. The Indians, while accepting US and British assistance, are unlikely to invite direct US or UK military presence in the area unless there is a renewal of hostilities in the Sino-Indian border region.

(4) Prospects for settlement of the India/Pakistan Kashmir dispute, while increasing slightly since Nehru's death, remain dim. A by-product of this dispute and of the general Indo-Pakistani hostility could have far-reaching effects in spheres of immediate US interests. The prospect of continuing US/UK military aid to India has caused strong resentment in Pakistan. To counter both the presumed threat from India and the perennial danger of pressure from the USSR, Pakistan probably will continue to improve her relations with Communist China. It is doubtful, however, that Pakistan will go so far as to withdraw from SEATO or CENTO despite her threats to do so.

(5) The USSR's political relations with Japan are likely to remain at an impasse. The USSR will continue to reject Japanese claims to the southern Kuriles and to insist upon abrogation of the defense treaty with the United States as a precondition for normalizing Soviet/Japanese relations with a peace treaty. The USSR would probably relax somewhat its present unyielding position, however, if it detected in Tokyo signs of a willingness to loosen ties with the United States.

(6) The communists desire to establish control in Laos and South Vietnam at an early date. The USSR is not disposed to make heavy sacrifice or to jeopardize other objectives vis-à-vis the West in order to make immediate advances in an area which is of more direct concern to North Vietnam and Communist China. The USSR is likely, therefore, to refrain from military actions and seek to avoid a US/USSR confrontation rather than accept the risks involved in a substantial effort to sustain the Pathet Lao and Viet Cong. The threat of large-scale intervention by ChiCom military forces will continue behind the communists' activities in this area as well as in Korea. Communist infiltration,

subversion, support and control of so-called "wars of national liberation" in SE Asia could increase. The ChiComs are not likely, however, to resort to direct intervention as long as they calculate that their ends can be achieved through means short of overt war. They will not hesitate, as illustrated by their actions in Tibet and on the Sino-Indian border, to resort to overt military action when they believe it is necessary and when in their opinion the risk of military confrontation with the United States is low. Effective action to halt infiltration, insurgency and subversion will continue to be an urgent requirement. While military limitations and concern over retaliation by the United States will deter Communist China from attempting a military conquest of Taiwan, they could undertake certain limited military action in the Taiwan Straits area to test Nationalist Chinese defenses and to probe US determination.

f. *Latin America*

(1) Latin America will continue to be a primary target for Soviet and ChiCom penetration. Their efforts will almost certainly intensify during the period, and they will continue to push their campaign to:

(a) Isolate the United States from its traditional allies;
(b) Nullify hemispheric unity;
(c) Infiltrate and subvert vulnerable countries;
(d) Strengthen and exploit their present foothold in Latin America.

(2) The Soviets and ChiComs will continue to use Cuba as a base from which to expand communist influence further into the Western Hemisphere and as a significant factor in world-wide negotiations. Cuba will be closely watched by Latin American and other nations as a measure of the relative strength and resolution of the United States and the Soviet Union. Periodic crises will almost certainly continue to occur in Latin America throughout the period. For the most part, based on the assumption of continued US support, the area will almost certainly remain US-oriented, although in the face of internal and external communist pressures, some nations can be expected to adopt an increasingly independent position. In addition to the already established Cuban communist government, the coming to power of a communist government by one or more of the Latin American republics during this time frame is possible. In this precarious political situation, the communists will seek advantage in whatever promising revolutionary developments occur.

4. *The Soviet Bloc Threat*

a. *General.* While striving to improve Soviet Bloc security, especially that of the USSR, the Soviet rulers will attempt to advance toward their over-all objective of achieving a communist world under Soviet leadership.

b. *Soviet Economic Problems and Outlook*

(1) A number of serious long-run problems in the Soviet economy have recently reached an acute stage. Over-all growth is lagging, various sectors of the economy are intensifying competition for scarce resources, agricultural production is falling far short of needs, large wheat purchases in 1963 have greatly aggravated the hard-currency deficit, and gold stocks are nearing a critically low level. This situation is due in part to chronic Soviet mismanagement, but mainly to the burdens imposed on the economy by a series of programs too ambitious for available resources. The demands of defense and space have greatly encumbered economic growth since 1958. Recently, industry has been adversely affected, as well as agriculture and the production of consumer goods.

(2) Soviet leaders have now launched a new effort to cope with their most intractable economic problem—the stagnation of agriculture—through a large expansion of the chemical industry, especially for the production of fertilizer. They apparently expect to finance this program from the expansion they anticipate in the economy, from cutbacks in some non-defense programs, and from large and long-term Western credits. But it is also thought that the Soviets will make every effort to hold down defense and space expenditures so as to release scarce resources for investment in the civilian economy.

(3) While defense expenditures could decline, it is thought more likely that they will continue to grow, though at a slower pace than in the recent past. In the short term, the Soviet leaders have the option of reducing force levels, but in the long term they must consider the advisability of curtailing or stretching out one or more programs for advanced weapons.

(4) The Soviets will make sustained efforts to expand trade with the West, and particularly to obtain large and long-term Western credits. This will help foster continued restraint in the tone of Soviet foreign policy, though not major concessions of substance.

c. *Attitude Toward War*

(1) Soviet thinking about military policy is influenced by a general outlook which asserts that historical forces are moving inexorably in the direction of communism. Soviet leaders see military power as serving two basic purposes: defense of their system and support for its expansion. Thus, one of the most important objectives of Soviet military policy is to deter general war while the USSR prosecutes its foreign policies by means short of actual hostilities involving Soviet forces. Military power is constantly brought into play in direct support of these policies, through the threats which give force to Soviet political demands, through the stress on its growing power which is intended to gain

respect for the Soviet state and its communist system, and through the military aid and support rendered to allies, friendly but neutral regimes, and anti-Western movements. As long as the relative strategic balance of forces is in favor of the West, it is highly unlikely except through miscalculation or misadventure, that the Soviets would initiate general war. There is, however, good evidence that the Soviets, in recognition of this imbalance, are striving to enhance their capabilities relative to the West.

(2) The Soviets wish to have the forces to fight wars effectively should they occur. Except for so-called "wars of national liberation," their political outlook, their military programs of recent years, and intelligence on their current intentions all suggest that the Soviet leaders do not regard war as desirable. They realize their deterrent must be credible in the sense that it rests upon powerful military forces. Moreover, they recognize that deterrence may fail in some key confrontation in which, despite their best efforts to retain control over risks, either they or their opponents come to feel that vital interests are under challenge. Against this contingency they wish to have a combination of offensive and defensive capabilities which will enable them to seize the initiative if possible, to survive enemy nuclear attack, and to go on to prosecute the war successfully. Although logically they must think that a deliberate Western attack on them is improbable, they appear to have genuine apprehensions.

(3) Devoted as they are to the need for implacable struggle against the "capitalist" world until communist domination is assured, and to the view that power—in its broadest economic, military and political sense—is the key ingredient in this struggle, the Soviets see their priority objective as constantly trying to change the East-West balance of power and the world conception of that balance in their favor. To this end they persistently endeavor to enhance the components of their economic, military, and scientific strength and no less important, their political position in the world arena. Soviet boasts of military prowess and superiority over the West are designed to back up their political initiatives by exploiting present and future Soviet power potential. At the same time, the Soviets do what they can to undermine and denigrate the power of the West in these respects.

(4) Fundamental hostility toward the non-communist world defines one limit of Soviet foreign policy; so long as it persists, the USSR will regard international issues as opportunities progressively to weaken and undermine its opponents, and not as occasions for conciliation which would protect the interests of all parties. The other limit, which puts a check upon this aggressiveness, is the Soviet leaders' awareness that their own nation and system would face destruction in a general

nuclear war. Both their statements and their actions in recent years have demonstrated their unwillingness to run any considerable risks of this eventuality. This does not mean, however, that they would always estimate the risks correctly, nor does it mean that they would abandon interests they considered vital in order to avoid grave risk of nuclear war. Barring the development of a decisive weapon system, the Soviets almost certainly consider that neither side will deliberately initiate a general war or react to any crisis in a manner which would gravely risk such a war, unless vital interests were considered to be in jeopardy.

(5) It is believed that the Soviets are unlikely as a matter of general policy, to assume the military and political risks involved in using their own forces in overt military operations to achieve local gains. They would probably employ Soviet forces, as necessary, if some Western military action in areas adjacent to a communist country threatened the integrity of the Soviet Bloc itself. Even in the latter case, however, they would attempt to use their forces in a way calculated to achieve their local objectives, to end hostilities rapidly and to control risks of escalation. At a much lower level, they will almost certainly encourage and support the use of force by pro-communist forces when they believe that a local situation is ripe for forceful exploitation and that the challenge to Western interests is not direct enough to involve uncontrollable risks of a direct encounter between United States and Soviet forces.

(6) This estimate of Soviet views on general and local war is generally consistent with their officially announced positions. They also distinguish a category of "Wars of national liberation, or popular uprisings." They are carefully vague, however, in discussing the forms their support would take, and in particular, have neither promised nor hinted that Soviet forces would join in the fighting. Soviet actions, however, indicate that it is not their intent to usher in a new phase of vigorous Soviet incitement of such conflicts everywhere or of maximum military assistance to "national liberation" forces.

(7) It seems likely that Soviet emphasis on "national liberation" warfare is intended in part to meet Chinese criticisms of the USSR. Despite Chinese pressures, it does not appear that the USSR will give full political and material support nor commit its prestige to all armed anti-Western movements in the under-developed areas. It is believed that the Soviets will continue to follow an opportunistic policy in this regard.

d. *Future Trends in Soviet Military Programs*

(1) *Strategic Attack Forces.* In the buildup of strategic strike forces, the Soviets have recently been placing major emphasis upon weapons for inter-continental attack, particularly ICBMs. It is believed that the Soviet ICBM force will grow in numbers and improve in quality, as will

their missile submarine force, and they will continue to possess a significant though reduced force of bombers. In the ICBM force, qualitative improvement will be emphasized; it is believed that the Soviets will introduce follow-on systems characterized by better accuracy, larger payloads, better reliability, and easier handling and maintenance. It is believed that they will also attempt to improve survivability by deploying a greater proportion of their ICBMs in hard sites, by providing their submarines with the recently developed submerged launch ballistic missiles which have longer range than their present surface launched missiles and by increasing the readiness of their strategic forces. If current estimates are correct, it would appear that the Soviets would not be able during the period of this plan to pursue successfully a strategy of attacking US nuclear striking forces prior to launch to such an extent that damage inflicted by US retaliatory strikes could be considered acceptable, but they will have a force capable of attacking major US cities and a portion of US nuclear delivery forces or, alternatively, of varying the relative weight of effort on these two target systems. Similarly, the Soviet Union probably would have a significant capability for retaliation even after an initial US attack. It is believed that Soviet strategic attack forces intended for Eurasian operations are nearing planned levels. The large missile forces deployed primarily against Europe will probably remain at about their present size, but survivability will be enhanced through hardening and possibly by the introduction of ground mobile systems. The medium bomber force will probably decline in size over the next several years, but capabilities will probably improve with the continued introduction of supersonic aircraft. Thus, the Soviets will maintain massive forces for strategic attack in Eurasia and will improve these forces.

(2) *Strategic Defense Forces.* Although the Soviets are aware of planned reductions in US bomber forces, this threat will remain a matter of great concern for the period of this estimate. The massive defenses deployed over the past several years provide a measure of the Soviets' concern with this problem, and evidence indicates that the Soviets are continuing to strengthen these defenses. The total number of interceptor aircraft will probably decline, but a larger percentage of the remaining force will be all-weather types. Deployment of the SA-3 for low-altitude defense probably will continue in order to supplement the existing medium and high altitude defenses around the more important targets and astride what the Soviets consider to be the more likely peripheral penetration routes. It is possible that more attention will be given to sheltering the civil population from fallout, but in view of construction needs in the economy, it is doubted that a large-scale shelter program will be undertaken. The Soviets might hope through development and deployment of an antimissile system to offset US strategic

superiority to some extent. The available evidence leads to the conclusion that the Soviets have not yet been successful in developing effective and reliable systems for defense against strategic missiles. It is believed that the Soviets would not regard as acceptable for wide-scale deployment any ABM system that does not have continuous readiness and an almost instantaneous reaction time together with a very high level of accuracy, reliability, and discrimination. Considering the effort devoted to ABM development, it is possible, though by no means certain, that the Soviets will achieve such a system within the period of this appraisal. When and if a satisfactory system is developed, the Soviet leaders will have to consider the great cost of large-scale deployment. They would almost certainly wish to defend key urban-industrial areas and they may seek to defend some portion of their ICBM force in order to strengthen their deterrent. Beyond these generalizations, the extent to which they would commit resources to ABM defenses cannot be estimated.

(3) *Soviet Ground Forces.* The Soviet ground forces are formidable and modern, with a large number of combat strength divisions backed up by a large mobilization potential. All presently existing divisions have been at least nominally converted to one of three types: tank, motorized rifle, or airborne. The modernization program has made heavy demands on resources in short supply in the USSR, and it is believed that Soviet ground force capabilities are still adversely affected by quantitative and qualitative deficiencies in equipment. During the past several years, the Soviets have reduced the total number of their divisions and have also reduced the proportion maintained at high levels of combat readiness. It is estimated that the total number of Soviet divisions lies in the range 110–140 and that 60–75 of these are now maintained at combat strength, i.e., at 85 percent or more of total authorized wartime personnel strength. The remainder are at either reduced strength (60–70 percent of authorized personnel) or at cadre strength (25 percent or less). The modernization of Soviet ground forces will continue. The extent of improvement, however, will be closely related to trends in total size; the larger the forces which the USSR, elects to retain, the more it will have to contend with obsolescence and shortages. The Soviets may, therefore, choose to maintain a smaller number of ground divisions which could be kept at a higher state of readiness. If the Soviets decide that they must seriously respond to the contingency of non-nuclear warfare, they will probably provide increased combat support as well as increased service support. Present trends in the ground weapons development program point to a continuing emphasis on firepower and mobility. The Soviets could probably have the numbers of tactical nuclear weapons which they would consider requisite for theater forces within two or three years, unless prior-

ity is given to air and missile defense warheads. Soviet procedures for the control and use of such weapons are likely to improve significantly. More and better general purpose vehicles and increased reliance on pipelines will reduce somewhat the Soviet dependence on rail lines for logistic support. In recent years, Soviet theater forces have acquired important tactical missile capabilities, including unguided rockets and ballistic and cruise missiles. Nuclear and toxic chemical bombs and warheads have been provided for tactical use; it is believed that their release is kept under strict political control. During the past year, the Soviets appear to have modified somewhat their expectation that any major conflict in Europe would either be nuclear from the start or would inevitably escalate. Their recent writings indicate that some thought has been given to the possibility of non-nuclear war in Europe. While Soviet capabilities to conduct non-nuclear warfare remain formidable, efforts to gear their theater forces for nuclear operations have had some adverse effects on conventional capabilities.

(4) *Strategic Deployment Capability.* In recent years, the USSR has increased its concern with areas remote from its borders, and the Cuban venture shows that it can deploy small ground and air contingents to distant areas and maintain them once deployed. However, there is no evidence that the USSR has established any special military component trained and equipped specifically for independent small scale operations, and it is severely limited in airlift, sealift, and naval support suitable for distant, limited military operations. It is possible that over the next few years the Soviets will seek to improve their capabilities for such operations through the designation and training of appropriate forces, and the development of equipment specifically for their use and logistic support. They may attempt to overcome their geographic disadvantages for applying such forces by negotiations with neutralist countries to utilize available facilities for refueling and maintenance of Soviet military aircraft or naval ships.

(5) *Naval Forces.* Much of the impetus for change in the Soviet Navy has come from the USSR's concern over the threat posed by US carrier task forces and missile submarines. The Soviets now have operational about 45 ballistic missile submarines—nine of them nuclear-powered—which carry a combined total of about 125 short-range (350 nm) missiles designed for surfaced launching. The USSR is developing longer range missiles for launching from submerged submarines. In addition, the Soviets have developed submarine-launched cruise missiles, which are probably designed primarily for use against ships but could be employed against land targets. In mid-1967, the Soviets will probably have more than two dozen nuclear-powered ballistic missile submarines, and about 20 nuclear-powered cruise missile submarines. By that time, they will probably have initiated routine submarine patrols

within missile range of the United States. The USSR's capabilities to conduct naval warfare in the open seas rest primarily upon the submarine force, which is capable of mounting a large scale torpedo attack and mining campaign against Allied naval targets and sea communications in the eastern North Atlantic and northwestern Pacific. Its capabilities for operations near the continental United States are more limited, but are growing. Capabilities against carrier task forces have been improved by the conversion of jet bombers to employ anti-ship missiles, by the introduction of submarines equipped with cruise-type missiles, and by increased air reconnaissance of open ocean areas by Long Range and Naval Aviation. The Soviets have also placed increasing emphasis on improvement of ASW forces in coastal areas and in the open seas. It is believed the Soviet Navy is capable of carrying out fairly effective ASW operations in coastal areas, but that it has a negligible ASW capability in the open seas. Despite the effort which they almost certainly are devoting to this problem, it is believed that over the next five years, the USSR will be able to achieve only a limited capability to detect, identify, localize, and maintain surveillance on submarines operating in the open seas.

(6) *Tactical Aviation and Missiles.* It is believed that the Soviets will continue to modernize Tactical Aviation, improving its ground attack capabilities in particular. It is expected that the rate of modernization will increase over the next few years, and that tactical aircraft with much improved range and payload characteristics will be introduced. It is expected that there will be a gradual decline in total numbers of tactical aircraft. The numbers of guided missiles in Soviet theater forces will probably remain about constant, but new and improved systems will probably be introduced. It appears likely that additional free rocket launchers will be assigned to divisions. Field force air defense capabilities will improve over the next few years through the modernization of Tactical Aviation and probably through the introductions of the SA-3 or follow-on SAM systems into ground formations. It is believed that a transportable ABM system for field force defense against ballistic missiles having ranges of several hundred nm could probably achieve operational status during 1964. There is no basis for determining the extent to which such a system may be deployed, but it seems likely that considerable improvement of defenses against aircraft would be a prerequisite to deploying an ABM vulnerable to aircraft attack.

(7) *Nuclear Weapons.* In the extensive 1961–1962 nuclear test series, the Soviets probably satisfied their most pressing weapons test requirements. Research and development in this field over the next few years will probably continue to focus upon the exploitation of these test results, and their translation into weapons. The Soviet weapons stockpile still consists largely of weapons developed from tests conducted

before the moratorium of 1958. It is estimated that, in general, a minimum of about two years is required after testing before a new nuclear weapon begins to enter stockpile. Thus, some weapons developed in the 1961–1962 test series are probably now entering inventory, with priority probably given to strategic weapons, particularly ICBM warheads. Probable trends in stockpile weapons include higher yields for strategic weapons and a broader spectrum of weapons for tactical use. As the stockpile of fissionable materials grows, restrictions on the availability of weapons for tactical use and for strategic defense will ease.

(8) *Chemical Warfare.* It is believed that the USSR now possesses a substantial chemical warfare capability based on extensive stocks of CW agents, a variety of chemical munitions, including warheads for tactical rockets and missiles, and a wide range of defensive equipment. The Soviet CW research and development program continues to be active on a scale generally comparable with that in the US. Current efforts are focused on developing new toxic agents and munitions for their delivery. The lack of a satisfactory method for timely nerve agent detection remains a major weakness. Many studies potentially applicable to discovery and development of nonlethal incapacitating agents are in process, and a new agent of this type could appear at any time.

(9) *Space Weapons.* On the basis of evidence presently available, it is not possible to determine the existence of Soviet plans or programs for the military use of space, apart from the Cosmos photographic satellites, which probably perform military support functions. However, it is believed the USSR almost certainly is investigating the feasibility of space systems for offensive and defensive weapon systems. Soviet decisions to develop military space systems will depend on their expected costs and effectiveness as compared with alternative systems, possible political advantages or disadvantages, and the Soviet estimate of US intentions and capabilities in comparable fields. For accomplishing military missions it is believed that within this decade, orbital weapons will not compare favorably with ICBMs in terms of reaction time, targeting flexibility, vulnerability, average life, and positive control. In view of these considerations, the much greater cost of orbital weapon systems, and Soviet endorsement of the UN resolution against nuclear weapons in space, it is believed that the Soviets are unlikely to develop and deploy an orbital weapon system of military significance within the period of this estimate. If they should nevertheless do so, developmental testing should be observable at least a year or two prior to their attainment of an accurate, reliable system. In the defensive weapons field, it is believed that the Soviets intend to develop a capability to counter US military satellites. By modification of existing equipment, including air defense early warning radars and ballistic missiles, the Soviets probably could develop a limited anti-satellite capability within

a few months after a decision had been made to do so. Evidence indicating that the Soviets have made such a decision is not available. The Soviets could also be working toward a system designed specifically for satellite interception, but it is almost certain that no such system is operational at present. The use of co-orbiting satellites or other advanced techniques during the period of this estimate seems much less likely.

(10) Soviet Bloc leaders probably continue to view their combined military power as adequate to meet military situations in Eurasia in which the nuclear capabilities of the Western Powers are not involved. They probably also conclude that they possess sufficient military power to deter the West from launching general war except under extreme threat to vital national or common interests. They almost certainly conclude that in the event of general war their military power would be unable to prevent unacceptable damage to the Soviet Union.

e. *Deterrence.* The Soviets see the present situation as one in which both sides are deterred from deliberately initiating general war or from knowingly initiating courses of action which would involve grave risk of such a war. They undoubtedly recognize the superiority of the United States in strategic power, but they are confident that they possess a credible deterrent based on both their massive capabilities against Eurasia and their growing intercontinental striking forces. Thus, the Soviet leaders do not regard the deliberate initiation of general war as a feasible course of action either for themselves or for the West. Moreover, despite increased Soviet attention to the possibility of limited wars with the West, it is believed that they will remain very reluctant to commit their own forces to such wars. In this situation the Soviets would take the opportunity to conduct aggressive maneuvers of many sorts and to undertake a comprehensive effort aimed at attaining a military technological breakthrough.

(1) In strategic terms, this line of policy suggests that presently, and for some time to come, the Soviet strategic forces will be numerically inferior to those of the US and more vulnerable to attack. The Soviet leaders must recognize, therefore, that the US would enjoy a considerable advantage should it strike first, and that the relative invulnerability, the fast reaction time, and the mobility of US strategic power make a Soviet first strike completely irrational. Nevertheless, in assessing the military balance, the Soviets are confident that they possess a credible deterrent based on both their massive capabilities to devastate Eurasia and their growing intercontinental striking power. Thus, the Soviets see the present situation as one in which both sides are deterred from deliberately initiating general war or from knowingly initiating courses of action which would involve grave risk of such a war. The increasing nuclear capability of the US and USSR will continue to have a restraining influence on both sides and will influence the type of conflict and tend to reduce the level and intensity of conflict which might occur.

(2) Soviet decisions as to force structure and military programs over the next several years are likely to be made in the context of a situation in which, although the US enjoys a clear strategic advantage, a condition of rough mutual deterrence exists. The Soviets will seek to improve their strategic capabilities vis-à-vis the US; however, policy decisions will be influenced by the continuing strain on economic resources, and the pressure arising from competition with the US in scientific and technological developments with military applications. Such decisions will be greatly influenced also by the Soviet estimate of the political situation, the opportunities which it affords, and the contribution which military power can make to the realization of these opportunities.

(3) It is believed that in these circumstances the primary concern of Soviet policy will be to continue to strengthen their deterrent against US attack primarily through a gradual buildup of ICBMs, hardening of sites, and increased mobility through missile submarines. At one time the Soviets may have considered an attempt to achieve capabilities sufficient to neutralize US strategic forces in a first strike, and they almost certainly have also considered the lesser goal of achieving rough parity with the US in intercontinental weapon systems. In the aftermath of Cuba they may have considered a substantial increase in their military effort. Evidence does not indicate, however, that the Soviets are presently attempting to match the US in numbers of intercontinental delivery vehicles. Recognition that the US would detect and match or overmatch such an effort, together with economic constraints, appears to have ruled out this option. On the other hand, available evidence on the development of large nuclear warheads and compatible delivery vehicles strongly suggests that the Soviets may be seeking to improve their position relative to the West by increasing the destructive power of their numerically inferior intercontinental strategic attack forces.

(4) Continuation of present lines of policy will ensure the Soviets of a growing credibility for their deterrent. However, the dynamism of Soviet policy depends to a great extent on the proposition that the balance of forces in the world is shifting in favor of the communist world. The Sino-Soviet rupture has already badly damaged this thesis, as has the inability of the Soviets to match the West in military power. It is conceivable that at some point a Soviet leadership would come to believe that they had to forego their expansionist aims, unless they could greatly improve their relative military strength, or at least refurbish the world's image of this strength. They might even be willing to make new economic sacrifices or assume some risks in order to accomplish this. What precise programs they might undertake in pursuit of such an aim cannot now be stated, but it cannot be ruled out that changes in the scale or character of Soviet programs could come about in this way.

(5) On the question of how a general war might begin, most Soviet military writings assume deliberate, surprise attack by the US, although some consider escalation from limited war and a few allow for the possibility that general war would begin accidentally. The criticality of the initial period of a nuclear war and the importance of surprise have led some military writers to advocate a form of pre-emptive action by the USSR: i.e., a "spoiling" or "blunting" action launched coincident with or slightly before an enemy attack. However, known doctrinal discussions do not consider a Soviet first strike. In the standard scenario, the USSR survives a nuclear attack, regains the initiative, and goes on to prosecute the war.

(6) Current Soviet doctrine holds that a general war will inevitably involve the large-scale use of nuclear and other weapons of mass destruction, beginning with a strategic exchange which may decide the course and outcome of the war in its initial phase, a relatively brief but not clearly defined period of time. To the Soviets, the importance of this phase implies the necessity to use all available forces at the outset of a general war; the doctrinal writings which are available have noted and rejected such US concepts as controlled response and damage limiting strategies. Moreover, no restraint is evident in targeting concepts for the initial phase of a general war; while enemy nuclear striking forces are evidently to be the primary targets of Soviet nuclear strikes, powerful nuclear blows are also to be directed against communication and control centers, industrial and population centers, and groupings of enemy armed forces.

(7) Despite the primary role attributed to nuclear and missile forces, current Soviet doctrine envisions the commitment of large theater forces virtually at the outset of a general war. It is argued that, even if the war is relatively short, large forces of all types would be required to defeat comparable enemy forces, to overrun base areas, and to occupy territory in Eurasia. Moreover, it is also held that the conflict may be protracted rather than brief and that, in this case, extensive theater campaigns would be required. Thus, current Soviet doctrine supports a military policy emphasizing strategic attack and defense capabilities, but supports as well the maintenance of large general purpose forces for use in all phases of general war.

(8) It is believed that debate continues, not only over subsidiary propositions, but over central tenets of doctrine as well. Certain key issues, such as the decisiveness of the initial phase, evidently remain unresolved. Moreover, certain vital questions seem to have been ignored. For example, while purporting to deal with a global war in which all types of weapons are employed, the current military writings to which there is access, concern themselves almost exclusively with

theater forces in Europe. Adequate consideration is not given to the effects of a strategic nuclear exchange on subsequent operations. Virtually no attention is given to the way in which a general war might be brought to a successful conclusion; it seems to be assumed either that US society would collapse as the result of the initial nuclear attack, or that in a long war the Soviet system would prove the more durable.

f. *Miscalculation.* Soviet strategy recognizes that, while general war is unlikely, it cannot be excluded as the result of miscalculation by either side or as the outcome of a crisis in which both sides become progressively committed. The Soviets are unable to be certain in advance what the circumstances surrounding the beginning of a general war would be. A miscalculation could occur if the Soviets misjudged either the importance to the West of an issue and the actions which the West might take in support of its position, or even the consequences of the policies being pursued by a third party associated with the Soviet Union. On the other hand, such a crisis might arise should the West miscalculate in a similar way.

g. *Pre-emptive attack.* If the Soviet leaders were ever absolutely certain that the West was irrevocably committed to an imminent strategic nuclear attack against them, there is little question that they would themselves strike pre-emptively. Such certainty, however, on the part of any country about the intentions of another is extremely unlikely. The Soviet leaders probably conclude that it would be impossible to count upon incontrovertible advance evidence that the enemy was irrevocably committed to an imminent attack. Moreover, for the Soviet Union, the compulsion to strike first, when the threat of hostile attack is still ambiguous, declines as US missile systems become more important and less vulnerable and the advantage to be derived from a first strike consequently decreases. This trend of Soviet thinking is suggested by assertions that an aggressor cannot neutralize the retaliatory capability of a powerful opponent. Nevertheless, a surprise attack—that is to say, one delivered in a period of no particular tension and after entirely secret military preparations—is the only one which would give the Soviet Union a chance of destroying any significant part of the Western nuclear strike capability before it could be launched. Therefore, in spite of its unlikelihood, it remains a possible, though improbable course of action for the Soviet Union.

h. *Escalation.* A number of Soviet statements in recent years have expressed the view that limited war involving the major nuclear powers would inevitably escalate into general war. While such statements are intended in part to deter the West from local use of force, this official view also reflects a genuine Soviet fear of the consequences of becoming directly engaged in limited war involving Soviet and US forces. This probably also extends to involvement of Soviet forces with certain Allied forces in highly critical areas, notably Western forces in the European area. Nevertheless, they might employ their own forces to achieve local gains in some area adjacent to Bloc territory if they judged that the West, either because it was deterred by Soviet nuclear power or for some other reason, would not make an effective military response. They would probably employ Soviet forces as necessary if some Western military action on the periphery of the Soviet Bloc threatened the integrity of the Bloc itself. Should the USSR become directly involved in a limited war with the US or Allied forces, it is believed that the Soviets would not necessarily expand it immediately into general war, but that they would probably employ only that force which they thought necessary to achieve their local objectives. They would also seek to prevent escalation both by restraints in the employment of their own forces and by political means. In view of the increasingly grave consequences of escalation, it is believed that over the next few years the Soviets will remain very reluctant to commit their own forces to limited warfare against Western forces. Despite recent Soviet references to the possibility of limited war involving tactical nuclear weapons, it is considered highly unlikely that the USSR would introduce such weapons into a limited conflict. The Soviet doctrinal debate, as far as it is known, has not dealt with limited war; it is therefore possible that discussion has been limited by official attitudes. Public Soviet statements have usually insisted that a limited war which involved the major nuclear powers would inevitably escalate into general war. Official pronouncements to this effect have almost certainly been designed in large part to deter the West from the local use of force, but they probably also reflected Soviet fears of becoming involved in limited war. The Soviets now appear to be modifying their position to allow for the possibility that even a limited war involving the major nuclear powers would not necessarily escalate to general war. They may now be persuaded that in the present strategic situation, the initial military reactions to a local crisis would be limited, and that it is therefore, not in the Soviet national interest to be doctrinally committed to inevitable escalation.

5. *Chinese Communist Threat*

a. *General.* Communist China's foreign policy will probably continue generally along current lines. Peiping will remain strongly anti-American and will strive to weaken the US position, especially in Asia, but is unlikely, knowingly, to assume great risks. Communist China's military force will probably not be used overtly except in defense of its own borders or to assert territorial claims against India. However, in the event that military operations against Communist Asian allies constitute, in the ChiCom view, a threat against ChiCom territory, their military forces may be employed overtly. Subversion and covert support of local revolutions will continue to be Communist China's primary mode of operation in Southeast Asia and, to a necessarily more limited degree, elsewhere in Asia, Africa, and Latin America.

b. *Modernization of Armed Forces.* The modernization of the armed forces, which was progressing steadily until about 1960, has practically ended, except for the continued introduction of radar and certain other electronic equipment. Domestic fabrication of fighter aircraft and submarines has ceased and inventories are being reduced by deterioration and cannibalization. In general, the Army has been less affected than the other Services.

c. *Advanced Weapons*

(1) The intelligence data available do not permit a high degree of confidence in estimating the future development of the Chinese nuclear weapons program, and this appraisal is made in light of this general caution.

(2) The Chinese Communists have given high priority to the development of nuclear weapons and missiles. If the normal number of difficulties are encountered a plutonium device might be tested in late 1964 or 1965, or even later depending upon the extent of difficulties. Beginning the year after a first detonation, the single reactor thus far identified could produce enough material for only one or two crude weapons a year. The Chinese have a few bombers which could carry bulky weapons of early design.

(3) Communist China is probably concentrating on a medium-range ballistic missile (MRBM) system of basically Soviet design, either the [*less than 1 line of source text not declassified*]. The earliest date either missile would be ready for deployment is believed to be 1967. It is unlikely that a compatible nuclear warhead would be available until 3 or 4 years after a first detonation.

(4) The detonation of a nuclear device would boost domestic morale. Although it is possible that the ChiCom leaders would experience a dangerous degree of over-confidence, it is more likely that they will concentrate on furthering their established policies to:

(a) Utilize their nuclear capability to enhance their political position as a world power, particularly with respect to the developing nations,

(b) Force their way into world disarmament discussions and other world councils,

(c) Overawe their neighbors and soften them for Chinese-directed communist subversion, and

(d) Tout Chinese-style communism as the best route for an underdeveloped nation to achieve industrial and scientific modernity. In pursuing these policies, increased confidence of ChiCom leaders would doubtless be reflected in their approach to conflicts on the periphery of Communist China.

d. *Domestic Production.* Communist China almost certainly intends to achieve domestic production of all necessary weapons and matériel for its armed forces. It has a long way to go before reaching this goal, however. The Chinese at present are probably unable to produce even MIG-17s entirely by themselves, and it will be a number of years before they can design and produce more advanced types of military aircraft. Indeed they may have chosen instead to concentrate their limited resources on missiles. Their wholly domestic naval shipbuilding capacity is likely to be restricted to surface ships of the smaller types during the next few years.

e. *Military Policy.* The decline in the relative effectiveness of Communist China's military equipment and weapons is likely to temper its policy, especially in circumstances where it might confront US armed power or sizable US-equipped Asian forces. However, the Chinese Communist Army will continue to be the strongest in Asia and will provide a powerful backing for Chinese Communist foreign policy. The Sino-Soviet dispute will probably place additional demands on Chinese military dispositions and capabilities, since one of the consequences of China's new "independence" from the USSR will be the need to keep a closer watch than previously on the long China-Russian border which the Chinese still consider a "difficult" and "unsettled" question. Her slowly developing nuclear weapon and missile capability will increase an already considerable military advantage over Asian neighbors. However, for the foreseeable future she will not approach the advanced weapons might of the United States or USSR, particularly in the field of long-range striking power. For this reason, among others, the ChiComs would be unlikely to attribute a decisive importance to modern weaponry. They would probably continue to rely primarily on a huge ground force and, unless confident of Soviet support, would try to avoid hostilities which might escalate into nuclear war. Considering the chances of retaliation, it is difficult to conceive of any situation in which Communist China would be likely to initiate the use of nuclear weapons in the next decade or so.

f. *Foreign Policy*

(1) Communist China's foreign policy objectives are the preservation of the regime and the protection of its existing boundaries. For these purposes the ChiComs are willing to go to war, almost regardless of the odds. If US or Allied troops approached its borders through Laos, North Vietnam, or North Korea they would almost certainly be ready to commit their forces openly, unless in the particular circumstances they saw greater advantage in more covert military operations. The acquisition of Taiwan falls in the second rank of objectives—those for which they are fully prepared to use overt military force, but only when the prospects of success are judged to be high. To achieve this goal, they are

prepared to run fewer risks and are particularly anxious to avoid direct conflict with the United States. They almost certainly will not attempt to seize by military force either Taiwan or any of the major offshore islands which they believe the United States would help defend. It is not believed that the explosion of a nuclear device, or even the acquisition of a limited nuclear weapons capability, would produce major changes in ChiCom foreign policy in the sense that they would adopt a general policy of open military aggression, or even become willing to take significantly greater military risks.

(2) China's leaders would recognize that their limited capabilities had not altered the real power balance among the major states and could not do so in the foreseeable future. In particular, they would recognize that they remained unable either to remove or neutralize the US presence in Asia. Nevertheless, the Chinese would feel very much stronger and this mood would doubtless be reflected in their approach to conflicts on their periphery. They would probably feel that the United States would be more reluctant to intervene on the Asian mainland and thus the tone of Chinese policy will probably become more assertive. Further, their possession of nuclear weapons and missiles would reinforce their efforts to achieve Asian hegemony through political pressures and the indirect support of local "wars of liberation." Such tactics would probably acquire greater effectiveness, since the Chinese feat would have a profound impact on neighboring governments and peoples. It would alter the latter's sense of the relations of power, even if it made little immediate change in the realities of power, and to a greater or lesser degree would probably result in increased pressures to accommodate to Chinese demands.

g. *Spread of Communism.* For the broader and longer range goal of spreading communism throughout the underdeveloped world, Communist China is probably not prepared to accept any substantial risk, although it must be noted that it tends to estimate the risks involved in supporting "wars of national liberation" much lower than does Moscow. It apparently does not intend to undertake overt conquests of foreign lands in the name of communism, but intends to let indigenous revolutionaries do the fighting and "liberating". The Chinese Communists are actively training at home and abroad foreign nationals in guerrilla and political warfare, and are actively engendering revolutionary movements to the extent of its limited capabilities with equipment, funds, propaganda and support in international affairs.

[Here follow Part III. Military Objectives, Part IV. Strategic Concept, and Part V. Basic Undertakings.]

44.   Letter From the Director of the White House Office of
Emergency Planning (McDermott) to Secretary of Defense
McNamara[1]

Washington, August 12, 1964.

Dear Mr. Secretary:

The Emergency Planning Committee, appointed by the President on February 14, 1962,[2] and composed of representatives of the Department of Defense, the Bureau of the Budget, and the Office of Emergency Planning, has been engaged in a review of various aspects of nonmilitary emergency preparedness planning. I have previously reported to you on the operations of this Committee (July 19, 1962, and March 11, 1963).[3]

A major area of concern to the Committee has been the lack of a clearly defined system for the *central management of resources under emergency conditions,* including nuclear attack. The Office of Emergency Planning was directed by President Kennedy to prepare a plan for such a system in order to assure that, in an emergency, resources would be used with maximum effectiveness in the national interest. Recommendations on this matter were incorporated in a report which was approved by the Committee and submitted to President Johnson for approval. A copy of the report is enclosed.[4]

I have received a memorandum from President Johnson, dated June 30, 1964, in which he states that:

"The report on the management of resources under emergency conditions, approved by the Emergency Planning Committee, deals with an extremely critical area of our total preparedness effort. I am pleased to note the progress being made in this field.
"The concept of an Office of Defense Resources, to be activated by the President in an emergency, is approved. This is a key element in further progress in this area of preparedness and I believe you should proceed with the development of the measures necessary to bring this, and any related programs, into an early state of standby readiness."[5]

---

[1] Source: Washington National Records Center, OSD Files: FRC 330 70 A 4443, 381 National Resources (Jan–May) 1966. No classification marking.

[2] Not further identified.

[3] Neither identified.

[4] The 11-page report (plus 1-page organizational chart), entitled "Central Management of Resources After Nuclear Attack," undated, is not printed.

[5] This 3-paragraph memorandum is in the Washington National Records Center, OSD Files: FRC 330 70 A 4443, 381 National Resources (Jan–May) 1966. The final paragraph reads: "I also agree with the advisability of selecting an Emergency Designee to head the Office of Defense Resources, when and if it is activated. Your recommendations regarding qualified persons who might be considered for this important emergency assignment will be appreciated."

The proposed organizational structure for the postattack central management of resources for mobilization and recovery will be developed with two primary considerations in mind: (1) the need for a central policy and coordinating organization reporting to, and acting on behalf of, the President; and (2) the need to make maximum use of the departments and agencies with emergency preparedness assignments under Executive Orders. Future work in this area of emergency preparedness will take full advantage of the capabilities of existing agencies.

The Department of Defense has an important role in this undertaking. It is counted upon to provide the leadership in the fields of civil defense, and military requirements. It will also contribute substantially to program development in other fields such as manpower, material resources, and communications.

I am calling a meeting on August 31, at 10:00 a.m., in Room 474, Executive Office Building, at which the basic concept and approach involved in central resources management will be presented to all agencies with mobilization responsibilities. After that meeting, there will be a period of active interagency staff work directed toward the early development of programs that can be made operational as quickly as possible in an emergency.

I will appreciate a letter designating someone qualified to speak for your Department to represent you at the August 31 meeting.[6]

Sincerely,

Ed

---

[6] An August 21 letter from Vance to McDermott designated Solis Horwitz as the Defense representative. (Ibid.) An undated, handwritten note by Vance on the letter printed here requested Horwitz to draft such a letter to McNamara.

45.   Memorandum for the Record by Charles E. Johnson of the
National Security Council Staff[1]

Washington, August 14, 1964.

SUBJECT

   Satellite Reconnaissance

Mac told me this morning that he had had a good long talk with
McCone on the above subject. McCone had told him that he planned to
go "quite a long way" in briefing the top Europeans that should be
filled in on our program. He will be in England in September and from
there will go to the other countries involved. He will probably take Bud
Wheelon with him to assist in the briefings.

Mac appeared satisfied with this arrangement and said that the
timing was such that it might be helpful in case we had to make use of
the information in some way during the next couple months.

Mac asked me to stay in touch with this matter and to pass the
word that he would like to see the briefing materials before McCone
leaves.

I called Bud Wheelon and told him of this talk and of Mac's request
that I stay in touch with him. He had not been filled in by the Director
and expressed his appreciation for receiving the information. He picked
up the ball right away and said that he would take the initiative in having the briefing materials prepared both on our program and the Soviet
program. I was unable to reach Garthoff and Scoville, both of whom are
on leave, and will try again on Monday.

Mac also suggested that I fill in Peter Jessup with the thought that
he might put this on the agenda for a "303 meeting".

C.E.J.

---

   [1] Source: Johnson Library, National Security File, Charles E. Johnson Files,
Reconnaissance Satellites, Box 11. No classification marking. A copy was sent to Spurgeon
Keeny.

46.   Memorandum From the Executive Secretary of the National Security Council (Smith) to President Johnson[1]

Washington, August 17, 1964.

In his presentation this afternoon to the Platform Committee, Secretary McNamara, if asked, plans to make public for the first time that in 1960–61 we eliminated from our nuclear stockpile [*number not declassified*] large weapons averaging [*less than 1 line of source text not declassified*] each) and replaced them with [*number not declassified*] smaller weapons. The result was a 45 percent reduction in the total yield of our stockpile.

(The reduction was personally approved by President Eisenhower in 1960 on the unanimous recommendation of the Joint Chiefs and Defense Secretary Gates.)

The information Secretary McNamara wants to use will make public the size of our nuclear stockpile[2] in the 1960–61 period and, along with information which the Joint Committee now has, will make it possible for experts to estimate our present stockpile.[3]

1. Secretary McNamara feels strongly that the information should be made public.

2. McGeorge Bundy agrees that the only way to reply to misinformation is to make public more details about our nuclear stockpile than has been done before.[4]

3. AEC Chairman Seaborg acknowledges that the decision to make public this information is not for the Commission to make but he wants to make clear that the information is Restricted Data and up to now has been closely held. The Commission this morning will make a decision to declassify the information, contingent on your decision.[5]

---

[1] Source: Johnson Library, National Security File, Subject File, President's Campaign, Defense, Stockpile, Box 41. No classification marking.

[2] President Johnson underlined the words, "will make public the size of our nuclear stockpile," and at the end of this phrase he drew a line to the margin where he wrote "opposed."

[3] At the end of this paragraph, the President added by hand three question marks.

[4] In the margin next to this paragraph the President wrote: "Why reply."

[5] On the morning of August 17, the AEC Commissioners made a determination for McNamara that the megaton total of the U.S. nuclear weapons stockpile could be declassified. (Seaborg, *Journal*, vol. 9, pp. 88, 89)

I will talk to McNamara about it.

Tell McNamara to go ahead and tell Seaborg that I approve of declassification.[6]

BKS

---

[6] Neither option is checked. In the margin the President wrote: "size of weapons, size of stockpile, why give Russians info dying to get." On the afternoon of August 18, Bundy told Seaborg that the President had decided not to reveal the megaton stockpile figures that the Atomic Energy Commission had declassified on a contingency basis. Seaborg, who "felt a study of the pros and cons should be made first," agreed with President Johnson. (Ibid., p. 94)

---

47. Memorandum From the President's Special Assistant for National Security Affairs (Bundy)[1]

Washington, August 18, 1964.

MEMORANDUM FOR

The Secretary of State
The Secretary of Defense
The Attorney General
The Director of Central Intelligence

SUBJECT

Measures for Strengthening the Counterintelligence Posture of the United States

Reference is made to the two memoranda from the Director of Central Intelligence dated August 5, 1964,[2] in response to my June 17 request for reports concerning certain recommendations which were made on the subject by the President's Foreign Intelligence Advisory Board on November 22, 1963,[3] following its review of the Dunlap espionage case:[4] (1) memorandum enclosing the report of the United States

---

[1] Source: Johnson Library, National Security File, Intelligence File, Foreign Intelligence Advisory Board, Vol. 2 [3 of 4], Box 6. Top Secret. The date is handwritten. Copies were sent to the Director of the Defense Intelligence Agency, the Director of the Federal Bureau of Investigation, and the President's Foreign Intelligence Advisory Board.

[2] Both of these memoranda from McCone to Bundy are ibid.

[3] The June 17 request was not found, and the PFIAB recommendations have not been identified.

[4] Sergeant Jack Dunlap, a National Security Agency courier, was under investigation for passing documents to Soviet authorities, when he committed suicide on July 22, 1963. After his death, highly classified documents were found in his home.

Intelligence Board on implementing actions taken with respect to Recommendations 4, 6, 7, 9, 10, 12, 13 and 21 of the President's Board;[5] and a report on actions pursued by the U.S. intelligence community, in lieu of establishment of the interdepartmental mechanism proposed in Recommendation No. 11 of the President's Board, to assure adequate measures to provide guidance, coordination and exchange of information among U.S. agencies in the counterintelligence field;[6] and (2) memorandum presenting the joint report of the Department of State and the Director of Central Intelligence with respect to Recommendations 14 through 17 of the President's Board.[7]

The two memoranda are being referred to the President's Foreign Intelligence Advisory Board for consideration in the course of its continuing review of foreign intelligence and related activities of the United States.

Noting the reported status of actions being taken to meet the objectives of recommendations which the Board has made in this important area it is requested that the Director of Central Intelligence, in consultation with member agencies of the United States Intelligence Board, continue to place priority emphasis upon counterintelligence programs and procedures to protect sensitive intelligence data, sources and methods against espionage penetration attempts on the part of hostile intelligence organizations.

It is also requested that the joint consideration by the Secretary of Defense and the Director of Central Intelligence with respect to Board Recommendation No. 7 be completed and a report furnished to this office and to the President's Board by October 1, 1964.

McGeorge Bundy[8]

---

[5] Attached as Tab A to one of the August 5 memoranda (see footnote 2 above).

[6] Attached as Tab B to the same August 5 memorandum (see footnotes 2 and 5 above).

[7] Attached to the other August 5 memorandum (see footnotes 2, 5, and 6 above).

[8] Printed from a copy that bears this typed signature.

48.   Editorial Note

During 1964 the White House Office of Emergency Planning began to put together a long-range civil emergency preparedness program. The completed 73-page study, entitled "A Report to the President: Civil Emergency Preparedness; Program Status and a Five-Year Projection," dated August 31, 1964, included an introductory section outlining the roles of the Office of Emergency Planning and of other departments and agencies, and the concepts underlying its proposed 5-year future program. The bulk of the report consisted of a statement of the 5-year objectives and status covering government in an emergency and the resources availability and their management. Also included was a summary treatment of civil defense. A copy of the report is in the National Archives and Records Administration, RG 59, Central Files 1964–66, DEF 1 US.

Attached to this copy of the report is a September 16 covering memorandum from Edward A. McDermott, Director of the Office of Emergency Planning, to the heads of 34 agencies and departments, which noted that President Johnson had approved the general outlines of the program contained in the report. McDermott promised to "work closely" with the agency and department heads "in translating this guidance into specific work programs and in developing the funding programs necessary to achieve the indicated levels of preparedness."

---

49.   Memorandum for the Record by Director of Central Intelligence McCone[1]

Washington, September 1, 1964.

SUBJECT

Discussion with the President—1 September 1964

Following the NSC meeting (memorandum of the meeting prepared by Dr. Cline and attached),[2] I had a private meeting with the

---

[1] Source: Central Intelligence Agency, DCI (McCone) Files, Memo for the Record, 7/9/64–10/10/64, Box 2. Top Secret. Drafted by McCone on September 2.

[2] Not found.

President. This meeting was in lieu of my attendance at the regular Tuesday luncheon which was to involve political matters and therefore my presence was not required.

[Here follows discussion of items 1–4.]

5. The President asked about the Patman article[3] and the consequences. I said the article was due to aggressiveness on the part of the Committee Staff and that great damage had been done. I felt that certain inquisitive writers such as Ross and Wise[4] would now attempt to find out what the Foundation did with the money, [1-1/2 lines of source text not declassified] and I thought the consequences would be very serious. Furthermore [less than 1 line of source text not declassified] would become involved. I hoped this would not occur but I thought it would. The President asked what we intended to do about it. I said there was little we could do except keep quiet [2 lines of source text not declassified].

---

[3] Reference is to the disclosure by Congressman Wright Patman (D–Texas) at a public hearing of his House Small Business Subcommittee on August 31 that the Central Intelligence Agency had secretly given money to the J.M. Kaplan Fund, a private foundation in New York City. See The New York Times, September 1, 1964, pp. 1, 19.

[4] Reference is to David Wise and Thomas B. Ross, The Invisible Government (New York: Random House, 1964).

---

50. Letter From the Deputy Secretary of Defense (Vance) to Director of Central Intelligence McCone[1]

Washington, September 4, 1964.

Dear John:

I looked over your memorandum of September 1, the memorandum of General Carter of August 27, and the report of Dr. Wheelon dated August 31, 1964 that you have approved.[2] I must call your atten-

---

[1] Source: Central Intelligence Agency, DCI (McCone) Files, 06 Sept 1961–30 March 1965, Box 8. Secret; [codeword not declassified]. Attached is a September 10 letter from McCone to Vance returning Vance's September 4 letter because "I don't wish this letter in my file." He suggested that he and Vance could discuss this matter "personally and alone. It appears to me," McCone went on, "the man charged by the President with the responsibility of running an organization should run it in accordance with the policies and procedures which best conform to the particular organization, not the policies and procedures established in some other department of government."

[2] None found.

tion to the fact that the direction issued by General Carter does not reflect our agreement in one very important detail. As you remember, you and I had agreed that an SETD (systems-engineering-technical-direction) contractor would be hired and that the work of integration and technical direction would be conducted by the contractor and not by CIA personnel. You may find the definition of systems engineering technical director given in DOD Directive Number 5500.10 to be of interest.

As used in these rules, "contractor" means the person under contract to the Department of Defense to perform the work described in each rule, and its affiliates; "system" means system, subsystem, project or item. The term "systems engineering" includes a combination of substantially all the following activities: determination of specifications, identification and solution of interfaces between parts of the system, development of test requirements or plans and evaluation of test data, and supervision of design work. The term "technical direction" includes a combination of substantially all the following activities: preparation of work statements for contractors, determination of parameters, direction of contractors' operations, and resolution of technical controversies.

General Carter interpreted this agreement to state:

Coordination, liaison, project integration and engineering support will be provided to DD/S&T by the systems engineering contractor, who will have direct access to all other contractors.

Clearly, this is inconsistent with our agreement.

My difficulties are increased by the interpretation given to this already weakened and not acceptable condition by Dr. Wheelon's memorandum where under paragraph 3.d. the systems engineering contractor is made responsible only for developing plans, specifications, etc., for all phases of the project on an integrated basis. Thus, the plan becomes contradictory with our agreement. I am sure that upon review of this plan you will agree with me.

Sincerely,

Cy

51.   Telegram From the Executive Secretary of the National
        Security Council (Smith) to the President's Special Assistant
        for National Security Affairs (Bundy)[1]

Washington, September 16, 1964, 1432Z.

CAP 64320. This is preliminary CIA comment on Khrushchev's weapon statement:

"1. On 15 September Khrushchev told a visiting delegation of Japanese socialist members of parliament that the Soviet Union has developed a 'monstrous new, terrible weapon.' He stated that on 14 September he had been shown a weapon of terrible destruction by military men, scientists and engineers. He is quoted as having said, 'I have never seen anything like it. It is a method of destroying and exterminating mankind. It is the strongest and most powerful of existing weapons. Its power is limitless.'

2. After mentioning the weapon, Khrushchev launched into an attack on Chinese border claims and accused Mao Tse-tung of spreading warlike sentiments. Earlier Khrushchev has recalled the tragedy of the Japanese people, the first in history to suffer the atomic bomb. Alluding to the Chinese, Khrushchev said that he who says that the atomic bomb is a paper tiger is crazy.

3. The choice of audience, and the context in which Khrushchev's statement regarding the new weapon was delivered, suggest that he intended the threat implied by this new development to be taken as directed primarily against the Chinese.

4. While Khrushchev gave no specific clues concerning the nature of the weapon, we did have an indication four months ago that Khrushchev wanted us to know beforehand that he was going to make such an announcement.

5. Last May [less than 1 line of source text not declassified], two Soviet KGB officers deliberately revealed themselves as such to a CIA officer, and told him that they knew he was a CIA officer. The spokesman for the two then asked twice 'very positively' that the CIA officer inform Washington that the Soviet Government was soon to make a very important announcement on development of a Soviet military capabil-

---

[1] Source: Johnson Library, National Security File, Subject File, Nuclear Weapons, USSR, Vol. I, Box 34. Secret; Noforn; Flash. There is no indication where the cable was sent, but on September 16 Bundy accompanied the President aboard Air Force One to Seattle, Washington, with stops en route at Great Falls, Montana, and Vancouver, Canada. (Ibid., President's Daily Diary) An identical typewritten draft from which this cable was prepared is ibid., National Security File, Subject File, Nuclear Weapons, USSR, Vol. I, Box 34.

ity which 'would not be used against the West but would be very effective against the Chinese.' The spokesman said he was not authorized to reveal the details.

6. The delay between this tip-off is that Khrushchev wanted us to know that the announced claim of a new weapon, when it came, would be directed at the Chinese and that we should not be concerned by it. It also is possible that Khrushchev had information indicating that the Chinese were going to claim a nuclear capability this year and timed the announcement to blunt the political effect of such a development.

8. We have no information on any specific Soviet weapon development which would equate to Khrushchev's description.

9. It is improbable that a new delivery system was the subject of his remarks since the Soviets have long claimed the ability to deliver their largest nuclear weapons by missile and to attack from any direction, although a January 1960 Khrushchev statement referring to a 'fantastic weapon' then in the hatching stage may have referred to the 100 megaton bomb. It seems improbable that his present 'new weapon' would refer to such a previously well publicized capability. It is unlikely in the absence of appropriate nuclear tests that the Soviets have had the opportunity to develop significantly larger nuclear weapons that could be used with confidence.

10. It is similarly difficult to conceive of radiological weapons that would fit Khrushchev's description. It is now possible, through appropriate selection of weapons and burst altitude, to contaminate very large areas with lethal radioactivity. These effects probably could be somewhat enhanced by alterations in weapon design, perhaps including the salting of weapons with materials such as cobalt. Such capabilities would not appear to be new or very significantly superior to those now possessed by the major nuclear powers.

11. In the biological warfare field, we have no information that agents capable of the extermination of mankind have been developed. Other scientific developments with weapons potential, such as lasers, do not appear to meet the mass destruction criteria of Khrushchev's description.

12. If in fact a monstrous new weapon exists, Khrushchev's statements imply that it is in the developmental rather than production state. If the weapon is 'very effective' against the Chinese but not against the West, anti-personnel weapons such as biological or radiological weapons, are suggested. We have, however, no evidence of spectacular developments in the fields."

Recommendations on U.S. public reaction will follow.

52.   Memorandum From the Joint Chiefs of Staff to Secretary of Defense McNamara[1]

JCSM–809–64   Washington, September 17, 1964.

SUBJECT

   Deep Underground Command Center (DUCC) (S)

1. Reference is made to a memorandum by the Deputy Secretary of Defense, dated 21 August 1964, subject as above.[2]

2. Within the context of the reference, the Joint Chiefs of Staff were requested to advise the Secretary of Defense as regards what functions they believe the Deep Underground Command Center (DUCC) should be capable of performing, and the number of people they believe the facility must house in order to perform these functions and to support the facility.

3. The Joint Chiefs of Staff believe that, if a DUCC is approved and constructed as an element of the National Military Command System (NMCS), it should be capable of performing those functions which support the Joint Chiefs of Staff in their role as principal military advisors to the President. If the President and his civilian and military advisors are to relocate to the DUCC, the facility must have the capability of performing the following pre-attack military functions as they pertain to international crisis situations and general nuclear war:

a. To maintain a minimum data base on the world-wide status of forces, Single Integrated Operational Plan, and force generation levels to ensure that the President will have adequate information to support a decision to authorize, if necessary, the use of nuclear weapons.

b. To maintain a capability to receive from external sources pertinent information on surveillance and analysis of the world situation, and indicator/warning data and current intelligence; and to maintain minimum facilities to conduct intelligence briefings on information and data received.

c. To provide an effective means of: (1) communications with the commanders of the unified and specified commands; and (2) negotiations with allied and foreign governments and the United Nations.

---

[1] Source: Washington National Records Center, OSD Files: FRC 330 70 A 4662, 381 DUCC (10 Jan 64) 1963 and 64 Papers. Top Secret.

[2] Vance's August 21 memorandum to the Joint Chiefs of Staff summarized JCSM–446–64, "Proposed Deep Underground Command Center," May 25; went on to express some views on the proposed center; and concluded by asking the JCS to advise OSD of the "functions they believe the facility must be capable of performing and the number of people they believe the facility must house in order to perform those functions and to support the facility." Copies of JCS–446–64 and Vance's August 21 memorandum are ibid.

d. To receive, process, and use, as available and as necessary, information from the National Military Command Center and existing Alternate Command Centers and Command Posts of the NMCS and other government agencies.

e. To maintain a state of readiness, including a current data base, to translate during the period of tactical warning from a standby condition to a fully capable primary Command Center to the extent permitted by the facilities provided, and prescribed by pertinent directives.

4. During the trans-attack and post-attack periods of a general nuclear war, a DUCC may be required to operate independently with information received directly from sources external to the Washington complex. In order to provide for this contingency, the DUCC must have the capability, within the context of a minimum facility, of performing the following functions in addition to those specified in the above paragraphs:

a. To receive and display information on the military and political situation in order to determine as quickly and accurately as possible the time, magnitude, and objective of the attack.

b. To disseminate decisions, orders, and instructions as to the appropriate action to be taken in response to an attack or threat of attack.

c. To communicate, by the surest and most effective means possible, with the major elements of the World-Wide Military Command and Control System.

5. Communications requirements vary considerably between critical international crises and general war. A need exists for an extensive world-wide network of reliable communications during crisis situations. After general war begins, the emphasis would then switch to survivable communications among the major command centers of the World-Wide Military Command and Control System primarily for the strategic direction of the military forces. However, there would remain a need for communications with the principal civil defense centers, and for negotiations with the principal adversary. Therefore, it appears that the functions of command communications would require that the DUCC be equipped with communications which approximate the capability now planned for the Alternate National Military Command Center.

6. It appears that the concept and capability reflected in the National Emergency Airborne Command Post would represent the minimum capability required in a DUCC to serve as an emergency command post for decision-making by the President. It is envisioned that the decision group, which would relocate to the DUCC, would comprise the National Command Authorities with a minimum number of

advisory personnel, and that they would remain in the DUCC in a post-attack situation only until the National Command Authorities could be relocated to a site from which the functions of government could more adequately be discharged. Basically, however, advisory information would be provided the DUCC by existing and surviving alternate command facilities equipped with larger data bases. A minimum data base would be maintained in the DUCC and staff support, to the extent feasible, would be provided to the decision group.

7. The determination of the precise number of people the DUCC must house in order to support the total mission of the facility, including the operation of the national government in crisis situations as well as the conduct of general nuclear war, would necessitate considerable liaison with the White House, and other departments and agencies of the national government. However, the Joint Chiefs of Staff believe that approximately 50 military personnel would be required to perform their part of the above functions in the manner described in the preceding paragraph. The figure does not include personnel for facility maintenance, communications, security, and housekeeping support for which about 175 additional people can be identified at this time. Additional functions and personnel possibly would be required to operate the national government in accordance with the desires of the President, and to the extent outlined in the reference. These latter requirements should be provided by the appropriate Departments and Agencies concerned, in order that the composite functional and personnel requirements, and hence the optimum size of the facility, may be established.

For the Joint Chiefs of Staff:
Earle G. Wheeler[3]
Chairman
Joint Chiefs of Staff

---

[3] Printed from a copy that indicates Wheeler signed the original.

53.   Circular Telegram From the Department of State to Certain Posts[1]

Washington, September 18, 1964, 4:22 p.m.

498. Joint State–Defense–USIA Circular. Reference: Circular 495.[2] Secretary McNamara issued following statement today on weapons developments announced by President yesterday:

Begin Text:

As you know, President Johnson announced yesterday that the United States is able to intercept and destroy armed satellites. I would like to give you, within the limits of military security, some additional information about this capability.

The two anti-satellite systems which the President discussed are operated by the Army and the Air Force. They are under the operational control of the Continental Air Defense Command. They make use of certain Navy facilities as well.

The Army system uses the Nike Zeus missile while the Air Force system employs the Thor missile. Both systems utilize the data from our global space detection and tracking network which includes various radars, sensors and computers.

The Army program to develop an anti-satellite capability was begun in May of 1962 and the Air Force program early in 1963.

It is especially significant that both the Army and the Air Force successfully intercepted satellites a year after I directed them to achieve this capability. The Army system was operational on August 1, 1963, the Air Force system on May 29, 1964.

The two systems have been effectively tested and have intercepted satellites in space, their missiles passing so close as to be within the destruction radius of the warheads.

The bases at which these anti-satellite systems are deployed is classified information.

---

[1]   Source: National Archives and Records Administration, RG 59, Central Files 1964–66, DEF 12–1 US. Unclassified; Immediate. Drafted by Thomas P. Dillon (P/PG) on September 18; cleared by Kirby (OASD/PA), Grant G. Hilliker (S/S), and Jay Warner Gildner (USIA/IOP); and approved by James L. Greenfield (P). Sent to all EUR and ARA posts and to 22 others.

[2]   Circular telegram 495, September 17, transmitted the text of remarks President Johnson made that day in Sacramento, California, on the steps of the State Capitol. (Ibid.) The President's remarks are printed in *Public Papers of the Presidents of the United States: Lyndon B. Johnson, 1963–64*, Book II, pp. 1086–1090.

To date, we have invested $80,000,000 to achieve this capability. This figure does not include the funds we are spending on items like the Space Detection and Tracking System and the Anti-Intercontinental Ballistic Missile system.

The family of over-the-horizon radars also announced yesterday by President Johnson is one of the most dramatic examples of new developments.

These new systems will bounce radar signals off the ionosphere and send them to the earth far beyond the horizon. Missiles being launched reflect or otherwise influence these signals which are received back at the transmitting station or at other points far beyond the horizon. These signals are then processed by electronic techniques to provide target detection and identification. Capabilities also exist against aircraft.

More than $50,000,000 has been invested in this program to develop and produce installations for these missile and aircraft detection systems. This radar will provide detection of missiles within seconds of launch at a distance of several thousand miles. *End Text.*

If transcript Q and A period, now being prepared, reveals additional relevant material posts will be informed.[3]

Rusk

---

[3] Selected questions and answers at Secretary McNamara's press conference were transmitted in circular telegram 500, September 18. (National Archives and Records Administration, RG 59, Central Files 1964–66, DEF 12–1 US)

54.   Memorandum From the President's Special Assistant for
        National Security Affairs (Bundy) to President Johnson[1]

Washington, September 23, 1964.

RE

Summary of the existing plans for emergency use of nuclear weapons

On March 26 you approved recommendations from McNamara and the Joint Chiefs to put into effect updated instructions for expenditure of nuclear weapons in emergency conditions.[2]

This instruction covers four emergency situations. Two of them are essentially defensive and would allow the use of nuclear weapons only against military targets in the air or at sea. These are: 1) active defense against air and space nuclear attack on the U.S., and 2) naval and air action against an imminent seaborne missile attack on the U.S.

In these two cases the commanders could act without contacting the President if the necessary delay would make it impossible for them to prevent the imminent attack.

The other two cases are 1) retaliation to a nuclear attack on the U.S., and 2) reply to a major assault on major U.S. forces at sea or in foreign territory. In these two cases every effort to contact the President must be made (with the qualifying phrase in the second case: "every effort consistent with the preservation of his command"). The authorized retaliation for an attack on the U.S. is a strategic attack on the Soviet Union. The authorized retaliation in the other case is against hostile forces but not repeat not against the Soviet Union itself.

The instructions reveal an interesting difference between situations in which nuclear weapons would do enormous civilian and industrial damage and situations in which they would be used in the upper atmosphere

---

[1] Source: Johnson Library, National Security File, Intelligence File, Meetings, Records Memoranda on Use of Nuclear Weapons, Box 9. Top Secret. During the 1964 Presidential election campaign, Barry Goldwater, the Republican Party nominee, made statements about nuclear weapons pre-delegation. In response, President Johnson in a speech in Seattle, Washington, on September 16, said that he alone exercised control over the use of nuclear weapons. The text of his speech is in *Public Papers of the Presidents of the United States: Lyndon B. Johnson, 1963–64*, Book II, pp. 1078–1081. In a September 22 memorandum to the President, Bundy outlined two alternative positions the President could take on the issue. First, he could hold to the position of his Seattle speech, but because Bundy believed that position was not accurate and was open "to the charge of deception," he preferred a second option, that "you should make a statement in which you make clear that there are indeed very specialized contingencies for which certain Presidential instructions already exist." (Johnson Library, National Security File, Intelligence File, Meetings, Records Memoranda on Use of Nuclear Weapons, Box 9)

[2] See Document 24.

or on the high seas. In the latter cases commanders have latitude to decide that the delay in contacting the President would be excessive. This is in line with a belief which Eisenhower had that when the destructive force of nuclear weapons would hit only military forces, the decision on their use was a very much less serious matter. It is possible that we ought to take account of this distinction in anything we say in the next few days.

McG.B.

55.   National Intelligence Estimate[1]

NIE 11–8–64   Washington, October 8, 1964.

SOVIET CAPABILITIES FOR STATEGIC ATTACK

The Problem

To estimate probable trends in the strength and deployment of Soviet forces for strategic attack and in Soviet capabilities for such attack through mid-1970.

Scope Note

This estimate covers those Soviet military forces which are suitable for strategic attack. Other major aspects of the Soviet military strength are treated in separate estimates on air and missile defense, on theater forces, on the nuclear program, and on the space program. Trends in the USSR's overall military posture and in Soviet military policy are examined in an annual estimate, the next issuance of which will be in the first quarter of 1965.

---

[1]   Source: National Archives and Records Administration, RG 263. Top Secret; Controlled Dissem. A cover sheet, prefatory note, title page, and table of contents are not printed. According to the prefatory note, the CIA and the intelligence organizations of the Departments of State, Defense, the Army, the Navy, and the Air Force; Atomic Energy Commission and National Security Agency participated in the preparation of this estimate. Representatives of the State Department, DIA, NSA, and AEC concurred; the FBI representative abstained, the subject being outside his jurisdiction. Attached is an October 8 memorandum from McCone to recipients of NIE 11–8–64, indicating that dissemination of the NIE "has been carefully limited because of the extreme sensitivity of the information therein" and stressing that there should be "absolutely no reproduction of this Estimate" and "no revelation of its existence . . . to unauthorized persons."

Summary and Conclusions

A. Major changes in Soviet programs for the development of strategic attack forces have become apparent during the past year. In 1962–1963, certain ICBM and ballistic missile submarine programs came to an end, and a pause ensued in the growth of these forces. At the same time, the pace of ICBM research and development increased markedly. More recently, the USSR has resumed ICBM deployment in a new and improved configuration, and the probable advent of a new submarine which we believe is designed to carry ballistic missiles probably marks the start of yet another deployment program. (Para. 1)

B. Soviet military policy in recent years has been to build up strategic offensive and defensive capabilities, maintain and improve large general purpose forces, and pursue research and development programs in advanced weapons. In our view, the primary concern of Soviet military policy for the next several years will continue to be the strengthening of the USSR's strategic deterrent. The evidence to date does not indicate that Soviet deployment programs are directed toward a rapid numerical buildup. We do not believe that the USSR aims at matching the US in numbers of intercontinental delivery vehicles. Recognition that the US would detect and match or overmatch such an effort, together with economic constraints, appears to have ruled out this option. (Paras. 2–4)

C. A stress on qualitative factors suggests that the Soviets see technological advance in weapons as a means by which they can improve their strategic position relative to the West. In the ICBM force, for example, major qualitative improvements currently being achieved include hardening and dispersal (which will sharply increase the number of aiming points), as well as better accuracy and larger payloads. (Paras. 4–5)

D. By the end of the decade, Soviet intercontinental attack capabilities will rest primarily upon an ICBM force of some hundreds of launchers, supplemented by a sizable missile-submarine fleet and a large but reduced bomber force. These forces will represent a marked improvement in Soviet retaliatory capability and a considerable strengthening of the Soviet deterrent. In the light of current and programmed US military capabilities, however, we do not believe that the Soviets will expect to achieve, within the period of this estimate, strategic attack capabilities which would make rational the deliberate initiation of general war. (Para. 5)

The ICBM Program

E. Major developments since mid-1963 include a proliferation of test facilities at Tyuratam, flight-testing of two third-generation ICBM systems (the SS-9 and SS-10), and the beginning of construction of hard, single-silo ICBM launchers, probably for one or both of the new systems. The deployment of second-generation ICBMs has probably ceased, and a pause between the second- and third-generation programs has slowed deployment. We believe that the Soviets now have about 200 operational ICBM launchers, and that the total number of operational launchers in mid-1965 will approximate the low side of the 250–350 range previously estimated. These figures do not include R&D launchers at Tyuratam.[2] (Paras 6–8, 10–18, 31)

F. Research and development on third-generation systems has been generally successful. The SS-9 system appears to be an outgrowth of the SS-7 with improved accuracy and a larger payload. We have little information on the characteristics of the SS-10. Both new systems could enter service in 1965. We believe that work is underway on still other ICBM systems, which we cannot as yet identify. We continue to believe that the Soviets are developing a very large ICBM, capable of delivering [*less than 1 line of source text not declassified*]. We estimate that it could enter service in the period mid-1966 to mid-1967. In addition, the Soviets might be developing a new, small ICBM employing improved propellants. If they are, it could become operational as early as 1967. (Paras. 19–26)

G. The Soviets are now emphasizing deployment of single-silo hard launchers for ICBMs, and we expect this emphasis to continue. We expect third-generation deployment to include the expansion of both second-generation complexes and the initiation of additional new complexes. (Paras. 9, 27)

H. The growth of the Soviet ICBM force over the next several years will be influenced by a number of factors. In economic terms, the program must compete for funds with other military and space activities and with the civilian economy. In the technical field, we believe that research and development is proceeding on additional, follow-on ICBM systems, and we doubt that with these in the offing the USSR will fix upon any one or even two existing systems for urgent deployment on a large scale. We are also mindful that the interruptions that marked second-generation deployment programs may recur. In strategic terms, the Soviets evidently judge that an ICBM force in the hundreds of launchers, together with their other strategic forces, provides a deterrent. On

---

[2] The Assistant Chief of Staff, Intelligence, USAF, considers the estimate of the numbers of launchers operational now and expected in mid-1965 is too low. He estimates that the Soviets now have about 240 operational launchers, including about 20 at Tyuratam and a 10 percent allowance for unlocated launchers. He believes the total number in mid-1965 will be between 275 and 325. See his footnote, page 11, para. 10. [Footnote in the source text. This footnote on page 11 notes that there were 197 identified operational launchers, and explained the rationale for increasing the estimate to 240.]

the basis of the evidence now available to us, we do not believe that they are attempting to deploy a force capable of a first-strike which would reduce the effects of US retaliation to an acceptable level.[3] At the same time, we expect them to continue a vigorous R&D effort in the hope of achieving important technological advances, in both the offensive and defensive fields, which would alter the present strategic relationship in a major way. (Para. 30)

I. We estimate a Soviet ICBM force of 400–700 operational launchers for mid-1970; in our previous estimate, we projected this force level for mid-1969. By mid-1970, we believe that the force will include most or all of the launchers now deployed, some 125–200 single-silo SS-9/10 launchers, and 10–20 launchers for very large ICBMs. We believe that the attainment of as many as 700 operational launchers by mid-1970 would be likely only if the Soviets begin deploying a new, small ICBM at a rapid rate about 1967. The Soviet ICBM force which we estimate for mid-1970 will represent a substantial increase in numbers and deliverable megatonnage. Further, the trend to single silos will increase the number of aiming points represented by individual launch sites from about 100 at present to some 300–575 in mid-1970, the bulk of them hard. This will greatly improve the survivability, and hence the retaliatory capability, of the force.[4] (Paras. 32–37)

J. In the past few years the Soviets have improved the readiness and reaction time of their ICBM force. Our evidence now indicates that from the normal state of readiness, the soft sites which constitute the bulk of the present force would require 1–3 hours to fire. Hard sites would require about half an hour or less. A higher state of alert (i.e., 5–15 minutes to fire) can be maintained at most soft sites for a number of hours and at most hard sites for days. (Paras. 38–40)

K. There is ample evidence that the Soviets designed their soft ICBM systems to have a refire capability. We have re-examined the factors likely to affect refire time, and conclude that it would require little longer to fire the second missile than the first. Our present estimate of

---

[3] The Assistant Chief of Staff, Intelligence, USAF, considers that the Soviets may already have directed their intensive military R&D effort toward achievement of an effective first-strike counter-force capability before the close of this decade. Considering the length of time covered by this estimate and the number of unknowns involved, he believes this is a possibility which should not be disregarded. [Footnote in the source text.]

[4] The Assistant Chief of Staff, Intelligence, USAF, considers the ICBM force by mid-1970 could range from approximately 600 to as high as 900 operational launchers depending on whether a new, small, easily deployed system is introduced. (See his footnote to table on page 18.) An ICBM force of this size would increase the number of aiming points represented by individual launch sites to approximately 400–700 in mid-1970. [Footnote in the source text. This footnote on page 18 develops the rationale for higher projections of launchers.]

refire time is 2–4 hours, considerably less than previously estimated. We believe that, on the average, two or more missiles are provided per soft launcher for initial firing, refire, and maintenance spares. We believe that hard ICBM sites do not have a refire capability. (Paras. 41–43)

L. We have little evidence on the hardness of Soviet ICBM sites. Given the many uncertainties in this area, only a very tenuous estimate can be made, but our best judgment is that Soviet hard ICBM sites have a hardness in the 300–600 psi range. This implies a design overpressure in the 200–400 psi range, somewhat higher than previously estimated.[5] (Paras 49–50)

M. Qualitative improvements in the force can be expected as new ICBM systems enter service. Currently operational ICBMs have CEPs on the order of 1–2 n.m. The SS-9 will probably have an accuracy of 0.5–1.0 n.m. with radio assist, or 1.0–1.5 with all-inertial guidance. By mid-1970, the Soviets could achieve accuracies on the order of 0.5 n.m. or better. The SS-9 will probably carry a payload [*less than 1 line of source text not declassified*] as compared with [*less than 1 line of source text not declassified*] for second-generation ICBMs. We do not believe that the Soviets have yet developed penetration aids or multiple warheads, but they may do so in the future, particularly if the US deploys antimissile defenses. (Paras. 44–48)

MRBMs and IRBMs

N. Deployment programs for the 1,020 n.m. MRBM and the 2,200 n.m. IRBM are now ending, and almost certainly will be completed by mid-1965. We estimate that at that time the MRBM/IRBM force will have a strength of about 760 operational launchers, 145 of them hard. The bulk of the force (about 90 percent) is deployed in western USSR, with the remainder in the southern and far eastern regions of the USSR. This force is capable of delivering a devastating first strike or a powerful retaliatory attack against targets in Eurasia, and can attack such areas as Greenland and Alaska as well. Some of the MRBM/IRBM launchers are probably intended to support ground operations. (Paras. 51–55)

O. We doubt that the Soviets will expand their MRBM/IRBM force during the period of this estimate. It is possible, however, that operational capabilities will be improved by the introduction of a new missile system, which probably would be deployed in single-silos. Such a system, employing unproved propellants, could become operational in the 1966–1968 period and would probably replace some of the soft launchers now operational. (Paras. 56–59)

---

[5] The Assistant Chief of Staff, Intelligence, USAF, considers that, given the uncertainties involved, no meaningful estimate of the hardness of Soviet hard sites can be made. However, he believes that the design overpressure of Soviet hard sites is no greater than the 100–300 psi previously estimated. [Footnote in the source text.]

Missile Submarine Forces

P. The Soviets now have operational some 40–50 ballistic missile submarines, including 8–10 nuclear powered. Most of these submarines are equipped with 350 n.m. missiles and must surface to fire. One or two are equipped with a new 700 n.m. submerged-launch missile, and others will probably be retrofitted. The USSR also has operational about 30 cruise-missile submarines, including 11–14 nuclear powered. The majority are equipped with 300 n.m. missiles designed for low altitude attack, primarily against ships. The remainder carry a newer 450 n.m. version of this missile, which probably has an improved capability to attack land targets. Current Soviet missile submarines carry relatively few missiles: the ballistic missile classes, two or three, and the cruise missile types, up to eight. The entire present force has a total of 120–140 ballistic missile tubes and 135–150 cruise-missile launchers. (Paras. 60–71)

Q. We believe that the Soviets have under construction a submarine which we estimate to be the first of a new nuclear-powered, ballistic missile class. We estimate that it will employ the submerged launch 700 n.m. missile, and have a few more missile tubes than current classes. The first unit will probably become operational in 1965. Beyond this new class, we consider it unlikely that the Soviets will develop an entirely new follow-on ballistic missile submarine system within the period of this estimate, although they will probably continue to improve existing systems. We believe that they will also continue to construct cruise-missile submarines. By mid-1970 the Soviet missile submarine force will probably number 100–130 ships, about half of them cruise-missile submarines and about half ballistic. (Paras. 72–75)

R. In the past year, limited numbers of Soviet missile submarines have engaged in patrols in the open oceans. We expect a gradual expansion of this activity. By the end of the decade, Soviet missile submarines will probably be conducting regular patrols throughout the North Atlantic and Pacific, and possibly into the Mediterranean. (Para. 76)

Long-Range Bomber Forces

S. We have no recent evidence of major changes in the capabilities and structure of Soviet Long-Range Aviation (LRA). The force now includes some 190–220 heavy bombers and tankers and 850–900 mediums. It is being improved primarily through the continued introduction of Blinder supersonic dash medium bombers and through modification of older bombers for air-to-surface missile delivery, for aerial refueling, and for reconnaissance. Use of both medium and heavy bombers of the LRA in support of marine operations has increased. (Paras. 80–86)

T. Considering noncombat attrition factors and the requirements for Arctic staging and aerial refueling, we estimate that the Soviets could put somewhat more than 100 heavy bombers over target areas in the US on two-way missions. Recent trends lead us to believe that medium bombers do not now figure prominently in Soviet plans for an initial bomber attack against North America. Nevertheless, should they elect to do so, we believe that at present the Soviets could put up to 150 Badgers over North American target areas on two-way missions. We have serious doubt about how effectively the Soviets could launch large-scale bomber operations against North America. We consider it probable that initial attacks would not be simultaneous, but would extend over a considerable number of hours.[6] (Paras. 91–97)

U. The Soviets will probably maintain sizable bomber forces, which will decrease gradually through attrition and retirement. Although continued Soviet work on advanced transports could be applied to military purposes, we think it unlikely that the Soviets will bring any follow-on heavy bomber into operational service during the period of this estimate. We believe that Blinder medium bombers, some equipped with advanced air-to-surface missiles, will be introduced during much of the period of this estimate. By mid-1970, Long-Range Aviation will probably include some 140–180 heavy bombers of present types and 300–500 mediums, mostly Blinders.[7] (Paras. 87–90)

Space Weapons

V. Although the USSR almost certainly is investigating the feasibility of space systems for use as offensive and defensive weapons, we have no evidence that a program to establish an orbital bombardment capability is seriously contemplated by the Soviet leadership. We think that orbital weapons will not compare favorably with ICBMs over the

---

[6] The Assistant Chief of Staff, Intelligence, USAF, considers this paragraph seriously underestimates the manned aircraft threat to the continental US. In the event war should eventuate and the USSR attacks the US with nuclear weapons, he believes this will be an all-out effort aimed at putting a maximum number of weapons on US targets. He therefore estimates that the number of heavy and medium bombers, including Badgers on one-way missions, could exceed 500. See his footnote on page 32, para. 94. [Footnote in the source text. This footnote on page 32 essentially repeats the information presented in this footnote.]

[7] The Assistant Chief of Staff, Intelligence, USAF, believes the Soviets will continue to consider manned strategic aircraft an important adjunct to their ICBM force. He estimates that the USSR will introduce a follow-on heavy bomber. He further estimates the heavy bomber force will remain at about 200 or somewhat larger, depending on the timing of the expected follow-on bomber, and that by mid-1970 the medium bomber/tanker force will probably still include about 650–850 aircraft. See his footnote to table on page 31 following para. 90. [Footnote in the source text. This footnote on page 31 presents a table showing the estimated annual numbers of heavy and medium-range bombers through mid-1970.]

next six years in terms of effectiveness, reaction time, targeting flexibility, vulnerability, average life, and positive control. In view of these considerations, the much greater cost of orbital weapon systems, and Soviet endorsement of the UN resolution against nuclear weapons in space, we believe that the Soviets are unlikely to develop and deploy an orbital weapon system within the period of this estimate. (Paras. 98–103)

[Here follow the Discussion section (Parts I–VII, pages 9–37) and Annexes A and B (pages 38–49 and following page 49).]

56.   National Intelligence Estimate[1]

NIE 4–64   Washington, October 21, 1964.

LIKELIHOOD OF A PROLIFERATION OF BW
AND CW CAPABILITIES

The Problem

To assess the capabilities and intentions of additional countries to achieve biological and lethal chemical warfare capabilities during the next three years or so.

Scope Note

This estimate excludes the USSR and its Warsaw Pact allies, since these countries have been considered in NIE 11–10–63: "Soviet Capabilities and Intentions with Respect to Chemical Warfare," dated 27 December 1963, Secret;[2] and NIE 11–6–64: "Soviet Capabilities and Intentions with Respect to Biological Warfare," dated 26 August 1964, Secret.[3] These estimates also contain general information on BW and CW agents, delivery systems, military doctrine, and defense measures.

---

[1] Source: Johnson Library, National Security File, National Intelligence Estimates 4, Arms and Disarmament, Box 1. Secret; No Foreign Dissem; Controlled Dissem. A cover sheet, prefatory note, title page, and table of contents are not printed. According to the prefatory note, the CIA and the intelligence organizations of the Departments of State and Defense and the National Security Agency participated in the preparation of this estimate. Representatives of the State Department, DIA, and NSA concurred; the AEC and FBI representatives abstained, the subject being outside their jurisdiction.

[2] Not found.

[3] A copy is in the Johnson Library, National Security File, National Intelligence Estimates 11–64, USSR, Box 3.

Our consideration of BW agents includes all those suitable for use against personnel, livestock, crops, and matériel; consideration of CW agents excludes incapacitating and riot control agents, and smoke, flame, and defoliant chemicals.

This estimate does not concern itself with BW or CW as instruments for clandestine use in assassination, small-scale terrorism, and the like.

Summary and Conclusions

A. For any reasonably modernized state, and even for many of the less developed nations, there are few obstacles in the way of acquiring at least some BW and CW capability. The technology underlying BW and CW is widely known or easily obtainable through open sources; the physical facilities required to develop and produce agents are in great part quite easily adaptable from existing chemical and pharmaceutical facilities; the means of delivery comprise a wide range of conventional weapons and even non-military equipment; and, overall, the costs are relatively small, at least for an offensive capability appropriate to most states' conceivable needs. (Paras. 8–12)

B. Yet despite these considerations, there is not now a trend toward the proliferation of BW or CW capabilities in the world. Such proliferation could occur during the next few years, notably through a snowballing process of mounting fear and suspicion, and of action and reaction on the part of particular sets of adversaries among the middle and smaller powers, but proliferation cannot now be judged likely. (Paras. 17–24)

C. A number of factors work to restrain BW and CW proliferation. The very fact that many states could achieve a capability with relative ease gives these weapons the quality of a two-edge sword. Prudence would dictate that countries deciding to acquire an offensive or retaliatory capability should also undertake to develop a defensive capability, and the requirements of doing so would add to the price, almost prohibitively if adequate provision were made for civilian needs. Most military doctrine on CW, and even more so on BW, lays emphasis on the defensive aspects of the problem, which is some evidence of a reluctance to be the first user. And finally, there exists an almost universal popular moral and psychological abhorrence of these forms of munitions, which adds to official reluctance to contemplate their use. (Paras. 2–7, 17–24)

[3 paragraphs (20 lines of source text) and 4-line table not declassified] (Paras. 1, 16)

G. Almost any semi-industrialized country could easily acquire *token* native capabilities in either field (i.e., enough for one or two attacks on important targets). Any country could quietly acquire through commercial channels at least a token capability in the less toxic World War I-type CW agents. (Paras. 1, 16)

H. Present evidence does not warrant an estimate that any nation is now determined to achieve a meaningful operational capability in either BW or CW during the next few years. We believe that most states will remain reluctant to do so. Nonetheless, some may proceed toward this goal, as a deterrent or retaliatory measure in case a potential adversary develops a capability, as a supplement to nuclear weapons, or possibly as the best available substitute for them. [3 *lines of source text not declassified*] (Paras. 17–24)

[Here follow the Discussion section (pages 4–8); Part II. Capabilities (pages 8–9); Part III. Intentions (pages 9–11); and Appendix (page 13).]

57.   National Intelligence Estimate[1]

NIE 4–2–64   Washington, October 21, 1964.

PROSPECTS FOR A PROLIFERATION OF NUCLEAR WEAPONS
OVER THE NEXT DECADE

The Problem

To estimate the capabilities and intentions of additional countries to develop and produce nuclear weapons over the next decade and to estimate the consequences thereof.

Conclusions

A. France has already developed deliverable nuclear weapons. Communist China has conducted its first nuclear test.[2] The other

---

[1] Source: Johnson Library, National Security File, National Intelligence Estimates 4, Arms and Disarmament, Box 1. Secret; Controlled Dissem. A cover sheet, prefatory note, title page, and table of contents are not printed. According to the prefatory note, the CIA and the intelligence organizations of the Departments of State and Defense and the National Security Agency participated in the preparation of this estimate. Representatives of the State Department, DIA, NSA, and AEC concurred; the FBI representative abstained, the subject being outside his jurisdiction.

[2] Separate estimates on both the French and the Chinese nuclear weapons programs are scheduled for publication later in 1964. [Footnote in the source text. The People's Republic of China conducted its first nuclear test on October 16, 1964.]

nations which we now believe may develop nuclear weapons in the next decade are India, and perhaps Israel and Sweden. (Paras. 1, 19, 23, 26)

B. India's decision as to whether to start a nuclear weapons program will depend on its evaluation of a number of domestic and foreign factors including the scope and pace of the Chinese program, any changes in Sino-Soviet relations, and outside assurances. On balance, we believe the chances are better than even that India will decide to develop nuclear weapons within the next few years. India now has the basic facilities necessary for a modest weapons program, including a plutonium separation plant. India could produce by 1970 about a dozen weapons in the 20 KT range. Thereafter, when reactor capacity is expected to increase substantially, India's ability to produce fissionable material will increase proportionately. (Paras. 12–19)

C. [6 lines of source text not declassified] (Paras. 20–23)

D. Sweden will continue its peaceful nuclear program, but we believe the chances of its developing nuclear weapons during the next decade are less than even. (Paras. 24–26)

E. Soviet and US policies have had some effect in hindering the proliferation of nuclear weapons. [4-1/2 lines of source text not declassified] (Para. 41)

F. In terms of broad international implications, the impact of the proliferation which is already occurring—in France and Communist China—will be far greater than the impact of the further proliferation by smaller powers which we can foresee. In military terms, basic power relationships between the USSR and the US are not likely to be changed significantly. But the French and Chinese nuclear programs will make relations within and between alliance systems increasingly difficult in years to come. Communist China's recent detonation of its first nuclear device will have an important impact throughout Asia, and in Southeast Asia will reinforce Chinese efforts to achieve Asian hegemony through political pressures and indirect support of local "wars of liberation." (Paras. 45–46)

G. The military impact of proliferation among the smaller powers would derive primarily from the possibility that more aggressive activities by these states could lead to confrontations involving the major powers. US and Soviet involvement in such crises could create the potential for escalation, but both countries would have incentives to urge prudence and caution on all parties. (Paras. 47–48)

H. The chances of unintentional or unauthorized explosion of nuclear weapons will rise as the number of countries possessing them increases. Although the odds are strongly against it, there is some possibility that the accidental firing of a nuclear warhead into the territory of one of the major powers could touch off an immediate nuclear exchange. An accidental nuclear explosion might, particularly if property and many lives were lost, restrain some countries not involved in the accident from undertaking a weapons program. In the country where the accident occurred, domestic opposition might become strong enough to cause abandonment of a weapons program already underway, as well as create intense pressure for the withdrawal of any nuclear weapons stationed in the area by allied nations. (Paras. 49–50)

[Here follows the Discussion section, which includes: I. General Considerations (pages 4–7); II. Survey of Individual Countries (pages 7–15); III. Policies of the Present Nuclear Powers Toward Proliferation (pages 15–16); and IV. Broad Implications of Nuclear Proliferation (pages 16–17).]

58.   Memorandum for the Record

Washington, October 29, 1964.

[Source: Department of State, INR/IL Historical Files, November 12, 1964. Secret; Eyes Only. Extract—2 pages of source text not declassified.]

59.   Letter From Director of Central Intelligence McCone to
       Secretary of Defense McNamara[1]

Washington, November 16, 1964.

Dear Bob:

A few weeks ago you asked me to examine and report to you personally on the history of Air Force dissents to national intelligence estimates.[2] The examination resulted in the attached report,[3] which I submit to you in complete confidence. It indicates Air Force dissents have been numerous and, in recent years, far exceeded the dissents of the Army, the Navy or DIA.

The most disturbing issue, of course, has been the Soviet ICBM's. You will note in Tab B that the Air Force has consistently taken the position of crediting the Soviets with a greater current and prospective capability than the other members of the intelligence community. In retrospect the Air Force has been wrong though the estimates have taken a somewhat downward trend in recent years. It is interesting that in February, 1960 the Air Force estimated the Soviets would have 250 ICBM's in mid-61 and 800 in mid-63. This is far above what actually occurred. Incidentally, the community's estimates of 140 to 200 ICBM's in mid-61 and 350 to 450 in mid-63 proved to be high. Again in August of 1960, the Air Force estimate of 950 ICBM's in mid-64 and 1200 in mid-65 is obviously high. In our most recent exercise (October 8th, 1964), the Air Force was about 20% above the community with respect to the current situation but I note that as they look into future years they consistently project a greater capability than the accepted view of the balance of the community.

With respect to heavy bombers, there have been consistent differences. However I find that in July, 1962 the community, as indicated in Tab C, lowered the estimate on Soviet Bisons and Bears. The Air Force dissented and in this instance the Air Force appears to be correct, as the community estimate was somewhat low. I think the community and Air Force views in this area are now compatible.

Tab D sets forth an Air Force dissent on capabilities of the Soviet Theater Forces. They here took the position that Soviet doctrine maintains that nuclear weapons will play a dominant role in all phases of

---

[1] Source: Central Intelligence Agency, Executive Registry Subject Files, Job 01676R. Top Secret; [codeword not declassified].

[2] This request has not been further identified.

[3] The attached report, which apparently includes Tabs B–E referenced below, has not been found.

a general war and that the initial phase of such a war may be decisive. The Air Force dismisses the concept of a non-nuclear war of substantial proportions.

With respect to the main trends in Soviet capabilities and policies (Tab E), the community has concluded that the Soviet's objective is the attainment of a substantial deterrent and pre-emptive attack capabilities. The Air Force dissents from this view and takes the position that the Soviet rulers are endeavoring to attain at the earliest practical date a military superiority over the United States which would be decisive.

There are other dissents relating to the introduction of new bombers, the attitude toward nuclear propelled aircraft, which are of lesser importance than the four mentioned above.

I wish you to handle this communication on a very personal basis as the existence of the study would obviously create misunderstanding within the community which might better be avoided.

Sincerely,

John A. McCone[4]

---

[4] Printed from a copy that bears this typed signature.

60.   Letter From the Acting Deputy Under Secretary of State for
       Political Affairs (Thompson) to the Secretary of Defense's
       Assistant for Atomic Energy (Howard)[1]

Washington, November 20, 1964.

Dear Mr. Howard:

Your letter of September 18, 1964,[2] requests the views of this
Department on a proposed Department of Defense Dispersal Plan for
nuclear weapons in the FY '65 stockpile.

There are certain underlying aspects of nuclear weapons planning
which the Department of State considers it important to explore further
with the Department of Defense, in order to establish a more adequate
basis for our future appraisal of detailed dispersal plans such as this
one. I have some suggestions to this end below. For the present, in view
of the wide variety of pending action decisions which need to be made
in connection with the FY '65 plan, the Department has no objection to
its being forwarded to the President.

I wish to make clear, however, that the Department of State does not
concur in the FY '65 planning figures shown for support of non-U.S.
forces with nuclear weapons. We consider this to be a matter for subsequent and separate consideration, as indicated most recently in Secretary
Rusk's letter of July 28, 1964, to Secretary McNamara.[2] It remains our
view that additional major dispersals of nuclear weapons in support of
non-U.S. forces should await joint State/Defense consideration of the
concept of tactical nuclear warfare in Europe, although we continue of
course to stand ready in exceptional circumstances to consider individual dispersal actions pursuant to the provisions of NSAM 197.[3]

In this general connection, it is also the view of the Department of
State that prior to final decision on the proposed FY 65 dispersals to U.S.
forces in Europe, highest-level consideration and evaluation should be
given to the following foreign policy aspects of the matter:

---

[1] Source: Washington National Records Center, OASD/ISA Files: FRC 330 68 A 4023,
471.6 1964 Oct–Dec. Top Secret; Restricted Data. A copy indicates that the memorandum
was drafted by Scott George (G/PM) on November 19 and was cleared in G/PM, S/P, and
EUR/RPM. (Ibid.) The letter was forwarded to John A. McNaughton (DOD/ISA) under
cover of a November 27 memorandum from Captain F. Costagliola (USN), Howard's
principal military assistant, for action.

[2] Not found.

[3] NSAM No. 197, "Improved Procedure—Communication to Other Countries of RD
on Weapons," October 23, 1962. (National Archives and Records Administration, RG 59,
S/S–RD Files: Lot 71 D 171)

1. To the extent dispersal of additional weapons to U.S. forces causes our NATO allies to gain the impression that more nuclear weapons
are essential for an effective defense by U.S. forces, we can reasonably
expect pressures to mount for further dispersals to non-U.S. forces.

2. To the extent we increase the magnitude of the disparity between
weapons held by U.S. forces and those held in support of non-U.S.
forces, we lay a basis for possible serious discord in the Alliance.

It is requested that these foreign policy aspects of the proposed dispersals to U.S. forces in Europe be considered in the Department of
Defense at appropriate level prior to transmittal of planning figures to
the White House and that the transmitting memorandum to the
President make note of the State view expressed in the preceding paragraph, as well as of the fact that this Department does not concur in the
planning figures for dispersal to non-U.S. forces.

As to the further State–DOD exploration referred to above, it would
be most useful if a number of inter-related subjects in this general area
could be discussed by the special committee composed of Mr.
McNaughton, General Goodpaster and myself.[4] I am therefore proposing that the following be considered at an early date by that group:

1. If we are to share in meaningful recommendations to the
President on nuclear weapons questions of this sort, my present feeling
is that some earlier State participation in the whole process is needed.
Dealing with the final dispersal plan alone, as important as this is, is not
wholly adequate, since it touches only one late-stage aspect—the
parceling out of a total stockpile amount which necessarily had to be
agreed at a considerably earlier date. One possibility I think should be
considered would be for the Department to comment from a foreign
policy point of view on proposed FY '66 and subsequent stockpile figures during the process of preparing a recommendation to the
President.

2. As discussed above, the FY '65 plan envisages a large increase
over presently-authorized levels for nuclear support of non-U.S. members of NATO. The Department of State has previously taken exception
to planned increases of this magnitude, pending joint consideration of
a concept for tactical nuclear warfare which would put the proposed
weapons support and our various commitments into some more meaningful context than presently exists. A continued piecemeal approach to
this matter, under NSAM 197, is not satisfactory, except as a temporary
expedient, and we consider it increasingly important that we come to
an agreed national policy on tactical nuclear weapons in Europe as a

---

[4] Documentation on this interagency Committee on Nuclear Weapons Capabilities,
as it was called, is in *Foreign Relations,* 1964–1968, volume XI. Llewellyn Thompson served
as chairman of the Committee.

basis on which to decide pending and future dispersal actions. [4 *lines of source text not declassified*]

I am of course aware that a number of studies have been and are now being conducted by various offices within the Department of Defense. Indeed we have had close and full association with many of these efforts, and this has been most helpful to us. What is still needed, however, is to press on until we have distilled a consensus within the Executive Branch on the vital policy issues underlying the potential employment of tactical nuclear weapons. Until that point is reached I do not believe we have adequate basis to make major decisions on further dispersal of such weapons in support of non-U.S. forces.

3. While our previous comments have been primarily directed toward the question of nuclear support of non-U.S. forces, this is clearly only a facet of the total problem, and we need therefore to address continuing study to the inter-relationship of U.S. and non-U.S. forces in NATO Europe as regards nuclear weapons. With respect to the ADM question mentioned above, for example, it would be helpful to know more about the concept and planned mode of operation which underlay the dispersal of ADMs to U.S. forces in Europe. This would undoubtedly have relevance to the problem of ADMs for non-U.S. forces, especially since it is our understanding that the ADMs for which dispersal to allied forces is planned are being held for the present by U.S. theatre forces. Circumstances and details undoubtedly differ with respect to other present and planned weapons systems, and my only point here is to emphasize that decisions on arming and equipping U.S. forces must be reckoned with in terms of the possible effect on non-U.S. forces. Thus, while we must of course continue to think in terms of the concern expressed in NSAM 305[5] about growth of excessive stockpiles abroad in support of non-U.S. forces, it is unrealistic to think solely in those terms, since the problem of nuclear weapons for allied forces cannot be dealt with in isolation, and any continued buildup of nuclear support for U.S. forces obviously increases political and other pressures for similar treatment for allied forces. One great merit of the national policy on tactical nuclear weapons in Europe to which I refer above is that it would serve as a background against which to make decisions in this area as required, whether U.S. or non-U.S. forces are involved.

Sincerely,

Llewellyn Thompson

---

[5] NSAM No. 305, June 16, 1964, concerns the nuclear weapons dispersal authorization for FY 1964. (Johnson Library, National Security File, National Security Action Memoranda)

61.   Memorandum From the Chairman of the Joint Chiefs of
        Staff (Wheeler) to Secretary of Defense McNamara[1]

CM–267–64   Washington, November 23, 1964.

SUBJECT

    Draft Memorandum for the President on Strategic Offensive Forces, Continental
    Air and Missile Defense Forces and Civil Defense by FY 1966–1970 (U)[2]

    1. I have forwarded, by JCSM–973–64,[3] the comments of the Joint
Chiefs of Staff on the subject draft memorandum for the President.
Except as noted below, I agree with the views expressed in
JCSM–973–64.

    2. In light of the offensive-defensive approach to the problem of
determining the optimum balance of the major components of our general nuclear war posture, and the recent studies of this problem as a single package, I have reached certain new conclusions with respect to
these forces and activities.

    3. My personal views concerning these forces, including the six
major issues in this area of the FY 1966–1970 program, are indicated
below:

    a. *Development and Deployment of a New Manned Bomber*

    I believe that it would be prudent to maintain a force of manned
strategic aircraft throughout the foreseeable future, and support the Air
Force PCP's and the strategic aircraft program as expressed in
JCSM–791–64 of 12 September 1964[4] and JCSM–925–64 of 31 October
1964.[5] Should you nevertheless continue to feel that there should be a
delay in the decision whether to proceed with the Project Definition
Phase, I then recommend that you reconsider the two-year moratorium
proposed in your memorandum. The advantages inherent in increased
dispersal and in the speed of AMSA as compared to the B-52, and the

---

    [1] Source: Washington National Records Center, OSD Files: FRC 330 69 A 7425, 381
Strategic Retaliatory Forces (9 Jan 64) Sep–Nov 1964. Top Secret.
    [2] Reference is to a lengthy November 5 draft memorandum from McNamara to Presi-
dent Johnson on "Recommended FY 1966–1970 Programs for Strategic Offensive Forces,
Continental Air and Missile Defense Forces, and Civil Defense." (Ibid.)
    [3] Dated November 20. (Ibid.)
    [4] This JCSM deals with proposed program changes for the Advanced Manned Stra-
tegic Aircraft (AMSA), AMSA Avionics, and propulsion system for the AMSA. (National
Archives and Records Administration, RG 218, JCS Files, 7000.1 (2 Sep 64) Sec 2)
    [5] Entitled "The Strategic Aircraft Program." (Ibid., RG 200, Defense Programs and
Operations, AMSA—Memo to the President, Oct.–Nov. 1964, Box 43)

smaller tanker requirement of AMSA in relation to a strategic version of the F-111, appear to me to weigh in favor of a new manned bomber, while recognizing the economies apparent in a B-52/SRAM combination. Considering the uncertainties regarding extension of the life of the B-52 until FY 1975 or beyond, and the estimated ten-year interval from go-ahead on PDP to attainment of a 200 AMSA force, it would appear desirable to go ahead in the near future with a decision to proceed with the Project Definition Phase in order to keep a timely option, and minimize the risk of a temporary degradation of our manned bomber capability. Pending such a decision, I recommend that advanced avionics and propulsion development be expedited, that the prerequisite phase proposed by the Air Force be completed as soon as practicable and that the decision with respect to initiating the formal Project Definition Phase be made at that time.

b. *The Size of the Strategic Missile Force*

As indicated in your memorandum for the President, even with a $30 billion balanced damage limiting program, U.S. fatalities associated with an early urban attack would be very heavy. I believe we should take every reasonable step to ensure that we maintain a substantially greater assured destruction capability than the Soviets. I am concerned by the effect upon our relative superiority if we reduce the previously approved Minuteman force from 1200 to 1000, with a substantial impact being felt in the early years, and also phase out many of our Atlas and Titan missiles. I concur with your recommendation to phase out Atlas and Titan-I by the end of this fiscal year provided we retain the previously approved Minuteman program, with as many as practicable of the added 200 being scheduled in the next two years. My views in this regard are influenced by the greater hardness of Minuteman as compared to all of these missiles, the reduced time required for launch of Minuteman, and doubt as to whether Atlas-F will be capable of demonstrating adequate reliability in the operational test program in a reasonable time prior to retirement. The $515 million saving as a result of the Atlas and Titan-I phase-out should provide an appreciable portion of the funds required for the additional 200 Minuteman missiles.

c. *The Over-all Level of the Anti-Bomber Defense Program*

Although a balanced defense requires a major reorientation of our effort, I believe we should avoid significant reduction of our present over-all capability against the Soviet manned bomber threat until that threat is appreciably reduced. A shift of funds and effort from less effective to improved systems is desirable, but should be accomplished without significant drop in total capability.

(1) I would be inclined to phase out the DEW Line Extension aircraft and radar picket ships in order to shift the funds into support of more

advanced systems, recognizing the possibility that by outflanking our warning systems Soviet bombers could deliver many megatons more quickly following their missile attack. It would appear that this risk is limited by current utilization of USAF airborne radar resources to perform random patrols, and that increased utilization could reduce the risk further. The calculated risk involved emphasizes the need for expediting improved warning systems such as over-the-horizon radar and AWACS.

(2) With regard to the century series interceptors, in my opinion, a decrease should not be made prior to evidence that the anticipated 1967 reduction in the Soviet bomber is a fact, or sufficient numbers of either the F-12A or an interceptor version of the F-111 are available to cope with the threat. With respect to elimination of the F-89 aircraft now in the Air National Guard inventory, I believe that in view of their age and performance, the added risk involved could be taken if the resources thus gained were applied to more advanced systems.

d. *The Production and Deployment of a New Manned Interceptor*

In their action on JSOP–69 last March,[6] the Joint Chiefs of Staff recommended either the procurement of 18 IMI aircraft (CSAF) or the retention of the option to initiate the procurement of IMI by means of inclusion in the FY 1966 budget of the necessary funds for the first increment of procurement subject to a review of this position following completion of an integrated review of all components of air defense (CJCS, CSA, CNO and CMC). The CJCS Special Studies Group has completed the study of Alternate General Nuclear War Postures.[7] Although the question of whether the F-12A is preferable to an interceptor version of the F-111 has still not been resolved, I believe the Special Studies Group study justified the requirement for procurement of a new manned interceptor. Accordingly, I recommend that the FY 1966 budget include sufficient funds to permit the procurement of either 18 F-12A's or 18 F-111's, whichever are determined to be preferable in studies to be conducted between now and FY 1966.

e. *The Production and Development of the Nike-X Anti-Missile System*

Recent studies establish the need for balanced strategic offensive and defensive forces. At the present time, we have relatively strong

---

[6] Not further identified.

[7] In a January 9, 1964, memorandum to the Joint Chiefs of Staff, Secretary McNamara asked the Special Studies Group to "prepare a study of the effectiveness and cost of alternative possible U.S. postures for general nuclear war in the time period in which we could have a fully deployed Nike-X defense." He attached to this memorandum a 2-page terms of reference for the study. (Washington National Records Center, OSD Files: FRC 330 69 A 7425, 381 Strategic Retaliatory Forces (9 Jan 64) Jan–Jun 64) The completed study has not been found but was sent as an attachment to a September 19 memorandum from Wheeler to Secretary McNamara (CM–139–64). (Memorandum from the JCS to Secretary McNamara, October 30 (JCSM–912–64); ibid., Sep–Nov 1964)

strategic offensive forces and also weapon systems for defense against the Soviet manned bomber. However, until such time as we establish an anti-ballistic missile capability, we cannot attain any semblance of a balance in our offensive and defensive forces. The existing lack of ABM defense warrants the inclusion of approximately $200 million for pre-production funding in the FY 1966 budget, in order to begin to attain this capability at the earliest practicable time. In my judgment, this production decision should not be delayed for a year because of the existence of uncertainties concerning the preferred concept of its deployment, the relationship of Nike X to other elements of a balanced damage-limiting effort, the prospects for the fallout shelter system, or uncertainties concerning possible Soviet reaction to our improving our defensive posture.

f. *The Construction of Fallout Shelters for the Entire Population*

As indicated in the draft memorandum for the President, an effective nation-wide fallout shelter program would provide a high return for the money expended. This program offers defense against either bomber or missile attack and could reduce rural fatalities by over fifty per cent. In view of this relatively economical means of saving approximately twenty-two per cent of the total population, I do not believe we should restrict the FY 1966 funding for this program to the limited amount recommended in the draft memorandum. In my opinion, the Defense Department, with Executive Branch support, should lead the major effort to convince the Congress of the need for this program. I urge that the FY 1966 budget contain provision for the required development and for the maximum practicable support of construction necessary to provide fallout shelters for the entire population.

5. In summary, I concur generally with the views expressed by my predecessor with respect to continental air and missile defense forces in JSOP-69, and I am convinced that some increases in the force levels now programmed or recommended are well justified for our national security.

Earle G. Wheeler

62.   Letter From Secretary of State Rusk to the Chairman of the
Joint Chiefs of Staff (Wheeler)[1]

Washington, November 23, 1964.

Dear General Wheeler:

I appreciate your sending me a copy of the 1964 Report of the Net
Evaluation Subcommittee of the National Security Council.[2]

There are some findings of the report on which I should like to comment. First, I agree completely that political and psychological factors
will be important, and in some situations may be determining, in the
decisions to release nuclear weapons. It is for this reason that I have
always felt that we need not only a wide range of options, but also effective means for exercising initial and continuing control by the President,
over the use of all types of nuclear weapons. I believe it would be helpful, if it has not already been done, to brief the President on what can
and cannot be accomplished with existing systems and procedures in
exercising selective control over the use of tactical nuclear weapons in
Europe. We should then seek means of remedying deficiencies in present control systems.

Second, I was impressed by the description of the restrictions of
SACEUR's flexibility in the use of NATO forces in limited aggression
situations. I concur in the judgment that "situations may arise in which
the risk inherent in degrading NATO's general war posture in Europe is
more than offset by the advantages of bringing decisive conventional
forces to bear in a limited conflict." While we must exercise considerable care to avoid the impression among our allies that we are prepared
to contemplate a World War II conventional hostility limited to Europe,
or that we would not carry out our nuclear commitments, it is important that we place our emphasis on the more likely sort of contingencies,
with the expectation that in time our allies will agree with the wisdom
of such action. This suggests that SACEUR should prepare, by the way
of planning or training, more than he has in the past for contingencies
in which some degrading of his general war posture is permitted by
higher authority in order to cope with a limited conflict. In particular, I

---

[1] Source: Washington National Records Center, OASD/ISA Files: FRC 330 68 A 4023,
381 1964 Nov–Dec. Top Secret. A copy was sent to Secretary McNamara.

[2] The full report has not been found; a revised staff draft of Section V (Conclusions
and Recommendations), June 26, is enclosed with a memorandum from General Leon W.
Johnson to McCone, June 26. (Central Intelligence Agency, DCI (McCone) Files,
Miscellaneous Papers, 19 Sept 1963–08 Aug 1964, Box 8) In the third paragraph of the letter printed here, Secretary Rusk quotes from this concluding section and in the final paragraph summarizes another recommendation in the section.

would hope additional effort would be directed at the problem of unpremeditated conflict arising from the present unsettled situation in Central Europe. I understand that this, and other ideas to improve SACEUR's capabilities for situations less than general war are under continuing discussions among Ambassador Thompson, Mr. McNaughton and General Goodpaster. I hope that we will be able to reach a considered judgment about this matter at an early date.

Third, I fully endorse the position that there should be continuing inter-agency work on improving our crisis management capability, to include a timely development of contingency plans identifying the politico-military courses of action in anticipation of a crisis. Pursuant to an exchange of correspondence between the Secretary of Defense and me, we have established a small senior level coordinating committee precisely to fill this need. (A copy of that correspondence is attached for your information.)[3]

Fourth, I am entirely in accord with the suggestion that there should be close State–Defense collaboration in developing the portions of the JSCP and JSOP having to do with national and military objectives and strategic concepts. I suggest that our staffs discuss soon how this might most effectively be done. In this connection, I assure you that we will make every effort to avoid creating delays in the JSCP and JSOP timetables as a result of Department of State participation.

With warm regards,

Sincerely,

Dean Rusk[4]

---

[3] Not found.

[4] Printed from a copy that indicates Rusk signed the original.

63.   Letter From Secretary of State Rusk to Secretary of Defense McNamara[1]

Washington, November 28, 1964.

Dear Bob:

This is in response to your memorandum of November twentieth to Ambassador Thompson[2] which attached a series of draft Memoranda for the President covering various aspects of the Department of Defense Five Year Force Structure and Fiscal Planning (1966–70).[3]

May I take this occasion, as I have in the past, to state my profound admiration for the outstanding success you have had in bringing conceptual clarity to the presentation of DOD military programs and budgets. I have found once again this year in reviewing the draft Memoranda to the President a highly impressive exposition of US military programs and objectives. However, partly as a result of the complexity and volume of the material, and partly as a result of my involvement in other pressing matters, I will limit my substantive comments at this time to two particular draft memoranda leaving open the possibility of forwarding additional comments on subsequent memoranda at a later date.

With regard to the role of tactical nuclear forces in NATO strategy, I feel that your memorandum blocks out for the first time the beginning of a rational conceptualization of the role of tactical nuclear weapons in Europe. I do, however, have the following observations to make:

a. It seems to me of vital importance that we turn our attention to the consideration of the utility and limitation of the potential utilization of tactical nuclear weaponry in other areas of the globe. I particularly have in mind the Far East where we maintain the second largest overseas nuclear arsenal and where, insofar as Southeast Asia is concerned the prospect for a major US military involvement cannot be overlooked. While I appreciate the fact that various studies have been conducted

---

[1] Source: Washington National Records Center, OSD Files: FRC 330 69 A 7425, 110.01 FY–66 1964. Top Secret. The letter is stamped: "Sec Def has seen 12 Dec 1964." Another copy indicates that it was drafted by Seymour Weiss (G/PM). (Johnson Library, National Security File, Agency File, Defense Budget—FY 1966, Box 16) Attached to that copy is a December 8 transmittal memorandum from Llewellyn E. Thompson to McGeorge Bundy, which noted that although Secretary Rusk wanted to attend the budget meeting between Secretary McNamara and the President, he would be in New York attending sessions of the UN General Assembly. The budget meeting took place on December 11 (see Document 66).

[2] Not found.

[3] None of these draft memoranda has been found.

from time to time on the role of nuclear weapons in the Far East and Southeast Asia, I would like to suggest that an analytical technique similar to that contained in your October twenty-sixth draft Memorandum to the President which deals exclusively with Europe,[4] be applied to the Far East. If you believe it feasible, such an effort might be included within the studies to be conducted by the Special Studies Group of the Joint Chiefs of Staff as proposed in your draft Memorandum to the President. However, whether this or some alternative solution is favored by you, I would be prepared to make available Department of State personnel to participate in such a study which I believe should be conducted on a relatively urgent basis.

b. With regard to the European portion of the problem, which is so extensively treated in your draft memorandum, I believe that you and I are in essential agreement on the limitations which attach to existing strategic posture as well as to the political implications which would be involved in any major and precipitant change. I think the central political feature is the one which you identify in your paper, namely that our allies' declaratory policy is for a variety of reasons closely wedded to reliance on nuclear deterrence. How much confidence one may have in the assumption that our allies' declaratory policy would be effectively implemented once war was initiated is, as you so correctly point out, open to serious question. What is not open to serious question, however, is that our allies strongly adhere to this position and any attempt to move them gradually toward increased reliance on a major conventional defense, which you suggest, will require a combination of persistence and patience which will call for our best efforts. I, therefore, endorse your proposal for a joint State–Defense developed program to prescribe manner, pacing and tactics; I believe this can be accomplished as a logical extension of the work of the Thompson Strategy Group.[5]

With regard to your memorandum on Strategic Forces, I should like to make the following observations:

a. Your analysis of the effect of US strategic missile capability above that required for "assured destruction" concludes that a 200 missile reduction in the Minuteman program is acceptable. (We assume that target procurement figures cast two or three years ahead are provisional and subject to review in the light of what the Soviet Union is doing.) What is not entirely clear from your memorandum is the effect which such a reduction would have upon damage limitation in Western Europe. I can readily imagine that the result would be negligible; nevertheless, having repeatedly assured the Europeans that US forces cover

---

[4] Not found.

[5] See footnote 5, Document 60.

targets threatening Western Europe with approximately the same priority as those which threaten the US, we have assumed the obligation to demonstrate that we have in fact considered their interests. Especially in view of the fact that this proposal is likely to receive considerable publicity, during Congressional testimony if not before, I would like to be assured that in fact your analysis does demonstrate that the 200 missiles involved in the reduction, if procured and targetted against threats to Western Europe, would make no appreciable difference in a damage limiting sense. If this cannot be demonstrated, I believe you and I should consider the matter further. However, even if it can be demonstrated, I think it is of vital importance that the case be developed in whatever detail required in anticipation of our having to make the case to our allies on the assumption that they will learn of the proposed reduction. I would appreciate receiving your views on this matter at your earliest convenience.

b. I was not able to determine whether your projected 200 missile Minuteman reduction was based on a force availability which assumed existence of the MLF or made the contrary assumption. (The two charts in your memorandum appear contradictory on this point.) This is a factual question we should try to clear up before the proposed Minuteman reduction becomes public since it has obvious implications both in terms of Congressional presentation and foreign consideration of the MLF proposal.

c. With regard to the SRAM missile, it strikes me that it is important, particularly at this stage of our negotiations with our European allies on alliance nuclear arrangements, to avoid giving an erroneous impression that the US is re-launching itself upon the development of a Skybolt-type of missile. While I do not anticipate that there should be problems, given the clear technical differences between the SRAM and the Skybolt, nevertheless this distinction might initially be overlooked. It seems to me prompt joint State–Defense preparation is called for: (i) to develop a public presentation program designed to minimize misunderstanding on the part of our allies as to the relationship (or lack thereof) between the SRAM and Skybolt and (ii) to develop a US position in anticipation of the fact that the British and/or the French may express an interest in securing the new missile once its projected availability becomes known.

d. Perhaps the most complicated issue in your Strategic Forces Memorandum deals with the question of anti-ballistic missile programs. Indeed, I take it, it is in deference to these complexities that you have decided to postpone for another year the decision on deployment of this system. I have expressed to you in past years my very considerable interest in the question of an anti-ballistic missile weapons system.

I will not repeat my arguments, but I will say that I continue to feel that the possibility of developing a technologically feasible, as well as reasonably economic defense against ballistic missiles is a matter of immense political import. It has implications which extend to the nature of our alliance system as well as to future relations with the Soviet Union and secondary nuclear powers. In view of the fact that if your recommendation is accepted we will have delayed for one year the basic decision on deployment of an ABM system, I think it vitally important that State and Defense enter into an urgent joint study of the various political implications associated with a decision to deploy an ABM system. If you would designate a point of contact with whom we might deal on this matter, we will take the initiative in seeing that the issues which concern us are identified in such a way as to permit them to be given appropriate consideration as an integral part of the development of next year's Five Year Force Structure memorandum on this subject.

e. Finally, there are several specific and for the most part probably minor issues which relate to the Strategic Forces Memorandum which we would like to pursue at an early date. For example, reference is made to the prospective requirement for additional facilities in Turkey and Iran. This is a matter we would like to pursue with your staff to gain a fuller understanding of what you have in mind. Also, as a strictly non-substantive problem, I would like to propose that the title of your Strategic Forces Memorandum be changed from "Strategic Offensive and Defensive Forces" to "Strategic Retaliatory and Defensive Forces." This is simply reverting to the terminology of previous years. However, I feel that from a political point of view your earlier terminology had some distinct advantages in avoiding a connotation which could have unfavorable political implications. On these and other similarly minor specific points, I will have my staff contact your Comptroller staff with whom they have been working over the past year.

I might say in this latter regard, that I am deeply appreciative of the very excellent cooperation which your entire Comptroller staff, and in particular Dr. Enthoven, has accorded us. As a result of your staff's effort, I believe our understanding and appreciation of the problems identified in your Five Year Force Structure Memoranda has been immeasurably enhanced.

With warm regards,

Sincerely,

Dean

64.   Letter From the Director of the White House Office of
       Emergency Planning (McDermott) to Secretary of State
       Rusk[1]

Washington, December 8, 1964.

Dear Mr. Secretary:

In my memorandum of September 16, 1964, referring to the OEP report of August 31, 1964, to the President on "Civil Emergency Preparedness",[2] I indicated our intention to work closely with you on specific programs. One of these programs, included in the five-year projection, to which the President has given approval, is directed at correction of deficiencies in arrangements for headquarters emergency operating facilities.

This program has been developed, conceptually, in accordance with criteria provided by the Emergency Planning Committee (EPC) in its initial report which was approved by the President. The Committee concluded that maximum delegations should be made, preemergency, to officials outside of Washington and that protected emergency sites be provided within 15 to 35 miles from the White House. These sites are to be used day-to-day by organizational units related to emergency activities, including at least one individual who could act for the department or agency in an emergency.

The Department of State has been selected for inclusion in the first year's increment of the program. This determination is based on the importance of the mission of the Department and the fact that the Department does not have an emergency facility of its own. It is contemplated that the State Department site will also accommodate small emergency units of AID and the Export-Import Bank.

The use of the Special Facility[3] by State is not in accord with the established policy governing the use of this already overcrowded facility, and would in an emergency, I am sure, be less satisfactory from an operating point of view.

Our staffs have had preliminary discussion on this proposal. We realize that accomplishment of our objectives may present problems

---

[1] Source: National Archives and Records Administration, RG 59, Central Files 1964–66, DEF 1 US. Confidential.

[2] See Document 48.

[3] According to a December 15 memorandum from Joseph F. Vaughan (G/PM) to Jeffrey C. Kitchen (G/PM), the "Special Facility" was at "High Point," which in an emergency was to be the relocation site for the non-military "seat of government." (National Archives and Records Administration, RG 59, Central Files 1964–66, DEF 1 US)

and further staff attention is necessary with respect to such things as the size and use of facilities, location, and funding. I would appreciate receiving as soon as possible your favorable reaction to this proposal and designation of the appropriate staff of your Department with whom my representatives may work.

Sincerely,

Edward A. McDermott

---

65.   **Memorandum From Secretary of Defense McNamara to President Johnson**[1]

Washington, undated.

SUBJECT

Defense Department Budget for FY 1966

With but minor exceptions, I have now completed my review of the Department of Defense military program and financial budget for FY 1966. The program, which I recommend for your approval, will require new obligational authority and expenditures for Military Functions, Military Assistance and Civil Defense as shown below (in billions):

	FY '64	FY '65	FY '66
NOA	$51.0	49.7[a]	49.0
Expenditures	51.2	49.8[b]	49.8

[a] Congress cut $1.2 billion from the $50.9 NOA request.

[b] This estimate, part of the Mid-Year Review, although $1.4 billion below the original budget estimate, continues to appear too high.

The military forces supported by this budget are summarized in the attached tables at Tab A.[2] The recommended force structure was based

[1] Source: Johnson Library, National Security File, Agency File, Defense Budget—FY 1966, Box 16. Secret. Another copy of the memorandum is dated December 10. (National Archives and Records Administration, RG 200, Defense Programs and Operations, Final Memos re Budget, Dec. 1964, Box 40)

[2] Not found.

on requirements for national security and was not limited by arbitrary or predetermined budget ceilings. In my review of the budgets proposed by the Services, I have attempted, as last year, to eliminate all non-essential, marginal, and postponable expenditures, with the objective of minimizing the costs of supporting the required forces.

In developing the program and reviewing the budget proposals, I have had the continuing counsel and assistance of the Joint Chiefs of Staff. Although the force structure does not include all the forces or force modernizations recommended by the Joint Chiefs of Staff or individual members thereof, the Joint Chiefs of Staff agree that the program supported by this budget will increase our over-all combat effectiveness and will provide effective forces in a high state of readiness for defense of the vital interests of the United States. Tab B lists specific comments of the Chiefs on my proposals.[3]

The recommended program has been reviewed with the Secretary of State, the President's Special Assistant for National Security Affairs, the Director of the Bureau of the Budget, and the President's Science Advisor. They are in agreement with my recommendations except with respect to the following programs:[4]

1. *Minuteman II Retrofit.* I favor delaying by six months the previous schedule for retrofitting Minuteman II missiles into Minuteman I silos, to insure adequate time for the development of a highly reliable missile system. The Director of the Bureau of the Budget agrees that funds should be appropriated on this basis, on the understanding that further delay may be necessary and funds will be released only to support a retrofit schedule which is optimized from the point of view of missile reliability and cost.

2. *CX-(HLS) Transport Aircraft.* Your Science Advisor is not convinced that the development of this new, large transport aircraft is required. He believes that the same over-all lift capability can be provided at lower cost with less airlift, if more roll-on roll-off ships are constructed and used as forward floating depots. I agree that we should make greater use of the new roll-on roll-off ships and have included four in the FY 1966 budget, but I am convinced that additional airlift is also needed and that it can be supplied most economically by developing the CX-(HLS). I recommend that we include funds for the develop-

---

[3] Not attached, but presumably an undated, 6-page "Summary of JCS Recommendations on the Draft Presidential Memorandum" in the Johnson Library, National Security File, Agency File, Defense Budget—FY 1966, Box 16.

[4] The Secretary of State expresses concern about the effect the proposed reduction in the Minuteman program (from 1200 to 1000) may have upon damage limitation in Western Europe. I have assured him that the effect would be small. [Footnote in the source text.]

ment in the FY 1966 budget, but initiate, jointly with the Science Advisor, a study to determine by April 1, 1965 the best mix of airlift and sealift in the forces. Dr. Hornig concurs in this approach.

3. *The Manned Orbital Laboratory (MOL)*. The Science Advisor and the Director of the Bureau of the Budget have doubts concerning the requirements for the MOL. I recommend, and both Dr. Hornig and Mr. Gordon agree, that funds for the project be included in the FY 1966 budget, but that they not be released until we are agreed that the program of military, engineering, and scientific experiments and steps toward operational capability is worth the cost and does not duplicate approved programs in any other agency. I am convinced that at least a major portion of the funds will be required to support a program of experiments involving heavy military reconnaissance payloads, manned or unmanned.

4. *TFX Production*. The Science Advisor has suggested stretching out the TFX production schedule to permit more of the Air Force planes to be equipped with the superior Mk II avionics. I disagree with this suggestion. The TFX with Mk I avionics is a far greater advance over the F-100's and F-105's, which would have to be retained longer in the force if the TFX schedule were stretched, than the TFX with Mk II avionics is over the TFX with Mk I avionics.

The budget at present contains no provision for an increase in military pay in FY 1966. The increase called for by the comparability formula which I presented to the Congress in my posture statement last year would be about $250 million.

We are still working on a number of minor budget issues. I do not anticipate that decisions on these matters will materially affect the budget totals.

I will be ready for a meeting with you and the Joint Chiefs of Staff on December 21, 22, or 23 to discuss our final proposals.

Robert S. McNamara

66.   Memorandum From the President's Special Assistant for National Security Affairs (Bundy) and Spurgeon Keeny of the National Security Council Staff to President Johnson[1]

Washington, December 10, 1964.

SUBJECT

  Papers on the FY '66 DOD Budget

1. Secretary McNamara has submitted the attached memorandum (Tab 1)[2] on the FY '66 DOD budget for consideration at the meeting with you tomorrow at 12:45 p.m. This is the only vital paper for tomorrow, and the most important stuff is in the first 2 pages. The views of the Chiefs on all aspects of the budget are summarized in Tab B to this memo,[3] and Bob hopes you will read them.

2. The Defense budget is in extremely good shape and there are really no major items seriously at issue. The four items in the memorandum are by their nature difficult problems that by common agreement are being called to your attention. I understand, however, that Mr. Gordon and Dr. Hornig are in general satisfied with the solutions suggested in the memorandum and there should not be a very extended discussion on these items.

3. There are a number of major actions involved in the current budget that are not reflected in the attached memorandum since they are not in dispute. These issues include the following: the reduction in the Minuteman force, the decision not to go ahead with an advanced manned bomber, the decision not to deploy an anti-ballistic missile system, the decision not to proceed with an advanced manned interceptor, the decision to eliminate the "shelter incentive" plan from the civil defense program, the decision to eliminate the MMRBM, and the decision to go ahead with a deep underground command and control center for the Pentagon and the White House. I am attaching for your information at Tab 2 a background paper on recommended strategic offensive and defensive forces that covers these and other issues.[4] This is not essential reading for tomorrow, but it is a most important basic paper on

[1] Source: Johnson Library, National Security File, Agency File, Defense Budget—FY 1966, Box 16. Top Secret.

[2] Not attached, but presumably Document 65.

[3] See footnote 3, Document 65.

[4] Not attached, but presumably a lengthy December 3 draft memorandum from McNamara to President Johnson on "Recommended FY 1966–1970 Programs for Strategic Offensive Forces, Continental Air and Missile Defense Forces, and Civil Defense" in the Johnson Library, National Security File, Agency File, Defense Budget—FY 1966, Box 16.

our overall strategic posture, and I think you will want to read it when you have time.

4. I am also attaching at Tab 3 a very interesting draft memorandum on the role of tactical nuclear weapons in NATO strategy that was prepared as background for the FY '66 budget submissions.[5] Although this paper is preliminary in nature, it has been recognized by the State Department and the BOB as an important policy statement that will affect future budget decisions; it may be referred to in tomorrow's discussion (see page 2 for the Summary of McNamara's preliminary conclusions).

5. Finally, I attach at Tab 4 a copy of a memorandum on nuclear materials production schedules through FY 73.[6] In view of the conflict between declining DOD weapons requirements and AEC production aspirations, this subject will present problems in the AEC budget this year and may also be discussed at tomorrow's meeting.

McG. B.

SMK[7]

---

[5] A 54-page Defense study, "The Role of Tactical Nuclear Forces in NATO Strategy," October 26; not printed.

[6] Not attached, but presumably a 2-page memorandum from McNamara to President Johnson, December 8, plus detailed Tables I–IV and two graphs (figures 1 and 2), in the Johnson Library, National Security File, Agency File, Defense Budget—FY 1966, Box 16.

[7] Only Keeny initialed; Bundy's initials are typewritten.

---

67. Paper Prepared in the Department of Defense[1]

Washington, undated.

SUMMARY OF FORCE STRUCTURE CHANGES

I. Strategic Retaliatory Forces

[table (11 columns and 6 rows of source text) not declassified]

---

[1] Source: Johnson Library, National Security File, Agency File, Defense Budget—FY 1966, Box 16. Top Secret. A December 14 covering memorandum from Cyrus Vance to President Johnson notes that the attached paper was prepared in response to President Johnson's request of December 11. The President's request has not been further identified.

1. Since 1961 we have increased the number of weapons on alert threefold and alert megatonnage more than threefold. We have now reached a plateau both in weapons and megatons, with future planned reductions in bombers offset by increases in missiles. Our remaining bomber/tanker forces in FY 1970, armed with over [*less than 1 line of source text not declassified*] can send [*1-1/2 lines of source text not declassified*].

2. The only major disagreements the Chiefs have with this program are: (a) that they prefer an ultimate force of 1200 Minuteman missiles instead of the 1000 we have recommended—if next year it seems desirable to increase the number of Minuteman missiles from 1000 to 1200, we have the option to do so; and (b) the Chiefs also recommend a faster rate of development of a potential follow-on bomber.

II. Continental Air and Missile Defense Forces

1. No major changes are planned in these forces. There will be some phase down of older interceptors and redundant radars. We are not approving the procurement of a new manned interceptor (YF 12-A) or the Nike X anti-missile missile, but we are planning to spend $400 million in FY 1966 to continue the development of the Nike X and retain the option to decide to deploy either the Nike X or the YF 12-A in subsequent years.

2. The Chiefs prefer to include pre-production funds for the YF 12-A and the Nike X, which would make possible their deployment nine months to a year earlier.

III. General Purpose Forces

	FY 61	FY 62	FY 63	FY 64	FY 65	FY 66	FY 67	FY 68	FY 69	FY 70
Combat Ready:										
Army Divs.	11	14	16	16	16	16	16	16	16	16
Marine Divs.	3	3	3	3	3	3	3	3	3	3
Marine Air Wings	3	3	3	3	3	3	3	3	3	3
A.F. Tactical Fighter Wings	16	23	20	21	22	23	23	24	24	24

1. A substantial part of our increase in defense expenditures over the past four years has gone into the increase in the number and strength of Army combat ready divisions and Air Force tactical fighter wings. The latter are now being equipped with F-4s and in FY 1966 we will make our first large procurement of the F-111 (TFX).

	FY 61	FY 62	FY 63	FY 64	FY 65	FY 66	FY 67	FY 68	FY 69	FY 70
Attack Carriers	15	16	15	15	15	15	15	15	15	14
Antisubmarine Warfare Carriers	9	10	9	9	9	9	9	9	9	9
Nuclear Attack Submarines	13	16	16	19	23	31	41	47	52	56

We are planning to reduce the number of carriers from 15 to 14 in FY 1970 and to 13 in FY 1972. This reduction is already being reflected in our procurement of carrier aircraft. While we are not increasing the number of antisubmarine carriers (ASW) we are making great qualitative improvements in all our ASW capabilities and are adding to the force nuclear attack submarines whose primary mission is ASW.

2. The JCS, except for the Chief of Staff, Army, approve the programmed number of Army divisions. Except for the Chief of Naval Operations and the Commandant of the Marine Corps, they approve the reduction in the number of the tactical carriers. They approve the tactical air force program except that the Chief of Staff, Army and the Chief of Naval Operations believe that 21 wings would be adequate as contrasted with the 24 we are programming. They recommend building six nuclear attack submarines in FY 1966 instead of the four, and sixteen destroyer escorts instead of the ten we recommend; three of the Chiefs also recommend construction of a nuclear powered guided missile frigate in FY 1966.

IV. Airlift and Sealift

	FY 61	FY 62	FY 63	FY 64	FY 65	FY 66	FY 67	FY 68	FY 69	FY 70
30-day airlift to:										
SE Asia (thousands of tons)	14.7	20.0	23.6	25.4	29.0	36.1	48.5	54.8	67.0	78.9
Europe (thousands of tons)	32.0	42.4	50.3	54.4	61.1	73.6	96.6	108.1	128.8	150.1

1. We have greatly increased the totally inadequate strategic airlift which we possessed in 1961. We are beginning to receive deliveries of operational C-141s, the new jet transport plane. We now propose to initiate development of a new, much larger, and more economical transport jet plane known as the CX(HLS). If we procure only the three squadrons of CX(HLS) now programmed, we will increase our 30-day airlift to Southeast Asia from 15,000 tons in FY 1961 to 79,000 tons in FY 1970 and to 89,000 tons in FY 1971.

The Joint Chiefs of Staff concur with these recommendations. We plan to further increase the strategic mobility of our forces by starting construction in FY 1966 of four fast forward deployment ships.

68.   **Memorandum From Director of Central Intelligence McCone to the President's Special Assistant for National Security Affairs (Bundy)**

Washington, December 15, 1964.

[Source: Johnson Library, National Security File, Agency File, Central Intelligence Agency, Vol. 11, Box 9. Secret. 2 pages of source text not declassified.]

69.   **National Intelligence Estimate[1]**

NIE 11–3–64   Washington, December 16, 1964.

SOVIET AIR AND MISSILE DEFENSE CAPABILITIES
THROUGH MID-1970

The Problem

To evaluate the capabilities of the Soviet air and missile defense forces, and to forecast probable trends in Soviet air and missile defense programs through mid-1970.

Conclusions

A. The combination of area and point defenses provided by the USSR's present force of interceptors and short-range surface-to-air missile (SAM) systems affords a good defense for major target areas against medium and high altitude bomber attacks. However, the air defense system has limited low altitude capabilities, and special difficulties are posed by supersonic aircraft and air-to-surface missiles (ASMs). We believe that a major Soviet effort during the remainder of this decade will be focused on meeting these particular problems. (Para. 55)

---

[1] Source: Johnson Library, National Security File, National Intelligence Estimates 11–64, USSR, Box 3. Top Secret; Controlled Dissem. A cover sheet, prefatory note, title page, and table of contents are not printed. According to the prefatory note, the CIA and the intelligence organizations of the Departments of State and Defense, the Atomic Energy Commission, and the National Security Agency participated in the preparation of this estimate. Representatives of the State Department, DIA, AEC, and NSA concurred; the FBI representative abstained, the subject being outside his jurisdiction.

B. We believe that improvements in the Soviet air defense system over the next few years will make progressively more difficult successful penetration by manned bombers to major target areas. Successful penetration by manned bombers will require increasingly sophisticated forms of attack. Soviet air defense capabilities can be degraded by the increasingly complex forms of attack which the West will be able to employ, including air-launched missiles, penetration tactics, electronic countermeasures, and low-altitude attack. Despite these limitations of their air defense system, the Soviets would expect to destroy a number of the attackers. We doubt, however, that they would be confident that they could reduce the weight of attack to a point where the resulting damage to the USSR would be acceptable. (Para. 57)

C. There are critical uncertainties in our knowledge of Soviet R&D and deployment in the antiballistic missile (ABM) field. From the evidence now available, however, certain general conclusions can be drawn: first, the Soviet R&D effort has been extensive and of long duration, and the USSR several years ago probably solved the technical problem of intercepting ballistic targets arriving singly or in small numbers; second, some initial ABM deployment activity was probably begun as long ago as 1960, but both the deployment and R&D programs were evidently interrupted and modified; third, the magnitude of R&D and the probable early deployment activity point to a strong Soviet desire to obtain ABM defenses rapidly; fourth, R&D continues, a new antimissile missile (AMM) has appeared, and some additional deployment activity may now be underway, but the USSR does not have any operational defenses against strategic ballistic missiles today. (Para. 58)

D. Much of our evidence indicates that the USSR has been exploring methods of ABM defense which differ in important respects from those now favored by the US. Low frequency radars may play an important role in the Soviet program. An early Soviet effort may have involved a missile designed to have dual capabilities against ballistic and aerodynamic vehicles. The new AMM which was recently displayed by the Soviets is probably designed to conduct exoatmospheric intercepts at considerable ranges, using a large nuclear warhead to achieve its kill. We believe, however, that the Soviets have probably not conducted many AMM firings to exoatmospheric altitudes, and that they have probably not attempted full system tests involving interceptions at these altitudes. (Paras. 37–42, 59)

Recent Defensive Deployments

E. The Soviets began construction of three defensive complexes at Leningrad in 1960–1961. We believe that the Leningrad system was originally designed to have a capability against ballistic missiles, and perhaps against aerodynamic vehicles as well. However, we believe that the initial design has been changed. We cannot determine the nature of this change, or whether it was caused by serious technical difficulties, a realization that the system was vulnerable to penetration aids, or important new developments in the state-of-the art. There are similarities between new construction at one of the Leningrad complexes and two recently discovered defensive complexes under construction in northwestern USSR. In light of these similarities, at least these three complexes may now be intended for the deployment of the same defensive system. (Paras. 46–47)

F. We are unable to associate the new complexes with any systems equipment, and any explanation for the mission of these complexes and the modified Leningrad complex is open to some doubt. There is some support for the belief that the complexes are for a SAM system to defend against aerodynamic vehicles. On the other hand, we have noted intensive Soviet research on missile defenses for several years and indications that the USSR has been working toward new and different ABM capabilities. In light of this factor and other considerations, we think there are also persuasive reasons for believing that the new complexes are related to missile defense. However, any judgment at this time on their mission is in our view premature. (Paras. 47, 50)

G. We have observed at Moscow three developments which may indicate ABM deployment there. A large radar now under construction could be the acquisition and early target tracking element of an ABM system. Other facilities also under construction could serve as the final target tracking and missile guidance element. SA-1 sites which are now being modified could be used as the AMM launch positions for the systems. However, the activities we have observed thus far may not be related, and some of them may represent improvements in Moscow's defense against aerodynamic vehicles or serve a space function. The missile to be employed is a major unknown; the recently displayed AMM could be used at Moscow to conduct exoatmospheric intercepts of ballistic missiles, perhaps at distances of several hundreds of miles from the city. In sum, we continue to believe that the Soviets may be deploying ABM defenses at Moscow, but we do not yet understand how the installations we have observed would function as an ABM system. (Paras. 41, 51–54)

ABM Prospects

H. If ABM deployment activity is now underway at either Moscow or the other locations we have noted, the USSR is likely to have some initial strategic ABM defenses operational within the next two years or so. Limited deployment, especially at Moscow, could be a special, highest-priority effort to defend the Soviet capital with an early and still unproved system. But widespread ABM deployment activity, whenever it occurred, would imply that the Soviets consider their ABM systems good enough to justify extraordinarily large new expenditures. It would indicate that the Soviets had achieved excellent R&D successes, and perhaps, that they had taken high-risk production and deployment decisions. We cannot exclude this possibility, but our evidence suggests that the Soviets have been proceeding cautiously since they modified their program. (Paras. 60–61)

I. In considering whether to provide ABM defenses for many of their urban-industrial centers and other targets, the Soviet leaders will have to weigh the great cost of such an effort against the likely effectiveness of the ABM systems available. Area defenses might offer considerable savings over point defenses, but we cannot be sure of this and in any event a major commitment of resources would be required. The Soviets may defer widespread deployment pending further R&D work on existing systems, or in the hope of achieving better systems at a later date. They might even decide that the cost of large-scale ABM deployment would not be commensurate with the protection it could offer against anticipated Western strike capabilities. We are certain that the Soviets will push ahead with their R&D effort, but we cannot forecast whether or when they will achieve ABM systems with capabilities and costs justifying widespread deployment. (Para. 62)

Antisatellite Capabilities

J. We believe that the Soviets are now constructing a series of large, new radars, most of which will probably be completed in 1966. We believe that some or all of these radars will be linked together as a space surveillance system. Such a system will, we think, have a capability considerably in excess of that required merely to detect the passage of US space vehicles. In our view, the chances are better than even that the Soviets intend to provide themselves, not only with a space surveillance system, but with an antisatellite capability as well.[2] If existing types of missiles were used in an antisatellite system, a nuclear warhead would probably be required, but a missile for non-nuclear kill could be developed in about two years after flight tests began. (Paras. 63–66)

[Here follow the Discussion section (Parts I–IX, pages 5–24) and Annexes A and B (pages 25–27 and following page 27).]

---

[2] The Director of Intelligence and Research, Department of State, believes that on the basis of available evidence, this affirmative judgment is premature. While he does not exclude the antisatellite function as a possibility, present evidence does not persuade him that the Soviets intend to develop and deploy within the next two years and at great cost an extremely complex antisatellite system. [Footnote in the source text.]

70.   Letter From the Deputy Assistant Secretary of State for
       Politico-Military Affairs (Kitchen) to the Director of the
       White House Office of Emergency Planning (McDermott)[1]

Washington, December 17, 1964.

Dear Mr. McDermott:

In the absence of the Secretary and Ambassador Thompson, I am responding to your letter of December 8, 1964,[2] concerning emergency operating facilities for the Department of State.

We are aware of the fact that our use of the Special Facility as an operational relocation site is contrary to the intended purpose of that installation. Consequently, we welcome your decision to include this Department's requirements in the initial phase of the recently approved five-year plan for providing protected emergency sites around the perimeter of the National Capital area. Pending the completion and occupancy of an alternative facility, we assume, of course, that there will be no change in current arrangements with respect to the availability of the Special Facility for our emergency operations.

Since this project will require major contributions from our management and budget staffs, we believe that our Bureau of Administration should participate actively in both its preliminary planning and developmental stages. Accordingly, Mr. Richard R. Brown, Special Assistant to the Assistant Secretary for Administration, as well as Joseph F. Vaughn of my staff, will be available for necessary consultation with your representatives.

We are most appreciative of the consideration which your Office and its predecessors have given to the emergency operational requirements of the Department of State.

Sincerely,

Jeffrey C. Kitchen[3]

---

[1] Source: National Archives and Records Administration, RG 59, Central Files 1964–66, DEF 1 US. Confidential. Drafted by Joseph F. Vaughan on December 15 and cleared by Brown (A).

[2] Document 64.

[3] Printed from a copy that bears this typed signature.

71.   Memorandum for the Record[1]

LBJ Ranch, Texas, December 22, 1964.

SUBJECT

> Conference between the President, the Secretary and Deputy Secretary of Defense, and the Joint Chiefs of Staff at the LBJ Ranch, Texas, on Tuesday, 22 December 1964, at 1020 CST

The following were present at the conference:

President Johnson
Secretary of Defense McNamara
Deputy Secretary of Defense Vance
General Wheeler
General LeMay
Admiral McDonald
General Johnson
General Greene
Major General Clifton (intermittently)
Colonel Forbes, JCS recorder

The main subject of this meeting was the Defense Department budget.

Mr. McNamara opened the meeting with a statement that the major issues have been considered and that the Secretary of Defense and the Joint Chiefs of Staff are agreed on about 95% of the items. Each Chief was then invited to discuss points he would like to bring up.[2]

General Wheeler listed three points which he considered a "package"—the Strategic Missile Force, the Fallout Shelter Program, and the Antiballistic Missile Program. He stated that he was concerned about the reduction from 1200 to 1000 Minutemen in this budget, especially since it is coming at the time we are phasing out[3] Atlas and Titan missiles.

There was an interruption and discussion of a telephone call to Secretary McNamara concerning Viet Nam.

---

[1] Source: Johnson Library, National Security File, Agency File, JCS, Filed by the LBJ Library, Box 29. Top Secret; Sensitive. Drafted by Clifton. A more detailed memorandum for the record (23 pages) of the same meeting, prepared by Colonel R.C. Forbes on January 25, 1965, is ibid.

[2] A December 17 memorandum to Secretary McNamara, signed by Lieutenant General Andrew J. Goodpaster for the Joint Chiefs of Staff, briefly summarized the Chairman's proposed comments at the upcoming December 22 meeting with the President on five issues: 1,200 Minutemen vs. 1,000, Nike X, National Fallout Shelter Program, Need for Military Pay Increase, and Level of Support. (Washington National Records Center, OSD Files: FRC 330 69 A 7425, 110.01 FY–66 1964)

[3] The word "Minuteman," immediately following this word was crossed out and initialed by Clifton.

Mr. McNamara gave a rather lengthy explanation of why he felt we could delay the decision on the 200 extra Minutemen missiles.

General Wheeler then spoke of the national fallout shelter program and his feeling that it should be speeded up if we are going to make our whole strategic force compatible with the protection of our own people. Secretary McNamara generally agreed with his point but stated that he felt that pushing ahead on civil defense while not pushing ahead with the antiballistic missile might not be of any great value. General Wheeler then pressed on with further support for the antiballistic missile and a proposal for $200 million for preproduction funding. Mr. McNamara made other statements which confirmed his view that the fallout shelter program and the antiballistic defense program should go together and that we are not ready at the moment to go ahead with either of these programs any more strongly than we are.

During the time that the President left the meeting, General Johnson and Secretary McNamara discussed post-D-Day aid to allies and the military assistance program as well as the military sales program. General Greene discussed Marine Corps Organized Reserves with Mr. McNamara.

At 1058 President Johnson rejoined the conference and General Wheeler continued his discussion. He made a strong plea for raising military pay this year. There was a lengthy discussion between President Johnson and other Chiefs on the pay situation. All of the Chiefs joined in on this subject and Secretary McNamara told the President that he would sit down with the Chiefs and examine the matter so all of them are talking on the same basis. There was a further discussion between General Wheeler and President Johnson on Congressman Rivers presenting a pay bill that they would have to testify about. In concluding this matter, President Johnson said that he would very carefully consider any recommendations from the Secretary of Defense and would discuss them with the Director of the Budget.

General LeMay then added a few words on the pay situation and reiterated the fact that there should be funds for the Project Definition Phase of the manned bomber and an improved interceptor for the Air Defense Command. He feels that the time lag is too long. Secretary McNamara stated that it was the Chiefs' view that it is too early to say that we don't need a new bomber and it is too early to say that we do need one. The Chiefs say that we should work on advanced engines, avionics, and Project Definition Phase. Secretary McNamara stated that his proposal would only delay this decision by five months.

Admiral McDonald then spoke about ship force levels, stating that antisubmarine warfare ships were short in the building program. The second point was gunfire support in connection with amphibious landing capabilities, and Secretary McNamara then agreed to put two additional rocket ships into the shipbuilding program.

Admiral McDonald then led a discussion on the replacement of major escort ships. General Greene then discussed the Marine Corps Organized Reserves at mobilization time. Mr. McNamara agreed that there were problems here but they needed to be sorted out. General Johnson then spoke about the fine equipment that we have in Viet Nam and out in the Far East and that the Army is doing well. This led to a discussion of the pay system, and finally General Johnson made a request for some more money for the Nike X.

Secretary McNamara adjourned the meeting at 1252.

Summary: The only positive decision I saw was the addition of two extra rocket ships and the determination that the Secretary of Defense should come forth with new recommendations on military pay.

The other problem areas that are open for further discussion are the manned bomber, the advanced manned interceptor; General Wheeler's "strategic package": Minuteman missiles, fallout shelters and the antiballistic missile; the Navy shipbuilding program of new ships.

CVC

72. Draft Memorandum From Secretary of Defense McNamara to President Johnson[1]

Washington, undated.

SUBJECT

Elimination of the Net Evaluation Subcommittee of the National Security Council

As part of a continuing effort to increase the efficiency and quality of various study programs, I have for some time questioned the value

---

[1] Source: National Archives and Records Administration, RG 59, Central Files 1964–66, DEF 1–1. Top Secret. Attached is a December 23 covering memorandum from McNamara to the Secretary of State, Chairman of the AEC, Chairman of the JCS, Director of Central Intelligence, Chairman of the Interdepartmental Intelligence Conference, and Chairman of the Interdepartmental Committee on Internal Security, asking for comments on his proposal to discontinue the Net Evaluation Subcommittee of the National Security Council. The draft memorandum and its attachments form Attachment B to a January 25, 1965, memorandum from Llewellyn Thompson to Secretary Rusk. See footnote 1, Document 74, and footnote 4 below.

of continuing the work of the Net Evaluation Subcommittee (NESC) of the National Security Council (established by NSC 5816).[2]

When the NESC was established by President Eisenhower in 1958, neither the Joint Chiefs of Staff Organization nor the Office of the Secretary of Defense included a capability for performing the type of study assigned to the NESC. The original directive charged the NESC with providing "integrated evaluations of the net capabilities of the USSR, in the event of general war, to inflict direct injury upon the Continental United States and to provide a continual watch for changes which would significantly alter those net capabilities." Subsequent directives have altered this task on an annual basis. For example, the most recently completed NESC study was an evaluation of a "war conducted in 1964 between the U.S., its Allies, and the Soviet Bloc based on current U.S. war plans."[3] Further, the over-all purpose of the report was to "evaluate the validity and feasibility of this type of analysis as a basis for providing guidance for political-military planning. . . ."

Having studied the 1964 Report, I do not feel that a brief survey of this type qualifies as a basis for planning guidance. As a broad survey of the problem, it is not without merit; but our strategic planning today is increasingly based upon more detailed studies of specific problem areas, such as those included on the Secretary of Defense's annual "Project List" and other studies conducted by the Joint Staff and military departments.

For example, the Special Studies Group (SSG) of the Joint Chiefs of Staff has developed a broader base of expertise than that of the NESC staff. Both groups have explored similar issues, used the same sources of input, obtained the same computer support and have performed the same type of analysis. Because of the close relationship of strategic studies to forces, the budget, and other on-going Defense Department studies, the usefulness of the SSG studies has been understandably greater than the annual survey of the NESC.

The economy involved in eliminating a major study group is obvious. We can, I feel, make better use of our limited study skills while simultaneously improving the product delivered to the consumer. Participation in DoD studies by other government agencies is, of course, welcomed when warranted by the subject matter. Similarly, we remain responsive to requests for study reports from other interested agencies of the government.

---

[2] Regarding NSC 5816, July 1, 1958, see Foreign Relations, 1958–1960, vol. III, pp. 118–119.

[3] See footnote 2, Document 62.

In summary, while the annual study program of the NESC had value and relevance in 1958, its contribution today is marginal when compared to the battery of specific studies which have become major functions of the JCS and DoD during the intervening years. It therefore appears logical to terminate the requirement for the NESC. Attached is a draft implementing directive for signature.[4]

---

[4] This undated draft directive reads: "Effective this date, the Net Evaluation Subcommittee of the National Security Council, having served its purpose, is discontinued. This directive supersedes NSC 5816."

---

73. Memorandum for the Record by Director of Central Intelligence McCone[1]

Johnson City, Texas, December 28, 1964.

Briefing of President Johnson at Johnson City, Texas, December 28, 1964

1. Reviewed the subjects covered in the briefing notes, Nos. 1 through 27[2] which should be made a part of this memorandum. In this connection, I emphasized the following:

Reduction in manpower of the Soviet armed forces represented a reappraisal and a new estimate but not a reduction. There was no evidence of a reduction through demobilization.

2. Emphasized that new ICBM's, bigger and better, indicated Soviet policy of qualitative improvement with no attempt to match the U.S. quantitatively. We cannot explain this policy except that they hope for a breakthrough in strategic offensive techniques which will offset U.S. quantitative advantage.

---

[1] Source: Central Intelligence Agency, DCI (McCone) Files, Memo for the Record, 1/1/65–12/28/65, Box 2. Secret; Eyes Only. Drafted on January 4, 1965. A typewritten note at the end of the memorandum indicates that it was dictated but not read by McCone. A handwritten notation at the end reads: "all backup & briefing papers destroyed."

[2] McCone's 16 pages of briefing notes of this meeting are attached to a January 11, 1965, letter from McCone to Bundy. In this letter McCone directed Bundy's attention particularly to the conclusions which had been placed at the beginning of the briefing notes. McCone continued: "They emphasize the dynamic character of the ongoing Soviet military program which is directed mainly at qualitative advances. Their purposes are obscure but it is obvious the Soviets are pursuing qualitative advances rather than quantitative additions to their capabilities." (Johnson Library, National Security File, Intelligence File, TKH Jan. 1964–Feb. 1965, Box 1)

3. Ground forces developing marine type units, are placing great emphasis on sealift and airlift, with apparent intent of developing a Commando capability for operations distant from the USSR. This is new because Soviet military forces have been landlocked since, and for that matter, prior to World War II.

4. The Soviet Air is relatively static. A new supersonic fighter plane being introduced but no evidence of supersonic long range bomber, although the Soviets have capability for such a development.

5. Air defense an enigma. After reviewing all evidence presented in attached papers, I concluded that Soviets were on an unexplained approach to either ABM or aircraft defense with a strong possibility that they had or were approaching a new technique. The status of construction in some of their facilities did not permit an accurate analysis of Soviet state of the art or air defense.

6. Soviets continue to expand special nuclear material production facilities, and I reviewed the figures in the paper, also photography of plant development.

7. In pointing out the extensive new Henhouse radar developments, I stated that these facilities, which were very expensive, exceeded requirements for tracking satellites, were not properly located for Early Warning, and therefore were quite possibly directed toward an anti-satellite capability to "blind" us from photographic intelligence gathering and we must be alert for this eventuality.

8. In summary, we were seeing a dynamic, progressive Soviet military program that was not being cut back, that was sophisticated, that was directed toward quality rather than quantity, and that there was a possibility of a breakthrough of some sort which would redress the present balance of power. This I said must not be overlooked and we must continually be on the alert for such a development.

[Here follow numbered paragraphs 9–12.]

The briefing was comprehensive. The President had few questions and very few remarks.

74. Memorandum From Acting Secretary of State Ball to Secretary of Defense McNamara[1]

Washington, January 28, 1965.

Dear Bob:

The Department of State has no objection to your raising with the President the question of discontinuing the Net Evaluation Subcommittee (NESC) of the National Security Council. The case you present in your draft memorandum of December 23 to the President[2] is a persuasive one and the Department believes the President would be well advised to consider whether he wishes to retain the Subcommittee, at least in its present form.

The participation of representatives of this Department in the preparation of strategic studies at the working level has been useful to this Department. Therefore, it is hoped that arrangements can be made to continue such participation.

Moreover, although surveys such as the last NESC study may not qualify as a basis for planning guidance, the Department believes that a similar broad survey of a possible major conflict between the United States and Communist China could serve a useful purpose in clarifying issues and highlighting areas which could usefully be the object of more detailed consideration.

If you agree, we suggest that Ambassador Thompson meet soon with Mr. Vance and General Wheeler to discuss these matters.

Sincerely,

George W. Ball[3]

---

[1] Source: National Archives and Records Administration, RG 59, Central Files 1964–66, DEF 1. Top Secret. The memorandum forms Attachment A to a January 25 memorandum from Llewllyn Thompson to Rusk, which summarizes the rationale for the reply to McNamara. Also part of this package is Attachment B (Document 72); an earlier, undated draft of the memorandum printed here; and a January 27 note from Read to Rusk explaining that he had received calls from McNamara's office urging action on McNamara's proposal to abolish the Net Evaluation Subcommittee and noting that all other agencies had concurred in the proposal.

[2] Document 72.

[3] Printed from a copy that indicates Ball signed the original.

75.   Memorandum From the Joint Chiefs of Staff to Secretary of Defense McNamara[1]

JCSM–84–65   Washington, February 4, 1965.

SUBJECT

Issues Regarding National Planning Raised by the 1964 NESC Report (U)

1. The Joint Chiefs of Staff have reviewed the 1964 NESC Report[2] pursuant to our meeting with you on 6 July 1964. This memorandum covers only those questions relating to national planning. Issues regarding NATO defenses were dealt with in JCSM–8–65, dated 8 January 1965, subject: "Issues Concerning NATO Raised by the 1964 NESC Report (U)."[3]

2. The 1964 NESC Report raised three major questions regarding planning:

a. Do the Joint Chiefs of Staff lack guidance for the preparation of military plans which could be provided by a Basic National Security Policy or other compilation of strategic planning guidance having national endorsement? (Pages 2–3, 33, NESC Report)

b. Should JSOP and JSCP sections dealing with national and military objectives and strategic concepts be discussed among planners of the Department of State, the Department of Defense, and other appropriate agencies? (Pages 4, 33–34, NESC Report)

c. Should US military and political departments undertake more extensive cooperation in identifying specific potential crisis situations and examining them in the light of the political-military measures which they might require? (Page 34, NESC Report)

3. With respect to the requirement for a Basic National Security Policy, its compilation into a single document is desirable in principle, but, at the present time, the Joint Chiefs of Staff do not lack policy guidance for the preparation of military plans. Necessary guidance is obtained through both face-to-face meetings and a continuing exchange of written memoranda with the Secretary of Defense. Guidance also results from meetings with the President, National Security Council meetings, National Security Action Memoranda, National Country Policy papers, and National Planning Task papers. Any effort to condense this guidance into a single document could result in a paper so

---

[1] Source: Washington National Records Center, OSD Files: FRC 330 70 A 1265, 381 NESC 1965. Top Secret; Sensitive. The memorandum is stamped: "Mr. Vance has seen."

[2] See footnote 2, Document 62. A handwritten note in the margin reads: "Mr. McNamara has only copy."

[3] A copy is in the National Archives and Records Administration, RG 218, JCS Files, 9050 (8 Jan 65) (1).

broad that it would be difficult to keep it meaningful and yet up-to-date. To the degree that such a document contained specific guidance, it could place inflexible restrictions on military planning and limit the scope of military advice on subsequent national security problems.

4. Lack of a Basic National Security Policy has not handicapped the Joint Chiefs of Staff in developing basic short-range (JSCP), mid-range (JSOP), and long-range (JLRSS) plans, as well as specific contingency plans. Reliance on these documents has permitted the Joint Chiefs of Staff to provide suitable military advice for specific purposes. It seems evident that questions such as "Are we prepared and preparing for the most likely kind of war?" (Page 2, NESC Report) should never be foreclosed by a master planning document.

5. With regard to the related problem of close coordination of military and political planning, interagency discussion of national objectives and national security policies would provide a useful exchange of ideas. The substance of approved documents such as National Security Action Memoranda, National Policy papers, and related military documents (e.g., JSCP, JSOP, and JLRSS) could provide a basis for these discussions, although it should be understood that the intent of the discussions is not to address these documents themselves or to suggest changes in them. Rather, such a process would give increased background knowledge and perception to the military and political officers concerned and could well provide for better inputs to future political and military plans. These discussions, conducted at the division chief/action officer level, would be informational in nature and supplemental to the liaison now carried out at higher levels. Political-military problem areas that are identified can be added to the list of National Planning Tasks.

6. As to the need to undertake a more extensive examination of possible crisis situations, the following provisions for political-military crisis planning are already in effect:

a. Bimonthly meetings between Department of State representatives and the Joint Chiefs of Staff.

b. Thursday planning group meetings attended by representatives of State, Defense, Joint Chiefs of Staff, and other appropriate agencies. This body monitors the current list of Policy Planning Tasks, including potential crisis situations.

c. Joint Staff participation in those Policy Planning Tasks which have military implications.

d. Preparation of National Policy Papers dealing with specific countries. There is input and participation by the Joint Chiefs of Staff in each of these papers. They constitute an additional area of State–Military cooperation which can contribute to crisis planning.

e. Finally, there are in existence some 200 contingency plans prepared by unified and specified commands as a result of both broad and specific directives in the JSCP. These plans represent the military planning for crisis situations in a wide variety of situations and a large number of countries and areas.

7. There is no evident need to provide additional organizations for crisis planning. This type of planning is being carried out along with other forms of planning for particular countries, areas, and circumstances. To segregate crisis planning from other planning would tend to make it less effective and could result in a failure to consider all appropriate factors. The principal need is to assure that timely and adequate planning is accomplished, and the recent establishment of an interagency group to facilitate the timely initiation and coordination of political-military planning should be of value in this regard.[4] Such a group will provide an important and necessary means of insuring that all relevant factors and views are considered in national security planning. Specifically, formal representation of the Joint Chiefs of Staff in such a group would permit a more effective contribution by them to national security planning. The modus operandi of this group will require further study and consultation between the participating parties.

8. In summary, the Joint Chiefs of Staff agree that:

a. Compilation of a Basic National Security Policy into a single document is desirable in principle, but, at the present time, they do not lack policy guidance for the preparation of military plans.

b. National objectives and national security policies should be discussed with the Department of State and other appropriate agencies at the division chief/action officer level. The Joint Staff has been authorized to set up meetings with the Department of State and other appropriate agencies for this purpose.

c. With regard to planning organization, participation by the Joint Chiefs of Staff in the high-level interagency group will facilitate the timely initiation and coordination of political-military planning.

9. The Chief of Staff, US Air Force, and the Commandant of the Marine Corps concur in the views expressed in paragraph 8, above, as an interim measure. However, they believe that, in the interest of improved national security, a Basic National Security Policy should be developed to guide interdepartmental planning. Further, they consider that reactivation of the NSC Planning Board would improve national security planning.

---

[4] In a March 1 memorandum to Secretary McNamara, Deputy Assistant Secretary of Defense Peter Solbert defined this interagency group as "the State–Defense group which Secretary Rusk proposed and to which you agreed, following the exchange of correspondence on the Latin American scenarios. Mr. Kitchen represents State, and Mr. Rowen has represented Defense. General Goodpaster represents the interests of the Joint Chiefs of Staff and has arranged for Joint Staff participation." (Washington National Records Center, OSD Files: FRC 330 70 A 1266, 381 National Defense (Alpha) E thru 1965)

10. In addition, the Commandant of the Marine Corps believes that the establishment of a National Command Center, in support of the Planning Board and manned by a suitable staff, would further improve national security planning and management.[5]

For the Joint Chiefs of Staff:

Earle G. Wheeler
Chairman
Joint Chiefs of Staff

---

[5] In a March 3 memorandum to General Wheeler, Secretary McNamara noted he generally agreed with the views expressed in JCSM–84–65. Concerning paragraphs 8–10, however, McNamara wrote: "I am inclined to the view that there is no pressing need for a BNSP in single document form and, at the moment, am not persuaded that the NSC Planning Board should be reactivated." (Ibid.)

---

76. Memorandum From the Joint Chiefs of Staff to Secretary of Defense McNamara[1]

JCSM–112–65   Washington, February 16, 1965.

SUBJECT

Draft Policy Paper—Chemical and Biological Warfare (U)

1. Reference is made to:

a. A memorandum by the Deputy Assistant Secretary of Defense (ISA), I–29945/64, dated 10 December 1964, subject as above, which forwarded a draft, "National Policy Paper—Chemical and Biological Warfare," for comment and recommendation, plus draft national policy paper.[2]

b. A memorandum by the Director, Correspondence and Directives Division, Office of the Secretary of Defense, dated 31 December 1964, subject as above,[3] which advised that the primary goal of the draft policy paper is the preparation of a National Security Action Memorandum (NSAM), that efforts should be focused accordingly, and that detailed comment on the background material is not required.

---

[1] Source: Washington National Records Center, OSD Files: FRC 330 70 A 1266, 385 Methods and Manner of Conducting War 1965. Secret.

[2] Neither the draft paper nor the December 10 memorandum attached to it is printed. (Ibid.) The words "plus draft national policy paper" were added by hand.

[3] Not found.

c. JCSM–184–64, dated 13 May 1964, subject: "Chemical and Biological Weapons,"[4] which forwarded to you draft responses to items of chemical and biological information requested by the Arms Control and Disarmament Agency.

d. JCSM–404–64, dated 13 May 1964, subject: "Chemical and Biological Weapons,"[5] which forwarded to you supplemental information for the coordinated State/Defense review of chemical and biological policy.

2. The draft national policy paper, forwarded by reference 1a, includes an abstract which contains specific statements of chemical and biological policy. The views of the Joint Chiefs of Staff on this abstract are reflected in the line-in line-out recommendations attached at Appendix A.[6]

3. In accordance with the request in reference 1b, a proposed NSAM based on the policy views of the Joint Chiefs of Staff, indicated in this revised abstract, is attached at Appendix B. In the event that substantive changes are considered necessary to the proposed NSAM, the Joint Chiefs of Staff request the opportunity to review and comment on such changes.

4. The draft paper in reference 1a was useful in the consideration of national policy for chemical and biological weapons. However, the source information contained in references 1c and 1d provides a more comprehensive consideration of chemical and biological operations and it is suggested that it be used as the primary source in support of the proposed national chemical and biological policy.

For the Joint Chiefs of Staff:

L.J. Kirn[7]
Rear Admiral, USN
Deputy Director, Joint Staff

---

[4] A copy is in the National Archives and Records Administration, RG 218, JCS Files, 320 (29 Oct 63).

[5] A copy is ibid., Sec. 2

[6] Neither Appendix A nor B is printed.

[7] Printed from a copy that indicates Kirn signed the original.

77. Memorandum From the Joint Chiefs of Staff to Secretary of Defense McNamara[1]

JCSM–129–65   Washington, February 26, 1965.

SUBJECT

Conceptual Approach to the National Military Command System (NMCS) (U)

1. Reference is made to:

a. A memorandum by the Assistant Secretary of Defense (ADM), dated 28 January 1965, subject as above.[2]

b. JCSM–4–64, dated 10 January 1964, subject: "Deep Underground Command Center (DUCC) (S)."[3]

c. JCSM–446–64, dated 25 May 1964, subject "Deep Underground Command Center (DUCC) (S)."[4]

d. JCSM–914–63, dated 2 December 1963, subject "Alternate Facilities and Supporting Communications Required for the National Military Command System (U)."[5]

2. Reference 1 a requested that the Joint Chiefs of Staff submit their views on a report, subject: "Department of Defense Command and Control Support to the President."

3. The Joint Chiefs of Staff are in broad general agreement with the principles and concepts developed in the study (see Appendix A hereto) and believe that the study provides an excellent basis for furthering rapport and understanding among the Joint Chiefs of Staff, the Office of the Secretary of Defense, and other governmental agencies concerned with planning for command and control at the national level. The first assumption in the terms of reference states that it is extremely unlikely that the President would leave the Washington area during a crisis situation. It is noted that the study nevertheless advocates the principle of multiplicity of centers for Presidential protection and infers that the likelihood of Presidential relocation would significantly increase as a crisis intensifies, even if the crisis is short of general war. The Joint Chiefs of Staff consider these points to be valid both prior to and after construction of a Deep Underground Command Center (DUCC); however, continued improvement of national command and control capabilities depends on a better understanding between all principals of the conditions under which the President might seek protection.

---

[1] Source: Johnson Library, National Security File, Agency File, JCS, Filed by the LBJ Library, Box 29. Top Secret.

[2] Not found.

[3] Document 3.

[4] See footnote 2, Document 52.

[5] See footnote 2, Document 3.

4. With regard to the alternate command centers of the National Military Command System (NMCS), the Joint Chiefs of Staff consider that:

a. The study's recommendation prejudges the conclusions of a separate study currently being undertaken by the Joint Chiefs of Staff regarding the optimum number of National Emergency Command Post Afloat (NECPA) ships required for the NMCS.

b. The National Emergency Airborne Command Post (NEACP) program, in which one or more of three EC 135 aircraft are maintained on continuous ground alert status, represents the minimum acceptable airborne command post posture.

c. There is firm need to assure, to the extent feasible, the survival of the Presidency during any future conflicts; and the circumstances of a future crisis or conflict may be such as to preclude the relocation of the President to one of the existing alternate facilities. In this light, the proposed DUCC represents a potentially effective means for assuring survival of the Presidency to an extent not now provided by the NMCS.

5. The Joint Chiefs of Staff:

a. Concur in the study's comments on the NEACP.

b. Agree in principle on the NECPA as an important element of the NMCS. In this connection, the Joint Chiefs of Staff are currently addressing the optimum posture for the NECPA and upon completion will forward their recommendations.

c. Consider that, if a DUCC is approved and constructed, the study's detailed concepts and principles regarding the DUCC generally provide a basis for determination of detailed functional requirements, concept of operation, and detailed design.

d. Are in general agreement with much of the detailed discussion in the body of the report regarding the role of the Alternate National Military Command Center (ANMCC). However, as indicated in Appendix B hereto, they do not feel that the study recognizes that the ANMCC is fully as valuable as the other alternates of the NMCS when its unique capabilities for supporting all levels of crisis and war are considered. Moreover, they have previously noted that it is essential to continue the ANMCC in its current role for the foreseeable future.

6. The Joint Chiefs of Staff recommend that:

a. The study be forwarded to the Special Assistant to the President for National Security Affairs, the Office of Emergency Planning, the Department of State, and the Central Intelligence Agency for comment regarding the principles and concepts underlying those parts of the study particularly applicable to their operations (see Appendix A).

b. They participate in any evaluation of the comments received by the Secretary of Defense from other agencies and in the identification of subsequent steps to clarify the conceptual approach to command and control.

For the Joint Chiefs of Staff:

Earle G. Wheeler[6]
Chairman
Joint Chiefs of Staff

Appendix A

Based on their analysis, it is the interpretation of the Joint Chiefs of Staff that the following constitute the underlying principles and concepts developed in the Study:

a. For all levels of crisis and war, the President needs utmost flexibility in many aspects of crisis management including centers to be used, immediate advisors, other staff elements to be informed, and options for military action.

b. In crises short of general war, the constitution of the Presidential advisory staff support (support which is estimative analytical, and advisory) is highly dependent upon the nature of the crisis. In contrast, capabilities for information support (defined by the study to include watch, monitoring, communications, decision implementation functions, and emergency action procedures) of the President and his advisors must be developed insofar as possible in advance of a crisis and can be developed more independently of a particular type of crisis. Advisory staff support and information support, although they must work closely together, can be somewhat separated both functionally and organizationally.

c. During intense crises and general war, protection of the President as an individual is as important or even more important than protection of the Presidency through use of legal successors. Although Alternate Decision Groups might be established and relocated, it is doubtful that the principals forming the groups will be named before the crisis and it is doubtful that more than one group will be formed.[7]

d. For crises less than general war, the President and his advisory group do not need an elaborate, national command center permanently staffed by representatives of several agencies; however, the

---

[6] Printed from a copy that indicates Wheeler signed the original.
[7] A handwritten note reads: "V.P.—I think 2 groups at least."

direction of the Armed Forces will be exercised through the National
Military Command System (NMCS).

e. During an intense crisis, protection of the President depends on his
seeking protection prior to the onset of general war. He will only occupy
a protected center if he can manage the intense crisis as well as he could
from the White House Cabinet Room.[8] (For Washington level support
during the intense crisis, the Presidential advisors located with the
President will primarily depend on their soft centers and their staffs in
Washington.) For managing the general war, it would be highly desirable
for the President to be collocated with his general war advisory staff support and the related information support. In light of these needs for both
intense crises and general war, the Alternate Command Centers of the
NMCS and other centers that the President might occupy must be capable of operating as national (versus departmental) command centers.

f. The basic missions of the alternate command centers of the
NMCS have the following priority:

(1) Support the President (located at the Center) during the intense
crisis and the strategic exchange phase of a general war.
(2) Support the President or an alternate decision group (located at
the Center) during the strategic exchange phase of general war.
(3) Locate the President after the onset of general war.
(4) After onset of general war, provide military information and
advisory staff support to the President or a legal successor located elsewhere.
(5) Protect information and advisory staff capability for the follow-
on phase of general war.

In assigning the above missions and priorities, the study concludes
that direction of the strategic exchange phase of a general war should
be directly from the Presidential location to the commanders of unified
and specified commands, their alternates, or successors.

g. Under a "no warning attack" at a time of international calm, only
marginal protection can be provided to the President or his designated
successors.

h. An alternate command center should be evaluated with respect
to the following criteria: survivability, accessibility, endurance, staff
support, communications support, flexibility, and cost. The study heavily emphasizes survivability and accessibility for individual centers and
a multiplicity of centers of comparable capability.

i. For the strategic exchange phase of a general war, the President
and the Presidential Group will be directly and primarily concerned
with military operations, civil defense, diplomacy and negotiations,
and informing and leading the public. The President can extensively

---

[8] Next to this sentence is written: "True."

delegate responsibility for nonmilitary resource allocation, economic mobilization, and maintenance of local law and order. Accordingly, during this phase, the advisory and information support to the Presidential Group should be preponderantly military.

j. The National Military Command Center (NMCC) should provide information support to the Secretary of Defense, the Joint Chiefs of Staff, non-Department of Defense officials, and their attendant advisory staffs. Under certain circumstances, the NMCC will provide advisory support. The NMCC must have the capability to "get information" from many sources (such as CINCs and Service Headquarters) and should not attempt to store all possible information, but only that essential for its primary mission, in its data base.

k. The NMCC and the Organization of the Joint Chiefs of Staff support the Secretary of Defense and the Joint Chiefs of Staff in exercising strategic direction of the Armed Forces. They should also support the President and his advisors in detailed monitoring and control of selected military actions when such actions may have grave national significance. A system built to satisfy only one of these roles will not necessarily be adequate for the other.

Appendix B

With regard to the Fort Ritchie Complex and the Alternate National Military Command Center (ANMCC), the Joint Chiefs of Staff reaffirm their previous position that these facilities are essential to our command and control capabilities in the foreseeable future. They concur with much of the analysis relating to the Alternate Joint Communications Center (AJCC) and the ANMCC and with many of the conclusions regarding their capabilities, functions, and relationships within our over-all national command and control capabilities. However, they are concerned that the study does not support these facilities strongly enough. Specifically:

a. The value of the ANMCC as one possible relocation site for the President or an alternate decision group is recognized (pages V–35, 36 and VI–36) but its capabilities for the strategic exchange phase are equated to [less than 1 line of source text not declassified]. This conclusion seems contrary to two principles in the study. First, survivability is stressed and the ANMCC is significantly harder than [less than 1 line of source text not declassified]. More important, the study stresses collocation of the President and his principal advisors with their supporting military staff. Such collocation could be achieved much more effectively at the ANMCC than at [less than 1 line of source text not declassified] or

Camp David. The study correctly proposes a multiplicity of sites available for relocation. If the individual sites for Presidential or alternate decision group relocation are compared, the Joint Chiefs of Staff would rate the effectiveness of the ANMCC as somewhere between that of a National Emergency Command Post Afloat ship and [*less than 1 line of source text not declassified*].

b. There is not sufficient stress within the study on the potential value of the ANMCC in supporting a decision group on board the National Emergency Airborne Command Post during the strategic exchange phase after Washington has been destroyed.

c. The study correctly recognizes the unique value of the ANMCC for the follow-on phase of a general war. However, since the dividing line between the initial and follow-on phases would be blurred at best, the study does not point out the great advantage of conducting both of these phases from the same location.

d. The study implies that a functional and technical analysis of the ANMCC would indicate potential savings. Such analyses are continuously taking place and they may equally indicate that, if the principles and concepts in the study are approved, additional investments in the AJCC would be warranted.

e. The report does not explicitly recommend continuation of a continuously manned ANMCC. The summary paragraphs discussing the AJCC (pages VI–72 and VII–10) are not consistent with the analyses and conclusions in the body of the report. For example, they indicate that "the ANMCC is not suited to use by the President or an alternate decision group during an intense crisis or the initial stages of a general war." If the report is rewritten, the body of the report should incorporate the above points and these summary paragraphs should be made consistent.

78.   Memorandum From the Joint Chiefs of Staff to Secretary of
Defense McNamara[1]

JCSM–131–65   Washington, March 1, 1965.

SUBJECT

Joint Strategic Objectives Plan for FY 1970–74 (JSOP–70), Parts I Through V
(Strategy and Objectives) and Part VI (Force Tabs and Analysis) (U)

1. The Joint Chiefs of Staff have approved, and forward herewith,
Parts I through VI of the Joint Strategic Objectives Plan for FY 1970–74
(JSOP–70).[2] The entire JSOP–70 is designed to provide military advice
by the Joint Chiefs of Staff for the development of FY 1967 budget justi-
fication for departmental FY 1967 program objectives as they pertain to
major combatant forces, and the basis for reassessment of the current
Department of Defense Five-Year Force Structure and Financial
Program.

2. Parts I through V consist of the following:

I Purpose—States the purposes of the JSOP and its various annexes.

II Strategic Appraisal—Analyses the world-wide threat through the
mid-range period.

III Military Objectives—Describes military objectives which are
considered necessary in support of national objectives.

IV Strategic Concept—Describes anticipated employment of forces
on a functional and geographical basis.

V Basic Undertakings—Describes basic undertakings envisioned
for the unified and specified commanders during the period.

3. Part VI contains the force tabulation of the major combatant
forces recommended to carry out the strategy presented in Parts I
through V. These forces are presented in the format specified by the
Assistant Secretary of Defense (Comptroller) in a memorandum dated
19 January 1965, subject: "Force Tabs of JSOP–70."[3] Amplifying views of
the individual Chiefs are attached as separate Tabs to the Force Tables.[4]
The further views of the Chairman, Joint Chiefs of Staff, will be forwarded by separate memorandum.[5]

---

[1] Source: National Archives and Records Administration, RG 218, JCS Files, 3130 (1
Feb 65). Top Secret; Restricted Data.

[2] Not attached, but copies are ibid., 3130 (1 Feb 65) Secs. 1A–3. Parts I and II of
JSOP–70 are printed as Document 43.

[3] Not found.

[4] Not attached, but copies are in the National Archives and Records Administration,
RG 218, JCS Files, 3130 (1 Feb 65) Secs. 1A–3.

[5] Not further identified.

4. A summary analysis of the personnel implications of force level changes and an order-of-magnitude summary of dollar costing of the objective force levels were considered by the Joint Chiefs of Staff in arriving at the recommended force objectives.

5. In arriving at the proposed force levels the present situation in Southeast Asia was only indirectly considered, and had little, if any, influence upon the JSOP–70 force levels. This is pointed out to identify a specific problem area that requires both a near term and long term solution. By separate action, the Joint Chiefs of Staff are addressing this problem and will provide you with their views on this subject.

For the Joint Chiefs of Staff:

Earle G. Wheeler[6]
Chairman
Joint Chiefs of Staff

---

[6] Printed from a copy that indicates Wheeler signed the original.

---

79.   Memorandum by the Counselor of the Department of State and Chairman of the Policy Planning Council (Rostow)[1]

Washington, March 5, 1965.

NOTIFICATION OF SECRETARY'S POLICY PLANNING MEETING
WEDNESDAY, MARCH 10, 1965, AT 10:00 A.M. IN THE
SECRETARY'S CONFERENCE ROOM

SUBJECT

Some Reflections on National Security Policy, February 1965[2]

Since I must leave for a trip to Germany on March 11 and I greatly desire the guidance of my colleagues, I have scheduled a meeting on

---

[1] Source: National Archives and Records Administration, RG 59, S/S–NSC Files: Lot 70 D 265, (General) National Policy Papers. Secret. According to a distribution list at the end of the memorandum, it was sent to Secretary Rusk, Under Secretary Ball, 19 senior Department of State officers, AID Administrator David E. Bell, and Jacob D. Beam, Assistant Director of the International Relations Bureau of ACDA.

[2] This is the title of Rostow's paper, Document 80.

this somewhat long paper for Wednesday, March 10.[3] It is an effort to outline the main directions for U.S. policy in the months and years ahead in the light of three quite general characteristics of the world scene:

a. The growing assertiveness of governments both within the Free World and within the Communist world;

b. The fact that this growing assertiveness in the Free World has not been accompanied by a development of military power (aside from U.S. power) capable of coping with either Soviet or Chinese Communist military strength; and

c. The fact that conventional nationalism does not permit nations to grip their major economic, security, and even regional political problems successfully.

Paragraph 11 (pages 22–25) sets out the major functional tasks of U.S. security policy that flow from this view of the world scene.

Part II then explores these questions:

a. The extent to which these functional tasks might be carried forward in the present environment by the creation or further development of regional organizations and devices in which the U.S. is integrally involved. Paragraph 15 (pages 31–32) underlines the special concept of regionalism suggested here and its twofold objective: "To permit nations to grip collectively problems that do not lend themselves to satisfactory solution on a national or bilateral basis"; and "To permit nations to deal with the U.S. (and, where relevant, other industrialized powers of the Free World) on a basis of greater dignity than bilateralism permits."

b. The appropriate degree and character of U.S. involvement on the world scene in the future, which is set out against an analysis of whether we are or are not in some sense "over-committed" (pages 44–48).

One operational question of some interest is raised by this analysis, not dealt with in the text: Would the further elaboration of regional economic development arrangements, symbolized by the emergence of an African Development Bank and the movement towards an Asian Development Bank, help meet the kind of criticism we now confront with respect to foreign aid by Senator Fulbright and others?

W.W. Rostow[4]

---

[3] Secretary Rusk attended this meeting on March 10 from 10:05 to 11:03 a.m. (Johnson Library, Rusk Appointment Book) No record of the discussion has been found.

[4] Printed from a copy that bears this typed signature.

80.   **Paper Prepared by the Counselor of the Department of State and Chairman of the Policy Planning Council (Rostow)[1]**

Washington, March 5, 1965.

SOME REFLECTIONS ON NATIONAL SECURITY POLICY
February 1965

Introduction

With the passage of time since the acute bipolar confrontations in Berlin and Cuba, in 1961–62, the shape of the world scene is altering. The environment in which we must seek to protect and advance the nation's abiding interests is changing its shape.

Briefly stated, we are somewhere between a cold war between two great blocs and a world of nation states; we are somewhere between a world organized rationally, respectful of the inescapable interdependencies of modern life, and the chaos of old-fashioned nationalism; we are somewhere between a world split on lines of wealth and race and differing stages of modernization and a community of partners in the spirit of the United Nations Charter.

If we are to use our limited but real margin of influence to produce from this lively, dangerous but not unhopeful, situation a world of nation states, organized in ways which respect their interdependencies, operating as a global community under the UN Charter, we need fresh bearings and, in some cases, new lines of action.

To set the stage for this exposition, it may be useful to present the problem we confront in the form of a series of paradoxes which characterize the essentially transitional passage of history through which we are passing and which we must seek, within our capabilities, to shape.

---

[1] Source: National Archives and Records Administration, RG 59, S/S–NSC Files: Lot 70 D 265, (General) National Policy Papers. Secret. Regarding the distribution and discussion of this paper, see Document 79. Rostow sent an earlier, February 15, draft of his paper to Secretary McNamara under cover of an undated, handwritten note, which asked for McNamara's "personal observations." "I don't do general papers often," Rostow wrote, "but I am convinced we need some such map of our problem now." (Washington National Records Center, OSD Files: FRC 330 70 A 1266, 381 National Defense 1965) In a March 27 letter to Rostow, McNamara replied that John McNaughton had told him that the Defense representatives at a planners' meeting on February 25 "indicated that your thesis was well worth exploring." McNamara added that he shared Rostow's concern that his approach "may be of somewhat limited value in the short run in Southeast Asia and other critical areas," but that he had directed McNaughton and his staff to assist him on this project. (Ibid.)

—Although the danger of overt Communist aggression, nuclear or conventional, has been evidently reduced, there is no indication that policy in Moscow or Peiping is restrained from the overt use of force by any factor other than credible opposing force—mainly U.S. military force.

—Although there has been in Western Europe and Japan a remarkable increase in economic power and political confidence and assertiveness, this revival has not been accompanied by a proportionate rise in nuclear or conventional military capacity; and, similarly, the rise of nationalist impulses and fragmentation within the Communist world has not been accompanied by an equivalent diffusion of nuclear or conventional military capacity away from Moscow and Peiping.

—There are strong forces at work on the world scene tending towards the diffusion of nuclear power, although the net security advantage of a small nuclear capability is, in almost every case, negative on any objective assessment.

—The most dangerous current military threat to the security of the Free World is subversion and guerrilla warfare in the developing nations, although in an industrial and atomic age this form of aggression is the most economical in men and resources and the most primitive.

—Although nationalism—often xenophobic in tone—is strong and rising in the developing nations, they lack a capacity to solve their security or economic problems on a national basis; and even on a regional basis they require intimate collaboration with the more advanced powers to solve their major domestic and security problems.

—Although the proportion of U.S. resources devoted to national security purposes (including foreign aid) has been declining, there is much talk of U.S. over-extension on the world scene.

It is against the background of these puzzlements that this paper, after summarizing the nation's interest, examines in Part One the environment we confront and the broad lines of policy required to resolve the paradoxes in a manner consonant with our interests; while Part Two comes to rest on the possible role of regional arrangements in this reconciliation and on the appropriate character of U.S. involvement on the world scene.

Part One

[Here follow the first two sections of Part One: "U.S. Interests and Objectives" (paragraphs 1–2) and "The Underlying Military Situation" (paragraphs 3–9).]

U.S. Policy

10. Thus, the central objectives of national security policy are to continue to maintain the capacity to project U.S. military strength around the borders of the Communist world, as a deterrent to Communist nuclear and conventional forces, in an environment of somewhat enflamed nationalism; to develop and maintain a political environment within which we can actively project our capacity to assist in the deterrence and defeat of Communist techniques of attraction and indirect aggression; to convert present conventional nationalist impulses into constructive courses of action which would permit the nations and peoples of these regions to grip their military, economic, and political problems more effectively and to do so in ways which enlarge their own capacity to shape their destiny; and on the foundations of a Free World where nationalist assertiveness is gradually organized in communal arrangements, where reactions against dependence are converted into the acceptance of responsible partnership, to work constructively to draw the presently Communist world into pacific relations to the world community.

11. In the light of this definition of objectives, the major tasks of U.S. national security policy can be set out under the following headings:

a. To maintain as basic insurance a U.S. nuclear and conventional military establishment of a scale and character sufficient, along with those of our allies, to deter overt aggression or to deal with it should deterrence fail in the various regions.

b. To maintain a political environment and a technical capacity which permits us to project our military power onto the European and Asian mainlands in a manner such as to deter overt aggression by the most economical means possible, or to deal with such aggression if it is mounted.

c. To mount programs, regional or national, as well as universal, designed to satisfy by other means the impulses of fear, pride and prestige now leading nations towards the development of national nuclear capabilities.

d. To create and maintain a political environment and to refine the methods and tasks required to frustrate effectively and to render unattractive as future tactics the forms of indirect aggression now being mounted against various parts of the Free World.

e. To damp the regional quarrels which threaten to disrupt various Free World regions and to expand opportunities for Communist influence and penetration.

f. Gradually to bring the more assertive and ambitious leaders in developing nations (Sukarno, Nasser) to an acceptance of their limitations and to policies of increased regional restraint and concentration on their domestic tasks by programs of constraint and incentive.

g. To damp and gradually to eliminate the frictions imposed by continuing colonial problems.

h. With respect to c–g, above, to refine our use of the tools of economic, technical, and military aid, which are a critically important, if limited, lever in damping the disruptive potential of reactive nationalism in the developing world.

i. Against a background of such policies (designed to discourage among Communists the view that the present environment offers important opportunities for expanding their power and influence) to work constructively with the forces of fragmentation within the Communist world, by moves which exploit limited areas of overlapping national interest which may exist, and to draw nations presently under Communist regimes into the orbit of the world community. The critical effort in this field will be, of course to work steadily in the direction of a Central European settlement which would reconcile German unity with effective measures for European security and arms control—an historical process in which the political liberalization of Eastern Europe and an expansion in its non-military ties to the West may play a central role.

j. To develop with the nations of Western Europe and Canada more effective means of dealing with North Atlantic problems and also to draw them, and, where appropriate, Japan, Australia, and New Zealand into policies of concert and support with respect to b–i, above.

This category of policy is evidently, critical in both the short run and the long run.

In the short run our world position depends on maintaining the essential structure of Atlantic unity, now precariously held together against Gaullist disruption, and moving forward in the critical fields of nuclear policy; trade and agricultural policy; and in monetary affairs. Failure in any of these areas of active negotiation could weaken the fabric of the Alliance.

In the long run, the acceptance of wider responsibilities on a world basis by our Atlantic allies and an acceptance of wider regional responsibilities by Japan, Australia, and New Zealand is essential to the execution of this strategy.

[Here follows Part Two: "Regionalism and the Appropriate Degree and Character of U.S. Involvement on the World Scene" (paragraphs 12–23).]

The Character of U.S. Involvement on the World Scene

24. The argument here is that, broadly speaking, we face in other regions of the world, each in a context that is unique, the same kind of problem that we have already confronted and in which we have done much pioneer work in the past generation with respect to the Atlantic world and Latin America. It is further assumed that there is no region in the world to whose evolution we can be indifferent, given the character of our national interest, although our regional interests vary and are of different weight.

25. Before concluding our observations on regionalism, it is worth posing a prior question; namely, whether or not the United States is now, in some meaningful sense, overextended on the world scene.

Do our military and economic commitments on the mainland or Eurasia, as well as in Africa and Latin America, constitute an increasing or intolerable strain on our resources?

Is the potential strength of our adversaries increasing relative to our own at a rate which justifies considering a retraction of U.S. commitment?

Is there some other sense in which we are over-committed?

So far as U.S. resources are concerned, Appendix B[2] makes clear that both over-all defense expenditures and foreign aid expenditures are a declining proportion of our annual output. Defense expenditures for FY 1965 are down to 7.5% of GNP, having fallen away from 9.5% a decade earlier; economic and military aid expenditures (excluding PL 480 and Export-Import Bank loans) are down to .48% of GNP from a figure of 1.1% in 1955. Economic assistance, at about the same absolute level as 1955 ($2 billion) has fallen from .51% of GNP to .32% of GNP. So long as the U.S. economy continues to expand at a reasonable rate there can be no serious anxiety about our capacity to sustain present military and foreign aid commitments or to expand them substantially, if necessary, without endangering the progress of our domestic life.

There is, of course, a continuing problem of assuring that outlays abroad in support of our security commitments do not endanger our balance of payments or the confidence felt in the dollar as a reserve currency. This real problem lends itself to resolution by many devices other than a retraction of defense outlays or foreign aid expenditures, notably because these expenditures are already substantially cushioned in their impact on the balance of payments and because national security should continue to enjoy a priority higher than, for example, long-term

---

[2] A table entitled "U.S. Defense Expenditure and Foreign Aid as Related to the U.S. Gross National Product and National Income at Factor Cost, 1946–1966"; not printed.

private investment in Western Europe or certain other private outlays abroad.

We could also be judged to be overextended if our potential adversaries were increasing their industrial capacity or military outlays at a rate which, if matched by us, could impose intolerable strains on our domestic life. This is, evidently, not the case. While there is no cause for complacency with respect to the evolution of either Soviet or Chinese Communist military capabilities, they do not appear to be evolving in ways or at a pace beyond our capacity to deter within the range of recent or existing percentage allocations of our over-all resources. We are most likely to be embarrassed by qualitative, rather than quantitative, changes in the military capabilities of our major adversaries.

What, then, accounts for recent discussions of "over-commitment"?

First, the rise of national assertiveness, in forms as various as Gaullism, the burning of libraries, and Buddhist antics in Saigon, has converged with the sense of release from Soviet nuclear blackmail after the Cuba missile crisis, to make the world appear both less tractable and less dangerous than it was in, say, the period 1961–62. There is a widespread, if ill-defined, feeling that if foreigners don't like us, let's pull back, and that some pull-back would be safe.

Moreover, our painful and frustrating experience in Laos and Viet Nam makes men search for solutions and perspectives which would permit our withdrawal while believing that no grave damage would be done to vital U.S. or Free World interests.

What passes for "over-commitment" is, in this sense, simply frustration in achieving our objectives by existing means in the turbulent and assertive environment we confront, compounded by Communist methods for expanding indirectly their power and influence in that environment, combined with a correct perception that other nations are seeking ways to solve their problems which involves less brute dependence on the United States than in the past.

There is a second sense in which we are very heavily committed, if not over-committed, as compared to earlier times. Every region on the planet is now part of a sensitively interacting world community. In the immediate postwar years, major decisions could focus on the Atlantic world, Japan, and relations with Moscow. Now not only have the countries of Latin America, Africa, the Middle East and Asia entered the game but Communist China and the individual countries of Eastern Europe appear on the stage with independent or quasi-independent personalities. This proliferation of states and emerging centers of power and influence diminish our capacity to influence or control given situations by means we have used in the past; and requires new methods and involvement of new kinds if we are to bring our residual margin of influence to bear on issues of vital interest. The number of U.S. relationships and problems capable of forcing a decision at the highest levels of the government has thus vastly multiplied. The working levels of government can be—and have been—expanded to deal with this phenomenon at home and in the field. But we can have only one President and one Secretary of State. And here the real burden of commitment and active engagement has been enlarged.

The burden of this paper is, then, that what we confront is not a question of continuing existing policies and commitments or pulling back. What we face is the task of transforming our relations with the nations of the Free World, region by region, in such a way as to permit them an enlarged role in their own destiny while permitting us to perform the minimum security, economic, and political functions required in their interests and in ours. This concept does involve a kind of selective relaxation of presence and pressure, as we encourage the nations themselves increasingly to take responsibility for assessing their interests and formulating responsible proposals for collective action. It does not, however, permit a significant withdrawal of U.S. security commitment and presence. And, as our experience with the OECD as opposed to the OEEC suggests, as well as our experience with CIAP, partnership in regional organizations (as opposed to dependence) tends to increase rather than to diminish the range and intimacy of contacts and common enterprise.

If all goes well, then, the present phase of rather anarchic nationalism abroad, with its counterpart in neo-isolationist impulses at home, should give way to relations of enlarging partnership in one region after the other.

That, in any case, is what the state of our environment and the character of our abiding interests appear to require. But it will not happen without a clear U.S. sense of direction, quiet leadership, and persistence.

81.   Memorandum From the President's Special Assistant for
       National Security Affairs (Bundy) to President Johnson[1]

Washington, March 11, 1965.

SUBJECT

Release of Nuclear Weapons to Air Defense National Guard Units

1. In the attached memorandum Secretary McNamara last year requested authority for emergency release of nuclear air defense weapons to National Guard units.[2] Under present arrangements, National Guard air defense units would be slow to act in an emergency due to administrative requirements for federalization. The requested authority would permit release of weapons and operational employment in accordance with emergency action procedures approved for regular forces.

I held up this action last year because of the risk of misunderstanding, in the light of the controversy over control of nuclear weapons. This is in fact a quite routine adjustment of emergency procedures, but it might not have seemed so in 1964. Secretary McNamara and the Joint Chiefs of Staff now feel that it should be approved, and I agree.

McG.B.

Approve[3]

Disapprove

---

[1] Source: Johnson Library, National Security File, Agency File, Department of Defense, Vol. II, 12/64, Box 12. Top Secret.

[2] Document 38.

[3] This option is checked. A March 12 memorandum from Bundy to McNamara confirmed that the President approved the recommendation. (Johnson Library, National Security File, Agency File, Department of Defense, Vol. II, 12/64, Box 12)

82. Memorandum From the Executive Secretary of the National Security Council (Smith) to All Holders of NSC 5816[1]

Washington, March 23, 1965.

SUBJECT

Discontinuance of the Net Evaluation Subcommittee

The President on March 11, 1965, approved the recommendation of the Secretary of Defense[2] that NSC 5816, "A Net Evaluation Subcommittee," be rescinded. The Subcommittee, having served its purpose with distinction, was discontinued on March 18 by National Security Action Memorandum No. 327.[3] The type of study which the Subcommittee has conducted since 1958 will be accomplished by other means.

Copies of NSC 5816 now in the custody of the member agencies may be destroyed or otherwise disposed of in accordance with the regulations of the member agency relating to the custody and destruction of classified materials and with Executive Order 10501,[4] as amended by Executive Order 10964.[5]

Bromley Smith

---

[1] Source: Johnson Library, National Security File, Agency File, National Security Council, Vol. I, Box 34. Top Secret; Special Limited Distribution. Regarding NSC 5816, see Document 72 and footnote 2 thereto.

[2] Secretary McNamara's recommendation to the President has not been found but probably followed closely his undated draft memorandum to the President, Document 72.

[3] A copy is in the National Archives and Records Administration, RG 59, S/S–NSC Files: Lot 72 D 316, NSAM No. 327. It reproduced almost verbatim the wording suggested by Secretary McNamara; see footnote 4, Document 72.

[4] E.O. 10501, "Safeguarding Official Information in the Interests of the Defense of the United States," November 5, 1953, Federal Register, vol. 18, pp. 7049, 7051–7054.

[5] E.O. 10964, "Amendment of Executive Order No. 10501, Entitled 'Safeguarding Official Information in the Interests of the Defense of the United States,'" September 20, 1961, ibid., vol. 26, pp. 8932–8933.

National Security Policy 229

83. **Letter From the Director of the White House Office of Emergency Planning (Ellington) to Secretary of Defense McNamara[1]**

Washington, March 31, 1965.

Dear Mr. Secretary:

I am pleased to enclose for your use revised "Guidance for Non-Military Planning"[2] which I reported on at Cabinet meeting March 25.[3] This provides new assumptions for use by Federal departments and agencies in the further development of their civil emergency preparedness. It supersedes the document of the same title issued October 31, 1963, by the Office of Emergency Planning.[4]

The new guidance has been brought up to date by the Committee on Assumptions for Non-Military Planning, established by the President. The Committee, as you know, consists of representatives from the Department of State, the Department of Defense, and the Central Intelligence Agency, with the Director of the Office of Emergency Planning serving as chairman. I am glad to take this opportunity to express my appreciation for the participation of your representative, the Deputy Assistant Secretary of Defense for Weapons Acquisition and Industrial Readiness, Mr. James Davis, and the members of the working group, Mr. Eckhard Bennewitz and Mr. Henry A. Damminger. The final document owes a great deal indeed to their substantive contributions and constructive comments.

The new guidance differs in several respects from the document it supersedes. It is more specific where lack of specificity was found to be a handicap to use. It also reflects a much greater emphasis on the necessity to prepare for less-than-nuclear situations up to and including large-scale conventional wars. There is corresponding reduction in the likelihood (but not the importance) of nuclear war.

It is important that civil emergency preparedness—both current arrangements and future plans—reflect this change of emphasis and other more specific planning factors covered in the guidance. I therefore suggest that you review your emergency plans and programs to assure their responsiveness to these contingency assumptions. If in the course

---

[1] Source: Washington National Records Center, OSD Files: FRC 330 70 A 1266, 384 Civil Defense Jan–June 1965. Secret.

[2] The subtitle of the publication is "1965 Issue"; not printed.

[3] No record of this meeting has been found.

[4] Not further identified.

of your review you discover the need for special situation assumptions, I will undertake to see that they are provided, working with the members of the Committee on Assumptions as appropriate.

Sincerely,

Buford Ellington

---

84. National Intelligence Estimate[1]

NIE 11–4–65   Washington, April 14, 1965.

MAIN TRENDS IN SOVIET MILITARY POLICY

The Problem

To review significant developments in Soviet military thinking, policy, and programs, and to estimate main trends in Soviet military policies over the next six years.

Scope

This estimate focuses upon broad trends in Soviet military policy and doctrine. It does not attempt to recapitulate existing NIEs on Soviet strategic attack, air defense, and general purpose forces. Our most recent detailed estimates on the size, composition, and capabilities of these principal components and the supporting elements of the Soviet military forces are as follows:

NIE 11–8–64; "Soviet Capabilities for Strategic Attack," dated 8 October 1964, Top Secret, Restricted Data (Limited Distribution)[2] and Memorandum to Holders of NIE 11–8–64, dated 7 April 1965.[3]

---

[1] Source: Johnson Library, National Security File, National Intelligence Estimates 11–65, USSR, Box 3. Secret; Controlled Dissem. A cover sheet, prefatory note, title page, and table of contents are not printed. According to the prefatory note, the CIA and the intelligence organizations of the Departments of State and Defense, the Atomic Energy Commission, and the National Security Agency participated in the preparation of this estimate. Representatives of the State Department, DIA, AEC, and NSA concurred; the FBI representative abstained, the subject being outside his jurisdiction.

[2] Document 55.

[3] No April 7 memorandum has been found, but for a May 10 memorandum on this subject, see Document 88.

NIE 11–3–64; "Soviet Bloc Air and Missile Defense Capabilities Through Mid-1970," dated 16 December 1964, Top Secret.[4]

NIE 11–14–64; "Capabilities of the Soviet General Purpose Forces, 1964–1970," dated 10 December 1964, Secret.[5]

Conclusions

A. Soviet decisions since Khrushchev's fall do not indicate any general alteration in his military policies. During the next six years, we believe that the main aim of the USSR's military policy and programs will remain that of strengthening the Soviet deterrent.[6] In the strategic field, we expect the USSR to increase the numbers and effectiveness of a variety of weapon systems and, in particular, greatly to improve retaliatory capabilities. These programs may include the deployment of anti-missile defenses. But we think it highly unlikely that the Soviets could achieve a combination of offensive and defensive forces so strong as to persuade the leadership that it could launch a strategic attack upon the West and limit to acceptable proportions the subsequent damage to the USSR. (Paras. 18, 46–52)

B. The Soviets will continue to press their dynamic military and space R&D programs. Soviet security considerations demand vigorous efforts to prevent a Western military technological advantage which might threaten the credibility of their deterrent. Beyond this, we believe that the Soviet R&D effort represents an attempt to achieve major technological advances in the hope of offsetting present Western strategic advantages. Should the Soviets achieve a technological advance which offered the prospect of significant improvement in military capabilities, they would seek to exploit it for political and military advantage, but their decisions as to deployment would involve a weighing of such advantage against economic considerations and US capabilities to counter. (Paras. 29–32)

C. With respect to theater forces, capabilities for nuclear combat will remain a prime Soviet concern. Certain recent trends, however, point to a growing concern with non-nuclear war, and we expect Soviet

---

[4] Document 69.

[5] Not printed. (Johnson Library, National Security File, National Intelligence Estimates 11–65, USSR, Box 3)

[6] The Director of the National Security Agency and the Assistant Chief of Staff, Intelligence, USAF consider that the intensity with which the USSR is pursuing a massive military research and development program—the specific content and progress of which are not clearly known to the US—portends far more than an intent merely to strengthen Soviet deterrent posture. They believe that attainment of strategic superiority continues to be the goal of Soviet political and military leadership and that the USSR is actively searching for ways and means of building toward parity and ultimate superiority. [Footnote in the source text.]

military policy to devote increasing attention to this contingency. Further, there is some evidence that the Soviets intend to develop greater capabilities for distant, limited military action, an area in which they are presently at a great disadvantage. (Paras. 40–43, 56–57)

D. The new Soviet leaders will continue to apply economic restraints to the expansion of military programs. The Soviet economy could support a substantially increased military effort. Nevertheless, the demands of costly military and space programs conflict directly with the requirements of the civil economy, and the newly announced agricultural program does not portend any early easing of economic constraints. Barring important changes in the international situation, we consider major shifts in the level of Soviet defense spending to be unlikely. (Paras. 20, 25–27)

E. Soviet military policy will also be heavily influenced by external developments. In Eastern Europe, if present trends toward autonomy continue, the Warsaw Pact will evolve toward a conventional military alliance, and the range of contingencies in which the USSR can rely on effective support from its Warsaw Pact allies will narrow. In Asia, the hardening of the Sino-Soviet dispute will probably force the USSR to recognize the military implications of China's hostility and ambitions, and the USSR will probably strengthen conventional forces in Soviet Asia. In Western Europe, the Soviets would consider their military problem to be sharply altered by any important changes in the political cohesion or military effectiveness of NATO. But the Soviets will continue to weigh the adequacy of military programs primarily against US capabilities, and to judge the desirability of proposed programs against probable US reaction. (Paras. 33–36)

F. Beyond the general mission of deterrence, we doubt that any single doctrinal design, meeting the tests of comprehensiveness and feasibility, will govern the development of Soviet military forces over the next six years. Old debates which seem certain to outlive Khrushchev's departure, the momentum of deployment programs, the clash of vested interests, attempts to capitalize on some technological advance, an urge to match or counter various enemy capabilities—these are some of the factors which are likely to inhibit any far-reaching rationalization of military policy around a single doctrine. (Para. 51)

[Here follows the Discussion section (Parts I–IV, pages 4–17).]

85.   Memorandum From the President's Special Assistant for
       National Security Affairs (Bundy) to Secretary of State Rusk
       and Secretary of Defense McNamara[1]

Washington, April 21, 1965.

The President would like to have it understood publicly that there
has been, and will be, no delegation of responsibility to the field for the
use of any war gases. To this end, he has recently informed a number of
private citizens that this is his policy.[2]

I would suggest that you refer to this policy in one of your public
statements during the next month, making clear that the policy is one of
long standing in the United States Government.

McG.B.

---

[1] Source: Washington National Records Center, OSD Files: FRC 330 70 A 1266, 385
Methods and Manner of Conducting War 1965. No classification marking. The date is
handwritten, and "Sec Def has seen 17 May 1965" is stamped on the memorandum. An
April 27 note in an unidentified hand on another copy indicates that the original was
handcarried from the White House on or about April 22 and given to Secretary McNamara and that this copy was given to Vance. (Ibid.)

[2] Not further identified.

---

86.   Study Prepared in the Department of Defense[1]

Washington, undated.

DEPARTMENT OF DEFENSE COMMAND AND CONTROL
SUPPORT TO THE PRESIDENT

[Here follow the Introduction and Chapters I–VI.]

---

[1] Source: Johnson Library, National Security File, Agency File, Department of Defense, Command and Control Support to the President, Box 20. Top Secret. The Introduction to the study indicates that it was prepared in response to a February 27, 1964, memorandum by Deputy Secretary of Defense Vance, which is included at the end of the study
as Annex A. The Introduction also identifies Rear Admiral Paul P. Blackburn, Jr., Chief of
the Joint Command and Control Requirements Group, Organization of the Joint Chiefs of
Staff, as chairman of the study; the other Defense members who prepared it; members of
an advisory group and working group; and consultants (pp. i–iii).

Chapter VII

Summary of Conclusions and Recommendations

The President increasingly becomes the focal point of crisis management as a crisis intensifies. He devotes more time to the crisis and considers selected operations in greater detail. The President needs and operates with extreme flexibility—flexibility in constituting his immediate decision group; in defining alternate courses of action that must be considered; in determining, to the extent feasible, the timing of the U.S. responses and therefore the time allowable for staff inputs; flexibility in seeking detailed information on selected military operations; in establishing and employing the organization and operational command chain including reducing the number of echelons of command; flexibility in determining the sensitivity of selected information relating to the crisis; in communicating with allied, neutral and enemy heads of state; and in establishing constraints or accepting risks in conducting the crisis.

The President will select the *Presidential Group* that will assist him in directing a given crisis. This has invariably been true in the past and it is reasonable to assume that it will continue to be so in the future. Since the Presidential Group will include personal advisors, and statutory advisors and their subordinates, it will reflect military, political, diplomatic, intelligence and other such interests that might be relevant to the crisis. As a crisis develops, the composition of the Presidential Group will normally grow and alter.

So far the U.S. has experienced only a very few of the infinite number of crisis situations with which command and control support arrangements must be prepared to cope. Crisis situations, far more intense than any yet experienced, but nevertheless short of a large scale intercontinental nuclear exchange, are possible. These should be given more consideration in the development of U.S. command and control arrangements. For example, as indicated below, consideration of *intense crises* can have a significant impact on plans for presidential protection.

During a crisis the President and the Presidential Group will probably use mission-oriented interagency groups to assist them in estimating the present situation, and in developing and evaluating alternate courses of action. These groups may be asked to consider broad or narrow aspects of the crisis. The President and the Presidential Group expect that such support has melded military, political, domestic and diplomatic factors. Accordingly, the constitution of the Presidential Group and their need for staff support implies the need for interagency staffing before estimates and advice are advanced to the Presidential Group.

For severe crises, the composition and extent of the advisory staff support to the President will be uniquely determined at the time of the crisis by the nature of the crisis including such factors as timing, areas and participants, scope of conflict, the opportunity and the need for secrecy, escalatory potential, and diplomatic constraints. On the other hand, the routine information support capabilities needed to support these individuals are much more predictable. These capabilities include communications and message distribution, provision of factual data on force status and plans, routine staff support in implementing and promulgating decisions, conferencing and display facilities, and the staff which operates and provides these capabilities. Accordingly, it is desirable and feasible to separate conceptually and organizationally the problem of providing the advisory staff support from that of providing the routine information support. It is difficult to improvise information support during a crisis and it is possible to anticipate the requirements for this support before the crisis. The reverse is true for staff advisory support.

Presidential councils are informal and consultative in nature. The President receives his information support through his advisors and, accordingly, crisis management would not be enhanced by establishment at the national level of an elaborate "National Command Center" manned by a large, permanent interagency staff.

Many avenues are available that would improve interagency effectiveness in crisis anticipation and management. The following are recommended: increased attention at all levels of the Joint Staff with crisis management, freer interaction at all levels between members of the Joint Staff and their counterparts in other agencies, greater interagency review of military and political contingency plans, increased interagency participation in war gaming and exercising, and increased attention within the Joint Staff on nonmilitary factors affecting crisis anticipation and management.

Within the military establishment the concept of handling crises within command posts or operations centers is well established. The NMCC is similar to, but both narrower and broader in its scope than the conventional operations center. It is narrower in that its support to decision makers is rendered through the medium of their staff advisors, and ordinarily it does not itself provide advisory staff support except when an emergency does not permit referral to such advisors. It is broader in that the principal users of NMCC information support are not only the Joint Chiefs of Staff and the Joint Staff, but also various elements of OSD and authorized persons in the White House, State Department and CIA.

The NMCC performs the functions of (1) warning and alert, (2) information support, and (3) implementation. Its principal suppliers of information to the NMCC are the operating forces, the service operations centers, and the DIA through the Intelligence Support and Indications Center.

The fundamental character of the NMCC is that of a DoD information support facility operated by the Joint Chiefs of Staff for the DoD as a whole. In the performance of its functions the NMCC should exchange information freely with analogous information centers elsewhere within the Government.

The management arrangements under which the NMCC operates should preserve its close working relationship with the Directorate for Operations in the Joint Staff and also should reflect its essentially informational character and DoD-wide scope.

Future development of the NMCC should emphasize evolutionary improvement as opposed to sweeping change. Such evolution will be helped by increased efforts to evaluate NMCC performances both in actual crises and in exercises. The establishment of suitable performance standards for the NMCC will also be helpful in its development.

Exercises of a variety of types and scope are necessary not only for the improvement of the NMCC but also to familiarize participating decision makers with its facilities and with command problems. For some of these exercises, senior members from all affected agencies and their staffs should participate.

At any stage of crisis or general nuclear war, enemy options range from a deliberate heavy attack against national command centers to strenuously avoiding these targets. In addition, there are a host of foreseeable and unforeseeable events that could lead to nuclear strikes on Washington or to Washington remaining completely undamaged. In providing for command and control support to the President, all of these contingencies must be considered. In providing survivability for the President, the worst cases must be planned for.

There are many factors militating against presidential relocation during crises short of general war. However, if the enemy decides to escalate a crisis to general war, he can easily destroy unprotected national centers without the President's receiving tactical warning. If tactical warning of an attack is received, it is not clear that the President's wisest course would be to seek immediate protection. Accordingly, capabilities should be provided for presidential protection in a highly survivable command center *during any phase of crisis.* This center must allow the President and the Presidential Group to manage intense crises short of general nuclear war as well as these can be managed from the White House.

The unique value of the President required that all possible measures be taken to insure his personal survival of an attack on the U.S. However, provision for a successor is also necessary. Accordingly, capabilities should allow relocation to a highly survivable center of an alternate Presidential Group headed by a presidentially designated alternate

Commander-in-Chief. The command and control support for this alternate group could be much more austere than those for a relocated President.

It is important to recognize the national-level character of those alternates that might be used by the President or an Alternate Decision Group as contrasted with the DoD-level role of the NMCC.

A DUCC in Washington would be the only facility that could adequately satisfy the presidential needs for accessibility combined with survivability and adequate staff support. However, since a DUCC cannot be operational for at least five years, in the interim only the NECPA ship and a National Mobile Land Command Post (NMLCP) come close to approximating the requirements of: adequate staff support; high volume (not necessarily survivable) communications between the alternate and soft Washington centers; continuous operation for a period of days or weeks; and high survivability of the alternate itself. The NEACP falls short of meeting the first three criteria: the ANMCC fails on the last.

For the time period before a DUCC could be operational, the study developed the following three different configurations of alternates ranging from most austere to the most adequate:

a. Two functionally similar NECPA ships
b. Three NEACP aircraft, plus (a) above
c. An NMLCP with a staff capacity somewhat less than an NECPA, plus (b) above.

The Study recommends alternative (b) above. An NMLCP is not recommended unless greater emphasis is placed on providing flexible capabilities for presidential relocation during intense crises short of general war.

The JCS assisted by DCA and the Navy should conduct a study that develops plans for remedying the operational defects of the current two-ship NECPA element. This study should: i) detail the functional needs and criteria for support of the Presidential Group during intense crises and during the strategic exchange phase; ii) compare the costs and schedules of significantly improving the *Northampton* or obtaining a replacement hull; and, iii) consider operating concepts with the current or new ships.

The operational concept and support plans of the NECPA and the NEACP should be revised to provide for greater endurance, survivability and accessibility. For the NECPA, this planning should include increased protection from various forms of attack, larger and faster transportation capability between Washington and the ships, and operations closer to the Washington area during crises. For the NEACP, the planning should include use of aerial refueling, permanent dispersal of the aircraft, capability for post-strike use of several bases that have prelocated logistics and communications support, and plans for locating the aircraft closer to Washington during severe crises.

Because of its relatively low survivability, the ANMCC is not suited to use by the President or an Alternate Decision Group during an intense crisis or the initial stages of a general war. The AJCC should be continued with primarily the following functions: act as a potential reconstitution site in the follow-on phases of a general war; provide a dispersed back-up to Washington communications; and support other NMCS centers for day-to-day operations and crises. A detailed functional and technical analysis of the current and planned AJCC should be conducted in order to develop a better understanding of how particular capabilities and costs contribute to each of these functions. The study should indicate potential savings.

---

87.   **Memorandum From the President's Military Aide (Clifton) to the President's Special Assistant for National Security Affairs (Bundy)**[1]

Washington, May 5, 1965.

Several of us have looked this over and find that it is a very logical study,[2] which fully appreciates the situation in regard to the President. The conclusions, as to the requirements for command and control support for the President, are sound.

The conclusions in Chapter VII are logical, and they would indicate the following actions:

(a) That the President choose a *Presidential Group* that will assist him in directing a crisis when it occurs.
(b) That further study be made of the means for the protection of the President during times of *intense crisis.*
(c) That interagency effectiveness in crisis anticipation and management be improved.
(d) That we should not attempt to establish a formal National Command Center with adequate staff support on a full-time basis, but

---

[1] Source: Johnson Library, National Security File, Agency File, Department of Defense, Command and Control Support to the President, Box 20. Top Secret.
[2] Document 86.

that we plan for the establishment of such a command center if it were to be needed.

Comments

(a) Someone in authority should take an active hand in lining up the proper Presidential support to go with the emergency plans, which are charged to the Office of the Military Aide at present. We have gone about as far as we can go with the present guidance. Fundamentally the President should have recommendations made to him as to the specific locations of his possible successors, including the Vice President, and see that appropriate staff assignments are made so that if a nuclear attack occurred, and the President were lost, the command function could be carried on by one or more successors.

The above includes the advance designation for certain members of the State Department, Defense Department, and the Joint Chiefs of Staff to go to the location of the Vice President, and that the Vice President and the agencies be so directed; and that the proper communications be established at these points when the Vice President goes.

(b) The Secretary of State and Secretary of Defense and you as the President's Special Assistant for National Security Affairs should review the "highly classified" command and control designations, and recommend to the President whether or not these should be continued. The last review was with President Kennedy, as far as I know.

(c) Most important, it behooves us to improve our own decision support to the President. As you can see from this study, decision support falls in several categories, including information, staff, etc. It is quite obvious from even the recent experience in the Dominican Republic situation that it takes from three to four days to extemporize a situation room and staff to meet a Presidential requirement even in a minor crisis in which our own security is not threatened. This could be improved with a little thought and some preparation on a more permanent basis. The staff and decision support of the President of the United States can be put on a better established basis now that we are so well acquainted with the working habits of the President, as well as his decision-making procedures.

I would suggest that the time has come for the White House to attain a capability to meet the crisis situations which appear to be a "norm" rather than an exception.

Recommendations

(a) That you designate a member of your staff to write a reply to Secretary Vance based on the above.

(b) That you designate a member of your staff to work out the basis for our own improvements in this area.

(c) That the President designate a member of his staff to supervise the "successor location" item of emergency planning.

C.V.C.

88.   Memorandum to Holders of National Intelligence Estimate 11–8–64[1]

Washington, May 10, 1965.

SOVIET CAPABILITIES FOR STRATEGIC ATTACK

The Problem

To review the evidence acquired since the publication of NIE 11–8–64, and to assess its implications for the Soviet ICBM forces through mid-1966.

Scope Note

NIE 11–8–64, "Soviet Capabilities for Strategic Attack," dated 8 October 1964, Top Secret Restricted Data, is a comprehensive estimate of Soviet capabilities in the field of strategic attack. This memorandum has been prompted by new evidence which requires us to review our judgments of Soviet ICBM programs and, in particular, the pace of ICBM deployment. A new estimate in the 11–8 series, which will deal with all Soviet strategic attack systems, will be issued in late 1965.

Discussion

1. In NIE 11–8–64, we estimated that deployment of second-generation ICBMs in soft sites and three-silo hard sites had come to an end, and that the Soviet ICBM program was moving into a new phase char-

[1] Source: National Archives and Records Administration, RG 263. Top Secret. A cover sheet and prefatory note are not printed. According to the prefatory note, the CIA and the intelligence organizations of the Departments of State and Defense, the Atomic Energy Commission, and the National Security Agency participated in the preparation of this estimate. Representatives of the State Department, DIA, AEC, and NSA concurred; the FBI representative abstained, the subject being outside his jurisdiction. NIE 11–8–64 is Document 55.

acterized by dispersed single silos. Subsequent evidence has confirmed these trends, but single silos apparently have been started at a faster pace than previously estimated.

2. We have now identified about 125 single silos, all begun since about January 1964. The actual number under construction is probably larger. When compared to past rates of starting ICBM launchers, the present level of activity is high; the largest number of ICBM launchers previously started in a single year was about 90. The building rate, however, is not without precedent nor does it represent what could be termed a maximum effort; at one point in 1963 about 140 ICBM launchers were under construction in a variety of site configurations, and MR/IRBM launcher construction was also continuing.

3. We believe that the most advanced of these launchers will not reach operational status until late 1965. This means that the mid-1965 operational ICBM strength will be about 225,[2] somewhat lower than our previous estimate of 235–260.[3] On the other hand, the pace of single-silo deployment could carry the force by mid-1966 beyond the high side of the previously estimated range of 285–320. Considering the estimated time to bring launch groups to operational status and making allowance for undetected launchers now under construction, our new estimate for mid-1966 is:

Soft Launchers	146[4]
Hard (3 silo)	78
Single Silo	<u>126–178</u>
TOTAL (Rounded)	350–400[2]

---

[2] These totals do not include R&D launchers at Tyuratam. There are now about 25 completed R&D launchers and we believe this number will increase to approximately 45 by mid-1966. We judge these launchers are not normally available for operational use, but varying numbers of them could be prepared to fire ICBMs at the US depending on the amount of advance notice. [Footnote in the source text.]

[3] The Assistant Chief of Staff, Intelligence, USAF, continues to hold to his footnote estimate in NIE 11–8–64, but considers the mid-1965 figure will be at the low side of his forecast spread of 275–325 (including Tyuratam launchers and a small allowance for unlocated second-generation operational launchers). The mid-1966 figure will somewhat exceed the high side of his forecast spread of 325–425 operational launchers in the field and at Tyuratam. [Footnote in the source text. Regarding this estimate in NIE 11–8–64, see footnote 2, Document 55.]

[4] This number does not include the SS-large, which we estimated in NIE 11–8–64 at 0–5 for mid-1966. Because this missile has not yet been tested, we no longer believe it could become operational by that date. [Foonote in the source text.]

The number of hardened ICBM launchers will increase from the present figure of 78 to 200–250 in mid-1966. The force will become more dispersed, with 150–200 separate hardened sites in mid-1966 in contrast with the present 26.

4. We cannot yet determine what missiles are intended for the new silos. The Soviets have tested two third generation ICBM systems, the SS-9 and the SS-10. We believe that the SS-9 which has followed a normal test program will be deployed in at least some of the silos. The SS-10 was test fired eight times between April and October 1964 but, for reasons we cannot explain, there have been no test firings since. It too may be deployed in some of the silos.

5. Finally, there is evidence pointing to the development of other missiles, including one which is probably small, at the test range. Thus, it is possible that some of the silos are intended for a new ICBM, which has not been identified in test firings.[5] If so, the deployment of the launchers so far in advance of the flight tests of the missile would represent a departure from previous Soviet practice. Such an innovation would imply confidence that no major changes in the weapon system will be required; it could stem from a desire to reach a planned ICBM force level more quickly than would otherwise be possible. An intensive and successful test program would be necessary for this missile to become available for extensive deployment as early as mid-1966. Thus it is possible that many of the new silos listed as operational in mid-1966 will at that time lack missiles.

6. It is not now clear how far the Soviets will push the current deployment program or whether it will be succeeded by follow-on programs. Though by mid-1967 the Soviets almost certainly will have more than the 330–395 operational launchers estimated in NIE 11–8–64, it is yet too early to revise our estimate that the Soviets will achieve a force of 400–700 ICBM launchers over the next five years. We expect, however, that evidence collected before the publication of NIE 11–8–65 this far will help to clarify Soviet goals.[6]

---

[5] We are unable to determine whether this missile would employ solid or liquid propellants; we believe that storable liquids are likely. [Footnote in the source text.]

[6] The Assistant Chief of Staff, Intelligence, USAF, sees no basis in current evidence for change to his footnote in NIE 11–8–64, which projected 600–900 operational ICBM launchers by mid-1970. [Footnote in the source text. Regarding this estimate in NIE 11–8–64, see footnote 4, Document 55.]

89.   Memorandum From R.C. Bowman of the National Security
        Council Staff to the Executive Secretary of the National
        Security Council (Smith)[1]

Washington, May 24, 1965.

SUBJECT

    National Command System

I have attached two JCS papers that you might like to scan. I have
not heard any more about the command system study since I spoke to
you about it in February.

JCSM 129[2] indicates the Chiefs' general agreement with the study
with the exception that they felt it underrates the Alternate Command
Center at Fort Ritchie. At that time the Chiefs deferred judgment on the
Command Post Afloat.

In the second paper, JCSM 364 (17 May),[3] they concluded that two
command ships are essential, and that the capabilities of the USS
Northampton should be improved. The Chief of Naval Operations disagreed, and argued that one ship was sufficient.

In the last analysis, the value of any command facility must be
determined to a great extent by the probability that the President will,
in fact, make use of that facility.

RCB[4]

---

[1] Source: Johnson Library, National Security File, Agency File, JCS, Filed by the LBJ
Library, Box 29. Top Secret.

[2] JCSM–129–65, February 26, "Conceptual Approach to the National Military Command System"; not printed.

[3] JCSM–364–65, "National Emergency Command Post Afloat"; not printed.

[4] A typed note under Bowman's initials reads: "Please return." Bowman wrote a
note at the bottom of the page: "It is long overdue that we take a positive hand in this &
some other related command control matters. RCB"

90.   National Security Action Memorandum No. 334[1]

Washington, June 1, 1965.

TO

The Secretary of State
The Secretary of Defense
The Chairman, Atomic Energy Commission

The President has noted the request for nuclear weapons dispersal authorization for FY 1965/1966 contained in the Department of Defense memorandum dated May 24, 1965,[2] and has taken the following actions in connection therewith:

1. The Atomic Energy Commission is authorized to:

a. Transfer to the Department of Defense, on call by the Secretary of Defense or his designee, sufficient numbers of separable nuclear components and complete atomic weapons to provide in Department of Defense custody as of June 30, 1966, up to a [*number not declassified*] nuclear elements. [*less than 1 line of source text not declassified*] which are planned to be dispersed until end FY 1966 and which do not appear in the approved stockpile for FY 1966.

b. Transfer additional weapons to the Department of Defense custody on a one-for-one basis, but not to exceed [*number not declassified*] weapons, to replace weapons recalled by the Atomic Energy Commission to support modernization, quality assurance and retirement programs;

c. Replace, on a one-for-one basis to the extent practicable, any nuclear components, complete atomic weapons, or non-nuclear components in the Department of Defense custody which become irretrievably lost or damaged beyond repair.

2. The Department of Defense is authorized to:

a. Obtain custody of up to a total of [*number not declassified*] elements;

b. Disperse atomic weapons in the United States without limit providing the total number of nuclear components and complete atomic weapons in Department of Defense custody does not exceed that authorized in paragraph 2a above;

c. Disperse nuclear weapons to areas outside the United States in the numbers indicated in the last column of Appendix A hereto[3] of the

---

[1] Source: Johnson Library, National Security File, National Security Action Memoranda, NSAM 334, Box 7. Top Secret; Restricted Data.

[2] Not found.

[3] Neither Appendix A nor B has been found.

representative FY 1966 dispersal plan with the provisos that: (1) The total in each area may be exceeded by 10% in the event of unforeseen contingencies, (2) weapons for which dispersal in support of non-U.S. NATO forces is authorized for planning purposes only will be dispersed in support of U.S. forces in the areas pending additional and specific dispersal authorizations on a case-by-case basis and (3) the grand total of weapons outside the US (areas under foreign sovereignty and areas under U.S. control other than U.S.) will not [*less than 1 line of source text not declassified*]. Such dispersals will be subject to the yield restriction outlined in NSAM 143 and the policy with regard to PAL devices contained in NSAM 160.[4] To the maximum extent possible, weapons earmarked for ultimate use in support of forecast allied nuclear capabilities will be dispersed and made available for U.S. forces, pending attainment of a capability by the allies.

d. Continue to disperse nuclear weapons and provide nuclear weapon support to non-U.S. forces in accordance with the current authorizations for dispersal as tabulated in the column "Non-US Forces—Authorized FY 1964" (Column C) of Appendix B hereto.

3. It is understood that the currently authorized area level of nuclear warheads to be stored in Europe is adequate in numbers and megatonnage to meet requirements now recognized for use by U.S. or non-U.S. NATO forces. There will necessarily be changes required in the stockpile due to such things as modernization, redistribution among users, and possible changes in force dispositions. It is expected that the next and succeeding dispersal plans focus principally on changes of this sort as far as Europe is concerned, and that any recommendation for significant net increases in the European stockpile beyond the level authorized by this NSAM will be made only on the basis of new circumstances.

McGeorge Bundy[5]

---

[4] NSAM No. 143 is entitled "Nuclear Weapons for NATO Forces." NSAM No. 160, June 6, 1962, is entitled "Permissive Links for Nuclear Weapons in NATO." Both are in the Kennedy Library, National Security Files.

[5] Printed from a copy that bears this typed signature.

91. Memorandum From the Director of the White House Office of Emergency Planning (Ellington) to President Johnson[1]

Washington, August 2, 1965.

This is a summary of readiness to put into effect civilian mobilization measures as necessary to support an increased military commitment to Vietnam.

—The Nation faces the present situation with greater economic strength and preparedness to mobilize our civilian effort in support of national defense than ever before in our history.

—The Defense Production Act of 1950[2] contains authority to meet the immediate problems of the buildup. It provides for priorities and allocations and other actions for expediting defense production. Authorities for price and wage stabilization have expired. Legislative proposals are ready if needed.

—The Director of the Office of Emergency Planning coordinates, on behalf of the President, all mobilization activities of the Executive branch. Executive Order 10480[3] gives him the priorities and allocations authorities conferred upon the President by Title I of the Defense Production Act.

—The Defense Materials System provides machinery for expediting and allocating materials for defense production. It is administered by the Business and Defense Services Administration (Department of Commerce) under redelegation from the Director of OEP. It successfully supports Defense, AEC, and NASA programs today, and can be expanded.

—Although the economy may be able, in general terms, to accommodate a stepped-up military effort, there will be instances where specific industries, materials, components, or facilities will require action under the Defense Production Act to facilitate production.

—The state of our strategic and critical materials stockpiles, having a market value of about $8 billion, is very good. Sixty-three of the 77

---

[1] Source: Washington National Records Center, OSD Files: FRC 330 70 A 1266, 384 (July–Dec) 1965. Secret. An August 9 covering memorandum from Bundy to McNamara briefly summarized the memorandum and concluded: "You need not be reminded of the importance of the relationship between Defense and OEP in developing prompt and adequate contingency plans, but it might be useful to ensure that the procedures and lines of communications are in good shape."

[2] P.L. 81–774, approved September 8, 1950. (64 Stat. 798)

[3] E.O. 10480, August 14, 1953, established procedures for the administration of the Defense Mobilization Act of 1950. (*Federal Register*, vol. 18, August 20, 1953, pp. 4939, 4941–4944)

stockpiled materials equal or exceed stockpile objectives for limited or conventional war. Although the inventories for the remaining 14 materials are adequate to meet a limited war of short duration, they should be brought to the level of established stockpile objectives, and we are taking steps to this end without unduly affecting markets.

—We are in touch with the Council of Economic Advisors and other agencies to watch economic indices affecting mobilization.

—Economic stabilization measures are of two types—indirect controls and direct controls. Indirect include: taxes, credit controls, and other monetary measures within the responsibility of the Treasury Department and the Federal Reserve Board. Some of these measures are part of our day-to-day economic system.

Direct controls include those for prices, wages and salaries, and rents as well as rationing. Authority for such controls does not exist today. Legislative proposals are kept ready, but capability to administer these controls does not exist since substantial national organizations would be required. Preliminary plans and arrangements have been developed as a part of our regular preparedness. A national organization could be established and in operation in a period of 60–90 days.

—No major national manpower problem is foreseen. Manpower shortages, to the extent they would exist, would be in critical skills and localized. These shortages could generally be met through existing voluntary manpower measures already established by the Department of Labor and endorsed by the National Labor-Management Manpower Policy Committee. Care will have to be exercised in meeting military requirements for medical personnel to minimize the effect on civilian communities. Selective Service is ready to meet increased calls for military personnel.

—In the transportation field there are three areas of possible shortages: ocean shipping (where the Maritime Administration has already pulled 14 ships from the National Defense Reserve Fleet), air cargo, and rail freight. Shortages occur in rail freight today. Necessary action to meet national defense requirements can be taken by the President under existing law.

—To evaluate the potential economic and industrial impact of increased defense spending, and to plan effectively the mobilization effort, we *must* have a clear and detailed statement from the Department of Defense on the size, composition, and phasing of defense requirements. I will review this matter with the Secretary of Defense so that we can provide coordinated civilian support.

Buford Ellington

92. Letter From Secretary of State Rusk to the Deputy Secretary of Defense (Vance)[1]

Washington, September 3, 1965.

Dear Cy:

The Department of Defense study, *Command and Control Support to the President*, transmitted with your letter of March 6, 1965,[2] contributes significantly to the development of a comprehensive Executive Branch approach to crisis management. The President's command and control support requirements are of obvious concern to the Department of State and to me personally.

I am of the personal view that much of the prevailing thinking about the problems of conducting essential governmental processes after sustaining a nuclear attack is inadequate and dated and fails to grapple realistically with the formidable obstacles which would confront officials surviving such an encounter. Of necessity, this basic reservation colors and qualifies some of the comments which follow.

Many of the observations and recommendations contained in this study confirm the validity of present State/Defense understandings and arrangements which have enhanced the President's ability to give direction to politico-military operations. I have in mind particularly the exchange of personnel between our Operations Center and the National Military Command Center, the monitoring by one department of the other's significant message traffic, and other machinery for managing crisis situations at the Presidential level. Moreover, the study emphasizes the value of such activities as the recently inaugurated State–Defense–CIA cooperation in politico-military contingency planning and in the development and conduct of major JCS exercises.

We also note that the current study reinforces the previously advanced justification for the construction of a Deep Underground Command Center (DUCC). The National Military Command System's *Master Plan* and the *JCS Continuity of Operations Plan*[3] contemplate State Department representation in both the sea and airborne alternates, as well as the ANMCC. We will give further study to operational concepts

---

[1] Source: Washington National Records Center, OSD Files: FRC 330 70 A 1265, 031.1 White House (23 Jan 65). Secret.

[2] For the conclusion of the study, see Document 86. The letter of March 6 was not found.

[3] Neither further identified.

and physical arrangements applicable to State Department functions both at and in support of such command posts.

Under its terms of reference, the DOD study group was instructed to state projections of Presidential support obtainable from non-DOD sources in "general terms" only. We concur in the view that a Presidentially directed response to varying crisis levels, up to and including general war, requires the marshalling of a wider range of governmental resources than those of the Department of Defense. Hence we believe that there is a need to explore more specifically the conceptual requirements for non-DOD command and control support to the President which will supplement the analysis of Department of Defense support developed by the DOD study group. Initially, such an undertaking would appear to call for a careful stock-taking by other key agencies of their own responsibilities and capabilities in this field. The Department of State, accordingly, will initiate a study along these lines at an early date. We hope such a study will contribute to government-wide understanding of the components of a total "national command" concept.

We shall be giving study to improving our own Command and Control System in the days ahead. Undoubtedly this work will include consultations between our respective Departments and joint consideration of pertinent materials, including the present study. If this exercise results in additional suggestions or proposals which might be worth your consideration in connection with review of command and control procedures, we will be in communication with you.

With warm regards,

Sincerely,

Dean

93.   National Intelligence Estimate[1]

NIE 11–6–65   Washington, September 16, 1965.

SOVIET CAPABILITIES FOR CONCEALING STRATEGIC WEAPON PROGRAMS

The Problem

To estimate Soviet capabilities for secretly developing and deploying strategic weapon systems and to examine factors bearing on Soviet intentions in this regard, over the next few years.

Scope Note

In this estimate, we assume that Western collection efforts will continue at approximately their present levels. Soviet capabilities for concealing strength under terms of an inspection agreement have not been considered, since these capabilities would have to be assessed in detail in relation to each of the many possible forms which such an inspection agreement might take. We have, however, considered in general the effect which arms control might have upon Soviet concealment.

In this estimate "concealment" is defined as an effort designed to limit Western knowledge of Soviet military programs. Its usual aim is to induce an *underestimate* of Soviet capabilities. It would also hamper targeting and reduce Western ability to develop countermeasures to Soviet weapons systems.

The Estimate

1. By definition, if the USSR should achieve complete and successful concealment of weapons systems, the fact would be unknown to US intelligence unless and until the Soviets chose to reveal it. It cannot, of course, be conclusively proven that successful concealment of this sort has not happened. It must be acknowledged at the outset that successful concealment is and will remain a possibility.

2. The Soviets have instituted concealment measures in all phases of their strategic weapons programs. The extent of these efforts and

---

[1] Source: Johnson Library, National Security File, National Intelligence Estimates 11–65, USSR, Box 3. Top Secret; Controlled Dissem. A prefatory note and cover sheet are not printed. According to the prefatory note, the CIA and the intelligence organizations of the Departments of State and Defense, the Atomic Energy Commission, and the National Security Agency participated in the preparation of this estimate. Representatives of the State Department, DIA, AEC, and NSA concurred; the FBI representative abstained, the subject being outside his jurisdiction.

their success have varied from program to program and even within programs. In general, however, the Soviets have been most successful in denying information on strategic weapons programs in the research and development phase. They have been less successful as a program progresses to systems testing, and have not, we believe, been able to conceal any large-scale deployment programs.

3. To some extent, these concealment efforts of the Soviets represent an extension of the devotion to secrecy that permeates their society. This factor alone would account for the rigorous physical security measures protecting strategic weapons facilities from observation by nearby inhabitants, as well as by clandestine agents or attachés.

4. Such concealment efforts as the Soviets have undertaken appear to have been directed toward hiding precise locations in operational deployment of a system and denying information on its characteristics. They clearly know of some of the various advanced intelligence collection methods employed by the US and almost certainly suspect the existence of others. But complicating Soviet concealment efforts is the variety of collection programs employed by the West which, in the process of all source analysis, results in a total body of intelligence greater than the sum of its parts. Thus, to be effective, a Soviet effort completely to conceal a strategic weapon program would require a complex and generally costly variety of safeguards. We believe that they now have insufficient incentive to undertake such an effort.

5. On the other hand, it is unlikely that Soviet efforts to conceal certain aspects of their strategic weapons programs will diminish, and they may increase. We cannot predict the extent to which contemplated improvements in US collection capabilities may be offset by an intensification of Soviet concealment efforts. But even if the Soviets undertake no additional measures, we consider it unlikely that our ability to detect, identify, and assess a new weapon system in the pretesting stage of development will improve. For the foreseeable future, new Soviet weapon systems are likely to have been under development for several years before they are detected in testing or in deployment, and the increasingly complex technology of modern weapons will probably lengthen further the time between initial research and deployment.

6. We believe that the Soviets have, or could develop, greater capabilities for concealment than they have practiced, and it is possible that their policy will change. If they should come to believe that the credibility of their deterrent is well-established, they may increase concealment activity in order to improve their retaliatory capabilities. While it is difficult to foresee technological breakthroughs, we consider it improbable that they could successfully conceal the deployment of strategic weapons in such numbers as to alter significantly the present strategic relationship.

7. The preceding paragraphs have discussed Soviet concealment primarily in the context of past and present conditions, that is, without an arms control agreement. In general, we do not foresee that an arms control agreement would significantly affect either US intelligence capabilities or Soviet concealment capabilities except as specific provisions might facilitate or discourage particular modes of intelligence collection or inspection. The effectiveness of any specific provisions of the agreement would depend on their content and the machinery for enforcing them, and cannot be estimated in the abstract. Certain general considerations can, however, be set forth.

8. The conclusion of an arms control agreement would probably signify that the Soviets had decided to accept, at least for a time, the strategic balance envisaged in the agreement. However, the Soviets might conclude such an agreement in hopes of freezing US strategic forces while secretly trying to build up their own. In the first case, they might subsequently decide that, because of international developments or for other reasons, they required substantially larger forces. In such circumstances they might choose to abrogate an agreement openly rather than to attempt to evade its provisions; they took a similar action during the Berlin crisis of 1961 when they ended the moratorium on nuclear testing. If they decided to abrogate, they would almost certainly make secret preparations for a resumption of the arms competition in advance of the announcement.

9. Nevertheless, under certain arms control agreements, the Soviets might see concealment as offering a strategic advantage which was worth the risk. If, for example, the US and the Soviet Union should be limited by an agreement to small numbers of strategic nuclear delivery vehicles, possession of even a few additional vehicles could significantly change the strategic equation. Depending on the provisions of the agreement, and the rules for policing it, they might assess the risk of detection as small, but they could hardly dismiss it as non-existent. And they would have to consider that if the concealed forces were detected, the arms control agreements would be abrogated in circumstances politically disadvantageous to them, and the West would make strenuous efforts to redress any real or presumed disparity.

10. If the Soviets should employ concealment to violate the arms control treaty, we believe that their aim would be to change the strategic balance. Any smaller stakes would hardly justify the risks. Such an effort would imply a Soviet decision to accept the complexity and cost of an all out concealment effort, thus degrading the reliance we could have in our detection capabilities. Even in the face of determined Soviet concealment efforts, there is a good chance that violations involving large scale testing or deployment would be detected, but this cannot be guaranteed. In view of our limited capabilities to detect the early pha-

ses of weapons programs, we cannot assure detection sufficiently timely to preclude attainment by the Soviets of a significant lead in acquiring an increased strategic capability.

11. Our capabilities for detecting smaller accretions to Soviet strategic strength are much less certain, especially in an arms control environment, and, depending upon the terms of any arms control agreement, even small accretions could be significant. Some such accretions might be detected but we cannot give assurance that any would be.

---

94.   National Intelligence Estimate[1]

NIE 11–12–65   Washington, September 22, 1965.

REACTIONS TO CERTAIN US BALLISTIC MISSILE
DEFENSE PROGRAMS

The Problem

To estimate the immediate and longer term foreign reactions to a US decision to deploy ballistic missile defenses.

Assumptions

1. The US will within the next year or so announce a decision to initiate deployment of ballistic missile defenses, either:

a. A small program, along with such other defensive measures as a fall-out shelter plan. This program would be intended and officially described as a defense against a light, unsophisticated ballistic missile attack, or

b. A much larger program, together with other defensive measures more extensive than those envisaged under the smaller program. This larger program would be clearly intended to provide a substantial, but not complete, defense against a Soviet strategic missile attack.

---

[1] Source: Johnson Library, National Security File, National Intelligence Estimates 11–65, USSR, Box 3. Secret; Controlled Dissem. A prefatory note and cover sheet are not printed. According to the prefatory note, the CIA and the intelligence organizations of the Departments of State and Defense, and the National Security Agency participated in the preparation of this estimate. Representatives of the State Department, DIA, and NSA concurred; the AEC and FBI representatives abstained, the subject being outside their jurisdiction.

2. Either program could be subsequently expanded.

3. The US will not have an initial operational capability under either program until the early 1970s.

Discussion

1. Most countries would make no distinction between the two assumed programs. They would not believe a US claim that it was deploying such costly ballistic missile defenses simply to guard against a minor threat; they would look on the smaller program as merely the first stage of a larger one. Accordingly, immediate reactions would be influenced more by the decision to deploy than by the size of the program.

2. In the non-Communist world, initial reactions to the US decision would depend to some extent on how the program was publicly presented. If it were announced as a logical development in the US military effort and as a response to Soviet progress in the ABM field, and especially if there were prior consultations with friendly governments, reactions in general probably would be mild and not unfavorable. There would be, nevertheless, some unfavorable reactions, but we believe that these too would be generally mild, of short duration, and unlikely to have a significant effect on the relations of these countries with the US.[2]

I. The USSR

3. Any such program would certainly be reported fully in US news media, particularly the military-industrial trade journals. In addition, the purpose and nature of the program would be described in public announcements and in news reports attributed to official sources. Thus, the Soviets probably would correctly estimate the general capabilities of either of the assumed programs, but they would be unlikely to accept official US explanations that the smaller program was intended primarily to counter the type of threat which may eventually be posed by Communist China. The Soviets almost certainly would see any US program for ballistic missile defenses as a move to reduce the effectiveness of their strategic attack forces and would take into account its effect upon their strategic position.

4. In assessing the significance of the US decision, the Soviets would be influenced by the value which they attach to ballistic missile defenses and, to a degree, by the status of their own program. The magnitude of the Soviet ABM effort points to a strong desire to obtain missile defenses rapidly. We believe that the Soviets have no

---

[2] See footnotes to paragraphs 12 and 15 for the reservation of the Director of Intelligence and Research, Department of State. [Footnote in the source text.]

such defenses operational at present, but we know that they are pushing ahead with their R and D effort. They have made, moreover, a stronger attempt in the last year or so to convey the impression that they have succeeded in developing effective ABM systems. If the Soviet program were progressing well at the time the US decision is announced, they probably would take a calmer view of the US move than if their program were lagging. It is possible that they would see the US announcement as having been precipitated by recent Soviet claims in the area of missile defense.

5. The Soviet assessment would go beyond the military significance of the US decision and consider as well political motivations. The Soviets would first of all view the decision as evidence that the US was intent upon maintaining its strategic position vis-à-vis the USSR. While they would recognize that their own ABM program had contributed to the US decision, they would judge that the US in this instance was willing to see, or at least saw no way to avert, a continuation of the arms race. Further, it is conceivable that they would view the decision as a move to force them to make military expenditures which would keep their economy under strain. They might even interpret it as a sign that the US considered nuclear war somewhat more likely in the longer term, particularly if the announcement came at a time of crisis in, for example, Vietnam. Associated expenditures for a shelter program would probably strengthen the voice of those advocating this interpretation. The Soviets would be likely to interpret the coupling of the US announcement with a disarmament proposal for, say, reducing strategic delivery vehicles as part and parcel of a scheme designed to restrict their strategic capabilities.

6. In the propaganda field, the Soviets almost certainly would charge the US with reducing the prospects for disarmament, and probably would accuse the US of seeking to increase its capabilities for nuclear war. Over the longer term, however, the Soviets probably would stress two propaganda lines: one, that the concept of "Fortress America" was again gaining ascendancy in the US; the other, that Soviet missile defenses were superior to those of the US, and that the latter could not cope with a Soviet strategic missile attack.

7. In their military planning, the Soviets probably have already taken into account the likelihood that the US would develop an ABM capability. Nevertheless, they would feel compelled to respond to the US move in several ways. Programs which they would consider include: improving the penetration capabilities of their strategic ballistic missile systems; expanding their ICBM and SLBM development programs beyond present plans; adopting targeting concepts consistent with a smaller number of key targets, whose defenses they would seek to saturate; placing greater emphasis on strategic

bomber systems and cruise missile submarines, in order to complicate the US defenses; seeking to develop space weapons; and finally, intensifying work on their ABM program. It should be noted, however, that the Soviets will probably undertake some of these advanced weapons programs even if the US implements no ballistic missile defense program.

8. Alternatively, it is possible that, in view of internal Soviet policy debates stemming from the resource demands of the military, the US decision might increase pressures on the Soviet leaders to stabilize some aspects of arms competition. In this context, a simultaneous new offer on arms control might have some prospects. We rate the chances of a positive Soviet reaction, however, as low.

9. In any event, we believe that the US decision to deploy ballistic missile defenses, by itself, would not significantly worsen US-Soviet relations. Nor would it be likely to have any direct or basic effect on Soviet policies in existing problem areas, i.e., Vietnam or Berlin. And we believe that the US decision would not change any of the key determinants of Soviet policies toward Western Europe or Communist China.

II. Communist China

10. The Chinese missile and nuclear programs are in such early stages of development that the US decision would have little immediate impact on them. We have estimated that the Chinese could not have an ICBM strike capability until sometime after 1970. Meanwhile, the Chinese would be likely to persist in their efforts to develop a shorter range nuclear capability and proceed to experiment and explore in the field of advanced weapons. If in time, however, the Chinese would come to judge the US ballistic missile defenses as highly effective, they might make only a token deployment of any crude ICBM or submarine-launched ballistic missile system which they might develop, while continuing R and D on more sophisticated systems. We believe that the US decision in itself would not cause the Chinese to develop a submarine-launched cruise missile fleet to threaten the US, a program which they might in any event undertake.

11. In the political field, Peking would exploit those exaggerated impressions of China's military strength which would arise from the public discussion of the smaller program as a defense against China. At the same time, the Chinese almost certainly would claim that the US was stepping up its efforts at "nuclear blackmail." The US decision, however, might increase the anxieties of the Chinese leaders that the US intends ultimately to attack China.

III. Western Europe

12. We believe that the West European reactions to the US decision would be generally mild.[3] There would be some initial, unfavorable public commentary, stemming primarily from concern over a possible intensification of the arms race and a further diminution of the prospects for East-West détente. This concern would probably be heightened by Soviet political reactions and, particularly, by fears that the USSR would make drastic responses of a military nature; misconceptions about the limitations and military significance of ballistic missile defenses might add to these fears. The announcement of the decision might be used in some quarters as proof of a shift in US policy toward a "Fortress America" concept, and in others as evidence that the US was beginning to think nuclear war more likely over the longer term. There would also be, however, a large amount of apathy regarding the decision, since most West Europeans of all political leanings regard the likelihood of general nuclear war as remote. In addition, if adequate explanations were given by the US in advance or at the time of the public announcement, unfavorable reactions caused by such attitudes could be dampened.

13. Those West European officials who assert there already is a growing divergence between US and West European strategic interests would probably cite the US decision as further justification of their position. If the US announcement of the smaller program emphasized defense against Communist China, critics of US policy would allege that increasing American involvement in Asia would, sooner or later, compel the US to reduce its commitments to Western Europe. De Gaulle

---

[3] The Director of Intelligence and Research, Department of State, believes that this net judgment is overly reassuring concerning the adverse reactions which could be set in motion, in varying degrees, in official circles in France, Germany, and England.

If Western Europe should remain without ballistic missile defenses, while both the US and the USSR were deploying them, important elements in Europe would come to feel that constraints to the initiation of nuclear war had diminished, that latent apprehensions over US judgments in the use of its weapons might be justified, that the multibillion dollar US expenditures for home defense reflected a further diversion of US strategic interest and support from the NATO alliance, that possibilities for security arrangements outside the transatlantic framework should be reopened, and that Europeans should in any case disengage themselves from any involvement in US-USSR confrontations outside of Europe.

These reactions would occur in a political context which could generate greater claims in Bonn for an increased strategic role, greater conviction in Paris that it could succeed in disrupting existing NATO ties, and greater pressures in London to move away from political support of the US in favor of a more independent role in East-West relations.

While these problems may not be insurmountable, the Director of Intelligence and Research, Department of State, believes that they would be of greater significance in both the short and longer term than this estimate allows. [Footnote in the source text.]

and his supporters would assiduously propagate such views. On the other hand, those governments and officials who favor close relations with the US and continue to place their trust in US willingness to defend Western Europe against a Soviet attack would probably support the US decision. They would regard the deployment of ballistic missile defenses as enhancing American capabilities to deter the USSR. They would probably see no lessening in the ability of the US to inflict unacceptable damage on the USSR, even if the Soviets responded by strengthening their offensive missile forces or intensifying work on their ABM program. Over the longer term, we see little likelihood that the West Europeans would conclude that improved US defenses weakened the deterrents to the outbreak of nuclear war. In general, we believe that the deployment of ballistic missile defenses by the US would not be a major factor in US-West European relationships in the foreseeable future.

14. The UK would probably be interested in acquiring missile defenses, but it would not be prepared to spend much money on a deployment program until a highly effective system was available. Although the West German Government would also support the US decision, Bonn would probably be disquieted by the contrast between a nascent US strategic missile defense and its own defenselessness against Soviet missiles. Some West German officials might argue that the risks of general war would no longer be shared equally with the US, and they would be encouraged in this argument by de Gaulle. Thus, the already growing West German desire for more influence in the nuclear strategy of the Western Alliance might in the longer term be further strengthened by the US decision. These same West German officials might even express a desire to acquire missile defenses, but the majority view in the government would probably be against such a step, at least until there was convincing proof that such defenses would actually be effective against the Soviet threat to West Germany.

IV. Asia

15. Asian reactions to the US decision probably would be mixed, but generally mild.[4] Since most Asians are more concerned with the Chinese Communist threat than with that posed by the USSR, the fact that the US rated the Chinese nuclear threat as requiring an "anti-Chinese" ballistic missile defense would tend to heighten fears of Communist China in some quarters. On the other hand, some Asians would be likely to view the US decision as further evidence of a contin-

---

[4] Taking into account the negative considerations adduced in paragraphs 15 and 16, the Director of Intelligence and Research, Department of State, believes the net assessment reflected in this sentence may be overly reassuring. [Footnote in the source text.]

uing US policy to contain China. At the popular level, there would be even more apathy about the US action than in Western Europe, and any unfavorable public reactions probably would be short-lived. Those Asian governments and officials who now support most US policies would accept the US decision, and those who do not would oppose it. We believe that, on balance, the US decision would have no basic or significant effect on US relations with the Asian nations.

16. Over the longer term, as Chinese strategic capabilities became more apparent, India and Australia might wish to obtain ballistic missile defenses from the US, but high costs would probably discourage them. The geographic situation of Taiwan would make its defense against ballistic missiles most difficult; nevertheless, the GRC might seek to acquire such defenses. The Japanese, although not presently as concerned as some other Asians that China poses a military threat to them, might develop an interest in obtaining ballistic missile defenses.

V. Other Areas

17. We believe that most of the Latin American and African governments and their peoples would not react strongly, if at all, to the US decision. They would probably see the US move as another manifestation of American military power. In general, however, any US action implying that Communist China had the capability to attack the US with ballistic missiles would considerably upgrade China in the opinion of the Latin Americans and Africans.

VI. Possible Threats From Other Countries

18. There are, at present, no countries other than the USSR and Communist China which might acquire missile forces which could attack the US and which might have the motivation to do so. The possibility will always exist, nevertheless, that the Soviets or perhaps the Communist Chinese would attain a highly influential relationship with some radical rebel government in the Western Hemisphere, such as was the case with Cuba in 1962, and exploit this relationship to establish missile bases threatening the US.

95.   Letter From Secretary of State Rusk to the British Ambassador (Dean)[1]

Washington, September 25, 1965.

Dear Pat:

On August 12, you provided me with a talking paper which expressed the interest of your Government in holding discussions with representatives of the United States on various aspects of a possible deployment of a United States anti-ballistic missile defense system.[2] I fully appreciate the interest of your Government in this problem.

We have been engaged in an examination of the political implications of a possible deployment decision; our preliminary study of these implications has not yet been completed. Meanwhile, our Department of Defense has certain additional technical studies in progress that could bear on a U.S. decision.[3]

Accordingly, it is our view that discussions of this question, in which we believe other members of the Alliance may be interested as well, would be more useful if they were held after we have progressed somewhat further with both our technical studies and our analysis of possible political implications.

I shall be in touch with you when we have completed more of our homework.

With warmest regards,

Sincerely,

Dean

---

[1] Source: National Archives and Records Administration, RG 59, Central Files 1964–66, DEF 12. Top Secret. The letter forms Tab A to a September 14 action memorandum from Llewellyn E. Thompson to Secretary Rusk, which indicates that the letter was drafted in G/PM.

[2] This talking paper, entitled "Anti-ballistic Missiles," is attached as Tab B to Thompson's memorandum (see footnote 1 above). It is not printed.

[3] Acting Secretary of Defense Vance's September 4 letter to Secretary Rusk, attached as Tab D to Thompson's September 14 memorandum, noted that the Department of Defense agreed in principle to talks with the British on anti-ballistic missile deployments, but preferred "to postpone setting a date until we have reached a more definite position on the deployment of an ABM system." Tab C is identified as Secretary Rusk's August 23 letter to McNamara, asking for the position of the Department of Defense on this question; this letter has not been found.

96. Memorandum From the Acting Deputy Under Secretary of State for Political Affairs (Thompson) and the Assistant Secretary of State for European Affairs (Leddy) to Acting Secretary of State Ball[1]

Washington, September 29, 1965.

SUBJECT

Letters from Prime Minister Wilson on Nuclear Weapons Arrangements

The two letters suggested for Tuesday luncheon discussion (Tab B) stem from the President's recent approval of the SACLANT ASW nuclear weapons dispersal plan which is the subject of attached State–DOD correspondence (Tab C).[2] In brief, this plan calls for the storage in the UK of nuclear depth charges, intended for anti-submarine use by UK, US, [*less than 1 line of source text not declassified*] forces which would be operating pursuant to NATO planning and under SACLANT command.

The UK has no objection to the NATO plan as such, but wishes to clear up two questions satisfactorily before the storage provisions of the plan are implemented. These questions were addressed in two letters rather than one because there is no real connection apart from the tie-relationship suggested. The proposals are these:

1. The first letter proposes that the long-standing US-UK Memorandum of Understanding[3] be amended to show accurately what NATO-commanded US and UK forces are to come within its terms.[4]

2. The second letter proposes a US-UK understanding to the effect that nuclear weapons will be released [*less than 1 line of source text not*

---

[1] Source: National Archives and Records Administration, RG 59, Central Files 1964–66, DEF 12. Top Secret. Drafted by Scott George (G/PM) on September 24 and concurred in by Jerry C. Trippe (L/EUR), Vincent Baker (EUR/RPM), and Thomas M. Judd (EUR/BNA).

[2] The two August 5 letters from Prime Minister Wilson to President Johnson are attached as Tab B, not printed. Copies of the two letters were forwarded to Secretaries Rusk and McNamara under cover of a September 3 memorandum from McGeorge Bundy, also attached, with the suggestion that they discuss the letters at a Tuesday lunch in the near future. Tab C was not found.

[3] Reference is to a U.S.-U.K. agreement on nuclear weapons dating from the Truman administration, which had been renewed and revised by succeeding U.S. Presidents. Most recently, in a letter to Prime Minister Wilson, December 8, 1964, President Johnson reaffirmed the understandings, which were detailed in a memorandum enclosed with the President's letter to Prime Minister Home, February 28, 1964. The President's December 8 letter has not been found, but for his February 28 letter and the enclosed memorandum, see *Foreign Relations, 1964–1968*, vol. XII, Document 226.

[4] The first August 5 letter details the proposed changes in the text of the U.S.-U.K. Memorandum of Understanding, and attached to this letter is an undated text of the Memorandum of Understanding, which includes the proposed British revisions.

declassified] only at such time as they are also being released to UK forces.

This matter was discussed extensively within the Department, with the Department of Defense and the White House staff, and with the British Embassy prior to the sending of the letters. It is our view that the President should accept the proposals made, replying to the Prime Minister with separate letters of assent. We believe also that action should be taken concurrently to inform [*less than 1 line of source text not declassified*] of certain conditions governing release of weapons, i.e. (1) there is to be no alert loading of any aircraft under the SACLANT plan; U.S. custodial requirements are such that weapons can be released [*less than 1 line of source text not declassified*] only upon granting of Presidential release of U.S. weapons for NATO use and (2) in terms of the SACLANT plan, this means that weapons will be released [*less than 1 line of source text not declassified*] only when they are also being released for UK use. This action could in our view best be taken by the Department after consulting the British Embassy. The background and reasons for these recommendations are set forth in the annex at Tab A.[5]

Recommendation:

That you take the foregoing line when the matter is discussed with the President.[6]

---

[5] Entitled "US-UK Understandings Concerning Use of US Nuclear Weapons," undated; not printed.

[6] Ball initialed his approval of the recommendation.

97.   National Intelligence Estimate[1]

NIE 11–8–65   Washington October 7, 1965.

SOVIET CAPABILITIES FOR STRATEGIC ATTACK

The Problem

To estimate the strength and capabilities of Soviet strategic attack forces through mid-1967, and to estimate general trends in these forces over the next decade or so.

Note

Estimates of Soviet strategic attack capabilities for the present and the next few years can be made with high confidence; those for the period five to 10 years in the future are, of course, highly tentative. The Soviet planners themselves may not yet have set clear force goals for the 1970–1975 period. Even if they have, it seems certain that such decisions will be modified repeatedly in response to changes in military technology, in other Soviet weapons programs, in US forces, in resource availability, and in the general Soviet view of world affairs.

Conclusions

A. Over the next 10 years, we estimate a considerable strengthening of Soviet strategic attack forces, particularly in retaliatory capabilities, with chief emphasis on ICBMs. We do not believe, however, that the Soviets will expect to achieve, within the period of this estimate, forces which would make rational the deliberate initiation of general war. We believe that they will continue to adhere to the concept of a deterrent force. A stress on qualitative factors suggests that the Soviets see technological advance in weapons as a means by

---

[1] Source: National Archives and Records Administration, RG 263. Top Secret; Controlled Dissem. A cover sheet, prefatory note, title page, and table of contents are not printed. The cover sheet indicates that this NIE supersedes NIE 11–14–64, December 10, 1964. (Ibid., National Intelligence Estimates 11–64, USSR, Box 3) According to the prefatory note, the CIA and the intelligence organizations of the Departments of State and Defense, the Atomic Energy Commission, and the National Security Agency participated in the preparation of this estimate. Representatives of the State Department, DIA, AEC, and NSA concurred; the FBI representative abstained, the subject being outside his jurisdiction.

which they can improve their strategic position relative to the West. (Paras. 4–7)[2][3]

B. *ICBM Force*. The present Soviet ICBM force of 224 operational launchers represents a formidable capability in terms of deliverable megatonnage but it is a predominantly soft, concentrated force. Apparently recognizing its vulnerability, the Soviets are now deploying ICBMs in dispersed single silos. Within the next two years, the number of ICBM launchers will approximately double, but the number of separate launch sites will increase from about 100 to at least 300. (Paras. 8–10, 25, 31)

C. We estimate that the Soviet ICBM force in 1975 will be somewhere between 500 and 1,000 operational launchers. A force near the high side of the range would probably consist primarily of small ICBMs in single silos. By contrast, a force near the low side, though including substantial numbers of small, single silo launchers, would probably incorporate greater qualitative improvement and significant numbers of larger ICBMs, perhaps with multiple warheads and penetration aids. It is possible that within the next 10 years the Soviets will deploy a rail mobile ICBM system. (Paras. 23, 26–30)[4]

D. *MRBM/IRBM Force*. During the past year, the Soviet MRBM and IRBM force leveled off at about 735 operational launchers, some 135 hard, deployed at almost 200 sites. It is capable of delivering a devastating first strike against targets in Eurasia, but like the present ICBM force it is soft and concentrated. By 1975, the Soviets will probably have replaced the major portion of the force with new solid-fueled missiles deployed in dispersed hard sites and on mobile launchers. The flexibility and survivability of such a force may lead them to conclude that the same target system could be covered with fewer launchers. We estimate

---

[2] Deterrence is defined as the prevention from action by fear of the consequences. Deterrence is a state of mind brought about by the existence of a credible threat of unacceptable counteraction. [Footnote in the source text.]

[3] The Assistant Chief of Staff, Intelligence, USAF, would reword the last two sentences as follows:

"We believe they will continue to adhere to the concept of a deterrent force so long as they continue to be in a posture of strategic inferiority, but the intensive Soviet military R and D effort raises the possibility that Soviet leaders already are focusing on achievement of a strategic superiority which would enable more aggressive pursuit of their political aims, perhaps within the time frame of this estimate." [Footnote in the source text.]

[4] The Director, Defense Intelligence Agency, and the Assistant Chief of Naval Operations (Intelligence), Department of the Navy, do not concur in the high side of the estimated ICBM launcher spread for mid-1975, believing it to be too high. See their footnote to paragraph 27.

The Assistant Chief of Staff, Intelligence, USAF, estimates that the Soviet ICBM force in 1975 will include at least 1,000 operational launchers and could well be above that figure. [Footnote in the source text.]

that in the 1970–1975 period Soviet MRBM/IRBM strength will stabilize at some 350–700 launchers. (Paras. 38, 40, 42–46)

E. *Missile Submarines.* The Soviet Navy has 43–48 ballistic missile submarines, including 8–10 nuclear-powered, with a total of 120–140 tubes. Construction of ballistic missile submarines of current classes ended in 1963. We estimate, however, that the Soviets will produce a new class which could become operational in 1968. It will almost certainly be nuclear powered and will probably carry more missiles than are carried by current classes, perhaps 6–12. A new submarine-launched ballistic missile with a range of about 1,000 n.m. will probably enter service in two or three years, and by 1975 a 2,000 n.m. missile may be available. At that time the Soviets will probably have some 60 ballistic missile submarines, including about 20 of a new type. Only recently have Soviet ballistic missile submarines regularly carried out ocean patrols; this activity will increase, and by 1975 about 25 percent of the force will probably be on station. (Paras. 47, 49, 51, 53–54, 65)

F. In recent years, the USSR has emphasized construction of cruise missile submarines. The Soviet Navy now has 39–43, including 16–18 nuclear-powered with a total of 195–210 launchers. These submarines were initially intended to counter naval task forces, but their mission may be expanded to include land targets. Construction appears to be tapering off, but will probably continue at a reduced rate for several years. By 1975, the Soviets will probably have 60–70 cruise missile submarines, possibly including some of a new type. At that time, they will probably also have available new types of cruise missiles. (Paras. 47, 55–57, 65)

G. *Bomber Force.* Long Range Aviation, a force of some 200 heavy bombers and 800 mediums, is in general much better suited for Eurasian than for intercontinental operations. This force will decrease gradually through attrition and retirement. The Soviets may develop another new aircraft of medium bomber range, but we believe it unlikely that they will introduce a follow-on heavy bomber into Long Range Aviation. By 1975, the heavy bomber force will probably be reduced to about 50 aircraft, and the medium bomber force to some 250–500, comprised largely of Blinders.[5] (Paras. 66, 70, 72–76)

H. *Space Weapons.* Our evidence does not indicate that the USSR is developing offensive space weapons, but it is almost certainly investi-

---

[5] The Assistant Chief of Staff, Intelligence, USAF, believes the Soviets will continue to consider manned strategic aircraft an important element of their intercontinental striking forces. He estimates that the USSR will introduce a follow-on heavy bomber into Long Range Aviation. He further estimates that in 1975 LRA will still include 150–200 heavy bombers and 450–600 medium bombers, up to half of which could be a follow-on to the Blinder. [Footnote in the source text.]

gating their feasibility. We do not believe that they will deploy such weapons within the next 10 years. This conclusion is based upon our judgment that such systems will not compare favorably in cost and effectiveness with ground-based systems and, to a lesser extent, upon our view that the Soviets would see political disadvantages in deploying weapons in space. The USSR has, however, orbited reconnaissance and communications satellites, and is probably developing other military support systems. (Paras. 83, 86, 87)

[Here follow the Discussion section (Parts I–VII, pages 5–31), Annex A (pages 33–45), and Annex B (following page 45).]

---

98. National Intelligence Estimate[1]

NIE 11–14–65   Washington, October 21, 1965.

CAPABILITIES OF SOVIET GENERAL PURPOSE FORCES

The Problem

To estimate the strength and capabilities of Soviet general purpose forces through mid-1967, especially against the Central Region of NATO, and general trends in those forces over the next ten years.

Conclusions

A. The new Soviet political leaders appear to have modified Khrushchev's policy of curbing military costs at the expense of the general purpose forces. This change is probably attributable primarily to international tensions arising from the war in Vietnam, but it also reflects the increased influence of the ground force marshals. (Paras. 1–9)

B. Revisions in the force levels, organization, and deployment of the general purpose forces are virtually certain to occur in the course of the next

---

[1] Source: Johnson Library, National Security File, Charles E. Johnson Files, NIEs [2 of 2]. Secret; Controlled Dissem. A cover sheet, prefatory note, title page, and table of contents are not printed. The cover sheet indicates that this NIE supersedes NIE 11–14–64, December 10, 1964. (Ibid., National Intelligence Estimates 11–64, USSR, Box 3) According to the prefatory note, the CIA and the intelligence organizations of the Departments of State and Defense and the National Security Agency participated in the preparation of this estimate. Representatives of the State Department, DIA, AEC, and NSA concurred; the FBI representative abstained, the subject being outside his jurisdiction.

ten years. The Soviets will probably improve the capabilities of their general purpose forces for non-nuclear war. The provision of more advanced weapon systems will increase the military effectiveness of the general purpose forces, but will also increase their cost. Over the longer term we foresee some reductions in personnel strength designed to hold this increasing cost within limits acceptable to the Soviet leadership. (Paras. 10–12)

C. We estimate that the USSR now has about 108 line divisions which are capable of participating in the initial operations of a war. These divisions have virtually all of their equipment. Their peacetime manning levels range from at least 90 percent of war strength in the Soviet forces in Eastern Europe to about 60 percent in the interior of the USSR. We estimate that the USSR has an additional 31 cadre divisions manned at an average of about 20 percent of full strength. Our confidence in these figures is higher than last year as a consequence of more intensive study and new information. (Paras. 13–27)

D. The Soviets have significantly increased their tactical rocket and missile support in the past year. Further increases are likely, as well as the introduction of systems of improved range and mobility. We believe that as the capabilities of tactical aircraft improve the numbers of aircraft in Tactical Aviation will gradually decline.[2] (Paras. 28–36)

E. During the past year there has been a marked increase in the tempo of Soviet naval activity; a larger number of units have operated at a distance from Soviet waters. We believe that Soviet naval capabilities for operations far from home bases will continue to increase over the next ten years with the introduction into the forces of more long-range submarines and support ships. (Paras. 47–53, 59)

F. The USSR is seriously concerned about the Polaris threat to the homeland and has intensified efforts to improve its antisubmarine warfare capabilities. We estimate that, even so, the Soviet capability to detect, identify, and destroy submarines operating in the open seas will remain severely limited for the next several years. (Paras. 54–57)

G. The Soviets have shown increasing interest in airborne and amphibious capabilities in support of theater operations. Over the next

---

[2] The ACS/Intelligence, USAF is unable to reconcile Conclusion B, which estimates a probable improvement in capabilities of Soviet general purpose forces for non-nuclear warfare, with this conclusion that there will be a further increase in tactical missiles which are cost-effective only with nuclear/CW warheads, but a reduction in Tactical Aviation, which has an iron bomb as well as a nuclear and air defense capability. He notes further that reduction of Tactical Aviation as predicted in each of the past several years has not materialized. He would substitute the following for the final sentence:

"Barring a marked change in the overall structure and size of Soviet general purpose forces we believe that the numbers of aircraft in Tactical Aviation will remain about the same as at present, and introduction of new aircraft will provide improved capabilities." [Footnote in the source text.]

ten years they will probably improve these capabilities and seek to develop some capability for distant limited military action. (Paras. 60–66)

H. The Soviets and their Warsaw Pact allies have 45 divisions and about 2,900 combat aircraft immediately available for employment against the Central Region of NATO. We believe, however, that if the Soviets planned to attack NATO they would reinforce these forces, if circumstances permitted, with additional ground and air forces from the western USSR. (Paras. 67–76)

Discussion

I. Soviet Policy Toward the General Purpose Forces

1. Despite the rapid and costly development of Soviet forces for strategic attack and defense, the general purpose forces remain the largest and most expensive element in the Soviet military establishment. Khrushchev, concerned with economic growth and consumer satisfaction, sought to check rising military costs. Because he gave priority to strategic attack and defense, he could accomplish this only by reducing the share of the military budget allocated to the general purpose forces. In 1960 he initiated drastic reductions in their strength. As the result of military opposition, which was strengthened by the Berlin crisis in 1961, these reductions were suspended, but Khrushchev continued to press for further cuts in the general purpose forces.

2. Khrushchev's policy of cutting back the general purpose forces was based on a strategy of deterrence which placed first reliance on strategic rocket forces. These forces, he held, would also be most effective should deterrence fail, since a general nuclear war would be of short duration and its outcome would be determined by the initial nuclear exchange. Subsequent operations, in his view, could have only minor effects, and large scale theater operations would be inconceivable in the aftermath of a massive nuclear exchange.

3. Khrushchev's views were strongly opposed by the military establishment in general. The more conservative marshals vigorously defended the utility of large general purpose forces, contending that large-scale and protracted land campaigns would be indispensable for victory in a general nuclear war; they concluded, not that these forces had no further role to play, but rather that they faced new and demanding requirements. The position eventually adopted by most important Soviet military leaders, including Marshal Malinovskiy, was a compromise. This accepted the decisiveness of nuclear weapons and the probability that a general war would be short, but it also held that such a war might be protracted and that the requirement for large theater forces continued into the nuclear era.

The Policy of the New Leadership

4. The men who displaced Khrushchev face the same problems that confronted him regarding the proper allocation of Soviet resources. They are no less concerned than he to promote economic growth and to strengthen Soviet strategic attack and defense capabilities, but they appear to have relaxed the pressure which he exerted to limit expenditures for the general purpose forces. This change is probably attributable primarily to the increased international tensions arising from the war in Vietnam, but it reflects also the increased influence of the Soviet marshals.

5. The recent restoration of Marshal Chuykov to command of the ground forces is the most definite indication of a change in policy. He is a strong advocate of the maintenance of large ground forces. His bold public defense of his views when he was relieved of that command in 1964 made his return to it unlikely unless there had been a change in policy in the direction which he advocated. Consequently we believe there will be a slight increase in the strength of Soviet general purpose forces, and that they will number some two million men by the end of 1965.[3]

6. Khrushchev's fall was accompanied by expressions of military disapproval of his preoccupation with nuclear armed missiles to the detriment of other military requirements. Ever since 1961 there have been indications of a growing acceptance of the possibility of non-nuclear conflict between nuclear powers. In June of this year Marshal Rotmistrov, predicting a nuclear stalemate between the US and the USSR, suggested that the ground forces might again become the decisive factor, in either a nuclear or a non-nuclear situation. Twice within the past six months Marshal Malinovskiy has spoken of the possibility of a non-nuclear war. Marshal Sokolovskiy recently observed that a situation of nuclear stalemate requires constant reappraisal of the relative roles of strategic and general purpose forces.

7. Thus the Soviet conviction that any conflict between nuclear powers must inevitably and quickly escalate into general nuclear war is now undergoing some modification. We believe that the Soviet leaders are increasingly prepared to contemplate the possibility of non-nuclear warfare between nuclear powers. Nevertheless, they almost certainly still consider that any conflict with NATO in Europe would carry grave risk of escalation to general nuclear war.

8. There has been no perceptible weakening of Soviet insistence that the use of tactical nuclear weapons in limited war would trigger a

---

[3] The numbers and distribution of manpower in all the Soviet military forces will be discussed in NIE 11–4–66, "Main Trends in Soviet Military Policy," scheduled for completion in April 1966. [Footnote in the source text. See Document 131.]

strategic exchange. While this doctrine serves deterrent purposes in part, it also represents an apparent Soviet conviction that escalation under such circumstances would be well-nigh uncontrollable. We do not believe that Soviet doctrine regarding the limited use of nuclear weapons will change in the foreseeable future, and we consider it highly unlikely that the USSR would initiate the use of such weapons in a limited conflict. If the Western powers were to do so, we believe that, doctrine notwithstanding, the Soviets would seek to prevent escalation to general war.

9. There have been no major changes in deployment of Soviet general purpose forces during the past year. However, after the collapse of border talks between the USSR and Communist China in August 1964, Soviet forces on the Manchurian border were strengthened by a motorized rifle division which was probably redeployed from the western USSR. Moreover, within the past year, internal shifts in the Far East moved elements of two other Soviet divisions closer to the Chinese border. Khrushchev's successors have avoided reopening the territorial issue, and the border problem appears to have lapsed into a state of armed quiescence. However, the Soviet units moved there in last year's crisis remain in position.

Trends to 1975

10. Revisions in the force levels, organization, and deployment of the general purpose forces are virtually certain to occur in the course of the next ten years. Such changes are more likely to result from technical military and economic considerations than from external political developments. A substantial relaxation of tensions between the USSR and the West would tend to aggravate tensions between the USSR and Communist China, and vice versa. Hence the Soviet authorities are not likely to find in the development of the international situation any warrant for a substantial reduction in general purpose forces, although the degree of tension may have marginal effects, as in the Berlin crisis of 1961.

11. Economic considerations will continue to be a major factor affecting the development of the general purpose forces. The provision of more advanced weapon systems will increase their military effectiveness, but will also increase their cost. Over the longer term we foresee some reductions in personnel strength designed to hold this increasing cost within limits acceptable to the Soviet leadership.

12. The principal changes over the next decade will probably be in the structure of the general purpose forces, particularly if the Soviets should decide to emphasize preparation for contingencies other than general nuclear war. Such a decision would imply, among other changes, a smaller number of larger divisions and increased provisions

for combat and logistic support. Some restructuring along these lines is probable, but it is likely to occur only very gradually.

[Here follow Parts II–VI, pages 5–21, and Tables I–VI, pages 22–25.]

---

99.   Editorial Note

In addition to studying many scientific and technical issues, the President's Science Advisory Committee (PSAC) also created panels to make recommendations on specific national security subjects. One of these was a Strategic Military Panel; see Document 101. Another was an Anti-Submarine Warfare (ASW) Panel, which Donald F. Hornig, the President's Special Assistant for Science and Technology, established in May 1964 following conversations with Secretary of Defense McNamara. The ASW Panel met June 29–July 1 and August 12–13, 1965, to prepare a report on ASW problems, such as those likely to be posed by the People's Republic of China, for the PSAC. (Status Report on Activities of the President's Science Advisory Committee and Its Staff, September 10; Johnson Library, White House Confidential File, FG 726, PSAC, Box 407) Attached to this Status Report is a September 18 memorandum from Hornig to President Johnson indicating that at its September 19–21 meeting, the PSAC would among other things have a final discussion of the work of the ASW Panel, which was writing a report that "will recommend major changes in the forces, in the tactics, and in the research and development program if the forces are to be effective."

A draft report prepared by the ASW Panel was forwarded to McNamara under cover of a 6-page letter from Hornig to McNamara, October 23. The report has not been found, but Hornig's covering letter summarizes many features of it in detail. (Ibid., National Security File, Agency File, Office of Science and Technology, Vol. 1 [1963–65], Box 42) Under cover of an October 25 memorandum to McGeorge Bundy, Hornig forwarded a copy of his letter to McNamara, and noted that "In many respects the results [of the report] are disturbing, although they follow the pattern of conclusions by previous expert panels." Bundy replied in an October 26 letter that he was "very much interested" in reading Hornig's letter to McNamara and hoped "you and your people will be able to follow up on it." (Both ibid.)

The PSAC's Status Report, dated November 9, indicated in part that the preliminary report of the ASW Panel had been forwarded to the

Defense Department "and is the subject of great controversy at this time. The principal areas of controversy relate to force levels. It appears that the DOD will establish a task force to examine in great detail the questions raised by this report." (Ibid.)

In a December 14 memorandum to President Johnson on ASW forces, which Hornig noted the President had requested, Hornig opposed the purchase of ten destroyer escorts (DE-1052s) and advocated reducing the purchase of nuclear submarines (SSNs) from five to three in the FY 1967 budget, which would save $413 million. "In my view," Hornig added, "our security would not be reduced." His memorandum laid out in some detail his reasons for these recommendations. (Ibid.)

For an extract from the final Report by the Anti-Submarine Warfare Panel, see Document 124.

---

100.   Memorandum From Secretary of Defense McNamara to the Director of Defense Research and Engineering, Department of Defense (Foster)[1]

Washington, October 22, 1965.

As we discussed during the last Nike-X briefing,[2] I believe it is important that we include in the FY 67 Research and Development program sufficient funds to:

(1) Assure the development of a "short leadtime" anti-ballistic missile defense directed against the Chinese threat,
(2) An "optimum" anti-ballistic missile defense directed against the Chinese threat,
(3) An "optimum" anti-ballistic missile defense against a Soviet attack on our offensive weapon system launchers.

Unless Mr. Vance or I specifically approve the additional expenditures in writing, do not include in the anti-ballistic missile Research and

---

[1] Source: National Archives and Records Administration, RG 218, JCS Files, 3212 (29 Oct 65) IR 4878. Top Secret. A copy was sent to Secretary of the Army Stanley R. Resor. An attached November 4 covering note by R.C. Forbes and J.E. Mansfield of the Joint Secretariat to the JCS (JCS 2012/259–1) notes that McNamara's memorandum was being circulated for information.

[2] Not further identified.

Development programs for FY 67 any funds to be expended on production engineering, procurement of components for deployment, or any other activities associated with deployment.

Robert S. McNamara[3]

---

[3] Printed from a copy that indicates McNamara signed the original.

---

101.   Report Prepared by the Strategic Military Panel of the President's Science Advisory Committee[1]

Washington, October 29, 1965.

PROPOSED ARMY–BTL BALLISTIC MISSILE DEFENSE SYSTEM

I. Introduction

The Panel has reviewed the current Army–BTL proposal to deploy a ballistic missile defense system capable of defending the United States against unsophisticated or light ballistic missile attacks. The Panel understands that the system, which consists of a high altitude, area defense for the entire country and a limited deployment of terminal Nike-X defense for high value targets, is primarily directed against a future Chinese nuclear capability and is intended to insure that the United States will be essentially invulnerable to Chinese nuclear attack for a considerable period of time. At the same time, the system is specif-

---

[1] Source: National Archives and Records Administration, RG 218, JCS Files, 3212 (29 Oct 65) IR 4878. Secret; Restricted Data; Privileged. An attached October 29 covering letter from Hornig to McNamara notes, among other things, that "I have had an opportunity to study this problem closely and am in full agreement with their conclusions and recommendations. The President's Science Advisory Committee has endorsed the report and concurs in its recommendations." Also attached is a November 2 covering note by R.C. Forbes and J.E. Mansfield of the Joint Secretariat to the JCS (JCS 2012/259) concerning the distribution of Hornig's letter and its enclosure. Spurgeon Keeny forwarded the report to McGeorge Bundy under cover of a November 1 memorandum, noting that the panel was "representative of the full spectrum of political and military views on this problem." He added: "When I wrote the first draft of this report, I frankly didn't think there was any chance of getting an agreed-upon report. I think it very significant, therefore, that this group, each of whom takes this problem very seriously from his own point of view, finally agreed unanimously on the attached report." (Johnson Library, National Security File, Agency File, Office of Science and Technology, Vol. 1 [1963–65], Box 42)

ically designed to permit growth to meet more massive and more sophisticated forms of ballistic missile threat from any quarter.

If the decision to deploy is made in FY-1967, the Army estimates that the proposed system would have an IOC in 1970 and would be completely deployed by 1973 at a cost of from $8 to $12 billion, depending on the number of locations defended by terminal defense.

In its deliberations, the Panel was deeply conscious of the fact that deploying a ballistic missile defense system is one of the most important military systems decisions that the United States has ever had to face. There is full agreement that the threat to American and world security posed by the emerging Chinese nuclear capability will be extremely serious.

There would clearly be considerable military and political advantages in a defense system that could insure that this country would not be subject to Chinese blackmail threats and, more important, that would give the government greater flexibility in its dealings with the Chinese Communists by denying them even a minimal nuclear deterrent for a great many years to come.

With regard to the magnitude of the commitment, the concept of a secure defensive shield against Chinese strategic attack could in the long run involve much greater expenditures for continental defense than those required simply for the proposed limited deployment. Future extensive deployment of Nike-X terminal defense (particularly since "growth potential" is a design requirement) would probably follow. Moreover, to achieve a tight defense, substantial additional expenditures would be required for ASW and air defense to plug obvious loopholes in the proposed Army–BTL system. Finally, if as a consequence of deployment of the Army–BTL system we become interested in the possibility of defense against more massive threats, a substantial expansion of our civil defense program would surely have to be considered.

The Panel has examined on technical and military grounds whether the proposed Army–BTL system is designed correctly to match the evolution of the Chinese strategic nuclear threat.

At the same time, there appear to be far-reaching military, economic and political consequences of the decision to deploy ballistic missile defense that may be to the long-term net disadvantage of the United States. The proposed system would have considerable capability against the Soviet ICBM force in its present configuration. The Soviets must therefore react to U.S. deployment of such a system in order to maintain their deterrent (or their capacity for assured destruction) at the present level. This reaction would most logically involve the development and deployment of penetration aids in the Soviet ICBM force but might well also in the longer term push the Soviets to higher levels of strategic force deployment, to which we, in turn, might well react.

A decision to deploy could also have a significant effect on our allies in Europe and Asia. It is not clear whether it would increase their confidence in our resolve to defend them or their fear that we were abandoning them while constructing a Fortress America. The question would probably have to be faced as to whether we were prepared to assist our allies in obtaining a similar defense. Finally, a decision now to spend $8 to $12 billion to defend ourselves against a Chinese strategic threat would probably enhance China's military stature in the eyes of the world years before China could actually have a real nuclear strategic capability, and at a time when we have been attempting to minimize the significance of the Chinese threat. What effect this would have on the actions of our allies and neutrals in Asia requires careful examination.

Finally, the question arises why we should consider undertaking a massive expansion of our strategic defensive forces in the face of a relatively weak Chinese threat when we have not chosen to do so against our much stronger Soviet opponent. Our intent would presumably be to maintain a defensive military posture against the Chinese capable of denying them any deterrent capability whatever for at least a limited period of time. We never achieved this posture with respect to the Soviet Union; however, it may be possible to achieve it against the Chinese because of our great technological advantage.

In its deliberations, the Panel has attempted to focus on the technical aspects of the problem. The Panel recognizes, however, that some of the broader issues noted above must weigh heavily in any final decision on deployment of a ballistic missile defense system.

II. Chinese Threat

At present, the Chinese clearly have no ICBMs and, for practical purposes, no intercontinental aircraft. They do have fission bombs; a Chinese copy of a Soviet ballistic missile type submarine (although it may not have any missiles); short-range cruise missiles; and an active ballistic missile development program, which includes a missile test range of about one thousand nautical mile range, static firing stands, and probably Chinese copies of the Soviet SS-4/MRBM. They also have a very strong motivation both to expand their ballistic missile submarine force and to develop an ICBM capability.

The general thinking in the intelligence community is that the Chinese may have a limited ballistic missile submarine capability in the latter part of this decade and that an initial Chinese ICBM capability might appear as early as in the 1970–1975 time period. However, there is also agreement that it is not possible to estimate with any accuracy at this time the evolution of the Chinese nuclear strategic threat during the next decade.

III. Capabilities of the Army–BTL System against Chinese Threat

The proposed Army–BTL system, which basically consists of components originally designed to provide a full-scale defense against the Soviet ICBM threat, appears, on the one hand, inadequate to cope with an initial Chinese capability composed of submarine-launched ballistic and air breathing missiles and, on the other hand, more effective than necessary for defense against the early Chinese ICBMs.

The concept of the proposed system is that the high altitude area defense would essentially defend the entire country against unsophisticated small attacks and that terminal Nike-X defense, deployed only at "high value" targets, would cover any leakage and would also provide additional defense against submarine-launched ballistic missiles in the case of coastal cities.

The area defense component of the system could provide a very effective defense against the initial Chinese ICBM capability which probably would not be equipped with adequate penetration aids. It is designed to acquire targets at 1600 n.m. and to launch interceptors when the target is 1000 n.m. away so that interception takes place at ranges up to about 300 n.m. from the defensive missile launching sites and at altitudes of 300,000 feet or higher. [*3-1/2 lines of source text not declassified*] This should give relatively high confidence of kill against individual warheads with limited penetration aids.

The area defense component of the proposed system can be expected to cope with some 15 to 30 individual warheads directed against a given contiguous target area before exhaustion of its interceptors. Thus, although the defense can always be overwhelmed in any one area by a large attack, the area component could provide a very high confidence defense against an initial small Chinese ICBM force with limited penetration aids. However, since there is no discrimination in the area component of the system, it can probably be exhausted by the use of light relatively unsophisticated, unhardened, exo-atmospheric decoys. Although there is considerable debate as to exactly how simple it is to develop such decoys, it seems unlikely that the earliest Chinese ICBMs would be so equipped. However, this would be the natural path of Chinese development to counter an area defense, and one probably could not count on a very extended effective life of such a system.

The terminal defense component, which uses atmospheric discrimination and rapid response Sprint missiles, also would have no difficulty at defended locations in handling the initial Chinese ICBM threat since it was originally designed to deal with relatively sophisticated missiles. However, against the initial Chinese ICBM threat, the terminal defense component appears somewhat redundant, when coupled with the area defense system. With the development of exo-atmospheric decoys, widely dispersed, the terminal defense component would become essential for the system to be effective. In that situation, it seems clear that the constraints imposed on the offense to penetrate both area and terminal defense would exact a heavy price in payload on target, and it would probably take the Chinese many years to acquire this capability. It should be noted, however, that initially the Army–BTL system provides terminal defense for only a limited number of U.S. cities. Thus it must be recognized that, if the Chinese are able to penetrate our area defense, they can always damage us by attacking the "n + 1" city in any system designed to defend "n" cities. Therefore, only a deployment of terminal defense batteries much more extensive than that contemplated in the Army–BTL proposal can in the long term hope to accomplish the original objective of an essentially invulnerable defense of the U.S. against the Chinese; even such a defense can eventually be penetrated. Consequently, at some point in the future it would presumably be necessary to accept a "damage-limiting" and "assured destruction" posture with respect to the Chinese.

Considering the submarine threat, the Panel believes that both the area and the terminal components of the system are vulnerable to such attacks. Neither component has any capability against air breathing cruise missiles flying at low altitudes. The area system would also be ineffective against submarine-based ballistic missiles launched on minimum energy trajectories of less than 100 n.m. More important is the fact that a 350 n.m. missile, which is the normal armament of the Soviet G-class submarine of which the Chinese have produced one copy, would be invisible to the area defense when launched at 100 n.m. The defense would thus have to rely on the terminal component, which in turn could not cope with missiles launched at distances of less than about 50 n.m.

If our ASW is as ineffective as some people fear, this means that there is a loophole to the proposed system that could probably be exploited by the Chinese with what might be their initial capability. If, on the other hand, our ASW forces are more able and can be made more effective to handle the Chinese submarine threat than is now apparent, then the need for a defense against submarine-launched missiles is decreased. However, even if ASW becomes relatively effective, it would appear that some form of advanced "air defense" such as SAM-D will probably also be required to plug the loophole in the proposed Army–BTL system posed by submarine-launched ballistic and air breathing missiles. This raises the question as to whether a SAM-D-type system alone or in combination with an improved ASW posture is not the correct answer to the submarine threat.

IV. Capabilities of Army–BTL System against Soviet Threat

The proposed Army–BTL system clearly also has considerable capability against the present Soviet threat. No matter how much we advertise the fact that the defense is directed at the Chinese, the Soviet Union and the rest of the world will probably consider that the principal significance of the system relates to its impact on the U.S.-Soviet strategic nuclear confrontation.

At the present time, the area defense component of the proposed Army–BTL system would be quite effective against Soviet re-entry vehicles since the Soviet Union has apparently not yet decided to deploy penetration aids, nor is there even any evidence of a Soviet penetration aids development program. Rapid U.S. deployment of an area defense (in particular, the simplified system discussed below) might lead the Soviet deployment of penetration aids by a year or two if the Soviets were slow to react, and it might buy us a short but possibly significant strategic advantage. However, it seems extremely improbable that the Soviets would not soon be able to equip their force with the penetration aids required to overcome an area defense.

There do not appear to be any developments implicit in the proposed system that would in any way change the unfavorable exchange ratio with Soviet offensive forces previously estimated for the Nike-X terminal defense system although analysis of the combined area and terminal defense has not been carried out.

V. Impact of Ballistic Missile Defense Deployment on the U.S.-Soviet Strategic Confrontation

A decision to deploy the proposed Army–BTL system would probably not initially result in a major political reaction on the part of the Soviets since they seem to accept defensive systems as natural militarily. However, if they have either not decided to deploy a ballistic missile defense system of their own or have decided on only a limited deployment for the general Moscow–Leningrad area, our decision to deploy might well influence them to undertake a full-scale ballistic missile defense. More important, for the long term, it would appear that such a decision on our part might well push the Soviets to higher strategic force levels, both qualitatively and quantitatively. Such an increase in Soviet force levels would probably again put pressure on the U.S. to expand its strategic forces.

The possibility that the Soviets may announce during the coming year that they are actually deploying a ballistic missile defense system is an added problem that must be weighed in deciding whether or not to deploy a system of our own. Despite the accumulation of information that may relate to this activity, it is still uncertain as to what the Soviets are actually doing. The Soviets may already actually be engaged in a limited deployment of a ballistic missile defense system. In any event, it is clear that the Soviet activities that may be related to ballistic missile defense and, in particular, to deployment have been substantially expanded throughout the last year.

If the Soviet Union were to announce to the world the deployment of a ballistic missile defense, which it claimed was very effective, the domestic political pressures for a similar action on our part would certainly be increased. Moreover, if such announcement by the Soviets were to occur during a major confrontation with this country, it might have a significant impact on world opinion. On the other hand, the Soviet Union has frequently claimed successful development, if not deployment, of an effective ballistic missile defense and has, in fact, intensified through recent pronouncements and a much-publicized film that they have a ballistic missile defense capability. World reaction to all these claims has been minimal.

There is little question but that the proper military counter to a Soviet ballistic missile defense system would be to improve the capability of the U.S. strategic forces to penetrate, in particular by the incorporation of improved penetration aids in our existing missile force. This would have the effect of assuring that we maintain the same basic deterrence posture relative to the Soviet Union that exists at present.

The Panel believes the probability is sufficiently great that either the Soviets will announce, or we will discover, the existence of a deployed Soviet ballistic missile defense system in the next year or two so that there should be a greatly increased effort to assure that we are in a position to incorporate appropriate penetration aids in our strategic missile systems as rapidly as necessary. In the past, the Services, particularly the Air Force, have been slow in developing programs for the incorporation of penetration aids despite continued pressure from OSD. Programs for penetration aids, specifically aimed at countering potential Soviet ballistic missile defense systems, have now been evolved by the Services and we hope that rapid progress will be made.

VI. What Is the Proper Response to the Chinese Threat?

There is considerable uncertainty about the time schedule of the emerging Chinese strategic nuclear threat. One may imagine that it will appear late (i.e., after 1973, the time of complete deployment of the Army–BTL system, were the go-ahead given now) or it might appear early, say in 1970. This uncertainty in the threat raises serious questions regarding the deployment of the Army–BTL system, and we discuss these questions below.

Because of the possible early threat, the Panel is concerned with the length of time required for deployment of the proposed system. In fact, the time to achieve the performance as predicted in the proposed Army–BTL system may be considerably longer than assumed, considering the advanced technology involved.

The Panel believes that it may be technically feasible to obtain a useful area defense against the plausible initial Chinese ICBM capability with shorter deployment time and at much lower cost than that of the proposed Army–BTL system. The high cost of the Army–BTL system is largely a consequence of overdesign in the attempt to build a growth capability into the system by means of a terminal component that is not really required initially. For example, the use of the very expensive MSRs at the Zeus missile farms is closely coupled to the requirements for terminal defense.

The Panel considered a simplified area defense in which the Minimar and MSR radars were omitted from the system. Acquisition could be achieved by VHF (~150 megacycles) or UHF (~ 400 megacycles) radars such as those used in SPADATS; and the defensive Zeus missiles could be controlled by MTRs, or by inertial guidance. The effects of blackout, including self blackout, particularly on the VHF radars, as well as the feasibility of using light decoys to penetrate the defense, would have to be considered in detail in evaluating such a system. A system of this variety would cost substantially less than the proposed Army–BTL system, perhaps as little as $1 billion, and could involve only "off-the-shelf" hardware. It could surely be deployed more quickly than the proposed Army–BTL defense.

Although the over-all capabilities of such a simplified system would clearly be less than the Army–BTL system, it would probably be as effective as the Army–BTL system in dealing with the early Chinese ICBM threat. The Panel believes that more detailed study will probably show that such a simplified system is feasible and that it can in fact be rapidly deployed. The ability to deploy such a system would provide an effective hedge against an early Chinese ICBM deployment. With this hedge, we would have more time to resolve the uncertainties in our intelligence on the Chinese nuclear strategic threat and in the technology of ballistic missile defense.

It is also important to recognize that our massive strategic offensive forces provide additional safeguards against the early Chinese ICBM threat. In the face of these U.S. forces, a few unhardened and easily located Chinese ICBMs would not constitute a very plausible blackmail threat or deterrent capability. Provided our defenses against the Chinese submarine missile threat are effective, the U.S. by taking preemptive action could be protected with a high level of confidence against the initial Chinese ICBM force. The level of confidence in such a preemptive disarming attack would of course decrease as the level of the Chinese ICBM force increases.

In this context and with a rapidly-deployable simplified system as a hedge, the Panel believes that we will have sufficient time to react to the Chinese ICBM threat as it becomes more apparent. In addition, there is an actual danger that a premature decision to deploy a defensive system would permit the Chinese to build around it if they are not already firmly committed to their future strategic systems. They might, for example, give additional emphasis to submarine or ship-launched missiles instead of undertaking an ICBM program. Moreover, the sooner the Chinese are clearly faced with the problem of having to penetrate a high altitude area defense the sooner we can expect them to introduce exo-atmospheric penetration aids into their evolving ICBM force.

For all of the reasons discussed above, the Panel does not believe that there should be a decision this year to deploy the proposed Army–BTL system.

VII. Possible Alternative Courses of Action

The Panel is aware that a number of alternatives to an actual decision in connection with the FY-1967 budget to deploy the Army–BTL system are being considered in DOD.

One such proposal is to make a firm decision to deploy the Army–BTL system at a time dictated by the future evolution of the Chinese strategic nuclear threat. On this basis the actual funding of the deployment decision would be delayed for at least one year. This proposal is presumably based on the idea that the announcement of such a decision would be of some domestic value in allaying criticism that the Administration was not reacting to the Chinese threat and to undercut the impact of any Soviet announcement that they were deploying such a system. The Panel believes that this proposal would present us with all of the problems inherent in the decision to deploy a ballistic missile system without doing anything to advance the day when a defensive system would be available. Moreover, it would tend to tie us unnecessarily to a specific system at a time when technology is changing very rapidly. The Panel finds very little to recommend this proposal.

A second proposal that is being considered is to postpone the formal deployment decision but to spend some $200 million in FY-1967 for long lead time items. It is argued that this action would, in essence, save one year in both the IOC and full deployment times if it is subsequently decided to deploy the Army–BTL system. On examination, it appears that the $200 million in question is essentially equivalent to the full first-year expenditures for the deployment of the system. This expenditure really amounts to building up in FY-1967 the organization that would be necessary in FY-1968 to spend $1.2 billion. This type of operation would make it more difficult next year to decide against deployment. This action would also tie us very closely to the specifics of the proposed Army–BTL system and would make it much more difficult to continue objective study of the problem since efforts would of necessity be focused on the very difficult management problem of building an organization capable of directing the single most complex military system ever undertaken. Although it is argued that this action would defer the political repercussions that may be involved in a formal deployment decision, the world at large would probably interpret this action as a decision on our part to deploy the Army–BTL system.

On balance, the Panel does not believe it would be wise to initiate the program for the procurement of long lead time items in the absence of a decision to deploy.

VIII. Recommendations

On the basis of the above considerations, the Panel recommends that:

1. A decision should *not* be made this year to deploy the proposed Army–BTL system.

2. A commitment should *not* be made this year to deploy the proposed Army–BTL system at a future date to be determined by the evolution of the Chinese strategic nuclear threat.

3. The proposed $200 million in pre-production funds for the proposed Army–BTL system should *not* be spent in FY-1967.

4. The DOD should intensify its study of the problem of countering short-range, submarine-launched, ballistic and air-breathing missiles which may well be the initial Chinese nuclear strategic threat.

5. The DOD should design and evaluate a simplified area defense system which would be relatively inexpensive, use off-the-shelf components, and be rapidly deployable.

6. The DOD should continue the R&D program in support of the proposed Army–BTL program and should carry out any necessary test and evaluation of components for a simplified area defense system. The DOD should also continue support of general technology relating to ballistic missile defense, in particular in the field of re-entry phenomena.

7. The DOD should vigorously continue its efforts on penetration aids against either a potential Soviet area or terminal defense system.

Dr. Marvin Goldberger, Chmn.	Dr. Wolfgang K.H. Panofsky
Dr. Hans A. Bethe	Dr. Jack P. Ruina
Dr. Lewis McA. Branscomb	Dr. Kenneth M. Watson
Dr. Sidney D. Drell	Dr. Jerome B. Wiesner
Dr. Richard L. Garwin	Mr. Spurgeon M. Keeny, Jr.
Dr. Richard Latter	

102. Editorial Note

In their book, *How Much Is Enough? Shaping the Defense Program, 1961–1969* (New York: Harper & Row, 1971), Alain G. Enthoven and K. Wayne Smith, who worked in the Systems Analysis Office of the Department of Defense during the Kennedy and Johnson administrations (Enthoven serving as the newly-created Assistant Secretary of Defense (Systems Analysis) from 1965 to 1969), summarized the strategic thinking of Department of Defense officials.

In determining strategic force requirements, the two wrote that U.S. defense officials decided that the "assured destruction" capability of U.S. strategic offensive nuclear forces would be sufficient to destroy 20 to 25 percent of the Soviet population and 50 percent of Soviet industry. This was a "judgment reached by the Secretary of Defense and accepted by the President, by the Congress, and apparently by the general public as well." Studies by the Systems Analysis Office concluded that following a Soviet nuclear attack, U.S. retaliation with 100 1-megaton-equivalent U.S.-delivered nuclear warheads would kill about 37 million people (15 percent of the total Soviet population) and destroy 59 percent of Soviet industrial capacity. Doubling the megaton delivery to 200 would increase the percentages to 21 percent fatalities and 72 percent industrial capacity destroyed. Higher levels would increase the destructive percentages, but the returns would be sharply diminishing compared with the expense involved. (Ibid., page 207) The studies of the Systems Analysis Office also concluded that the number of U.S. and Soviet citizens killed in a nuclear exchange would be very high, regardless of whether the United States had no ABM defense system, an ABM defense of 25 cities, or defense of some 52 cities. (Ibid., pages 184 ff.)

The figures cited by Enthoven and Smith in their book, as well as additional estimates presented in their tables, were publicly known and debated at the time. Indeed, Enthoven's office likely developed the estimates for Secretary McNamara, who used the same figures in his annual posture statements to Congress. See, for example, *Statement of Secretary of Defense Robert S. McNamara Before the Senate Armed Services Committee on the Fiscal Year 1969–73 Defense Program and 1969 Defense Budget* (prepared January 22, 1969), page 57. For additional references to assured destruction of the Soviet population and industrial capacity, see Documents 103, 128, 139, 160, 200, and 210.

103. Draft Memorandum From Secretary of Defense McNamara to President Johnson[1]

Washington, November 1, 1965.

SUBJECT

Recommended FY 1967–71 Strategic Offensive and Defensive Forces (U)

I have completed my review of our general nuclear war posture and our programs for the strategic offensive and defensive forces over the FY 1967–71 period. The estimated costs for the Previously Approved, the Service Proposed, and my Recommended Programs are presented below:

	FY 66	FY 67	FY 68	FY 69	FY 70	FY 71	Total FY 67–71
			(TOA in millions of dollars)				
Previously Approved	6399	5796	5488	5348	5259		
Service Proposed	6552	7458	9459	10919	11393	11306	50535
SecDef Recommended	6392	6254	5995	5692	4888	4512	27341

This year we have given special attention to an analysis of threats over and above those projected in the latest National Intelligence Estimates of Soviet strategic offensive and defensive forces. We have done so because recent technological progress on our part, which if duplicated by the Soviets and incorporated in their strategic forces, could pose a new and much more severe threat to our Assured Destruction capability than postulated in the NIEs. This threat would arise, for example, if the Soviet Union were to deploy simultaneously a force of new ICBMs equipped with highly accurate, multiple, independently aimed re-entry vehicles (MIRVs) and a reasonably sophisticated anti-ballistic missile system. Although we do not now consider this to be a likely contingency, it does lie within their technical capabilities over the next ten years and could require some major changes in our strategic offensive forces in the future.

There are seven major issues involved in our FY 1967–71 programs for the general nuclear war forces. The first five are related primarily to the threat projected in the latest National Intelligence Estimates. The last two are associated with the possibility of a more severe threat. These issues are:

---

[1] Source: Washington National Records Center, OSD Files: FRC 330 70 A 1265, 031.1 WH PDM Oct 1965. Top Secret; Restricted Data. An earlier, July 14, draft is in the National Archives and Records Administration, RG 218, JCS Files, 7000 (14 Jul 1965) IR 3879. Regarding an October 1 draft, see footnote 2, Document 105.

1. To what extent should qualitative improvements (in range, payload, etc.) be made in the Minuteman force?

2. Should an effective manned bomber force be maintained in the 1970s; if so, what aircraft should be selected for the force?

3. Should an anti-ballistic missile system be deployed; if so, when and of what type?

4. Should we produce and deploy a new manned interceptor?

5. What should be the future size and scope of the Civil Defense program?

6. Should development of new penetration aid packages for the Polaris and Minuteman missile forces be accelerated?

7. Should full-scale, accelerated development of the Poseidon missile designed for use in Polaris submarines be initiated?

After considering the alternatives open to us, I have concluded that we should:

a. Maintain the Minuteman force at the previously approved level of 1,000 missiles, with the entire force to consist of the improved Minuteman II and III[2] missiles by FY 1972. The FY 1967 cost of replacing Minuteman I with Minuteman II and III will amount to $1.0 billion, with a total cost of $2.9 billion for FY 1967–71.

b. Continue Engineering Development of the Poseidon missile designed for use in Polaris submarines. The FY 1967 cost will be $210 million and the total development cost will be about $1.1 billion, to achieve an Operational Availability Date (OAD) of August 1970.

c. [6-1/2 lines of source text not declassified] I estimate the FY 1967 costs of the Air Force R&D program at $73.8 million, and the Polaris R&D program at $41.3 million. These development programs will permit us to deploy penetration aids, if needed, within intelligence lead times on Soviet Anti-Ballistic Missile (ABM) development.

d. Replace 345 B-52 C-F and 80 B-58 bombers with 210 FB-111 dual purpose (i.e., tactical and strategic) aircraft incorporating the minimum modification to the F-111A necessary for strategic mission capability, including the Short Range Air-to-Surface Missile (SRAM). FB-111 is estimated for the fourth quarter of 1968 and the build-up is to be completed by June 1971. The FB-111/SRAM program will involve $48 million for R&D and $317 million for procurement in FY 1967. The FY 1967–71 costs of the recommended bomber program will be about $400 million more than the previously approved program. However, retaining the B-52 C-F beyond 1972 would have required an additional $600 million of modification expenditures.

___

[2] Minuteman III designated Minuteman with multiple independently aimed re-entry vehicles (MIRVs). [Footnote in the source text.]

Therefore, the FY 1967–71 costs of the recommended program are about $200 million less than the cost of retaining the force of 600 B-52s.

e. Disapprove initiation of full-scale development in FY 1967 of the Advanced Manned Strategic Aircraft—development and deployment of 200 of these aircraft would cost about $8.9 billion, $11.5 billion in five year systems cost.

f. Disapprove an Army recommendation for a full-scale deployment of Nike-X at a cost of $12.7 billion from FY 1967–71 and an FY 1967 cost of $212 million. This proposal involves an ultimate investment cost of $15.7 billion and annual operating costs of $861 million.

g. Continue the development of the Nike-X system at an FY 1967 cost of about $400 million, including FY 1967 funds for development of a long range exo-atmospheric interceptor missile. This will give us an option to deploy a light anti-ballistic missile defense system designed against small or unsophisticated attacks such as the Chinese Communist will probably be capable of in the mid-late 1970. Such a program would have an investment and five-year operating cost of between $5 and $8 billion. The production and deployment decision can be deferred for at least one more year.

h. Disapprove an Air Force proposal to deploy 12 squadrons of F-12 as an improved manned interceptor—initial investment costs for such a program would approximate $4.4 billion.

i. Extend the approved Civil Defense Program, including the expanded program for shelter survey and the shelter prestocking program, at an FY 1967 cost of $184 million.

The recommendations form the basis for my FY 1967 budget for the strategic offensive and defensive forces. The remainder of this paper will discuss the rationale behind the recommendations:

[Here follows a table of contents.]

A. The General Nuclear War Problem

Last year in my memorandum to you on the same subject I pointed out that our general nuclear war forces should have two basic capabilities:

1. To deter deliberate nuclear attack upon the United States and its Allies by maintaining a clear and convincing capability to inflict unacceptable damage on an attacker, even if that attacker were to strike first;
2. In the event such a war nevertheless occurred, to limit damage to our population and industrial capacity. The first of these capabilities we call "Assured Destruction" and the second "Damage Limitation".

Assured Destruction involves the maintenance on a continuous basis of a highly reliable ability to inflict an unacceptable degree of damage, even after absorbing a first strike, upon any single aggressor or combination of aggressors, independently of warning, and at any time during the course of a strategic nuclear exchange. This capability is the vital first objective which must be met in full by our strategic nuclear forces since it would ensure, with a high degree of confidence, that we could deter under all circumstances a calculated, deliberate nuclear attack upon the United States. Although we cannot and need not state with precision what kinds and amounts of destruction we would have to be able to inflict on an aggressor in order to provide this assurance, whatever that level may be, it must be provided regardless of the costs or the difficulties involved.

Once high confidence of an Assured Destruction capability has been provided, we should then consider additional forces and measures which would allow us to reduce the damage to our population and industry in the event deterrence fails. The level of the threat against which we might design Damage Limiting postures may range all the way from that posed by a minor nuclear power—for example, the Chinese Communists in the 1970s—to that posed by the Soviet Union in a carefully synchronized first strike against our urban areas.

With respect to the Damage Limiting problem posed by the Soviet nuclear threat, I believe it would be useful to restate briefly certain basic considerations which have guided our programs over the last several years:

First, against the forces we expect the Soviets to have during the next decade, it would be virtually impossible for us to be able to ensure anything approaching perfect protection for our population, no matter how large the general nuclear war forces we were to provide, even if we were to strike first. The Soviets clearly have the technical and economic capacity to prevent us from achieving a posture which could keep our fatalities below some tens of millions; in a Soviet first strike they could do this at an extra cost to them substantially less than the extra cost to us of any additional Damage Limiting measures we might take.

Second, since each of the three types of Soviet strategic offensive systems (land-based missiles, submarine-launched missiles and manned bombers) could, by itself, inflict severe damage on the United States, even a "very good" defense against only one type of system has only limited value.

Third, for any given level of Soviet offensive capability, successive additions to each of our various Damage Limiting systems have diminishing marginal value. The same principle holds for the Damage Limiting force as a whole; as additional forces are added, the incremental gain in effectiveness diminishes.

With respect to the Damage Limiting problem posed by an Nth country nuclear threat, e.g., Communist China in the 1970s, it now appears to be technically feasible to design a defense system which would have a reasonably high probability of avoiding any substantial damage. The deployment of such a system might also contribute to our objective of control of proliferation by strengthening the credibility of a possible U.S. commitment to come to the assistance of a friendly nation confronted by an Nth country nuclear threat. It might also deter the threatened or actual use of nuclear weapons by Nth countries acting independently of the Soviet Union.

It was with these considerations in mind that we have carefully evaluated the major alternatives available to us in meeting the two strategic objectives of our general nuclear war forces—Assured Destruction and Damage Limitation.

B. Capabilities of Our Forces Against the Expected Threat

In order to assess the capabilities of our general nuclear war forces over the next several years, we must take into account the size and character, of the forces the Soviets are likely to have during the same period.

1. The Soviet Strategic Offensive-Defense Forces

Summarized in the table below are the Soviet strategic offensive forces indicated in the latest, but still preliminary, National Intelligence Estimates for mid-1965–1967, and 1970. Shown for comparison are the U.S. forces in being or recommended for the same dates. A detailed tabulation of the U.S. forces can be found on Table I (page 39) of the Appendix.[3]

U.S. vs Soviet Strategic Nuclear Forces

	Mid-1965		Mid-1967		Mid-1970	
	U.S.	USSR	U.S.	USSR	U.S.	USSR
ICBMs[a]						
Soft Launchers	0	146	0	142-148	0	40-150
Hard Launchers	854	78	1054	278-328	1054	460-650
Mobile	0	0	0	0	0	0
Total	854	224	1054	420-476	1054	500-800
MR/IRBMs						
Soft Launchers	0	600	0	575	0	390-420
Hard Launchers	0	135	0	135	0	160-200
Mobile	0	0	0	0	0	50-100
	0	735	0	710	0	600-720
SLBMs	464	120-140	656	120-190	656	120-220
Bombers and Tankers[b]						
Heavy	630	205-220	465	185-215	255	155-195
Medium	305	770-820	78	540-725	150	300-550
Tankers	620	0	620	0	620	0
Total	1555	975-1040	1163	725-940	1025	455-745

---

[a] Excludes test range launchers having some operational capability of which the Soviets are estimated to have 34 in the mid-1965 to 55–60 in the mid-1970 period.

[b] Soviet aircraft figures include tankers as well as bombers. U.S. medium bombers include FB-111s in 1970. The range of the FB-111 and the number of weapons it will carry are markedly greater than those of the Soviet medium bombers.

[3] Tables I–IV constituting the Appendix are not printed.

While we have reasonably high confidence in our estimates of the size and composition of the Soviets' strategic offensive and defensive forces for the near future, many details concerning the technical and lethal characteristics of their weapon systems are less certain. Also, estimates for the latter part of this decade and the early part of the next decade are, of course, subject to great uncertainties.

a. Intercontinental Ballistic Missiles

At present the Soviet ICBM force is deployed on 224 operational launchers, 146 of which are soft and 78 of which are hard and configured in a triple-silo pattern. As reported last year the ICBMs—all of which are liquid fueled—are designated the SS-6, SS-7, and SS-8.

The Soviets are constructing at least two types of single silo launch sites. We believe that the large payload (9,000–11,000 lbs) liquid fueled SS-9 ICBM system, which we expect to become operational in 1966, will be deployed in the larger silos and that the SS-11 ICBM, a small storable liquid fueled missile, also estimated to become operational in 1966, is intended for the smaller silos. While we have anticipated the development of a solid-fuel Soviet ICBM system, we are certain that as of this time, a full-scale flight test program for such a missile has not been undertaken. Accordingly, with the cessation of SS-6/7/8 deployment programs, major additions over the next few years to the operational ICBM force would consist of the SS-9 and SS-11.

By mid-1967, the Soviet ICBM force is estimated to total between 420–476 operational launchers. Compared with the Soviet missile force at mid-1965, this would be an increase of 60 to 70 SS-9 ICBM launchers and 140 to 180 SS-11 ICBM launchers.

In our estimates last year, we projected a Soviet ICBM force of some 400–700 operational launchers for mid-1970. Because of the relatively early introduction of the single silo basing configuration our present estimate for mid-1970 is a minimum of 500 and a maximum of perhaps 700 to 800 operational launchers, with the bulk of the force probably consisting of small payload missiles.

While it is possible that the Soviet ICBM force could expand in the later years of this decade at a higher rate than we now estimate, present-deployment trends and economic, strategic and technical considerations would not appear to support a higher estimate.

b. MRBMs/IRBMs

Deployment of the MRBM (1020 n.mi.) and IRBM (2200 n.mi.) forces appears to be completed with about 735 operational launchers, 135 of which are hard. We estimate that the size of this force will remain relatively constant through the mid-1967 period. Improvements through mid-1970 will probably include the deployment of solid fueled missiles (although no flight test program has been identified), some mobile units phasing out of the soft sites.

c. Submarine-Launched Ballistic Missiles

The trend in Soviet submarine construction is still not very clear. However, new programs under development or in production are not likely to affect Soviet missile submarine strength for the next few years. The Soviet Navy now has some 43 to 48 ballistic missile submarines with a total of 120–140 tubes. Only 8 to 10 of these submarines are nuclear powered and only 2 or 3 of these carry the 700 n.mi. SS-N-5 submerged launch missile. All of the other operational Soviet ballistic missile submarines contain the 300 mile surface-launch SS-N-4 missile. Only recently have the Soviet ballistic missile submarines regularly carried out ocean patrols, but these appear to be to staging areas rather than to strike stations.

Because of construction lead times, no change in the force level of Soviet ballistic missile submarines is now projected through mid-1967. However, it is estimated that by 1968 the Soviets could have a nuclear powered submarine capable of launching 6 to 12 salvo-fired, 1,000 n.mi. missiles. By mid-1970 they could have as many as seven of these boats.

Although the Soviets do not appear to consider the cruise missile submarine as primarily a strategic attack system, they now have 39 to 43 such boats equipped with 350 n.mi. missiles, 16 to 18 of which are nuclear powered. We estimate that the Soviets will continue to build a limited number each year of both conventional and nuclear cruise missile submarines.

d. Manned Bombers

There is still no evidence that the Soviets intend to deploy a new heavy bomber in the late sixties. The force currently consists of some 200 heavy and 800 medium bombers, some of which are used as tankers. It is estimated that the Soviets will continue to maintain their heavy bomber force through mid-1967 although attrition would reduce this force to about 75 percent of the current level by the end of the decade. It is estimated that the medium bomber force will continue to decline gradually as older aircraft are phased out faster than the new Blinders are delivered.

As indicated last year, the Soviets' capability for intercontinental bomber attack remains limited. Considering the requirements for Arctic staging, refueling and noncombat attrition, we estimate that the Soviets could currently place only slightly more than 100 heavy bombers over target areas in the U.S. on two-way missions. While we believe that medium bombers do not figure prominently in Soviet plans for an initial attack on the U.S., a limited force of Badgers could attack targets in Greenland, Canada, Alaska and the extreme northwest U.S. on two-way missions.

e. Air Defense Fighters

The current operational strength of the Soviets' fighter-interceptor forces is estimated at 3,800 aircraft, of which more than 70 percent are older models. However, these aircraft are gradually being replaced by new generation fighters with both all-weather and air-to-air missile capabilities. There is also evidence that high-speed Mach 3 follow-on interceptors are in an early development stage.

f. Surface-to-Air Missile System

The SA-2 deployment within the USSR was virtually completed in 1963–64 with some 800–900 sites, less than we had previously estimated. However, there is evidence that through a successive series of modifications, the low altitude intercept capability of some of these sites has been improved to about 1,500 feet. The SA-3 system, estimated to have been designed against the low altitude threat (also 1,000 feet), continues to be deployed at a slow pace and is not expected to grow much beyond its current size of about 110 sites.

g. Anti-Ballistic Missile Defenses

We had at one time estimated that the Soviets were constructing an anti-missile defense system which might be operational at Leningrad as early as mid-1965 and at Moscow about mid-1967. Numerous indications point to Soviet difficulties with this program with a series of changes and modifications in related facilities and equipment at their test ranges. Activity at deployment locations has been sporadic, rather than part of an all out, high priority effort.

While we had previously thought that all these activities were primarily anti-missile defense oriented, currently the weight of the evidence suggests that two distinct programs are underway—a probable anti-ICBM system around Moscow, and a long-range surface-to-air interceptor missile system deployed across the northwest approaches.

The components of the probable anti-ICBM system around Moscow are a long-range exo-atmospheric intercept missile, the "triad" electronic facilities at several of the SA-1 complexes, the large phased array radar southeast of Moscow orientated toward our ICBM threat corridor, and the dual early-warning tracking radars sited at two locations on the northwest periphery. (The latter also have the capability to track satellites.) None of these facilities has been completed. An initial operating capability within the primary ICBM threat corridor might be achieved by late 1967. A capability against the Polaris would require at least another year or two.

With regard to the latter system, construction is proceeding at Leningrad and three additional places on the northwest periphery.

Considering the location, distribution, and orientation of these sites, the number of missile launch positions, and the apparent simplicity of the electronics facilities, the evidence suggests this may not be an effective ABM defense, although this conclusion is by no means certain. This system might be effective against high-performance aircraft, cruise missiles, and possibly have a limited capability against short-range ballistic missiles.

2. The Chinese Communist Nuclear Threat

There is no evidence that the Chinese Communist are currently engaged in an ICBM development program. However, as a result of earlier Soviet assistance, their technical and industrial capabilities would permit them to undertake a development program which could result in an initial operational capability in the early to mid-1970s. If they did so, it is estimated that they would develop and deploy missiles of the MRBM class, possibly in the late 1960s and early 1970s, before they deployed ICBMs.

The Communist Chinese currently have one "G" class ballistic missile submarine. It is estimated that a missile for this submarine could be available in the 1967–68 time period.

The Chinese also have bombers capable of delivering nuclear weapons:

Aircraft Type	Number	Operational Radius
TU-16 Badger	2	1650 mi.
TU-4 Bull	13	1450 mi.
IL-28 Beagle	270	500 mi.

It is estimated that a significant Chinese Communist nuclear threat to the continental United States will not develop any earlier than the 1975–1980 period.

3. Adequacy of the Strategic Offensive Forces for Assured Destruction

Although no one can state with any degree of certainty how a general nuclear war between the United States and the Soviet Union might evolve, for purposes of evaluating the Assured Destruction capabilities of our forces under all foreseeable circumstances we must assume that the Soviets strike first in a well-coordinated surprise attack. As shown in the table below, even if the Soviets in the 1970 period were to assign their entire available missile force to attacks on our strategic forces (reserving only refire missiles and bomber-delivered weapons for urban targets), more than half of our total forces would still survive.

	Total Forces	Total Surviving
Missile Weapons		
Number	[*]	[*]
Megatons	[*]	[*]
Bomber Weapons		
Number	[*]	[*]
Megatons	[*]	[*]

[* *entry in table not declassified*]

Of these surviving forces, [*1 line of source text not declassfied*]. The destructive potential of these forces in a nuclear attack [*less than 1 line of source text not declassfied*] is shown in the next table.

Soviet Population and Industry Destroyed as a Function of the
Number of 1 MT Warheads Delivered
(Assumed 1970 Total Population of 240 Million; Urban
Population of 140 Million)

Delivered Warheads	[*headings not declassified*]				
100	[*]	[*]	[*]	[*]	[*]
200	[*]	[*]	[*]	[*]	[*]
400	[*]	[*]	[*]	[*]	[*]
800	[*]	[*]	[*]	[*]	[*]
1200	[*]	[*]	[*]	[*]	[*]
1600	[*]	[*]	[*]	[*]	[*]

[* *entry in table not declassified*]

The figures on population fatalities and industrial damage have been revised on the basis of recent data. At the lower levels of attack, population fatalities are somewhat higher and at all levels of attack, industrial damage is lower than the figures used last year. The major change is in industrial damage figures and results from a redefinition of Soviet industrial capacity. Last year these figures were based on a combined index of War Support Industries and Gross Industrial Product. Since Soviet War Support Industries are very concentrated geographically, small numbers of weapons showed large percentages of industrial damage; the new figures are based on Gross Industrial Product only, a more consistent measure of overall Soviet industrial capacity.

The delivery and detonation of [*4-1/2 lines of source text not declassified*]. Beyond this point, additional increments of warheads delivered do not appreciably change the results. In fact, when we go beyond about [*1 line of source text not declassified*].

It is clear, therefore, that our strategic missile forces alone would be sufficient to inflict unacceptable damage on the Soviet Union, even after absorbing a well-coordinated Soviet first strike against our strategic offensive forces. Indeed, I believe that an ability to deliver and detonate [*less than 1 line of source text not declassified*] would furnish us with a completely adequate deterrent to a deliberate Soviet nuclear attack on the United States or its Allies.

[*2-1/2 lines of source text not declassified*] Thus, the strategic missile forces recommended for the FY 1967–71 period would provide an Assured Destruction capability against both the Soviet Union and Communist China simultaneously.

4. The Role of the Manned Bomber Force

Given current expectations of cost, effectiveness, vulnerability to enemy attack before or after launch, and simplicity and controllability of operation, missiles are preferred as the primary weapon for the Assured Destruction mission. Their ability to ride out even a heavy surprise nuclear attack and still remain available for retaliation at times of our own choosing weighs heavily in this preference. On the basis of the latest intelligence, we are quite confident that the Soviets do not now have, and cannot have in the near future, the ability to inflict high levels of pre-launch attrition on our land-based missiles, or any attrition on our submarine-based missiles at sea.

However, for purposes of analysis we have estimated the additional forces which would be required if our missile forces turned out to be less reliable and suffered greater pre-launch attrition than presently estimated. To simplify the analysis we have taken a hypothetical case in which our missile forces would be barely adequate for the Assured Destruction task, given the expected missile effectiveness and allowing no missiles for other tasks. (In fact, as I have indicated, our approved missile forces are much more than barely adequate for this task and therefore already have built into them a good measure of insurance.) The table below shows the cost of insuring against various levels of unexpected missile degradation by buying either additional missiles or bombers to attack the targets left uncovered as a result of the assumed lowered missile effectiveness. Against the current Soviet anti-bomber defenses we have measured the cost to hedge with B-52s armed with gravity bombs since the FB-111/SRAM would be a more expensive alternative. Conversely, against an improved Soviet anti-bomber defense, the FB-111/SRAM was used as providing a cheaper hedge than the B-52 armed with either gravity bombs or SRAM.

Costs To Hedge Against Lower Than Expected Missile Effectiveness
(Ten Year Systems Costs in Billions of Dollars)

Assumed Degradation to Missile Effectiveness (Realized/ Planned)		Cost to Hedge With:	
	Additional Missiles	B-52/Gravity Bombs (Against Current Soviet Anti-Bomber Defenses)	FB-111/SRAM (Against Improved Soviet Anti-Bomber Defenses[a]
1.0	—	—	—
.8	.8	1.3	5.4
.6	2.0	2.6	7.7
.4	4.5	4.0	9.6
.2	12.0	5.3	11.5

[a] Assumes the Soviets deploy somewhat less than the equivalent of a force of 300 F-111 with ASG-18, GAR-9 in the western Soviet Union.

Only when missile effectiveness falls to less than about 50 percent of the expected value are bombers more efficient than additional missiles for insurance purposes. Against current Soviet defenses, the B-52 G and H force is adequate to hedge against complete failure of the missile force for Assured Destruction. Against possible future Soviet defenses, we must be willing to believe that our missile effectiveness could turn out to be as low as about 30 percent of our planning value before we would wish to insure by bombers rather than by additional missiles.

Similar arguments could be developed with respect to greater than expected Soviet ballistic missile defense effectiveness. There, too, it would be necessary to assume very large and expensive Soviet ballistic missile defense programs before bombers became a preferred form of insurance. (Later in this memorandum I discuss the far less likely contingency where the Soviets simultaneously deploy a force of MIRVed ICBMs and a sophisticated ABM system.)

Accordingly, for the Assured Destruction mission, manned bombers must be considered in a supplementary role. In that role they can force the enemy to provide defenses against aircraft in addition to defense against missiles. This is particularly costly in the case of terminal defenses. The defender must make his allocation of forces in ignorance of the attacker's strategy, and must provide in advance for defenses against both types of attack at each of the targets. The attacker, however, can postpone his decision until the time of the attack, then strike some targets with missiles alone and others with bombers alone, thereby forcing the defender, in effect, to "waste" a large part of his resources. In this role, however, large bomber forces are not needed. A few hundred aircraft can fulfill this function.

The present strategic bomber force consists of some 600 operational B-52s and 80 B-58s. Some 345 of the operational B-52s are the older C through F models. Last year we had planned to keep these aircraft operational through 1972 by a program of life extension modifications and capability improvements, at a cost of about $1.3 billion. To keep them operational through FY 1975 would cost another $606 million for modifications, and even then we could not be certain about their life expectancy. Thus, these older B-52s will eventually have to be phased out of the force, leaving a total of 255 operational B-52Gs and Hs. These later models of the B-52 can be maintained in a satisfactory operational status at least through FY 1975 and the modifications necessary to ensure this have already been included in the previously approved program.

Shown in the following table are the characteristics of three aircraft which might serve as replacements for the B-52s, compared with the B-52C, the B-52H and the B-58.

	B-52C	B-52H	B-58	FB-111A+	FB-111M-3	AMSA
Maximum Speed (knots)						
at high altitude	495	495	1147	1270	1270	1270
sea level	390	390	610	790	790	790
Ferry Range (unrefueled) N.M.	7450	9454	4250	5320[a]	5960[a]	8800
Combat Range (1 refuel) N.M.						
All subsonic[b]						
Full Tanker	7400	9500	6602	7450	8150	9150
Down Loaded Tanker	—		5152	5950	6700	7750
Part supersonic[c]						
Full Tanker		—	4567	5400	7250	8100
No. of SRAMs	N.A.	18	N.A.	5	5	18

[a] With four drop fuel tanks, and 2,000 lb. fly away kit
[b] With 1,000 n.mi. low level penetration
[c] With 1,000 n.mi. high altitude supersonic leg

The FB-111A is a bomber version of the F-111 with the minimum changes required to make it suitable for the strategic bombing role. The FB-111M-3 is a larger version of the F-111. It would have a longer fuselage, a maximum takeoff gross weight of 130,000 lbs compared with 111,000 lbs for the FB-111A and would carry a crew of 3 instead of 2. It would also have about a 10 percent greater combat range. The AMSA is an entirely new and larger aircraft which has yet to be developed. The characteristics and cost of the AMSA were discussed in considerable detail in my memorandum on this subject last year.

The first operational FB-111s could be available in FY 1969 and the first FB-111M-3s about a year later. For a force of 210 U.E. aircraft, the FB-111M-3 would cost about $800 million more than the FB-111As, including development and production. The most significant operational factor in favor of the FB-111M-3 over the FB-111A is the availability of space for a crew of 3 instead of 2. The larger crew could spread the heavy workload and reduce the strain involved in strategic missions. The FB-111, however, would have essentially the same performance as the fighter version and could be easily used in that role. The FB-111M-3 would have less range with the same payload in that role because of its greater weight, and could not operate as efficiently from the shorter runways for which the F-111A was designed.

The Air Force proposes:

a. The production and deployment of a force of 210 (U.E.) FB-111As and the phase out of the 345 B-52 C-Fs.

b. The initiation of a contract definition phase for an AMSA in FY 1967 at an expenditure of $11.8M looking towards an Initial Operational Capability in FY 1974 at a total development cost of about $1.6 billion.

c. The procurement of short range attack missiles (SRAM) for the B-52 Gs and Hs as well as the FB-111A at an additional cost of about $400 million.

I fully support the first of these Air Force proposals. I believe, however, that we can safely phase out the B-52 C-Fs on a somewhat faster schedule than that proposed by the Air Force. I also propose to hold the FB-111A configuration as close as possible to the fighter version so that it would, indeed, be a dual purpose aircraft—strategic and tactical. The role of the manned bomber in the strategic offensive mission, as we see the threat today and over the next five years, simply does not warrant any large expenditure on new manned bombers at this time.

To hedge against currently unforeseen requirements to replace the B-52 G and H series with a manned aircraft capable of effective penetration against possible advanced Soviet bomber defenses, system studies and advanced development of subsystems suitable for an Advanced Manned Strategic Aircraft (AMSA) should continue. There does not appear to be sufficient reason to start an engineering development program for AMSA now because of the high cost of the system, and because the recommended bomber force offers adequate insurance against the range of threats for which we have any current evidence.

With regard to the Air Force's third proposal, no immediate decision to equip the B-52s with SRAM is needed until we have a more substantial indication of an improvement in Soviet low altitude terminal defenses. However, the capability to install SRAMs on B-52s should be developed.

Although not proposed by the Air Force, I also believe we should plan to phase out the remaining B-58 medium bombers in FY 1971 when the build-up of the new FB-111 force is completed. We now have 80 operational B-58s and this number would decline through attrition to about 70 by FY 1971. Their primary advantage resides in a supersonic dash capability. Once the FB-111 enters the force the uniqueness of this feature of the B-58s will be lost, and their contribution to the strategic offensive forces will become marginal.

In summary, the objective of forcing the enemy to split his defense resources between two types of threats could be performed adequately by B-52 bomber forces considerably smaller than those now programmed. However, introduction of a dual-purpose FB-111 would provide added insurance at a relatively small cost. A mixed force of B-52G-Hs together with some FB-111/SRAM now appears to be a reasonable choice since the SRAM with its low level standoff capability and range of about 25 nautical miles can force the enemy to build expensive terminal bomber defenses or be vulnerable to low altitude attack. Even against very advanced terminal defenses the small size and low weight of SRAM would allow the U.S. to saturate or exhaust the defenses with large numbers.

The cost of the manned bomber force I recommend compared to the cost of continuing the current forces is shown in the table below:

	FY 1967	FY 1971	FY 1975
	(Costs in Billions of Dollars)		
Current Force Extended			
Forces			
B-52	600	600	600
B-58	80	70	64
Cost (Cumulative '67–)		$8.6	$17
Recommended Bomber Force			
Forces			
B-52	600	255	255
B-58	80	0	0
FB-111	0	210	210
Costs (Cumulative '67–)		$8.4	$14

5. Adequacy of the Strategic Offensive-Defense Forces for Damage Limitation

The ultimate deterrent to a deliberate nuclear attack on the United States or its Allies is our clear and mistakable ability to destroy the attacker as a viable society. But if deterrence fails, either by accident or miscalculation, it is essential that forces be available to limit the damage of such an attack to ourselves or our Allies. Such forces include not only anti-aircraft defenses, anti-ballistic missile defenses, anti-submarine defenses, and civil defense, but also offensive forces, i.e., strategic missiles and manned-bombers, used in a Damage Limiting role.

a. Damage Limitation Against the Soviet Nuclear Threat

With regard to the Soviet Union, the potential utility of all Damage Limiting efforts, including the use of our strategic offensive forces in that role, is critically dependent on a number of uncertainties:

1. Future developments in their general nuclear war posture;
2. Their response to our efforts at Damage Limiting; and
3. If deterrence fails, the precise timing of a nuclear exchange as well as their objective in such an exchange.

In order to illustrate some of the major issues involved in this problem, we have tested a range of possible Damage Limiting programs against different possible future Soviet threats. In practice, of course, uncertainty about the direction in which the Soviet posture was developing would lead us to maintain a flexible approach, matching the scope of our deployment of forces to our evolving knowledge of the Soviet threat. Nevertheless, these cases help to develop an appreciation of the possible future costs and benefits of such programs.

For the purpose of this analysis we have used two hypothetical Soviet threats, the strategic offensive portions of which are shown below:

	1967	1970	1975
Soviet Threat Ia			
ICBMs	380	560	740
Bombers/Tankers	840	560	420
SLBMs	156	185	225
Soviet Threat III			
ICBMs	390	1040	1550
Bombers/Tankers	825	570	500
SLBMs	174	270	300

Threat Ia is basically an extrapolation of the latest intelligence estimates, reflecting some future growth in both offensive and defensive forces. Threat III is a large Soviet response to our deployment of a ballistic missile defense with much greater than expected growth in both offensive and defensive forces. It includes a large number of big, land-based missiles equipped with penetration aids designed to overwhelm our defenses. Threat III also assumes that the Soviets respond defensively to our Damage Limiting efforts with an extensive deployment of a reasonably sophisticated ABM system around 25 of their major urban areas.

The major defensive components of the four U.S. Damage Limiting postures considered in this analysis are shown below:

U.S. Posture Components	Alternative U.S. Damage Limiting Posture Against:			
	Soviet Threat Ia		Soviet Threat III	
	Posture A	Posture B	Posture C	Posture D
Nike-X				
Sprint msls	4896	10536	4896	10536
Zeus msls	544	1052	544	1052
Terminal Bomber Defenses				
SAM-D Btrys	47	74	47	74
Air Defense				
F-12 Interceptors	54	54	108	108
Cities w/Terminal Defenses	20	47	20	47

Postures A and B are tailored against Soviet Threat Ia; Postures C and D against Threat III. In addition, all Postures contain additional offensive missiles for Damage Limitation. However, because Threat III is stronger than Ia, Postures C and D would require more of these missiles than Postures A and B.

The interaction of the various Soviet threats and the four alternative Damage Limiting programs is shown on the table on page 18.[4] The program costs shown on that table represent the value of the resources required for each of the alternative postures. The costs for Assured Destruction represent the resources required to ensure that we can, in each case, deliver and detonate the equivalent of [less than 1 line of source text not declassified]. The costs for Damage Limiting represent the value of the additional resources required to achieve the various postures shown on the table. The last two columns of the table show the U.S. fatalities which would result under two alternative forms of nuclear war outbreak.

---

[4] Reference is to the immediately following table.

Costs of U.S. Damage Limiting Postures and Soviet Damage Potential

	Program Costs FY 66–75 (Billions of Dollars)		Soviet Damage Potential in Terms of Millions of U.S. Fatalities[c][d]	
	Assured Destruction	Damage Limiting Increment	Soviet First Strike	U.S. First Strike[e]
1970				
S.U. Expected Threat				
U.S. Approved Program			130–135	90–95
1975				
S.U. Threat Ia				
U.S. AD[a] Posture plus App'd Civil Defense Prog.	$16.8	$1.4	130–135	95–105
U.S. AD[a] Posture plus Full Fallout Shelter Prog.	16.8	3.6	110–115	80–85
U.S. DL[b] Posture A	16.8	28.1	80–95	25–40
U.S. DL[b]	16.8	35.7	50–80	20–30
S.U. Threat III				
U.S. DL[b] Posture C	28.5	24.8	105–110	35–55
U.S. DL[b] Posture D	28.5	32.3	75–100	25–40

[a] AD is Assured Destruction.

[b] DL is Damage Limiting. U.S. postures A and C include Nike-X deployments with Sprint defenses at 20 cities; postures B and D represent Sprint defenses at 47 cities. Other components of postures A and B are balanced against Soviet Threat Ia; C and D are balanced against Threat III.

[c] The higher fatality estimate shows the full Soviet damage potential for a well coordinated Soviet attack attempting to maximize fatalities. The ranges reflect variations possible in Soviet targeting doctrine, in technological sophistication, in possible errors in attack planning, and in uncoordinated or disrupted attacks.

[d] Rounded to the nearest five million.

[e] Assumed that Soviets do not launch at U.S. urban targets until after impact of U.S. missiles.

In the first case, we assumed that the Soviets initiate nuclear war with a simultaneous attack against our cities and military targets. In the second case, we assume that the events leading up to the nuclear exchange develop in such a way that the United States has no better alternative than to strike first.

The ranges of fatalities estimated in the table reflect some of the possible variations in Soviet targeting doctrine, technological sophistication, possible errors in attack planning and in the degree of the disruption to Soviet attack coordination. The higher end of the ranges of fatalities shown for each case represents the full damage potential (a well-planned, well-coordinated attack to maximize fatalities) under the given scenario. The lower end of the ranges of estimates represents likely degradations in execution and targeting, rather than lower bounds on the possible effectiveness of Soviet weapon systems. All estimates assume that the Soviets have missile penetration aids which are as sophisticated as our own are expected to be in the same time period.

The first line on the table shows the Soviet damage potential against the currently approved U.S. program in 1970. It illustrates the projected performance of the currently approved bomber defenses, the Civil Defense program and the strategic offensive forces. Without these programs, the damage potential could be 160 million or more U.S. fatalities in a mixed Soviet attack on military and civilian targets. A full Soviet attack directed against our urban areas only would not increase this total by very much.

As shown on the second line of the table, the situation is not substantially changed by the assumed Soviet buildup (Threat Ia) between 1970 and 1975. A Full Fallout Shelter Program, at a cost of about $3.6 billion would reduce fatalities by about 15–20 million in all three cases. Damage Limiting Posture A (cost—$28.1 billion) might reduce fatalities to somewhere between 80 and 90 million and Posture B (cost—$35.7 billion) to between 50 and 80 million in an early urban attack. But the benefits of these Damage Limiting programs could be substantially offset, especially in the case of a Soviet first strike, if the Soviets were to increase their offensive forces to the levels assumed in Threat III.

Even larger Soviet responses than that of Threat III cannot be ruled out by what we know of Soviet technology and resource constraints. Whether or how the Soviets actually will respond depends on how strongly they desire a reliable threat against the United States and on the alternative military and non-military uses for the resources involved.

Our own uncertainty about how well our Damage Limiting forces would work is likely to remain large. Some, but by no means all of the uncertainties are reflected in the table on page 18.[5] It is difficult to quantify the operational conditions of nuclear war. Degradations in our missile defense reliability or in our offensive missile accuracy might have substantial effects. For example, if our operational missile aiming error were 50 percent higher than we assumed against Soviet hard missiles, the expected Soviet damage potential after a [*less than 1 line of source text not declassified*] (even with Posture B) would be [*less than 1 line of source text not declassified*] U.S. fatalities instead of the [*less than 1 line of source text not declassified*] shown on the table. Even more important to the outcome of a [*less than 1 line of source text not declassified*] is the question of the speed and nature of Soviet response. We estimate that the Soviets have the ability to place their missiles on alert during a crisis, and, in the case of their hard missiles, to keep them at 5 to 15 minute readiness for extended periods. Accordingly, there is always the possibility that they might get warning of our attack and launch at least their ready missiles at our cities before the impact of our missile attack. In that case, U.S. fatalities, even if [*less than 1 line of source text not declassified*] and provided for Damage Limiting Posture B, would be [*less than 1 line of source text not declassified*].

The costs of the various Damage Limiting programs would, of course, be spread over a period of years. Even so, they would reach $5 to $6 billion per year in the early 1970s. To maintain or improve the postures shown (against an evolving Soviet threat) might involve continuing an annual expenditure of $3 to $5 billion.

On the basis of our analysis of the major Damage Limiting program alternatives in relation to the Soviet nuclear threat, I have reached the following conclusions:

1. Against likely Soviet postures for the 1970s, appropriate mixes of Damage Limiting measures can effect substantial reductions in the maximum damage the Soviets can inflict, but only at substantial additional cost to the U.S. above the requirements for Assured Destruction. Even so, against a massive and sophisticated Soviet attack on civil targets, we cannot have high confidence of reducing fatalities below [*less than 1 line of source text not declassified*].

2. Efficient Damage Limiting against the kinds of postures available to the Soviets, considering their technology and resources, requires a mix including a full civil defense Fallout Shelter Program, ballistic missile defenses, and improved bomber defenses. Against a very rapid buildup of the Soviet missile forces based in hard silos, additional U.S. missile payload may have to be added.

---

[5] Reference is to the table entitled "Costs of U.S. Damage Limiting Postures and Soviet Damage Potential," printed above.

3. Feasible improvements in missile accuracy, and the use of MIRVs where applicable, can greatly increase the efficiency of our offensive forces against hard Soviet targets. However, the effectiveness of offensive forces in Damage Limiting is sensitive to the timing of a nuclear exchange.

4. Assuming that the Soviet bomber threat will remain at least as great in numbers and sophistication as we currently estimate, a decision to attempt to achieve a significant Damage Limiting capability against Soviet attack would imply the inclusion, as one element of a balanced posture, of a force of improved interceptor aircraft. The choice between the F-12 and the F-111, and the desired force size would depend on the threat, the level of Damage Limiting effectiveness aimed at, and the timing of the decision.

5. Recent analyses suggest that a system employing long range exo-atmospheric interceptors (above 300,000 ft. altitude) in addition to lower altitude interceptors may complicate even a sophisticated attacker's ballistic missile penetration problem and improve system performance relative to the performance of an ABM system employing only lower altitude interceptors. However, there are still many unresolved questions about the design and performance of a system employing both exo-atmospheric and lower altitude interceptors.

6. Our offensive forces are likely to remain the primary agent for limiting damage to our Allies.

7. Dominating the entire problem of the extent and kind of efforts we should make to limit damage is the great uncertainty about Soviet responses to those efforts. Accordingly, we should not now commit ourselves to a particular level of Damage Limiting against the Soviet Union—first, because our deterrent makes general war unlikely, and second, because assuring with high confidence against all reasonably likely levels and types of attack is very costly, and even then, uncertain. Our choices should be responsive to the observed development of the Soviet threat and our evolving knowledge of the technical capabilities of our own forces.

b. Damage Limitation Against an Nth Country Nuclear Threat

During the last year, the potential of an Nth country nuclear threat to the United States has become more real and the feasibility of a defense against it more promising. As pointed out earlier, the Chinese Communists have detonated two nuclear devices and could develop and deploy a small force of ICBMs in the mid to latter part of the 1970s. About seven other nations are economically and technologically capable of producing nuclear weapons within the next ten years.

Obviously, the threat of greatest concern to the United States is that posed by the Chinese Communists. The development and deployment of even a small force of ICBMs might seem attractive to them as a token but still highly visible threat to the U.S., designed to undermine our military prestige and the credibility of any guarantee which we might offer to friendly countries. An effective defense against such a force might not only be able to negate that threat but might also prevent their use of nuclear weapons for aggressive purposes and possibly discourage their production and deployment of such weapons altogether.

Recent studies have convinced us that the development of an area ABM defense weapon is feasible and, indeed, we have reprogrammed some $22 million of FY 1965 funds to initiate this development. The area defense weapon, a long range missile interceptor designated DM15X2, would, of course, be used in combination with other components of the Nike X system. Furthermore, other elements of a Damage Limiting posture might also be required—anti-bomber defense, ASW, civil defense.

In order to illustrate the problem of defense against an Nth country nuclear threat, we have analyzed three Damage Limiting postures in relation to two levels of threat in the mid-1970s. The major ABM components of these postures are shown below:

Major Components of Illustrative Missile Defenses Against Light Attack

	Posture A	Posture B	Posture C
Cities With Local Defense	22	16	25
Major Components			
TACMAR Radars[a]	0	6	6
VHF Radars[b]	0	6	6
Missile Site Radars (MSR II)[c]	75	14	26
Area Interceptors	0	960	1176
Sprint Interceptors	3480	576	1088

[a] Austere version of multi-function array radars, with reduced tracking capacity and reduced ability to discriminate decoys.
[b] Included in this illustration as insurance for TACMARs.
[c] MSRs acquire targets for and control area interceptors, and control Sprint.

Posture A provides terminal ABM defense for 22 cities using MSRs and Sprint interceptors, but no area defense. Postures B and C both include an area defense of the entire country, based primarily on TACMAR radars for long range acquisition of targets, and area interceptors with high-yield warheads for long-range X-ray kills of re-entry vehicles. Posture B also includes terminal defense for 16 cities. Posture C provides terminal defense for 25 cities and a heavier area defense.

The effectiveness (and cost) of the defenses could be increased further by strengthening them in any of a number of ways. Against attacks employing no penetration aids, increasing the number of long range interceptor missiles might be preferred. Against more sophisticated or larger attacks, the number of Missile Site Radars might be increased from one to two at each point defended with Sprint, the capabilities of the TACMAR radars might be increased, or the number of cities with terminal defenses might be increased.

Defense against Nth country aircraft involves area protection—insuring that no enemy aircraft regardless of its target or direction of attack can be sure of success. A minimum defense could be provided by situating our current interceptor aircraft around the periphery of the country. The force required for the peacetime air surveillance mission would provide a relatively effective defense against small attacking bomber forces in the northeast and north central sections. For other sections of the country appropriate deployments of Airborne Early Warning and Control (AEW&C) aircraft could reduce significantly the probability of penetration. To achieve higher effectiveness, this minimum area air defense could be supplemented, first by improved surveillance capability—to insure against enemy aircraft approaching U.S. airspace undetected, and secondly, by the introduction of more advanced interceptors capable of intercepting attacking aircraft with higher probability, and further from our borders.

Fallout shelters are designed primarily to protect against collateral fallout from counter-military attacks, weapons aimed at other urban-industrial areas or weapons deliberately exploded upwind of population targets in order to avoid terminal defenses. The "area" defense described above might be very effective in denying the last of these tactics, especially against small attacks. The other two sources of fallout are also relatively much less important in light attacks. This suggests that, against small unsophisticated attacks, something less than a Full Fallout Shelter Program may be appropriate in a light Damage Limiting posture.

ASW might be particularly important in defending against Nth country threats. Submarine delivery of relatively short range cruise or ballistic missiles may represent the earliest form of a Chinese threat against the United States. Preliminary results indicate that currently programmed ASW forces are already adequate to handle any foreseeable Chinese threat. This problem is addressed in a separate memorandum on ASW.

Much more analysis of light defense postures is required before we are in a position to choose appropriate combinations of the various components.

To illustrate the potentials of a "light" defense, we have examined the cost and performance of Postures A and C against small ICBM attacks of the sort that the Chinese Communists might be able to mount in the latter part of the 1970s (approximately 10 to 25 warheads over the U.S.) (Posture B has been omitted since it is simply a scaled-down version of Posture C.) The results of this analysis are summarized below.

U.S. Posture	Five Year Systems Costs ($ Billions)	Millions of U.S. Fatalities	
		10 Attacking Missiles	25 Attacking Missiles
Approved Program (Extended)		6	12
Posture A	8.7	3	6
Posture C	8.2	0–1	0–2

The costs shown are for the ABM components of the program only; they include investment, operating and future R&D. The fatalities shown represent expected fatalities assuming missiles carrying the equivalent of 1 MT warheads. The lower bound of zero for Posture C represents the defense effectiveness against a very unsophisticated attacker or even an attack on major U.S. cities with a somewhat more sophisticated payload. The upper bound represents an attack (with the more sophisticated payload) designed to maximize the number of fatalities even if it means avoiding major U.S. cities. The table above does not deal explicitly with contribution of our offensive forces to Damage Limiting against Nth countries. Their contribution, however, would be substantial both in terms of the retaliatory threat they would pose and in terms of their effectiveness in pre-emptive counter-military strikes.

This table brings out two important points: (1) Posture C, which includes an exo-atmospheric missile, is far superior on a cost-effectiveness basis than Posture A which does not; and (2) the successful development of the exo-atmospheric missile would, for the first time, give hope of achieving a high confidence defense against a light ICBM attack, not just for a few selected cities, but for the entire nation.

The effectiveness of light Damage Limiting postures against future Soviet threats has not yet been analyzed. It appears clear, however, that the largest Soviet threats examined earlier in this memorandum could simply exhaust the defense in a Soviet counter-urban first strike. Against smaller Soviet postures, or Soviet attacks degraded in numbers or coordination by prior U.S. counter-military attacks, offense penetration aids and tactics might produce significant variations in outcome. Penetration aids such as re-entry vehicles hardening and exo-atmospheric chaff would have important effects for attack levels of about 100 to 200 Soviet missiles.

The problem of designing light Damage Limiting postures is not yet well understood. On the basis of information and analysis available at present I have reached the following tentative conclusions:

1. A light anti-ballistic missile system using TACMAR radars, exo-atmospheric interceptors with large yield weapons, and a terminal Sprint defense at a small number of cities, offers promise of a highly effective defense against small ballistic missile attacks of the sort the Chinese Communists might be capable of launching within the next decade. Such a defense would have initial investment and five year operating costs (including R&D) of about $5 to $8 billion, depending on the number of cities defended by Sprint and the density of the area coverage.

2. With such a defense the presently Approved Civil Defense program may be appropriate. Analysis is needed of the interaction of light active defense programs with Civil Defense.

3. It appears likely that such a defense would remain highly effective against Chinese capabilities at least until 1980, even if the presence of this defense did not, in the first place, deter them from developing a strong ICBM capability.

4. Once fully deployed, this defense system could be strengthened to increase its effectiveness against larger or more sophisticated threats—by adding more long range interceptors, by improving the TACMARs, or by increasing the number of cities with terminal defenses.

5. On the basis of our present knowledge of Chinese Communist nuclear progress, no deployment decision need be made now. But the development of the essential components should be pressed forward vigorously.

C. Adequacy of Our Assured Destruction Forces Against a Higher Than Expected Soviet Threat in the 1970s

At the beginning of this memorandum I noted that we had given special attention this year to an analysis of Soviet threats over and above those projected in the latest National Intelligence Estimates, and that we have done so because of certain recent U.S. technological developments which, if duplicated by the Soviet Union, could have a major impact on our Assured Destruction capability. I also stated that this capability is the vital first objective which must be met in full by our strategic nuclear forces under all foreseeable circumstances and regardless of the costs or difficulties involved.

Perhaps the worst possible threat the Soviets could mount against our Assured Destruction capability would be the simultaneous deployment of a force of several hundred SS-9 ICBMs equipped with highly accurate MIRVs and a reasonably sophisticated ABM system equipped with exo-atmospheric area defense missiles. Our MIRV re-entry vehicle [*less than 1 line of source text not declassified*] is already well along in development and we now propose to produce and deploy it in part of the Minuteman force. We have also started development of an exo-atmospheric missile. We believe the Soviets are developing an exo-atmospheric defense missile, but we have no evidence that they are developing MIRVs. In fact, we have no evidence that they have done much work on missile penetration aids, which involve a technology which we believe would logically precede the development of MIRVs. Past experience with Soviet developments of this type indicates an intelligence lead time of three to four years. However, the lead time for MIRVs might be significantly shorter.

Although we have no reason to believe at this time that the Soviets will actually deploy a MIRVed ICBM force and an effective ABM defense during the next five to ten years, the impact of such an action on our Assured Destruction capability would be of such significance that we must carefully examine its implications and take whatever measures may be necessary to hedge against that possibility.

Four paragraphs omitted in this copy.[6]

Our [*less than 1 line of source text not declassified*] can be translated into a requirement for [*less than 1 line of source text not declassified*] of delivered U.S. payload. Whether this requirement can be fulfilled by the programmed forces depends on the scale and technology of Soviet offensive and defensive forces, and on Soviet targeting doctrine. In the analysis which follows, it is assumed that the Soviets use all but 100 of their ICBMs against our land-based missiles and that they use their remaining ICBMs, their SLBMs, and their bombers against other military and civilian targets. Reliabilities, yields, and CEPs of Soviet weapons are assumed to have conservative (pessimistic for the U.S.) values throughout. We have also assumed that the U.S. would have no missile defense during the period under consideration.

---

[6] As on the source text. The text of these four paragraphs has not been found.

1. Base Case: No Soviet MIRVs, No Soviet ABMs, High Range of NIE on Missile Numbers

Soviet Missile Forces and United States Reliable
Payload Surviving Soviet First Strike

	July 66	Jan 70	July 72
Soviet ICBMs	350	738	800
U.S. Reliable Surviving Payload (KP)			
Minuteman	[*]	[*]	[*]
Polaris	[*]	[*]	[*]

[* entry in table not declassified]

In both 1966 and January 1970 the Soviets are assumed to execute high value (and high risk) attacks against launch control facilities. Such tactics maximize the expected Soviet kill of U.S. missiles. This factor has little effect in 1966 when the Soviet SS-9 CEP is estimated at 1.0 n.mi.; but in January 1970, with an SS-9 CEP of 0.5 n.mi., attacks on launch control facilities have a major impact and account for the relatively low U.S. surviving payload. By July 1972, all surviving Minuteman missiles could be launched by the airborne launch control center and the Soviets therefore would have to attack launch facilities.

In view of this apparent sensitivity to the availability of an airborne launch control center, an analysis was done for July 1968 assuming no airborne launch control center. Under these conditions, surviving land-based payload was reduced to [less than 1 line of source text not declassified]. With the Polaris contribution, this is still more than enough for the Assured Destruction task. The Soviet attack in this situation was concentrated on the Minuteman launch control centers and accounted for disablement of over 500 Minuteman missiles. This emphasizes the importance of timely development of the airborne launch control center. Funding for both development and procurement of this system has been approved.

In summary, the table above shows that the Soviets cannot undermine our Assured Destruction capability without MIRVs or ABM or unless they build many more missiles than the high range of the NIE.

2. Intermediate Case: Soviet MIRV But No ABM

Here we assume that instead of continuing to deploy new missiles, as projected in the high NIE, the Soviets level off at 650 launchers in January 1969 and begin to retrofit MIRVs on the SS-9, with as many as 15 re-entry vehicles [less than 1 line of source text not declassified] per booster. In effect, we give the Soviets the same IOC date for MIRV as we project for the United States. We also assume that the Soviets use the MIRVs against our land-based missile forces.

	July 66	July 69	July 70	July 71	July 72
Soviet ICBMs					
Total	350	650	650	650	650
MIRVed SS-9s					
(included in total)	0	25	100	150	200
U.S. Reliable Payload Surviving (KP)					
Land-Based					
1. No Soviet CEP					
Improvement	[*]	[*]	[*]	[*]	[*]
2. Very low Soviet					
CEP (at 1, 200 feet	[*]	[*]	[*]	[*]	[*]
Sea-Based					
Polaris	[*]	[*]	[*]	[*]	[*]

[* *entry in table not declassified*]

The table shows that if the Soviets *do* achieve a CEP of 1200 feet with their MIRVs, a force of [*less than 1 line of source text not declassified*] could wipe out our land-based missile forces. The extreme sensitivity of these calculations to CEP is illustrated by the fact that a force of 150 MIRVed SS-9s with a CEP of [*less than 1 line of source text not declassified*] rather than 1200 feet, would (in case #2 shown on the table) leave [*less than 1 line of source text not declassified*] surviving in 1971 rather than [*less than 1 line of source text not declassified*].

In summary, a Soviet MIRV deployment could pose a serious problem to the survivability of our land-based force, provided they achieve CEP improvements on the same schedule we project for ourselves. A Soviet MIRV deployment alone would not affect our sea-based missile force which, in itself, could deliver [*less than 1 line of source text not declassified*].

3. Extreme Case: Soviet MIRV With ABM

Here we assume that the Soviets deploy an anti-ballistic missile defense simultaneously with a MIRVed ICBM force. The ABM defense would consist of a force of about 4000 to 4500 exo-atmospheric area defense missiles [*less than 1 line of source text not declassified*], deployed in such a way as to counter most effectively a "rank order" U.S. missile attack against Soviet cities. (Such a force so deployed would be able to engage 3000 targets, provided the [*1-1/2 lines of source text not declassi-*

fied].) The Soviets MIRVed ICBM force would be the same as described in the Intermediate Case with a 1200 foot CEP. Again, we assume that the Soviets would use their MIRVed SS-9s against our land-based missiles. The results of these calculations are shown below:

	Jul 69	Jul 70	Jul 71	Jul 72	Jul 73
Soviet ICBMs					
Total	650	650	650	650	650
MIRVed SS-9s					
(incl. in total)	25	100	150	200	200
Soviet ABM					
Reliable Area Interceptors	800	1300	1900	2400	3000
U.S. Payload Surviving (KP)					
Minuteman	[*]	[*]	[*]	[*]	[*]
Polaris	[*]	[*]	[*]	[*]	[*]
U.S. Payload					
Penetrating (KP)	[*]	[*]	[*]	[*]	[*]

[* *entry in table not declassified*]

This case illustrates the effect of a hypothetical—very strong and very early—but possible Soviet threat. The assumed Soviet ICBM forces reflect the maximum feasible MIRV capability. Although the assumed Soviet ABM defense does not include terminal defenses, its effectiveness is overestimated since U.S. payloads are based on the currently programmed forces and U.S. tactics used in these calculations have not been optimized in the light of that defense. For example, if our attack were to be concentrated only on a part of the Soviet urban target system, the results would be much better for the U.S.

But, as I noted earlier, the simultaneous deployment by the Soviet Union of both a MIRVed ICBM force and an ABM defense would require major changes in U.S. strategic offensive forces since the MIRVs would degrade the effectiveness of our land-based missiles to a point where the ABM defense would become effective against the residual strategic forces, i.e., the sea-based Polaris. Although we do not now believe that the Soviets could achieve such a combined MIRV–ABM capability in the time schedule shown in the table above, or that they would be willing to incur the very high costs of such a program, it does lie within their technical capabilities in the decade of the 1970s. Accordingly, we should now take whatever steps are needed to place ourselves in a position to counter this threat if it should develop.

4. Alternative Hedges Against a Soviet MIRV–ABM Threat

In general, there are two broad classes of alternatives available to supplement our presently planned strategic offensive forces, if this should become necessary. The first is to proliferate hard, fixed-base missiles (such as Minuteman) with relatively low cost per unit of alert payload in inventory, but high cost per unit of payload surviving a Soviet MIRVed, low-CEP, ICBM attack. The second includes sea and land based mobile systems, and "super hardened" and "hard defended" fixed missile sites, which have relatively high costs per unit of alert payload in inventory and are relatively insensitive to the Soviet offensive threat. The characteristics of four of these alternatives are shown below:

	Payload (pounds)	CEP (feet)	Range (n. mi.)
Minuteman II	1,500	[*]	5,500
Improved Capability Missile	7,500	[*]	5,500
Polaris A-3	1,100	[*]	2,500
Poseidon	3,000	[*]	2,000

[* *entry in table not declassified*]

The ICM is assumed in the calculations which follow to be deployed in new, [*less than 1 line of source text not declassified*] silos. The Poseidon would be retrofitted into Polaris submarines.

The comparative ten-year costs of these systems, per thousand pounds of payload, are given in the following table for inventory missiles, alert missiles, and missile surviving the counter-military attacks of the most likely (NIE) Soviet threat and an extrapolation of the high, unlikely, threat discussed in the "Extreme Case" above. In this calculation, the low Soviet attack inflicts 10 percent damage on U.S. land-based forces and the high Soviet attack 90 percent.

Ten-Year Costs Per Thousand Pounds of Payload ($ millions)			
		Reliable and Surviving:	
In the Inventory	On Alert & Reliable	Low Soviet Attack	High Soviet Attack
Minuteman II	3.1	4.4	4.9	44.0
ICM	2.7	3.8	4.2	38.0
Polaris A-3	9.2	20.4	20.4	20.4
Poseidon	5.6	12.5	12.5	12.5

The costs of Polaris submarines and of Minuteman facilities have already been incurred and hence are not included. The Poseidon and ICM figures include development costs. The ICM costs are for a force of 600 missiles, while the Poseidon costs are based on retrofitting all 41 of the Polaris submarines. The Polaris and Poseidon costs are based on the 56 percent of the Polaris force which we plan to have on station at all times.

If the Soviets do not develop MIRVs and choose to emphasize ABM defense, or if they achieve a major breakthrough in their ASW capability, fixed-base missiles are generally preferred to mobile missiles. The Air Force is now studying the development of follow-on, land-based missiles of considerably increased size and payload which could be available in the time period with which we are concerned. One such missile, the above-mentioned ICM, could be retrofitted to existing Minuteman silos or be deployed in new, harder [less than 1 line of source text not declassified] silos. Even against the MIRV threat, ICM might become attractive if it could be effectively defended at a sufficiently low cost.

The U.S. response to a Soviet deployment of an ABM defense unaccompanied by a MIRVed ICBM force would be the incorporation of appropriate penetration aids on our strategic missiles. Against area defense interceptors, chaff cloud penetration aids can be provided for U.S. missiles (so that an Assured Destruction capability is maintained) at a cost to us of less than 10 percent of the cost of an ABM defense to the Soviets. The lead time for the Soviets to mount an ABM defense is greater than the time for us to produce and deploy penetration aids, provided we take timely action to develop them. A capability for employing terminal penetration aids is already being incorporated in our strategic missile forces. We now propose to develop area penetration aids for the Polaris A-3, the Minuteman and the Titan missiles, and improved terminal penetration aids for Minuteman III which will use the [less than 1 line of source text not declassified]. A decision actually to deploy these new penetration aids is not required now. If the Soviets do attempt a large ABM defense we will still be able to make appropriately timed decisions to produce and deploy the necessary penetration aids before the Soviets could achieve an extensive deployment.

Against a combined Soviet MIRV–ABM threat, it is clear from the above table that the most efficient of the alternatives available to us would be to develop Poseidon and retrofit it into Polaris boats. The timing of the development and of the decision to produce and deploy would depend upon how this threat actually evolved. To bring out this problem in its starkest form, we have assumed for the analysis which follows the same Soviet threat used previously in the "Extreme Case". The numbers of additional surviving, reliable Poseidon missiles needed to guarantee our Assured Destruction capability after FY 1970 are shown in the table below—using first, the MIRV re-entry vehicle [*less than 1 line of source text not declassified*] already well along in engineering development and second, using the advanced MIRV [*less than 1 line of source text not declassified*] which is in the early stages of advanced development.

	Jul 69	Jul 70	Jul 71	Jul 72	Jul 73
Soviet ICBMs					
Total	650	650	650	650	650
MIRVed SS-9s					
(incl. in Total)	25	100	150	200	200
Soviet ABM					
Reliable Area Interceptors	800	1300	1900	2400	3000
Additional Surviving, Reliable Poseidon Missiles Needed For Assured Destruction:					
With MK 12	—	—	[*]	[*]	[*]
With MK 100	—	—	[*]	[*]	[*]
Surviving, Reliable Poseidon Missiles Added If:					
Poseidon OAD/1969	—	[*]	[*]	[*]	[*]
Poseidon OAD/1970	—	—	[*]	[*]	[*]
Poseidon OAD/1971	—	—	[*]	[*]	[*]

[* *entry in table not declassified*]

The last block of this table shows the number of survivable, reliable Poseidon missiles which could be added to the force, time-phased for three different initial "operational availability dates (OAD)". In each case, [*less than 1 line of source text not declassified*] would be retrofitted with Poseidons; to retrofit the remaining 10 boats would be too expensive and other alternatives such as the construction of new boats might be more attractive. Considering the fact that we are dealing here with an extremely high and very unlikely threat, I believe that an initial OAD date of 1970 would provide us an ample margin of safety. Last year I recommended the initiation of the Poseidon development but without any fixed schedule. In the light of the foregoing analysis, I now recommend that its development schedule be tied to an OAD date of 1970.

5. Command and Control for Polaris

Although Poseidon appears to be the best hedge against an early, simultaneous deployment of MIRV and ABM by the Soviets, further study of the sea-based missile post-attack command and control problem is needed, especially if we are to place even more reliance on such a force. At present, the primary communication system for Polaris submarines in the Atlantic consists of two VLF transmitters and a number of repeaters dependent on them. These transmitters are extremely vulnerable, as is the command post at Norfolk, Virginia from which they are keyed. Emergency communications facilities are also soft, consisting primarily of HF/LF transmitters. [2 lines of source text not declassified]

[1 paragraph (13-1/2 lines of source text) not declassified]

A number of alternative systems are currently under study. However, it is not yet clear which of them offers the most promise for a survivable communications system, and a decision now to develop any one of them on a crash basis would be premature. Because of its importance to an Assured Destruction capability which depends heavily on a sea-based missile force, this study effort must and will continue to receive a very high priority.

D. Specific Recommendations on Major Issues

1. Qualitative Improvements to the Minuteman Force

The Air Force now agrees that a 1971 force of 1,000 Minuteman is adequate in context with the total U.S. strategic offensive forces now programmed and in the light of the expected (i.e., the NIE) threat. However, the Air Force also recommends the development of an Improved Capability Missile (ICM) for deployment in the FY 1973–74 time period as a replacement for some of the Minuteman. As brought out in the foregoing analysis, the ICM must be considered in conjunction with the Poseidon and in relation to the higher-than-expected Soviet threat. Accordingly the principal issue concerning the Minuteman force at this time is the production and deployment of new re-entry systems.

Last year it was decided to replace, eventually, all of the Minuteman I with the Minuteman II, which has much greater accuracy, payload, and versatility. Minuteman II, for example, promises a single shot kill probability against a [1-1/2 lines of source text not declassified]. In addition, its greater re-targeting capability reduces the number of missiles that need to be programmed to achieve one reliably delivered warhead. Finally, its booster is compatible with MIRV. For these reasons I recommend that all the Minuteman I's be replaced by end FY 1972.

The effectiveness of the Minuteman force can be further improved by the production and deployment of two new re-entry systems which we now have under development. One of these, the MK 17, promises a kill probability against [less than 1 line of source text not declassified] for the MK 11 now being installed in the Minuteman II. The other, the MK 12/MIRV, will [*5 lines of source text not declassified*]. The recommended force is shown below:

	1965	1966	1967	1968	(End Fiscal Year) 1969	1970	1971	1972	1973	1974
Minuteman I	800	800	700	550	400	250	100			
Minuteman II		80	300	450	550	570	600	700	700	700
Minuteman III					50	180	300	300	300	300

Specifically, I recommend:

a. Production and deployment of the MK 17 and the MK 12/MIRV re-entry vehicles at an FY 1967–71 cost of $122 million and $220 million, respectively. For FY 1967, $6.5 million will be required for the MK 17 and $10.2 million for the MK 12/MIRV for the procurement of long lead time items to ensure an IOC date of January 1969 for both systems.

b. Development and production of a trajectory accuracy prediction system (TAPS) for Minuteman II and III at a total FY 1967–71 cost of $48 million, of which $25.7 million will be required in FY 1967.

c. Production and installation of a Secure Status System, to provide cryptographic equipment at the Minuteman launch control centers and Minuteman launch facilities for the secure transmission of status information, at a total FY 1966–71 cost of $92 million of which $1.1 million will be required in FY 1966 and $10.4 in FY 1967.

d. Production and installation of a computer memory system which will allow routine checkouts to be performed in the Minuteman launch facilities, thus freeing the missile-borne computers for the guidance task. This additional computer capacity in the missile itself will be required when the MK 12/MIRV is installed on the Minuteman. The total FY 1966–71 cost is estimated at $77 million of which $2.1 million will be required in FY 1966 and $13.4 million in FY 1967.

2. Maintenance of an Effective Manned Bomber Force in the 1970s

The Air Force has proposed the procurement of a force of 210 (U.E.) FB-111As, the phaseout of the B-52 C-Fs, the procurement of SRAM for both the FB-111A and B-52 G-Hs, and the initiation of a contract definition phase for AMSA in FY 1967. For reasons discussed in the foregoing analysis, I make the following specific recommendations:

a. Approval of the Air Force proposal to procure an FB-111 force of 210 U.S. aircraft at a total FY 1966–71 systems cost of $1.9 billion (including $1.6 billion for initial investment), with the first two wings to be operational by end FY 1969 and the full force operational by end FY 1971. Some $28 million will be required in FY 1966 and $336 million in FY 1967 for the procurement of the first 33 aircraft.

b. Development and production of the SRAM for the FB-111s only, at an FY 1967–71 cost of $316 million of which $51 million will be required in FY 1967. These amounts include the costs of adapting the SRAM avionics for the B-52, thus retaining the option to deploy that missile on the B-52 G-Hs if that should prove desirable at some time in the future.

c. Phase out the B-52 C-Fs faster than recommended by the Air Force with an additional savings over the next five years of $800 million. The total savings compared with the previously approved program would be $1.1 billion over the same period.

d. Phase out the B-58s by end FY 1971 as the FB-111 buildup is completed. In view of this recommendation, I recommend that we not go ahead with the installation of a Terrain Following Radar on the B-58, as proposed by the Air Force, with an FY 1967–71 saving of $97 million.

e. Disapproval of the Air Force proposal to initiate a contract definition phase for AMSA in FY 1967, but approval of continuation of advanced development work on the avionics so that adequate technology will be available when and if a decision for full scale development work on the avionics so that adequate technology will be available when and if a decision for full scale development becomes necessary. This will require an additional $11 million in FY 1967. Prior year funds will be sufficient to complete advance development work on the propulsion system and the airframe.

3. The Character and Timing of a Deployment of an ABM Defense

As indicated in the foregoing analysis, there is no system or combination of systems within presently available technology which would allow us to deploy, now, an ABM defense with a reasonable expectation of keeping U.S. fatalities below tens of millions in a major Soviet first attack. Moreover, although our analysis suggests we could design an ABM defense with a high degree of effectiveness against a light attack such as the Chinese Communists may be able to mount some time in the late 1970s, the timing of the threat is such that a production and deployment decision can be safely deferred for at least another year.

Accordingly, I recommend:

a. Disapproval of an Army proposal for a full scale deployment of Nike-X at an FY 1967–71 cost of $12.7 billion and an FY 1967 cost of $212 million. The total investment cost of this proposal would be $15.7 billion and the annual operating costs about $861 million.

b. Continued development of the Nike-X system, including the development of the recently approved, long-range exo-atmospheric interceptor (DM-15-X2), at an FY 1967 cost of $403 million. ($22 million of FY 1965 Emergency Funds have been provided to initiate the DM-15-

X2 development.) This recommendation will give us an option to deploy a light anti-ballistic missile defense system designed against small or unsophisticated attacks if and when that should become necessary.

c. Continuation of the Defender program designed to increase our knowledge of ballistic missile defense, at an FY 1967 cost of $130 million.

4. Production and Deployment of a New Manned Interceptor

The major issue in the entire anti-bomber defense area is the production and deployment of a new manned interceptor. The Air Force proposes a force of 12 squadrons (216 U.E. aircraft) of the F-12 to begin deployment in FY 1969 and complete deployment by FY 1973. Although this force would provide greatly increased combat effectiveness, its very great cost ($6.6 billion in FY 1967–71 period) would be consistent only with a decision to seek a very large and effective Damage Limiting program against the Soviet Union, and then only if the Soviets increased their bomber threat in both numbers and quality. Neither of these conditions is in prospect at this time. Accordingly, I recommend:

a. Continuation of the YF-12A flight test program with the three aircraft now available. These aircraft have been equipped with the ASG-18/AIM-47A fire control and air-to-air missile systems, the performance of which is being improved with FY 1966 funds.

b. Continued study of the use of the F-111 in the manned interceptor role.

c. Continued efforts to define the Airborne Early Warning and Control System (AWACS) capability with a view towards the eventual development of such an aircraft.

d. Continued work on overland radar technology in support of the AWACS program.

e. Extension of the presently approved manned interceptor program through the FY 1967–71 period.

f. Continued development of the SAM-D terminal bomber defense system, primarily for field Army defense but also for potential use in CONUS defense if required.

These efforts will provide an option for improving our anti-bomber defenses, if they should be needed some time in the future.

5. The Future Size and Scope of the Civil Defense Program

All of our analysis indicates that a Civil Defense effort of at least the magnitude of our currently approved program ($150–200 million per year) would be an efficient component of any Damage Limiting program. However, we are still uncertain how many useful shelter spaces the present program will provide. We currently estimate the deficit at 74 million spaces by 1970, although the number could be much larger. If we were to eliminate this deficit, principally by providing dual-purpose shelter space in new construction, the total cost to the Government of a nation-wide fallout shelter program would be about $3.7 billion. Every increase of 10 percent above the estimated deficit could add $200–500 million to the cost of that program.

In any event, shelter construction lead time is shorter than that for the other components of a major Damage Limiting program. When and if we decide to deploy such a program, sufficient time will be available to provide any additional fallout shelters needed. Moreover, the prospect of an area missile defense for the entire country has reopened the question of the relationship between passive and active defense. If we were to decide to orient our Damage Limiting efforts primarily to the Nth country threat, it would appear that a large expansion of the Civil Defense Program would not be competitive with additions to the active defenses.

Accordingly, I recommend:

a. Disapproval of the Army's proposal to initiate a dual-purpose fallout shelter development program in FY 1967 at a cost of $10 million. A decision on such a program should be deferred until we know better the extent of the deficit and the direction which our Damage Limiting efforts will take.

b. Continuation in FY 1967 of a Civil Defense Program of essentially the same scope as proposed to the Congress for FY 1966, including: the small shelter survey effort; the Community Shelter Planning Program; architectural and engineering advice to private builders; the provision of ventilation kits to increase the capacity of existing shelter spaces, and the shelter provisioning program—at a total FY 1967 cost of $184 million.

6. Accelerated Development of New Penetration Aids

Although we still do not know whether the Soviets will actually deploy an extensive ABM system during the next five or six years or how sophisticated it might be, the adverse impact of such a deployment on the effectiveness of our strategic missile forces might be sufficiently great to warrant the installation of penetration aids on our missiles. This measure would be even more imperative if the Soviets were also to deploy a MIRVed ICBM force at the same time. Accordingly, I recommend:

a. Initiation of engineering development of area penetration aid packages for all Minuteman missiles and a terminal penetration aid package for the Minuteman III (which will use the MK 12/MIRV) at a total FY 1966–71 cost of $178 million, of which $24.3 million will be required in FY 1966 and $73.8 million in FY 1967.

b. Continuation of: engineering development of an area penetration aid package for the Polaris A-3; the development program to harden the A-3 re-entry vehicle to give it added protection against an exo-atmospheric defense missile; and the development program to provide a lofting capability for the A-3 missile system to vary its trajectory and make its interception more difficult. (A terminal penetration aid package has already been developed for the A-3 missile.) The FY 1967–71 costs of these development programs is estimated at $93 million of which $41.3 million will be required in FY 1967.

c. Provision of $30 million in the FY 1967 budget for the production of penetration aids for the Minuteman I and II, to be held in reserve until the actual decision to produce is made. This decision need not be made before September 1966. Production decisions on penetration aids for Minuteman III and Polaris A-3 need not be made until FY 1968.

7. Accelerated Development of the Poseidon Missile

For reasons discussed in the previous section of this memorandum, I believe it would be prudent at this time to place ourselves in a position to deploy a force of Poseidon missiles in the early 1970s if required. Accordingly, I recommend:

a. The full scale, accelerated development of the Poseidon missile on a schedule which would provide for its operational availability in 1970. The total cost of this development program is estimated at about $1.1 billion of which $210 million will be needed in FY 1967. No decisions on actual production or the number of Polaris submarines to be retrofitted with this missile need to be made now—installation of 352 missiles on 22 submarines would cost $700 million in addition to the development cost.

b. Initiation of engineering development of penetration aids for the Poseidon, at a total estimated cost of about $100 million, $10 million of which will be required in FY 1967.

c. Disapproval at this time of the Air Force proposal to develop an ICM (the development cost of which would approximate $1.3 billion), although study of this missile should continue.

104.   Memorandum From the Joint Chiefs of Staff to Secretary of Defense McNamara[1]

JCSM–807–65   Washington, November 6, 1965.

SUBJECT

  Nike-X Deployment Study (DEPEX) (U)

1. (S) Reference is made to:

a. A memorandum by the Director of Defense Research and Engineering, dated 16 October 1965, which requested review of the Army Nike-X Deployment Study (DEPEX).[2]

b. JCSM–589–65, dated 30 July 1965, which indicated a desire by the Joint Chiefs of Staff to comment on the Army Program Change Proposal (PCP) A–5–026, which requested $188.2 million for preproduction funding of the Nike-X system.[3]

c. A report by the Strategic Military Panel of the President's Science Advisory Committee (PSAC) on the "Proposed Army–BTL Ballistic Missile Defense System," dated 29 October 1965.[4]

d. A memorandum by the Secretary of Defense, dated 22 October 1965,[5] which provides instructions to the Director of Defense Research and Engineering pertaining to the antiballistic missile R&D program for FY 1967.

2. (S) As indicated in reference 1b, the Joint Chiefs of Staff have, in connection with their review of DEPEX, considered the Army PCP A–5–026 which requests the necessary resources to initiate the production and deployment planning required to meet the desired Nike-X initial operational capability (IOC) date of October 1970. Inasmuch as these are inseparable elements of the deployment consideration, comments submitted herein are consolidated.

3. (S) The Joint Chiefs of Staff believe that the requirement for an effective ballistic missile defense is a very real and urgent one. The existing and growing Soviet ballistic missile capability, the increasing probability of a Soviet ballistic missile defense deployment, plus the potential Chinese People's Republic (CPR) threat, all emphasize the necessity for proceeding with a US ballistic missile defense at the

---

[1] Source: National Archives and Records Administration, JCS Files, 4714 (1 Oct 65) IR 4060. Secret.

[2] Not found.

[3] Neither found.

[4] Document 101.

[5] Document 100.

earliest practicable date. The Joint Chiefs of Staff consider that the phased deployment concept for Nike-X, presented in DEPEX, represents a logical approach toward the attainment of the necessary capability. It would provide an initial defense against the over-all ballistic missile threat, permit controlled growth within fairly level budgetary expenditures, while providing the necessary decision latitude required for a program of this magnitude.

4. (C) The requirement for a balanced assured destruction and damage-limiting capability against the total threat remains valid and is a strong factor in any recommendation to undertake deployment of a ballistic missile defense. The deployment phasing proposed in DEPEX will permit parallel effort in other complementary systems to achieve the required balance in assured destruction and damage-limiting elements.

5. (C) The deployment phasing in DEPEX also provides a planning base and opportunity for continuing review by the Joint Chiefs of Staff and other Department of Defense agencies as decision points are reached for Nike-X deployment. The Joint Chiefs of Staff will address the subject of deployment of Nike-X in JSOP–71.

6. (S) The Joint Chiefs of Staff have reviewed the PSAC report (reference 1 c) and have the following comments thereon:

a. The Joint Chiefs of Staff believe that the type of limited capability system advocated in the PSAC report would provide an inadequate defense against the over-all ballistic missile threat and would fail to exploit available technology. A return to components of the earlier Nike Zeus system type proposed by the PSAC would not shorten the four-year span from production approval to system IOC but would result in deployment of an inferior and inadequate system.

b. The Nike-X system considered in DEPEX has been developed to overcome the widely recognized limitations of the earlier concepts of a ballistic missile defense system.

c. The Joint Chiefs of Staff do not agree with the recommendations of the PSAC report which would delay the IOC for the Nike-X system for at least another year. It is their view that PSAC has placed undue emphasis upon the limited threat of the CPR and has based its conclusions regarding ballistic missile defense upon incomplete military and political considerations that go beyond the scope of scientific appraisal of the Nike-X system. The Joint Chiefs of Staff consider that our strategic defense posture in regard to the Soviet threat could be placed in jeopardy by delay in the IOC of the Nike-X system. This is a military risk that should not be accepted.

d. The Joint Chiefs of Staff are convinced that the US national posture would be seriously impaired if it failed to consider and counter all aspects of the threat. It was for this reason that the Army's DEPEX study recommended employment of other defensive measures as well as

Nike-X. The PSAC report on the one hand seems to expect Nike-X to do this alone and on the other hand proposes a much less capable ballistic missile defense at some later date.

e. Failure of the United States to deploy a ballistic missile defense could be considered by the Soviets as an opportunity to redress the existing strategic balance which they could ill afford to pass by. Accordingly, the Joint Chiefs of Staff consider that our failure to proceed with a ballistic missile defense might well encourage the Soviets into further acceleration of their current offensive-defensive efforts.

7. (U) The Joint Chiefs of Staff have noted the instructions provided the Director of Defense Research and Engineering in reference 1 d, above.

8. (S) CINCONAD has reviewed DEPEX and concurs in its recommendations and additionally recommends that a Canada-US deployment option be adopted as a planning concept and goal. The Joint Chiefs of Staff are examining also a recommendation of the Chief of Staff, US Army, that Presidential approval be obtained for a program of cooperation with Canada for terminal defense against ballistic missiles, and recommendations on this option will be forwarded separately.

9. (S) For the reasons indicated above, and as stated in both JSOP–70[6] and reference 1 b, above, the Joint Chiefs of Staff strongly support the action required to preserve the option of attaining a Nike-X IOC date of 1970. As stated by the Army, the resources requested in the preproduction PCP are those required to maintain this option. Accordingly, the Joint Chiefs of Staff recommend that:

a. The Army PCP A–5–026 be approved with sufficient FY 1967 preproduction funds to preserve the IOC date in 1970 for the Nike-X system as outlined in DEPEX.

b. Phase I (BC) (US only) deployment of Nike-X, with provisions for Phase II deployment, be used for planning purposes as outlined in DEPEX.

c. The Nike-X deployment phasing outlined in DEPEX be used by the Joint Chiefs of Staff, the Services, and other Department of Defense agencies as the common base for studies and analyses pertaining to FY 1968 program developments to counter the total strategic ballistic missile threat.

For the Joint Chiefs of Staff:

A.H. Manhart[7]
Major General, USA
Vice Director, Joint Staff

---

[6] Document 43.

[7] Printed from a copy that indicates Manhart signed the original.

105.   Letter From Secretary of State Rusk to Secretary of Defense
        McNamara[1]

Washington, November 13, 1965.

Dear Bob:

I have reviewed the draft memoranda on the Five Year Force Structure for FY 67–71 which you forwarded to me on October 28.[2] As in past years, I am immensely impressed at the very high caliber of your analyses. I find these memoranda extremely useful in obtaining a better understanding of the current status of our force posture and likely future problems. In this connection, I would like to note that your staff, in particular Alain Enthoven and his people, have been most cooperative in providing us with an appreciation of the emerging problem areas.

I would like to comment on several issues which I believe to have major significance for our national security policy. The first deals with our NATO policy.[3] You and I continue to be in agreement that the position which the US has evolved over the past several years concerning the importance of a realistic non-nuclear capability in Europe remains an important tenet of US policy. In this connection, the further work which you are now having done within the Department of Defense to define more precisely both the requirements for and the capabilities of a non-nuclear military effort in Europe will undoubtedly prove useful. But the problem to which I believe we must both address ourselves is the priority of effort which we wish to apply to a series of policy issues which currently confront us within the alliance.

I know you are fully aware of the numerous problems which currently bear on our European relations. First and foremost among these are the German/nuclear sharing issue and the future role of France within NATO. Clearly these matters are so important that they should take first priority in our diplomatic relations with Europe. While giving primary attention to the solution of these problems, I agree we should

---

[1] Source: Washington National Records Center, OSD Files: FRC 330 70 A 1265, 031.1 White House PDM Oct 1965. Top Secret.

[2] Reference is to a set of draft memoranda from McNamara to President Johnson prepared during October 1965, which outlined the military force structure for the FY 1967 defense budget. (All ibid.) The memorandum on recommended FY 1967–71 strategic offensive and defensive nuclear forces is dated October 1. For text of a later version, see Document 103. The October 28 transmittal memorandum is in the Washington National Records Center, OSD Files: FRC 330 70 A 1265, 031.1 WH PDM Oct 1965.

[3] This issue was covered mainly in McNamara's October 13 draft memorandum to the President on "NATO and the United States Five-Year Force Structure and Financial Program." (Ibid.)

continue to pursue other important objectives, including those relating to what the US considers to be an appropriate strategy and force posture for the alliance.

However, we are not likely to persuade our allies fully to adopt our judgments on force posture, at least in the short run. It could be seriously counterproductive if we were to press our views with regard to emphasis on a major non-nuclear option to the point that it further complicated our political problems. While I personally cannot accept the point of view, there would be those in Europe who would question our resolve to defend Europe in the event of Communist attack if they interpreted our emphasis on a non-nuclear buildup as reducing the importance we attach to a nuclear deterrent.

I note that you feel that there may be some inconsistency in our retaining the current US military posture in Europe (or in CONUS-based support) if we cannot bring our allies to a full acceptance of our views on strategy with resultant major improvements to their own non-nuclear force posture. Despite the limited sympathy of the Europeans with our strategic views, we have managed to induce our allies to develop forces which do contain a capability for a considerable non-nuclear effort. This, together with our present nuclear options, represents a strong deterrent, and a significant war-fighting capability. While I agree that we should work toward elimination of inadequacies in our allies' force postures, it seems to me that we are going to have to accept some imbalances for the time being. Thus, I do not see that the threat to reduce, even less so, the actual withdrawal of a portion of US forces from Europe, as is touched upon in one of our memoranda, would serve our policy interests during the next several months while we pursue the German/nuclear sharing problem and the problems which will undoubtedly arise out of the evolving issue with regard to France's role in NATO.

I personally hope that full discussion of the nuclear problem in connection with the NATO nuclear force issue will serve to close the gap between us and our allies on strategy, particularly as the European leaders come to understand fully the issues involved in the use of nuclear weapons.

There are other related matters which bear on our NATO policy which are treated in your memoranda and on which I might briefly comment:

a. With regard to the constraints on a further tactical nuclear weapons buildup, I agree that the general guidelines established by NSAM 334[4] should be maintained. However, I would hope that we

---

[4] Document 90.

could have some additional clarification concerning the relationship to NSAM 334 levels of certain specific proposals, such as the ADM and 155 Howitzer programs, and any others you may see arising in the early future. My staff will be following up on these problems.

b. If the question of land-based MRBM's is again surfaced in NATO, it will be necessary for us to work out carefully the tactics for handling this matter with our allies. I gather you feel that the military case for such weapons is not persuasive. For our part, we see some political problems which would result from a land-based deployment of such weapons, though we have not recently reviewed our position on this matter. This is clearly an issue which requires continuing close contact between State and Defense. The outcome of current discussions on the ANF/MLF problem will have a bearing on this.

c. I agree in principle on the desirability of shifting the QRA role from aircraft to Pershings, as Pershings demonstrate the necessary capability, but anticipate this may raise certain political problems. At such time as you are prepared to make a specific proposal with regard to this shift, I would appreciate an opportunity to review it and to work out with you the precise tactics for presenting the proposal to our allies.

d. Your proposed command and control study seems to me to have very considerable merit. This question has generated so much interest among allied governments in the past, that any US study of this issue can be expected to arouse considerable attention in the future. Accordingly, I suggest that our staffs work out very carefully the terms of reference and the method for proceeding with this study, and upon its completion that we consider together its political implications before it is presented to NATO.

As a matter which bears upon our NATO policy but obviously has broader implications as well, I have been impressed by the increasing reliance which our strategy places on the ability to deploy US forces to various trouble spots around the world. I appreciated the degree to which your efforts have been directed toward improving the ability of the US to project its military power where it is required and to do so in ways designed to support our foreign policy. In the face of growing demands on US forces, I feel it is important that we stay abreast of the status of our deployment capabilities and accordingly, I have asked Alex Johnson to keep in touch with your staff on this matter.

The third major issue on which I should like to comment deals with damage limiting programs and especially the ABM. I want to make clear that I do not believe that foreign policy problems should in any way prevent us from deploying a system that could contribute significantly to the defense of the US at such time as you believe such a program is feasible and necessary. Nevertheless, there will be certain political problems that will have to be dealt with if a decision is made to deploy an ABM. As you know, the UK already has asked to discuss the political implications of an ABM deployment with us, and other countries have shown some interest. I would like to see us take advantage of the additional time afforded by the deferral of the ABM deployment to discuss the political aspects of the ABM program as it affects our allies. This will require additional studies both by State and Defense, and the joint development of a course of action. I propose that we address ourselves to that task without delay. I am, therefore, suggesting that Alex Johnson get in touch with appropriate people in Defense on this matter at an early date.

There are several other issues which I can only briefly touch upon in this letter, but I believe you and I should set aside time to discuss them at greater length, and I would hope in the fairly near future:

a. While we need to do some very hard thinking about how the military assistance program can be improved, the foreign policy significance of MAP is such that I would not want to proceed on the assumption that major adjustments in rationale, scope or content of that program can be made until such changes are thoroughly and carefully examined.

For example, in your draft memorandum to the President on this subject, certain conclusions are advanced about the ability to reduce reliance upon indigenous forces and the MAP support for such forces on the assumption of a changing threat and the further assumption that the growing US capability can to a degree substitute for indigenous forces. This issue requires very careful examination. The extent to which we wish to assume such responsibility, even provided the governments in question were prepared to accept such a change, is by no means a clear or easy issue to decide. Moreover, in view of the more immediate problems which appear to confront us in connection with meeting our overseas obligations (a point which I have alluded to above), it is not entirely clear to me whether or when we can assume such increased responsibilities.

A second major question concerns the relationship between the military aid which should be provided Pakistan and that for India. While I fully agree that the relationship between these two countries must be carefully scrutinized before we decide upon the content and levels of future military aid, I feel we cannot settle this question at the present time. This illustrates what to me is a very troublesome question about MAP, namely to what extent do we take any part in military efforts which might encourage other nations to engage in local arms races or to use violence in neighborhood quarrels. Until such broad issues are resolved we should leave open the specific MAP allocations to India and Pakistan.

I suggest that Alex Johnson discuss with Dave Bell and appropriate people in Defense how we might best proceed to examine in greater depth these and other issues which surround the military assistance program so that they might formulate proposals for you and me to consider at an early date.

b. I noted last year my interest in having a further exposition of the tactical nuclear problem as it affects theaters other than Europe. Particularly with our growing commitment in the Far East, it seems to me that we need a great deal more insight into the utility of and limitations on the possible use of tactical nuclear weapons in that theater. While your memorandum to the President on tactical nuclear weapons this year alludes briefly to this problem, I am convinced that a great deal more work needs to be done. Since the questions of tactical nuclear weapons so intimately relates political and military considerations, I believe this is an effort which might jointly be undertaken by State and Defense. I would welcome your views on this entire problem.

Finally, we would like to work with your staff, as in the past, on your presentation to Congress of the five year military program. My staff is available to be of as much help as possible in insuring that this presentation takes full account of the political issues involved in our relations with other countries. Perhaps we can be particularly helpful in working with you to develop the review of the world-wide situation which normally opens your presentation.

In view of the fact that I will be out of the country until November 24,[5] during which time I presume there will be further discussions on your draft memoranda within the Executive Branch, I am taking the liberty of sending a copy of this letter to Messrs. McGeorge Bundy, Charles Schultze and Dave Bell.

With warm regards,

Sincerely,

Dean[6]

---

[5] Secretary Rusk traveled to several Latin American nations en route to and from the Second Special Inter-American Conference at Rio de Janeiro. He returned to Washington on the evening of November 24.

[6] Printed from a copy that indicates Rusk signed the original.

106. National Intelligence Estimate[1]

NIE 11–3–65   Washington, November 18, 1965.

SOVIET STRATEGIC AIR AND MISSILE DEFENSES

The Problem

To estimate the capabilities and limitations of Soviet strategic air and missile defense forces through mid-1967, and general trends in these forces through 1975.

Conclusions

A. Confronted by powerful Western strategic attack forces, the USSR is sustaining its vigorous effort to strengthen its defenses. We believe that the Soviets are responding to those challenges to their security that they can now see or foresee from aircraft, ballistic missiles, and earth satellites. (Paras. 1–5)

Air Defenses

B. The Soviets have achieved a formidable capability against aircraft attacking at medium and high altitudes, but their air defense system probably is still susceptible to penetration by stand-off weapons and low-altitude tactics. The Soviets probably foresee little reduction in the bomber threat over the next ten years. To meet this challenge, they are improving their warning and control systems and are changing the character of their interceptor force through the introduction of new high-performance, all-weather aircraft. In addition, there are recent indications that the Soviets are now employing light AAA in some areas for low-altitude defense. (Paras. 3, 4, 8–19)

C. The Soviets probably will continue to improve and to rely on the SA-2 as the principal SAM system. We believe that they will develop an improved or new SAM system for low altitude defense; such a system would probably be deployed more extensively than the SA-3. Deployment of a long-range SAM system probably is now underway in the northwestern USSR and probably will be extended

---

[1] Source: Johnson Library, National Security File, National Intelligence Estimates 11–65, USSR, Box 3. Top Secret; Controlled Dissem. A cover sheet, prefatory note, and table of contents are not printed. According to the prefatory note, the CIA and the intelligence organizations of the Departments of State and Defense, the National Security Agency, and the Atomic Energy Commission participated in the preparation of this estimate. Representatives of CIA, State Department, DIA, NSA, and AEC concurred; the FBI representative abstained, the subject being outside his jurisdiction.

to other peripheral areas and to some key urban locations in the interior.[2][3] (Paras. 20–26)

Ballistic Missile Defenses

D. For nearly ten years, the Soviets have given high priority to research and development of antimissile defenses. We estimate that they have now begun to deploy such defenses at Moscow. These defenses could probably achieve some capability as early as 1967, but we think a more likely date for an initial operational capability is 1968. We do not yet know the performance characteristics of this system, or how it will function. (Paras. 27–34)

E. The Soviets will almost certainly continue with their extensive effort to develop ballistic missile defenses to counter the increasingly sophisticated threat that will be posed by US strategic missile forces. We cannot now estimate with confidence the scale or timing of future Soviet ABM deployment. We believe, however, that the Soviets will deploy ABM defenses for major urban-industrial areas. By 1975, they could deploy defenses for some 20 to 30 areas containing a quarter of the Soviet population and more than half of Soviet industry. (Paras. 36–37)

Antisatellite Defenses

F. The Soviets could already have developed a limited antisatellite capability based on an operational missile with a nuclear warhead and existing electronic capabilities. We have no evidence that they have done so. In any event, we believe that the Soviets would prefer to have a system which could track foreign satellites more accurately and permit the use of non-nuclear kill mechanisms. We estimate that the Soviets will have an operational capability with such a system within the next few years. We believe, however, that the Soviets would attack a US satellite in peacetime

---

[2] Lieutenant General Joseph F. Carroll, USAF Director, Defense Intelligence Agency, Major General John J. Davis, the Assistant Chief of Staff, Intelligence, US Army, and Major General Jack E. Thomas, Assistant Chief of Staff, Intelligence, US Air Force, believe that the many uncertainties stemming from analysis of available evidence does not permit a confident judgment as to the specific mission of the new defensive systems being deployed in northwest USSR. They acknowledge that available evidence does support a conclusion that the sites in the northwest may be intended for defense against the aerodynamic threat. However, on balance, considering all the evidence, they believe it is more likely that the systems being deployed at these sites are primarily for defense against ballistic missiles. [Footnote in the source text.]

[3] Rear Admiral Rufus L. Taylor, Assistant Chief of Naval Operations (Intelligence), Department of the Navy, and Lieutenant General Marshall S. Carter, USA, Director, National Security Agency, do not concur in the degree of confidence reflected in this judgment. Although they concur that the deployment activity is more likely a long range SAM system than an ABM system, they believe that the evidence at this time is such that a confident judgment is premature. [Footnote in the source text.]

only if, along with a strong desire for secrecy, they were willing for other reasons to greatly disrupt East-West relations.[4] (Paras. 38–41)

[Here follow the Discussion section Parts I–V, pages 4–14) and Annex (page 15).]

---

[4] Mr. Thomas L. Hughes, the Director of Intelligence and Research, Department of State, believes that the Soviets would conclude that the adverse consequences of destroying or damaging US satellites in peacetime would outweigh the advantage of such an action. He therefore believes it highly unlikely that they would attack US satellites in peacetime. [Footnote in the source text.]

---

107. Memorandum From Spurgeon Keeny of the National Security Council Staff to the President's Special Assistant for National Security Affairs (Bundy)[1]

Washington, December 10, 1965.

SUBJECT

    CIA Memorandum on Status of Soviet ICBM Force

The attached CIA memorandum on the status of the Soviet ICBM program[2] does not contain any new worries, and I am not really clear as to why it was issued at this time.

The estimates are essentially the same as those contained in the most recent NIE on Soviet Capabilities for Strategic Attack (NIE 11–8–65, dated October 7, 1965).[3] Actually, the specific estimate in the attached that, in mid-1966, there will be about 315 operational ICBM launchers (of which 90 will be of the new single-silo type) lies at the bottom of the range of 310–364 (of which 90–140 would be new single-silo type), as estimated for mid-1966 in the '65-NIE. The estimate in the attached of 440 launchers in mid-1967 is about in the middle of the range of 420–476 launchers estimated for that time in the '65-NIE.

The estimates in the '65-NIE were up somewhat from the '64-NIE[4] which estimated that in mid-1966 there would be 285–320 launchers

---

[1] Source: Johnson Library, National Security File, Intelligence File, TKH April–December 1965, Box 7. Top Secret.

[2] Entitled "Soviet ICBM Single Silos Nearing Operational Status," December 8; not printed.

[3] Document 97.

[4] Document 55.

and in mid-1967 there would be 330–395 launchers. The change in the '65-NIE reflected the firm information on the introduction by the Soviets of complexes of single-silo launchers which one might compare with our own Minuteman system. The numbers in the attached, however, are within the range predicted in the '64-NIE for mid-1966 and only 10 percent higher than the range predicted for mid-1967.

The Soviet build-up does of course make the option of a disarming preemptive strike less and less plausible. However, this has been recognized in DOD planning for a couple of years. As you know from the most recent DOD budget exercise, DOD planning has now passed far beyond numbers like these. We are now worrying about much more massive missile deployments coupled with possible Soviet MIRVs (multiple independent reentry vehicles) and the extensive deployment of a Soviet ABM system.

To give you a little perspective as to how bad things have looked in the past, I would remind you that the '58-NIE[5] estimated that the Soviets would have around 315 ICBMs in mid-1961, and that the '59-NIE[6] estimated that they would have this number in mid-1962, and that the '61-NIE[7] gave them this capability around mid-1964.

This isn't to say you shouldn't still be scared, but I don't see anything new in the attached to contribute to this emotion.

Spurgeon

---

[5] Presumably a reference to NIE 11–5–58, August 19, 1958; for a summary, see *Foreign Relations*, 1958–1960, vol. III, pp. 135–136.

[6] Reference may be to NIE 11–8–59, February 9, 1960; see ibid., pp. 325–330.

[7] Presumably a reference to NIE 11–8–61, June 7, 1961; see ibid., 1961–1963, vol. VIII, Document 29.

108. Memorandum From Secretary of Defense McNamara to the Secretary of the Air Force (Brown) and the Chairman of the Joint Chiefs of Staff (Wheeler)[1]

Washington, December 18, 1965.

SUBJECT

B-52 Airborne Alert (U)

I have carefully considered your reclamas on the discontinuation of the B-52 airborne alert.[2] A staff evaluation of your proposal is contained in the enclosure to this memorandum.[3] I believe that the very great improvements in the survival potential of our Strategic Retaliatory forces, resulting mainly from the deployment of Minuteman and Polaris, make an airborne alert no longer necessary. Moreover, in view of the improvements in our intelligence and warning systems since the airborne alert was established, I believe that the airborne alert is no longer the way to get maximum effectiveness out of the bomber force, even in the face of surprise attack.

This decision is intended to provide adequate resources to support B-52 training requirements. SAC should continue to fly the amount of airborne alert type indoctrination flights the Joint Chiefs of Staff consider optimum within the resources provided for the normal flying program. The airborne alert spares stockpile and missile (Hound Dog) spares need no longer be reserved for airborne alert.

Robert S. McNamara[4]

---

[1] Source: Washington National Records Center, OSD Files: FRC 330 70 A 1266, 381 (Alpha) A thru D 1965. Secret. Drafted by Ike Selin (OASD (SA)/SP) on December 10; rewritten on December 11, 13 (twice), and 14; and revised by McNamara on December 18.

[2] In a December 8 memorandum to McNamara, which responded to McNamara's decision to discontinue SAC airborne alert operations on July 1, 1966, Brown summarized the Department of the Air Force reclama (attached to his memorandum) as recommending the reduction of the airborne alert to the flying of "six aircraft on continuous alert with an on-shelf capability for one-eighth of the B-52 fleet for ninety days" and "a less desirable alternative which eliminates one year's provision of long lead items." (Ibid.) In a December 9 memorandum to McNamara (JCSM–872–65), the JCS made a similar recommendation. (Ibid.)

[3] Not printed.

[4] Printed from a copy that indicates McNamara signed the original.

109.   **Memorandum From Acting Director of Central Intelligence Helms to the President's Special Assistant for National Security Affairs (Bundy)**

Washington, December 28, 1965.

[Source: Johnson Library, National Security File, Subject File, President's Foreign Intelligence Advisory Board, Box 41. Secret. 2 pages of source text not declassified.]

---

110.   **Editorial Note**

Despite initial opposition from the Joint Chiefs of Staff, during 1964 and 1965 the civilian leadership in the Department of Defense proceeded to develop plans for the construction of a Deep Underground Command Center (DUCC) in the Washington, D.C., area and continued to ask the Joint Chiefs of Staff for their views. Regarding this internal debate and the evolving plans on this issue, see Documents 3, 4, 52, 77, and 92.

The Department of Defense also promoted this project in Congress, and included funds for further research on the specific size, operations, and functions and for its construction in the Army's portion of the military construction authorization bills in early 1964. Aware of the Joint Chiefs of Staff's reservations and believing the issues were too complex and sensitive, the House Armed Services Committee did not approve funds for the Deep Underground Command Center but instead created a special subcommittee to study the issue thoroughly. (Memorandum from Deputy Director of Defense Research and Engineering Eugene G. Fubini to Deputy Secretary Vance, February 25, 1964; Washington National Records Center, OSD Files: FRC 330 70 A 4662, 381 DUCC (10 Jan 64) 1963 and 64 Papers) The appropriations for FY 1965 as enacted by the Congress did not include funds for construction or research for this facility, and the chairmen of key Congressional committees also rejected the Department of Defense proposal to use other authorized funds for feasibility studies. (Letters from Vance to Representative George H. Mahon, September 30, 1964, and to Senator Carl Vinson, October 1,

1964; letter from Vinson to Vance, October 1, 1964; letter from Mahon to Vance, October 6, 1964; and letter from Senator Carl Hayden to McNamara, October 9, 1964; all ibid.)

The Department of Defense deferred action temporarily (letter from Vance to Vinson, October 9; ibid.) but continued to study the cost and configuration of the proposed facility. In early 1965, for instance, the Office of the Director of Defense Research and Engineering made tentative recommendations for possible sites. (Memorandum from James M. Bridges, Special Assistant (Command and Control), to Harold Brown, March 4, 1965; ibid., 381 1966) A large map of the Washington, D.C., area outlining proposed layouts for the DUCC, and a table comparing tunnel length for two DUCC configurations are attached to a March 8 memorandum to Brown. (Ibid.)

The House Armed Services Committee reduced the Defense Department's FY 1966 request for $26.2 million for the DUCC to $6 million, which would permit the Pentagon "to more fully develop plans and to again present the actual construction authorization request" next year. (Letter from Congressman L. Mendel Rivers to McNamara, May 25; ibid.; FRC 330 70 A 4443, 381 DUCC (10 Jan 66) 1965 & 1966 Papers)

In its response, the Department of Defense informed the House Committee that it proposed, among other things, to dig one shaft to "advance both the design and construction time and permit research and development efforts associated with the rock properties at the site to proceed concurrently. This would permit us to obtain early verification of our current estimates of subsurface rock conditions (based on preliminary test drillings) which have a direct bearing upon the cost and technical problems associated with the major construction of entrance and exit tunnels and the main underground facility." (Letter from Assistant Secretary of Defense (Installations and Logistics) Paul R. Ignatius to Rivers, June 14; ibid.)

Nevertheless, the Department of Defense's interest in the project gradually waned. When, for example, the Joint Chiefs of Staff proposed to obtain, among other things, the President's views "as to the nonmilitary functional and personnel requirements of those departments and agencies of the National Government" to be provided for in the DUCC, they were much later informed that no response would be made to their proposal. (JCSM–985–64 to Secretary McNamara, November 27, 1964, and memorandum from Maurice W. Roche to the JCS, August 10, 1965; both ibid., FRC 330 70 A 4662, 381 1966)

Moreover, Congress authorized only $4 million for this project in FY 1966, and letters from four Committee Chairmen told the Defense Department "not to go ahead with any designs without

Congressional approval." (Memorandum from Assistant Secretary of Defense Robert N. Anthony to McNamara, February 16, 1966; ibid., FRC 330 70 A 4443, 381 DUCC (10 Jan 66) 1965 & 1966 Papers) Although McNamara had earlier approved an FY 1967 request to Congress for $21,898,000 for the DUCC, he expressed "doubt that we should proceed to spend $4 million until after Congress acts on '67" (handwritten note to Ignatius, February 18, on Anthony's February 16 memorandum), and he shortly decided not to seek Congressional clearance for continued planning for the DUCC project and agreed to divert the Army specialists engaged on the DUCC to other military construction projects. (Handwritten notation, March 3, on Ignatius' memorandum to McNamara, February 25; ibid.)

Congress again failed to provide funding for the Deep Underground Command Center in the Department of Defense budget for FY 1966, but Vance agreed to ask the Congress to authorize FY 1967 funds for early initiation of work on the facility. (Memorandum from Ignatius to Vance, April 15, and unsigned April 15 note from Vance's office to Ignatius; both ibid., FRC 330 70 A 4662, 381 1966) Nothing seemed to come of this initiative, however, and no later documentation on the Deep Underground Command Center has been found.

111.   Memorandum by the Deputy Secretary of Defense (Vance)[1]

Washington, January 6, 1966.

MEMORANDUM FOR

The Secretaries of the Military Departments
The Chairman, Joint Chiefs of Staff
The Director of Defense Research & Engineering
The Assistant Secretaries of Defense
The Assistants to the Secretary of Defense
The Director, Defense Intelligence Agency

SUBJECT

DoD Human Resources Intelligence Collection Study and Outline Plan (U)

REFERENCES

(a) JCSM–422–65, subject as above, dated 29 May 1965[2]
(b) DoD Directive 5105.21, "Defense Intelligence Agency," dated 1 August 1961[3]
(c) DoD Directive TS–5105.29 "Defense Intelligence Agency (Intelligence Activities)," dated 21 February 1963[3]

I have reviewed the Defense Intelligence Agency (DIA) Study and Plan on Human Resources Intelligence (HUMINT) Collection which was forwarded by reference (a).

The Outline Plan contained in reference (a) is approved. DIA will assume technical direction and coordination of HUMINT activities within DoD. I expect that implementation of the approved Outline Plan will result in resource economies in the form of an increased scope of HUMINT operations or in a release of resources for use in other Defense programs.

The Department of the Army will assume responsibility for conducting over-all DoD individual HUMINT training in accordance with policies and instructions promulgated by DIA under provisions of reference (b). Authorities and responsibilities set forth in reference (c) remain unchanged.

---

[1] Source: Washington National Records Center, OSD Files: FRC 330 70 A 6649, 350.09 1966 Jan– . Top Secret.

[2] Entitled "DOD Human Resources Intelligence Collection Study and Outline Plan." (National Archives and Records Administration, RG 218, JCS Files, 2010 (11 Dec 64) IR 5156) The Outline Plan itself, however, is not attached to this JCSM and was not found. JCSM–422–65 gives among other things a general description of the contents of the Plan: Volume I "summarizes the study and the appraisal of the subject area listing conclusions and recommendations;" Volumes II and III provide a "thorough examination of human resource intelligence collection activities;" and Volume IV contains the Plan, which "provides for the definition of optimum resource levels and the maintenance of balance on a continuing basis among the related DOD organizational units."

[3] Not found.

The Secretary of the Army, in collaboration with the Secretaries of the Navy and Air Force, is requested to develop a plan for DoD-wide HUMINT training within 120 days. A copy of the completed plan should be provided the Joint Chiefs of Staff for their comments.

I endorse the Study finding that the successful accomplishment of sensitive HUMINT missions will be mainly dependent upon the caliber of personnel assigned to the program. Consequently, I wish to underscore the importance of assuring that only highly competent personnel are assigned to HUMINT duties by the military departments, DIA, and other DoD components involved.

Cyrus Vance

---

112. Memorandum From Secretary of Defense McNamara to the Chairman of the Joint Chiefs of Staff (Wheeler)[1]

Washington, January 22, 1966.

SUBJECT

Minuteman Force Posture (U)

In my draft memorandum for the President on Strategic Offensive and Defensive Nuclear Forces, dated October 16, 1965,[2] the planning figures of 700 Minuteman II and 300 Minuteman III were used. These figures were based on an extrapolation to 1970 of the present Soviet target system and the present philosophy that underlies the US Single Integrated Operations Plan (SIOP). The calculations that lead to these figures take proper account of other programmed U.S. strategic forces in the same time period, e.g., the Polaris force. However, no account has yet been taken in these calculations of the implications of possible Soviet anti-ballistic missile (ABM) defenses.

The immediate questions that should be answered this year are:

---

[1] Source: Washington National Records Center, OSD Files: FRC 330 70 A 4443, 381 SRF 1966. Secret. Drafted by Ike Selin (OASD(SA)SP) on January 3 and rewritten by F.S. Hoffman on January 12. An attached January 21 covering memorandum from Enthoven to McNamara further explains the purpose of the studies proposed in the memorandum and recommends McNamara's signature.

[2] Not found; for text of the November 1, 1965, draft memorandum, see Document 103.

1. What is a proper mix of Minuteman II and Minuteman III missiles, and hence how may MK 12 and MK 17 re-entry vehicles should be procured for use on Minuteman missiles?

2. How should penetration aids to accompany MK 12 re-entry vehicles be distributed through the Minuteman III force, against various possible Soviet ABM threats?

Clearly, these are complex questions. Overall U.S missile force postures will depend on the types of Soviet ABMs we assume. The distribution of Minuteman II/Minuteman III will depend on the Polaris/Poseidon mix, and will be affected by possible development and eventual deployment of a small re-entry vehicle of the MK 100 type for Minuteman. Perhaps most importantly, the desirable mix of Minuteman II/Minuteman III will depend on the strategic objectives we assign to the U.S. offensive forces, as reflected in the type of SIOP assumed to govern the use of these forces in the time periods and environments of interest.

In addition to providing very important source material for rather near-term Minuteman force posture decisions, I expect that a study of these questions would be of significant aid in a number of other areas:

a. Strategic Operations against ABMs, including use of TAPS and other elements of a Minuteman control system.

b. Design of MIRVs that might have to be used against hard targets as well as against defended cities.

c. Compatibility of Assured Destruction and of Damage Limiting criteria in designing force postures that include MIRVs and that must penetrate ABMs.

I should like you to perform such a study in stages. The first stage will be to consider the types of SIOP, and hence the type of SIOP guidance, that might seem appropriate for the employment of U.S. missile forces against a Soviet target list protected by ABM defenses. To be specific, I suggest you consider SIOP guidance for the programmed U.S. forces at end FY 1971, against National Intelligence Estimates of Soviet strategic offensive forces and two Soviet ABM threats:

1. An ABM deployment consisting of some 1,000 area interceptors;

2. An ABM deployment consisting of some 1,000 area interceptors plus 1,000 terminal interceptors, deployed at the 25 largest Soviet cities in rough proportion to their population.

The second stage will be to carry out two calculations:

1. A simple, pilot analysis of the performance of the programmed force, against the particular ABM threat and in the face of a specific Soviet attack. The programmed force would be operated under the SIOP guidance resulting from Stage I of the study.

2. An Assured Destruction calculation to measure the number of fatalities that could be inflicted by this U.S. force against the same

Soviet threat if the entire U.S. force were applied to Soviet urban-industrial targets.

After my review of the results of the first two stages, I would like to specify a small number of alternative combinations of U.S. force postures, Soviet offensive threats and ABMs, and scenarios. For each such combination, an evaluation of both the Damage-Limiting capability and of the Assured-Destruction capability of each U.S. posture will be requested.

I would like to receive the SIOP guidance requested above, together with the rationale behind it, by February 15, 1966. This discussion may assume a good knowledge of the present SIOP on the part of my staff. It should discuss how a SIOP in the face of an ABM would differ from our present plan. It can be in outline form, but it should be complete enough to allow a simulated laydown of arbitrary mixes of the U.S. strategic weapons available in 1971, against a Soviet target list of the size and structure that might be predicted for that time on the basis of National Intelligence Estimates. For this purpose, details of the assumed Soviet SBM are not highly relevant. Much more important are questions of targeting philosophy, such as, for instance, the desirability of attacking ABM radars as part of a counter-military task, and the desirability of choosing urban-industrial targets on a rank-order basis, instead of on a basis of maximum total fatalities.

Robert S. McNamara[3]

---

[3] Printed from a copy that indicates McNamara signed the original.

---

113.   Letter From the Ambassador at Large (Thompson) to the Assistant Secretary of Defense for International Security Affairs (McNaughton)[1]

Washington, February 1, 1966.

Dear John:

The Secretary has concluded that we should give consideration to offering the Russians a reciprocal exchange of information on our

---

[1] Source: Johnson Library, National Security File, Subject File, Nuclear Weapons, USSR, Vol. I, Box 34. Secret.

respective procedures for insuring control of nuclear weapons. Although it is obvious that propaganda underlies the clamor recently raised by the Soviets alleging inadequacies of American control over nuclear weapons stockpiled with Allied forces, it is possible that the top Soviet leaders are not fully aware of the extensiveness and effectiveness of these controls. We doubt that the Russians would agree to such an exchange of information, but the very fact of such an offer on our part would provide us with a counter to their propaganda charges of alleged neglect toward nuclear control. They would also be aware that unwillingness to discuss their own procedures would increase their vulnerability on this propaganda front. Finally, raising the idea of such an exchange might also cause the top leaders to familiarize themselves more thoroughly with our procedures, and might even lead them to review and to tighten their own arrangements.

We therefore believe that we should consider making such an offer, in terms which would put on record a reaffirmation of the seriousness with which we regard the problem and a refutation of their erroneous statements regarding our controls. In case of Soviet acceptance of the offer, we believe it should be possible to provide information—without disclosing data which must be kept secret—which will strengthen our case, we may elicit some useful information from the Soviet Union, and we would have opened a dialogue in an area of important mutual concern. We believe it would be possible to engage in such an exchange without getting into questions about aspects of our custodial control procedures which might be unconvincing to the Russians; it is clear that they will not be so forthcoming with respect to their own arrangements, if, indeed, they will discuss them at all—as to place us in the position of being more reticent than they. If they do not agree to a reciprocal exchange of information, as is likely, we can still provide them information on our control procedures if we wish.

While the Soviets have placed the main emphasis in their propaganda on our nuclear weapons stockpiled with and for the use of Allied forces, we believe it would be preferable to focus our comments on the general subject of insuring Presidential control, so as not to accentuate questions of trust with respect to Allies. (This would, incidentally, also blunt Soviet suspicion that we were only attempting to smoke out questions of Warsaw Pact nuclear supporting arrangements.)

Enclosed are a draft note proposing such an exchange; and an illustrative draft of a statement[2] setting forth some information on our control arrangements, which could be passed to the Soviet Government.

---

[2] Neither printed.

We would of course want to inform such Allies as Germany and the United Kingdom in the first instance, and NAC, in advance.

I would appreciate Defense's comments and concurrence on the proposition and the enclosed drafts.

Sincerely,

Tommy

---

114.   **Memorandum From R.C. Bowman of the National Security Council Staff to the President's Special Assistant for National Security Affairs (Bundy)[1]**

Washington, February 9, 1966.

SUBJECT

    AEC Review of Nuclear Control Procedures

Commissioner Palfrey has indicated to Chuck Johnson that he intends to approach you personally for a reconsideration of your decision not to give the AEC [less than 1 line of source text not declassified].[2] It might be just as well to take care of this before you leave.[3]

As I mentioned in my last memo,[4] there are indications that the AEC intends to make a major move into the area of Presidential control. They are currently holding up the [3 lines of source text not declassified].

The [less than 1 line of source text not declassified] is a classic case in that it raises all of the key issues in the area of Presidential control.

---

[1] Source: Johnson Library, National Security File, Subject File, Nuclear Weapons, Dispersals (General), Vol. I, Box 33. Top Secret; Closely Held. A handwritten note by Bromley Smith reads: "Bundy handled by phone with Seaborg."

[2] Reference is to two agreements on nuclear warheads for Canadian forces in Canada and Europe negotiated in August and September 1963. See Foreign Relations, 1961–1963, vol. XIII, Document 455, footnote 2.

[3] Reference is to Bundy's planned resignation as the Special Assistant to the President for National Security Affairs at the end of February.

[4] Presumably a reference to Bowman's December 2, 1965, memorandum to Bundy, which presented four options on this issue and asked for guidance from Bundy, who was "the only one with access to all of the info on the Presidential command and control arrangements." (Johnson Library, National Security File, Subject File, Nuclear Weapons, Canada, Vol. I, Box 33)

344 Foreign Relations, 1964–1968, Volume X

[*5 paragraphs (10 lines of source text) not declassified*]

Since the [*less than 1 line of source text not declassified*] is dealing with defensive weapons, these questions are less critical in this context. But the release of this Agreement with its comprehensive list of issues might open up a great debate over the President's emergency powers.

As you are aware, the [*less than 1 line of source text not declassified*] provides for [*8 lines of source text not declassified*].

A letter from the Deputy Secretary of Defense to the President on 6 December 1963[5] indicated that it was the view of State, Defense and Justice that [*6 lines of source text not declassified*].

If the AEC were given access to the [*less than 1 line of source text not declassified*] they might challenge [*7 lines of source text not declassified*].

As you are aware, [*6 lines of source text not declassified*].

Recommend that you dissuade the AEC from further efforts to review Presidential command arrangements and confine their activities to safety provisions for the weapons in the field.

RCB

I conclude that the President and SecDef must themselves serve as the reviewing authority for Presidential nuclear control procedures. This is one of those rare cases in which national security will not permit any further checks and balances.[6]

---

[5] Not found.

[6] The postscript is handwritten.

115.   Memorandum From the Deputy Under Secretary of State for
        Political Affairs (Johnson) to the Assistant Secretary of
        Defense for International Security Affairs (McNaughton)[1]

Washington, February 17, 1966.

SUBJECT

    Special Committee[2]

    Attached is a copy of the minutes of our Strategy Discussion Group
Meeting last Tuesday. I thought that this was a very useful discussion as
it enabled us to get on the table some of the issues that have been concerning all of us with respect to the future direction of the Special
Committee.

    I was particularly struck by the fact that we face a very real dilem-
ma as we proceed with future meetings of the Working Groups. On the
one hand, if we are to make the Special Committee a useful and meaningful activity, which is an objective we share, we will have to engage
the other members in a thorough discussion of current nuclear planning
ultimately focused on the question of specifying how the Europeans can
become more effectively involved in nuclear planning and crisis consultation. On the other hand this seems certain to involve not only the
release of sensitive military information but also disclosure of sensitive
political relationships between heads of government; most importantly,
it will require our coming to grips with the question of just how much
of a voice we are prepared to give our allies in the planning of nuclear
forces and in consultations regarding their use. Although in general we
want to be forthcoming, there is obviously a point beyond which we are
not prepared to go. Moreover, the decision as to the extent to which it is
in the US national interest, both generally and specifically, to so engage
our allies, can only be made at the highest levels of government.

    On the basis of the foregoing considerations, it seems to me the fol-
lowing guidance should be applicable for all US personnel in the conduct of meetings and discussions under aegis of the Special Committee
and its Working Groups:

    1. That US staff, in preparing proposals for internal US review, be
guided by the principle of maximum allied participation in the various
stages of nuclear planning and consultation, but

---

    [1] Source: National Archives and Records Administration, RG 59, Central Files
1964–66, DEF 1 US. Secret. Drafted by Leon Sloss (G/PM). Also addressed to General
Goodpaster (JCS representative on this Special Committee) and Assistant Secretary of
State for European Affairs Leddy.

    [2] Regarding the origins of this committee, see footnote 4, Document 75.

2. That such proposals clearly identify instances that will require disclosure of sensitive military or political information or which will lead to commitments for any significantly increased allied involvement in any aspect of US nuclear planning and consultation, so that,

3. These proposed disclosures and commitments may be subject to explicit review by our Strategy Group and we may take whatever actions for securing subsequent approval as may appear appropriate (including specifically forwarding proposals to our respective superiors and the President where this is indicated).

If you agree with the preceding suggestion, I propose that our Group meet again early in March to conduct the review suggested in 3. above, as well as to consider other related business.

UAJ

Attachment

Memorandum of Conversation[3]

Washington, February 15, 1966, 4 p.m.

SUBJECT

Strategy Discussion Group Meeting

PARTICIPANTS

State:	DOD/ISA—Mr. McNaughton
	DOD/ISA—Mr. Wyle
G—Mr. Johnson	DOD/ISA—Gen. Seignious
G/PM—Mr. Weiss	
G/PM—Mr. George	JCS—Lt. Gen. Goodpaster
G/PM—Mr. Sloss	JCS—Capt. Matthews
EUR—Mr. Leddy	JCS—Col. Donaldson
EUR—Mr. Schaetzel	
EUR—Mr. Spiers	DCA—Gen. Starbird
EUR—Mr. Baker	
EUR—Mr. Gilman	
S/P—Mr. Owen	

1. Working Group I.

Colonel Donaldson of the Joint Staff reported on the first meeting of Working Group I (Intelligence and Data Exchange) which was held in Paris on February 7–8. He characterized the meeting as being generally very successful, and no major issues arose. Agreement was reached

---

[3] Drafted by Sloss on February 17. The memorandum is marked as an uncleared text. An attached distribution list is not printed. The meeting was held in the Deputy Under Secretary's Conference Room.

on a questionnaire to be sent to the Standing Group, SACLANT and SHAPE which would develop information on current arrangements for exchange of intelligence and related data. The initial scope of the Working Group is to consider data related to the use of nuclear weapons in the NATO area only. The terms of reference of the Working Group were broadened to include data on allied forces as well as intelligence data. At the next meeting the members of the Working Group will exchange papers on what data they believe their Heads of Government will need for consultation regarding the use of nuclear weapons. In response to a question by Mr. Johnson, Colonel Donaldson indicated that the data to be exchanged will include political as well as military information.

Mr. Johnson noted that it appeared that this Working Group will quickly get into issues involving high level political relationships between Heads of Government which would directly concern the President. He asked whether the Working Group was receiving adequate political guidance. Colonel Donaldson noted that Mr. Gannett of EUR was working with the US representatives of the Working Group. Mr. Johnson noted that it was important that we did not start down paths which would commit the President to provide information, or to enter into consultations which he might not be willing to undertake. He noted that, based on his experience with crisis situations, he felt sure the President will want to maintain freedom of action as to whom he consults with, about what, and under what conditions. For example, the President would not be likely to relish the idea of 14 colored phones ringing in his office during an acute international crisis. General Goodpaster noted that at the military level also the question of exchange of military information will require very careful looking at; he would not want exchange of military information to be automatic.

2. *Working Group II.*

General Starbird reported on the initial meeting of Working Group II which was held in Paris, February 8–10. The Working Group agreed to submit three questionnaires designed to obtain an inventory of current communication resources in NATO. The first questionnaire is directed at Supreme Commanders and is designed to elicit information on the communication capabilities which they have between each other and to the NAC, the Standing Group and national authorities. The second questionnaire is directed to national authorities, and is designed to elicit information on communication capabilities between national authorities and NATO civilian and military bodies. The third questionnaire is directed to communications capabilities between member nations. Questionnaires are being addressed to all 14 NATO countries. They will not go into communication capabilities below the level of the

Supreme Commanders. Working Group II hopes to hold a meeting with Working Group I once the questionnaires are completed to provide the results of their survey and to obtain guidance from Working Group I as to what data Heads of Government may wish to exchange.

General Starbird noted that the committee effort so far is largely "marking time" until they can receive inputs from Working Groups I and III. Nevertheless, the following issues have already emerged:

(a) There is a problem with respect to release of data by the US on the capabilities of secure voice equipment. General Starbird has requested USIB to reexamine a previous decision not to release such data to NATO.

(b) It is clear that certain countries will not be in a position to release data on certain sensitive communication facilities (e.g., Heads of Government communication capabilities between the US and the UK cannot be released unilaterally by the US).

(c) The UK, supported by Canada, took the position that consultation would obviously be centered in NAC and was initially opposed to sending out a questionnaire relating to communications between governments. General Starbird convinced them that the effort to elicit information would not prejudge the means of consultation, and they finally agreed to the third questionnaire.

Mr. Johnson asked what the US philosophy was on the use of NAC for consultation. Mr. McNaughton and Mr. Spiers replied that it is considered as an option, but not the only one and this is one of the questions to be explored by the Special Committee. Mr. Johnson noted that he considered secure written communications to be generally preferable to secure voice, General Starbird pointed out that Ambassador Cleveland had noted the possible requirement for secure voice between the NATO PermReps and their Heads of Government.

3. Working Group III.

Mr. McNaughton summarized the arrangements being made for Working Group III which meets February 17–18 in Washington. He pointed out that ISA already had recommended to Mr. McNamara against the inclusion of substantive conclusions in the report from Working Group III to the Special Committee, and Mr. McNamara has agreed. Mr. McNaughton said they were not sure what bilateral discussions would take place, but clearly Mr. McNamara would have to talk with Minister Healey about F-111's, and would want to talk to Minister Von Hassel about German aid for Turkey. He would probably also want to talk to the Turkish Defense Minister about Mr. McNaughton's forthcoming visit to Turkey.

As to where the Special Committee is to go from here, Mr. McNaughton acknowledged that they are faced by a dilemma. On the one hand, there really is a desire on Mr. McNamara's part to get the

Europeans (and when Mr. McNamara says the Europeans, what he really means is the Germans and, specifically, Von Hassel) more heavily involved in the details of nuclear problems. But, as we get further into detail, we run into areas where the US just doesn't have all the answers as yet, or if we do, the answers raise major policy issues. For example, the problems involved in deploying ABMs and ADMs in Europe. Mr. McNamara wants a follow-on meeting in April which would deal with tactical nuclear forces. Mr. McNaughton couldn't predict where they would go from here. They would probably want to establish groups of experts to meet between meetings of the Working Group, but they had made no final decision on this as yet.

Mr. Johnson asked what the philosophy was on the approach to the meetings and specifically whether they want to string them out or come to conclusions rapidly. Mr. McNaughton pointed out that here again there was a dilemma. If Working Group III went on for too long, it could become an institution and be subject to attack by the French. On the other hand, they certainly wanted to extend its life beyond the June Ministerial Meeting, again with the French in mind. How long the Working Group III meetings are extended really depends on how well the first few meetings go. He thought that Mr. McNamara and Minister Healey were optimistic. Mr. Johnson said that he favored keeping it going as a Working Group as long as it was productive.

Mr. Schaetzel said that it is important to make a record to show that we really tried to make the group succeed, but if we prolonged it indefinitely, it would play into French hands. Mr. McNaughton's view was we should certainly keep the group going for a while, but not forever. He also noted that it was the Germans' clear view, as expressed in the paper they sent us, that they do not want the Special Committee to compete with the hardware solution. Mr. Spiers noted that much of the problem arises from UK pressure to make the Special Committee a substitute for a hardware solution. Mr. Johnson stated that this UK position is counterproductive. Mr. Johnson summarized the objectives as expressed by the group as being "without prejudice to the hardware solution to make the Special Committee as meaningful as possible and to keep it going so long as it was being productive." Mr. Weiss noted there was a dilemma between providing enough information and sense of sharing to keep the Europeans engaged, while at the same time not committing the US government to consultation procedures and planning that we are not prepared to follow through on.

Mr. McNaughton then noted several possible proposals that had been made for involving the Allies in nuclear planning. These include (a) placing national representatives at SAC, (b) hot lines between national governments, (c) joint studies of such subjects as MRBMs, ABMs and ADMs, as suggested in Mr. Leddy's memorandum,[4] and (d) examination with the allies of the requirements for the next generation of weapons systems.

At this point, Mr. Johnson asked whether we were trying to press our conclusions with respect to force structure and strategy on the allies. Mr. McNaughton acknowledged that to some extent Mr. McNamara does want them to reach the same conclusions as we have reached. (For example, that there is no need for additional MRBMs.) But, he also said Mr. McNamara was mindful of the need not to overdo this. Mr. McNaughton said that he very much agreed with the approach suggested in Mr. Leddy's memorandum to set up groups of experts under Working Group III to discuss specific problems. The problem was what subjects could we get into and which subjects should we avoid because we didn't have all the answers, or couldn't provide the necessary information. Mr. Spiers noted that a number of useful proposals had now been made which would involve the allies in nuclear planning and suggested that we set up a US Working Group under the aegis of the Strategy Discussion Group to examine these proposals and to develop a US position on what we were prepared to offer.

Mr. McNaughton again emphasized that Mr. McNamara thinks of the objectives of Working Group III principally in terms of the Germans. Ideally, he would like to see US-UK-German discussion of these issues for the principal purpose of educating the Germans and of involving Minister Von Hassel more in the details of nuclear planning. Mr. McNaughton noted the strong objections of the Italians to trilateral meetings, and asked State how serious we felt these Italian objections were.

Mr. Schaetzel replied that there is no question that this a real problem and that we cannot ignore the Italian objections if we want to keep them committed to NATO. He pointed out that the people in Italy who raised these objections were real friends of the US and supporters of European unity. Mr. McNaughton asked how can we proceed fruitfully to achieve our objectives with the Germans? Mr. Schaetzel suggested that we should meet with the Germans bilaterally rather than trilaterally. Mr. McNaughton expressed the view that this was not as effective. Mr. Johnson stated that State had no question but that the Germans were the key target, but we, nevertheless, had the problem of how to deal with the Italian objections to trilateralism.

Further expounding on Mr. McNamara's views with respect to the Special Committee, Mr. McNaughton said that Mr. McNamara does see it as a possible alternative to a hardware solution, that he is anxious to push on to conclusions as rapidly as possible but that he (Mr. McNaughton) has cautioned Mr. McNamara about pushing too fast.

---

[4] Not further identified.

General Seignious, seconded by General Goodpaster, pointed out that this first set of briefings would give the Europeans a great deal to absorb. General Goodpaster went on to express his view that this sort of discussion with the Germans was quite productive based on their experience with the German military. However, he pointed out that it was going to take time for them to absorb US thinking on these complex issues. Mr. Weiss and Mr. Johnson agreed that it was going to take time. General Goodpaster also stressed that the Joint Chiefs would want to take a very careful look at the proposal to put national representatives at SAC.

Mr. McNaughton said that he personally liked the idea of discussing the ABM problem with the Germans, but thought that their conclusion would be that ABM was just fine for Germany and what do we do then? Mr. Schaetzel supported the idea of discussing ABMs with the Germans and the British and felt they would be most interested.

General Goodpaster said it was his view that the important thing is not what we discuss, but to engage the Allies in real discussions. He personally felt, based on his discussions with the German military, that there were some real possibilities in the Special Committee if we really engage the Allies in detailed discussion. He also felt it was healthy for them to know that we do not know all the answers.

Mr. McNaughton said that the idea of technical experts groups was a good one and that we ought to discuss this at the Working Group III meeting this week. General Seignious suggested that the expert groups might well occupy themselves in absorbing the material presented at the briefings. In response to a question from Mr. Sloss, Mr. McNaughton said that they were not in a position to distribute the material from the JCS briefings. Thus, it was agreed that it would be useful to bring experts here from the other member countries to study the briefing materials in greater detail.

4. Action

a. Mr. Spiers was asked to take the leadership in developing and analyzing proposals for involving the allies in nuclear planning and consultation.

b. Mr. Weiss was asked to participate with Defense in developing the first draft of a paper on tactical nuclear weapons to be presented to the next meeting of Working Group III.

c. Mr. McNaughton said he would explore further with Mr. McNamara the idea of experts groups to meet between meetings of Working Group III.

**116.   Memorandum From the Chairman of the Joint Atomic
Energy Intelligence Committee (Chamberlain) to the
Chairman of the U.S. Intelligence Board (Raborn)[1]**

Washington, undated.

SUBJECT

    JAEIC Comments on the Report of the Foreign Weapons Evaluation Group
Meeting of 27 February 1966

1. The subject report is attached for your information.[2]

2. On 27 February the Foreign Weapons Evaluation Group (Bethe Panel) met to consider recent analysis of a class of Soviet thermonuclear devices with yields in the 3–25 MT range that were tested during the 1961–62 test series. [*3-1/2 lines of source text not declassified*]

3. The Joint Atomic Energy Intelligence Committee (JAEIC) agrees in general with the principal findings of the Panel, which are as follows:

a. [*14 lines of source text not declassified*]

b. [*11 lines of source text not declassified*]

c. [*4-1/2 lines of source text not declassified*]

d. The recent Soviet model studies do not warrant any changes to the previously estimated yield-to-weight ratios of Soviet devices.

4. JAEIC notes that additional work is underway to consider other design models that might reasonably explain the technical data on these Soviet devices. It is hoped that after further analysis a more definitive statement about the characteristics of these and other Soviet devices may be possible.

Donald F. Chamberlain

---

[1] Source: Washington National Records Center, OSD/AE Files: FRC 330 69 A 2243, 99 USA–USSR Weapons Evaluation (Bethe). Secret; Restricted Data. An attached March 14 transmittal memorandum from James S. Lay, Executive Secretary of the U.S. Intelligence Board, to its Chairman, mentions, among other things, that this report was not scheduled on the agenda of a USIB meeting unless specifically requested by a Board member before March 21.

[2] Not printed; the 5-page report, dated February 28, was signed by Hans A. Bethe, Chairman of the Foreign Weapons Evaluation Group.

117. **Memorandum From the Assistant Secretary of Defense for Systems Analysis (Enthoven) to Secretary of Defense McNamara**[1]

Washington, March 2, 1966.

SUBJECT

Programmed Future Strategic Ballistic Missile Force Capabilities (U)

Enclosed is a summary table drawn from an evaluation of the programmed U.S. missile force against likely estimates of the future Soviet target system. These estimates are based upon the median estimates of this threat presented in the N.I.E. on Soviet capabilities for strategic attack (N.I.E. 11–8–65).[2] Enclosed also are tables containing the detailed assumptions for the analysis. Most of the previous calculations that you have seen for this time period have treated the U.S. Assured Destruction capability in the face of a maximum plausible Soviet threat. By contrast the enclosed calculations are relevant to the U.S. combined Assured Destruction/Damage Limiting capability against a more likely Soviet threat. These calculations strongly suggest that U.S. capabilities to attack the likely Sino-Soviet target system will increase sharply over the period 1966 to 1971. By 1971 our ballistic missile force alone, operating in pre-emption, would be able to destroy the major part of their strategic offensive forces. To compare the 1971 force with the current force, we have assumed that [*8-1/2 lines of source text not declassified*]. In terms of residual opposing weapons, instead of average kill against the target systems, the performance is even more impressive. When bomber weapons are also included in U.S. counter-military strikes, this effectiveness would be further enhanced.

The calculations summarized above utilized a targeting procedure as much like that of the SIOP as we could make it. We used a median threat without ABMs or extremely high numbers of Soviet hardened missiles to test the ability of our missile forces to destroy military targets for the Damage Limiting mission. We are now in the process of calculating performance when targeting is designed to minimize Soviet damage potential, instead of following [*2 lines of source text not declassified*].

---

[1] Source: Washington National Records Center, OSD Files: FRC 330 70 A 4662, 381 SRF 1966. Top Secret. A stamped notation, dated April 6, reads: "Sec Def has seen."

[2] Document 97.

I expect to use the calculations in this paper in the next Presidential Memorandum on Strategic Offensive and Defensive Forces, and compare the results with others that assume larger missile forces withheld for the urban-industrial task. Additionally, since the results are so striking, a copy of the enclosed table has been made available for the back-up book for your congressional testimony. I will, of course, send you the full paper if you are interested in pursuing this any further.

Alain Enthoven

Enclosure

TABLE I

SINO-SOVIET TARGET LIST

[*table (6 columns and 12 rows) not declassified*]

TABLE II

U.S. FORCES—INVENTORY BOOSTERS

	1966	1967	1969	1971
Minuteman I	800	700	400	100
Minuteman II	80	300	550 [*]	600 [*]
Minuteman III	0	0	50	300 [*]
Titan II	54	54	54	54
Polaris A2/A3 (66% At Sea)	512	656	656	656

[*number and text in table not declassified*]

TABLE III

OPERATIONAL FACTORS[1]

System	SIOP-4 Non Reprog.[3] Rel.	CEP	1967 Non Reprog. Rel.	CEP	Yield
Minuteman I	[*]	[*]	[*]	[*]	[*]
Minuteman II	[*]	[*]	[*]	[*]	[*]
Minuteman III					
Titan II	[*]	[*]	[*]	[*]	[*]
Polaris A2/A3 (66% At Sea)	[*]	[*]	[*]	[*]	[*]

System	1969 Reprog Rel	Non Reprog Rel.	CEP	1971 Reprog Rel.	Non Reprog Rel.	CEP	Yield
Minuteman I		[*]	[*]	[*]	[*]	[*]	[*]
Minuteman II	[*]	[*]	[*]	[*]	[*]	[*]2	[*]
Minuteman III	[*]	[*]	[*]	[*]	[*]	[*]2	[*]
Titan II		[*]	[*]	[*]	[*]	[*]	[*]
Polaris A2/A3 (66% At Sea)	[*]	[*]	[*]	[*]	[*]	[*]	[*]

[* entry in table not declassified]
1 All reliability estimates are from Blue Lance.
2 BSD Estimates of operational CEP.
3 Non-Reprogrammable Reliability. Reprogramming of missiles for unreliability is an operation in which new missiles are assigned and launched to cover the targets of missiles that have failed in launch. The amount of the total unreliability for which reprogramming is possible depends on the stage in missile flight at which success or failure is reported (e.g., lift-off or cut-off). Non-reprogrammable reliability is the reliability of the missile after the last report.

TABLE IV

OVERALL SUMMARY OF RESULTS

BALLISTIC MISSILES ONLY

[table (13 columns and 10 rows) not declassified]

118.   Memorandum From the Joint Chiefs of Staff to Secretary of Defense McNamara[1]

JCSM–147–66   Washington, March 7, 1966.

SUBJECT

Military Strategy for Fiscal Years 1968 Through 1975

1. JCSM–15–66,[2] dated 10 January 1966, subject: "Changes and Revisions in Content and Transmittal Procedures of the Joint Strategic Objectives Plan (JSOP), Parts I–V and Part VI (U), "informed you of certain procedural changes instituted by the Joint Chiefs of Staff regarding the JSOP.

2. Transmitted herewith are:

a. A résumé of the view of the Joint Chiefs of Staff concerning over-all military strategy for the period 2–10 years hence (Appendix A).

b. Tentative major force-level decision-issues which the Joint Chiefs of Staff will address in Part VI of the JSOP (Appendix B).[3]

c. Parts I–V of JSOP 68–75[4] (Appendix C, forwarded separately).

3. Force levels considered necessary to implement this strategy together with supporting rationale will be forwarded as Part VI of JSOP 68–75 about mid-March 1966. At that time, the Joint Chiefs of Staff will provide you with their analyses and recommendations on the major decision-issues listed in Appendix B.

4. The Joint Chiefs of Staff recommend that the separate force analyses of the draft memorandums for the President, prepared for the upcoming budget year, be developed within the context of the over-all military strategy contained in Appendix A as supported by the more detailed treatment in JSOP 68–75. They further recommend that Appendix A be utilized as the principal basis for your draft memorandums for the President on over-all US military strategy and force levels for Fiscal Years 1968 through 1975.

---

[1] Source: National Archives and Records Administration, RG 218, JCS Files, 3130 (10 Dec 65) Sec 1 IR 5216. Top Secret. The memorandum forms Enclosure A to a report by the J–5 to the Joint Chiefs of Staff, February 28 (JCS 2143/268–2), which was revised on March 7 or later to indicate revisions in Enclosure A and Appendix A to Enclosure A, several pages of which bear the typed note: "Revised by Decision—7 March 1966" or "Revised" followed by the March 1, 3, or 4 dates.

[2] Enclosure A to JCS 2143/268–1. [Footnote in the source text. JCSM–15–65 has not been found.]

[3] Not found.

[4] Enclosure A to JCS 2143/260. [Footnote in the source text. JSOP 68–75 has not been found.]

5. Without attachments, this memorandum is Unclassified.

For the Joint Chiefs of Staff:
Earle G. Wheeler[5]
Chairman
Joint Chiefs of Staff

Appendix A[6]

MILITARY STRATEGY FOR FY 1968 THROUGH 1975 (U)

Part I

Introduction

General

1. (U) The basic missions of the US Armed Forces are two: (1) to deter or deal decisively with any military attack against the United States and its possessions and (2) to protect and project US interests on a global basis in support of national goals.

National Goals

2. (U) Five major goals[7] of US foreign policy are:

a. To deter or defeat aggression at any level, whether of nuclear attack or limited war or subversion and guerrilla tactics.
b. To bring about a closer association of the more industrialized democracies of Western Europe, North America, and Asia in promoting the security and prosperity of the Free World.
c. To help the less developed countries carry through their revolution of modernization without sacrificing their independence.
d. To assist in the gradual emergence of a genuine world community, based on cooperation and law, through the establishment and development of such organs as the United Nations, the World Court, the World Bank and Monetary Fund, and other global and regional institutions.
e. To search for means of reducing the risk of war, of narrowing the areas of conflict with the communist world, and of encouraging the re-

---

[5] Printed from a copy that bears this typed signature.

[6] Top Secret. A title page and table of contents are not printed.

[7] Department of State pamphlet "Five Goals of U.S. Foreign Policy," 24 September 1962; and Department of Defense "Commanders Digest," 12 February 1966. [Footnote in the source text. The text of the former, issued as Department of State Publication 7432, is printed in Department of State *Bulletin,* October 15, 1962, pp. 547–558. The Department of Defense publication has not been found.]

emergence in communist countries of the nationalism and individualism which are already changing and dividing the once-solid communist bloc.

3. (C) The United States must take an active part in shaping a world compatible with freedom or yield to the communist powers a major opportunity to shape the world to our disadvantage. The role of US military forces in this concept is (1) primarily, to deter the use of hostile force and, if deterrence fails, to enable the United States together with its allies to defeat the enemy, and (2) secondarily, to participate in non-war diplomatic, economic, and psychological operations to the degree their unique capabilities and their primary role permit. Derived from the national goals and fundamental military role for US forces are basic military objectives.

Military Objectives

4. (S) Four basic military objectives of the United States are:

a. Protect and defend the United States and preserve both its status and freedom of action as a dominant world power. The military forces required to achieve this objective must first be capable of deterring or dealing effectively with any military attack against the United States.
b. Be capable of supporting US world-wide interests. The military forces of the United States should be able, in conjunction with allied and friendly forces as available, to deter or deal effectively with any military attacks against other areas essential to US security.
c. Support US foreign policy and diplomatic efforts abroad. Included herein are military programs to assist friendly governments in the prevention and defeat of subversion, insurgency, and aggression which threatens their survival. Concomitant tasks of US forces are the capability to protect US property as well as US and selected nationals and their properties as required. This responsibility extends, as appropriate, to ensuring the freedom of the sea, air, and space regions for the United States and friendly powers and to denying their use for purposes adverse to US interests.
d. Maintain active forces in a high state of readiness, strategically deployed, mobile, and adequately supported to conduct military operations so as to achieve US objectives, minimize damage to the United States and her allies, and force a conclusion of hostilities on terms advantageous to the United States and its allies, while keeping hostilities at the lowest scale of conflict commensurate with the achievement of US objectives.

Strategic Considerations

5. (TS) The over-all strategic concept designed to support US national goals and achieve US military objectives is to prevent or to defeat aggression wherever and whenever US national interests are adversely affected. This requires (1) a military posture of sufficient strength and flexibility to permit exercise of the initiative by the United States in the conduct of military, political, and economic affairs and (2)

the coordination and exploitation to best advantage of all instruments of national power. Deterrence, collective security, and flexible response are the basic elements of this concept.

6. (C) Deterrence of a nuclear exchange is the first responsibility of US strategy since national survival is clearly at stake; at the same time, US strategy must also provide for the capability to deter aggression at any lesser level of conflict. To insure deterrence, US forces must be clearly capable of making both direct and indirect attack on the United States or its interests grossly unattractive and unprofitable. The military capability to control, defeat, or destroy the enemy and the firm resolve of the United States to use its forces if required must be obvious as well as real.

7. (C) Collective security involves the acquisition, the development, and stability of those allies who can now or ultimately will contribute to US security interests world-wide.

8. (S) Flexible response is essential to the prevention of conflict escalation and is, therefore, an inextricable element of deterrence. Flexible response requires a combination of modern, mobile, and balanced forces which will permit the exercise of a wide range of options to employ military forces under varying conditions and threats to achieve US objectives.

9. (C) Translation of these considerations into a force structure depends on the interaction in the world environment between US national goals and the threat to their accomplishment.

Part II

Global Strategic Appraisal

Threat

1. (U) Today's world appears to be somewhere between (1) a bipolar world and a polycentric world; (2) an environment in which the USSR and the Chinese People's Republic (CPR) are challenging Free World interests and an environment in which the CPR is challenging USSR as well as Free World interests; (3) a globe divided on lines of ideology and political organization and on lines of race and economic development; and (4) a world of law organized to respect the interdependencies of modern life and a world of conflict disorganized by competing ideologies and social turmoil.

2. (S) The most dangerous threat to US interests is posed by the strategic nuclear forces of the Soviet Union. This threat is so serious—regardless of the estimated intentions of Soviet leaders—that it must receive primary cognizance in the formulation of military strategy and in the development of adequate countering force levels. Concurrently, it must be recognized that, without ever resorting to a strategic nuclear

attack, the USSR and/or the CPR could expand the communist-dominated world until the United States and its allies are finally isolated and subjected to piecemeal domination.

3. (S) The USSR now has the capability to conduct a massive nuclear attack against Eurasia with manned aircraft, surface-to-surface missiles, and submarine-launched missiles. The Soviet strategic offensive force of ICBMs, SLCMs/SLBMs, the heavy bombers, and some medium bombers can wreak enormous damage on the United States in a first strike but cannot at the present time destroy enough of the US strategic nuclear force to preclude retaliatory destruction of the Soviet Union as a viable society. Additionally and apart from Soviet nuclear capabilities, the USSR/Warsaw Pact and the CPR have significant conventional forces which pose major threats to the Free World.

4. (TS) Without a clear belief that they would emerge as the dominant world power, Soviet leaders are not likely to initiate deliberately a strategic nuclear exchange. This does not preclude the possibility of strategic nuclear war through escalation or miscalculation. Further, the United States cannot safely discount the possibility that Soviet leaders might launch a pre-emptive strike if they considered themselves irretrievably committed in a confrontation or if they believed a nuclear attack on the USSR was imminent.

5. (S) The fact that the United States and the USSR each has the ability to inflict extensive destruction on the other, regardless of which strikes first, has a paradoxical impact on the formulation of military strategy. It decreases the likelihood of strategic nuclear war but increases the necessity that the United States maintain a balanced strategic nuclear force superior to that of the Soviet Union. It increases the importance of conventional military power but inhibits its application in direct confrontation between major powers because of the risks of escalation. It diminishes the role of lesser powers in high-intensity conflicts but enlarges their role in mid- and low-intensity conflicts.

6. (S) The US and USSR strategic nuclear capabilities are expected to remain superior to those of any other nation for the period of this appraisal, provided no unbalancing arms control or disarmament agreements are negotiated. The actual and potential nuclear capability of the United Kingdom is not considered to be in competition with US interests. France's nuclear efforts are weighted more toward a political and psychological effect than toward a direct military threat and are aimed primarily at gaining leadership in Europe. However, in the current worldwide environment and considering the militant and sometimes irrational orientation of Chinese communist officials, the growing nuclear capability of the CPR—although expected to remain less than that of France for the next decade—constitutes a significant political, psychological, and military threat to US security interests.

7. (TS) The CPR has initiated a long-range, broad-based program in support of nuclear weapons development. A weaponized version of their 1964 fission device probably is available now in limited numbers, and Communist China at this time has some bombers—but no missiles—capable of delivering nuclear weapons. There are indications of some developmental work on ICBMs and construction of missile launching submarines; however, the CPR appears to be concentrating first on obtaining MRBMs. By 1970, the CPR could have sufficient medium range missiles and warheads to threaten peripheral states. Hence, nuclear attack and nuclear blackmail become feasible CPR courses of action in the Western Pacific-Asian area. Additionally, the CPR may be able to pose a limited nuclear threat to the United States and to the USSR by the early 1970's. Communist China certainly will attempt to exploit these capabilities, as well as its large conventional forces, to threaten its neighbors and to undermine US commitments in the Asian area without, however, subjecting its growing potential to serious risk.

8. (S) There is no longer a communist bloc in the traditional sense of a monolithic structure subservient to Moscow. Independent factions are developing because of the growing tendency of East European countries to emphasize national rather than ideological and bloc ambitions as well as because of the increasingly bitter Sino-Soviet dispute which has its deepest roots in national rather than ideological differences. The trend in Europe toward independent national policies probably will be enhanced by increased East-West trade and other forms of communications stimulated by historical orientation. Although there may be some temporary accommodations for purposes of expediency, the Sino-Soviet rift is likely to persist and, in the absence of overt war between the United States and either the USSR or the CPR, to crystallize. Competition between the USSR and CPR may intensify their activities in areas of interest to the United States; on the other hand, the rift, for as long as it continues, lessens the magnitude of the otherwise combined military threat to the United States.

9. (S) There has been a trend toward a general stabilization of the US-USSR relationship—although this trend could be reversed suddenly. Contributing to this stabilization are the maturing of the Soviet society, the continued economic advancement of West Europe and Japan, and the divisive tendencies within the communist group of nations.

10. (C) This stabilization of US-USSR relations has significant ramifications:

a. The focal point of the cold war is shifting to the underdeveloped two-thirds of the world.

b. The cold war has become less linear and more triangular, with the CPR, the USSR, and the United States—each with its allies—at the apexes.

c. The Soviet Union and the CPR, without disavowing their intent ultimately to achieve world domination, have reoriented their strategies; i.e., the Soviets' espousal of "Wars of National Liberation" and the Chinese communists' doctrine of "People's Wars" to wear down, isolate, and destroy opposing advanced states.

11. (C) The underdeveloped world is particularly susceptible to communist insurgency because of the prevailing militant and immature nationalism coupled with the instability inherent in the modernization process. The coming decade is likely to be critical because of revolutionary trends stemming from the inability of governments to cope with social and economic problems; further, exacerbation of this situation by the disruptive competition between the USSR and CPR for influence in these areas must be anticipated. Whether the continuing conflicts in the underdeveloped regions will be primarily military or primarily political and economic will depend on two factors: (1) the success of the current US military effort in Vietnam and (2) the ability of the Free World to execute effective political, economic, psychological, and military preventive programs.

12. (S) In summary, of all the forms of warfare, general nuclear war, although the most dangerous threat, is the least probable for the next decade. Continued low-intensity conflict, particularly in the underdeveloped portion of the world, is almost certain. Limited war in the underdeveloped areas is a continuing possibility because (1) militant and immature nationalism prevails in many states; (2) there remain many traditional unresolved issues between neighboring states and races; and (3) there will be the possibility of escalation of Soviet or CPR-instigated insurgencies. Limited war in the developed portion of the world is unlikely because (1) the dangers of escalation are magnified by the intimate involvement of both US and USSR interests and (2) the relative postures of the advanced states are sufficiently balanced that each would be reluctant to initiate a limited war without explicit US or USSR backing which is considered unlikely in the absence of extreme provocation (e.g., a serious threat to the allied position in Berlin or Western military intervention in an East German uprising).

13. (S) Fundamental to the entire question of the likelihood of conflict is recognition that the most important single factor in deterring Moscow, Peking, or their allies from the use of force in any portion of the conflict spectrum is opposing military power—the existence of superior US strategic nuclear capabilities and US military presence at, or an obvious capability to deploy military power rapidly to, the point of contest. With its allies the United States is presently superior militarily and has the potential to exert superior military force globally if it decides that the situation merits the requisite military, political, and economic decisions. Nevertheless, the Sino-Soviet schism bears so impor-

tantly on US strategic planning that, should there be a USSR-CPR accommodation, the basic threat and consequent Free World force posture will have to be reassessed.

Balance of Military Power

14. (S) At present the balance of strategic military power appears to favor the United States. There are a number of factors, however, which could lead to upsetting this favorable balance, such as unmatched technological breakthroughs in nuclear strategic systems by the USSR, failure to consider basic US-USSR disparities in deciding on force levels, unverified arms control agreements or unbalanced arms reductions, and major shifts in alliances and alignments.

15. (TS) The Soviet Union is improving its strategic nuclear posture relative to that of the United States. It undoubtedly will seek continued qualitative and quantitative force improvements and may be seeking to enhance its relative posture through arms control agreements. Primary Soviet efforts have focused on a build-up of ICBMs; the hardening and dispersing of missile sites; developing active air and missile defense systems; an increased mobility of land-based and sea-based ballistic missile systems. There is evidence that the Soviets are deploying a ballistic missile defense (BMD) system, and are working on larger nuclear warheads with compatible delivery vehicles; and they have the capability to develop and deploy multiple independently guided re-entry vehicles (MIRVs). The Soviets probably could attain an operational capability with a MIRV in the period 1970–1975. They could already have developed a limited antisatellite capability based on an operational missile (e.g., the SS-4) with a nuclear warhead and on existing electronic facilities. A breakthrough or major advance in any of these areas could alter, in their favor, the present ratio of the US-USSR strategic nuclear postures unless the United States, through its own vigorous development and modernization program, keeps pace.

16. (TS) There are three basic disparities between the United States and the USSR which must be considered in determining the minimum US strategic nuclear force levels. First, the Soviet Union, as a closed society, has an advantage in thwarting intelligence collection; it can secretly increase its forces quantitatively and qualitatively with less chance of detection than if the United States made the same attempt. Second, the Soviet Union probably has less inhibitions about executing a first strike. Third, there are significant differences in population distribution which, in conjection with higher missile payload capacities, favor the Soviet Union. Hence, equality in US and USSR strategic nuclear forces is less than parity for the United States when the asymmetry in intelligence, in population distribution, and in willingness to strike first are considered.

Thus, the strategic nuclear advantage must be clearly in our favor both actually and in the view of potential enemies.

17. (C) Arms control is a desirable objective for national security policy if it actually reduces the likelihood of the outbreak of war. However, an arms control or disarmament agreement which resulted in a state or a group of states improving its military posture vis-à-vis other states probably would be more destabilizing than stabilizing. There is ample evidence that the USSR and other communist states do not subscribe to the idea of arms control in the same way Western governments do, to include the traditional and doctrinal attitude of communist states toward treaties and agreements. A fully adequate verification system in effect prior to implementation of any arms control or disarmament agreement is essential to US security.

18. (TS) Comprehensive or threshold test ban treaties are cases in point. There are serious gaps in US hard intelligence about Soviet knowledge and capabilities in the newest weapon effects areas; in fact, there are indications that the USSR already may have made gains in nuclear weapons technology beyond current US capabilities. Should probable Soviet developments in BMD systems with drastically improved nuclear effects warheads be deployed prior to compensating accomplishments by the United States, the military balance of power could be critically upset in favor of the USSR. Vigorous nuclear testing within the restrictions of the present Limited Test Ban Treaty is necessary to permit the United States to increase effectiveness and better to assure survival of its offensive nuclear weapons and defensive systems against the effects of the improved Soviet nuclear weapons. To stop or even further to limit testing would foreclose the possibility of attaining essential knowledge of BMD, of improved silo hardening, of better penetration aids, and of other strategic weapon technology for the United States.

19. (TS) Space competence is important to national security just as it is to national growth and prestige. In recent Moscow parades, the Soviets displayed what they alleged to be an orbital missile. Despite a number of Soviet allusions to "orbital rockets," probably advanced for propaganda purposes, it is not believed that the USSR has an orbital bombardment capability, and there is no evidence of an intention to develop such systems. It is estimated that the Soviets will not deploy offensive weapons in space within the next ten years. However, it is clear that Soviet space technology is well advanced, and their current peaceful objectives in this medium sooner or later may be accompanied by hostile demonstrations or acts seeking to obtain a military advantage in space. A lack of parallel or countervailing space capabilities would place the United States at a disadvantage, regardless of its earth-based strategic deterrent strength.

20. (S) A significant destabilizing element in the world environment is the potential proliferation of nuclear weapons capabilities. There are a number of countries which have the capability to become members of the "Nuclear Club" if they make such a decision, with India, Israel, and Sweden being the most likely to do so in the short run. In the long run, the FRG and Japan probably will become the serious contenders. Such nuclear proliferation as may occur over the next ten years is not likely to affect materially the existing thermonuclear duopoly. Although widespread independent national nuclear capabilities are basically deleterious to US security interests, it may not be within the reasonable power of the United States to preclude nuclear proliferation. Even though multilateral nuclear partnership arrangements tend to reduce unilateral US military flexibility, the political and psychological requirements of national policy may be such as to override the military disadvantages. Hence, considering all factors, additional nuclear sharing arrangements may become desirable in specific instances to maintain favorable power relationships.

21. (TS) Evidence indicates that the Soviets can support substantial toxic chemical warfare (CW) operations and that research on improving toxic nerve agents and efforts to develop nonlethal incapacitating agents is continuing. The Soviets have a variety of chemical munitions and delivery vehicles for dissemination of chemical agents and they possess a wide range of good defensive CW equipment. While Soviet CW munitions probably will be used in the tactical sense, the Soviets have consistently grouped toxic agents with "weapons of mass destruction" in political and classified military writings. Decision to use such weapons probably will be taken at the highest political level in the Soviet government.

22. (S) Another factor which could affect the world balance of power in the mid-term is a weakening of alliances, together with a concomitant realignment and greater independence of action within and among the major power sectors. As Western nations grow stronger economically, as their sense of nationalism increases, and as the fear of nuclear war recedes, the Western alliances are becoming less united, and the member states are more inclined to base their individual military forces on national interests rather than alliance requirements. The resurgence of nationalism in East Europe and the broadened relations between Eastern and Western Europe probably will militate against success of Soviet efforts to achieve any additional military, economic, or political integration of the Warsaw Pact. While both East and West European alliance systems can be expected to become less unified, it appears that the communist alliance system will suffer greater disintegration as its members improve their economic status.

23. (S) Coupled with the foregoing trend in the alliance structure of the communist and noncommunist camps is the move toward progres-

sive withdrawal and decreasing military presence in colonial areas by former colonial powers. As colonial power presence has diminished, a corresponding vacuum has developed. France, the Netherlands, and Germany are no longer Asian powers. The United Kingdom is gradually withdrawing militarily from the overseas areas. The power equation has been drastically altered in Africa, although France, Belgium, Portugal, and the UK will retain some presence and influence on that continent. To maintain a power balance, the United States has had and probably will continue to have to fill such military vacuums to varying degrees.

24. (C) The United States, Western Europe, and the Soviet Union each appear economically capable of increasing significantly their military efforts. Since 1945, the US gross national product has risen from approximately $330 billion (in 1964 prices) to $675 billion in 1965 while defense expenditures, as a percentage function of GNP, have declined from 12.9 percent in 1954 to 7.9 percent in 1965. Although the balance of payments problem has an adverse impact on US forward deployment and military assistance programs, the United States is in a better economic position than either the USSR or the CPR to support increased military expenditures and to engage in economic warfare. The economy of West Europe is certainly such that it could support an increased military defense effort as well as simultaneously provide substantial assistance to underdeveloped areas.

25. (C) The increasing economic gap between the developed and underdeveloped areas of the world contributes significantly to international tensions. Economic modernization is a slow, painful process which requires a major effort just to keep up with the population growth. There are already three billion people in the world, most of them living in underdeveloped regions. The United Nations Population Commission estimates that, if present trends continue, the world population will be nearly 7.5 billion by the end of this century. Low agricultural output is a significant limitation in the underdeveloped world. The ability of the United States to produce and distribute food can become an even more significant element of national power. The ability and success of the Free World vis-à-vis that of the communist world to foster democratic capitalism versus communism in the underdeveloped areas will impact on peace and stability during the mid-range period, as well as over the long run, on the balance of world power.

119.   Memorandum From the Joint Chiefs of Staff to Secretary of
        Defense McNamara[1]

JCSM–167–66   Washington, March 22, 1966.

SUBJECT

    Joint Strategic Objectives Plan for FY 1968–1975 (JSOP 68–75), Part VI, Analysis
    and Force Tabulations (U)

1. (U) The Joint Chiefs of Staff have approved and forward herewith Part VI, JSOP 68–75.[2] Parts I–V, JSOP 68–75 were forwarded by
JCSM–147–66, dated 7 March 1966.[3]

2. (U) Part VI, JSOP 68–75, contains the military advice of the Joint
Chiefs of Staff relative to the force level objectives they recommend for
the mid-range period. It includes an assessment of the current
Department of Defense Five-Year Force Structure and Financial
Program, and examines alternatives and risks. Phasing required to
achieve their recommended force levels and weapon systems development programs for the period FY 1968–1975 is also included. Particular
emphasis is placed on these issues which must be addressed in conjunction with the FY 1968 budget.

3. (S) JSOP 68–75 force objectives were assessed on the basis that
requirements which exceed the capabilities of the recommended permanent active establishment would be met either by some combination of partial mobilization, full mobilization and extension of terms
of service, or by temporary activation of additional forces. Since the
decision to meet these requirements without the selective call-up of
reserves appears to be a continuing one, certain temporary adjustments in the force recommendations may be required. These temporary active force adjustments for the nearer time frame, relating
specifically to the reserve call-up alternative and keyed to operations
in Southeast Asia, are reflected in the Force Tables or, as appropriate,
by annotation. Further temporary adjustments may be required as a
result of extended deployments and other operations relative to
Southeast Asia.

4. (U) As indicated in JCSM–147–66, dated 7 March 1966, specific
major decision issues which require resolution in the FY 1968–1975 force
programs are set forth in Appendices A and B hereto.[4]

---

[1] Source: National Archives and Records Administration, RG 218, JCS Files, 3130 (10
Feb 66) Sec 1 IR 4932. Top Secret; Restricted Data.

[2] Not found. See Document 118.

[3] See Document 118 and footnote 4 thereto.

[4] Neither found.

5. (U) The views of the Chairman, Joint Chiefs of Staff are contained in the separate memorandum attached herewith.[5]

6. (U) Without attachments, this memorandum is downgraded to Secret and removed from the Restricted Data category.

For the Joint Chiefs of Staff:
Earle G. Wheeler[6]
Chairman
Joint Chiefs of Staff

---

[5] Document 120.

[6] Printed from a copy that indicates Wheeler signed the original.

---

120.   Memorandum From the Chairman of the Joint Chiefs of Staff (Wheeler) to Secretary of Defense McNamara[1]

CM–1279–66   Washington, undated.

SUBJECT

Joint Strategic Objectives Plan for FY 1968–75, Part VI (U)

1. (U) JCSM 167–66[2] forwarded Part VI of the Joint Strategic Objectives Plan for FY 68–75.[3] As indicated in the Force Tables of Part VI and the footnotes thereto, the Joint Chiefs of Staff did not reach complete agreement on certain programs. There are, however, fewer divergencies in JSOP 68–75 than in past JSOPs. It is also noted that where there are differences of opinion on force levels, these are in many cases differences in timing rather than in concept or substance. Finally, our experiences associated with the war in Vietnam were heavily weighted in the deliberations and resultant recommendations on General Purpose forces.

2. (U) My views on the major program issues contained in the various programs are indicated in the following paragraphs.

3. (TS) *Strategic Offensive/Defensive Forces*

Studies, analyses and war games completed during the last year indicated trends that are not favorable to the United States. In order to

---

[1] Source: National Archives and Records Administration, RG 218, JCS Files, 3130 (10 Feb 66) Sec 1 IR 4932. Top Secret.

[2] Document 119.

[3] Not found; see Document 118.

maintain a credible deterrence we must take great care to assure that we retain clearly superior strategic offensive forces over the USSR. This concern is reflected in the unanimous agreement among the Joint Chiefs of Staff on an IOC of FY 1974 for a follow-on manned bomber, deployment of Poseidon commencing in FY 1971 and an IOC of FY 1973 for an Advanced ICBM. I agree with these recommendations.

I continue to believe that our defensive forces are inadequate in their damage limiting role and in their contribution to a credible deterrence. I accord top priority to the acquisition and deployment at an early date of a ballistic missile defense, and fully agree with the unanimous recommendation of the Joint Chiefs of Staff to commence deployment of Nike-X in FY 1972. While some questions such as point defense of our offensive forces have not been resolved, I do not believe we should delay the decision to deploy Nike-X.

I continue to support the requirement for a follow-on manned interceptor. Although the Joint Chiefs of Staff are not agreed on the ultimate numbers of F-12s to be deployed, they are agreed that deployment of the F-12 should commence in FY 1972. In view of the intelligence lead times and the USSR capability to deploy supersonic long range bombers, I consider it prudent to include sufficient funds in the FY 1968 budget to permit deployment of 12 F-12s in FY 1972. The force levels after FY 1972 should be dependent on future evaluations of the USSR bomber threat. I continue to believe, along with the majority of the Joint Chiefs of Staff, that except for normal attrition we should not decrease the number of Century series interceptors in our Continental Air Defense Force prior to the occurrence of a reduction in the strategic bomber threat or the deployment of a follow-on manned interceptor.

4. (S) *General Purpose Forces*

In agreement with the other members of the Joint Chiefs of Staff (less the Chief of Staff, US Army), I recommend a force level of 27-1/3 division forces. While our recent experience would tend to substantiate an increase in permanent active Army divisions, I join with the Chief of Staff, Air Force and the Commandant of the Marine Corps in deferring judgment on the number and mix of active divisions and brigades until the resolution of the Southeast Asia situation is clearer as well as our future NATO commitments and the resolution of questions concerning rapid deployment and rapid reinforcement. For these same reasons I also defer judgment on the number of sustaining support increments in the permanent active structure.

The war in Vietnam, gold flow considerations and uncertainties regarding overseas bases all support the unanimous recommendation of the Joint Chiefs of Staff for a force level of 16 attack carriers and 16 attack carrier air wings in FY 1969. I am in agreement with these force levels. I continue to support, as do the other members of the Joint Chiefs of Staff (less the Chief of Staff, Air Force), the increase in antisubmarine carriers from 9 to 11.

With regard to the number of Air Force tactical fighters, our experiences in Southeast Asia and the results of studies indicate an increase in total numbers is required. Recognizing the divergencies of views on total numbers of tactical fighters required, I believe that a reasonable program would be to level off at 30 tactical fighter wings (about 2200 aircraft) pending a more thorough study of our total national tactical air requirements.

5. (S) *Air and Sealift Forces*

I support the approved program for the C5A of 96 aircraft in FY 1972. Beyond FY 1972, I join with the other members of the Joint Chiefs of Staff (less Chief of Staff, Air Force) in deferring judgment on increased force levels pending a better understanding of our strategic mobility requirements for rapid deployment and rapid reinforcement.

6. (U) Accordingly, I recommend approval of the force levels which are supported unanimously by the Joint Chiefs of Staff together with the force levels I have indicated in the above paragraphs for certain of the programs on which there are divergent JCS views. With respect to divergencies not addressed in the above comments, I will provide my views in the review of Presidential Memorandums or programming documents.

Earle G. Wheeler[4]

---

[4] Printed from a copy that bears this typed signature.

121. **Memorandum From the Director of Defense Research and Engineering, Department of Defense (Foster) to the Assistant Secretary of Defense for International Security Affairs (McNaughton)**[1]

Washington, April 7, 1966.

SUBJECT

Determination of a DoD Position on Chemical and Biological Warfare

As you are aware, the Department of Defense has been participating since November 1963 in an interagency effort to develop a national policy on Chemical and Biological (CB) Warfare. This effort was initiated at the instigation of the Arms Control and Disarmament Agency with the approval of the Special Assistant to the President for National Security Affairs (Mr. McGeorge Bundy).[2] Before even posing the question of a national policy a Defense position had to be established and efforts in this direction have been going on with JCS and several offices of OSD contributing. The various actions were closely coordinated with members of your Policy Planning Staff and with Mr. Barber.

My staff have reviewed the progress to date for me, and I find that the thrust of the effort has essentially evaporated. Rather than resurrect the effort and proceed from where we left off, we should make a fresh start. The only stipulations I would suggest are that (1) we concentrate on arriving at a DoD position irrespective of whether we proceed from there to an official national policy position, and (2) we start with face-to-face discussions rather than the distribution of memoranda.

I cannot overemphasize the importance of a DoD position. Lack of this is reflected in ambiguity and indecision in the CB planning of the military departments and OSD offices. If we are to spend our resources wisely, an agreed upon position has to be generated. Dr. MacArthur of my staff is quite willing to assume responsibility for the coordination of the OSD position provided you are in agreement. If you would nominate a senior member of your staff, Dr. MacArthur would like to meet with your nominee at an early date and agree on a course of action.

Finn Larsen[3]

---

[1] Source: Washington National Records Center, OASD/ISA Files: FRC 330 70 A 6648, 384 1966 Jan– . Secret.

[2] Reference is probably to an ACDA memorandum from William C. Foster to the Committee of Principals, October 29, 1963, and Bundy's memorandum to Foster, November 5, 1963. (Both in the Kennedy Library, National Security Files, Departments and Agencies Series, ACDA, General 7–11/63)

[3] Larsen signed for Foster above Foster's typed signature.

122. **Memorandum From the Deputy Director of the Arms Control and Disarmament Agency (Fisher) to the Committee of Principals' Deputies**[1]

Washington, April 19, 1966.

SUBJECT

Chemical and Biological Warfare Policy (U)

Since November 1963, in compliance with a request of the Special Assistant to the President for National Security Affairs, this Agency has been conducting studies on the arms control and disarmament aspects of chemical and biological warfare. Concurrently, in response to the same directive the Departments of State and Defense have been conducting studies concerning those areas relating to CB weapons where they have prime responsibility and interest. The ultimate objective of these related studies is to formulate an agreed inter-agency statement of policy which could be developed into national policy guidance.

The attached paper, titled "Chemical and Biological Warfare Policy", which is forwarded for your consideration and comment, represents the tentative conclusions of this Agency on policies which the U.S. should adopt with respect to these weapons. It reflects the hypothesis that the spread of lethal chemical and biological weapons to states which do not now possess them is, prima facie, not in the national interest. Part III, titled "Basic Elements of Policy" proposes policies flowing from the hypothesis that are designed to minimize the risk that U.S. actions in the field of CB weapons might encourage other nations to acquire capabilities to use these potentially destabilizing weapons.

While it is believed that the suggested policies are in the national interest, there may be compelling military and political factors which militate against their adoption. It is requested, therefore, that in commenting on the attached draft, implications of the policies relating to military capabilities and international relations be emphasized. Your comments on arms control aspects would also be welcome.

In light of the delay since inter-agency studies on CB weapons were inaugurated, early action on this matter would be appreciated.

Adrian S. Fisher

---

[1] Source: Washington National Records Center, OASD/ISA Files: FRC 330 70 A 6648, 384 1966 Jan– . Secret. An attached April 22 memorandum from McNaughton to the Chairman of the JCS requests comments on the ACDA paper by May 20.

Attachment

CHEMICAL AND BIOLOGICAL WARFARE POLICY[2]

I. Purpose

To propose for discussion a policy for the US to adopt with respect to chemical and biological weapons. Attention is focused on those aspects of policy which relate to arms control and disarmament.

II. Background and Scope

Background

Since November 1963, in response to a request by the Special Assistant to the President for National Security Affairs, this Agency has been studying the arms control aspects of CB weapons. Also in November 1963, the Department of State proposed an inter-agency review of the entire CB field, with its goal a statement of related national policy.[3]

Since that time, two draft policy papers on CB warfare have been prepared and circulated for informal comment, one by the Department of Defense in December 1964,[4] and one by the Department of State, in May 1965.[5] While each of these papers has helped to narrow down the pertinent problems which require resolution, ACDA's concern is that neither one stresses the issue of proliferation commensurate with the evolving threat as we see it. ACDA views the spread of chemical and biological weapons of mass destruction to states not now possessing them, particularly the developing states, as not in the national interest and as a threat to world peace. Although studies made in early 1964 estimated CB proliferation not to be imminent, there have been an increasing number of signs since that time, particularly from Israel, the UAR, Iraq and Indonesia, which may indicate the beginnings of a dangerous trend.

Scope

The policies discussed in this paper are designed to minimize the risk that US actions in the field of CB weapons might encourage other

---

[2] A table of contents is not printed.

[3] Memorandum from U. Alexis Johnson to McGeorge Bundy, November 15, 1963. (Kennedy Library, National Security Files, William H. Brubeck Series, Disarmament 11/63)

[4] See footnote 2, Document 76.

[5] Not further identified.

nations to acquire capabilities to use these destabilizing weapons. They reflect, for the most part, official statements and policy decisions on such matters as use of CB weapons, sales of CB munitions to foreign nations, technical assistance and public information in the CB field, all of which have proliferation implications.

We have also suggested a definition for the term "CB Weapons of Mass Destruction", which appears without definition in the US draft outline of a GCD treaty[6] and for which an agreed definition would be necessary in the event proposals for the control of CB weapons are entertained as separable measures. It is our view that all CB weapons are not "weapons of mass destruction" as frequently categorized.

In addition, this paper suggests an approach to the difficult problem of control of CB weapons. In so doing, it recognizes that first priority must continue to be placed on the prevention of nuclear war, and that efforts to control CB weapons should not hinder or delay our efforts to halt the spread of nuclear weapons.

Our immediate objective in proposing these policies is to present the proliferation aspects of chemical and biological weapons for discussion and comment by interested agencies of the Government. Our ultimate intent is to arrive at an agreed position which can be incorporated into the national policy recommendations that will result from the current inter-agency review of the whole field of chemical and biological weapons.

A collateral, but important, objective of this paper is to be prepared for the unexpected introduction of the question of control of CB weapons at a future disarmament conference, or to take advantage of an opportune time for Western initiative.

III. Basic Elements of Policy

A. Definitions—

1. The term "CB Weapons of Mass Destruction" refers only to lethal chemical and biological weapons; it excludes all other CB weapons such as the non-poisonous tear gases, "CN" and "CS," and any analogous weapons having the primary purpose of only temporary incapacitation without residual injurious effect.

2. Smoke, flame and incendiary agents should not be considered as CB weapons.

---

[6] The quoted phrase appears in the "Outline of Basic Provisions of a Treaty on General and Complete Disarmament in a Peaceful World," submitted by the United States to the UN Disarmament Commission on April 29, 1965. For text, see *Documents on Disarmament, 1965*, pp. 115, 116.

B. Use—

The US should continue to adhere to its declared policy of "no-first-use" of chemical and biological weapons of mass destruction, but this policy should not extend to those non-toxic CB weapons, as specifically designated by the President, which cause only temporary incapacitation without residual injurious effect.

C. Non-Proliferation—

1. *Assistance to Others*—The US should not assist any other state or groups of states to acquire CB weapons of mass destruction.

2. *Discouraging Acquisition*—The US should take no actions that would encourage any other state or group of states to acquire CB weapons of mass destruction and should, as appropriate, discourage such acquisition.

3. *Information Exchange*—While the US should continue for the present to honor its existing cooperative arrangements with the UK, Canada, Australia, and France, it should not enter into agreements with any additional states dealing with the exchange of technical data on CB weapons of mass destruction.

4. *Public Information*—The US should maintain close control of information about CB programs. CB information released to the public should be limited to that necessary to establish the distinction between lethal and non-lethal CB weapons and to justify military use of tear gas where such use is necessary for humanitarian reasons.

D. On Seeking Agreements—

1. *Non-Proliferation*—Efforts to achieve a CB non-proliferation agreement should not be sought publicly or with the USSR until after a nuclear non-proliferation agreement has been achieved. Thereupon, the US should support efforts to forestall the acquisition of CB weapons of mass destruction by additional nations and should be prepared to enter into international agreements designed to achieve that objective. In the event that a nuclear non-proliferation agreement can not be obtained, the desirability of a CB non-proliferation agreement should then be considered in the light of conditions prevailing.

2. *CB Free Zones*—The US should support the creation of CB Free Zones after the establishment of Nuclear Free Zones. When an NFZ has been established then the US should support expansion of the denuclearized zone so as to also exclude CB weapons of mass destruction from the designated zone. Should the issue of CB Free Zones be pressed before NFZ's are established, the question of US support would be contingent on conditions then prevailing.

3. *Ban on "First-Use"*—Although the US should continue to adhere to its declared "no-first-use" policy on CB weapons of mass destruction, it should not so bind itself by international agreement, unless such action by the US would assist materially in obtaining adherence by other nations to a more comprehensive agreement, such as a CB non-proliferation agreement, which the US may wish to support.

4. *Other Agreements*—Other, more far-reaching agreements looking towards the eventual elimination of chemical or biological weapons of mass destruction from the arsenals of all nations should be sought when adequate means of verification are available to protect national security.

[Here follows Part IV, Discussion, pages 7–23.]

---

123. Memorandum From Spurgeon Keeny of the National Security Council Staff to the President's Special Assistant (Rostow)[1]

Washington, April 19, 1966.

SUBJECT

Proposed Exchange with the Soviets on the Control of Nuclear Weapons

I think you should be aware of the proposal discussed in the attached correspondence for reciprocal exchange with the Soviets of information on procedures for insuring control of nuclear weapons. Although I think that it will be submitted to the White House routinely for clearance if State decides to go ahead with it, Secretary Rusk might bring up the matter at some future Tuesday luncheon.

The proposal was originally made by Ambassador Thompson in a letter to John McNaughton (attached—Tab A),[2] and Bob McNamara has approved a draft note and statement (attached—Tab B).[3] The JCS oppose the proposed exchange for reasons summarized in paragraph 7 of their statement (attached—Tab C).[4]

---

[1] Source: Johnson Library, National Security File, Subject File, Nuclear Weapons, USSR, Vol. I, Box 34. Secret.

[2] Document 113.

[3] Letter from McNaughton to Thompson, April 19; not printed.

[4] Identified as a February 26 memorandum from the JCS to McNamara; not found.

In principle, I think this proposal is a good idea. In practice, however, I am afraid that, unless it is handled extremely carefully, it could create some real problems that would be counterproductive. The points in paragraph 7 of the Chiefs' paper are illustrative of the kinds of problems that might be involved in such an exchange.

The most serious problem is that such a dialogue would naturally lead to questions about the nature of Presidential control and our arrangements with our allies. While one obviously could refuse to discuss the subject or give only very general replies, this could have the effect of creating additional suspicions rather than reassuring the Soviets. If it became known to Congress that such an exchange had taken place, this might lead to renewed interest on the part of various Congressional committees such as the Joint Committee on Atomic Energy as to the details of Presidential authority for the release of nuclear weapons. This is a subject on which the President is very sensitive for obvious political reasons and about which the less said the better.

At the same time, I think there may be merit in the idea of reassuring the Soviets about our control procedures and informing them of some of the specific equipment, such as Permissive Action Links (PALs), that we might wish to encourage them to incorporate in their own weapons. If we decide to go ahead with this project, I would recommend that we simply give the Soviets the specific information that we think they should have, rather than instituting a dialogue or exchange on this subject. In transmitting the information, we could indicate that we would of course be interested in a similar reassurance on their own procedures but not make this a precondition or part of a dialogue on the subject.

I have discussed the problem along the above lines with Ambassador Thompson and called to his attention the special area of Presidential interest in the proposal. He indicated that he wants to give the matter further thought to decide whether it should be pursued at all at this time. I have also asked Ben Read to make sure that any action State decides to take on this proposal be cleared with the White House.

Spurgeon

124. **Report by the Anti-Submarine Warfare Panel of the President's Science Advisory Committee**[1]

Washington, April 28, 1966.

I. PREFACE

A. *Charge to the Panel*

The Panel (membership attached as Appendix A)[2] was formed in May 1964 by the Special Assistant to the President for Science and Technology and asked to review our Nation's present and planned capability in Anti-submarine Warfare (ASW).

The ASW Panel was to assess for the President:

1) the extent and nature of the submarine threat,
2) the technical possibilities for coping with this threat,
3) the extent to which the programs we are undertaking or are projecting will take advantage of the available technical opportunities for coping with the submarine threat, and
4) the organization for developing and applying the technical means for solving ASW problems.

The PSAC ASW Panel examined the Navy's ASW program during the period May 1964–July 1965. This report was completed in August 1965.[3] Time has not stood still since that date, and in particular the Navy has accelerated or undertaken many important efforts that implement in part certain of the Panel's recommendations. For example, the Navy has expanded its exercise program and continued to develop an improved analytical capability; the Captor program has been accelerated; much greater coherence is seen in the torpedo-countermeasures program; greater emphasis has been given to anti-ship torpedoes; etc. The Panel is aware of these developments, in broad outline, but for the most part it has not investigated these matters in sufficient detail to attempt to revise the report to take into account new progress. The Panel believes that its assessment of the total ASW program remains valid and that its recommendations require further action.

B. *Panel Activities*

In carrying out its mission, the Panel undertook to examine all relevant technical areas, recognizing that this involved many aspects of

---

[1] Source: Johnson Library, National Security File, Agency File, Office of Science and Technology, Vol. 1 [1966], Box 42. Top Secret. A title page is not printed.

[2] Not printed.

[3] See Document 99.

technology and a wide variety of naval programs. We also sought to take full advantage of the wealth of experience accumulated by our naval personnel and by other technical groups, both through an examination of their writings and through personal contacts and discussions. Finally, we sought to gain as much first hand experience as our schedules would allow with the current operational and R&D ASW equipment and with our ASW forces.

In so doing, the Panel has considered the present families of ASW platforms: 1) submarines, 2) surface ships (destroyers), 3) fixed-wing aircraft, and 4) helicopters; ASW sensors: 1) fixed acoustic surveillance systems, 2) submarine-borne active and passive sonar, 3) ship-borne active and passive sonar, 4) variable-depth sonar (VDS) either towed or free-swimming, 5) helicopter-dipped sonar, 6) sonobuoys, 7) airborne magnetic anomaly detection (MAD), and 8) radar; ASW weapons: 1) MK-37, MK-44 and MK-46 acoustic homing torpedoes, 2) mines, and 3) nuclear armed torpedoes or depth charges, including such delivery methods as anti-submarine surface launched rockets (ASROC), submarine launched rockets (SUBROC), and drone anti-submarine helicopters (DASH); and ASW fire-control and data-processing techniques and equipment.

In addition to these primary technical areas, the Panel has examined in some depth the Naval organization for R&D in ASW, including in particular the Navy's programs and techniques for developing, testing and evaluating systems and equipment. The Panel has also been concerned with manning requirements and training, ship automation, reliability and serviceability, the methods by which ASW effectiveness is measured, and the rationale for force-level determination. The Panel explored deeply with the Navy the detailed nature of the intelligence available on the Soviet submarine threat, and some members of the Panel went more extensively into the total store of intelligence.

Members of the Panel participated in ASW carrier task force exercises, visited shore-based sound surveillance systems, flew in shore-based and carrier-based fixed-wing aircraft and in helicopters, sailed on destroyers hunting submarines, spent several days on nuclear-powered killer-submarines (SSKN) of the most advanced types (Plunger-Thresher), and witnessed trial firings of Polaris missiles from nuclear powered ballistic missile submarines (SSBNs). The Panel also visited naval laboratories and facilities, as well as the headquarters of ASW, both Atlantic and Pacific. In addition, the Panel has had constant contact with the staffs of DDR&E and the Department of the Navy, as well as a joint meeting with a United Kingdom ASW panel under Dr. John Kendrew.

Thus, we believe that we have examined the relevant technical areas. We have benefited greatly by our contacts with naval personnel and by the work of other technical groups. Although we were able to visit many naval establishments and to examine much equipment first-hand, we were not able to do so to the extent that we would have liked and have instead had to rely to a great extent on the available technical data. We believe that the available data have been provided by the Department of Defense and the Navy; as we received these data we were gradually led to the conclusion that one of the primary weaknesses in our ASW program was the scarcity of technical and scientific personnel in positions which carried real management responsibility and/or authority.

In this report, the technical material and supporting arguments are to be found in Sections III through VII; conclusions and recommendations are contained in each of these sections; however, the major ones have been extracted and are to be found in the summary section (Part II). A first reading of the material should include at least Parts II and III.

II. SUMMARY

A. The Submarine Threat

The submarine threat to the United States is very substantial and will remain so indefinitely. As a measure of its intensity, we can note that the Soviet Union has a fleet of approximately 350 long range submarines of which 40 are nuclear and 310 conventional; that China has already built one and will probably build more copies of the Soviet diesel-electric G-class submarine which is capable of firing short range ballistic missiles while surfaced; and that such lesser powers as Indonesia and Egypt have been given Soviet submarines and can, therefore, pose a threat to elements of our naval forces in limited wars. Without question, submarines will with time become available to more and more nations perhaps including South American nations.

We found it useful to classify the submarine threat in the following important categories:

1. Submarines carrying nuclear weapons which can be used against CONUS by the Soviet Union now and by China in perhaps five years, as a deterrent force.

2. USSR submarines which would be used against our Naval forces (i.e., carrier and amphibious landing force) and against merchant shipping which might be carrying out theater support in a limited war.

3. Submarines of small powers which might be used as in para 2. Although we do not have detailed knowledge of the technical characteristics of the newer Soviet submarines, we have some quantitative data to support the conclusion that, with the possible exception of the most recent classes whose acoustic characteristics are not well known, current Soviet submarines are relatively noisy—except, of course, when

they work on battery. In addition, nuclear submarines may possess a very small separate machinery plant to allow long endurance "creep" operation at reduced noise level. This does not mean that the Soviets may not now be developing relatively quiet nuclear subs, as we have done, or even fuel-cell powered quiet submarines. In fact, it is hard for us to assume otherwise since the Soviets certainly have the technical capability to do so and they are surely aware of the fact that noise is a key weakness in their subs.

B. Our Capability

Our capability in ASW depends on a composite of sensors, ordnance, platforms to carry the sensors and ordnance, and tactics for their utilization. The sensors which are used for detection and classification, location, and tracking of submarines include active and passive sonar, MAD, radar, and even visual sighting. These sensors must work in the open ocean, which is a complex medium with poorly determined properties that vary with both time and location. The platforms in which the sensors are installed include surface ships, submarines, fixed-wing aircraft, helicopters, sonobuoys, as well as fixed platforms in our coastal water and other critical areas. The effectiveness of each element, or combination of elements, of course, also depends strongly on the technical characteristics and the tactics of the enemy submarines.

No one device or tactic plays a predominant role in our capability to detect, classify, locate and kill enemy submarines, and our capability is indeed a result of the combined use of the elements which make up our ASW forces. We do not foresee at this time any single new invention, development, or discovery which would by itself drastically alter this interdependence. The Panel does recognize that if large surface-effect naval vessels such as the Captured Air Bubble (CAB) ship could be successfully developed, they would, because of their great speed, be substantially less vulnerable to submarines than present types of vessels. It also recognizes that a reduction in the noise output of USSR submarines would greatly reduce our over-all effectiveness, but would affect the elements of our ASW forces differentially to different degrees.

Assessing our ASW capability for various threats is an extremely difficult task. It cannot be done convincingly by combining in a simple way the performance capability of each of the many elements that make up our ASW forces. It must depend in good part on empirical data from imaginatively and carefully designed naval tests and exercises. These are costly and difficult to design, execute and evaluate, but are nevertheless essential if we are to have any confidence in any assessment of our ASW capability. Although efforts to test and evaluate our ASW forces have been greatly expanded in the past two years, and the quality of the at-sea exercises shows continuing improvement, much still needs to be done in this very difficult aspect of ASW. As a result, we are now in the position that any such assessments are largely based on incomplete, inconsistent and fragmentary data; and any reliable quantitative assessments of our over-all capability is virtually impossible at this time.

Quantitative evaluation is fundamental not only in assessing our over-all capability, but also in assessing the desirability of various courses of action at all levels in the ASW program, from exploratory development, to component selection, to force design and procurement, to the selection of tactics and ASW strategy. Unless the marked improvement in this area which we have observed over the past two years continues and is expanded, we shall be forced to continue to rely too heavily on judgment in areas in which the rapidity of technological advance has provided opportunities and problems well beyond the scope of past military experience. Although the design, execution and evaluation of appropriate analytical studies, naval tests and exercises are difficult, they must be pursued with increased vigor.

In assessing our capabilities, we note that some of the individual components of our ASW forces, such as nuclear powered submarines (SSNs), are clearly qualitatively superior to their Soviet counterparts. We are impressed by the dedication and general quality of the officers in our ASW forces. These forces can clearly cope with the existing submarine threat from any of the smaller nations, although not without some losses. We note also that the Navy has carried out successfully numerous difficult intelligence missions, using components of the ASW forces, but the analysis of our ASW capabilities against the Soviet threat is still a complex problem. We can, however, say that our currently programmed (5 year) ASW forces would have extreme difficulty in denying to the Soviet Union a submarine-launched nuclear second strike capability which is a substantial augmentation of their land-based strategic nuclear forces.[4] Our active ASW is not good enough and our detection net is too soft do this.

By addressing ourselves to the specific threat, we may be able to acquire the capability of denying the Chinese a credible nuclear deterrent as long as the Chinese deterrent is based solely on a few G-class subs with short-range missiles aimed at West Coast targets. A detailed study of this threat and of possible techniques to counteract it is clearly warranted.

Although we believe that being prepared for an all-out non-nuclear war in Europe in the style of World War II may be somewhat unrealis-

---

[4] We note that since the publication of the draft of this report, greater emphasis has been devoted to the concept of [less than 1 line of source text not declassified] and more emphasis to the question of coercing the USSR through blockades at sea; neither of these changes in emphasis is evaluated in this report. [Footnote in the source text.]

tic, we emphasize that in most of the information provided to the Panel, a large fraction (1/2 to 1/3) of currently programmed ASW forces was justified primarily for this purpose. Nevertheless, our capability is poor to protect against substantial loss in sustained conveying of groups of 50 to 150 slow merchant ships in the face of a concerted attack by a Soviet submarine force. The fact that the Navy was unable to present to the Panel a current carefully-thought-out and realistic convoy doctrine or policy (and probably has an insufficient number of torpedoes if the USSR uses countermeasures) is symptomatic of the uncertainty even the Navy has in this matter.

Regarding the protection of carriers, amphibious forces and replenishment groups against the USSR submarine force, we appear to be placing a great deal of reliance on the effectiveness of the SQS-26 sonar used in bottom-bounce and convergence zone modes. Our limited (and inadequate) collection of oceanographic data does not support confidence in the bottom-bounce and convergence zone operations over large areas of the oceans and this leads us to doubt that detection will be achieved with a consistency sufficient to permit effective escort protection in many of the situations postulated for its use. Moreover, we believe that the potential effectiveness of our SSN/SS barriers has been overestimated, principally because enemy attacks, variations in enemy tactics, and even simple torpedo countermeasures have not been realistically assessed. Thus, we conclude that our carriers, amphibious forces, and replenishment groups are likely to be much more vulnerable to submarine attack, either by the USSR or by the smaller nations possessing USSR submarines, than has been stated in Memoranda to the President and presentations to the Congress on the basis of the Official Navy Study Cyclops II. In the case of small nations, for which submarine effectiveness is alleged to be very poor because of the inexperience of native crews, we note in particular that identification of the nation to which a W-class submarine belongs poses difficult technical and political problems and that the operational readiness of these submarines could rapidly be enhanced through appropriate use of "volunteer" crews.

C. ASW Expenditures

Considering the total submarine threat to the U.S., the very costly, but, in our view, inefficient program we mount to counter the important categories of the threat, and considering the high cost and low effectiveness of adding to our force structure many of the platforms, devices, techniques, etc., now being considered by the Navy, we conclude that some portion of the budget originally planned for the further operation and acquisition of present types of systems should be re-allocated to improvement programs to increase those systems substantially in effectiveness from their present marginal levels. Many of these systems, in fact, have considerable potential for improvement. Further acquisition of larger numbers of marginal or ineffective systems would provide far less ASW defense for our dollar than will such improvement programs.

D. ASW As A Systems Problem

The structuring and utilization of the various elements in our ASW forces constitute a systems problem in its most challenging form. The interdependence of the elements with each other must be appreciated and accounted for. Major commitments either for development or deployment in any one area must be made in the light of an assessment of the net contribution of each element to the over-all system. We cannot afford to neglect systems analysis and management here, even though they are far more difficult than in the strategic military areas where they have been very effectively utilized. On the contrary, because of the greater complexities and the greater number of subtleties involved, it seems to us that an over-all systems approach to ASW would be more fruitful, would reduce unnecessary duplication and redundancy, and could provide more insight than it does in those areas where it is more easily applied. How else can we possibly measure the increase in effectiveness we get for each dollar spent in ASW, or even the relative value of investing in different elements of our ASW forces, or the priority which we should assign to different development projects?

E. ASW Management

The responsibility for ASW in the Navy now is diffused through the many bureaus, laboratories, etc., in the Navy, and we find little evidence of *effective* testing, analysis, evaluation or decision-making concerning our over-all ASW forces. Rather, we have the impression that our ASW posture is largely a residue of tradition, of history, and of considerations of "balanced forces" rather than response to the realities of the current and projected threat and the current and projected technology. It is quite natural that past history, tradition, and internal forces within the Navy would have strong influences, but they cannot be allowed to overwhelm whatever hard data, analysis, test results, etc., one can bring to bear on the problem. Clearly, the Navy recognizes its dilemma and has tried in the last year to focus much of the responsibility for ASW in two newly created positions: the Director of ASW Programs under the Chief of Naval Operations, and the Manager of ASW Systems Projects under the Chief of Naval Matériel. Although we support these actions as steps in the right direction, we consider them inadequate to cope with the problem in spite of the obvious competence, dedication, and serious intent of the individuals chosen to occupy these positions. The new offices do eliminate in part the excessively piecemeal approach of the old organization, but they seem to have inadequate technical staff and insufficient line authority and responsibility in ASW.

We conclude that the Navy is not yet organized to maximize its ASW capability, and that to do so would require a major reorganization which would recognize and treat ASW as a technical system and provide greater management focus for responsibility and authority. In order to achieve marked improvements in our ASW effectiveness per dollar spent, there must be a high-level organizational element within the Navy with a strong technical staff which would have the responsibility for examining *all* the elements of ASW and their interrelationship, and would also have the authority to control the major portion of the resources allocated to ASW. It would be only too easy simply to recommend a Polaris type management system for handling ASW. But we recognize that the ASW problem is characterized more by its differences than by its similarities to the Polaris system. We do, however, recommend that the Department of Defense develop a management system for ASW which will have the substance and authority that the Special Projects Office had; but this will evidently require more effort and more technically competent people to manage adequately this more complex and more varied field.

F. Major Conclusions and Recommendations

1. *General.*

The Panel has heard the Navy on a number of occasions on matters relating to the rationale underlying force level development, threat and desired capabilities of Naval forces. The Panel was convinced that the information that was presented to it was inadequate and that the rationale underlying the development of forces has not been adequately developed. In its deliberations the Panel has arrived at a number of conclusions in this area that do not coincide with those of the Navy, and strongly believes that the Navy should devote much greater efforts to the development of a rationale for the employment of ASW forces and of justification for its development and procurement programs.

Our primary general conclusion is that our over-all ASW capability is very poor in relation to what we should expect from a program which costs the nation approximately $3B per year. The principal reason seems to us to be an inability to take full advantage of technical opportunities available to us, which is directly traceable to management policy which in effect gives excessive emphasis to quantity, to the relative neglect of quality (technical performance, availability, reliability, ease of maintenance, etc.) in force development. This is reflected most clearly in a relative lack of *effective* operational tests and evaluation of components and systems, and hence in a lack of a realistic factual basis on which decisions might be based. This is further reflected in a collection of components that are not well matched, or capabilities for individual components that are clearly out of phase. (The mismatch between destroyer sonar detection ranges, fire control accuracy, and weapon acquisition range is one example. Another is the lack of balance between torpedo countermeasures capability, which is practically nonexistent, and other characteristics of torpedoes such as range, lock-on range, etc., which have been continually improved. Another is the lack of balance between sonobuoy detection capability, which utilizes narrow band spectral analysis (LOFAR) of low frequency line structures, but is not directional, and correlation analysis using sonobuoy (CODAR) localization which depends on broad band noise with average higher frequencies and hence much greater attenuation. A final example is the great emphasis placed on anti-submarine torpedoes and the relative lack of effort on anti-shipping or anti-surface ship torpedoes.) These deficiencies will not be corrected by further procurement of the present systems. Thus, the Panel does not endorse several major components of the present ASW procurement program, and instead, concludes that a major effort should be made to improve the quality of our ASW posture rather than increase the numbers of those components that are often inadequate to their mission.[5] An increase in the numbers of such components over the next five years at the proposed rate means only a modest increase in total numbers, but it is questionable whether this will correspond to an equivalent increase in over-all effectiveness. However, the institution of several major developmental programs over the next five years is almost certain to lead to a very major improvement in our ASW capabilities in the period five to fifteen years from now, provided that these programs are well executed.

In adopting this conclusion, the Panel recognizes that over the next five years major improvements in our ASW posture can come about only as the result of improving the presently-existing components. In addition, the proposed developmental programs, if they are to be properly executed, will require a major reorganization in the management of ASW.

In concluding that many of the proposed increases or replacements in present ASW forces are not justified, the Panel examined the threat, with the results which follow:

a. *General War with USSR.* The Panel recognizes the capability of the USSR to use surface-launched ballistic missiles (SLBM) and surface-launched cruise missiles (SLCM) in an attack on the Continental United

---

[5] The Panel is aware that current budgeting procedures result in R&D and procurement programs being considered quite separately, but believes this to be unwise, especially for systems which are not normally replaced over an interval of from 15 to 20 years. [Footnote in the source text.]

States (CONUS). The limited size of such attacks, plus the possibility of early detection and warning, reduce the attractiveness to the USSR of this as a first strike alternative. The USSR SLBM and SLCM's could be used in a second strike as a follow-on to their first strike or in the event of a first strike by the U.S. Our present ASW forces might detect the build-up for a first strike, but have a limited capability for interdicting one. The U.S. capability would diminish and could become largely ineffective in the event the Soviets elected to use such submarine forces as a second strike. A numerical build-up of our SSN and DE-1052 destroyer forces over the next five years would lead to only minor improvements in both our capability to detect or interdict.

b. *Non-nuclear War with USSR.* The Panel believes that the large number of Soviet submarines would lead to very large U.S. and allied shipping losses during the early months of such a war—perhaps sufficiently great to materially reduce the effectiveness of allied ground forces, though the Panel has not examined this point in detail. An increase in the number of ASW components could *possibly* produce a proportional decrease in shipping losses in convoys, but the Panel believes that alternative tactics to convoy operations could also decrease such losses.

c. *General War with Communist China.* The Panel believes that the Chinese Communists could deploy in five years a small number of missile-carrying submarines which would pose a threat to West Coast cities and act as a deterrent against our use of nuclear weapons. While such a threat is not decisive, it does provide China with a negotiating tool. The Panel believes that development of [*less than 1 line of source text not declassified*] techniques *may* effectively neutralize this threat. The development of [*less than 1 line of source text not declassified*] tactics will require extensive operational tests. Success in these tests should lead to increased consideration of a forward Sound Surveillance System (SOSUS) and to the development of special [*less than 1 line of source text not declassified*] aids.

d. *Limited War.* The Panel concludes that there is a definite threat to carrier task forces and to amphibious forces in limited war situation. Such forces are vulnerable primarily because of inadequate sensors.

In view of these considerations, the Panel recommends acceleration in certain development programs, changes in the organization of the R&D program, and reduction in several procurement (or replacement) programs.

[Here follow Sections (or Parts) III–VII.)

125.   Memorandum From the Joint Chiefs of Staff to Secretary of Defense McNamara[1]

JCSM–296–66   Washington, May 5, 1966.

SUBJECT

The Foreign Intelligence Effort of the United States

1. The Director, Defense Intelligence Agency, in response to a memorandum for you by the Chairman, President's Foreign Intelligence Advisory Board, dated 19 April 1966,[2] subject as above, has prepared a reply and forwarded it to the Joint Chiefs of Staff for their consideration.

2. The Joint Chiefs of Staff have reviewed the draft memorandum and consider that it is responsive to the request.

3. The Director, Defense Intelligence Agency, consulted with the offices of the Director of Defense Research and Engineering, the Assistant Secretary of Defense (Administration), the Assistant Secretary of Defense (International Security Affairs), the Assistant Secretary of Defense (Systems Analysis), the commanders of the unified and specified commands, and the Services and considered their views.

4. The Joint Chiefs of Staff recommend that a memorandum, substantially the same as that contained in the Appendix hereto, be forwarded to the Chairman, President's Foreign Intelligence Advisory Board, on a "Special Handling—Not Releasable to Foreign Nationals" basis.

5. Without attachment, this memorandum is Unclassified.

For the Joint Chiefs of Staff:
John C. Meyer[3]
Major General, USAF
Deputy Director, Joint Staff

---

[1] Source: Washington National Records Center, OSD Files: FRC 330 70 A 6649, 350.09 1966 Jan– . Top Secret; Noforn; Restricted Data.

[2] Not found.

[3] Printed from a copy that indicates Meyer signed the original.

Appendix

Draft Memorandum From the Joint Chiefs of Staff to the Chairman of the President's Foreign Intelligence Advisory Board (Clifford)

SUBJECT

Principal Intelligence Gaps and Deficiencies (C)

1. (C) In your memorandum of 19 April 1966, you requested my views and comments regarding the principal gaps and deficiencies which, in my opinion, inhibit performance within the Department of Defense of its responsibilities and functions which significantly affect the national security.

2. (S) In the light of the above criterion, I have endeavored to identify and select those questions to which intelligence is currently not able to supply a fully satisfactory response and each of which is of such importance as to represent either a significant area of strategic uncertainty in force-oriented and strategic planning or a significantly inhibiting factor in the conduct of military operations. In this process, I have solicited the views of the major components of the Department of Defense, including the commanders of the unified and specified commands.

3. (TS) The following is a list of those subject areas which represent important gaps and deficiencies measured against the needs of the Department of Defense for intelligence support. This list is not exhaustive but is intended rather as a statement of those unanswered questions which, because of their importance, currently assume an exceptional degree of prominence within the Department of Defense. The items are not listed in order of importance; each is significant in its relation to major elements of the Department of Defense mission.

a. *Soviet Capabilities and Intentions with Respect to Multiple Independent Reentry Vehicles (MIRV).* Significant Soviet capability to employ MIRV will affect the force requirements and technological planning for future US ballistic missile defenses (BMDs).

b. *Soviet Capabilities and Intentions with Respect to BMD.* There is substantial evidence that the Soviets are deploying a BMD. The capability and characteristics of such a system are not known to us at this time; however, depending upon its effectiveness, such a system could drastically affect the strategic balance and US deterrent capability. BMD developments against short-range (battlefield) and medium-range ballistic weapons are also of concern.

c. *Soviet Allocation of Fissionable Material.* The wide range in the estimate of nuclear material available to the Soviets and the manner in which this material is allocated to major categories of nuclear weapons, such as strategic bombs, strategic missiles, and battlefield weapons, creates uncertainties in assessment of Soviet capabilities. Consequently, US planning must be based on assumptions the validity of which cannot be stated with adequate confidence.

d. *Soviet and ChiCom Nuclear Weapons Development Program.* More information is needed on the scope and direction of both Soviet and ChiCom nuclear weapons development programs. Although we have monitored individual Soviet nuclear tests over the past years and estimated their design parameters, we have inadequate over-all intelligence on Soviet broad objectives for the future. On ChiCom nuclear weapons development, we appear able to maintain a degree of surveillance over their testing program, but we continue to lack sufficient information on the broad objectives of their weapons program; in particular, we lack sufficient indication of their intentions and capabilities to develop deliverable weapons and to minimize weapons diameters.

e. *Soviet and ChiCom Capabilities and Intentions With Respect to Nuclear Weapons and Delivery Systems.* The present and future capabilities of the Soviets and ChiCom to employ nuclear weapons directly affect US war plans and tactics. For example, we lack information on the Soviet intent and capability to deploy a solid propellant ICBM, field a mobile ICBM, develop new strategic aircraft, or employ ballistic missile submarines and on the ChiCom intent and capability to produce strategic delivery systems. Insufficient knowledge forces planning to be based on assumptions which, if incorrect, can invalidate plans, affect national security, and waste resources.

f. *Soviet Activities in Enhanced Nuclear Weapons Effects (Specifically Hot X-Rays) (S-RD).* Specific knowledge of Soviet work in these areas is needed for US strategic missile development and hardening antiballistic missile planning and for establishing concepts of operation.

g. *Soviet Capabilities and Intentions in Space.* There is a deficiency in our present ability to detect launch, including zero orbit and the first orbit of Soviet space vehicles and their potential military application, and to provide early detection and subsequent tracking of altered orbits of such vehicles. In addition, the Soviet Union has conducted several sophisticated space experiments about which the United States had no foreknowledge and has not yet duplicated. Some knowledge of the technological advances which made this possible would assist our space program, particularly the manned orbiting laboratory.

h. *Surveillance of ChiCom Military Movements as an Indicator of Intentions in Southeast Asia.* The situation in Southeast Asia could be altered rapidly by the introduction of large numbers of Red Chinese into the North Vietnam area. One of the first indications would be a buildup of ground and air forces in Southern China and naval surface and submarine forces in adjacent sea areas. We are not getting intelligence coverage of these areas with the timeliness, frequency, and quality required.

i. *Soviet and ChiCom Capabilities in Support of Protracted Operations.* More knowledge is needed of those aspects of force structure and logistics support capabilities that determine the size of committed forces and the duration for which they can be committed. In the case of the Soviet Union, this consideration applies to both nuclear and nonnuclear operations and will similarly apply to Communist China when that country attains significant nuclear capability.

j. *Effectiveness of the Soviet's Stored Obsolescent Weapons.* Information is lacking regarding the total capability represented by obsolescent Soviet weapons in storage and their ability to reactivate, man, and support them. In particular, their ability to obtain pilots for tactical aircraft is not known.

k. *Communist General Purpose/Tactical Military Capability.* There is a persistent over-all deficiency in intelligence available on communist general purpose/tactical forces. Specific deficiencies include current and future information on detailed order of battle, combat and service support, mobilization capability, electronic surveillance and reconnaissance capabilities, tactical air support, tactical nuclear weapons and doctrine, and tactical air defense capabilities and systems, ground and air, low and high altitude (with special regard for future air defense systems). This over-all deficiency embraces considerations of timeliness, accuracy, and degree of detail and particularly the posture and capabilities of mobile weapons systems. It continues to inject significant uncertainties into force-oriented and strategic planning and into the establishment of readiness postures.

l. *Soviet Antisubmarine Warfare (ASW).* There is insufficient information available on Soviet antisubmarine warfare capabilities to enable an assessment of the threat posed by this capability against nuclear powered ballistic missile submarines.

m. *Soviet and ChiCom Research and Development.* The principal gap in scientific and technical intelligence, which has the most significant effect on our national security, has been the inability to obtain definitive information on applied development projects and programs in the time period between the end of general research and the appearance of development testing or deployment.

n. *Soviet and ChiCom Capabilities and Intentions with Respect to Biological and Chemical Warfare.* Lack of specific knowledge of biological and chemical warfare activities prevents our effective defense planning for offensive and defensive material and for establishing operational posture.

o. *Soviet and ChiCom Mapping, Charting, and Geophysical Data.* The principal intelligence gap and deficiency for the DOD mapping, charting, and geodetic community is the almost complete inability to penetrate the rigidly controlled society of the communist world for the procurement of communist-produced topographic, charting, and geophysical materials. Both countries have completed major programs of effort during the last ten years covering the fields of topographic mapping, aeronautical and nautical charting, and geophysical activities such as geodesy, gravity, and geomagnetics. We have obtained practically none of these data. These deficiencies have a pronounced influence on the geodetic positioning of targets and will directly bear on the success or failure of military operations.

p. *Counterinsurgency Intelligence.* There is a general deficiency in detailed basic and operational intelligence on newly emerging countries, particularly in Africa South of the Sahara, and in other areas such as Latin America which are potentially vulnerable to insurgency. Contingency operations must be planned which require detailed data on external and internal subversive elements and infrastructure; the degree of loyalty and capability of indigenous defense forces; biographic data on potential leaders, both loyal and subversive; and basic information on accurate graphics, key communications, public utilities, and other operational and supporting facilities.

q. *Lack of Reliable Information on Plans, Policies and Intentions of Communist Countries.* This deficiency continues to be one of the most difficult to solve and, additionally, continues to pose a great strategic, as well as political, uncertainty in military planning and preparedness.

r. *ChiCom Economic, Industrial, and Technological Base.* There is inadequate information on the extent of development of the ChiCom economic, industrial, and technological base and its ability to support political, military, and subversive activities in Asia, Southeast Asia, and other areas. Additionally, much is needed on the ChiCom role relating to other communist countries, and the apparatus by which it influences them, especially North Vietnam.

4. (U) In addition to the above, as you are well aware, we are beset with many intelligence deficiencies and problems associated with the conduct of military affairs in Southeast Asia. Although of immediate importance, these have not been specifically delineated in the above list since they have been, and are continuing to be, comprehensively addressed in response to a White House memorandum signed by Mr. McGeorge Bundy to the Secretary of State, the Secretary of Defense, and

the Director of Central Intelligence, dated 4 January 1966, subject: "Review of the US Foreign Intelligence and Related Activities in Selected Areas of Southeast Asia and the Far East," and which was based on the PFIAB report to the President, dated 9 December 1965, same subject.

5. (U) On behalf of the Department of Defense, may I assure you of our continued and wholehearted cooperation.

---

126.   Letter From the Director of the White House Office of Emergency Planning (Bryant) to Secretary of State Rusk[1]

Washington, May 10, 1966.

Dear Mr. Secretary:

On June 17, 1964 the then Director of the Office of Emergency Planning in a letter to you furnished information on the Supply-Requirements Study for Nuclear War and Reconstruction[2] being carried out by various departments and agencies under guidance from this Office.

The initial aspect of this work dealt primarily with the development and testing methods and techniques. We subsequently undertook a more definitive study which could serve as the basis for reaching decisions about nuclear war stockpile objectives.

This study has now been completed, and I am enclosing a set of documents which describe it.[3] The economic guidelines contained in the tables of the enclosed material should now be used by your Department and other participating departments and agencies carrying out the analyses of individual materials needed to reach decisions about nuclear war stockpile objectives.

A set of the documents is also being sent to Mr. Edmund Getzin, Chief of Industrial and Strategic Materials Division, with a request that he review them prior to a meeting that we will have with department and agency representatives later this month. Mr. Getzin is your repre-

---

[1] Source: National Archives and Records Administration, RG 59, Central Files 1964–66, DEF 1–2 US. Secret.

[2] Document 33.

[3] Attached are a 15-page OEP study, "Supply-Requirements Study for Nuclear War & Reconstruction," and a 4-page Appendix; not printed.

sentative on the Interagency Working Group on National Supply-Requirements Studies. Members of the Working Group are responsible for coordinating the preparation of analyses of individual resources and materials within their respective agencies.

The work on the analyses should advance as rapidly as possible. The schedule for carrying it forward will be established at the meeting of the Working Group on National Supply-Requirements Studies. The continued cooperation of your Department in this endeavor will be greatly appreciated.

Sincerely,

Farris Bryant

---

127. Memorandum From the Joint Chiefs of Staff to Secretary of Defense McNamara[1]

JCSM–344–66   Washington, May 21, 1966.

SUBJECT

Chemical and Biological Warfare Policy (U)

1. (U) Reference is made to:

a. A memorandum by the Assistant Secretary of Defense (ISA), I–22689/66, dated 22 April 1966, subject as above.[2]

b. A memorandum by the Deputy Director, US Arms Control and Disarmament Agency (ACDA), for the Deputies to the Committee of Principals, dated 19 April 1966, subject as above.[3]

c. JCSM–112–65, dated 16 February 1965, subject: "Draft Policy Paper—Chemical and Biological Warfare (U)."[4]

---

[1] Source: Washington National Records Center, OASD/ISA Files: FRC 330 70 A 6648, 384 1966 Jan– . Secret. A September 1 covering memorandum from McNamara to the Chairman of the JCS indicates McNamara's concurrence with the JCS view that a national policy on chemical and biological weapons should be established. He added that he had directed his staff to prepare a recommended Defense position for JCS comment during October and to use the draft NSAM included with JCSM–112–65 (Document 76) in developing the position.

[2] See footnote 1, Document 122.

[3] Document 122.

[4] Document 76.

2. (S) In reference 1a, the Assistant Secretary of Defense (ISA) requested the Chairman, Joint Chiefs of Staff, to provide comments on an ACDA paper, attachment to reference 1b, which sets forth that agency's tentative conclusions on policies which the United States should adopt with respect to chemical and biological weapons. The Deputy Director, ACDA, believes that, while the suggested policies are in the national interest, there may be compelling military and political factors which militate against their adoption.

3. (S) The Joint Chiefs of Staff, in response to a request from the Office of the Assistant Secretary of Defense (Administration), provided, in Appendix B to reference 1c, a proposed National Security Action Memorandum (NSAM) on chemical and biological weapons. No action has been taken on the proposed NSAM. The Joint Chiefs of Staff continue to hold the view that a national policy on chemical and biological weapons should be established as a matter of priority. They further believe that policy matters regarding arms control and disarmament aspects should not be considered until such time as a national policy has been established or, at least, until a DOD position is determined.

4. (S) The proposed NSAM forwarded in reference 1c continues to reflect the views of the Joint Chiefs of Staff. Accordingly, they recommend that:

a. The proposed NSAM contained in reference 1c be used as the basis for establishing the DOD position on the chemical and biological warfare policy issue in question.

b. Efforts be made to attain a national policy as soon as possible.

c. The Joint Chiefs of Staff be afforded an opportunity to comment on any possible DOD revisions to their proposed NSAM, as well as to participate in the review of any over-all State/Defense/ACDA interagency policy proposals prior to final adoption.

d. ACDA and other interested governmental agencies be advised that no action within the Department of Defense will be taken on the ACDA paper in reference 1b until such time as, preferably, a national policy on chemical and biological weapons has been established or, at least, until such time as a DOD position is determined.

For the Joint Chiefs of Staff:
Earle G. Wheeler[5]
Chairman
Joint Chiefs of Staff

---

[5] Printed from a copy that indicates Wheeler signed the original.

128.   Memorandum From the Assistant Secretary of Defense for
        Systems Analysis (Enthoven) to Secretary of Defense
        McNamara[1]

Washington, May 23, 1966.

SUBJECT

   Interaction of U.S. Assured Destruction and Damage Limiting Forces (U)

Last year's Memorandum to the President on Strategic Offensive
and Defensive Forces[2] paid particular attention to larger-than-expected
threats to our Assured Destruction capability. These threats were postulated without explicit study of their desirability or feasibility from the
Soviet viewpoint and without evidence of Soviet trends in those directions from intelligence indicators. Postulation of such threats furnishes
an appropriate analytical tool for an extreme test of our Assured
Destruction capability; nevertheless there is a risk that it may obscure
possible U.S. opportunities to influence Soviet behavior. Taking larger-
than-expected threats as "given" fails to credit our Damage Limiting
forces with the virtual attrition that they in fact exact of the Soviets in
planning their own forces.

The Soviets apparently view our forces, as we do theirs, as a potential first strike threat. They therefore must design their capabilities to
protect their own Assured Destruction capability against a U.S. first
strike. To the extent that Soviet resources are thus expended, and hence
diverted from alternative uses in improving the U.S.S.R.'s Damage
Limiting posture, our own Assured Destruction task becomes easier.

It is in our interest for the Soviets to spend sizable sums in guard-
ing their Assured Destruction capability, provided these expenditures
are primarily reflected in *defensive* measures such as missile launch facility hardening, missile dispersal or missile mobility, rather than in
increases in their offensive forces' payloads. Diversion of Soviet
resources to defensive measures would reduce the cost of maintaining
our relative Assured Destruction position for a given level of Soviet
expenditure on strategic programs and would also contribute to U.S.
and Allied Damage Limiting by reducing their ability to inflict damage
on us.

The implications for U.S. policy concern the value of continuing to
maintain a counter-military threat against the Soviet strategic offensive

---

[1] Source: Washington National Records Center, OSD Files: FRC 330 70 A 4662, 381
SRF 1966. Top Secret. "Sec Def has seen, 24 May 1966" is stamped on the memorandum.

[2] Document 103.

forces; specifically they concern the value of achieving low CEP to force the Soviets to adopt very expensive vulnerability-reducing methods such as mobility and hard point defense. Although Soviet responses cannot be predicted with confidence, a Soviet response that optimized their Assured Destruction capability against a U.S. threat with much lower CEP than we have now, would result in a reduction in Soviet first strike Damage Limiting capability over a wide range of Soviet Assured Destruction budgets.

An illustration of the pressure imposed by U.S. strategic offensive forces on Soviet forces was made in the DDR&E study, "A Summary Study on Strategic Offensive and Defensive Forces of the U.S. and U.S.S.R." of September 8, 1964.[3] The study contains an analysis (p. 68) showing that if the Soviets optimized their Assured Destruction capability against a small U.S. counter-military offensive capability they could purchase large, soft missiles at $1.33 million per kilopound ($M/KP). The cost to the Soviets of the same payload *triples*—to $4M/KP—if survivability through hardening and dispersal must be purchased. Virtual attrition seems to be exerting major influence on Soviet force planning, as shown by the Soviets' large scale deployment of SS-11s and by their pursuit of small and mobile missile technology.

My staff has undertaken a further analysis of the pressures that programmed U.S. forces indirectly bring to bear on the Soviet Damage Limiting capability. This analysis proceeds in three steps.

In the first step, a Soviet force is designed to negate the U.S. Assured Destruction capability in a Soviet first strike assuming that the Soviets were not in fact concerned with maintaining an effective Assured Destruction capability. It is basically the approach used in the extreme cases of last year's Draft Presidential Memorandum.

Then, the programmed U.S. forces are applied against this Soviet posture, and surviving Soviet forces strike U.S. urban targets. Resulting U.S. fatalities are so low that the assumed enemy posture could not constitute a high-confidence (to the U.S.S.R.) Soviet Assured Destruction capability.

Finally, at the same Soviet budget level used in the first step, a new Soviet force is designed for first strike Damage Limiting, subject to a constraint on Soviet second strike Assured Destruction stemming from the pressure exerted by our capabilities. This constraint markedly reduced the Soviets' ability to erode our Assured Destruction capability within the fixed Soviet budget level.

---

[3] This 192-page study and Appendix are not printed. (Washington National Records Center, OSD Files: FRC 330 69 A 7425, 381 Strategic Retaliatory Forces (9 Jan 94) Sep–Nov 1964)

Analysis

Soviet First Strike Only Damage Limiting Threat. A re-examination of SS-9 requirements, taking all reliabilities into account, indicates that the Soviets would need some 350 SS-9s, each carrying 10 MK-17 MIRV's, to achieve high expected damage against programmed U.S. land-based forces with high confidence. Assuming the existence of such a Soviet capability, and applying reasonable adjustments to National Intelligence Projections for Planning (NIPP) factors to reflect the assumed introduction of MIRV, the expected damage against U.S. forces is .92 with a 1500 foot SS-9 CEP, but only .77 with a 2100 foot CEP. (We now project a CEP of 3000 feet for the SS-9 in 1970, with no evidence of an appreciable Soviet effort to reduce this figure.) These missiles alone cost some $9 billion (about $1.5 M/KP) beyond the cost of the remainder of Soviet Offensive forces.

Next, we design a least-cost Soviet defense to keep Soviet fatalities at [*less than 1 line of source text not declassified*] of their total population in the face of a counter-urban attack by the surviving U.S. forces. This fatality level corresponds to the delivery of [*less than 1 line of source text not declassified*] warheads in the absence of Soviet defenses, and roughly equates to the level that might be expected from leakage through a very good defense against a U.S. retaliatory attack. This defense consists of 1800 area interceptors and 1000 terminal interceptors at 15 cities, at a total five-year cost of approximately $6.4 billion plus a non-recurring cost for research and development, tooling and production facilities, etc., which is irrelevant to this calculation. Of this cost, approximately 80 percent is for area defenses. This is consistent with results obtained in analyses of light Nike-X deployments.

Thus, for a total increment of some $15 billion over a base U.S.S.R. budget, the Soviets can reduce the Assured Destruction capability of our programmed missile forces to a highly unsatisfactory level through 1969–1974. The base budget is the cost of their R&D program, their missile programs, their SLBM programs, their bomber program and their air defense programs.

Assured Destruction Capability of the Soviet Force. We have analyzed a pre-emptive U.S. strike as a Soviet planner might do, in evaluating the Soviet Assured Destruction capability. The programmed U.S. forces are laid down in a pre-emptive strike against the Soviet intercontinental strategic military target system designed above (i.e., the MIRVed SS-9s plus the other Soviet ICBMs, SLBM bases, intercontinental bomber bases, etc.). If the Soviet area defenses did not cover their SS-9 missile fields, as would be the case with the present locations of the SS-9 silos, U.S. fatalities would be less than 10%. If the Soviet area missile defense is assumed to protect Soviet military targets and to operate without leakage residual Soviet forces are estimated to inflict 22% U.S. fatalities (200 equivalent one MT weapons) in the absence of U.S. ABM. Thus the Soviet deterrent would depend entirely on the precise siting and effectiveness of their ABM as a component of hard point defense. (Even a very light U.S. ABM deployment would be able to negate the remaining Soviet forces.)

Soviet First Strike Damage Limiting with Assured Destruction Constraint. As a last step, the Soviets take measures to maintain their Assured Destruction capability. They are allowed to replace the forces assumed above with more survivable forces at the same cost as the Soviet Damage Limiting force. The resulting posture (shown in table below is very similar to the missile force predicted in the NIPP), but the SS-9s are assumed to carry MIRVs. Additional mobile missiles and an area only defense are also purchased at the expense of Soviet terminal defenses. The SS-9s and the area defenses can be considered as the Damage Limiting increment added to the Assured Destruction backbone of their posture.

If this *entire force* is sent against the U.S. in a Damage Limiting first strike (i.e., no part is withheld for a later Assured Destruction capability), the residual U.S. missile forces can still deliver more than [*less than 1 line of source text not declassified*] equivalent weapons against the U.S.S.R. instead of the [*less than 1 line of source text not declassified*] equivalents that the U.S. could deliver against the Soviet Damage Limiting only posture. Again, this figure exceeds the [*less than 1 line of source text not declassified*] equivalent criterion for an effective U.S. Assured Destruction capability that was suggested in last year's Presidential Memorandum.

TABLE 1: Soviet Intercontinental Forces of the Damage Limiting Posture (#1) and of the Assured Destruction Posture (#2)

Launchers	69	70	71	72	73	74
Posture #1						
Soft SS-7 (1x2)	102	80				
Hard SS-7 (1x3)	70	70	70	70	55	30
Hard SS-9 MIRV (1x1)	300	350	350	350	350	350
Posture #2						
Soft SS-7 (1x2)	102	80				
Hard SS-7 (1x3)	70	70	70	70	55	30
Hard SS-9 MIRV (1x1)	125	125	125	125	125	125
Hard SS-11 (1x1)	300	375	425	475	525	550

Conclusions

The Soviets, by viewing our forces as a first strike threat to their Assured Destruction capability, must spend much more to achieve a first strike Damage Limiting capability. This does not argue that the Soviets are incapable of achieving both a satisfactory (to them) Assured Destruction capability and a Damage Limiting capability. But it does mean that, by carefully designing our own forces, we can foreclose any "easy" roads to Damage Limiting for the Soviets. Furthermore, low U.S. CEPs prevent simple proliferation of hard ICBM silos from being a useful Soviet response; Soviet mobility or defense would be required. Thus, a simple increase in total Soviet offensive payload is not a likely response to the strong U.S. counterforce capability.

Characteristics of U.S. Damage Limiting forces that place this constraint on Soviet forces should, therefore, receive continued attention. For example, the high accuracy attainable with the MK-17 (rather than the MK-11A) can be thought of as making an indirect contribution to Assured Destruction.

Proposed changes in U.S. forces (such as the addition of large payload missiles) should be evaluated in light of possible Soviet responses, and especially in light of the constraints they impose on the Soviet mix of Assured Destruction and Damage Limiting. Analyses not based on such consideration are likely to be incomplete, and the decisions based on such incomplete analyses, misleading.

In this year's Presidential Memorandum, I propose to include an interaction analysis. Thus, in addition to postulating Soviet threats and finding what forces would be required to overcome them, various possible new U.S. systems—both for Assured Destruction hedges or for Damage Limiting—will be considered in terms of the effects they would be likely to have on the U.S.S.R.

Alain Enthoven

129.   Memorandum for the Record[1]

Washington, May 27, 1966.

The President and the Vice President met with the NSC Staff on Friday, May 27, largely to get acquainted. The President began the meeting by outlining his philosophy of our foreign policy. He made these points:

1. We have to stay strong militarily, not because we want to use force but just because we have now learned that force is sometimes necessary to keep peace. "My father used to tell me that love would solve 95% of the world's problems but that you had to be strong to solve the other 5% because some people do not understand the language of love and friendship." Later in the meeting he came back to this theme. Thinking about the $60 billion defense budget, he said "Think what wonders I could perform with that money if I could put it into agriculture and health and education."

2. This strength is not to set up a fortress America. In this world which is now 3 billion people and will be 6 billion in not too long a time, we just can't survive by keeping to ourselves. So in our own interests we have to worry about the other fellow.

3. More than that we can't rest while other people are miserable in such numbers. "They are human beings just like we are. They laugh like we do. They cry like we do when they are hurt. They eat like we do, although not so well. They need clothes and shelter like we do." So a nation blessed with the riches ours has can not sit back while others like ourselves are in misery.

The Vice President spoke generally on the same theme of circulating the ideals of the Great Society into a world wide effort against poverty, disease, and illiteracy.

The President picked up one of the Vice President's remarks and said he wanted to make very clear his position on Vietnam. He said he obviously was under all kinds of pressure to "get out with General Fulbright, go in with General Goldwater, and General Gavin wants me to 'hunker up like a jackass in a hailstorm'." He said he had looked at all the choices. He didn't see how any President of the United States could do other than what he has chosen to do. He admits he could be wrong. But having decided on this course, he is absolutely determined to see it through. No one should be under any illusion that we will be pulling out.

---

[1] Source: Johnson Library, National Security File, Harold H. Saunders Files, NSC, SIG, IRG, 4/1/66–8/31/66. Secret. Prepared by Saunders on July 13.

The President said he was very happy with the memos, analyses, and recommendations coming from the staff. What he would like to see more of now is "ten new ideas" in his reading folder every night. He said these were beginning to flow but he wanted more and more of them.

H.S.

130. Memorandum From Spurgeon Keeny of the National Security Council Staff to the President's Special Assistant (Rostow)[1]

Washington, May 31, 1966.

SUBJECT

CIA Intelligence Report on the Status of the Anti-Missile Defense System for Moscow

Bromley Smith asked that I prepare a note for you commenting on the attached report which summarizes the current status of our knowledge of the anti-missile defense system in the Moscow area since he felt it might have considerable impact on our own military planning.

This is not a new development. Information on this system has been accumulating for several years. There has been agreement in the intelligence community for over a year and a half that it was almost certainly intended for some sort of anti-ballistic missile defense and that it was probably based on the use of relatively high-yield weapons for exoatmospheric defense. The principal new piece of information reported in the memorandum is that the Soviets are now beginning to construct missile launchers, probably for the Galosh missile, at several of the radar sites associated with this system. This move had been anticipated for several months since launchers were observed under construction at the prototype installation at the Sary Shagan anti-missile development center.

---

[1] Source: Johnson Library, National Security File, Intelligence File, TKH Jan.–July 1966, Box 1. Top Secret; [codeword not declassified]. An attached undated note from Bromley Smith to Rostow notes that this statement on Soviet ABMs also affected the ACDA proposal Rostow had spoken about that morning. Smith added that the President's attention should be directed to this data during the preparation of the military budget.

The central question is how effective the Moscow ballistic missile defense would be against US strategic missiles in the late 1960s and early 1970s when it would presumably be fully operational. While it is impossible to give a precise answer to this question since we can only guess how the Moscow system would operate, I think it is possible to make some significant general observations on the system's capabilities that indicate quite persuasively that by itself the Moscow system would not be particularly effective even in the defense of Moscow and would have only a small perturbation on our over-all war plans.

1. *Physical Vulnerability.* The Moscow system is extremely soft and hence highly vulnerable to a well-planned large-scale attack. It appears to depend for early warning and initial tracking on the Hen House radars located at Olenegorsk in northern Murmansk and Skrunda on the Baltic coast. Both of these radars are very soft and essentially undefended. The large Dog House radar at Moscow, which may be back-up early warning and tracking radars for the system, and the radars at the triads which probably do the final tracking of the incoming missile and the tracking of the defensive missiles are also extremely soft. Finally, the defensive missiles will fire from exposed above-ground launchers.

2. *Penetrability.* By the 1969–70 period our programmed penetration aids for Minuteman-Polaris will probably be very effective against a Moscow-type system (high altitude intercept). By dispensing chaff and decoys, each missile will present the defense with some 7 to 21 separate re-entering targets even when very high-yield warheads are employed. Hence, a very small number of our offensive missiles would probably overwhelm the system.

3. *Fire Power.* The Moscow system will not have a high rate of fire. So far, we see only some 64 missile launchers under construction. When the entire projected deployment of 8 double triads is completed (some of this is not yet really started), the total system would consist of only 128 launchers. This is very small compared to the requirements of a really effective ABM system and the Soviet threats McNamara has hypothesized in his US force level projections. For example, in his Memorandum for the President in connection with the FY-1967 budget for strategic offensive-defensive forces,[2] McNamara examined a worst-possible Soviet threat in the early 70's in connection with the decision to initiate deployment of the Poseidon missile to increase the fire power of the Polaris submarine fleet. In this analysis he assumed that the Soviets put MIRVs (multiple independent re-entry vehicles) on enough of their ICBM force to completely eliminate our Minuteman force in a pre-emptive strike. (I would note that there is no evidence that the Soviets have

---

[2] For a draft, see Document 103.

done anything leading towards a MIRV capability.) McNamara also assumed that our penetration aids programs would all fail catastrophically and that aircraft would be unable to inflict any damage on the Soviet Union because of SAM defenses. He then assumed that the Soviets would deploy 4,500 exoatmospheric ABM interceptors which could effectively engage 3,000 separate incoming targets. Even in the face of this concatenation of extreme threat assumptions, he concluded that with the added fire power of Poseidon we would still be able to approximate the amount of damage required to meet his criteria of assured destruction.

Although it is not discussed in the attached document, the big area of disagreement about Soviet ABM capabilities in the intelligence community is over the functional identity of the so-called Leningrad–Tallinn system which has been suspected, particularly by DIA, as being a possible ABM system. This system is now being deployed at a number of locations from the Baltic to the Urals. CIA is now almost certain that this system is in reality a long-range air defense system to supplement or replace the SA-2 system. DIA is now in the process of reevaluating their position on this system. I agree with CIA.

In summary, there is nothing particularly new in the attached report. Although we are beginning to accumulate details that may indicate how the Soviet system actually works, we are fundamentally in the same position concerning Soviet capabilities and intentions in this area that we have been in for the last year or two. There is no question that the Soviets are interested in ABMs and are undertaking at least a limited deployment at Moscow. We have not, however, seen real evidence of a massive national deployment or of a really effective system at Moscow by the standards we are now considering.

In line with Bromley's concern, I believe that this information will not have any special impact on the DOD since they have already assumed much worse threats in their military planning. I also do not believe the information on the Moscow system will have any special impact on Congress since McNamara has already briefed the Congress on an estimated Soviet ABM threat that is, if anything, more extensive than the current facts indicate. (See attached extract from McNamara's classified testimony.)[3] I would emphasize that the above views are my own. They are based on what I think we have seen and not what the Soviets might do in the future. There is no agreed-upon or disagreed-upon net evaluation within the US Government of the effectiveness of the Soviet ABM system and our ability to penetrate it. To correct this sit-

---

[3] Not printed; the excerpt is from McNamara's testimony on February 7 before the House Subcommittee on Defense Appropriations on the FY 1967–1971 Defense program and the FY 1967 Defense budget.

uation, Bob McNamara has just (May 21) directed Johnny Foster (DDR&E) to prepare such a study,[4] working with the Services and cooperating with CIA and Don Hornig's office. Although the organization of the study has not yet been worked out, Don Hornig and I together with some of our consultants, who are extremely well informed on this subject, will be involved in the review of the study. The study is now tentatively scheduled for completion on August 1, 1966.

Spurgeon

Attachment

Washington, May 18, 1966.

INTELLIGENCE MEMORANDUM[5]

USSR Pushing Ahead With Antimissile Defenses for Moscow

Summary

The Soviets are pushing ahead with deployment of antimissile defenses. Probable launch positions now are being constructed at one of the four ABM electronic sites which form an arc to the north and west of Moscow. The missile has not yet been identified. While there is no evidence of deployment elsewhere, the Soviets can be expected to extend ABM defenses to the same areas where the extensive deployment of new long-range surface-to-air missile defenses is under way.

---

[4] In this memorandum McNamara asked Foster to work with other Service Secretaries, the Director of Central Intelligence, and the President's Science Adviser in preparing an "authoritative report" on "the character, geographical deployment, and potential effectiveness, by year for each of the next five years, of the Soviet anti-ballistic missile system" and "the capabilities of each of our major ballistic missile systems to penetrate the Soviet anti-ballistic missile system, by year for each of the next five years, and the level of confidence we can attach to these capability estimates." (Washington National Records Center, OSD Files: FRC 330 70 A 4662, 471.94 Penetration 1966)

[5] Prepared by the Office of Current Intelligence and coordinated with OSI, OPR, and ONE. [Footnote in the source text.]

131.   National Intelligence Estimate[1]

NIE 11–4–66   Washington, June 16, 1966.

MAIN TRENDS IN SOVIET MILITARY POLICY

The Problem

To review significant developments in Soviet military thinking, policy, and programs, and to estimate main trends in Soviet military policies over the next five years or so.

Scope

This estimate assesses broad trends in Soviet military policy and doctrine. It does not attempt to recapitulate existing NIEs on Soviet strategic attack, strategic air and missile defense, and general purpose forces. Our most recent detailed estimates on the size, composition, and capabilities of these principal components and the supporting elements of the Soviet military forces are as follows:

NIE 11–8–65: "Soviet Capabilities for Strategic Attack," dated 7 October 1965, Top Secret, Restricted Data (Limited Distribution).
NIE 11–14–65: "Capabilities of Soviet General Purpose Forces," dated 21 October 1965, Secret.
NIE 11–3–65: "Soviet Strategic Air and Missile Defenses," dated 18 November 1965, Top Secret.[2]

Summary and Conclusions

A. There has been no basic change in established Soviet military doctrine or force structure, but recent trends point to adjustments in Soviet defense policy. The present political leaders seem more attentive than was Khrushchev to professional military advice, and they have been willing to authorize increases in both defense expenditures and military manpower. Current military writings reveal a search for ways to broaden the options available to the USSR in the application of its military power. (Paras. 1–5)

B. The Soviets retain their belief in the primacy of strategic attack and defense forces, both for deterrence and for foreign policy support.

---

[1]   Source: Johnson Library, National Security File, National Intelligence Estimates 11–65, USSR, Box 3. Secret; Controlled Dissem. A title page, prefatory note, and table of contents are not printed. According to the prefatory note, the CIA and the intelligence organizations of the Departments of State and Defense and the National Security Agency participated in the preparation of this estimate. Representatives of CIA, State Department, DIA, and NSA concurred; the AEC and FBI representatives abstained, the subject being outside their jurisdiction.

[2]   Documents 97, 98, and 106.

In addition, however, they now show increasing interest in improving the capabilities of their general purpose forces to meet contingencies short of general nuclear war. We believe this interest is in part responsive to past developments in US and NATO capabilities and to US advocacy of flexible response. Additional factors include the tensions arising from the Vietnam war and the resulting US military buildup, as well as Chinese hostility towards the USSR. (Paras. 6, 7, 12–14)

C. A sharp increase in Soviet defense expenditures is evidently to occur this year. We attribute it primarily to planned expansion in military R and D and to the cost of long lead-time deployment programs for strategic systems which were authorized in previous years. It probably also stems in part from some recent increase in operating costs, including military manpower. The Soviet leaders have probably authorized further growth in military and space expenditures during the 1966–1970 Five Year Plan period. We believe, however, that in the interests of their ambitious economic programs they will seek to limit the growth in defense spending to no more than the average rate of growth in GNP. (Paras. 3, 4, 17–22)

D. The Soviet leaders probably expect to achieve a substantial improvement in their strategic position vis-à-vis the US during the next several years. Chief among their current strategic attack programs is the rapid deployment of ICBMs in dispersed and hardened silos, which will add substantially to the survivability and retaliatory capability of the force. Major current air and missile defense programs include improved means of warning and control, better defenses against aircraft and aerodynamic missiles, and what we believe to be ABM defenses under construction. Through these and other programs, we think the Soviets are working to alleviate their present strategic inferiority, and to gain greater assurance of deterring the US in the various crises and confrontations they must allow for as they contemplate possible developments in the world situation.[3] (Paras. 26, 30, 31, 36)

E. The past restructuring of Soviet theater forces for general nuclear war has resulted in certain characteristics which could be serious handicaps in non-nuclear warfare, particularly if at all prolonged. We estimate that the Soviets will undertake gradual improvements in their general purpose forces which will make them somewhat better suited

---

[3] Colonel Harry O. Patteson, for the Assistant Chief of Staff Intelligence, USAF, would add the following sentence to this paragraph:

The intensity with which the USSR is pursuing a massive military research and development program—the specific content and progress of which are not clearly known to the US—could portend far more than an intent merely to strengthen Soviet deterrent posture and could well be aimed at attainment of a strategic military position which the US would recognize as providing the USSR with a credible first strike damage limiting capability as well as an assured destruction force. [Footnote in the source text.]

than at present for conventional operations. Ground units will probably be provided with greater tactical mobility and improved combat and logistic support, becoming more quickly responsive and better able to engage in sustained combat. The Soviets will also maintain a large and versatile tactical air component. They will continue to expand their naval presence in the open oceans, and will acquire greater capabilities to move unopposed military forces to distant areas. The Soviets may regard improved general purpose forces as having increased relevance as their strategic capabilities grow, but we do not think they expect alterations in the strategic situation so great as to permit them to undertake substantially more aggressive courses of action.[4] (Paras. 32–35, 37)

F. Soviet military policy will continue to be heavily influenced by external developments. In recent years Soviet forces in the Sino-Soviet border area have been strengthened in minor ways, and we expect a gradual increase in Soviet military strength confronting China. In Eastern Europe the USSR continues to develop the forces of its Warsaw Pact allies, despite their increasing tendency to assert their independence. The USSR is thus far disposed toward caution with respect to the present weakening of NATO, perhaps because of concern over the possible loosening of constraints on a revival of independent German power. But the Soviets weigh the adequacy of their military programs primarily against US capabilities, and they will continue to be sensitive to major new developments in US military policy and forces. (Paras. 8–11, 14)

G. Within the USSR, a high level of effort in military R and D will almost certainly be continued, despite resource allocation problems. The Soviets probably regard such an effort as imperative in order to prevent the US from gaining a technological advantage and also to gain, if possible, some advantage for themselves, but in deciding to deploy any new weapon system they would have to weigh the prospective gain against the economic costs and the capabilities of the US to counter it. (Paras. 15, 23)

H. We do not expect that Soviet military forces will come to be structured according to some quite new and clear-cut strategic doctrine. This will almost certainly be prevented by such factors as the momentum of existing programs, the multiplicity of claims on resources, and the differing views of various groups as to priorities. (Para. 5)

[Here follows the Discussion section (pages 5–16).]

---

[4] Colonel Harry O. Patteson, for the Assistant Chief of Staff Intelligence, USAF, believes the Soviet longer term goal is a combination of capabilities which would yield a credible first strike capability against US forces and thus permit substantially more aggressive courses of action. [Footnote in the source text.]

132.   Memorandum From the Central Intelligence Agency to the 303 Committee[1]

Washington, June 22, 1966.

SUBJECT

The Asia Foundation: Proposed Improvements in Funding Procedures

1. Summary

The Asia Foundation (TAF), a Central Intelligence Agency proprietary, was established in 1954 to undertake cultural and educational activities on behalf of the United States Government in ways not open to official U.S. agencies. Over the past twelve years TAF has accomplished its assigned mission with increasing effectiveness and has, in the process, become a widely-known institution, in Asia and the United States. TAF is now experiencing inquiries regarding its sources of funds and connections with the U.S. Government from the aggressive leftist publication, *Ramparts*.[2] It is conceivable that such inquiries will lead to a published revelation of TAF's CIA connection. In the present climate of national dissent and in the wake of recent critical press comment on CIA involvement with American universities, we feel a public allegation that CIA funds and controls TAF would be seized upon, with or without proof, and magnified beyond its actual significance to embarrass the Administration and U.S. national interests at home and abroad. Some immediate defensive and remedial measures are required [*2-1/2 lines of source text not declassified*].

[*3 paragraphs (11 lines of source text) not declassified*]

In the long run, we feel TAF's vulnerability to press attack can be reduced and its viability as an instrument of U.S. foreign policy in Asia can be assured by relieving it of its total dependence upon covert funding support from this Agency. In the belief that TAF contributes substantially to U.S. national interests in Asia, and can continue to contribute if its viability is sustained, CIA requests the Committee's study and attention to possible alternative means of supporting it.

[*6 pages of source text not declassified*]

---

[1] Source: Department of State, INR/IL Historical Files, Minutes of 303 Committee, 6/22/66. Secret; Eyes Only.

[2] Regarding a later revelation by the magazine, see footnote 2, Document 176.

133.   Memorandum From Charles E. Johnson of the National
        Security Council Staff to the President's Special Assistant
        (Rostow)[1]

Washington, July 1, 1966.

Walt—

The FY 1968 Nuclear Weapons Stockpile proposal has been ill-starred. When it came in in January,[2] Mac looked at it but got away before we could get the Bureau of the Budget analysis and paper work completed. Bob Komer sent the package to the President in March recommending approval. It is not clear whether the President or Joe Califano looked at it, but we were requested to return the package to the Pentagon to get Secretary McNamara's signature on it and also to obtain the formal concurrence of the Joint Chiefs. This was done about the middle of March and ever since Cy Vance and General Wheeler have been in negotiation, characterized more by its heat than its light.

The new proposal does not carry the Secretary's signature (it is also signed by Vance),[3] and it is my recommendation, as well as Keeny's, that we should not at this time press for a McNamara signature. Gen. Wheeler did concur in the submittal but the JCS price was to force deferring the retirement of [number not declassified] weapons previously scheduled for retirement in FY 1968 as a result of joint action by BOB and Vance's staff.

I have no doubt, and the BOB staff agrees, that the [number not declassified] weapons will be retired either in FY 1969 or possibly in FY 1968. I would not be surprised to see this matter disposed of next Fall in connection with the Secretary's budget memorandum projecting weapons requirements through 1975.

Keeny and I have both gone over this package and recommend that it be sent forward to the President.

Charles E. Johnson[4]

---

[1] Source: Johnson Library, National Security File, Memos to the President, Walt Rostow, Vol. 8. Top Secret; Restricted Data.

[2] The January 1966 proposal has not been found.

[3] Reference is to a June 6 letter from Vance and Seaborg to the President. A copy is in the Washington National Records Center, OSD Files: FRC 330 70 A 4662, A–400.23 1966.

[4] Printed from a copy that bears this typewritten signature.

134. Memorandum for the Record[1]

Washington, July 8, 1966.

SUBJECT

Minutes of the Meeting of the 303 Committee, 8 July 1966

PRESENT

Mr. Rostow, Ambassador Johnson, Mr. Vance, and Mr. Helms

Mr. Bill Moyers and Mr. Cord Meyer were present for Items 1 and 2

[Here follow a list of additional participants and discussion of agenda item 1.]

2. The Asia Foundation

a. Mr. Meyer capsuled the substantial accomplishments of The Asia Foundation and the endorsements it has received throughout the years. Ambassador Johnson supported these statements. Mr. Meyer pointed specifically to the vulnerability of The Asia Foundation cover and how a gadfly publication such as *Ramparts* had the capability to inflict considerable damage and apparently that was their intention.

[*1 paragraph (4 lines of source text) not declassified*]

c. There was some discussion of the real costs of a full endowment solution. Mr. Vance felt that the sum requested was too small. The others agreed that Mr. Meyer was instructed to arrive at a more appropriate figure which could then be checked with the principals for a telephonic vote.[2]

d. Mr. Meyer then went on to point out that this was only one conspicuous example of a problem which would grow larger, and he specifically mentioned the need of a new institution created by legislation and based on [*less than 1 line of source text not declassified*] lines which could provide general support grants to this and similar organizations whose activities are of proven value to the United States abroad.

e. He cited a speech by Eugene R. Black at the recent Wesleyan University commencement dealing with grants in aid.[3] It was empha-

---

[1] Source: Department of State, INR/IL Historical Files, Minutes of 303 Committee, 8/5/66. Secret; Eyes Only. Prepared by Jessup on July 9. Copies were sent to U. Alexis Johnson, Vance, and Helms.

[2] [*text not declassified*] (Department of State, INR/IL Historical Files, Minutes of 303 Committee, 9/15/66) [*text not declassified*] (Memorandum to Rostow, October 6; Johnson Library, National Security File, Intelligence File, CIA Budgets & 303 Committee, Box 2) [*text not declassified*]

[3] A Presidential adviser on financial matters and former president of the World Bank, Black proposed the creation of an American council for education and industrial arts to manage some of the nation's overseas programs. (*The New York Times,* June 5, 1966, p. 38)

sized that substantial private contributions and those of foundations are inhibited, if not precluded, by CIA association with such organizations as The Asia Foundation. Mr. Rostow pointed out that the CIA had many times taken up the slack when other agencies were unable to come up with funds. Mr. Meyer's suggestion was greeted with considerable interest, and Mr. Helms suggested that any committee on this subject be headed in the White House in order to give it sufficient impetus. Mr. Moyers agreed to approach Mr. Harry McPherson[4] and urged that talks continue between Mr. Meyer, Mr. McPherson and other interested parties.[5] It was noted that although the committee would not operate under 303 aegis, its determinations and findings might well have a bearing on future proposals before the 303 Committee.

[Here follows discussion of other agenda items.]

Peter Jessup

---

[4] Special Counsel to the President.

[5] In his October 6 memorandum (see footnote 2 above), Jessup also reported that progress among Moyers, McPherson, and Thomas L. Farmer (AID General Counsel) to create a new institution to deal with such funding "has been extremely slow with the press of other business."

---

135. Memorandum From the President's Special Assistant (Rostow) to President Johnson[1]

Washington, July 11, 1966, 10:15 a.m.

1. Defense and AEC resubmit for your approval *the proposed FY 1968 Nuclear Weapons Stockpile*,[2] and certain related adjustments to the FY 1967 stockpile as previously approved by you on April 19, 1965.[3] The requirements set forth are consistent with the long-range Defense fore-

---

[1] Source: Johnson Library, National Security File, Memos to the President, Walt Rostow, Vol. 8. Top Secret; Restricted Data.

[2] See Document 133.

[3] The President's approval has not been further identified. Documentation on the background to this approval is in the Washington National Records Center, OSD Files: FRC 330 70 A 1265 Atomic–400.23 (6 Mar 65).

cast (through 1974) of weapons and special nuclear materials presented in your current Budget.

2. The stockpile proposal was first submitted to you last January and it was returned to Defense to obtain formal JCS concurrence (although the JCS had previously concurred informally in the proposal). The JCS looked again at certain of the figures and some minor changes have resulted in the new submittal, largely resulting from a decision to stretch out the retirement of certain tactical and strategic bombs that are becoming obsolete and the retirement of the Nike Hercules warheads.

3. An important aspect of the new proposal is that the approved FY 1967 stockpile figure is being reduced from [*numbers not declassified*]—a reduction of [*number not declassified*]. The proposed FY 1968 stockpile will be further reduced [*number not declassified*] to a total of [*number not declassified*]. Thus, the current proposal will cause a net reduction of [*number not declassified*] from the currently authorized stockpile total—or a reduction of nearly [*number not declassified*] from the total you approved in April 1965. The reduction of megatonnage of yield would be proportionately larger because a large number of high yield weapons are being retired. At the same time, however, we are getting a more modern stockpile better tailored to specified military missions.

4. The recommended stockpile is within the projected availability of special nuclear materials, and the number of new weapons is within AEC capability to produce. There are potential plutonium requirements in the possible deployment of the [*less than 1 line of source text not declassified*]. Poseidon/Minuteman warheads which, if approved, would substantially increase plutonium and weapons fabrication requirements in future years. On the basis of present estimates, however, there will be enough plutonium available by the end of FY 1967 to meet the *firm* Defense special nuclear requirements through 1974, not including the above possible additional requirements.

5. The Bureau of the Budget has reviewed this proposal. BOB believes that some obsolete weapons should be retired on a faster schedule than is now being proposed. It does not recommend that you disapprove this stockpile action, but BOB will make this a budget issue for discussion with Defense this Fall. There is no immediate major cost impact from maintaining the approximately [*less than 1 line of source text not declassified*] in the inventory in FY 1968. The important thing will be to make sure that the [*less than 1 line of source text not declassified*] do not become a part of the permanent base that is used for estimating requirements.

6. I recommend that you approve the proposed stockpile and sign the attached memoranda to Defense and AEC.

W.W. Rostow[4]

Approved[5]

Disapproved

See me

---

[4] Printed from a copy that bears this typed signature.

[5] This option is checked. For the President's July 12 memorandum to Secretary McNamara, see Document 136. A similar memorandum to AEC Chairman Seaborg, July 12, is in the Johnson Library, National Security File, Memos to the President, Walt Rostow, Vol. 8.

---

136.   **Memorandum From President Johnson to Secretary of Defense McNamara**[1]

Washington, July 12, 1966.

SUBJECT

FY 1968 Nuclear Weapons Stockpile

I approve the proposed Nuclear Weapons Stockpile for the end of FY 1968 submitted to me by the Department of Defense and the Atomic Energy Commission on June 6, 1966.[2]

Accordingly, I approve a total of [*number not declassified*] complete nuclear weapons ([*number not declassified*] nuclear warhead elements) as the stockpile composition for the end of FY 1968. I also approve a total of [*number not declassified*] complete nuclear weapons ([*number not declassified*] nuclear warhead elements) as the adjusted stockpile composition for the end of FY 1967. This will mean a planned production by the Atomic Energy Commission of [*number not declassified*] nuclear warhead elements and a planned retirement of [*number not declassified*] nuclear warhead elements during FY 1968, resulting in a net reduction of [*number not declassified*] nuclear warhead elements during FY 1968 under the adjusted FY 1967 stockpile.

---

[1] Source: Washington National Records Center, OSD Files: FRC 330 70 A 4662, A–400.23 1966. Top Secret; Restricted Data.

[2] See footnote 3, Document 133.

I have directed the Atomic Energy Commission to produce and retire those quantities of atomic weapons and atomic weapons parts necessary to achieve and maintain the approved FY 1968 stockpile. I have also directed the production of the additional weapons required for quality assurance and reliability testing.

I authorize you, in coordination with the Atomic Energy Commission, to make such changes in the total stockpile not to exceed ±10% of the specifically stated numbers of nuclear warhead elements to be produced and retired in FY 1967 and FY 1968, as may be necessary to adjust production schedules to meet AEC material availabilities or production capability. I further authorize you to make minor changes (±10%) in strategic, tactical, air defense or anti-submarine warfare warhead totals that may be required because of adjusted delivery assets or changes in military requirements. Any changes indicative of a major shift in defense policy or AEC production capability will be submitted for my approval.

Lyndon B. Johnson

137. Memorandum From the Director of Defense Research and Engineering, Department of Defense (Foster) to Secretary of Defense McNamara[1]

Washington, August 2, 1966.

SUBJECT

Transmittal of Study Report—Penetration Capability of U.S. Missile Forces versus Soviet ABM Defense 1967–1973

REFERENCES

(1) Memorandum, Secretary of Defense to DDR&E dated 21 May 1966 requesting study of U.S. Missiles ability to penetrate Soviet Defenses[2]
(2) Memorandum, DDR&E to Secretary of Defense dated 8 June 1966 outlining study approach[3]

Attached are Summary Volume I and Volume II of the Penetration Study[4] prepared by my staff in response to your request of May 21, 1966. Volumes III and IV are separate reports prepared as inputs to my staff for the purpose of this study by CIA and DIA respectively, entitled "Soviet Anti-Ballistic Missile Capabilities" and "The Soviet Anti-Ballistic Missile Program and Deployment";[3] these are available through Special Activities Office control.

The results of the study, for a "high" estimate of the projected number of Anti-Ballistic Missile interceptors show that the U.S. can maintain approximately [*less than 1 line of source text not declassified*] in the Soviet Union through 1973, in agreement with studies presented by ASD(SA) in the draft 1968–1972 Strategic Offensive and Defensive Forces Presidential Memorandum,[5] if a *simple, unsophisticated* model of defense capability is assumed. On the other hand, if the Soviets are assumed to have the capability to operate these forces in a coordinated manner, using "preferential" defense of some locations at the expense of others and to operate some of their long range interceptors in a precommitted "loiter" mode to intercept reentry objects [*less than 1 line of source text not*

---

[1] Source: Washington National Records Center, OSD Files: FRC 330 70 A 4662, 471.94 Penetration 1966. Top Secret.
[2] See footnote 4, Document 130.
[3] Not found.
[4] These two volumes, entitled "U.S. Strategic Missile Force Penetration Capability versus Soviet ABM 1967–1973," August 1, and four annexes are not printed.
[5] Reference may be to a July 26 (for comment) draft. (National Archives and Records Administration, RG 200, Defense Programs and Operations, Draft Memoranda to the President, 1968–72, Tab 8, Box 71) For text of a later draft, September 22, see Document 139.

declassified], then they may limit their fatalities to about [*number not declassified*] through 1971 and to substantially less than that thereafter against the presently programmed U.S. Missile Forces.

As indicated in the Introduction and Threat discussions in the report, the study results are strongly influenced by the Threat projection, about which there remains considerable uncertainty. These uncertainties involve questions as to: 1) which of the two systems that the Soviets are building that can have ABM capability will be proliferated as the main ABM component; 2) what the rate of interceptor build-up will be; 3) what mode of defense (as discussed above) their interceptors will operate in; 4) how effective their first strike on U.S. Missile Forces will be (including the possibility of MIRV or Terminally Guided Reentry Vehicle), and 5) the success of the U.S. in continuing to have accurate intelligence on interceptor deployment.

The study results, in general, are U.S. conservative in that the choice of assumptions regarding the reference case ABM deployment rate, the lack of defense command and control constraints, the Soviet Offense effectiveness, and the effects of simplifications needed to model the engagements for computation all tend to provide an upper bound to Soviet ABM effectiveness. Alternatively, changes in certain key assumptions could reduce the level of Soviet[6] fatalities significantly, under certain circumstances. These assumptions are 1) that the U.S. penetration aids will be effective in drawing interceptors; 2) that the Soviets do not have mobile interceptors about which we are unaware and that we will continue to obtain intelligence regarding their fixed sites and 3) that the U.S. will develop changes to its SIOP to have a planned option for nearly 100% utilization of Missile Forces for Assured Destruction by 1970.[7] In the early 1970's, when the major part of the U.S. reentry systems can be in the form of small warheads, the dependence on penetration aids effectiveness can be reduced.

The U.S. does not presently have in its inventory any missile payloads that individually "penetrate" Soviet Defenses. Our "penetration aids" are in reality [*8-1/2 lines of source text not declassified*].

There are other penetration aids that can potentially "penetrate" if the details of the defense are known and which therefore are not particularly sensitive to the *numbers* of interceptors. Penetration in this way involves [*6 lines of source text not declassified*]. Thus while U.S. defense design has had to worry in detail about these tactics, the offense has not yet been able to plan to use them with confidence. As the Soviet defense

---

[6] McNamara inserted the word "Soviet" by hand.

[7] In the margin next to this third assumption, McNamara wrote: "aren't all the calculations based on this assumption?"

design matures and as we begin to get sufficient intelligence about their systems to probe for weak spots, such "penetration" tactics will probably become available with confidence and be cheaper to apply than is the exhaustion tactic. These penetration concepts are undergoing exploratory development under the ABRES program and the bus deployment techniques now being developed for payload dispersal on Minuteman III and Poseidon are both well suited for quick adoption of payload variants.

As soon as you have had a chance to review the contents of the report, I would be glad to set up a meeting with you, Cy, Alain and Harold to discuss its implications.

John S. Foster, Jr.

138.　Editorial Note

Following completion of its report on the central management of resources under emergency conditions, including nuclear war (see Document 44), the White House Office of Emergency Planning (OEP) placed more emphasis on the study of emergency conditions in a limited war situation. In May 1966 a draft of a Resource Mobilization Plan for Limited War was completed and submitted to the Department of Defense and other government agencies for review and comment. As summarized in a May 20 letter from OEP Director Farris Bryant to McNamara, the Plan, among other things, "provides for an Office of Defense Resources, including the organizational and staffing arrangements, together with general operating procedures and emergency actions which would be put into effect upon the activation of ODR by the President." It also "recognizes the role of private industry in any mobilization effort, realizes the need for flexibility to meet the demands of a situation which are not precisely predictable, and places a heavy burden on the Federal Departments and Agencies in their respective areas of responsibility." (Washington National Records Center, OSD Files: FRC 330 70 A 4443, 381 National Resources (Jan–May) 1966)

In a May 24 memorandum to the Chairman of the Joint Chiefs of Staff, the Department of Defense's General Counsel, and several Assistant Secretaries of Defense, Solis Horwitz requested review of and comments on the proposed Plan. (Ibid.) The Joint Chiefs of Staff soon concurred in the plan. (Memorandum to Secretary of Defense McNamara (JCSM–386–66), June 9, 1966; ibid., 381 National Resources (Jun–1966)) In a July 2 letter to Bryant, Deputy Secretary of Defense Vance concurred in "the basic concept for such an emergency agency, its organizational structure, planned emergency actions to be taken by its director, and the proposed legislation and executive order for its establishment," but outlined "several substantive items" which needed "clarification and correction prior to issuance of the plan to make an organization such as the proposed ODR fully effective." (Ibid.)

Under cover of an August 30 letter to McNamara, Bryant enclosed a copy of the Resource Mobilization Plan for Limited War, as revised in July 1966, following comments by the Department of Defense and other Federal departments and agencies, along with a revised Annex A to the Plan, "which contains the classified Office of Defense Resources emergency plan actions." Bryant noted that these documents were to "be used as a guide by your Department in preparing the supporting plans for resource mobilization." Because the Plan was prepared under the OEP's continuing responsibility for the development of civil emergency preparedness measures, however, Bryant added that distribution of the Plan "at this time should not be given any special significance." (Ibid.)

---

139. Draft Memorandum From Secretary of Defense McNamara to President Johnson[1]

Washington, September 22, 1966.

SUBJECT

Recommended FY68–72 Strategic Offensive and Defensive Forces (U)

I have reviewed our Strategic Offensive and Defensive Forces for FY68–72 in preparation for the FY68 budget. The tables on pp. 3–4 summarize our force goals. Detailed force and financial summaries are displayed in the tables attached to this Memorandum.[2] I recommend that we:

---

[1] Source: Johnson Library, National Security File, Agency File, Department of Defense, FY 68–72 Strategic Offensive and Defensive Forces, Box 18. Top Secret.

[2] Neither the tables on pp. 3–4 nor the attached tables is printed.

1. Complete development of and deploy a MIRVed Poseidon, for $700 million in FY68, and $3.2 billion in FY68–72. Plan on a total force of 31 Poseidon submarines.

2. Maintain 1000 Minuteman missiles, consisting by FY72 of 600 Minuteman IIs and 400 IIIs, the latter with improved third stages and Multiple Independent Re-entry Vehicles (MIRVs), for $1.1 billion in FY68, $3.6 billion in FY68–72.

3. Procure area penetration aids for all Minuteman and terminal penetration aids for Minuteman III, at an FY68 cost of $125 million and a total of $214 million in FY68–72. Complete development of Polaris penetration aids and preserve a 1970 Operational Availability Date (OAD), but disapprove a JCS recommendation for procurement in FY68 of penetration aids for Polaris. Procurement of these would cost $333 million in FY68–72.

4. Adopt a 1.5 crew-to-aircraft ratio and a 43% alert rate for the strategic bomber force instead of continuation of JCS recommended 1.8 crew ratio and 53% alert rate; approve in principle a bomber dispersal plan and an increase in the number of B-52s per base to 30 where savings will result. The estimated savings are $100–200 million in FY68, and about $1 billion in FY68–72.

[Here follow 2 pages of tables.]

I. The General Nuclear War Problem

Our strategic nuclear forces should deter attack on the U.S. and its Allies and, if deterrence fails, limit damage to our society and those of our Allies. To accomplish these objectives, we design our forces around two related concepts; Assured Destruction—that is, the clear and unmistakable ability to destroy the societies of the USSR and/or the Chinese People's Republic (CPR) even after a surprise attack; and Damage Limiting, which entails the ability to reduce by both offensive and defensive means the damage an enemy can inflict on the U.S. and its Allies.

Deterrence must work over a range of situations. It must prevent not only a massive surprise attack, but also Soviet escalation to general nuclear war from local war. The Assured Destruction capability is designed to deter a potential aggressor, even in crisis situations when the alternatives to initiating nuclear war might otherwise lead him to go to war.

The Soviets seem to view our forces, as we do theirs, as a potential first strike threat. The recent deployment of the new, relatively small SS-11 ICBM in hardened and dispersed silos and Soviet interest in small and mobile missile technology reflect their concern to protect their strategic offensive forces against a U.S. first strike. Our force structure planning should take account of the interactions implied by their interest in having a protected retaliatory force.

Three broadly different posture alternatives are available. First, we could seek only an Assured Destruction capability (although we would in any case achieve a substantial Damage-Limiting capability in the process of building an Assured Destruction capability). Second, we might add a light Damage Limiting increment that would give some protection against probable types of Soviet attacks, and more complete protection against small attacks that the CPR may be able to mount in the 1970s. Third, we might try to add a major Damage Limiting capability to keep U.S. fatalities very low against the heaviest possible Soviet attack, and regardless of Soviet force structure responses.

Plainly, we must and will maintain whatever forces are needed to meet the Assured Destruction objective, while keeping flexibility to meet unpredictable changes in the threat. Under the second option, we would choose Damage Limiting programs that insure against the failure of deterrence under many, but not all, circumstances. The third alternative is certain to be very expensive. Moreover, because its rigid objective is probably infeasible, I reject this option.

Relative U.S.-USSR Strategic Capabilities. The table on the following page compares estimated Soviet strategic offensive forces with those of forces the U.S. programmed for the same years.

U.S. vs Soviet Strategic Nuclear Forces[a]

	1966		1968		1971	
	U.S.	USSR	U.S.	USSR	U.S.	USSR
ICBMs[b]						
Soft Launchers	0	142-146	0	135-145	0	10-100
Hard Launchers	934	168-218	1054	465-550	1045	630-900
Mobile	0	0	0	0	0	20-0
TOTAL	934	310-364	1054	600-695	1045	660-1000
MR/IRBMs						
Soft Launchers	0	574	0	546	0	286-300
Hard Launchers	0	135	0	135	0	185-265
Mobile	0	0	0	0-24	0	75-150
TOTAL	0	709	0	681-705	0	546-715
SLBM Inventory						
Launchers	512	121-136	656	121-148	656	127-244
Bombers and Tankers[c]						
Heavy	600	150-165	510	130-155	255	100-130
Medium	80	515-675	76	370-500	210	245-410
Tankers	620	180-205	620	155-205	620	90-165
TOTAL	1300	845-1045	1206	655-860	1085	435-705

[a] From National Intelligence Projections for Planning (NIPP), except for the number of hardened ICBM launchers. Recent ICBM deployment rates lead to the figures in this table, rather than the NIPP projections of 514–582 ICBMs for mid-1968, and 499–844 for mid-1971.

[b] Excludes test range launchers, having some operational capability, of which the Soviets are estimated to have 47 in mid-1966, 49–50 in mid-1968, and 60–65 in mid-1971.

[c] We estimate that the Soviets could send somewhat over 100 heavy bombers and no medium bombers over the continental United States on two-way missions. U.S. medium bombers are FB-111s in 1971, with range and payload markedly greater than those of the Soviet medium bombers.

The Soviets are building at least two types of single silo launch sites, a large one that we expect to hold the large payload (9,000–12,500 pound) storable liquid fueled SS-9 ICBM system, operational in limited numbers in 1966, and a small one probably intended for the SS-11, a small payload (1,000–2,000 pound) storable liquid fueled missile, also operational in 1966.

The Soviets have recently increased the rate of deployment of the SS-11 missile launchers to a level about 20 percent above their previous maximum. As a result I estimate that they will have between 600 and 700 operational launchers in FY68 instead of the 514–582 estimated in NIE 11–8–65, with the increase consisting of SS-11 missiles.

We have not yet observed any evidence of Soviet Multiple Independent Re-entry Vehicle (MIRV) programs, of Soviet penetration aid developments, or of the re-entry technology required for highly accurate missiles. We might not see such programs, however, until about three years before their deployment in significant force.

In addition to the offensive forces shown, two relatively large-scale Soviet defensive programs appear to be underway: a probable long range anti-ICBM system around Moscow (16–32 launchers expected to be operational in 1967 or 1968); and a system near Leningrad and across European USSR intended for either ballistic missile defenses, long range surface-to-air bomber defenses, or some combination of the two. Soviet defense priorities, as we assess them, suggest a probable emphasis on ABM. As an ABM, however, the technology of the Leningrad system appears to be much closer to some of the early systems considered by the U.S. than to Nike-X, except perhaps for the use of an X-ray kill warhead above the atmosphere.

The CPR Nuclear Threat. The earliest operational Chinese ICBM is not likely to appear till the mid-1970s. Given the utility to the CPR of being able to threaten her neighbors and U.S. Far Eastern bases, it seems likely that the Chinese would try first to develop and deploy an MRBM. Indeed, some test firings of medium range missiles have been in progress over the past several years.

The CPR also has one "G" class ballistic missile submarine for which a missile could be available in 1967–69, useful primarily as a threat to Asian targets. As a force to retaliate for a U.S. strike against the CPR, however, this system is vulnerable, since the "G" class boat's long transit time to the U.S. (40–45 days) would allow our Naval forces to destroy the submarine (or submarines) in the early 1970s.

The CPR also has almost 300 bombers capable of delivering nuclear weapons against Asian targets. But only 15 of these have ranges beyond 600 miles, and the Chinese are unlikely to undertake the costly development of a long range bomber to attack CONUS.

II. Adequacy of the Programmed Offensive Forces for Assured Destruction

Against the Expected Threat. Our Assured Destruction capabilities based on programs approved last year or on the programs I am now recommending can survive a well-coordinated Soviet surprise attack, even if the Soviets used all their available strategic offensive forces against our own.

U.S. Weapons Surviving Soviet First Strike, 1972[a]

[*table (5 columns and 6 rows) not declassified*]

---

[a] The RV mix for Poseidon in the 1972 recommended forces need not be decided now. In the above table, based on the expected threat, a mix of [*8-1/2 lines of source text not declassified*].

As shown, even after a Soviet first strike, some [*less than 1 line of source text not declassified*] U.S. weapons could be reliably launched against the USSR by either the programmed or recommended forces. [*3 lines of source text not declassified*] An even higher percentage of the recommended forces would reach their targets. The table below shows the damage potential of various sizes of U.S. retaliatory attacks in the absence of strong defenses.

[*table (6 columns and 7 rows) not declassified*]

I believe that a clear and unmistakable ability to inflict [*less than 1 line of source text not declassified*] will deter a deliberate Soviet attack on the U.S. or its Allies. Even if the Leningrad associated sites are an effective ballistic missile defense, or if the Moscow defense were deployed at other cities as well, the programmed U.S. missile force, with the penetration aid program of this and prior years, could inflict more than [*less than 1 line of source text not declassified*].

Although the Chinese may attain the capability to threaten U.S. bases and Asian neighbors, the CPR nuclear forces, between now and 1972, will not pose a threat either to U.S. retaliatory capability or to the viability of our society. [*5-1/2 lines of source text not declassified*]

[*1 paragraph (7 lines of source text) not declassified*]

Against Higher-Than-Expected Threats. We cannot now be sure that the USSR would not deploy a very heavy ABM in the FY68–72 time period. The effect of adding a very extensive Soviet ABM (which would cost them the equivalent of $25 billion over a five year period) is summarized below:

	FY69	FY70	FY71	FY72
Soviet ABM				
Reliable Area Interceptors	750	1350	1875	2475
Reliable Terminal Interceptors	675	975	1425	1800
[*1 row not declassified*]				

This illustration shows that the procurement of Poseidon to replace Polaris A-3 on 31 existing SSBNs and of Minuteman penetration aids, maintains our Assured Destruction capability at an adequate level. I am recommending that we include both these measures in the missile force.

Against a strong Soviet missile force with accurate MIRV but in the absence of an extensive ABM the Assured Destruction capability of the recommended missile force would not fall [*less than 1 line of source text not declassified*]. In fact, our sea-based forces alone could inflict [*less than 1 line of source text not declassified*] fatalities against such a Soviet threat.

The worst case against which we should hedge now—unlikely, but possible in the early 1970's—is one in which the Soviets deployed SS-9s with accurate MIRV as well as an extensive ABM defense. The Soviet ABM could destroy our offensive re-entry vehicles directly, and also force us to equip missiles with penetration aids at the expense of lethal payload. The Soviets might also defend preferentially, protecting some targets with more interceptors than expected, thus complicating our targeting problem.

The Soviets might deploy MIRV on SS-9s as follows:

	FY69	FY70	FY71	FY72	FY73
Number of SS-9s with MIRV	0	0	50	100	150

Each SS-9 is assumed to carry six MIRV with a yield of three megatons per re-entry vehicle, with a CEP of 2,000 feet in FY 1971 and 1,500 feet thereafter. Against the combined threat with both the heavy ABM deployment and MIRV on SS-9s, penetration aids for Poseidon would be desirable, and the recommended force therefore would include 31 SSBNs converted to Poseidon, penetration aids for both Minuteman and Poseidon, as well as the other elements of the previously approved missile force. If the Soviets do not employ sophisticated tactics such as preferential defense, the Soviet fatalities that could be inflicted by the recommended missile force against the combined threat are as follows:

	FY69	FY70	FY71	FY72	FY73
Soviet Fatalities	*[numbers not declassified]*				

More extreme threats are possible, but they are so unlikely, given the state of Soviet technology and the high cost to the USSR of mounting such forces, that they do not warrant taking now any actions in addition to those included in the recommended U.S. force. I will, however, discuss below some available hedging actions for our missile force. In any case, even against the most extreme threat, the combined Assured Destruction capability of the Recommended U.S. Missile Force and the Programmed Bomber Force is clearly adequate, and would amount to [*less than 1 line of source text not declassified*] fatalities.

Our offensive forces make it dangerous and expensive for the Soviets to move in the direction of extreme threats to our Assured Destruction capability. The incremental 5 year cost to the USSR of the depicted SS-9 and ABM threats would be about $30 billion, approximately a forty percent increase in the present Soviet expenditure rate on strategic forces. Yet, evaluating the Soviet Assured Destruction capability with extreme conservatism, as a Soviet planner might do, this Soviet missile force with only these SS-9s, SLBMs, and the older missiles would inflict less than 10%

fatalities on the U.S. after a pre-emptive strike by programmed U.S. forces. If this was an unsatisfactory Assured Destruction capability for the Soviets and they reoriented their planning at the same budget level to maintain Assured Destruction, they would have to reduce their spending on ABM or MIRV. The USSR would have to reduce vulnerability to the very accurate programmed U.S. offensive forces, by expensive measures such as further dispersal of missile payload (the SS-11 deployment appears to be the beginning of this), by hard point defenses (HPD), or by adoption of mobile missile basing schemes thereby reducing the total Soviet missile payload that would otherwise be available at a given budget level. The reduction in Soviet missile payload, in turn would make the U.S. Assured Destruction task less expensive or, alternatively, the development of higher-than-expected threats even less likely.

Of course, the Soviets could increase their strategic budget. But we can, in planning our forces, foreclose any seemingly "easy" and cheap paths to their achievement of a satisfactory Assured Destruction capability and a satisfactory Damage Limiting capability at the same time.

III. Missile Hedges Against a Soviet MIRV-ABM Threat

If it became desirable to supplement our planned strategic offensive forces, we could either (1) add hard, fixed-based missiles—such as an undefended advanced ICBM—with relatively low cost per unit of alert payload in inventory, but high cost per unit of payload surviving an attack; or (2) add sea- or land-based mobile systems or fixed-site missiles with hard point defense, all of which have relatively high costs per unit of alert payload in inventory, but are relatively insensitive to the Soviet offensive threat.

This distinction is illustrated in the following table with Minuteman representing the first class of offensive forces and Polaris representing the second class. In this calculation the low Soviet attack inflicts [*less than 1 line of source text not declassified*] on U.S. land-based forces and the high attack inflicts [*less than 1 line of source text not declassified*].

Ten-Year Costs Per Thousand Pounds of Payload
(Millions of Dollars)

	In The Inventory	On Alert & Reliable	Reliable and Surviving Low Soviet Attack	Reliable and Surviving High Soviet Attack
Minuteman II	4.5	6.2	6.9	62.0
Polaris A-3	14.2	31.8	31.8	31.8

Future candidate systems in these two classes are considered below:

1. Poseidon: To hedge against an extreme threat, we could consider construction of new Poseidon submarines in addition to the recommended conversion of Polaris A-3 to Poseidon submarines. If long lead time items were switched from the SSN to the SSBN programs in FY67, 10 new Poseidon submarines could be constructed and delivered, 5 each in FY71 and FY72, at $1.46 billion in FY68 and $2.4 billion in FY68–72.

2. Advanced ICBM: We are studying new ICBMs of increased payload, and basing schemes to protect the missiles against the MIRV threat. These studies are essential to determining the utility of an advanced ICBM as part of the force mix. Definitive results are not expected in time for the FY68 budget. A decision on an Advanced ICBM before completion of these studies would be premature. By end FY73, 50 Advanced ICBMs could be available in a mobile or defended configuration. Undefended, they would cost $1.8 billion to develop and $15 million per missile to deploy. Annual operating costs for 300 missiles would be about $600 thousand per missile, including flight testing. Ten year costs of a mobile or defended ICBM might be approximately twice as high.

3. Interim Minuteman Defense: Although hard point ballistic missile defenses would be intended for an advanced ICBM, they could be deployed as an interim measure in FY71 or FY72 to protect Minuteman, if the extreme Soviet threat appeared. For $240 million in FY67–68 Nike-X production funds, Minuteman could be defended on the following schedule:

	FY71	FY72	FY73
Minuteman Squadrons with Terminal Defense	0	6	6
Sprint Interceptors	0	1000	2000
Zeus Interceptors	0	500	500

The FY68–72 costs of this defense would be approximately $5.3 billion, and the defenses could also be useful for an Advanced ICBM.

4. Ballistic Missile Ships (BMS): A ballistic missile ship was studied extensively in connection with various proposals for an Allied Nuclear Force. Built to look like a merchant vessel, such a ship would rely on deception, speed, or fleet defense for protection. The vulnerability of this system is, of course, the principal reservation. Long lead time funding of some $86 million would maintain the option of procuring ballistic missile ships on the same schedule as that of new Poseidon submarines. If the option were exercised, FY68–72 costs would be $1.4 bil-

lion for 10 ships and $2.6 billion for 20. About $0.8 billion of the $2.6 billion is for Poseidon missiles, which could be later used in Poseidon submarines.

I believe that it is not necessary to commit ourselves now to exercising our options on any of these hedges.

IV. The Manned Bomber Force

Strategic bombers might be called on in the future to support conventional operations on a much wider scale than they are doing now in Southeast Asia. Moreover, the Assured Destruction capability of our strategic missile force will almost certainly deter the Soviets from a surprise attack except, perhaps, in an extreme crisis or an escalating war. In these cases we would have received sufficient warning to put the strategic bomber force on high alert. Our bombers should therefore be primarily designed for such situations, rather than for all-out immediate use in spasm nuclear exchanges.

Our bomber threat appears to affect enemy force planning, just as do our missiles. Bombers force the enemy to divert resources to defend against aircraft as well as against ICBMs. In this role, they have their chief advantage; and in this role, they are not needed in large numbers.

Reductions in manned aircraft operating expenses would be consistent with this view of the bombers role. A 43% alert rate, down from 53%, will be sustainable with the recommended new 1.5 crew ratio. At this rate, our alert bombers could deliver more than [*less than 1 line of source text not declassified*] against the present Soviet defenses, and [*number not declassified*] against the projected, improved FY71 defenses. Location in the interior of the U.S. is desirable, where suitable bases exist, to protect against a future sea-launched missile threat. In general, B-52s should have the ability to disperse in times of crisis and be distributed with 30 per home base where economies will result. By May 1967, the Air Force will have completed a basing study to determine the feasibility of these basing concepts.

Such operating adjustments will provide a large enough surviving bomber fleet to meet the entire Assured Destruction payload requirement, will save $200–400 million annually, and will probably make it possible to extend the B-52 G/H's life to FY77 without additional modification. This will allow an added margin of safety in the timing of some of our strategic missile development and procurement decisions.

V. Strategic Forces and Damage Limiting

Damage Limiting forces, unlike those for Assured Destruction, cannot and need not work with near perfection under all conditions, but should insure against the most probable risks, including those posed by the growth of Chinese nuclear forces. The implications of Soviet reactions for our own choices of Damage Limiting forces must also be taken into account.

Evaluation of Damage Limiting Programs Against the Soviet Threat. So long as we have secure retaliatory forces, any kind of nuclear war with the Soviets is unlikely. Of the ways in which one might start, a surprise attack in normal times is especially unlikely; it would be much more likely to arise from a crisis or limited war, giving both sides enough strategic warning to increase their alert status. The Soviets might start a nuclear war for fear of a pre-emptive strike by the U.S., as part of a massive attack on Western Europe, or to prevent the loss of a limited war. In each case, the Soviets could be expected to try to preserve as much as possible of Soviet society and military power. Thus, they might devote a large part of their strategic offensive forces to reducing the U.S. offensive threat.

The Damage Limiting ability of various U.S. postures will be evaluated under the following kinds of wars:

[*3 paragraphs (20 lines of source text) not declassified*]

The Soviet damage potential against the U.S. in three kinds of war is depicted, with the Soviet threat in 1976 assumed to consist of 1000 ICBMs, 211 submarine launched missiles, and 46 heavy bombers.

United States Fatalities

	Comb. Military-Urban Attack By USSR	Withheld Urban Attack Collateral Fatalities	Withheld Urban Attack Remaining Urb. Damage Potent.	U.S. Pre-emptive Strike
1971 U.S. Approved Program	30-45%	3-5%	18-19%	28%
1976 U.S. Approved Program Extended	22-45%	2-4%	20%	24%

Two factors tend to decrease U.S. fatalities between 1971 and 1976: the gradual decline in the Soviet bomber threat, and improved U.S. counter-military capabilities. Without programmed U.S. defenses, however, the USSR's damage potential could be over 100 million (50%) U.S. fatalities in a mixed Soviet attack.

We have also analyzed the effects if the U.S. initiated either of two balanced Damage Limiting programs, assuming at this point that we evoked no response from the USSR except for provision of penetration aids for projected Soviet missiles. (Soviet responses are considered below.) Posture A includes Nike-X with a limited Sprint defense at 25 cities, an improved bomber defense using F-111s, and expanded civil defense. Posture B includes a heavy Sprint defense of 52 cities. Incremental expenditures for these postures, measured from the Approved Program as a base, are shown in the following table.

Costs of Alternative Defense Postures (In $ Billions)

	Approved Program Level-Off		Damage Limiting Increment Over Approved Programs Posture A		Posture B	
	Dev+Inv	Annual	Dev+Inv	Annual	Dev+Inv	Annual
Civil Defense	0.8	0.1	0.8	0.0	0.8	0.0
Nike-X	1.4	0.0	8.0	0.3	17.5	0.6
Air Defense	0.4	1.3	1.5	-0.3	1.5	-0.3
TOTAL	2.6	1.4	10.3	0.0	19.8	0.3

The table below compares the performance of the Approved Program with that of Postures A and B.

[table (5 columns and 4 rows) not declassified]

[9-1/2 lines of source text not declassified] These figures underscore the importance of improved civil defense.

The light defenses of Posture A are sensitive to large Soviet counter-urban attacks, although they keep the damage level below that of the Approved Program. The heavier and much more costly Posture B defense is less sensitive to the size of the counter-urban attack.

Interaction of U.S. and USSR Force Planning. U.S. offensive forces, apparently viewed by the Soviets as a potential first strike capability, exert pressure on the Soviets to protect their retaliatory forces. The effect of U.S. defensive measures—say, an ABM—on the Soviets, almost sure-ly, would be to move them to offset the U.S. defense by expanding their offensive force. Our encouraging prospects in the development of U.S. anti-submarine defenses, however, may discourage major Soviet reliance on SLBMs. The long term viability of these measures, and their implications for ASW force requirements are under study.

The following table shows the results if the Soviets choose to restore their Assured Destruction capability against U.S. Damage Limiting Postures A and B; because of the prospect of U.S. ASW defenses, possible Soviet land-based responses are assumed. The assumed response to Posture A is procurement of 200 large mobile missiles at a 10 year cost of about $10 billion; to Posture B, 650 missiles at a cost of about $20 billion. Results of equal expenditures on defended missiles would be similar.

[table (5 columns and 6 rows) not declassified]

Addition by the Soviets of relatively invulnerable missiles as a Soviet response to a U.S. Damage Limiting program can regain their retaliatory potential against a U.S. first strike without fully restoring Soviet first strike potential against the U.S.

[2 paragraphs (21 lines of source text) not declassified]

VI. Specific Recommendations on Major Force-Oriented Issues

Poseidon Deployment. Because Poseidon is so much more effective per dollar than Polaris A-3 and because Poseidon provides insurance against a higher-than-expected Soviet threat, I believe that we should ultimately convert 31 Polaris submarines to Poseidon. A fleet of 31 Poseidon boats will have [less than 1 line of source text not declassified] of a fleet of 41 Polaris A-3 boats. Only an unexpectedly serious Soviet ASW threat that would require dispersal of our forces on a larger number of SSBNs could change this. Disposition of the last 10 submarines, which cannot economically be converted to Poseidon, need not be decided now. We are studying the option to deploy new Poseidon submarines after the last conversion of the 31 now planned.

We plan on an operational availability date (OAD) in 1970 for the Poseidon missile carrying Mark-3 re-entry systems. Possible Mark-3/Mark-17 mixes will be re-evaluated yearly as new estimates of the Soviet ABM are made and a capability to deploy a MK-17 MIRV on Poseidon will be preserved. The total FY68 cost of the Poseidon program is $700 million; and the FY68–72 R&D, investment, and operating costs are $3.2 million.

[1 paragraph (2-1/2 lines of source text) not declassified]

Last year I commented on some of the command and control vulnerabilities of the FBM force. The Navy has generated a number of alternative solutions to these problems on which recommendations will be made this October.

Minuteman. I have approved the inclusion in the Minuteman III program of an improved [less than 1 line of source text not declassified] at an additional FY67–72 cost of $400 million. When Minuteman III becomes operational, there will already be 600 Minuteman IIs in the force. Rather than replace these with Minuteman IIIs prior to the completion of the Force Modernization Program in early 1972, we will take as a tentative planning objective a force consisting of 600 Minuteman II and 400 Minuteman III, with additional Minuteman III to be procured thereafter as replacements.

Since all 600 Minuteman IIs will be available by July 1969, I am also recommending a rate of 40 [less than 1 line of source text not declassified] Mark-17s per month, which will lead to the complete replacement of all Mark-LLAs by end FY70. [3-1/2 lines of source text not declassified] By buying full complements of warheads [*less than 1 line of source text not declassified*] in FY68, we will maintain the flexibility to tailor Minuteman III re-entry packages to Soviet defenses and target systems. In succeeding years we will adjust production quantities to avoid having excess reentry systems.

[*1-1/2 lines of source text not declassified*] I am also approving development of a [*less than 1 line of source text not declassified*] at an FY68 cost of $25.6 million and an FY68–72 development cost of $288 million to achieve an IOC by end FY71.

Titan. As newer missiles phase into the force, Titan II will lose its unique advantages, while remaining expensive to operate. The end FY66 Titan II inventory can support a follow-on test (FOT) program of 6 launches per year without cutting into the operational force until the end of FY70, at which time it would be necessary to phase down approximately one squadron per year. I recommend that the $18 million in FY67 funds for 6 new Titans not be released.

Penetration Aids. The effectiveness of penetration aids against Soviet ABM defenses is now under review. Pending completion of that review, I recommend that production of the penetration aids for the Minuteman programs be approved.

[*1 paragraph (8-1/2 lines of source text) not declassified*]

The FY68 cost of the Minuteman penetration aid program is $91 million, with a total cost of $230 million in FY68–72. Disapproval of deployment of the Polaris A-3 penetration aids will save $218 million in FY68, and a total of $333 million in FY68–72.

Missile Flight Test Programs. We have re-examined our ballistic missile flight test programs, with two major conclusions:

—The number of missiles in operational flight tests (OT) should be determined on the basis of the number of significantly different missile configurations, rather than as a fixed percentage of the total force.
—FOTs should be viewed as providing data for updating our estimates.

These considerations suggest an optimum OT rate of approximately 40 launches per configuration, and an FOT rate of 20 per configuration per year, yielding savings of approximately $330 million during FY66–71, without appreciable loss to our knowledge of systems effectiveness, compared with the previously approved program.

Strategic Bomber Forces. A study of B-52G/H lifetime based on the recommended lower crew ratio and considering possible modifications, suggests that our B-52s will be able to operate effectively even after 1975 against projected or even better-than-expected Soviet air defenses. Therefore, I do not believe that an AMSA development program must meet an initial operational capability date of FY74, even if it is decided that the B-52 should be followed by an AMSA. However, as an insurance program, I have started concept formulation to define and evaluate a suitable bomber design.

I recommend that 3 squadrons of Hound-Dog A be retired in FY67, and the remaining 6 squadrons in FY68; Hound-Dog B should be retained pending the outcome of the Terrain Matching Guidance (TERCOM) development program. This program will maintain enough Hound-Dogs for their SIOP mission, primarily to attack area bomber defenses and lower-priority airfields, while resulting in FY67–71 savings of approximately $30 million.

[1 paragraph (5-1/2 lines of source text) not declassified]

Nike-X Deployment. The following table shows the components entering the Nike-X defenses of Postures A and B, and their cost, in addition to the $1.4 billion of RDT&E funds to be spent:

	Limited Defense Posture		Heavy Defense	
	No. of Units	$ Billions	No. of Units	$ Billions
Radars				
TACMAR Radars	7	$1.7	3	$1.0
MAR Radars	0	0	8	2.2
VHF Radars	6	.3	6	.3
Missile Site Radars	26	3.4	40	7.9
DM-15-X2 Interceptors	1200	1.1	1200	1.1
Sprint Interceptors	1100	.7	7300	3.1
Total Investment Cost		$7.2		$15.6
FY67-76 Operating Cost		$1.0		$ 1.8
AEC Costs		$ .7		$ 2.0

[2 paragraphs (12 lines of source text) not declassified]

In view of the uncertainty of Soviet targeting and force structure response, and given the substantial cost and relative ineffectiveness of either Posture A or Posture B, I disapprove the JCS recommendation to deploy Nike-X for a FY72 IOC.

Deployment of a New Manned Interceptor. The Soviets would probably use their bombers primarily in attacks on urban areas rather than on time-urgent military targets, since the time to reach target is so much longer for bombers than for ballistic missiles. Therefore, air defense is an important component of a Damage Limiting posture.

The F-12 and F-111 interceptors, equipped with the improved ASG-18/AIM-47 fire control and missile systems, and used with an effective Airborne Warning and Control System (AWACS), would be better than the present force in operating from degraded bases, countering concentrated bomber attacks, operating independently of a vulnerable fixed ground environment, and dealing with bombers attacking at low-altitude or carrying air-to-surface missiles.

With strategic warning we estimate that 32 UE F-12s or 48 UE stretched F-111As could achieve the same number kills before weapons release as the current force which has a 10 year cost of $3.0 billion. The 10 year systems cost for the 32 UE F-12 force have increased from the previously estimated $1.9 billion to $2.9 billion. Estimates for the F-111 force remain at $1.5 billion. The F-111 force therefore appears substantially more efficient than the F-12s against the currently projected threat. Supplementary calculations indicate that it is comparable in efficiency to the F-12 force against possible future threats.

The 48 UE F-111 force would operate from 4 main bases, 8 dispersal bases and 30 recovery/recycle bases. Sixteen combat support aircraft, that would be flushed with the interceptors, would carry missiles, ground support equipment, spares, and personnel to support the F-111 turn-around at the recycle bases. With 42 AWACS aircraft to provide airborne control, we could reduce the present ground environment, retaining only enough radars and BUIC centers for peacetime control.

The investment costs for this force include $676 million for the F-111 and $790 million for AWACS. Since the modernized force would ultimately have operating costs about $250 million per year lower than the present posture, the additional investment costs would be recouped by FY78.

Given the advantage of the F-111 interceptors—an aircraft already in long term production—and in the absence of a decision to deploy Nike-X, the decision to modernize our air defense structure can be deferred for one year.

The F-12 development program will be reoriented in FY 67 and FY 68 to include further design studies for the F-111 interceptor, cost studies, and adaptation of the Navy AWG-9 fire control system for ADC use, using the YF-12 as a test bed. The AWACS development program which supports both tactical and CONUS defense missions, will be continued as a high priority effort.

SAM-D. We have a new surface-to-air missile system (SAM-D), in Advanced Development oriented primarily toward Field Army air defense and Fleet air defense but with potential application to CONUS defense. These efforts will define a building block approach to the system, and reduce costs. At this stage of development, a deployment decision would be premature. We are also examining the utility of Nike-X in a surface-to-air role. Preliminary results are encouraging.

Civil Defense. The Damage Limiting Postures A and B include an expanded Civil Defense Program with dual purpose shelters in new non-federal public and private construction in addition to the shelters resulting from the present shelter survey and stocking program, but no special purpose shelter construction. The table shown below summarizes the protection offered by this program and compares it with the Approved Program, considering the location of shelters and limits on the movement of population.

The Approved Program extended to 1976 would cost $1.5 billion. Last year we proposed a one year, $10 million experimental program to evaluate shelter development in new construction. This program would give us information on the feasibility of incorporating dual purpose shelters in new construction, and on the necessary incentive schemes to stimulate shelter development. Although this proposal was not approved by the Congress, continued study indicates that such a program would provide for an efficient, controlled Expanded Civil Defense Program over time by incorporating shelters in new public construction and that this expansion can be matched to the deficits that will remain after conclusion of the shelter survey program. It is presently estimated that for $800 million we could add 50 million useful spaces, and save an additional 3 to 4% of our population over the approved program. An additional $1 billion spent on special purpose shelter construction, to meet the residual deficit, would save less than one percent of the population, and would not be warranted.

	Approved Program		Expanded Program	
	Number of Shelter Spaces In Millions	Percent of Population With Protection Factor of 40 or more[a]	Number of Shelter Spaces In Millions	Percent of Population With Protection Factor of 40 or more[a]
1966	140	35%	N.A.	N.A.
1971	230	64%	240	70%
1976	280	67%	330	88%

[a] The protection factor is the factor by which the outside radiation dose is reduced by the shelter.

Accordingly, I am recommending $186.3 million for the FY68 Civil Defense program to include $10 million for an experimental shelter development program. Pending completion of the experiment, I am including a nominal $25 million for shelter development in FY69. The further development of this program will depend on the results of this experimental program.

[1 paragraph (17 lines of source text) not declassified]

140. Letter From the Chairman of the Policy Planning Council (Owen) to the President's Special Assistant (Rostow)[1]

Washington, September 27, 1966.

Walt:

This is a personal note to express my concern that we may not be grappling seriously and urgently enough with the question of an ABM freeze.

My purpose here isn't to pass judgment on the issue, but to stress the need for doing more than we are now doing, in order to be able to reach a deliberate decision on that issue before such a decision is forced on us by a series of inter-acting Soviet deployment and ad hoc U.S. budgetary decisions.

In the broadest sense, the question is where trends in strategic offensive and defensive weapons (on which we recently had an excellent DOD briefing in the Thursday group) are taking us, and whether there is any alternative to drifting into the more dangerous and unstable strategic world which these trends may foreshadow. We may not be able to find an alternative (such as a viable ABM freeze), but we ought to be looking for one before events carry us further downstream. We ought not to assume that because the Soviets are now deploying ABM's they might not draw them back if we proposed some alternative means of meeting both sides' security needs.

The bureaucracy may be too unwieldy to meet this in time without a prod from the President. Failing this, all you are likely to get is a staffing out of possible ABM weapons effects by various ABM weapons proponents. (We are currently arranging to get the DOD study and briefing to which you were exposed and which Bob Ginsburgh was kind enough to tell me about.) This doesn't fully meet the President's need as he reaches for decision, however.

Proposal: I would urge setting up a Wise Man's Group, made up of inside and outside talent, which would work full-time on this problem, on the QT, in order to present to the President a careful evaluation of alternative courses—before the range of options is precluded by the march of events, here and in the U.S.S.R.

Henry Owen[2]

---

[1] Source: Johnson Library, National Security File, Name File, Spurgeon Keeny Memos, Box 5. Secret.

[2] Printed from a copy that bears this typed signature.

141. Memorandum From Spurgeon Keeny of the National Security Council Staff to the President's Special Assistant (Rostow)[1]

Washington, October 11, 1966.

SUBJECT

Henry Owen's Memo to You on the ABM Problem

I share Henry Owen's serious concern about the ABM deployment issue (see attached memo).[2] I think, however, that he grossly underestimates the extent and seriousness of the consideration that is and has been given to this difficult problem within the U.S. government.

I have followed this question for the past six or eight years and in general have been impressed during the past few years with the relatively high level of sophistication of the analysis in OSD of the role of ABMs in our strategic offensive-defensive posture. I think Henry is wrong in his impression that Defense is being forced into a decision without giving the question serious or sophisticated attention. The issue is certainly not being handled simply as "a series of interacting Soviet deployment and ad hoc U.S. budgetary decisions." I think it most unfair to state that without a prod from the President "all you are likely to get is a staffing out of possible ABM weapons effects by various ABM weapons proponents." Henry has obviously been talking to the wrong people. Finally, this problem has been a central issue in arms control thinking in ACDA and the rest of government for the past few years.

With regard to Henry's specific proposal, I am not sure what he would really want the "Wise Man's Group" to do at this point or just who he thinks he could get to work fulltime on this problem. The proposal seems somewhat reminiscent of the Gaither Panel of 1957.[3]

With regard to independent review of the issue, I would note that for the past six years I have been working on this problem with a very good PSAC panel made up of the most knowledgeable scientists on the subject.[4] This group has given and is currently giving useful independent evaluations of ABM proposals, intelligence on the Soviet program,

---

[1] Source: Johnson Library, National Security File, Name File, Spurgeon Keeny Memos, Box 5. Secret. A copy was sent to Ginsburgh.

[2] Document 140.

[3] Documentation on the Gaither Panel is in *Foreign Relations*, 1955–1957, vol. XIX, pp. 464 and 620 ff.

[4] Reference apparently is to the Strategic Military Panel of the President's Science Advisory Committee; see Document 101.

and the broader strategic issues involved. On the basis of my experience with this and other panels, I would emphasize the difficulty of getting useful advice on a problem of this extreme complexity unless there are specific government proposals or alternatives framed in advance. Therefore, since it is now apparent that McNamara will not propose an ABM deployment or the introduction of other major new strategic systems as part of the FY-1968 budget, I would particularly question the utility of organizing a new "Wise Man's Group" at this time. Such a review might be useful before we make a final commitment on this subject (next year?), but I think we should think the plan through very carefully before launching another Gaither Panel exercise.

Spurgeon

---

142.   **Editorial Note**

In a telephone conversation on October 16, 1966, President Johnson and Secretary of Defense McNamara first discussed the Nuclear Non-Proliferation Treaty. That part of their conversation is summarized in *Foreign Relations, 1964–1968*, volume XI, Document 162, footnote 4. McNamara then went on to report that he had just gone over the fiscal year 1968 defense budget estimates submitted by the military services. The President interjected, "Hold on and let me get my hat," and McNamara responded, "you'll need more than your hat; [you'll need] a storm shelter."

McNamara then reported that these military estimates totaled $98 billion. That figure he found "just unbelievable and there's no damned reason in the world for it and it won't come out that way." When President Johnson asked what the military asked for last year, McNamara said it was about $75 or $72 billion. The President said that $10 billion had been added, and McNamara agreed but said that that would be reduced. "But the $98 billion is just unbelievable. The next 60 days are just going to have to be budget cutting days." "I've just got a helluva task on my hands," he shortly commented. Working with Deputy Secretary Vance, McNamara concluded, "I can get it down to a reasonable level by Christmas time, but it's going to take every minute between now and Christmas to do it." (Johnson Library, Recordings and Transcripts, Recording of Telephone Conversation Between President

Johnson and Secretary McNamara, October 16, 1966, 7:03 p.m., Tape F66.29, Side A; this transcript was prepared specifically for this *Foreign Relations* volume)

---

143.   National Intelligence Estimate[1]

NIE 11–8–66   Washington, October 20, 1966.

SOVIET CAPABILITIES FOR STRATEGIC ATTACK

The Problem

To estimate the strength and capabilities of Soviet strategic attack forces through mid-1968, and to estimate general trends in these forces over the next 10 years or so.

Summary and Conclusions

A. The Soviets retain their belief in the primacy of strategic attack and defense forces, to deter the US and to support their foreign policy. Soviet strategic attack forces will continue to include a variety of weapon systems, with chief emphasis upon ICBMs. The Soviets are building forces which we believe will give them, in the next year or two, greatly increased confidence that they have a retaliatory capability sufficient to assure the destruction of a significant portion of US industrial resources and population. They will probably also seek, through both strategic attack and defense programs, to improve their ability to reduce the damage the US can inflict on the USSR should deterrence fail and war in fact occur. We do not believe, however, that the Soviets will

---

[1] Source: National Archives and Records Administration, RG 263. Top Secret; Controlled Dissem. A cover sheet, prefatory note, title page, and table of contents are not printed. According to the prefatory note, the CIA and the intelligence organizations of the Departments of State and Defense, the NSA, and the AEC participated in the preparation of this estimate. Representatives of CIA, State Department, DIA, NSA, and AEC concurred; the FBI representative abstained, the subject being outside his jurisdiction.

Attached is an October 20 memorandum from Helms to recipients of this NIE, which notes that because of the "extreme sensitivity of the information" in this NIE, the President wanted its dissemination to be "carefully limited." Helms stressed "that there be absolutely no reproduction of this Estimate, and that no revelation of its existence be made to unauthorized persons."

expect to achieve by the mid-1970's strategic capabilities which would make rational the deliberate initiation of general war.[2]

B. *ICBM Force.* The Soviets now have about 335 operational ICBM launchers. We estimate that the USSR will have some 670–765 operational launchers in mid-1968. This is considerably more than we anticipated in our last estimate and reflects our belief that construction of launchers has been started at a higher rate than ever before.

C. In mid-1968, about half the operational launchers will be for the small and relatively inaccurate SS-11. This missile is suitable mainly against large, soft targets such as cities. Deployment of the SS-9, a large missile more suitable for attacking hard targets, is also continuing, though at a slower rate than the SS-11.

D. The present Soviet stress on dispersed single silos, especially those for the SS-11, probably reflects decisions taken several years ago to improve sharply the survivability and thus the retaliatory capabilities of the ICBM force. In mid-1968 about 80 percent of the total launchers will be hard.

E. The Soviets might not find it advantageous to build ICBM forces much larger than those we estimate for 1968. On the other hand, they might consider their deterrent to be significantly more convincing and their military power improved if they can acquire an ICBM force about as large as that of the US. We therefore estimate a Soviet ICBM force of some 800–1,100 operational launchers in mid-1971 and some 800–1,200 in mid-1976.[3]

F. A 1976 force of about 1,200 launchers would probably consist primarily of small, less expensive ICBMs. A force of 800 or so would probably incorporate greater qualitative improvements and significant numbers of larger ICBMs. Characteristic of future deployment will be hard silos and possibly mobile launchers. Qualitative improvements will

---

[2] Maj. Gen. Jack E. Thomas, Assistant Chief of Staff, Intelligence, USAF, believes that developments of the past year reflect a continuing Soviet dissatisfaction with a posture of strategic inferiority vis-à-vis the US and a determination to eliminate such inferiority. He would add the following to the final sentence:

". . . but programs already underway, plus a continuing strong R&D effort, reflect a Soviet determination to rise from a position of strategic inferiority to one of at least numerical parity with the US in the belief that such a posture would markedly enhance the aggressive pursuit of Communist aims." [Footnote in the source text.]

[3] Maj. Gen. Jack E. Thomas, Assistant Chief of Staff, Intelligence, USAF, believes that the Soviets could construct single silo ICBM launchers at a rate which would enable the USSR to achieve numerical parity with the planned US program by 1970.

He would delete the last sentence and substitute the following:

"We estimate a Soviet ICBM force of some 1,000–1,100 operational launchers by 1970–1971. If the USSR develops a MIRV capability, the launcher total may hold at around 1,000–1,200; otherwise, the Soviets probably will have upwards of 1,200 and perhaps 1,500 launchers by the mid-1970's." [Footnote in the source text.]

probably include much better accuracies and may include sophisticated reentry vehicles and penetration aids. The development of the force will probably be marked by interruptions and leveling-off phases as new, more effective systems are introduced and older systems are phased out.

G. We think that ICBM forces falling anywhere within these estimated ranges could be considered as meeting a broad Soviet criterion for a credible deterrent. Thus we intend our estimate of future force levels as a range of uncertainty, either side of which would reflect the same basic Soviet strategic concept. For a period so far ahead, however, much will depend on the interplay between US and Soviet decisions taken in the interim.

H. The Soviets have recently conducted feasibility tests of what may be a depressed trajectory ICBM or a fractional orbit bombardment system. We cannot determine which, if either, of these systems will be deployed. Either could become operational during 1968 but probably would not be deployed in large numbers.

I. *MRBM/IRBM Forces.* No major changes in the MRBM/IRBM force have been noted during the past year. We estimate that the current force comprises somewhat over 700 operational launchers, some 135 of them hard, deployed at about 200 sites. This force is capable of delivering a devastating attack against Eurasian targets but is predominantly soft and concentrated. We believe that throughout the period of this estimate the USSR will maintain some 500–700 MRBM/IRBM launchers. Qualitative improvements are expected to include solid propellant missiles, more hard launchers, and probably mobility for some portion of the force.

J. *Missile Submarines.* The Soviets presently have some 45 ballistic missile submarines (8–10 nuclear-powered) with a total of about 130 launchers, and an equal number of cruise missile units (21–23 nuclear-powered) with about 250 launchers. No new ballistic missile submarines have become operational since 1963. We believe, however, that a new class of ballistic missile submarine—which almost certainly will be nuclear-powered and may carry 8 or more missiles with a range of some 1,000 to 2,000 n.m.—will be operational by mid-1968. We estimate that by 1976 the Soviets will have some 60 to 70 ballistic missile submarines, including about 30 of the new type. We believe that production of cruise missile submarines will continue, but at a reduced rate, into the 1970's. We estimate that some 55–65 of these units will be operational in 1976.

K. Regular open ocean patrols by Soviet missile submarines have been stepped up in recent months. This patrol activity will probably continue to increase. By the early 1970's, as much as 30 percent of the ballistic missile submarine force may be on station in potential missile launch areas at any one time. This number could be augmented by whatever portion of their cruise missile submarine force the Soviets allocate to a strategic attack mission.

L. *Strategic Bomber Force.* Long Range Aviation is now composed of 950–1,000 bomber/tanker aircraft, 200–210 of which are heavies and the rest mediums. The primary mission of the heavies is intercontinental attack; at present, the Soviets could probably put about 100 heavy bombers over US target areas on two-way missions. The medium bombers are mainly for use against Eurasian targets, though a few squadrons might be employed for initial strikes against Alaska, Canada, Greenland, and Iceland. The Soviets could augment the force over North America by using medium bombers on one-way missions, but we think this unlikely. The Soviets may develop a new medium bomber during the period of this estimate, but probably not a new heavy. We estimate that by 1976 attrition and retirement will have reduced the heavy force to some 70–100 aircraft and the medium force to about 300–500.[4]

M. *Space Systems.* For some years the USSR has been orbiting several types of satellites including reconnaissance types. Within the next 5 to 10 years the Soviets will probably develop and employ a variety of space systems (such as navigation and communications satellites) to further support their strategic attack forces. The Soviets have long had the capability to orbit a nuclear-armed satellite and have frequently alluded to "orbital rockets." Recent feasibility tests could lead to a multiple-orbit bombardment system. For the foreseeable future, however, ICBMs are likely to be much more effective and far less costly. This, plus the political liability which would be incurred by orbiting a nuclear weapon, lead us to believe that the Soviets are unlikely to deploy a multiple-orbit bombardment system in space during the period of this estimate.

N. *Research and Development.* The Soviets continue to pursue a vigorous R&D program to develop and improve strategic attack systems. A high level of R&D activity is expected to continue. The USSR appears

---

[4] Maj. Gen. Jack E. Thomas, Assistant Chief of Staff, Intelligence, USAF, believes the Soviets will continue to consider manned strategic aircraft an important element of their intercontinental strike forces. He estimates the USSR has the capability and—considering the currently limited size of the Soviet ICBM force—the requirement for a major manned strategic bomber effort against the US in the event of general war, and could put as many as 400 heavy and medium bombers over US target areas.

He estimates the USSR is likely to introduce both a follow-on heavy bomber and a new medium bomber into LRA within the next few years. He concludes that in 1976 LRA will consist of about 200 heavy bombers and some 400–600 medium bombers of both new and old types. [Footnote in the source text.]

to be about as capable as the US of developing new strategic systems and subsystems which its leaders feel are important enough to justify the expenditure of resources. In deciding to deploy any new weapon system, however, the Soviets would have to weigh the prospective gain against the economic cost and the capabilities of the US to detect and counter it.

[Here follow the Discussion section (Parts I–VII, pages 6–34) and Annex A and B (pages 35–47 and following page 47).]

---

144.   Memorandum From Director of Central Intelligence Helms to the President's Special Assistant (Rostow)[1]

TCS 9594–66   Washington, October 27, 1966.

SUBJECT

   NIE 11–8–66, "Soviet Capabilities for Strategic Attack"[2]

1. Attached is the extremely sensitive, all-source National Intelligence Estimate, "Soviet Capabilities for Strategic Attack." In my judgment, its conclusions can be summarized as follows:

a. The Soviets are building powerful strategic attack forces along with the strategic defense and other elements of their military establishment. Their main object in building these forces is to deter the US and support their own foreign policy.

b. Over the past year, the Soviets have started to build ICBM launchers in larger numbers than ever before. By 1968, they will have a considerably bigger operational force than we anticipated in our estimate of a year ago. Most of the ICBMs will be in dispersed silos to protect them from attack. This force should give the Soviet leaders greater confidence in their deterrent because of its ability to inflict mass destruction upon the US even if the US were to strike first.

c. In their planning for the years beyond 1968, the Soviets must consider such things as the cost of building more ICBM launchers, their

---

[1] Source: Johnson Library, National Security File, Intelligence File, Miscellaneous CIA Intelligence Memoranda, Box 14. Top Secret; [classification marking not declassified]; Handle Via COMINT Talent Keyhole Channels Only. A copy addressed to President Johnson is in the National Archives and Records Administration, RG 263.

[2] Document 143.

technical ability to develop better systems, and the possible course of US military programs. They may decide that there is little strategic advantage in building an ICBM force much larger than the one they will have in 1968. On the other hand, they may seek to strengthen their deterrent and military power still more by increasing their ICBM force to about the size of the one now planned by the US. In either case, they will probably introduce new ICBMs with greater ability to survive US attack and greater effectiveness to strike at US forces. But the Soviet leaders almost certainly do not expect to build forces so powerful that they could launch a first strike against the US without receiving unacceptable damage in return.

d. The Soviet strategic attack forces will continue to include numerous missile submarines. In about 1968, the fleet will probably begin to have improved submarines with longer range missiles, more like US Polaris submarines than are present Soviet types. Missile submarines will increase their patrolling in the open seas, and in a few years a number of them may be on station within missile range of the US. The USSR will keep large numbers of bombers and missiles which could deliver massive attacks against Europe and Asia. It will continue to have a small force of bombers to use against the US.

e. The Assistant Chief of Staff, Intelligence, USAF, does not agree with certain major views expressed in the NIE. He estimates that "programs already underway, plus a continuing strong R&D effort, reflect a Soviet determination to rise from a position of strategic inferiority to one of at least numerical parity with the US in the belief that such a position would markedly enhance the aggressive pursuit of Communist aims." He considers that the Soviets will build somewhat more ICBM launchers than forecast in the NIE and that the estimate underplays the role of bombardment aviation in Soviet intercontinental attack capabilities.

2. This estimate on Soviet strategic attack forces will be followed within the next few weeks by estimates setting forth our latest findings on Soviet strategic defenses and Soviet general purpose military forces.

3. I commend the entire document to your attention, especially its Summary and Conclusions.

Dick

145.   Letter From Secretary of Defense McNamara to Secretary of
State Rusk[1]

Washington, November 17, 1966.

Dear Dean:

I am attaching for your comments a Defense draft NSAM on the
subject of chemical and biological warfare policy.[2] It has been prepared
in response to a State request for a Defense position.[3]

The draft states that the President does not now expect to authorize
first use of lethal CB weapons. With respect to incapacitants, it reflects
the actual situation as it now exists by stating that the President may
authorize their use in certain situations of national urgency. In my view,
we should keep this option open until we have better information concerning specific incapacitating agents, their military effectiveness, and
the political consequences of their use. Accordingly, I have asked the
members of my staff to conduct a study on the role of incapacitating
agents. The results of this study will be reflected in next year's Draft
Memorandum for the President on Theater Nuclear Warfare. In the
meantime, I believe policy guidelines such as those in the attached draft
NSAM would be appropriate and desirable.

I share your interest in reaching an early joint position which we
can recommend to the President. I would be happy to discuss the draft
policy with you at your convenience, if you wish.

Sincerely,

Bob[4]

---

[1] Source: Washington National Records Center, OASD/ISA Files: FR 330 70 A 6648,
384 1966 Jan– . Secret. Drafted by Commander Morris on November 1 and rewritten on
November 16. An attached November 17 memorandum from McNamara to the JCS notes
that the letter reflected the principal points made in JCSM–637–66 and offered "to discuss
the draft policy with you at your convenience, if you wish." A copy of JCSM–637–66,
"Chemical and Biological Warfare Policy," October 3, is in the National Archives and
Records Administration, RG 218, JCS Files, 3260 (10 Dec 64) S.2 IR 2095.

[2] Not printed.

[3] The State request was transmitted to the Department of Defense under cover of a
November 3 letter, but it has not been further identified. (Letter from Vance to Llewellyn
Thompson, November 16; Washington National Records Center, OASD/ISA Files: FRC
330 70 A 6648, 384 1966 Jan–)

[4] Printed from a copy that indicates McNamara signed the original.

146.   National Intelligence Estimate[1]

NIE 11–3–66   Washington, November 17, 1966.

SOVIET STRATEGIC AIR AND MISSILE DEFENSES

The Problem

To estimate the strength and capabilities of Soviet strategic air and missile defense forces through mid-1968, and general trends in these forces through 1976.

Conclusions

A. The Soviet leaders give a higher priority to strategic defenses than does the US; they allocate about equal resources to their strategic attack and their strategic defense forces. The Soviet object in building their strategic defenses is to contribute to deterrence and to foreign policy support, and to limit the damage the US could inflict on the USSR. The Soviets will continue to emphasize strategic defense throughout the next 10 years, and will pursue their efforts to meet the changing US threat. They will seek, through both offensive and defensive programs, to improve their strategic position relative to that of the US. (Paras. 1–5)

B. The Soviets have steadily improved their strategic defenses against aerodynamic vehicles over the last decade, by upgrading their air surveillance system and by developing and deploying both manned interceptors and surface-to-air missile (SAM) systems. Through these systems they have achieved a formidable capability against subsonic and low-supersonic aircraft attempting to penetrate at medium and high altitudes to principal target areas. Current systems are progressively less effective against higher performance aircraft, standoff weapons, and low-altitude penetrations. At present, Soviet strategic air defenses have virtually no effectiveness at altitudes below about 1,000 feet.[2] (Paras. 10–16, 20–22, 29–32)

---

[1]   Source: Johnson Library, National Security File, National Intelligence Estimates, Box 11. Top Secret; Controlled Dissem. A cover sheet, prefatory note, title page, and table of contents are not printed. According to the prefatory note, on the inside of the cover sheet, the CIA and the intelligence organizations of the Departments of State and Defense, the AEC, and the NSA participated in the preparation of this estimate. Representatives of CIA, State Department, DIA, NSA, and AEC concurred; the FBI representative abstained, the subject being outside his jurisdiction.

[2]   Rear Adm. E.B. Fluckey, Assistant Chief of Naval Operations (Intelligence), Department of the Navy, believes that the strategic defense manned interceptors have a greater capability at altitudes below 1,000 feet than indicated in the text, particularly in some sea approaches. [Footnote in the source text.]

C. The Soviets will be deploying over the next few years improved air surveillance radars, air defense communications and control systems, and defensive weapon systems with capabilities against aero-dynamic vehicles. They are now deploying an interceptor with improved low-altitude capabilities. We believe they will also deploy new interceptors with a better capability to defend against standoff weapons and higher performance aircraft. Although we think the Soviets will continue to work on the problem of defense against penetrations below 1,000 feet, we do not expect any system with such capabilities to be operational before about 1970. (Paras. 17–19, 23–28, 38)

D. Since 1964 the Soviets have been constructing complexes for a new missile system for strategic defense, which we call the Tallinn system. There are now probably 20–25 complexes (each with multiple launch sites) under construction. We believe all of these will become operational in 1967 and 1968. The deployment concept appears to include both forward defense on likely approaches to the industrial region of European USSR and local defense of selected targets. We believe that the rate at which new complexes have been started has increased in the past year or so, and that this system will be widely deployed throughout the USSR. (Paras. 33–34, 37)

E. The information available at present is insufficient for us to estimate with high confidence the capabilities and mission of the Tallinn system. Such evidence as we have leads us to believe that the system has significant capabilities against high-speed aerodynamic vehicles flying at high altitude and that its mission is defense against the airborne threat.[3] Depending on the characteristics of some components, however, the system could have capabilities against ballistic missiles. We have therefore assessed the potential of the Tallinn system in both the SAM and antiballistic missile (ABM) roles. (Para. 35)

F. In the SAM role, we believe the Tallinn system represents a considerable improvement over currently operational Soviet SAMs in terms of range (on the order of 100 n.m.), altitude (up to 100,000 feet), and ability to deal with supersonic targets (up to Mach 3 or 3.5). We

---

[3] Lt. Gen. Joseph H. Carroll, Director, DIA; Maj. Gen. Chester L. Johnson, Acting Assistant Chief of Staff for Intelligence, Department of the Army; and Maj. Gen. Jack E. Thomas, Assistant Chief of Staff, Intelligence, USAF, believe that the many uncertainties stemming from analysis of available evidence do not support a confident judgment as to whether the mission of the Tallinn-type defensive system is SAM, ABM, or dual purpose. They acknowledge that the available evidence does support a conclusion that these sites may have a defensive mission against the aerodynamic threat. However, on balance, considering all information available, they believe it is more likely that the systems being deployed are for defense against ballistic missiles with an additional capability to defend against high flying supersonic aerodynamic vehicles. [Footnote in the source text.]

do not believe it is the Soviet answer to the low-altitude threat. If the system was designed as an ABM, then data would have to be fed to the complexes from off-site radars in order for them to defend areas large enough to provide a strategic ABM defense. Some of the Tallinn complexes are in locations where they could take advantage of such data from known radars of appropriate types, but some are not. With such data, the Tallinn complexes may be capable of exoatmospheric intercept of incoming ballistic missiles at distances out to about 200 n.m., and thus each complex could defend a fairly large area. Without such data, the ABM capabilities of each complex would be seriously reduced and limited to local and self-defense. (Paras. 36, 51)

G. After an intensive ABM research and development program, the Soviets decided at least five years ago to deploy an ABM system at Moscow. This system (which we call the Moscow system) will achieve an initial capability in the next year or two, and all sites now under construction will be completed by about 1970. We believe that it is a long-range exoatmospheric system with a large kill radius, and that the primary purpose of its present deployment is the defense of Moscow. (Paras. 39, 43–47)

H. The Moscow ABM system probably will have a good capability against a numerically limited attack by currently operational US missiles. Its capabilities could be degraded by advanced penetration systems, and it could not cope with a very heavy attack. Furthermore, the system utilizes data from large radars for it to function most effectively. Without these radars, the capabilities of the system would be seriously reduced, though if the launch sites were designed to operate autonomously, the system could still intercept some missiles targeted against Moscow. The present deployment will cover only a part of the Polaris threat to Moscow. (Paras. 48–50)

I. We cannot now identify any wholly new ABM system in development and we do not expect any to become operational before the early 1970's. In view of the presently limited capabilities of the ABM defenses now under construction, we believe the Soviets will devote substantial efforts to upgrading their present hardware, developing improved ABM systems, and improving their detection and tracking capabilities. The Soviets might decide that ABM defenses for the general defense of the USSR are too costly. We think it likely, however, that they will extend their ABM defenses. But we think they will be cautious about committing themselves to a fixed policy with respect to ABM deployment over the long term. They will probably adjust whatever program they pursue on the basis of a number of factors, including the capabilities of present defenses to deal with penetration aids, the advances in ABM technology, the cost of additional deployment relative to the protection it is likely to afford, and the US reaction to Soviet strategic developments.[4] (Paras. 52, 55–60)

J. In the course of their ABM program, the Soviets have developed large radars which have good capabilities for tracking ballistic missiles and space vehicles. A number of radars of this type, now under construction, will become operational in 1967–1968. Although they do not all have the same functions, we believe that in the aggregate they will provide the USSR with a national space surveillance capability. Within the next 5 to 10 years the Soviets will probably develop and employ a variety of space systems (such as infrared detection and other types of warning) in support of their strategic defensive forces. (Paras. 40–42, 53–54, 62–63)

K. We have no positive evidence that the Soviets are developing antisatellite defenses, but we believe they have had an incentive to do so for some time. It would be technically possible for them to have a limited antisatellite capability already, based on existing radars and missiles and requiring a nuclear weapon to achieve a kill. When their new space surveillance radars are operational in 1967–1968, they could have a capability to destroy satellites by either nuclear or nonnuclear means after the satellites had passed over the USSR a few times. The Soviets may also explore techniques for neutralizing satellites without destroying them. A manned satellite inspection and antisatellite system could be developed in the 1970's. We believe, however, that the Soviets would seek to destroy or neutralize US satellites only if they believed general war were imminent. There might also be some other special circumstances in which they would use antisatellite systems in peacetime, such as an occasion in which they believed they were retaliating against US interference with their own satellites. (Paras. 61, 64–67)

L. Over the past decade or more the Soviets have developed an extensive civil defense program, which is now administered by the

---

[4] For the views of Rear Adm. E.B. Fluckey, Assistant Chief of Naval Operations (Intelligence), Department of the Navy, see his footnote to paragraph 58, page 20. [Footnote in the source text. This footnote reads: "Rear Adm. E.B. Fluckey, Assistant Chief of Naval Operations (Intelligence), Department of the Navy, believes that the Galosh system could be a part of a Soviet retaliatory assured destruction defensive weapons system. Moscow, at the hub of all defense and counter strike and the center of command and control, must avoid destruction long enough to provide time for decision, retaliation, damage assessment of the Soviet Union, and rapid communications with the outside world. Should the US strike first, the Soviets would have only about 10 minutes tactical warning, compared to our own short 15 minutes if the Soviets strike first. They may consider this reaction time insufficient and so are willing to expend substantial funds to cover Moscow with an effective ABM system to gain as much as 24 hours grace before fallout moving in from other attack areas would degrade their capability to decide and respond. Having attained this, they might decide that ABM defenses for the comprehensive defense of the USSR are too costly."]

Ministry of Defense. The current program is characterized by widespread public training, the use of simple shelters, and plans for urban evacuation in advance of hostilities. Shelter space is available for less than one-sixth of the urban population, and adequate shelter for key personnel only. We have detected no recent major changes in the priority or pace of the program and we have no indication that the Soviets would regard a stepped up civil defense effort as a necessary adjunct to extended ABM deployment. We anticipate continued slow but steady improvement in overall civil defense effectiveness. (Paras. 68–73)

[Here follow the Discussion section (Parts I–VI, pages 6–23) and an Annex (pages 24–27).]

147. Memorandum From Director of Central Intelligence Helms to President Johnson[1]

TCS–8649–66   Washington, December 1, 1966.

SUBJECT

National Intelligence Estimate 11–3–66, "Soviet Strategic Air and Missile Defenses," dated 17 November 1966

Attached is National Intelligence Estimate 11–3–66, "Soviet Strategic Air and Missile Defenses."[2] It is the third in our current series of estimates on Soviet military capabilities. In my judgment, its conclusions can be summarized as follows:

1. The crucial question in this estimate concerns the status of Soviet defense against ballistic missiles. We know the Soviets have been engaged in research and development in this field for more than ten years. The intelligence community is agreed that an anti-ballistic missile system has been under construction in the Moscow area since 1962 and will begin to be operational in the next year or two. It will probably have good capabilities against a limited-scale attack on Moscow by present US ICBMs. We

---

[1] Source: Johnson Library, National Security File, Intelligence File, Miscellaneous CIA Intelligence Memoranda, Box 14. Top Secret; Handle via Talent-Keyhole-COMINT Channels Jointly. An attached note from Rostow to President Johnson, December 4, 1 p.m., briefly summarized NIE 11–3–66 and added: "You will wish to read Dick Helms' evaluation of the evidence on Soviet ABMs plus, perhaps, the summary—or even more. It is the foundation on which tough decisions are coming up."

[2] Document 146.

believe that its effectiveness could be reduced by advanced penetration systems, and that it could not cope with a very heavy attack or with Polaris attacks from certain directions. At present there is no indication that this system is being installed anywhere else in the USSR. (I might add that I am confident that we could detect the installation of such a system elsewhere, perhaps two or three years before it reached operational status.)

2. There is, however, another new defense system under construction at a number of locations. It will begin to be operational next year. The intelligence community does not have enough information about this system to be certain of exactly what it is designed to defend against—whether ballistic missiles or aerodynamic vehicles. The general nature of the system, its equipment, and the pattern of its deployment lead me to believe it is an improved defense against high-speed, high-altitude aircraft, and also against the air-to-surface missiles that such aircraft may launch. But I cannot rule out the possibility that it is a defense against ballistic missiles. My views about this system are shared by the intelligence officers of the Department of State, the US Navy, and the Atomic Energy Commission, and by the Director of the National Security Agency.

Disagreement with these views is expressed by the Director of the Defense Intelligence Agency and the intelligence officers of the US Army and US Air Force. Their view is that while a confident judgment cannot now be made as to whether this system is for defense against ballistic missiles, aerodynamic vehicles, or both, it is more likely to be an anti-ballistic missile system with an additional capability to defend against high-flying supersonic aerodynamic vehicles. (Because of the uncertainties and our differences of view, we have included in the estimate an evaluation of the capabilities of this system in both roles.)

3. We are all agreed that the Soviets could have a limited anti-satellite capability now. Furthermore, they are building a space surveillance radar network which could support a much improved system. In a year or so they may be able to destroy our reconnaissance and other satellites by non-nuclear means; they may explore techniques for neutralizing satellites without destroying them. But we do not think they would actually try to neutralize or destroy US satellite unless they thought war were imminent or unless there were other special circumstances, such as an occasion in which they thought they were retaliating against US interference with their satellites.

4. The USSR has excellent defenses against present Western bombers operating at high and medium altitudes. Present systems will become less effective as the US introduces higher performance aircraft and air-to-surface missiles. The Soviets are working to improve their capabilities against these prospective threats, in part by developing much better interceptor

aircraft and air defense control systems. Their low altitude defense is now a major weakness and will remain so for at least the next several years.

This estimate on Soviet strategic defenses completes our present series on the main elements of Soviet military capabilities.

I commend the entire document to your attention, especially its more formal Conclusions.

Dick

---

148.   Letter From Secretary of State Rusk to Secretary of Defense McNamara[1]

Washington, December 1, 1966.

Dear Bob:

Thank you for the opportunity once again to review your five year force structure memoranda.[2] These documents continue to provide an invaluable summary of DOD programs and a concise analysis of the major issues related to future force plans. They also raise a number of important policy issues which bear on our foreign relations. In the following paragraphs, I would like to set forth my views with respect to certain of the memoranda. In some instances, I am suggesting specific follow-up actions. However, if you believe it would be desirable for us to discuss any of these matters before we undertake further specific staff action, I should be happy to do so.

A. Strategic Forces

Your memorandum on Strategic Forces raises two issues of particular interest to me:

---

[1] Source: Washington National Records Center, OASD/ISA Files: FRC 330 71 A 4919, 320.2 1967 Jan–March. Top Secret. A stamped notation indicates that McNaughton saw the letter. An undated, handwritten note on the letter by McNaughton reads: "Who was assigned action within DOD? ISA?"

[2] Reference is to draft memorandum to the President on recommended FY 1968–1972 national defense programs. These memoranda have not been found, but are elsewhere identified as Draft Presidential Memoranda on Strategic Offensive and Defense Forces, Land and Air General Purpose Forces, and Air and Sea Lift. (Memorandum from McNaughton to McNamara, January 8, 1967; ibid.)

1. What effect can we expect growing Soviet capabilities to have on their policy and actions and what implications does this have for US policies and our future military programs? (Included in this question is, of course, the possible deployment of a US ABM); and,

2. What international political implications should we expect to grow out of the improving Soviet strategic missile force, Soviet ABM deployment, etc., and how should those implications be handled?

Your memorandum to the President makes it quite clear that our own offensive systems are going to maintain our assured destruction capability under any circumstances. While it is clear that Soviet capabilities will become increasingly potent and secure I do not think the situation of mutual deterrence has changed fundamentally from that which we have had to face over the past several years.

However, I do think that we ought to consider whether the Soviets will assess the situation as we do. I do not think it probable that they will make an erroneous assumption, but we must make every effort to insure that the Soviets do not reach the conclusion that a more convincing second strike capability gives them greater latitude for the use of conventional military force.

Your memorandum provides an excellent summary of the present and projected strategic balance. However, in order to understand better the implications for our security policy of this complex and dynamic situation I would like to suggest that our staffs cooperate in examining in some detail the interaction of US and Soviet strategic capabilities past, present and future. Future projections should also take account of estimated Chinese strategic nuclear capabilities and how they affect the US-Soviet strategic relationship as well as the situation between the US and China. I would hope that such an analysis would illustrate, for a range of scenarios the major changes in the strategic nuclear balance from 1960 to the present and their military effects, and how this balance might change at specific future dates through 1975, as new capabilities appear on both sides.

This would provide a data base, which in conjunction with other factors, would permit a clearer assessment of the implications for our security position of projected US, Soviet and CPR postures, and the impact of these changes on our foreign relations. Among other things, a careful and detailed analysis might serve to sharpen our thinking and provide a better basis for discussions with our allies who are likely to be increasingly concerned, or at least uncertain, about the effect on their security of changing strategic capabilities.

I am asking Foy Kohler, in his new capacity as Deputy Under Secretary for Political Affairs, to discuss this suggestion with whomever you designate from DOD. In view of the sensitivity of the subject matter, I propose to limit participation in this analysis to a very small group in State, and I assume you will want to do the same with regard to DOD participation. It may well be that a presentation to the President of our analysis and conclusions might eventually be desirable. I am enclosing at Tab A a list of some of the issues[3] that I think might be illuminated by the proposed joint analysis, though I suggest this be considered as a point of departure, rather than a comprehensive or final description of the proposed analysis.

This leads to my second question. Even though we may be persuaded that mutual deterrence persists and the validity of our commitments is unchanged, the conclusions to be drawn from the new developments in both Soviet and US nuclear capabilities will not be immediately clear to all our allies, nor to third parties on the international scene. It will be important for us to think through what impressions we want to convey and how we wish to convey them. It is, therefore, imperative that we have a clear, consistent and agreed line within the government which can be followed both at home and abroad.

The ABM is a special, but integral part of the foregoing problem. I have emphasized previously my great interest in ABM developments and the political importance I attach to any decision regarding a US deployment, whether it be positive or negative. The clear evidence of a Soviet ABM program, and your recent public statement about it[4] place this matter in a new perspective. I believe it is certain that we will face growing Congressional and public pressures to begin an ABM deployment ourselves. I recognize that there are persuasive arguments for and against deployment, and the decision will not be an easy one. I want to emphasize, however, one point I have made in the past. I do not believe foreign policy problems should in any way prevent us from deploying an ABM system at such time as it is determined to be necessary for the security of the US.

Nevertheless, we can anticipate concern from some of our allies if we do make a decision to deploy. Thus, we will need to plan together very carefully how we approach our allies on this matter, and particularly how we deal with the difficult question of possible overseas deployment of such a system.

There will be several opportunities in the near future for a comprehensive US Government statement on the strategic balance including the President's State of the Union Message,[5] your annual presentation

---

[3] Not printed.

[4] Presumably a reference to McNamara's press conference in Austin, Texas, on November 9, at which he announced that the U.S. Government had good evidence that the Soviets were building an ABM system around Moscow.

[5] Given on January 10, 1967; for text, see *Public Papers of the Presidents of the United States: Lyndon B. Johnson, 1967*, pp. 2–14.

of the five year defense program to the Congress, and my contemplated foreign policy review, which I discussed with you several weeks ago. In addition, I believe we will need to cover the subject in some way at the NATO meeting in Paris this month. Finally, there is a pressing need for an agreed governmental line given the increasing interest shown in this subject by both the US and foreign press community.

In order to assure the international understanding and reception of these problems that we want, I am proposing that the enclosed set of guidelines (Tab B)[6] be utilized in preparing any statements, public or private, which will impact on international audiences. If you agree, our staffs might jointly refine these guidelines from time to time to keep them abreast of developments, referring to your consideration and mine any major unresolved policy issues. I would, of course, appreciate any suggestions you would care to offer for additions or adjustments to the guidelines I am enclosing. I am also sending copies of these guidelines to Bill Foster and Len Marks asking for their comments and suggestions.

B. General Purpose Land Air and Lift Forces

In reviewing your several memoranda on general purpose land, air and lift forces, two major questions appeared to me to warrant further comment:

1. Can we define more precisely the circumstances in which US conventional forces, including strategic lift, will have relevance in a future that will unquestionably include continuing military conflict and threats of violence in various parts of the world, and

2. How should US and allied military capabilities relate to one another?

As you have pointed out, it is not easy to establish future requirements for general purpose forces. The wide variety of possible contingencies, the uncertainties as to the scope and timing of future conflicts, and the diversity of the forces involved do not allow the sort of rigorous analysis that can be applied to strategic force requirements. It is just these general purpose forces, however, that provide us with the flexibility we require to pursue our foreign policy objectives.

Clearly we have today far more powerful mobile and balanced forces than we had six years ago, and I am impressed by the rate at which their development is proceeding. Nevertheless, the level of conflict in the world is frighteningly high, and while we have no mandate to police the world and no inclination to do so, our security is directly related to the security of others. Obviously, we must deal with the

---

[6] Not printed.

sources of conflict and try to eradicate them if possible before violence erupts. But there remains the problem of containing and settling conflicts that may occur and of minimizing direct involvement of US forces while maximizing their deterrent influence. I assume that it would assist in your force planning analysis if we were able to help define somewhat more clearly what appear to be the most likely future conflicts which may confront us, and their nature. We might also investigate more deeply the kind of settlement to such conflicts we would hope to see.

I have no illusions about the difficulty of this task and I doubt that we can expect precision in such definitions. But, perhaps we can go further than we have heretofore. I believe, for example, that my own staff can be set to work examining in greater depth the future international environmental and developing reasonable politico-military assumptions useful for force planning.

I gather from your memoranda that your own staff is looking at future contingencies with a view to establishing future logistics requirements. These two staff efforts seem to me to be logically related if indeed they are not complementary. Both of them also bear some relationship to the work of the interagency Contingency Coordinating Committee, which has developed a number of plans that might provide a point of departure.

Finally, one area which I believe has not received a recent and thorough examination, from either the political or the military points of view, is how and in what ways indigenous country military efforts should relate to US efforts. I have in mind questions ranging from the contribution US military assistance might make in reducing reliance on early use of US force to the future needs for bases, overflight rights and access to foreign territory. All of these are essential elements in planning the size and nature of our own conventional forces and especially of our future strategic mobility needs. Moreover, such an examination of indigenous capabilities in relation to our own seems to me central to the formulation of a concept for the role which US force should be prepared to play in the future.

I would like to suggest that our two Departments jointly address these problems. We have, by way of example, made an effort to identify some illustrative questions which might be analyzed (Tab C).[7] I wish to emphasize the fact that they are only illustrative, and again, I am asking Foy Kohler to pursue this line of inquiry with your representatives to see how far we can usefully carry such a joint analysis. Foy will of course have available the assistance from our geographic bureaus and

---

[7] Not printed.

policy planning staff which should be able to contribute significantly to this undertaking.

In view of my pending departure for Asia,[8] I have not had adequate opportunity to review all of your remaining memoranda to the President. Several appear, however, to raise important foreign policy questions warranting further comment.

Your memorandum on European Forces and Strategy is one which raises important foreign policy issues. However, since those are being addressed in connection with John McCloy's Report for the President,[9] I will not comment further at this time.

My views on the issues raised in your MAP memorandum, except insofar as they are touched on in this letter, will be provided to you in a separate communication.

I would prefer to withhold comment on the remaining memoranda until I have had a chance to review them more thoroughly, particularly your memoranda on Theater Nuclear Forces, ASW forces, and perhaps on Research and Development.

May I congratulate you and your staff for an impressive and extremely useful series of analyses.

As in the past, given their interest in these matters, I am sending copies of this letter to the Director of the Bureau of the Budget and to Walt Rostow.[10]

With warm regards,

Sincerely,

Dean

---

[8] On December 4 Secretary Rusk left on an extended trip to Asia and the Middle East. He arrived in Paris on December 13 and attended the December 15–16 NATO Ministerial meeting. (Johnson Library, Rusk Appointment Books)

[9] See Foreign Relations, 1964–1968, vol. XIII, Document 218.

[10] In the January 8 memorandum prepared for McNamara's reply to Secretary Rusk (see footnote 2 above), McNaughton commented that Rusk's "letter represents primarily an attempt at the staff level to effect changes in the preparation and coordination of the Draft Presidential Memoranda, so as to give State more influence in their formulation. This is obviously a delicate matter which I had best discuss privately with Foy, after hearing your views." In his January 19 reply to Rusk, McNamara responded that the two Departments had recently agreed on guidelines for all diplomatic posts on recent developments in strategic forces, "particularly ABM's" and that he had asked McNaughton to explore all the issues with Kohler. (Washington National Records Center, OASD/ISA Files: FRC 330 71 A 4919, 320.2 1967 Jan–March) For the agreed guidelines, see Document 163.

149.   Memorandum From the Joint Chiefs of Staff to Secretary of
        Defense McNamara[1]

JCSM–742–66   Washington, December 2, 1966.

SUBJECT

  Production and Deployment of the Nike-X (C)

  1. (U) Your informal memorandum, dated 29 November 1966,[2]
requested the comments of the Joint Chiefs of Staff on your draft memorandum for the President, subject: "Production and Deployment of the
Nike-X."[3] Detailed comments, in line-in/line-out form, are contained in
the Annex hereto.[4] These comments refine the factual data and are not
intended to produce a text which represents the judgments of the Joint
Chiefs of Staff.

  2. (S) The Joint Chiefs of Staff cannot agree with the over-all rationale in the draft memorandum in the following respects:

  a. They consider that your discussion of assured destruction and
damage limiting does not address the need for a suitable interrelationship between these two capabilities.
  b. They do not agree that Soviet decisions as to the future development of their offensive missile force are as directly dependent on the US
ABM decision as is implied in the draft memorandum.
  c. They believe that the problems and uncertainties of coping with
a US ABM defense would reduce the risk of a Soviet attack.

  3. (S) The Joint Chiefs of Staff reaffirm their recommendation that a
decision be made now to initiate deployment of Nike-X for an initial
operational capability in FY 1972.

  4. (U) Without attachment, this memorandum is downgraded to
Secret.

                                        For the Joint Chiefs of Staff:
                                        Earle G. Wheeler
                                        Chairman
                                        Joint Chiefs of Staff

<hr>

  [1] Source: Washington National Records Center, OSD Files: FRC 330 70 A 4662, 471.94
ABM (Nov & Dec) 1966. Top Secret.
  [2] Not found.
  [3] Not found. Reference may be to a later draft of a November 18 19-page paper, la-
beled "Draft II" but without a subject line. (Washington National Records Center, OSD
Files: FRC 330 70 A 4443, 471.94 ABM (November) 1966)
  [4] Not printed.

150. Draft Notes of Meeting[1]

Austin, Texas, December 6, 1966.

Notes on Meeting with the President in Austin, Texas, December 6, 1966 with Secretary McNamara and the Joint Chiefs of Staff

THOSE PRESENT WERE

The President
Secretary McNamara
Deputy Secretary Vance
General Wheeler
General Johnson
Admiral McDonald
General McConnell
General Greene
W.W. Rostow

Secretary McNamara reported that agreement had been reached between the Secretary of Defense, the Under Secretary, and Members of the Joint Chiefs on all but five major issues: the ABM defense system; advance strategic bomber; advanced ICBM; the Army force structure; and the appropriate number of nuclear fleet escort ships.

The latest Defense budget figures for submission to the President were these:

FY 1967 Vietnam Supplemental, $14.7 billion (NOA)
Overall Defense budget FY 1968—$77.7 billion (NOA)
Overall expenditures Fiscal 1967—$68.3
Overall expenditures Fiscal 1968—$74.6[2]

The President asked if the Joint Chiefs confirmed Secretary McNamara's statement. The Chairman so stated, and Admiral David

---

[1] Source: National Archives and Records Administration, RG 200, Defense Programs and Operations, Draft Memoranda to the President, 1968–72, Tab 8, Box 71. Top Secret; Eyes Only for the President. Drafted on December 10; no other drafting information appears on the notes.

[2] In a telephone conversation with President Johnson on December 23, McNamara reported among other things that the final defense budget figures were very close to what he had earlier given the President. They were: FY 1967 Supplemental (NOA) $12.9 billion, Overall FY 1967 Supplemental (NOA) $74.466 billion, FY 67 expenditures $67.950 billion, and FY 68 expenditures $73.1 billion. He added that he could still squeeze out $200–300 million from the FY 68 figures if required. The President replied, "That's wonderful; that's wonderful." McNamara concluded, "That's how we stand and you can consider this final." In response to the President's questions, he said the budget figures included the anti-missile missile but excluded the pay increase and what McNamara called "the construction stimulants." (Johnson Library, Recordings and Transcripts, Recording of Telephone Conversation Between President Johnson and Secretary McNamara, December 23, 1:01 p.m., Tape F6612.03, Side B; this transcript prepared specifically for this *Foreign Relations* volume)

McDonald added that in his experience the Secretary and the Chiefs have never been "so close together," except on the five specified issues.

General Wheeler then stated the case for the deployment of an ABM system. He said two new facts had to be taken into account: (1) the USSR was deploying an ABM system around Moscow, and they were deploying a system widely throughout the USSR which might have ABM capabilities; (2) they were installing at an accelerated rate hardened ICBM's, the S-11, a city buster. By 1971 they might have between 800–1100 ICBM's.

We do not know the objective of Soviet nuclear policy: whether it is parity with the U.S. or superiority. But, taken together, their new program could reduce our assured destruction capability; complicate our targeting; reduce confidence in our ability to penetrate; reduce our first-strike capability; and improve the Soviet capability to pursue aims short of nuclear war.

The Chairman then quoted from Secretary McNamara's paper[3] the latter's key judgment:

"After studying the subject exhaustively, Mr. Vance and I have concluded we should not initiate ABM deployment at this time for any of these purposes. We believe that:
"1. The Soviet Union would be forced to react to a U.S. ABM deployment by increasing its offensive nuclear force with the result that:
a. The risk of a Soviet nuclear attack on the U.S. would not be further decreased.
b. The damage to the U.S. from a Soviet nuclear attack, in the event deterrence failed, would not be reduced in any meaningful sense.
The foundation of our security is the deterrence of a Soviet nuclear attack. We believe such an attack can be prevented if it is understood by the Soviets that we possess strategic nuclear forces so powerful as to be capable of absorbing a Soviet first strike and surviving with sufficient strength to impose unacceptable damage on them (e.g., destruction by blast and radiation alone of approximately [*less than 1 line of source text not declassified*]). We have such power today. We must maintain it in the future, adjusting our forces to offset actual or potential changes in theirs."

General Wheeler expressed disagreement with this judgment. He said we cannot predict confidently how the Soviet Union would react to counter our deployment of an ABM system. The costs would constitute an important diversion of resources. The development of multiple warheads would reduce the kilotonnage of their nuclear payloads; they would face grave uncertainties in targeting against our ABM's. He said deterrence was not only technology, it was a state of mind. Our having

---

[3] Not found, but presumably an early draft of Document 160.

an ABM system would increase our deterrence capability no matter what they did.

On the other hand, a lack of a deployed ABM might increase the possibilities of war by accident; create an imbalance or a sense of imbalance between the U.S. and USSR; suggest that we are interested only in the offense; suggest also that the U.S. was not willing to pay to maintain its present nuclear superiority.

We would be denying to many of our own people a chance to survive a nuclear exchange: 30–50 million lives might be saved by Nike-X.

Therefore, the JCS recommends to the President that we initiate deployment of the Nike-X system in order to maintain the present overall favorable nuclear balance and give to us some or all of the following advantages:

—damage limiting capability;
—the imposition of new uncertainties should the Soviets contemplate initiating nuclear war;
—to demonstrate that we are not first-strike minded;
—and to maintain the kind of favorable power environment which helped us during the Cuba missile crisis.

Specifically the JCS recommends that we immediately decide to develop Option A to protect 25 U.S. cities. The cost in Fiscal 1968 would be $800 million; for the period Fiscal 67–76, $10 billion.

The President asked if there was any difference between the JCS and Secretary McNamara concerning the costs. Secretary McNamara said "No."

The President then asked if our position would be better if the Soviet Union did not react to our deployment. The Secretary agreed that our position would be better; but that it was "inconceivable" that the Soviet Union would not react to counter our deployment of an ABM system.

The President then asked what determined the difference in judgment between the Secretary and the JCS.

Secretary McNamara replied that the difference lay less in rational calculation than in the inherently emotional nature of the issue. It was extremely hard to make the case for a policy which appeared to be denying protection to our people, when the Soviet Union was willing to employ large resources to protect its people. He said he was fully aware that if the President decided against deploying an ABM system he would face a most difficult time politically and psychologically. Why, then, does he recommend against?

First, the Soviet Union has been wrong in its nuclear defense policy for a decade. They have systematically spent 2 or 3 times what we have on defense. It has not been worth it. Their defenses are not worth a damn. We still can impose unacceptable losses on them even after a first strike. Because they are making an error in deploying ABM's is no reason we should also make that error.

Second, we must be clear why it would be an error for us. If we go ahead with the $10 billion ABM program and they did not [2 lines of source text not declassified]. Therefore, they would have to do something about it. Their security would depend on their doing something about it. They would have to bring back their assured damage capability to something like 80 million U.S. fatalities under their planning case, which is [less than 1 line of source text not declassified]. As they did so, we could not hold to our initial $10 million [billion?] ABM system. We would have to expand in response to what they did, both our ABM and our offensive systems.

Secretary McNamara concluded that we would be launching ourselves and the Soviet Union into two decades of escalatory action in the nuclear field in which the costs on each side would prove to be of the order of $31–40 billion. We would each end up no better off than we are at present.

Secretary McNamara then said there are certain rational roles for a limited ABM system, in particular these four:

—to protect our offensive force, notably our Minutemen;
—to protect in the time frame 1975–85 against a ChiCom ICBM capability;
—to protect against an accidental firing of a single missile;
—to protect against a small blackmail Soviet attack.

In the face of the terrible dilemma faced by the President, Secretary McNamara is inclined to recommend, as a fallback from his judgment against the ABM system, a limited system with these four capabilities. On the basis of that system we could explore whether the Soviet Union was willing to negotiate a freeze acceptable to us.

The President then asked, "Is there any middle ground in this debate?" Secretary McNamara said that the emotionalism attaching to the ABM issue made middle ground hard to find.

The President asked what would the view be in the Congress?

Secretary McNamara said about 25% of the Congress—the Liberals—would oppose the ABM. Senators Russell, Stennis, etc., would strongly favor it, and they would have about 40% of the Congress with them. The balance of 35% would remain in the middle and be subject to persuasion. The President asked who might be on that middle ground. Secretary McNamara replied Senators like Kuchel and Javits.

He pointed out further that the Congress had been interesting itself in this matter for a long time. Last year they voted $165 million for

ABM's, and when he inquired what they had in mind, they didn't know; they merely wanted to move in that direction.

The President asked again, "What is a middle alternative?"

Secretary McNamara pointed out that we did not have to make a final decision one way or the other right now. For example, we had important technical problems to overcome with respect to the warheads for the Olympia ABM. We had to install at Kwajalein a quite revolutionary system for '69 tests of the ABM. It is quite risky in fact to start building [a] plant for the ABM system before those tests are complete. In short, there are technical reasons to go slow.

With these unsolved technical problems as a background, we could move forward with a limited system to get the four objectives Secretary McNamara had earlier stated. As for the fifth objective—population protection—we would not be able to walk away from that forever, but we would have some time to see if anything could be worked out with the Soviet Union to avoid the interacting escalation in the nuclear arms race that was otherwise inevitable.

Deputy Secretary Vance then added that he did not believe we could stand for long with Posture A, which promised to protect 25 cities. Under pressure from other cities and regions, the Congress would go for a full program. It would be wiser to face from the beginning that if we started down the road to population protection, it is really Posture B that we were undertaking—a $20 billion rather than a $10 billion program.

General Wheeler said that, given the lead time, we ought to begin to build factories now for certain of the components about which we are technically sure. We do not have that capability and it should not be delayed.

Secretary McNamara came back again to the point that a decision not to deploy would create emotional and political problems in the country, and that a decision to deploy merely to protect offensive forces would face the same emotional problem. There would be a strong impulse to protect people, not missiles. As for the factories, he said the components are complex; there are many parts to be tested.

Our experience is that the system will prove more expensive than we presently calculated.

General Johnson said the critical question was U.S. casualties. An ABM system would cut our casualties in a nuclear exchange. Secretary McNamara replied that he completely disagreed because the USSR would react to re-establish its assured damage capability.

General Johnson said that there were constraints on their ability if they did react. Secretary McNamara replied that both an Air Force study and an NIE had indicated that the Soviet Union could not afford not to react.[4]

The President wondered if the best opportunity for agreement among us would not be a decision to move ahead on a limited basis and to see what we can negotiate with the Soviet Union. Admiral McDonald said the Soviet Union was now moving ahead both with ABM's and to increase its offensive nuclear force. Secretary McNamara said that their defensive effort was wasted.

General McConnell said that their defensive effort was not wholly wasted. They had imposed heavy additional costs on the U.S. to assure our continued penetration ability.

Secretary McNamara said we have over-reacted. We have more than insured that we can still maintain our assured damage capability. The Soviet ABM's have not saved Soviet lives.

General McConnell said he can't forget that we are dealing with the descendants of Genghis Khan. They only understand force.

Secretary McNamara agreed and said that is why, at whatever cost, we must maintain our assured second-strike damage capability. Deputy Secretary Vance added that that is why we have gone ahead with Poseidon and other means to assure our ability to penetrate an ABM system.

Secretary McNamara asked if the JCS would wish to express any views if there were a press conference. The members of the JCS replied that none of them desired to meet the press.

The subject then turned to the second item in which there was disagreement; that is, the advanced strategic bomber (AMSA).[5]

---

[4] Neither of these documents has been further identified.

[5] See Document 151.

151.   Memorandum for the Record[1]

Austin, Texas, December 6, 1966.

1. AMSA

Mr. McNamara asked General McConnell to state the position of the Joint Chiefs with respect to AMSA. General McConnell said that the Chiefs wish to proceed to contract definition. He said he wanted to make very clear that this did not mean full-scale development. General McConnell said further that the Chiefs wish to do full-scale development of the engines required for an advanced manned strategic aircraft, but went on to point out that this engine would have uses for other aircraft as well as AMSA. He stated, thirdly, that the Chiefs wish to proceed with further avionic development for the AMSA. He said the Chiefs wish to proceed to contract definition so that we would be in a position to seek to obtain an IOC in 1974. General McConnell went on to say that it was his own personal belief that it would not be possible to get an IOC of 1974, even if we proceeded on the schedule recommended by the JCS. He said he believed that a more likely IOC would be 1976.

Mr. McNamara pointed out that he and Mr. Vance did not feel that we need an IOC of 1974. Further, he said it is not clear that we need a new manned bomber.

The President then asked General McConnell the difference between the FB-111 and the AMSA in respect of speed and other characteristics. General McConnell said the AMSA would have a slightly higher speed, more range, and a substantially greater bomb carrying capacity. He said the latter factor was of greatest importance. General McConnell said he wanted to repeat that he is not asking for full-scale development.

Mr. McNamara then said it is doubtful that we will need a new manned bomber because of difficulties associated with penetration of the Soviet Union during that time period. He also said that missiles plus the FB-111 force which the United States will have at that time may be enough to meet our force requirements.

Mr. McNamara said that it was his opinion, and that of Mr. Vance, that we did not need to move as fast as the Air Force is requesting, and

---

[1] Source: National Archives and Records Administration, RG 200, Defense Programs and Operations, Draft Memoranda to the President, 1968–72, Tab 8, Box 71. Top Secret. Drafted on December 7; no other drafting information appears on the memorandum, although it is on the stationery of the Deputy Secretary of Defense. This memorandum is a continuation of the record of the December 6 meeting in Austin (see Document 150).

that we should go forward with the development of engines and avionics which are not unique to the AMSA.

General McConnell then said he wanted to point out that the Air Force had done a number of studies which had indicated that a mixture of bombers and missiles is more cost effective than missiles alone.

The President said he would consider the matter and give his decision at a later date.

2. ICM

Mr. McNamara said that the difference between the recommendation of the Chiefs and that of himself and Mr. Vance was merely when we might need such an advanced intercontinental ballistic missile. He said we do not disagree that preliminary work should be started.

General McConnell stated that the Joint Chiefs recommend that we develop an ICM at a total cost in FY 1968 of $36 million. This $36 million would be broken down into $10 million for various component development, and the balance for contract definition. General McConnell said the Secretary of the Air Force would not go to contract definition but would spend $19 million for component development. General McConnell said the Joint Chiefs could live with a $19 million program.

Mr. McNamara responded that he thought we could work this out as he and Mr. Vance were recommending a program of $19 million, and the only question between the Joint Chiefs of Staff and Mr. McNamara and Mr. Vance was how fast we should proceed.

General McConnell emphasized that for the expenditure of $2-1/2 million in offense, we could cause the Soviets to spend $80 million in defense. Mr. McNamara pointed out that this was the very point he and Mr. Vance had been making in the ABM discussion.

3. Army Force Structure

Mr. McNamara said that the Army has recommended that two more brigades be authorized in the Active Army, with a possibility of adding another division to the Active Army force structure in Calendar Year 1967. He said the Army proposed that these additional forces be equipped with equipment taken from the Reserve. He pointed out that thus the effect of authorizing these additional forces would merely be one of substituting the deployment time of Active forces for Reserve forces. He then asked General Johnson to speak to this issue.

General Johnson said that normally we use Active forces to build a time bridge, during which time Reserve forces are called to active duty and brought to a point of training where they can be deployed. He said that with respect to part of our Reserve force, i.e., the Selected Reserve

Force, we have reduced the training time required before that force could be deployed from 14 to 11 weeks. He said we expect to reduce it further to reach a goal of 8 weeks.

General Johnson then said he wanted to point out that we had certain additional "bills" which had been laid before us: (1) the requirement of three divisions to meet NATO commitments; (2) 40,000 personnel to maintain the proposed barrier in South Vietnam; and (3) a corps contingency force of three divisions. He said that to meet these "bills" we have only five division forces in the continental United States in the Active Army. He said this caused him concern because of indications of possible aggressive action by the North Koreans, and the possibility that the situation might become more unstable in Cyprus and Jordan, and that the United States might be required to supply forces for these contingencies.

General Johnson said if he were queried by the Congress as to the adequacy of our ground forces, he would have to say we were very thin. He said, therefore, he recommends that the additional forces he has requested be authorized.

Mr. McNamara said that we are equipment limited—that this did not mean we did not have additional equipment, but that we had bought equipment for only the authorized force structure. He said, therefore, what General Johnson was talking about was merely shifting equipment from the Reserve to the Active Army, thus substituting a slight reduction in reaction time.

He said an alternative to General Johnson's proposal was the calling up of Reserves. He said further that he and Mr. Vance had raised with the Joint Chiefs last week the desirability of calling up Reserves, and they did not recommend we do so at this time. The President then asked each of the Chiefs whether they favored a call-up of Reserves at this time. Each of the Chiefs replied in the negative.

4. Navy Shipbuilding

Mr. McNamara stated that we were proposing to go forward with the construction of one DLGN, which had been authorized in the FY 1967 budget, and the construction of two DDG's. He said that Admiral McDonald would recommend that we add another DLGN in the FY 1968 budget. He pointed out, however, that he thought there was a broader issue that Admiral McDonald might wish to address—the entire shipbuilding program.

Admiral McDonald said he wanted to point out that there had been no major Navy escort ships constructed since 1962. He said last year the Department of Defense had supported two DDG's but no DLGN. He said he felt this year we ought to have one more DLGN over and above the one authorized by the Congress in FY 1967, and that if we did not put in another DLGN, we would end up in the same wrangle with the Congress that we had last year.

Admiral McDonald said the basic issue is how many nuclear escorts there should be per carrier. He said he and the Navy believe there should be two per nuclear carrier, while Mr. McNamara and Mr. Vance felt there should be only one. Admiral McDonald said he did not feel we were pushing too fast on nuclear power, because the Navy was asking for only these two DLGN's and was not asking for any other nuclear powered ships.

Admiral McDonald said he also wanted to mention the issue of nuclear submarines. He said nuclear submarines were one of the most important elements of our ASW program. He said currently we have 105 submarines in our ASW program, and that this figure was agreed to by both the Navy and the Office of the Secretary of Defense. He said the Navy feels that all of these submarines should be nuclear powered, but that up to now the Office of the Secretary of Defense believes that we should have only 68 nuclear submarines. Admiral McDonald said that in the past we had been constructing five nuclear attack submarines per year, and the Navy feels we should continue at five per year until we get a higher number.

Admiral McDonald said his main concern is what happens in 1968 and beyond, and that we need at least five per year for the next three years.

Mr. McNamara pointed out that the Navy hopes in 1968 to have a newer class of submarine. Therefore, he said both he and Mr. Vance have felt it advantageous to put two of the five submarines which were tentatively scheduled for FY 1968 over until next year, which would thus permit the Navy to take advantage of the newer technology that would be available in such a new class.

The President reserved decision on this issue.

The President on three different occasions during the discussions asked whether it was correct to state that, apart from the five issues which had been presented to him, the Joint Chiefs of Staff were in general agreement with the budget. Each of the Chiefs said that this was the fact. Admiral McDonald stated that he thought the Chiefs and the Secretary of Defense and Mr. Vance were closer together this year than any other year that he could remember.

152.   Letter From the Ambassador at Large (Thompson) to
        Secretary of State Rusk[1]

Washington, December 8, 1966.

Dear Boss:

Nick has asked that I inform you of the following since it might
bear on conversations you will be having in Paris.[2]

Yesterday, Secretary McNamara held a meeting attended by Nick, Foy,
Dick Helms, Don Hornig, Cy Vance and myself.[3] He showed us a memorandum which he had given to the President on the problem of production
and deployment of the Nike-X.[4] McNamara's long and thorough memorandum went into the pros and cons of the whole question. The President
had studied it and asked those of us at the meeting to prepare, individually, memoranda describing what we each thought Soviet reaction would be
to a light defense against Soviet missile attack which would cover 25 large
cities and a second heavier defense which would cover 50 cities.

This operation overlapped a discussion which I had with
Ambassador Dobrynin the day before.[5] I reported this to the meeting
and was authorized by the President[6] to pursue the matter with
Dobrynin. I enclose copies of the memcons.[7]

All of this has been very closely held here. My guess is that the
Soviets will take us up on this; but the matter is, of course, urgent
because of McNamara's budget problem. However, the Soviets will be
preoccupied with a meeting of the Central Committee and the Supreme
Soviet. One of the reasons we went as far as we did was to try to head
off any decision they may be making at the Supreme Soviet which will
approve their plan for 1967.

Sincerely,

Llewellyn E. Thompson[8]

---

[1] Source: National Archives and Records Administration, RG 59, S/AL Files: Lot 67
D 2. Top Secret. An attached December 8 covering memorandum from Thompson to Ambassador Bohlen indicates that the letter should be opened only by the Secretary.

[2] See footnote 8, Document 148.

[3] No other record of this meeting has been found.

[4] See footnote 3, Document 150.

[5] Regarding Thompson's December 6 conversation with Dobrynin, see *Foreign Relations, 1964–1968*, vol. XI, Document 168, footnote 2.

[6] The words "by the President" were typed in the margin and inserted in the text at this
point. Regarding the President's authorization, see ibid., vol. XI, Document 168, footnote 4.

[7] Not attached.

[8] Printed from a copy that bears this typed signature.

153. Letter From Acting Secretary of State Katzenbach to Secretary of Defense McNamara[1]

Washington, December 8, 1966.

Dear Bob:

Thank you for your letter of November 17 transmitting a Defense draft NSAM on chemical and biological warfare policy.[2] Our initial reaction is that there are large areas of agreement between your draft and the CB paper developed in State[3] and previously sent to Defense and other interested agencies. Both drafts are now being studied by members of my staff. After completion of this work, it may be useful to follow up on your suggestion to discuss any remaining issues. You will recall that Bill Foster stressed the desirability for developing basic national policy in the CB field in a letter to the Committee of Principals in October, 1963.[4] More recently, on April 19, 1966, Butch Fisher addressed a letter on the same subject to the Deputies.[5] In view of ACDA's continuing interest in our CB policy, I suggest that it would be desirable to invite Bill, as well as Dick Helms and Len Marks, to join the discussions. I will subsequently be in touch with you about a mutually agreeable time.

Sincerely,

Nick

---

[1] Source: Washington National Records Center, OASD/ISA Files: FRC 330 70 A 6648, 384 1966 Jan– . Secret.

[2] Document 145.

[3] See footnote 3, Document 145.

[4] See footnote 2, Document 121.

[5] Document 122.

154.   Memorandum From the President's Special Assistant for
         Science and Technology (Hornig) to President Johnson[1]

Washington, December 9, 1966.

SUBJECT

Policy on the Use of Biological Weapons

After an extensive review of the subject, your Science Advisory Committee has recommended in the attached memorandum (Tab A) that the U.S. Government publicly state that it is our policy not to initiate the use of biological weapons.

This recommendation was made prior to the recent adoption by the U.N. General Assembly (91 in favor including the U.S., 0 against, and 4 abstaining) of a Resolution (Tab B)[2] calling for the strict observance by all States of the principles and objectives of the Geneva Protocol of 17 June 1925 on the "Prohibition of the Use of Asphyxiating, Poisonous and Other Gases and Bacteriological Methods of Warfare."[3] This Resolution implicitly associates us with the principle of "no first use" of biological and chemical warfare agents. However, in our statement on the Resolution to the U.N. General Assembly, which made clear that riot control agents and defoliating chemicals are not covered by the Geneva Protocol, we failed to state explicitly what our policy on biological weapons is.[4]

I believe that our support of the U.N. Resolution goes a long way toward answering the criticism that the U.S. is the only major power that has not signed the Geneva Protocol and the charge that our use of riot gas and defoliants in Vietnam might escalate into chemical and biological warfare. I am afraid, however, that this improved position could be undercut by our failure to be explicit in stating that it is our policy not to initiate the use of biological weapons.

---

[1] Source: Washington National Records Center, OASD/ISA Files: FRC 330 70 A 6648, 384 1966 Jan– . Secret. Copies were sent to Moyers and Rostow. An attached December 10 covering memorandum from Hornig to Secretaries Rusk and McNamara asked for their Departments' views on the proposed "no first use" policy with respect to biological weapons. Also attached is a December 15 memorandum from Acting Assistant Secretary of Defense Townsend Hoopes to the Chairman of the Joint Chiefs of Staff asking for comments by the JCS on the PSAC recommendation no later than December 30.

[2] Not printed; for text of Part B of UN General Assembly Resolution 2162 (XXI), adopted December 5, see *Documents on Disarmament, 1966,* pp. 798–799.

[3] The United States did not ratify this treaty until 1975. For text, see 26 UST 571.

[4] Reference presumably is to the statement by U.S. Representative James M. Nabrit, Jr., on December 5; see *Documents on Disarmament, 1966,* pp. 800–802.

I understand that you will receive in the next few weeks a petition signed by several thousand scientists relating to our position on chemical and biological warfare.[5] This could be handled with the least fuss and controversy if a prior low-key statement of "no first use" for biological weapons were on the record.

I have discussed the problem with Secretary McNamara and Under Secretary Katzenbach, and they both agree that our public position would be much stronger if we clarified this point.

I recommend, therefore, that at a forthcoming press conference, probably in answer to a question, you make a brief statement (Tab C)[6] on the U.N. Resolution that would set forth explicitly that it is the policy of the United States not to initiate the use of biological warfare weapons. If you concur, I will clear the statement with DOD and State.

Donald Hornig

Tab A

Memorandum From the President's Special Assistant for Science and Technology (Hornig) to President Johnson

Washington, December 8, 1966.

SUBJECT

Use of Biological Weapons

Your Science Advisory Committee has reviewed the problem of biological warfare and has concluded that we should formalize our policy of "no first use" of biological weapons. In view of public uncertainty as to our policy in this field and the mounting domestic and international concern regarding the use of biological and chemical weapons, the Committee recommends that, at a suitable opportunity, an official statement be made along the following lines:

"As a matter of policy, the United States has never made military use of biological weapons and our policy will continue to be not to use such weapons unless they are first used against us."

In explaining the use of riot control agents and defoliants in Viet Nam, senior officers of your Administration have made clear that it is against our policy to initiate the use of chemical warfare. There has not,

---

[5] See Document 170.

[6] Not printed.

however, been comparable public statement concerning a policy of "no first use" of biological weapons.

The United States is the only major power that did not sign the Geneva Protocol of 1925, which essentially proscribed the first use of biological as well as chemical agents. In the absence of a publicly stated position, this leaves us particularly vulnerable to charges that it may be our intention to employ such agents.

On the basis of a continuing review over the past few years of the various biological agents, both "lethal" and "non-lethal," that are presently under study by the Defense Department, your Committee has concluded that the problems associated with these agents appear to outweigh any military advantages that might be attained by their use. In general, the risks associated with these weapons are so great and the uncertainties as to their military effects so large that your Committee believes it extremely unlikely that we would, in fact, consider initiating the use of these weapons in a military conflict.

The risk associated with massive use of biological weapons is essentially impossible to predict. In many applications there is the possibility of creating a new focus of endemic infection which might constitute a continuing hazard. In addition, we have scanty experience with the ecological consequences of disturbing the natural biological equilibrium of an area by the introduction of substantial quantities of viable, infectious organisms. Finally, there is at least a theoretical possibility that the use of biological agents on a large scale may result in mutations producing new strains of unusual virulence or even a new form of the disease for which treatment is not available.

At the same time, we have been presented with no scenarios, nor have we thought of any ourselves, in which the military value seems significant. This applies particularly to the so called incapacitating biological agents which are intended to make the subject very sick without killing him. It is not possible at this time to predict the reliability of any of these agents and some would have significant lethality when applied in massive doses to a large population. There is also considerable uncertainty as to how effective such agents might be in reducing the military potential of enemy forces in an actual combat situation.

For these reasons, your Science Advisory Committee concludes that a policy of "no first use" of biological weapons is sound and recommends that it would be advantageous to formalize it in a public statement.

Donald Hornig

155.   Memorandum From the Deputy Secretary of Defense (Vance) to President Johnson[1]

Washington, December 10, 1966.

There are five purposes for which we might want to deploy an anti-ballistic missile system (ABM). They are:

1. To protect against a Communist Chinese missile attack.
2. To protect against an accidental missile launch.
3. To protect against "nuclear blackmail," which could take the form of a light attack on a single target of moderate value.
4. To help protect our land-based strategic offensive forces.
5. To protect our cities against a large Soviet missile attack.

Today there are three options open to you.

a. Do nothing at this time except continue a vigorous research and development program.
b. Deploy a "thin" ABM system, which would meet Items 1 through 4 above.
c. Deploy a "thick" ABM system, which would meet Items 1 through 4 and would, in addition, give local protection to 25 selected cities. This option is recommended by the Joint Chiefs of Staff.

I will discuss each one of these options briefly.

a. The arguments in favor of Option a are: 1) it is unnecessary now to deploy a system against the Chinese threat because they are 8 to 9 years away from having any significant ICBM capability; 2) we have such missile superiority over the Soviet Union with our Polaris submarines which are essentially invulnerable, and our penetration aids for both sea and hardened land-based missiles, that it is unnecessary to protect our land-based strategic forces with an ABM; 3) the chance of an accidental missile launching is remote; 4) a blackmail attack is unlikely, because an attacker would know that he was risking all-out nuclear war which would destroy his country; 5) a system designed to protect our cities would ultimately leave us in essentially the same position as we are now vis-à-vis the Soviet Union, because they would be forced to react to preserve their assured destruction capability. In the end, each

---

[1] Source: Washington National Records Center, OSD Files: FRC 330 71 A 3470, ABM Memo and JCS View Folder 103. Top Secret. This memorandum was prepared in response to Secretary McNamara's paper discussed at the December 6 meeting; see Document 150 and footnote 3 thereto. For responses by Hornig and Rostow to this request, see Documents 156 and 157. Responses by Katzenbach, Thompson, and Helms are printed in *Foreign Relations, 1964–1968*, vol. XI, Documents 169, 170, and 171. Kohler's December 10 written statement is in the Washington National Records Center, OSD Files: FRC 330 70 A 4662, 471.94 ABM (Nov & Dec) 1966.

would have the capacity to kill [*less than 1 line of source text not declassified*] and we would have wasted $30 to $40 billion.

It has been argued that one need only expend about $10 billion to deploy a system which would give protection to 25 selected cities. This argument, however, ignores the fact that if we were to deploy such a system, the Soviet Union would be forced to take countermeasures in the same fashion as we have done. This would require us to thicken our system to meet such countermeasures. In the end, our commitment to defend our cities would force us into deployment of a very thick system at a total cost of between $30 and $40 billion.

Further, if we were to deploy a system protecting only 25 cities, the pressures in the Congress would be tremendous to extend such a system to protect other population centers not covered by the $10 billion system.

Finally, there are still difficult technical problems remaining to be solved, such as the development of the extended range Spartan missile and its associated [*less than 1 line of source text not declassified*] required for exoatmospheric intercept, the development of the high acceleration Sprint missile for local defense, the development of the very complex radars, and the integration of all of these into a reliable system.

The argument against this option is the probable attitude of the Congress and our people. The first reaction of most Americans will inevitably be in favor of an immediate start on deployment, if for no other reason than the Soviets are deploying an ABM system.

b. The second option, i.e., to deploy a "thin" system, would meet the first four objectives listed in the first paragraph of this memorandum, probably at a cost of between $4 and $5 billion. It would have to be made clear that this system would not be expanded to attempt to protect our cities against a heavy Soviet attack. This system would not only meet the first four objectives but, for a limited period of time, would also have the side benefit of reducing population losses in the United States against a Soviet attack by 20 or 30 million. This benefit would disappear in time as the Soviets improved their missiles—as we have done—by the development of penetration aids and multiple warheads. If this option were chosen, the deployment decision could be coupled with talks with the Soviet Union, seeking to reach an understanding with respect to the further deployment of both ABM's and offensive missiles. A decision in favor of this option would draw the teeth of much of the argument that the Soviets have a defense and we do not. However, there would be continuing pressures from some sources to expand to a "thick" system.

c. The third option would, as indicated above, deploy a system designed to meet the first four objectives and to protect 25 selected cities.

The Joint Chiefs of Staff have recommended that you decide in favor of this option. For the reasons given above, this would not produce a stable situation because the Soviet Union would be forced to react and thus would negate the effectiveness of the system. In the end, we would spend $30 to $40 billion in thickening this system, and would not be able to protect our country from devastation from a Soviet missile attack.

The Congress is divided on the issue of deploying an ABM system, but we believe that a substantial majority favor going ahead with some form of deployment. The group in favor of proceeding with an ABM deployment is led by Senator Russell and has strong backing in the Armed Services Committees of both Houses.

Cyrus M. Vance[2]

---

[2] Printed from a copy that indicates Vance signed the original.

---

156. Memorandum From the President's Special Assistant for Science and Technology (Hornig) to the President's Special Assistant (Rostow)[1]

Washington, December 10, 1966.

SUBJECT

Soviet Reaction to ABM Deployment

The following is a rather hasty paper. I hope, over the weekend, to put something more thoughtful together.

A key question is whether the Russians consider that we are responding to a large-scale deployment on their part, or whether they see us as escalating the competition.

The analysis shown to us *assumes* that a Soviet ABM deployment is under way. Now, while there is little doubt that the Moscow system is an ABM system, there is a real question whether the Tallinn system which is being deployed rapidly (23 sites as of 12/7/66) is for air defense or ABM use. The most recent NIE (10–26–66)[2] concludes that it is probably an air

---

[1] Source: Washington National Records Center, OSD Files: FRC 330 70 A 4662, 471.94 ABM (Nov & Dec) 1966. Top Secret. "Mr. Vance has seen" is stamped on the memorandum. Regarding the context for this memorandum, see footnote 1, Document 155.

[2] Not further identified.

defense system, although it may have marginal ABM capabilities. All of the people I have had look at the problem (the PSAC Reconnaissance Panel, Chairman Dr. Edwin Land, and Strategic Offense and Defense Panel, Chairman Dr. Marvin Goldberger) concur in this view (but DIA does not).

The essence of the problem is that the radars at the Tallinn sites are too small to give an area capability unless early warning and acquisition are performed by the Hen House radars at distant locations. But (1) the large Hen House radars are soft and undefended, and (2) some of the sites are not covered by Hen House radars; e.g. the last three discovered are too far East. If not used in conjunction with Hen House radars, this is a point defense system with a radius of coverage of about 30–200 miles. In that case, some of them are very poorly sited, e.g. one on a peninsula in the Crimea (Feodosiya) which would largely defend water, although it is excellently sited to bar intrusion by aircraft.

Therefore, I conclude that it would be incorrect to proceed from the assumption that a general deployment is underway in the USSR and we must take into account the possibility that the Soviets do not see themselves as having initiated one. In this case they would regard the deployment of a general system—even a "thin" one—if undertaken on anything like a crash basis as a new threat to their deterrence and would react strongly to it.

One might note, though, that for this same reason they might react favorably to proposals to mutually limit ABM deployments on a mutual example basis.

In judging possible Soviet reaction, one cannot underestimate the extent to which they apparently feel themselves "under the gun." My basis for saying that is that I am possibly the only American who has recently spoken directly to Marshal Malinovsky, the Minister of Defense (November 7, 1964)[3] and who has seen the reddening of his face when he says, "Your Mr. McNamara thinks he can overwhelm us with his thousands of rockets." For this reason I see their increased hard missile deployment rate as an effort to catch up and eliminate the threat of a first strike by us. I suspect they are keenly aware of our advantage in both missiles and aircraft and would react as strongly as they could if their deterrence were threatened.

Consequently, if we are to have any hope of stabilizing a race which in the end poses increasingly serious threats to both sides and becomes increasingly expensive, it seems unwise to start down a new road unless: (1) there is better evidence than we have now that we face a new threat, (2)

---

[3] No other record of this conversation has been found.

the deployment would give us a real military advantage (which it appears not to), (3) it can be done in a way which minimizes the provocation or new challenge unless there is reason to believe that the pressure would produce a "truce."

For all these reasons, I would continue to delay a deployment decision until the diplomatic possibilities have been more thoroughly explored and the intelligence has improved. If this is not practicable, I would start slowly on an experimental basis with a "thin" system—for the additional reason that there are still many technical problems to be solved before a sensible system can be put together.

One other factor should also be considered. Some will argue that the continued engagement of their technical talent in these areas will impoverish the civilian economy. The effect might be the reverse—that by being forced to work on priority problems of the greatest technical sophistication they will acquire a higher technological capacity than they would otherwise achieve—if fewer cars, consumer goods, etc. There is reason to believe that although their technology definitely lags ours in substantially all areas, their relative position may be improving (e.g. as shown by a comparision of their radars or aircraft with ours in 1950 and in 1966). I think it is clear that their best engineering, quality production and management is in the defense industries. But I have seen first hand that there is no shortage of highly trained scientists and engineers in the non-defense area (they train twice as many as we do). I have also noted that key people in science (e.g. Keldysh, President of the Academy), in the electronics, computer and communications industry have a defense or military background. Hence, one can hypothesize that there may in fact be a strong "spin off" such as we ascribe to DOD, NASA and AEC.

Don

157.   Memorandum for the Record[1]

Washington, December 10, 1966, 2:30 p.m.

SUBJECT

Soviet reaction to U.S. deployment of Nike-X, Postures A or B

1. A U.S. ABM program to reduce fatalities in a nuclear exchange to the range of 5–15 million would force the Soviet Union to respond to reestablish the credibility of its assured destruction capability—both to themselves and to the world. They regard this capability as the bedrock of their security, now secrecy has been virtually lost.

2. They would seek the cheapest way to accomplish this objective, given the severe resource allocation conflicts they now confront—and will continue foreseeably to confront.

3. The precise mix they would choose I cannot confidently predict; but it might well include ICBM's with very large warheads.

4. Among the ways they might envisage to achieve this objective will be negotiations to stabilize the nuclear arms race with the United States; although that route will confront at least three severe problems:

—inspection and sea-based ICBM's;
—warheads as opposed to launching vehicles, as the unit of measure in an agreement;
—the parity question: can they accept a freeze which appears to lock them into permanent nuclear inferiority?

They will carefully weigh the advantages and costs of an agreement against the advantages and costs of the next cheapest way to re-establish an adequate assured destruction capability.

5. I recommend that we war-game and staff out the problem stated in para. 4, as a matter of urgency.

WR

---

[1] Source: Washington National Records Center, OSD Files: FRC 330 70 A 4662, 471.94 ABM (Nov & Dec) 1966. Top Secret. "Mr. Vance has seen" is stamped on the memorandum. Regarding the context of this memorandum, see footnote 1, Document 155.

158.   Memorandum From the Deputy Secretary of Defense (Vance) to President Johnson[1]

Washington, December 13, 1966.

There are five major issues between the Joint Chiefs of Staff and Messrs. McNamara and Vance.[2]

1. Anti-Ballistic Missile.

The Joint Chiefs of Staff recommend deployment of the Nike-X to protect our population against a Soviet attack. The initial system is estimated to cost $10 billion with $800 million in FY '68. This system would be designed to provide a light area defense of the Continental United States *and a local defense of 25 selected cities.* The Joint Chiefs would preserve the option to expand the local defense system to 50 selected cities at an estimated cost of $20 billion using present cost factors. Messrs. McNamara and Vance believe that because of the usual cost under-estimation and engineering changes to overcome defects in systems tests, the necessary redesign to overcome Soviet countermeasures, the eventual cost of such a program would reach $30 to $40 billion.

Messrs. McNamara and Vance recommend against the deployment recommended by the Joint Chiefs because they believe the Soviets will take the necessary countermeasures to overcome our system just as we are doing to overcome theirs. They believe that ultimately the Soviet Union and the United States will end up in the same position after the unnecessary expenditure of millions of dollars. Messrs. McNamara and Vance believe that if any ABM system is to be deployed, it should be a "light" deployment, specifically and exclusively designed to satisfy the following four purposes.

a. To protect against a Communist Chinese missile attack.
b. To protect against an accidental missile launch.
c. To protect against nuclear blackmail which could take the form of a light attack on a single target of moderate value.
d. To help protect our land-based offensive forces.

Messrs. McNamara and Vance estimate the cost of such a system should run between $3 and $4 billion.

---

[1] Source: National Archives and Records Administration, RG 200, Defense Programs and Operations, Draft Memoranda to the President, 1968–72, Tab 8, Box 71. Secret.

[2] For their discussions of these issues with President Johnson in Austin on December 6, see Documents and 150 and 151.

2. Advanced Strategic Bomber (AMSA).

The Joint Chiefs of Staff recommend that we proceed to obtain a firm contractor proposal for the development of a new strategic bomber and that we begin engine development in FY '68 to achieve an initial operational capability in FY 1974. The Secretary of the Air Force estimates the FY '68 cost at $47 million, FY 67–72 cost at $1.2 billion and the total development cost at $1.5 billion (production costs are *not* included in these figures and would add several billions). General McConnell has stated that he is not asking for a decision to go into production. General McConnell has stated that the principal reason he believes we should have an AMSA is because it will have a substantially greater bomb-carrying capacity than the FB-111.

Messrs. McNamara and Vance recommend $26 million in FY '68 for continuation of component development, i.e. engines and avionics. They recommend disapproval of action to obtain a firm contractor proposal for system development because they do not believe an initial operational capability in FY 1974 is needed. They further believe it is doubtful we will need a new manned bomber because of difficulties associated with penetration of the Soviet Union in the mid and late 1970s. In addition, they believe that missiles, plus the FB-111 force which the United States will have at that time will be enough to meet our force requirements. Messrs. McNamara and Vance point out that the monies to be expended on engine and avionics development will give us an engine and avionics that could be used for other aircraft and therefore believe that the expenditure of such funds is wise and prudent.

3. Advanced ICBM.

The Joint Chiefs of Staff recommend $36 million of R&D funds in FY '68 for development of a propulsion and guidance system to meet a 1973 initial operational capability date. The $36 million would be broken down into $10 million for component development and the balance for contract definition. The Secretary of the Air Force would not go to contract definition but would spend $19 million for component development.

Messrs. McNamara and Vance recommend $19 million in FY 1968 which will permit us to carry on component development and begin system development next year if this should be desirable after review next summer. They see no need for an initial operational capability in 1973. At the recent meeting in Austin General McConnell stated that the Joint Chiefs could live with the $19 million program.

4. Army Force Structure.

Messrs. McNamara and Vance recommend a total 1968 land force 32-1/3 division force equivalents (27-1/3 Army, 5 Marine) with 18-1/3 active Army divisions and 4 active Marine divisions. The Chief of Staff of the Army would add 30,000 men to the active Army now, and possibly an additional 45,000 in March or April of 1967, to provide 2 additional brigades now and a whole division later in the active Army. The equipment for these forces would be borrowed from similar units in the Reserves. The purpose of this plan, as explained by the Chief of Staff of the Army, would be to reduce the time required to deploy such forces.

Messrs. McNamara and Vance do not believe this is necessary or that it would significantly reduce the deployment time of such forces. They pointed out at the meeting in Austin that an alternative to General Johnson's proposal would be the calling up of Reserve units. However, none of the Joint Chiefs of Staff believe that the Reserves should be called at this time. Although the Joint Chiefs of Staff support the position of the Chief of Staff of the Army, in fact, their support is lukewarm.

5. Major Fleet Escorts Ships (DLGN/DDG).

The Joint Chiefs of Staff recommend construction of one nuclear-powered guided missile frigate (DLGN) in FY 1968 for $151 million, construction of the DLGN already authorized by the Congress in 1967, and the construction of two guided missile destroyers (DDG) in FY 1968 for $167 million. Messrs. McNamara and Vance recommend construction of the two DDGs in 1968 and the FY 1967 DLGN. They point out that the latter will provide us with one nuclear-powered escort for each of the planned nuclear-powered aircraft carriers. They recommend against the 1968 DLGN because they believe one nuclear escort per nuclear carrier is enough. The Chief of Naval Operations believes we should plan two nuclear escorts per nuclear carrier. This is the nub of the controversy between the Navy and Messrs. McNamara and Vance. In addition, Admiral McDonald points out that there has been no major Navy escort ship construction since 1962. Admiral McDonald states that we are not pushing too fast on nuclear power because the Navy is asking only for these two DLGNs and not asking for any other nuclear-powered surface ships.

Cyrus M. Vance[3]

---

[3] Printed from a copy that bears this stamped signature.

159.   Memorandum From President Johnson to His Armed Forces Aide (Cross)[1]

Washington, December 21, 1966.

Under my responsibility to activate the Emergency Broadcast System, I direct that in the event the Commander in Chief, North American Air Defense Command, declares Air Defense Emergency Red condition, the White House Communications Agency shall be authorized to activate the Emergency Broadcast System and the Office of Civil Defense shall be authorized to follow with the dissemination of appropriate warning messages.

Lyndon B. Johnson

---

[1] Source: Washington National Records Center, OSD Files: FRC 330 70 A 4443, 384 Civil Defense (Aug–) 1966. No classification marking.

---

160.   Draft Memorandum From Secretary of Defense McNamara to President Johnson[1]

Washington, December 22, 1966.

SUBJECT

    Production and Deployment of the Nike-X

A number of events have occurred during the last year which, taken together, tend to bring to a head the long-standing issue of whether to produce and deploy a U.S. anti-ballistic missile defense:

1. The Soviet Union has accelerated the deployment of hard ICBMs beyond the rates forecast in the last year's NIE[2] (but not beyond the "higher than expected" case on which the U.S. Defense Program was based).

2. The Soviet Union has started the deployment of an anti-ballistic missile system around Moscow and a second type of system, which may have an ABM capability, in other parts of the country.

---

[1] Source: Washington National Records Center, OSD Files: FRC 330 70 A 4662, 471.94 ABM (Nov & Dec) 1966. Top Secret. Regarding earlier drafts, see footnote 3, Document 149, and footnote 3, Document 150. For an extract from a later version, January 17, 1967, see *Foreign Relations*, 1964–1968, vol. XI, Document 173.

[2] Presumably a reference to NIE 11–8–65, Document 97.

3. The Chinese Communists have launched and demonstrated a nuclear-armed, 400-mile range ballistic missile,[3] and there is some evidence that they may be preparing to test a booster in the ICBM range.

4. Our own anti-ballistic missile system, the Nike-X, has now reached a stage of development where it may be feasible to start concurrent production and deployment.

5. The Joint Chiefs of Staff have reaffirmed their recommendation that a decision be made now to deploy, with an initial operational capability in FY 1972,[4] a Nike-X system which would provide for area defense of the continental U.S. and local defense of 25 cities against a "low" Soviet threat.

6. The Congress for the first time since 1959 has appropriated funds to prepare for the production and deployment of an ABM defense system.

There are five somewhat overlapping but distinct purposes for which we might want to deploy an ABM system:

1. To protect our cities against a Chinese Communist missile attack in the 1970s.
2. To protect our land-based strategic offensive forces (i.e., Minuteman) against a Soviet missile attack.
3. To guard against nuclear armed missiles launched by accident towards the United States.
4. To discourage the use of "nuclear blackmail", i.e., the threat of attack with one or a few missiles against targets of moderate value.
5. To protect our cities (and their population and industry) against a heavy, sophisticated Soviet missile attack.

After studying the subject exhaustively, Mr. Vance and I have concluded that we should not initiate at this time an ABM deployment for the last purpose. We believe that:

1. The Soviet Union would be forced to react to a U.S. ABM deployment by increasing its offensive nuclear force with the result that:

a. The risk of a Soviet nuclear attack on the U.S. would not be further decreased.
b. The damage to the U.S. from a Soviet nuclear attack, in the event deterrence failed, would not be reduced in any meaningful sense.

The foundation of our security is the deterrence of a Soviet nuclear attack. We believe such an attack can be prevented if it is understood by the Soviets that we possess strategic nuclear forces so powerful as to be capable of absorbing a Soviet first strike and surviving with sufficient

---

[3] On October 27, 1966, the People's Republic of China successfully conducted a guided nuclear missile weapons test. For an excerpt from the communiqué issued by the PRC Government, October 28, see *American Foreign Policy: Current Documents, 1966*, pp. 676–677.

[4] See Document 149.

strength to impose unacceptable damage on them (e.g., destruction by blast and radiation alone of approximately [*less than 1 line of source text not declassified*]). We have such power today. We must maintain it in the future, adjusting our forces to offset actual or potential changes in theirs.[5]

There is nothing I have seen in either our own or the Soviet Union's technology which would lead me to believe we cannot do this. From the beginning of the Nike-Zeus project in 1955 through the end of this current fiscal year, we will have invested a total of about $4 billion on ballistic missile defense research—including Nike-Zeus, Nike-X and Project Defender. And, during the last five or six years, we have spent about $1.2 billion on the development of penetration aids to help ensure that our missiles could penetrate the enemy's defenses. As a result of these efforts, we have the technology already in hand to counter any defensive force changes the Soviet Union is likely to undertake in the foreseeable future.

We believe the Soviet Union has essentially the same requirement for a deterrent or "Assured Destruction" force as the U.S. Therefore, deployment by the U.S. of an ABM defense which would degrade the destruction capability of the Soviet's offensive force to an unacceptable level would lead to the expansion of that force. In that event, we would be no better off than we were before.

2. With respect to the other four purposes, a limited ABM deployment might offer sufficient advantages to justify the cost (estimated at about $4 billion to produce and deploy, and about $200 million per year to maintain and operate).[6] Such a deployment, which could be completed by 1973, might:

---

[5] Last year, as a hedge against a "higher-than-expected" Soviet threat—i.e., the deployment of a full-scale ABM defense and the incorporation of multiple, independently-aimed reentry vehicles (MIRVs) in their large, hard ICBMs—we proposed in the FY 1967 Budget, and the Congress supported, the following improvements in our strategic offensive forces:

1. The acceleration of the development of the Poseidon missile, including area penetration aids, on a schedule which could make it operationally available in the summer of 1970.

2. The production and deployment of the Minuteman III with three MK-12 multiple independently-aimed reentry vehicles each.

3. The production and deployment of the MK-17 reentry vehicle for the Minuteman II (the MK-17 promises a kill probability against [*less than 1 line of source text not declassified*] for the MK-11 now used on the Minuteman II).

4. The replacement of all Minuteman I by FY 1972.

5. Initiation of engineering development of new *area* penetration aids packages for all Minuteman missiles and of a *terminal* penetration aids package for the Minuteman III. [Footnote in the source text.]

[6] The cost to complete development, test and evaluation of the system is not included because we assume that this work would be done in any event. [Footnote in the source text.]

a. Hold U.S. fatalities from a Chinese Communist missile attack in the mid-1970s below two million, if their operational inventory reaches 75 missiles; or possibly zero, if the number does not exceed 25.

b. Ensure the survival of about 200–300 Minuteman in a heavy, sophisticated Soviet attack in the mid to late 1970s.

c. Provide a very high degree of protection against accidental attacks.

d. Virtually eliminate the threat of "nuclear blackmail".

e. Reduce, as a by-product, U.S. fatalities from a Soviet attack against our cities in the early 1970s, if the Soviets do not react immediately to our ABM deployment.

In the pages which follow I will explore in detail the foundation for these conclusions:

1. The Soviet Strategic Threat

The latest National Intelligence Estimate, dated Oct. 20, 1966,[7] indicated that the Soviets have accelerated the deployment of two hard ICBMs, the SS-11 and SS-9. (The SS-9 is a large, storable liquid-fueled missile, roughly the size of our Titan II, with a warhead yield of [*less than 1 line of source text not declassified*] and a CEP of [*less than 1 line of source text not declassified*]. The SS-11 is a small, storable liquid-fueled missile, about the size of our Minuteman, with a warhead yield of [*less than 1 line of source text not declassified*] and a CEP of [*less than 1 line of source text not declassified*]). The November 1965 NIE[8] estimated that by mid-1968 the Soviets would have operational about 100–110 SS-9s and 200–250 SS-11s; we now estimate that they will have 130–140 SS-9s and 320–400 SS-11s by that date.[9]

By mid-1971, we believe they could have a total of 800–1100 operational ICBMs on launchers, compared with last year's estimate of 500–800 by mid-1970. We believe the higher end of the range of estimates will prevail if the Soviets decide to emphasize quantity in an effort to match the size of our ICBM force, and the lower end if they choose to emphasize quality. In the first case, they would concentrate on the SS-11 which is a relatively simple and cheap missile. In the second case, they would place added emphasis on the SS-9 which is a more expensive and also, for certain purposes, a much more effective missile. The SS-11 because of its relatively poor CEP and small payload would have little value against hard targets such as our Minuteman silos, and it is therefore essentially a retaliatory weapon for use against cities. The

---

[7] Document 143.

[8] No November 1965 NIE discussed the SS-9 and SS-11.

[9] In addition to the SS-9s and SS-11s the NIE forecasts that the Soviets will have in mid-1968 273 other missiles, including missiles at the test ranges. [Footnote in the source text.]

Soviets also have some older ICBMs but these are already being phased out and few are expected to be left in the operational force by 1971. Although we still have no direct evidence of such an effort, the Soviets might also develop and install multiple independently-aimed reentry vehicles (MIRVs) on their SS-9s. However, an effective capability with such reentry vehicles would require much greater accuracies (lower CEPs) than have thus far been achieved by Soviet ICBMs. If they were to start now, they could probably achieve an operational capability by about 1971–72; and we would probably be able to detect the testing of such a system perhaps two years earlier. Improvements in both accuracy and penetration capability could also be made in the SS-11s, and in addition the Soviets might deploy a new solid fuel, highly accurate small ICBM.

We have known for some time that the Soviet Union was working on anti-ballistic missile defense. After several false starts, the Soviets now appear to be deploying one type of system (which is definitely designed for ballistic missile defense) around Moscow and another type of system, designated "Tallinn", (which may be designed for defense against manned bombers, or ballistic missiles, or both) across the northwest approaches to the Soviet Union and at a few other locations.

The Moscow system appears to consist of a series of complexes deployed at some of the outer ring SA-1 sites, about 45 n.mi. from the center of the city. Each complex has two "Triads" (one large and two small radars operating together) and 16 launchers apparently designed for the "Galosh" missile which the Soviets displayed in 1964. (Six complexes are under active construction and a seventh is now dormant.) In addition, there is a large phased-array radar southwest of Moscow (called Dog House) oriented towards our ICBM threat corridor and additional large phased-array radars (called Hen House) sited at two locations to the northwest. These three radars may be intended as forward acquisition radars for the Moscow system, while the Triad radars handle the target and interceptor missile tracking functions. The Moscow system could have an initial operational capability in 1967 or early 1968, and a full operational capability with six complexes (96 launchers) by 1970–71. (By that time the Soviets could also construct two more complexes to fill out the southern part of the ring, for a total of 128 launchers.)

The Galosh itself is a large, relatively slow acceleration missile probably designed for exoatmospheric interception much like our new extended range interceptor missile, which we now call "Spartan". We have no evidence thus far of a Soviet terminal defense missile such as our Sprint. If used for both area and terminal defense, the Galosh system would be very expensive, at least $15 million per missile on launcher (dividing the total investment cost by the number of missiles on launchers) where only 16 missiles are provided per complex. Even if two reload missiles were provided for each launcher, the cost per missile would still amount to about $6 million. But there is a real question whether the reloading speed of the Galosh (now estimated at 10–30 minutes after arrival of the missile at the launcher) would be fast enough to be of any use in a single engagement. Similarly, there is a question whether a single Triad, the radars of which are mechanically steered, could handle more than eight launchers. (We ourselves have abandoned this type of radar for ABM defense because of its grave limitations.)

With regard to the second defensive system, there is still disagreement within our Intelligence Community as to its primary purpose. One view is that it is primarily an advanced surface-to-air missile system designed against high altitude, high speed manned bomber attacks, and the pattern in which it is being deployed, the configuration of the sites and their equipment, and the characteristics of the radars, all lend credence to this view. Several "farms" of missile launchers are located in a barrier line across the northwestern part of European Russia and around Leningrad and Moscow, and some parts of the southern approaches. At least 22 complexes have been definitely identified, most of which consist of three launch sites, each with six launch positions and one radar. These could be operational by 1967–68, and more may be under construction. The local radars associated with the launchers are of limited capability and would appear to need the support of the much larger but vulnerable Hen House radars if the system is expected to perform with a reasonable degree of effectiveness in the ABM role.

If it is indeed designed as an advanced surface-to-air, anti-aircraft missile, it would be most effective in defending against high-altitude penetrating bombers of the B-70 or SR-71 type; it would be ineffective against low-altitude penetrating bombers such as the B-52 or FB-111. It is this incongruity, together with the fact that this type of ABM system would be much cheaper than the Galosh, which leads the proponents of the other point of view to believe that it is an ABM system, or at least has some minimal ABM capability. And while we know something about the geographical deployments of this system, and about its launchers and radars, we still know very little about the interceptor missile itself.

The latest intelligence estimates (NIE 11–3–66) concludes " . . . that the Moscow ABM system will have a good capability against a numerically limited attack on the Moscow area by currently operational missiles, but that its capabilities could be degraded by advanced penetration systems and it could not cope with a very heavy attack. Moreover, the present deployment will not cover all of the multi-directional Polaris threat to Moscow." With regard to the Tallinn system in the ABM role, the NIE concludes:

"Many of the Tallinn system complexes are so located that presently known Hen House or Dog House radars could not furnish useful target tracking data to them. Where this is the case, or if the Hen Houses or Dog House were destroyed or blacked out, the capabilities of the system would be seriously reduced and limited to local and self-defense. Thus, under these assumptions [including the alternate characteristics which would have to be assumed for the missile to give it an ABM capability][10] if Hen House or Dog House data were available, the Tallinn complexes could defend areas large enough to provide a strategic ABM defense; without such data, they could not."

In summary, we have firm evidence of Soviet *ICBM* deployment through mid-1968 and fairly good estimates through mid-1971. Our knowledge of Soviet *ABM* deployments is much more sketchy. We are reasonably certain that the deployment of the Galosh around Moscow will be completed but until we know more about the Tallinn type of system or see evidence of Galosh deployments around other cities, we can only conjecture about the ultimate scale, effectiveness and cost of the Soviet ABM effort. However, knowing what we do about past Soviet predilections for defensive systems,[11] we must plan our forces on the assumption that they will have deployed some sort of an ABM system around their major cities by the early 1970s. Whether made up of Galosh only, or a combination of Galosh and a Tallinn type system, or even some combination of Galosh and a terminal missile of the Sprint type, a full scale deployment would cost the Soviet Union something on the order of $20 to $25 billion.

2. History of the U.S. ABM Effort

In considering the issue of whether to deploy the Nike-X, it might be useful to review briefly the history of the U.S. ABM effort, the kind of system originally envisioned, the evolution of technology in that field and the attitudes of past Presidents, Secretaries of Defense, Chiefs of Staff, the Congress, etc.

The predecessor of the current ABM development program, the Nike-Zeus was begun in FY 1955. Up until the launching of the Sputnik

---

[10] Brackets in the source text.

[11] The Soviets for more than a decade have spent substantially more on air defense against strategic bombers than has the U.S. The bulk of the Soviet expenditure has been wasted—throughout the period the U.S. Strategic Air Command stated, and it was generally agreed within the United States Government, that approximately 85 percent of the U.S. incoming bombers could penetrate the Soviet defenses and reach their targets. [Footnote in the source text.]

in October 1957, the project proceeded at a leisurely pace. Congressional attitudes towards the program ranged from incredulousness regarding its operational feasibility (especially in view of the problems then being encountered in anti-bomber defense) to concern over a new "roles and missions" fight between the Army (Zeus) and the Air Force (Wizard).

In the aftermath of Sputnik a new sense of urgency developed with regard to all aspects of advanced military technology. From FY 1955 through FY 1957, a total of only $12.2 million was applied to Nike-Zeus R&D but in FY 1958 alone the total rose to $66 million and in FY 1959, to $237 million. By the spring of 1958, when the FY 1959 Budget was before the Congress, the Army had already proposed the production of initial sets of equipment. Secretary of Defense McElroy, however, argued that "we should not spend hundreds of millions on production of this weapon pending general confirmatory indications that we know what we are doing." His view prevailed for the moment.

It was not until the FY 1960 Budget that Nike-Zeus deployment became a real issue. The Army's initial request included $875 million for Zeus—$35 million for R&D, $720 million for procurement and $115 million for construction. President Eisenhower, however, sent to the Congress a request of $300 million for R&D and test facilities only. The House Appropriations Committee recommended the addition of $200 million "for the acceleration of the Nike-Zeus and/or the modernization of Army firepower." Secretary McElroy agreed to accept $137 million for the acceleration of Nike-Zeus and $63 million for Army modernization. The Senate approved these amounts and added $200 million more for Army modernization. The final enactment provided $375 million for Nike-Zeus and/or Army modernization.

In the fall of 1959, in connection with the development of the FY 1961 Budget, the Army proposed a new Nike-Zeus deployment plan consisting of 35 local defense centers (one for each defended area), 9 forward acquisition radars and 120 batteries. The typical battery was to consist of 50 missiles on launchers and 16 radars, a missile-to-radar ratio very close to that of the current Soviet Galosh system. An initial operational capability was to be achieved by FY 1964 and the entire program completed by FY 1969, with a total investment cost estimated at $13 to $14 billion, of which $1.5 billion would be required in FY 1961.

The system was designed around a relatively slow speed and limited range interceptor missile and mechanically steered radars. Because of the missile's slow speed, it had to be fired long before the incoming target reentered the atmosphere, thereby precluding the use of the atmosphere as a means of distinguishing real warheads from other objects such as decoys or tankage fragments; and the limited range of the missile reduced the potential kill radius. (Indeed, the plan called for the firing of three Zeus against each attacking ICBM.) Because the radars were mechanically steered (like the local Galosh radars), the traffic-handling capabilities of the system were low, leaving it vulnerable to saturation attacks.

This plan was rejected by President Eisenhower, who pointed out in his FY 1961 Budget message that:

"The Nike-Zeus system is one of the most difficult undertakings ever attempted by this country. The technical problems involved in detecting, tracking, and computing the course of the incoming ballistic missile and in guiding the intercepting Zeus missile to its target—all within a few minutes—are indeed enormous.

"Much thought and study have been given to all of these factors and it is the consensus of my technical and military advisors that the system should be carefully tested before production is begun and facilities are constructed for its deployment. Accordingly, I am recommending sufficient funds in this budget to provide for the essential phases of such testing. Pending the results of such testing, the $137 million appropriated last year by the Congress for initial production steps for the Nike-Zeus system will not be used."

The Joint Chiefs of Staff, with one dissenting vote, supported the President's position and the Congress agreed to limit the program to research and development.

The weaknesses in the Nike-Zeus system led in 1961 and 1962 to the development of a new and different system known as Nike-X. To help solve the problem of discriminating actual warheads from decoys and other objects, a new, high acceleration terminal defense missile, the Sprint, was designed. Because of its fast reaction time, this missile would permit the defense to wait until the enemy attack penetrated well into the atmosphere where the lighter objects, such as unsophisticated decoys, would be separated from the warheads, thus permitting the defense to concentrate more of its fire on the latter. To solve the problem of limited handling capacity, a new family of phased-array radars was developed. These radars employ a relatively new principle; instead of scanning the skies with an electronic beam by mechanically rotating the entire radar structure, the structure is covered with thousands of sensors and is kept stationary while the electronic beam does the rotating. Because an electronic beam can be rotated a million times faster than a mechanical structure, the phased-array radar has a far greater search and tracking capacity. In other words, it can simultaneously handle many more incoming objects, thus eliminating one of the major limitations of the old Nike-Zeus system.

With the phased-array radar and Sprint missiles, the defense battery could bring firepower to bear on all targets entering an area 20 miles high and 25 miles in radius. However, even if these batteries were deployed around all our major cities, a large part of the nation would still be left undefended and the attacker would have the option of ground-bursting his warheads outside the defended areas, thus producing vast amounts of lethal fall-out which could be carried by the winds over the defended areas. Moreover, a terminal (or local) defense compels the defender to allocate his resources in advance, leaving the attacker free to concentrate his resources against whatever targets he may choose at the moment of the attack.

To fill in this gap, we initiated in the spring of 1965 the development of a new long-range interceptor with a high yield, high temperature X-ray warhead. This missile, the Spartan, is designed to reach out over 400 nautical miles from its launcher and attack incoming objects at altitudes of up to 280 nautical miles. Its warhead is to be capable of destroying ballistic missile reentry vehicles at ranges of five to ten miles if they are hardened, and 10 to 100 miles if they are not. About a dozen properly located batteries of such a missile could provide some coverage over the entire United States. Together with the Sprint, it could provide a defense in depth, permitting all incoming objects to be attacked first well above the atmosphere and then the surviving objects a second time as they enter the atmosphere. Moreover, by overlapping the coverage of the Spartan batteries, some of the attacker's inherent advantage against terminal defenses alone could be overcome, since the defender at the moment of the attack would also have the choice of concentrating his resources over those targets he chooses to protect.

The deployment of an ABM system did not become a serious issue again until earlier this year. It was clear to us from the beginning, i.e., 1961, that the Nike-Zeus as then conceived would not be an effective ABM system against the type of ballistic missile attack the Soviets would be able to launch by the end of the decade. Accordingly, both in President Kennedy's and your administrations, we have steadfastly maintained that the development of a more effective ABM system should be pursued on an urgent basis but that no production or deployment should be undertaken until much more was known about the system's technical capabilities and its likely effect on the strategic situation generally. This view found substantial support within the Executive Branch and in the Congress up until recently, although an abortive attempt was made by some members of the Senate in 1963 to authorize an appropriation for the deployment of the Nike-Zeus. However, in acting on the FY 1967 Defense Budget, the Armed Services Committees and the Defense Appropriations Subcommittees of both Houses recommended, and the Congress appropriated, about $168 million to prepare for the production of the Nike-X system. It is, therefore, clear that the deployment of this system will be a major issue in the next session of the Congress.

3. *Technical Feasibility of the Nike-X System as Presently Visualized*

Attachment 1[12] provides a description of each of the major elements of the Nike-X system and its current development status. Briefly, the system would consist of a number of different types of phased-array radars and two types of interceptor missiles, which could be deployed in a variety of configurations:

a. Multi-function Array Radar (MAR)—a very powerful phased-array radar which can perform all the defense functions involved in engaging a large, sophisticated attack: central control and battle management, long-range search, acquisition of the target, discrimination of warheads from decoys or "spoofing" devices, precision tracking of the target, and control of the defense interceptor missiles.

b. TACMAR Radar—a scaled down, slightly less complex and less powerful version of the MAR, which can perform all the basic defense functions in a smaller, less sophisticated attack.

c. Perimeter Acquisition Radar (PAR)—a relatively low frequency, phased-array radar required for the very long-range search and acquisition functions involved in area defense. To achieve the full potential of the extended-range Spartan, the target must be picked up at much greater distances in order to compute its trajectory before the Spartan is fired.

d. Missile Site Radar (MSR)—a much smaller, phased-array radar needed to control the Sprint and Spartan interceptor missiles during an engagement. It can also perform the functions of the TACMAR but on a considerably reduced scale. Actually, a number of different sizes are being studied. This "modular" approach will permit us to tailor the capacity of the radar to the particular needs of each defended area.

e. The extended-range Spartan—a three stage missile with a hot X-ray, [*less than 1 line of source text not declassified*] capable of intercepting incoming objects at a range of over 400 nautical miles and at altitudes of up to 280 nautical miles. This missile makes use of some of the components of the old Nike-Zeus.

f. Sprint—a high-acceleration interceptor missile which can climb to 80,000 feet in 10 seconds. It is designed to make intercepts between 5,000 and 100,000 feet at a range of 25 miles.

In addition to these major elements of the system, an entire new infrastructure, including base facilities, communications, logistics support, etc., will be required. The exact cost of this infrastructure cannot be determined until a specific deployment plan is decided upon, but it would surely be substantial for any deployment.

---

[12] Not printed.

The technical principles involved in the radars are now fairly well established. One R&D MAR-type radar has been constructed at the White Sands Missile Range. A contract has been let for the power plant of a second MAR-type radar, which is to be constructed on Kwajalein Atoll. The Missile Site Radar is well along in development and the construction of one of these radars on Kwajalein Atoll has also begun.

Testing of the Sprint missile was started at White Sands in November 1965 with one complete success, two partial successes and three failures. The failures are attributed mostly to insufficient quality control but some of the missile's components may have to be redesigned. The tempo of testing will steadily increase during the current fiscal year and we are advised by our technical people that the missile will eventually reach its design goals. The nuclear warhead is also well along in development and does not appear to present any particular problem.

The Spartan is still on the drawing boards. It represents a very substantial redesign of the original Nike-Zeus and we will not know until it is flight tested a year and a half hence how well it will perform. However, we are less concerned with the missile itself than we are with its warhead. A significant number of development tests will have to be performed, all underground, before the design parameters can be established; and then we will have to proof test the resulting warhead, again underground. (The feasibility of a full yield test underground has still to be established, but it may be possible to use a scaled-down test.) Accordingly, there is still considerable technical uncertainty concerning the warhead. Although alternative warheads could be used on the Spartan, they would be less effective against a heavy, sophisticated attack.

Facilities for testing both the Sprint and the Spartan will be constructed on Kwajalein Atoll. These, together with the TACMAR and MSR and the programs for the computers will give us all of the major elements of the Nike-X system which are essential to test its overall performance against reentry vehicles fired from Vandenberg Air Force Base in California. (We feel we know enough about the PAR technology to be able to use the mechanically steered radars already on Kwajalein as simulators.) The system will be tested in stages, starting with the MSR and Sprint tests in January 1969, then the Spartan missile in July 1969 and the TACMAR radar between July and December 1970. Upwards of 100 test shots will be launched from Vandenberg to Kwajalein during the period 1969–72 to test the system thoroughly as a whole. The most important objective of this effort is to determine proper system integration and computer programming, since the individual components of the system will have already been tested ahead of time.

But even after this elaborate test program is completed, a number of technical uncertainties will still remain unresolved. Chief among these are the following:

1. Large Sophisticated Attacks. Notwithstanding the number of test shots planned, the ability of the system to cope with a large sophisticated attack will still remain to be demonstrated, except to the extent that such attacks can be simulated in the computers.

2. Discrimination of Decoys and Other "Spoofing" Devices. Although the MAR-type radars are specifically designed to deal with this problem, discrimination will always remain an unresolved issue. We have been studying and developing such devices for many years and we are now installing some of them in our offensive missiles. No doubt new devices and the counters to them will be invented in the future, and the contest between the offense and the defense will continue as it has in the area of manned bombers.

3. Blackout. Detonation of nuclear devices high in the atmosphere can seriously degrade the effectiveness of the defense's radars. These detonations can be either the defensive warheads (self blackout) or deliberate explosions of the incoming warheads (precursor blackout). They have the effect of producing an area in the atmosphere similar to an opaque cloud which the radars cannot see into or through. The size of the area is a function of how high the burst occurs and of the frequency of the radars. The blacked-out region is larger at higher altitudes and appears larger to lower frequency radars. At the lower altitudes, the blackout region is essentially the visible fireball. For the terminal defenses employing Sprint missiles in the lower atmosphere and radars in the microwave region (about 1200 megacycles), the blackout effects can be minimized and are well understood from previous testing.

For the area defense the problem is more severe. For one thing, the number of tests conducted by both the U.S. and the Soviet Union at the altitudes of interest for area defense (above 200,000 feet) is relatively small. In the U.S. tests, the data collected are not complete enough to answer all the technical issues, although our continuing study of the available data is increasing our knowledge of the blackout effects. However, we can never resolve all the uncertainties with the existing data. We know there will be blackout effects and we know that we can choose a radar frequency and proliferate radars to minimize them. But we do not know how many precursor nuclear blasts the Soviets would have to place over the United States to black out our radars. And, we do not know how much they learned from their nuclear tests. Consequently, we do not know precisely what their uncertainties would be in using this as an offensive tactic. We do know that the blackout effects can be offset by raising the frequencies of the radars, and we are doing this in the case of the PAR. However, because the area defense radars must detect small targets at long ranges and because the price of a radar set operating in this manner increases with the frequency, there is a limit on how far we can go in this direction to counter blackout.

4. Programming the Computers. The management of a sophisticated ballistic missile attack engagement presents an extremely complex problem. To control the phased-array radars and guide the missile, powerful computers and sophisticated "programs" are needed. The size of the computer varies with the type of radar. For the area defense (with PAR), computer speeds and capacities equivalent to the best of today's commercial computers are adequate. The MSR and the MAR will need much more powerful computers, development of which has been underway since 1962. However, it is not the computer itself which is our major concern, but rather the production of the "programs" which must be designed in advance to reflect every conceivable eventuality the system may confront. Our experience in programming the SAGE computers against manned bomber attacks has revealed some of the complexities, and the costs, of such an undertaking. Whether we can provide for all of the variables involved in such a vastly more complex problem as anti-missile defense has yet to be demonstrated. Here, again, we will have a much better idea of what is actually involved in programming the computers when the prototype system on Kwajalein is demonstrated in the 1970–72 period.

5. Production and Operational Problems. We have learned from bitter experience that even when the development problems have been solved, a system can run into trouble in production or when it is put into operation. All too often the development prototype cannot be produced in quantity without extensive re-engineering. Production delays are encountered and costs begin to spiral. Sometimes these problems are not discovered until the new system actually enters the inventory and has to function in an operational environment. The Terrier, Talos, and Tartar ship-to-air missiles are a good example; after spending about $2 billion on development and production of these missiles, we had to spend another $350 million correcting the faults of those already installed and we still plan to spend another $550 million modernizing these systems.

In this connection, it is worth noting that had we produced and deployed the Nike-Zeus system proposed by the Army in 1959 at an estimated cost of $13 to $14 billion, most of it would have had to be torn out and replaced, almost before it became operational, by the new missiles and radars of the Nike-X system. By the same token, other technological developments in offensive forces over the next seven years may make obsolete or drastically degrade the Nike-X system as presently envisioned. We can predict with certainty that there will be substantial additional costs for updating any system we might consider installing at this time against the Soviet missile threat.

4. Assuming the Nike-X System is Technically Feasible, Should it Be Deployed Now?

This question can be answered only within the context of the general nuclear war problem as a whole and our overall national security objectives. For many years the overriding objective of our national policy with regard to general nuclear war has been to deter the Soviet Union (or any other nation) from launching a surprise nuclear attack against us or our Allies. As long as that remains our overriding objective, the capability for "Assured Destruction" must receive first call on all of our resources and must be provided regardless of the cost and the difficulties involved. Programs designed to limit damage to our population and industrial capacity in the event the deterrent fails can never substitute for an "Assured Destruction" capability in this context, no matter how much we spend on them. It is our ability to destroy the attacker as a viable 20th century nation that provides the deterrent, not the ability to limit damage to ourselves.

What kind and amount of destruction we would have to be able to inflict on an attacker to provide this deterrent cannot be answered precisely. However, it seems reasonable to assume that in the case of the Soviet Union, the destruction of, say, [*2-1/2 lines of source text not declassified*]. Such a level of destruction would certainly represent intolerable punishment to any industrialized nation and thus should serve as an effective deterrent to the deliberate initiation of a nuclear attack on the United States or its Allies.

Once sufficient forces have been procured to give us high confidence of achieving our "Assured Destruction" objective, we can then consider the kinds and amounts of forces which might be added to reduce damage to our population and industry in the event deterrence fails. But here we must note another important point, namely, the possible interaction of our strategic forces programs with those of the Soviet Union. If the general nuclear war policy of the Soviet Union also has as its objective the deterrence of a U.S. first strike (which I believe to be the case), then we must assume that any attempt on our part to reduce damage to ourselves (below what they would estimate we would consider "unacceptable levels") would put pressure on them to strive for an offsetting improvement in their deterrent forces. Conversely, an increase in their "Damage Limiting" capability would require us to make greater investments in "Assured Destruction", which, as noted earlier in this memorandum, is precisely what we are now doing. It is in this context that we should examine the desirability of increasing our "Damage Limiting" capabilities against a heavy, sophisticated Soviet attack in the 1970s.

As I noted earlier, the major elements of the Nike-X system, as they are now being developed, would permit a variety of deployments; two have been selected for the purposes of this analysis. The first, which I will call "Posture-A", represents a light U.S. defense against a Soviet missile attack on our cities. It consists of an area defense of the entire continental United States, providing redundant (overlapping) coverage of key target areas; and, in addition, a relatively low-density Sprint defense of the 25 largest cities to provide some protection against those warheads which get through the area defense.[13] The second deployment, which I call "Posture B", is a heavier defense against a Soviet attack. With the same area coverage, it provides a higher-density Sprint defense for the 50 largest cities.

Shown on the following table are the components and the costs (which, if past experience is any guide, are understated by 50 to 100 percent for the systems as a whole) of Posture A and Posture B, together with the time frames in which the deployments can be completed:

| | Posture A | | Posture B | |
	Number	Invest. Cost ($ Billion)	Number	Invest. Cost ($ Billion)
Radars				
TACMAR	7	$1.9	3	$0.6
MAR	0	0	8	2.8
PAR	6	0.8	6	0.8
MSR	26	3.8	95	8.4
Invest. Cost		$6.5		$12.6
Missiles				
Spartan	1200	$ 1.7	1200	$ 1.7
Sprint	1100	0.7	7300	3.1
Invest. Cost		$2.4		$4.8
DoD Invest. Cost		$8.9		$17.4
AEC Invest. Cost		1.0		2.0
Total Invest. Cost (ex-R&D)		$9.9		$19.4
Annual Operating Cost		$0.38		$ 0.72
No. of Cities w / Term.Def	25		50	
IOC with Decision 1/67	FY 71		FY 71	
Deployment Completed	FY 74		FY 75	

---

[13] This is essentially the deployment now recommended by the Joint Chiefs of Staff. [Footnote in the source text.]

In addition, if technically feasible, we would have to provide some improvement in our defense against manned bomber attack in order to preclude the Soviets from undercutting the Nike-X defense; we would also want to accelerate the fallout shelter program. The investment cost (including R&D) of the former is estimated at about $1.5 to $2.4 billion and would provide for a small force of F-111 or F-12 type interceptors (e.g., 48 F-111s or 32 F-12s) and about 42 aircraft warning and control aircraft (AWACS). With the introduction of these new types of aircraft, we might be able to phase out most of the present interceptor aircraft and a large part of the ground-based aircraft warning and control network, thus producing an actual saving in operating costs over the longer term. The expanded fallout shelter program would cost about $800 million more than the one we are now pursuing. We would also need some of our anti-submarine warfare forces for use against Soviet missile submarines, but we are not yet clear whether these ASW forces would actually have to be increased over the currently planned levels. In any event, the "current" estimates of the investment cost of the total "Damage Limiting" package would amount to at least $10.5 billion for Posture A and at least $20 billion for Posture B ("final" costs for each of these Postures would probably be 50 to 100 percent higher).[14]

To test the contribution that each of these Nike-X deployments might make to our "Damage Limiting" objectives, we have projected both the U.S. and Soviet strategic nuclear forces (assuming no reaction by the Soviets to the U.S. ABM deployment) to FY 1976, by which time Posture B, the heavier defense, could be fully in place. These forces are shown on the table which follows:

---

[14] Even before the systems became operational, pressures would mount for their expansion at a cost of still additional billions. The unprotected, or relatively unprotected, areas of the U.S. (e.g., Alaska, Tampa, Birmingham, Sacramento) would claim that their tax dollars were being diverted to protect New York and Washington while they were left naked. And, critics would point out that our strategic offensive force is premised on a much larger Soviet threat (the "possible", not the "probable" threat); they would conclude that the same principles should be applied to our strategic defensive forces. For these and other reasons, I believe that, once started, an ABM system deployed with the objective of protecting the United States against the Soviet Union would require an expenditure on the order of $40 billion over a ten year period. [Footnote in the source text.]

Projected U.S. and Soviet Strategic Nuclear Forces, Mid-1976
(assuming no reaction by the Soviets to U.S. ABM deployment)

	U.S.	USSR
ICBMs (Hard Launchers)		
Large (Titan II/SS-9 Class)	27	276–249
Small (Minuteman/SS-11 Class)	1000	500–950
SLBMs		
Large (Poseidon Class.)	496	0
Small (Polaris/SSN-5 Class)	160	307–399
Total No. of BM Warheads	6931	1083–1608
Bombers (for U.S./Soviet Attacks)		
Heavy	255	70–110[a]
Medium	210	300–500[a]
ABM (Anti-ballistic Missile Defense)		
Area Interceptors		800–3250[b]
Terminal Interceptors		0–1500[b]
Air Defense		
Fighters	700	1700–2400[c]
SAM Batteries	116	1440–2400[c]

[a] Includes only heavy bomber force. Current NIE accepts only minimal use of Soviet medium bombers for CONUS attack.

[b] NIE does not estimate numbers.

[c] Numbers, per the NIE, assume some improved Soviet air defenses, some F-4 Fiddler-type interceptors with look-down radar and some Improved Hawk-type SAMs.

Note: Forces for other years are shown in Attachment 2.

The fatalities which these Soviet forces could inflict upon the U.S. (with and without a U.S. ABM defense) and the fatalities which the U.S. forces could inflict on the Soviet Union (with a Soviet ABM defense) are shown on the following table:

Number of Fatalities[a] in an All-out
Strategic Exchange (in millions), 1976[b]
Assumes No Soviet Reaction to U.S. ABM Deployment

U.S. Programs	Soviets Strike First, U.S. Retaliates		U.S. Strikes First, Soviets Retaliate[c]	
	U.S. Fat.	Sov. Fat.	U.S. Fat.	Sov. Fat.
Approved	100	[*]	80	[*]
Posture A	15	[*]	15	[*]
Posture B	10	[*]	5	[*]

[*entry in table not declassified]

[a] Fatality figures shown above represent deaths from blast and fallout; they do not include deaths resulting from fire storms, disease, and general disruption of everyday life.

[b] The data in this table and the table on page 21 are highly sensitive to small changes in the pattern of attack and small changes in force levels. [Reference is to the next table.]

[c] Assumes U.S. targets Soviet cities with Poseidon missiles and manned bombers.

The first case, "Soviets Strike First, U.S. Retaliates", is the threat against which our strategic forces must be designed. The second case, "U.S. Strikes First, Soviets Retaliate", is the case that would determine the size and character of the Soviet reaction to changes in our strategic forces, if they wish, as clearly they do, to maintain an "Assured Destruction" capability against us.

These calculations indicate that without Nike-X and the other "Damage Limiting" programs discussed earlier, U.S. fatalities from a Soviet first strike could total about 100 million; even after absorbing that attack, we could inflict on the Soviet Union about [number not declassified] fatalities. Assuming the Soviets do not react to our deployment of an ABM defense against them, which is a most unrealistic assumption, Posture A might reduce our fatalities to 15 million and Posture B, to about 10 million.

Although the fatality estimates shown for both the Soviet Union and the U.S. reflect some variations in the performance of their respective ABM systems, they are still based on the assumption that these systems will work at relatively high levels of efficiency. (In fact, for the purpose of these calculations we have assumed that the Soviet ABM system will be just as good as the Nike-X, even though we believe the system, or systems, which they are now deploying are, in fact, far inferior.) If these ABM systems do not perform as well as our technical people postulate, fatalities on both sides could be considerably higher than shown in the table above, or the costs would be considerably higher if major improvements or additions had to be made in the systems to bring them up to the postulated level of performance.

If the Soviets are determined to maintain an "Assured Destruction" capability against us and they believe that our deployment of an ABM defense would reduce our fatalities in the "U.S. Strikes First, Soviets Retaliate" case to the levels shown in the table above, they would have no alternative but to increase the second strike damage potential of their offensive forces. They could do so in several different ways: by deploying a new large, land-based ICBM (either mobile, or hardened and defended), or a new submarine-launched missile like our Poseidon, or by adding large numbers of hardened but undefended SS-9s or SS-11s. They have the technical capability to deploy any of these systems with highly accurate MIRVs (or single warheads) by the mid-1970s. Shown in the table below are the relative costs to the Soviet Union of responding to a U.S. ABM deployment with a land-mobile ICBM system:

Level of U.S. Fatalities Which Soviets Believe Will Provide Deterrence[a] (Millions)	Cost to the Soviets of Offsetting U.S. Cost to Deploy an ABM
22	$1 Soviet cost to $4 U.S. cost
33	$1 Soviet cost to $2 U.S. cost
44	$1 Soviet cost to $1 U.S. cost
55	$1-1/4 Soviet cost to $1 U.S. cost
66	$1-2/3 Soviet cost to $1 U.S. cost

[a] U.S. fatalities resulting from a Soviet second strike.

If the Soviets choose to respond to our ABM deployment with such a system (200 missiles against Posture A and 650 against Posture B), the results would be as shown below:

	Number of Fatalities in an All-out Strategic Exchange (in millions), 1976 (Assumes Soviet Reaction to U.S. ABM Deployment)			
	Soviets Strike First, U.S. Retaliates		U.S. Strikes First, Soviets Retaliate	
U.S. Programs	U.S. Fat.	Sov. Fat.	U.S. Fat.	Sov. Fat.
Approved (no response)	100	[*]	80	[*]
Posture A	90	[*]	75	[*]
Posture B	75	[*]	70	[*]

[*entry in table not declassified]

In short, the Soviets have it within their technical and economic capacity to offset any further "Damage Limiting" measures we might undertake, provided they are determined to maintain their deterrent against us. *It is the virtual certainty that the Soviets will act to maintain their deterrent which casts such grave doubts on the advisability of our deploying the Nike-X system for the protection of our cities against the kind of heavy, sophisticated missile attack they could launch in the 1970s. In all probability, all we would accomplish would be to increase greatly both their defense expenditures and ours without any gain in real security to either side.*

5. Deployment of Nike-X for Other Purposes

As I noted at the beginning of this memorandum, a limited, i.e., light, deployment of the Nike-X (estimated investment cost, about $3.5 billion) might offer a high degree of protection for our cities against the kind of ballistic missile attack the Chinese Communists may be able to launch in the 1970s; and, with some special additions (estimated investment cost, about $660 million), ensure the survival of a significant portion of our Minuteman force even against a heavy, MIRVed Soviet attack. Such a deployment would have an inherent capability to provide a very high level of protection against accidental and "nuclear blackmail" attacks. And, as a by-product, it would-also have some capability to reduce U.S. fatalities from a Soviet attack against our cities in the early 1970s, provided the Soviets do not immediately react to our ABM deployment.

Shown below are the components and costs of a "light" Nike-X deployment designed to achieve the foregoing purposes:

	Basic CONUS System	Hawaii & Alaska Increment	Minuteman Defense Increment	Total System
Radars				
PAR	3	1	1	5
MSR	13	2	2	17
Missiles				
Spartan	390	30	60	480
Sprint	120[a]	50	285	455
Investment Cost ($ Mil.)				
DoD	2835	404	561	3800
AEC	211	27	97	335
Annual Oper. Costs ($ Mil.)	148	27	27	202
IOC with Decision Jan. '67				1Jul71
Deployment Completed				1Oct73

[a] For defense of PARs

6. Defense Against the Chinese Communist Nuclear Threat

The Chinese Communist nuclear weapons and ballistic missile development programs are apparently being pursued with high priority. On the basis of recent evidence, it appears possible that they may conduct either a space or a long-range ballistic missile launching before the end of 1967. Such an event might suggest that the Chinese are aiming at an initial operating capability (IOC) for an ICBM as early as 1969, and that the threat to the United States is more imminent than is actually the case. In our judgment, it still appears unlikely that the Chinese could achieve an IOC before the early 1970s and deploy a significant number of operational ICBMs before the mid-1970s, or that those ICBMs would have great reliability, speed of response, or substantial protection against attack.

Nevertheless , it would seem prudent to initiate the deployment of a "light" Nike-X system (described in the preceding section) at this time. The effectiveness of this system in reducing U.S. fatalities from a Chinese Communist attack in the 1970s is shown in the table below:

	Chinese Strike First (Operational Inventory)	
	25 Missiles	75 Missiles
U.S. Fatalities: (In Millions)		
Without ABM	5	10
With ABM	0	1

This "light" defense could probably preclude damage in the 1970s almost entirely. As the Chinese force grows to the level it might achieve by 1980–85, additions and improvements might be required, but relatively modest additional outlays could probably limit the Chinese damage potential to low levels well beyond 1985.

7. ABM Defense of U.S. Offensive Missile Forces

In contrast to our sea-based Polaris/Poseidon forces, our land-based Minuteman forces (even though they are installed in hard underground silos) could become vulnerable to a Soviet surprise attack, if the Soviets continue to increase the size and, more important, greatly improve the accuracy of their ICBM forces. However, even assuming the strongest Soviet threat projected in the latest National Intelligence Estimates for mid-1974, and even assuming that the Soviets use all of their accurate ICBMs against our Minuteman forces, about 470 missiles would still survive. The "light" Nike deployment could increase the number of surviving missiles to 730. Together with the sea-based missile forces, we would have more than enough for "Assured Destruction", even if the Soviets deploy an extensive ABM system of the sort described in the latest National Intelligence Estimates.

But the most severe threat we must consider in planning our "Assured Destruction" forces is an extensive, effective Soviet ABM deployment combined with a deployment of a substantial hard-target kill capability in the form of highly accurate SS-11s or MIRVed SS-9s. By equipping their SS-9 boosters with six MIRVs (each with a CEP of 0.25 n.mi. and a yield of 3MT), the Soviets could destroy large numbers of our Minuteman missiles. An extensive, effective Soviet ABM system could then intercept and destroy a large part of our residual missile warheads. (These Soviet offensive and defensive threats are both higher than those projected in the latest National Intelligence Estimates.)

We could not count on more than two years of warning between the first intelligence indications of a Soviet MIRV development effort and the start of deployment of the system. Assuming that the Soviets start such a development immediately and press forward with their ABM deployment at a rate of 1000 interceptors per year (beginning in FY 1968), they might achieve the build-up shown below:

Greater-Than-Expected Soviet Threat

	FY 70	FY 71	FY 72	FY 73	FY 74
Soviet Threat to Minuteman					
SS-9	150	150	150	150	100
SS-9 MIRV	0	50	100	150	200
(Six 3-megaton RVs/Missile)					
SS-11 (improved accuracy)	300	550	800	925	925
Total No. of BM Warheads	450	1000	1550	1975	2225
Soviet ABM Defense					
Area Interceptors)	3200	4200	5200	6200	7200
Terminal Interceptors)					

The effect of such a deployment could be to reduce the number of U.S. Minuteman surviving attack to the levels shown below:

	FY 70	FY 71	FY 72	FY 73	FY 74
Minuteman Surviving[a]	710	340	205	120	90

[a] In addition, the Polaris and Poseidon force would survive.

To offset the possibility of such a decline in the damage potential of our land-based missile forces, we have authorized the development and production of the Poseidon. Should still additional offensive power be required, and such a requirement is not now clear, we are considering the development and deployment of a new Advanced ICBM (a large payload missile with an as yet undetermined basing system designed to reduce vulnerability to a Soviet MIRV threat). The deployment of the Nike-X as a defense of part of our Minuteman force would, however, offer a partial substitute for the possible further expansion of our offensive force.

Shown below is the contribution the "light" Nike-X deployment (described on page 22) might make to the survival of our Minuteman force against the greater-than-expected Soviet threat, compared with the "No Defense" case:

	FY 70	FY 71	FY 72	FY 73	FY 74
No Defense Case					
MM Surviving	710	340	205	120	90
Nike-X Defense					
ABM Interceptors	0	55	495	805	855
MM Surviving[a]	710	340	370	300	280

---

[a] Assumes the Soviets attack the defended Minuteman silos first. They might attack our radars first if they felt they had enough information on our defenses and were willing to gamble that we would delay launching our Minuteman for at least 15 minutes while their attack proceeded. In that case, the number of surviving Minuteman might be 90 fewer.

Thus, the "light" Nike-X deployment (with a total investment cost of about $4 billion and an annual operating cost of about $200 million) would be able to maintain the Minuteman force's retaliatory capability even against the higher-than-expected threat.

8. Capability of the "Light" Nike-X Deployment to Reduce U.S. Fatalities from a Deliberate Soviet Attack in the 1970s

As I noted earlier, a limited deployment of the Nike-X would, as a by-product, also help to reduce U.S. fatalities from a Soviet attack. Shown below is the contribution such a system could make in 1974 if the Soviets do *not* react to our ABM deployment:

Number of Fatalities in an All-out
Strategic Exchange (in millions), 1974

US Programs	Soviets Strike First, US Retaliates		US Strikes First, Soviets Retaliate	
	US Fat.	Sov. Fat.	US Fat.	Sov. Fat.
No ABM Def	100	[*]	80	[*]
Lt ABM Def (No Sov Reaction)b	85	[*]	65	[*]

[*entry in table not declassified]

b Projection of Soviet Strategic Forces based on latest NIEs.

But with a limited and low-cost reaction the Soviets could offset the benefits of this Nike-X deployment.

9. Effect of U.S. ABM Deployment on Relations with Other Nations

With regard to our NATO Allies, two questions arise: (1) What would be their reaction to our deployment of an ABM system?; and (2) Would they want to deploy such a system?

Some European governments and many European specialists in defense and arms control matters have exhibited a growing interest in ABM defense. At the insistence of several European countries, ABM defense was discussed at the recent NATO arms control experts conference. The European and Canadian attitude as expressed at the NATO meeting was generally hostile to a U.S. ABM deployment. The same attitude was expressed by the U.K. delegation at the recent U.S.-U.K. bilateral talks on ABMs. This reaction appears to be based on a desire to avoid an accelerated arms race which Europeans believe would upset the détente. There is also some fear on the part of the British that an ABM race would price them out of the nuclear business.

Even if the U.S. offered the Europeans a similar system, it is unlikely that they would accept; only Germany has expressed a mild interest thus far. This is so for several reasons. First, the cost (at least $6 billion, and probably more, for a meaningful system) would involve a substantial increase in their defense budgets. Second, the European preoccupation with deterrence rather than defense makes it unlikely that they would pay for such an ABM system. Third, the Europeans are unlikely to achieve the degree of political and decision-making unity which would be necessary to deploy an effective ABM system.

10. Attitude of U.S. Public Toward ABM Defense

Perhaps the most difficult problem we will have to face in a decision not to deploy at this time an ABM system for defense of our cities against a *Soviet* ballistic missile attack is the attitude of our Congress and our people. The first reaction of most Americans to the events I have described at the beginning of this memorandum will inevitably be in favor of an immediate start on production and deployment, if for no other reason than the Soviets are deploying such a system. More mature reflection on all of the factors involved in this vastly complex problem should convince at least the majority of the informed public that any attempt on our part to build an ABM defense which could keep our fatalities in a Soviet "second strike" below what the Soviets consider would deter a U.S. attack, would almost certainly force them to respond by increasing their offensive forces and would therefore be self-defeating. But a massive program will have to be undertaken to present all of the relevant information, and in an understandable form, to both the Congress and the general public. Without such an understanding, we cannot hope to gain their support for a sensible ABM program.

11. Conclusions

In view of the great uncertainties surrounding both the Soviet and Chinese Communist missile threats over the next five to ten years, and the advantages that even a limited ABM defense might offer in dealing with possible accidental and "nuclear blackmail" attacks, a "light" deployment of the Nike-X may be worth its cost. But none of the four purposes for which deployment of Nike-X might make sense would justify a crash program at this time. Even without an ABM defense, and even if the higher-than-expected Soviet threat develops, our surviving offensive missile and bomber forces could inflict at least [*less than 1 line of source text not declassified*] on the Soviet Union in 1974. Moreover, we do not know when, if ever, the higher-than-expected Soviet threat will develop. Nor do we believe that the Chinese Communists could have a significant number of ICBMs before the mid-1970s. (The possibilities of accidental or "nuclear blackmail" attacks probably would not, in themselves, justify even a "light" deployment of the Nike-X.) Finally, much work remains to be done in the development, test and evaluation of the Nike-X system.

Accordingly, Mr. Vance and I recommend that:

1. We *not* deploy the Nike-X system at this time for the defense of our cities against a Soviet missile attack.

2. We initiate, on an orderly basis, a "light" deployment of the Nike-X, specifically and exclusively designed to satisfy the first four purposes.

3. You approve a total program of about $ million for FY 1967 and $ million for FY 1968, including RDT&E, procurement, construction,

etc. (The Congress in FY 1967 provided a total of $614.7 million for Nike-X compared with $446.8 million in the budget request. The additional $167.9 million was for production.)

4. You authorize the Secretary of State and the Secretary of Defense to initiate negotiations with the Soviet Union designed, through formal or informal agreement, to limit the deployment of anti-ballistic missile systems.

---

161. Memorandum From the President's Special Assistant (Rostow) to President Johnson[1]

Washington, December 22, 1966, 4:10 p.m.

Mr. President:

You are aware of the debate about whether the massive Tallinn system is or is not ABM.

The latest evidence from the CIA,[2] summarized below, suggests it is not ABM-associated.

"The identification of six new complexes since July provides further evidence that the Tallinn system will be extensively deployed. Three of the new complexes are too far East to receive inputs from known ABM radars; this supports the view that the intended mission of the system is defense against aerodynamic targets. It is estimated that 75 complexes containing 240 launch sites will be deployed by 1971."

Walt

---

[1] Source: Johnson Library, National Security File, Intelligence File, TKH August 66–July 67, Box 1. Top Secret; Sensitive.

[2] Reference is to Intelligence Memorandum, "Extension of Long-Range SAM Deployment to Siberia, December 1966" (TCS–8524/66). (Ibid.)

162. Memorandum From the Joint Chiefs of Staff to Secretary of Defense McNamara[1]

JCSM–804–66   Washington, December 29, 1966.

SUBJECT

  Production and Deployment of Nike-X (C)

1. (C) The Joint Chiefs of Staff have reviewed your revised draft memorandum for the President, dated 22 December 1966, subject: "Production and Deployment of the Nike-X,"[2] and have noted the alternative proposal for Nike-X deployment recommended therein. They do not consider that detailed comments on the draft memorandum are required; however, they suggest that the draft memorandum should be amended to set forth more adequately a rationale supporting the recommended deployment.

2. (S) The DEPEX II deployment of Nike-X that the Joint Chiefs of Staff have recommended to you is designed to counter an evolving USSR and CPR threat to the United States. They consider that the proposed Nike-X deployment alternative will not be able to cope with all aspects of the evolving threat. They agree, however, that this modified deployment will provide some measure of area and city defense, provide partial protection of Minuteman sites, guard against the consequences of accidental launch of nuclear missiles toward the United States, and discourage the use of "nuclear blackmail."

3. (S) The inclusion of ABM systems in any arms control negotiations with the Soviet Union raises complex political, military and psychological problems, many of which stem from the developing communist Chinese nuclear capability. The Joint Chiefs of Staff consider that the military aspects of such negotiations should be carefully weighed prior to and during negotiations; they are prepared to provide appropriate advice as needed. In any event, deployment of Nike-X should not be delayed pending initiation or conclusion of arms control negotiations since, apart from the military requirement, implementation of the proposed deployment of Nike-X would provide the United States useful negotiating leverage.

4. (S) In summary, while the Joint Chiefs of Staff reaffirm their previous recommendations stated in JCSM–742–66, dated 2 December 1966, subject as above,[3] they support the proposed deployment of Nike-

---

[1] Source: Washington National Records Center, OSD Files: FRC 330 71 A 3470, ABM Memo and JCS View Folder 103. Secret.

[2] Document 160.

[3] Document 149.

X as a first step in attaining a critically-needed ballistic missile defense capability, recognizing and emphasizing that the ultimate deployment of Nike-X must be predicated on present and future developments in offensive and defensive strategic systems.

For the Joint Chiefs of Staff:
Earle G. Wheeler
Chairman
Joint Chiefs of Staff

### 163.	Circular Airgram From the Department of State to Certain Posts[1]

CA–4864	Washington, December 31, 1966, 2:16 p.m.

SUBJECT

Recent Developments in Strategic Forces

A. Purpose

1. This message provides background information and guidance concerning developments bearing on the strategic (nuclear) relationships of the US with the Soviet Union and Communist China.

2. Posts may, of course, employ freely what has been said publicly by US officials. (Paragraphs C1a, C2f, C5a, b, c, and C6b, c, d below.) The remaining material in sections B and C is available for informal discussions with officials of other governments if they themselves inquire.

---

[1] Source: National Archives and Records Administration, RG 59, Central Files 1964–66, DEF 1 US. Confidential; Priority. Drafted by Leon Sloss (G/PM) and Wreatham Gathright (S/P); cleared by Secretary Rusk, Sidney Sober (NEA), Samuel D. Berger (EA), Robert J. McCloskey (P), Paul J. Long (ACDA), Frederick D. Sharp (ARA), Foy Kohler (G) in substance, Allen C. Hansen (USIA), Vincent Baker (EUR/RPM), Richard Straus (EUR/CAN), Vladimir Toumanoff (SOV), John T. McNaughton (DOD/ISA), and Alain C. Enthoven (DOD/SA); and approved by Jeffrey C. Kitchen (G/PM). Sent to 43 posts and 4 military commands.

An undated draft of this airgram was transmitted under cover of a December 21 letter from Kohler to Vance explaining the need for this guidance to posts abroad on "the changes occurring in Soviet and Communist Chinese strategic capabilities and our reactions to them" in order "to avoid a series of incomplete and conflicting statements," and requesting DOD's "prompt concurrence or comments" on the airgram. A December 24 note attached to this draft indicates that Vance assigned McNaughton to prepare an alternative version and that Enthoven would supply certain information. (Washington National Records Center, OSD Files: FRC 330 70 A 4443, 471.94 ABM (December) 1966)

In view of the complexity of technical and other aspects and the need to relate inter-governmental exchanges with on-going studies and conclusions in Washington, it is requested that serious governmental inquiries be referred to Washington for guidance. We do not wish press stories out of other capitals about USG views on ABMs or our assessment of strategic facts. It is expected there will be further public discussion of these matters here in connection with presentations to Congress. Therefore suggest posts abroad not use this material for background briefings but refer press inquiries to Washington.

3. It is recognized that the material will not be equally useful or appropriate for all posts. Additional classified information will in due course be provided to allies.

4. Policy implications of the developments discussed below continue under review. On the one hand, this review may lead to further arms control efforts. On the other hand, further consideration is being given to US deployment of an anti-ballistic missile (ABM) system. The material below is not intended to prejudge or prejudice either approach.

5. Addressee posts are requested to report any significant and spontaneous host country press or other comments on strategic developments. Negative reports are not required.

B. General Considerations

1. *Objectives of US Strategic Forces*

a. Our strategic forces are the product of necessity rather than of aggressive designs against any nation. Changes in our strategic forces will not adversely affect US efforts for constructive interchange with the Soviet Union and with Communist China. Rather, further changes will afford a prudent basis for continuing such efforts.

b. We would much prefer to see strategic armaments remain at present levels and, indeed, would hope to reduce them. But to date, many of our efforts to halt the arms race have not borne fruit. We shall continue these efforts, but meanwhile, we must also continue to maintain the strength and flexibility essential to deterrence.

c. It is in our interest, and that of our allies, to preclude any possibility of miscalculation by the Soviet Union or Communist China. Preventing miscalculation and maintaining deterrence requires the continuing effectiveness of tactical nuclear and non-nuclear capabilities as well as strategic capabilities. In the Soviet case our purpose of maintaining a spectrum of capabilities is to assure that they are not tempted to exploit mutual deterrence at the strategic level by risking conflict at lower levels of the hostilities spectrum.

d. Over the past twenty years, the US has developed forces and arms control techniques to ensure that its military strength will remain constantly responsive to the peaceful purposes of deterring aggression and preventing the outbreak of war. Our concern is to preserve military stability, for it is from instability that tension, miscalculations and war could come.

2. *Present Trends in Perspective*

a. In the light of the foregoing objectives, the main points respecting on-going changes in strategic capabilities are as follows:

(1) Our purposes in maintaining strong strategic capabilities are peaceful.

(2) The effectiveness of the US strategic deterrent is not impaired by changes in Soviet capabilities, or by the ChiCom nuclear weapons effort.

(3) There is no gap in strategic technology, including anti-ballistic missile (ABM) technology in the Soviet Union's favor. In fact US ABM technology is more highly developed.

(4) Our nuclear guarantees to our allies remain valid.

(5) Changes in our own strategic capabilities do not reflect any change in our intentions vis-à-vis the Soviet Union or Communist China, but represent prudent measures to maintain deterrence.

(6) We have no intentions of increasing tensions; we are determined to maintain a strong strategic posture in the face of continuing Soviet and ChiCom efforts.

b. We desire these points to be understood by the Soviet Union and Communist China as well as others.

C. *Questions and Answers*

1. *What changes is the Soviet Union making in its strategic offensive and defensive capabilities?*

a. On November 10, 1966 Secretary McNamara stated publicly that the Soviet Union has initiated deployment of an anti-ballistic missile (ABM) system.[2] On December 6 he said that the Soviets appeared to have begun an accelerated build-up of Soviet intercontinental ballistic missiles (ICBMs) as well.[3]

b. In building up their ICBM force, the Soviets are continuing to disperse their missiles in hardened silos. The Soviets are evidently seeking to remedy to some extent the inferiority and vulnerability of their ICBM deterrent force. We do not find this surprising or alarming.

c. The first known Soviet anti-ballistic missile (ABM) deployments are in the Moscow area. These may become operational over the next

---

[2] Excerpts from McNamara's statement and responses to subsequent questions at this November 10 news conference in Johnson City, Texas, are printed in *American Foreign Policy: Current Documents, 1966*, pp. 504–506.

[3] Excerpts from McNamara's statement and responses to subsequent questions at this December 6 news conference in Austin, Texas, are printed ibid., pp. 506–508. A copy of his full statement released to the press on that occasion is in the Washington National Records Center, OSD Files: FRC 330 71 A 3470, ABM Memo and JCS View Folder 103.

several years. We regard this system as limited in technical sophistication and consider it inferior to our Nike-X anti-ballistic missile development. The Soviet Union has always invested heavily in defensive systems, and their initiation of anti-ballistic missile (ABM) deployment is consistent with past practice. However, we have concluded that they are expending their resources on a system we could readily overcome.

d. We do not know how far either of these trends in offensive and defensive capabilities will be carried. We shall maintain the effectiveness of our deterrent by retaining the capability to inflict very severe damage on the Soviet Union under any circumstances.

2. *What changes is the US making in its strategic capabilities?*

a. Our Minuteman and Polaris forces have been designed to provide a secure, survivable, non-provocative deterrent which would be capable of inflicting very severe damage on the Soviet Union even if it should initiate a first-strike. Our planned build-up of these systems is now almost complete. We are not now planning further increases in the number of Minuteman and Polaris launchers.

b. Because we had for some time foreseen the possibility of changes on the Soviet side, including the possibility of anti-ballistic missile (ABM) deployment, we have developed significant qualitative improvements. We now plan to introduce the Minuteman III and Poseidon ballistic missiles in the late 1960's to replace some of the older versions of Minuteman and many of the present Polaris ballistic missiles.

c. A principal qualitative change is that Minuteman III and Poseidon will be able to launch heavier payloads than our present missiles. These heavier payloads do not mean that we are planning to increase the megatonnage that could be directed against the Soviet Union. They will add to our ability to launch adequate numbers of devices such as decoys and multiple warheads which will ensure that we can penetrate Soviet defenses.

d. One point that should be recognized concerning changes in offensive capabilities is that the Soviet Union is introducing quantitative changes whereas the US is now pursuing qualitative changes. As a result, the Soviet Union can be expected to narrow the numerical gap in ICBMs that has for some time existed in our favor. However, more is involved than numbers in determining the effectiveness and significance of strategic forces. Although we could, if there were need, substantially increase our own number of launchers, qualitative superiority will continue to yield a number of advantages.

—A more flexible force;
—A more accurate force, which is able to employ relatively small warheads with greater effect than would be the case with larger warheads launched with lesser accuracy;

—A more survivable force which includes not only ICBMs dispersed in hardened silos but also a substantial, wholly invulnerable sea-based component.

—A force with a greater capability to penetrate defenses.

e. Although we do expect to maintain an overall numerical edge for some time, our emphasis on qualitative improvements will meet our deterrent needs in the face of the probable Soviet offensive build-up and its introduction of anti-ballistic missile (ABMs).

f. In his December 6 statement Secretary McNamara said:

"It is vital that these three major points are clearly understood by the American public:

"1. Even if the new intelligence estimate for mid-1968 proves accurate, the US, without taking any actions beyond those already planned, will continue to have a substantial quantitative and qualitative superiority over the Soviet Union in ICBMs at that time.

"2. The US has as many ICBMs today as the latest national intelligence estimate gives the Soviet Union several years hence.

"3. Our strategic offensive forces have today and will continue to have in the future the capability of absorbing a deliberate first strike and retaliating with sufficient strength to inflict unacceptable damage upon the aggressor or any combination of aggressors."

3. *How can we be sure that we can penetrate Soviet anti-ballistic missile (ABM) defenses?*

a. The type of anti-ballistic missile (ABM) defense that technology now permits—and this is true of Soviet technology as well as our own—does *not* represent a kind of impenetrable umbrella that could offer sure protection against incoming missile warheads.

b. The way to think of an anti-missile missile is a very advanced interceptor. In effect, it would be assigned to "shoot down" or neutralize an incoming warhead just as a SAM (surface-to-air missile) or fighter might be assigned to intercept a manned bomber.

c. Depending on the particular ABM techniques, this effort to intercept incoming warheads might take place outside the atmosphere, or it might occur after the warhead has reentered the earth's atmosphere. Both approaches might be involved, the one supplementing the other.

d. In confronting this kind of defense, we will employ a number of different techniques which we have been working on for some years. Obviously, we are not going to discuss these in detail. However, broadly speaking, they can be thought of as complicating the defense's tasks of identifying incoming warheads and of destroying them if they are identified.

e. A key point is that Soviet defenses would have to intercept a very large number of objects, including large numbers of warheads. In addition to attempting to cope with a large number of warheads, we are sure that they will not be able to distinguish effectively between what might be decoys or other penetration devices and what might be warheads. They would have to "shoot" at everything, and they would exhaust their supply of interceptors in doing so, if they were not already overwhelmed by the scale of attack. In effect, then, we can confront them with more targets than their interceptors could manage.

4. *What about deploying our own Nike X ABM?*

a. In the face of Soviet ABM deployment, we are giving priority to ensuring the effectiveness of our offensive deterrent force. In this way, we are precluding the emergence of an "anti-missile gap" which could occur if we could not penetrate their defenses.

b. As for the Nike X anti-ballistic missile (ABM) system which we are developing, we are satisfied on technical grounds that it is more advanced than the Soviet system. But like Soviet ABMs, Nike X would not provide "perfect" defense against a large-scale attack by a sophisticated missile force. A major deployment would be costly, and its potential effectiveness would depend in part on such uncertainties as the changes the Soviets might make in their own capabilities in response to such a deployment. Under some assumptions, US defenses would be relatively ineffective. Under other assumptions, US defenses might limit damage and reduce casualties.

c. A more limited deployment might be effective against some forms of light Soviet attacks or accidents and very effective against a Chinese Communist nuclear missile capability. It could also be designed to protect our strategic offensive forces. (The Soviet system, for example, can be expected to be highly effective against any small nuclear force.)

d. All of these considerations have a bearing on the question of deploying Nike X. The development effort is being continued, and we are continuing to examine the questions of whether to deploy and what level of defense might be sought. We have not at this time arrived at any decision.

5. *Would the US favor a freeze on ABM deployment?*

a. In his news conference of December 21, 1966 Secretary Rusk made the following statement in response to questions:[4]

"We would regret very much the lifting of the arms race to an entirely new plateau of major expenditures.

"As you know, we made earlier to the Geneva Conference proposals for freezes and limitations on the further production of offensive and defensive nuclear weapons.

---

[4] Text in Department of State *Bulletin,* January 9, 1967, p. 43.

"We would like to see some means developed by which both would not have to go into wholly new and unprecedented levels of military expenditure, with perhaps no perceptible result in the total strategic situation.

"This is a matter that is before the Geneva Conference. We and the Soviet Union are co-chairmen.

"I presume that there will be further contacts on this matter. But I cannot go into more detail at this point."

b. Secretary Rusk added that there has been no progress on the matter thus far at the Geneva Conference, that the Conference is to resume in February, and that he could not anticipate at this point what might be the results.

c. Our original freeze proposal to which Secretary Rusk referred was in the following terms:

"The US, the Soviet Union and their respective allies should agree to explore a verified freeze of the number and characteristics of strategic nuclear offensive and defensive vehicles. For our part, we are convinced that the security of all nations can be safeguarded within the scope of such an agreement and that this initial measure preventing the further expansion of the deadly and costly arms race will open the path to reductions in all types of forces from present levels."[5]

d. Several suggestions have been made for freezing or limiting anti-ballistic missile (ABM) deployment only, that is without a corresponding freeze on offensive systems. We have not proposed any of these approaches. They continue to be studied.

6. *How significant are Communist China's nuclear weapons and missile development programs?*

a. We had estimated that Communist China would be able to deploy medium range ballistic missiles (MRBMs) initially in the next several years. They have not tested a short-range guided missile with a nuclear warhead, and they thus seem to be progressing on a schedule consistent with our estimate.

b. While they do not yet have a militarily useful nuclear capability, they could pose a potential nuclear threat against their neighbors in Asia within a few years. At the time of the initial ChiCom nuclear test in 1964, President Johnson made the following statement concerning our defense commitments:

"The US reaffirms its defense commitments in Asia. Even if Communist China should eventually develop an effective nuclear capability, that capability would have no effect upon the readiness of the US

---

[5] The quotation is from President Johnson's message of January 21, 1964, to the Eighteen-Nation Disarmament Committee in Geneva. Text in *Documents on Disarmament, 1964*, p. 8.

to respond to requests from Asian nations for help in dealing with Communist Chinese aggression. The US will also not be diverted from its efforts to help the nations of Asia to defend themselves and to advance the welfare of their people."[6]

c. The President also announced that it would be our policy to provide support to non-nuclear countries threatened by ChiCom "nuclear blackmail".

d. In October 1966 in Malaysia the President made the following further statement: "The leaders of China must realize that any nuclear capability they can develop can—and will—be deterred. A peaceful China can expect friendship and cooperation . . . a reckless China can expect vigilance and strength."[7]

e. We would suppose that Communist China is interested in and possibly working on an intercontinental ballistic missile (ICBM) as well as on MRBMs, since an ICBM might be viewed as having political and psychological values from Communist China's standpoint. We can't predict when a token ICBM might be demonstrated. It is possible that Communist China might have a few ICBMs by the early 1970's.

f. As for our capabilities vis-à-vis the Communist Chinese, we will for the foreseeable future have such a marked superiority that it would be suicidal for them to attempt a nuclear attack on the US. They will have no prospect whatever of mounting a disarming strike against us. We, on the other hand, will continue to possess a vastly larger, much more reliable, and substantially more flexible force. In addition, we could for some years negate any ChiCom nuclear threat to the US, with a light anti-ballistic missile deployment if it should be determined that such a deployment would be desirable.

7. *Has the US considered the effects of ABM deployment on our allies?*

a. We have been giving this matter considerable attention. We have discussed aspects of the ABM question with a number of our allies and anticipate further discussion. To date, such discussions have been very general and have concerned such matters as the status of US ABM development, strategic and other implications of ABM deployment, and arms control aspects.

b. We have also been undertaking preliminary technical studies of the possible utility of ABMs for defense of other countries. Our purpose has been to obtain a better understanding of potential cost and effectiveness. Our analysis of such basic questions has not yet been com-

---

[6] President Johnson's statement on October 16, 1964; text in *Public Papers of the Presidents of the United States: Lyndon B. Johnson, 1963–64,* p. 1357.

[7] President Johnson's statement on October 30, 1966; text is ibid., *1966,* p. 560.

pleted. (FYI. We do not wish to encourage discussion of overseas deployment of ABM at this time. End FYI.)

c. We plan to keep our allies advised of our plans as we have in the past.

Rusk

---

164.   Memorandum From the Joint Chiefs of Staff to Secretary of Defense McNamara[1]

JCSM–812–66   Washington, January 3, 1967.

SUBJECT

Planning for Improving Survivability of the National Command Authorities (U)

1. (U) Reference is made to:

a. DOD Directive S–5100.30, dated 16 October 1962, subject: "Concept of Operations of the World-Wide Military Command and Control System."[2]
b. DOD Directive S–5100.44, dated 9 June 1964, subject: "Master Plan for the National Military Command System."[2]
c. JCSM–103–64, dated 25 February 1964, subject: "The Continuity of Operations Plan for the Organization of the Joint Chiefs of Staff (COOP–OJCS) (U)."[3]

2. (S) The references provide the concept and plans to insure the survivability of a command and control system and the necessary staff personnel to support the National Command Authorities (NCA) in the strategic direction of US military forces throughout the entire spectrum of cold, limited, and general war. Currently, there is no adequate plan to insure the survivability of the NCA or their authorized successors. The Joint Chiefs of Staff believe that a credible policy of controlled response requires that such a plan be prepared. Therefore, the plan outlined herein is submitted for your consideration and recommendation to the President.

---

[1] Source: Washington National Records Center, OSD Files: FRC 330 72 A 2468, 381 Cont of Govt Ops 1967. Secret. A stamped notation on the memorandum reads: "Sec Def has seen Brief."

[2] Not found.

[3] A copy is in the National Archives and Records Administration, RG 218, JCS Files, 3180 (28 Jan 64) Sec 1 IR 337.

3. (S) As reflected in reference 1c, present continuity planning by the Joint Chiefs of Staff provides the necessary flexibility to adapt to whatever relocation action the President may select in an emergency. However, there is no assurance that such relocation action will be initiated in sufficient time nor, if initiated in time, that it would ensure survival of the present NCA. Therefore, the Joint Chiefs of Staff believe that a plan should be developed to disperse designated successors to the NCA to existing facilities of the National Military Command System (NMCS) in the following manner:

a. Based on the established line of succession to the individual offices comprising the NCA, the following three groups of alternate NCA should be designated:

[3 paragraphs (20 lines of source text) not declassified]

b. The proposed alternate command groups have been kept small to improve their mobility. However, provision would be made for one or two individuals to accompany each member of the groups, if desired. For example, the Deputy Secretary of Defense has not been included in any of the groups in this concept in the event you desire that he accompany you.

c. According to the situation and Presidential desire, the groups of alternate NCA would relocate during a crisis escalation, one to each of the three alternate command centers of the NMCS. Command center communications would permit participation of the relocated groups in national deliberations.

[1 paragraph (8-1/2 lines of source text) not declassified]

4. (S) The Joint Chiefs of Staff believe that specific procedures should be established to execute this plan as a means of preventing all legal successors to the NCA, and their key advisors, from becoming casualties at the same time. Timely dispersal of designated persons in line of succession to the NCA to the alternate command centers of the NMCS is believed to be the best method for assuring that recognized NCA are available for direction of military operations. The persons designated by law as successors to the NCA should be briefed on the plan and made familiar with its procedures.

5. (U) The Joint Chiefs of Staff recommend that a memorandum substantially the same as that contained in the Appendix hereto,[4] which advocates the development of such a plan, be forwarded to the President, subject to the concurrence of the Secretary of State and the Director of the Office of Emergency Planning.

For the Joint Chiefs of Staff:
Earle G. Wheeler
Chairman
Joint Chiefs of Staff

---

[4] Not printed.

165. Memorandum From Spurgeon Keeny of the National Security Council Staff to the President's Special Assistant for Science and Technology (Hornig)[1]

Washington, January 4, 1967.

SUBJECT

ABM Deployment

The Administration is now considering a proposal to initiate in FY-68 the deployment of a "light" ABM defense of the United States. While there are many pros and cons to this complex question, I believe that on balance such a system is not only unnecessary at this time but, in fact, contrary to our net strategic interests.

The purpose of this "light" ABM system would be primarily to provide a high level of protection against any Chinese missile capability that would emerge in the 70s and to increase the survivability of our Minuteman force against a massive Soviet counterforce attack. It is not claimed that the system would be able to defend U.S. cities against a heavy, sophisticated Soviet missile attack.

My objection to the deployment of the proposed ABM system is not based on any difference with the DOD's evaluation of the system's technical capabilities. Although one cannot rule out the possibility of catastrophic failure of such a complex system, I know of no specific reason to question the conclusions that the proposed system is probably capable of providing effective defense against early Chinese ICBMs and of increasing the survivability of our Minuteman force. The DOD has accurately stated the limitations of such a system against a massive sophisticated Soviet attack. While I believe that the weight of evidence indicates that the Soviets are not undertaking a massive ABM deployment but only a rather pedestrian effort around Moscow, I consider the DOD's somewhat more cautious appraisal entirely reasonable in the circumstances. In any event, I am in full agreement with the DOD's conclusion that the appropriate U.S. response to a Soviet ABM deployment is an improvement of our penetration capabilities and not an ABM deployment.

Accepting then the stated limited objectives of the proposed system, I believe that it is by no means demonstrated that it is in fact necessary to initiate deployment of such a system in FY-68.

[1] Source: Johnson Library, National Security File, Agency File, Office of Science and Technology, Vol. 1 [1967], Box 42. Secret. Copies were sent to Rostow and Moyers. In an attached January 4 note to Rostow, Keeny noted that he prepared the memorandum to Hornig for his meeting with the President on the ABM problem at 5:30 p.m. that day. For Rostow's account of the meeting, see Document 166.

—*Protection against China.* I am not convinced that there is a real military case for deploying a system at this time against a future Chinese ICBM threat. While a limited ABM deployment would have an IOC of less than four years and could be fully deployed in six years, it is unlikely that the Chinese will have even a token ICBM capability before the mid-70s. If the Chinese seek to achieve an earlier direct nuclear threat to the United States, it will probably come in the form of short-range submarine-launched ballistic or aerodynamic missiles. Against this threat, the proposed "light" ABM deployment would be relatively ineffective since short-range ballistic or aerodynamic missiles could be directed against undefended targets on the coast or fly under the ABM defenses. More fundamentally, it is by no means clear that there is a military requirement for such a system even when the Chinese ICBM force comes into being. Our massive strategic forces provide us with a very high confidence capability to conduct a pre-emptive strike against a small force of soft ICBMs with relatively slow reaction times. Therefore, as a "blackmail" weapon against the U.S., such a Chinese force would appear to have little value and would in fact be an open invitation to a catastrophic disarming attack by this country against China. As a deterrent, such a Chinese force would also appear to have little value since the Chinese could not hope to use it without assuring the total destruction of China. We have pursued our policies in the past in the face of a tremendously larger Soviet deterrent force, and there does not appear to be any clear reason why we would not continue to do so in the future in the face of a very small early Chinese ICBM capability.

—*Protection of our Minuteman Force.* Although I believe there is no question that such a system would improve the survivability of Minuteman, it is by no means clear that there is any requirement to accomplish this on the proposed time scale. We are making a major investment in Poseidon and the upgrading of Minuteman to assure our penetration capabilities against the worst plausible Soviet missile and ABM threats through the mid-70s. The Soviet threat will in all likelihood not evolve this rapidly; and, even if it does, there will still be adequate time in the future to deploy defenses for our strategic forces. In this connection, it is by no means clear that the proposed system is in fact the most cost effective way to defend hard sites such as Minuteman. This question should be examined in detail as part of the broader study that is now under way to determine appropriate follow-on systems to Poseidon and Minuteman to maintain our strategic posture in the period after the mid-70s.

If the above were the only considerations, it might still be argued that the expenditure of $6 billion over the next five or six years would be a relatively small price to pay for the added insurance that such a system might give in the event that we have seriously misjudged

Chinese or Soviet capabilities or intentions. I believe, however, that a decision to deploy would probably have the following highly undesirable consequences that will be to our net disadvantage.

—*Soviet-U.S. Relations.* Despite our efforts to explain the limited objectives of our ABM deployment, the decision would very probably lead to a substantial escalation in Soviet strategic offensive and defensive armaments, which in turn would almost certainly escalate the level of our own forces. The latest NIE concludes that the future of the Soviet ABM deployment will in part depend on the Soviet reaction to our own strategic decisions.[2] Whatever the true nature of the present Soviet ABM deployment, I believe that a decision on our part to deploy an ABM system would assure that they will undertake an extensive ABM deployment. Moreover, this decision will put pressure on the Soviets to increase the level of their missile forces beyond whatever their present plans may be and to upgrade the penetration capability of their existing missile forces. This would in turn put pressure on us to increase our strategic forces and upgrade the capability of our ABM system. Even if such an arms race does not actually increase the immediate danger of war, it would certainly increase the tensions between the U.S. and the USSR. Although it is difficult to evaluate the impact of this development on internal Soviet affairs, the increasing demands of a major build-up in Soviet military expenditures will put increasing pressure on the present civilian Soviet leadership with the danger that there will be a trend back to Stalinist attitudes.

—*Western Europe.* The decision could have a very divisive effect on our relations with Western Europe. Despite our efforts to explain the limited purpose of our "light" deployment, it would probably prove very difficult to explain to Western Europeans why a similar deployment could not be helpful in protecting them from Soviet "blackmail," particularly since such a system might be technically quite effective against existing Soviet IRBMs targeted on Western Europe. If the Europeans should press us to assist them in developing their own ABM, there would appear to be real political problems in denying them this defense; and, despite any plans to the contrary, we would probably end up paying most of the bill. A more likely consequence, however, would be that the decision would feed the forces of neutralism in Western Europe to the detriment of NATO since it would be argued that Europe is now a defenseless pawn in an arms race in which they could not meaningfully participate.

—*Far East.* A decision of this magnitude based in large part on the Chinese threat would greatly enhance the image of Chinese military

---

[2] Document 146.

capabilities in the Far East. Despite our arguments that this will increase our flexibility in dealing with China, the net effect would probably be to increase substantially Chinese prestige with its neighbors. It would be extremely difficult to explain to Japan and India why they should not also have an ABM system to protect them from Chinese "blackmail," and there is little question that we would have to subsidize most, if not all, of the cost of such systems in these countries.

—U.S. Domestic Relations. Although it will be argued that any decision on this problem will remove it as a political issue, I believe that the proposed "light" defense will actually be a very poor solution from the point of view of domestic politics in that it will satisfy no one. On the liberal wing, the decision will be widely attacked as an unnecessary and dangerous expense further undercutting the prospects of the Great Society. On the conservative wing, the decision will be attacked as inadequate and as a devious device to avoid coming to grips with the real problem of providing real protection for the U.S. population against a Soviet attack. The majority of people, who are not really particularly interested in this problem anyway, will be presented with a spectacle of a major Administration decision which is attacked on all sides.

The effect of this decision on the plans for the Great Society may in fact be much greater than is now apparent. Although the estimated cost of $6 billion for the "light" defense (even if it in fact increases by a factor of two, as could easily be the case on the basis of past experience) would appear to be easily absorbed over the next six years, I believe that this is simply the first installment on a much larger system. I believe that the system at the proposed level is politically unviable and that it would be very difficult to prevent it from expanding over the next few years into the complete Nike-X defense system that the military really wants. It will be extremely difficult to explain to some parts of the country why they are not defended while other parts of the country are. Despite protestations as to the inherent limitations of such a system, there will be a major military-industrial lobby to explain the potential defense capabilities of an expanded system. It is estimated that the cost of such a system would be on the order of $20 billion, which again could easily increase by a factor of two. To this would have to be added the cost of a nationwide shelter program, an improved air defense program to balance the capabilities of the ABM system, and eventually radically improved strategic forces to compensate for the almost inevitable increases in Soviet strategic forces to compensate for our defensive effort.

—International Arms Control. The decision would come at a particularly unfortunate time from the point of view of arms control. There appear to be real prospects that in the next month or so we will come to agreement with the Soviet Union on a Non-Proliferation Treaty which is acceptable to our allies.[3] This treaty will be meaningless unless the major non-nuclear countries sign it. The fact that the United States and the Soviet Union concurrently undertake another major step in the escalation of nuclear armaments may well be seized upon by such countries as India and Japan as a reason for not signing the treaty. Beyond this, as the pace of the ABM development accelerates, I believe that a serious question will develop as to whether the Limited Test Ban Treaty[4] can survive since it will be argued with increasing vehemence that many of the problems associated with the effectiveness of such a system cannot be fully answered without further atmospheric testing.

In view of the above considerations, I recommend that—

1. We should *not* make a formal decision to deploy a "light" ABM defense in connection with the FY-68 budget.

2. We should state in the budget message that the subject is under continuing study and that, if a positive decision to deploy is reached, a supplemental request will be submitted.

3. We should encourage a continued Congressional and public discussion of this entire issue.

4. We should continue an intensive effort to involve the Soviets in serious discussions of this issue—with the objective of clarifying the nature of their present ABM system and obtaining agreement to freeze further deployment of ABMs for an agreed period of time.

---

[3] Documentation on the negotiations leading to this multilateral treaty, which was signed by several nations on July 1, 1968, is in *Foreign Relations, 1964–1968*, volume XI.

[4] Entered into force on October 10, 1963. (14 UST 1313)

166.   Record of Meeting With President Johnson[1]

Washington, January 4, 1967.

PRESENT

Secretary McNamara	The Vice President
Gen. Wheeler	John Foster
Gen. Harold K. Johnson	Secretary Harold Brown
Adm. David McDonald	Secretary Stanley Resor
Gen. John McConnell	Lt. Gen. Harold Mangrum
Cyrus Vance	Dr. Donald Hornig
Gen. Alfred Gruenther	Dr. George Kistiakowsky
Dr. James R. Killian	Mr. Robert Kintner
Dr. Jerome Wiesner	Mr. Bill Moyers
Herbert F. York	Mr. Walt Rostow

SUBJECT

ABM's

The President thanked those who had come from out of town for attending, and asked Secy. McNamara to pose the issue.

Secy. McNamara stated, in accordance with a draft paper which had been distributed,[2] that we faced essentially this choice with respect to an ABM system:

—do nothing;
—set up a limited so-called "thin" system with a capability: to protect against Chicom missiles; accidentally launched missiles; nuclear blackmail; and to furnish additional protection for our Minuteman;
—install a system capable of protecting our population against heavy sophisticated Soviet attack.

He stated that he would now solicit the views of the JCS, the Science Advisors to the President, and others.

He turned to Gen. Wheeler, who spoke for the JCS. Gen. Wheeler proposed, as the JCS had in the Austin meeting with the President,[3] that we install a Nike-X system on a scale capable of protecting 25 major population centers. This would provide a damage-limiting capability; introduce uncertainties about Soviet capabilities which would make them more cautious at a time of crisis; stabilize the nuclear balance; demonstrate that the U.S. was not first-strike minded; and deny the Soviet Union a first-strike capability.

---

[1] Source: Johnson Library, National Security File, Memos to the President, Walt Rostow, January 1–14, 1967, Vol. 18. Top Secret; Sensitive. Drafted by Rostow on January 6.

[2] Not found.

[3] See Documents 150 and 151.

The proposed Nike-X deployment could not cope with all attacks upon us, but it would provide substantial population protection. It would also provide the four benefits cited for the limited "thin" system.

In short, the JCS reaffirmed its previous position of support for Nike-X deployment to protect 25 population centers.

The views of the Science Advisors were then solicited by seniority, beginning with Dr. Killian.

Dr. Killian stated that he had addressed himself to this important matter, putting political considerations aside, although he was aware that they were extremely important. He was not persuaded about the need for the minimum first-step in the form of a limited system. Beyond the first step an ABM system would be "extremely dangerous." If politics required the first step, the thin system of Secy. McNamara was the most sensible. He hoped it would not be necessary. He recognized that it might, however, be an advantage to have committed ourselves to the first step in negotiating with the Soviet Union.

Dr. Kistiakowsky stated the issue was of very great importance. He agreed completely with the arguments of those who were against massive deployment of an ABM. The argument was complex, but in essence it was this: our system of deterrence is designed now to prevent a nuclear war. The mounting of an ABM system constitutes preparation for nuclear war. It would lead to a radical acceleration of the arms race, in which "all hope would be lost" for arms control agreements.

He felt the same arguments applied to a limited "first step." The international effects would be the same; but they would be stretched out over time. The pressure for expansion of the system would be great and irresistible.

Moreover, he did not believe it would even be effective against Chicom nuclear blackmail. They would prove ingenious and could turn, for example, to submarine-launched delivery systems, or to a dirty bomb exploded, say, 50 miles off shore.

He also doubted that the thin system was the optimum for protecting Minuteman against Soviet attack.

Therefore, he recommended against deployment while we undertook a major diplomatic effort to persuade the Soviet Union to stand down. Conceivably, we might put into the budget certain long lead time items for an ABM system to increase our bargaining leverage.

Dr. Wiesner stated that he supported the arguments presented by his two predecessors. An ABM system cannot buy defense against Soviet attack. He stated that U.S. and Soviet decisions to deploy ABM's would lead to greater casualties in a nuclear war, not less. There is a built-in tendency to overbuild in compensation for the erection of a defensive system. The history of Soviet anti-aircraft in relation to the expansion of our own Strategic Air Command illustrates this tendency. It is inherent in an offensive-defensive race.

With respect to Communist China, there is no need for an ABM system. We can rely on normal deterrence. [6 lines of source text not declassified]

The Chinese already have missile-carrying submarines, and our ABM's would provide no protection against them.

Finally, Dr. Wiesner said that the introduction of an ABM race would lead to great uncertainty and destabilize the arms race. We shall certainly overbuild in response to the Soviet ABM's. He noted that he had spent a great deal of his mature life working on defensive systems: first, anti-aircraft, than ABM's. He is now convinced that in the game of nuclear deterrence, defense doesn't work. The offense will always overcome. He noted the irony of his present position in opposition to the JCS since, at an earlier time, the JCS had strongly opposed him when he was supporting an air defense system. (General Wheeler noted that it was a different JCS.)

Dr. Hornig concurred with what had been said by his predecessors. He noted the issue had been reviewed by three Science Advisory panels. He concluded that it was not feasible to have an effective defense against missiles. The facts were that the Soviet Union had taken steps to deploy a limited system around Moscow. It was a poor system and penetrable. His own people believe the second system now being deployed in the Soviet Union is not ABM but air defense. Against this background and the problems of escalation inherent in an ABM deployment, he believed it unwise to take the major step recommended by the JCS.

As for a thin system, he believed that the balance vis-à-vis the Chinese was such that we did not require an ABM system for that purpose; although a thin system could help against an accidentally launched missile; against an Nth country with nuclear capability stirring up trouble; and it could provide some additional protection to our Minuteman.

If it were believed that it would help in our negotiations with the USSR for an ABM-missile freeze, he would tend to support a limited system. He would, however, proceed slower than the thin system proposed by Secy. McNamara until we had a definitive response from the Soviet Union.

Gen. Gruenther stated that he subscribed to the limited thin system outlined by Secy. McNamara. He would support this light deployment for the four purposes sketched by the Secretary.

He wished to underline the disagreement in the intelligence community about the functions of the Tallinn system; all hands did not agree that it was strictly anti-aircraft. He said that we should not put excessive hopes in diplomatic negotiations on this question. In saying that, he wanted it understood that he believed in arms control as the right solution to the security problem in a nuclear age; he was a member of Mr. John McCloy's advisory committee to ACDA. He was, simply, not optimistic about negotiating prospects.

Dr. York, former Director of Research and Engineering in the Department of Defense, stated his agreement with the science advisors. He supported a policy of: "Let's do nothing now." He said the case against full-scale deployment of Nike-X had been understated. The workings of the system could lead to an increase in casualties in a nuclear war. The most that might be said is that casualties might be cut.

What is certain, he said, is that the arms race would accelerate, and the net result would be, in the future, as in the past, that more American lives would be at risk each year. If the installation of our defensive system were the last move in the arms race, then, of course, less lives would be at risk. But that would not be the last move, and in the end, more U.S. lives would be in jeopardy.

As for the Soviet system, in his judgment, it is so ineffective that we can afford to defer a decision. He repeated: we should do nothing at this time.

We have a very vigorous R&D effort going forward. It creates a better potential ABM system each year. We should maintain that vigorous effort.

The President then asked Secy. McNamara to summarize. He said our choices are:

1. Do nothing.
2. The thin system with its four limited functions. It was estimated to cost $4.2 billion. We must count on the actual cost being 25 to 50% higher than that. It would cost $250 million a year to operate.
3. Installing Nike-X to protect the population in substantial numbers in 25 cities. This system is now estimated to cost $13 billion to build. We must expand that realistically to $20 billion. In fact, his estimate is that it would cost $40 billion in 10 years.

The argument against deployment was that the Soviet Union must build a system which will [less than 1 line of source text not declassified] and have enough striking power left to inflict such casualties on the U.S. that we would not strike the Soviet Union in the first place. An ABM system is not capable of reducing U.S. casualties to the point where the Soviet Union would not be able to carry out its policy in this matter.

The counter-argument is that we could try and protect our population to some degree. His view is that the effort to protect would lead to an offensive increase in the Soviet Union which would more than offset our initial effort to protect our population.

As for the limited thin system, it might play some role in pushing the Soviet Union into negotiations, but we could not guarantee that. It offered some protection against a Chicom attack. He said that he would be more concerned than he now is, with our policy of bombing North Vietnam, if the Chicoms had ICBM's. A thin system could protect us against the kind of missile accident that, statistically, might happen with the passage of time and the multiplication of missiles. He referred to the Mace incident of January 4.[4] It might also provide some protection against nuclear blackmail.

He felt the decision about a limited thin system was "marginal."

As for the case for doing nothing, the President had heard the pros and cons.

The President asked Secy. McNamara for his recommendation. He said he would prefer to withhold judgment now and present his view to the President later.[5]

The President then summarized: the Chiefs wish to go all the way; the scientists say No; but if we go we should go with a thin system because it might help our negotiations with the Soviet Union.

Secy. McNamara said it was his judgment that it would help; that the argument has some merit. There has been some evidence in the past 3–4 weeks. But the ABM problem is extremely difficult: once you start you are pregnant. It will be virtually impossible to stop.

The President then asked for a summary of intelligence on the Soviet system.

Secy. McNamara, asking Gen. Wheeler to correct him if he disagreed, stated that the assessment of Nov. 17, 1966, based on July information, showed disagreement in the intelligence community.[6] The majority agreed that a limited ABM system was being deployed around Moscow which was penetrable by heavy U.S. attack or through Polaris missiles. In addition, a wide-scale system was being deployed which might contain as many as 240 missiles by 1971. There was some evidence that this so-called Tallinn system was solely designed against aircraft; but others believed it was an ABM system, or dual purpose. In December we acquired new evidence that it is more probably anti-aircraft, since some units are not linked to the radar which is required to track missiles.[7]

---

[4] Reference is to an unarmed Mace missile launched from Eglin Base, Florida, on January 4, which strayed over the western tip of Cuba and landed in the Caribbean Sea after its destruction system failed and a U.S. jet fighter was unable to shoot it down.

[5] See Document 167.

[6] See Document 146.

[7] Not further identified.

Secy. McNamara concluded by stating that, in his view, it made no difference. No defensive system could be effective. He recalled that when he became Secretary of Defense he first investigated the ability of SAC to penetrate the Soviet Union. To his surprise he found that the best estimates indicated that [*1-1/2 lines of source text not declassified*]. The Soviet Union has spent 2-1/2 times as much as the U.S. on defense and has not gotten any serious protection for those expenditures. The Soviets have an irrational bias towards defensive systems. Their present deployments around Moscow are not militarily justifiable, but represent an instinctive, almost theological desire to protect Moscow as the center of Russian life.

The President again thanked those present. He stated he would take their views into account. He was particularly grateful for those outside the government who again showed their willingness to serve. When he came to make his decision he would do so with greater confidence because they had come. He had talked with others about this matter, including General Eisenhower.[8]

W.W. Rostow[9]

---

[8] In a telephone conversation with Senator Everett Dirksen shortly after this meeting, President Johnson said that Eisenhower had told him to get advice on the ABM issue from the Joint Chiefs, experienced military people like General Gruenther, former Presidential science advisers, and former Presidents. President Johnson also offered this summary of the meeting: "The net of it is all the Joint Chiefs, they say you've got to go all the way and the quicker the better and forty billion. All the scientists say you ought not to do anything." (Johnson Library, Recordings and Transcripts, Recording of Telephone Conversation Between President Johnson and Senator Dirksen, January 4, 1967, 7:54 p.m., Tape F67.01, Side A; transcript prepared in the Office of the Historian specifically for this *Foreign Relations* volume)

[9] Printed from a copy that bears this typed signature.

---

167.   Editorial Note

In the evening of January 4, 1967, Secretary McNamara telephoned the President. After a brief discussion of details on strategic stockpile sales in the defense budget, the two talked extensively about the ABM problem. When the President asked McNamara what he thought of the meeting with the Joint Chiefs and the former science advisers (see Document 166), McNamara replied:

"Well, the only reason I didn't give a recommendation when you asked for it, I didn't want them to hear what I say in view of you might decide differently . . . I still favor doing nothing as we initially recommended three or four weeks ago, but it would be a helluva political crisis if you did nothing. The forces pushing you to do something are very, very strong indeed. But I myself agree fully with Killian and the science advisers. I don't think we'll buy anything worth going ahead. But if we're to go ahead, then I think the best thing to do is the 'thin' system."

McNamara also mentioned that the President could ask for the views of the contractors who would profit from an ABM deployment. He said that he met with these high-level business executives about 2 weeks earlier, and "without qualifications" they were all opposed to an ABM system against the Soviet Union. When the President asked who these businessmen were, he gave their names. McNamara continued that these contractors were willing to support fully the "thin" system, however, and had worked out its technical capabilities, time schedule, amount of money required, and the protection it would provide against China and for the U.S. offensive systems.

President Johnson said that McNamara seemed to be saying that the full ABM system was "not worth the price," and McNamara replied, "To be absolutely honest with you, Mr. President, I don't." He believed, however, that Congress would "absolutely crucify him and through me you" if he testified against it, as he was prepared to do. But, McNamara continued, "I feel it's wrong."

The two discussed the difficulty in advocating a "thin" system, which would be a first step, and according to McNamara the Joint Chiefs would go along with a "thin" system on these terms. But the administration might be pushed, as McNamara put it, toward a heavy system costing $20 or $40 billion "that won't buy a damn thing." They also discussed proposing the "thin" system as a "contingency" and going to a full system if an agreement limiting ABMs could not be negotiated with the Soviet Union, but McNamara did not think much of this strategy.

President Johnson then asked, what if the administration started on a "thin" system and then got an agreement with the Soviet Union? "Oh, oh, yes, oh, yes, yes, yes, there's a real possibility of that, Mr. President," McNamara responded. He went on to summarize the Thompson–Dobrynin talks on ABM systems, and noted that he believed that the Soviets were willing to talk on the issue. Dobrynin had very recently given Thompson "a fair amount of information," from which McNamara theorized that the Soviets' ABM system was to protect Moscow "only as a symbol of all Russia, and that this Tallinn system probably is not an ABM system." Their ABM system might be extended "to Leningrad, Kiev, and a few other major centers," but the Soviets did not intend it to be "a very widespread deployment." Thus "it might be fairly simple to negotiate a limitation with them if we were willing to limit to something like Moscow. So I think there is a real possibility here of fruitful discussions."

At the end of their conversation, the President remarked, "So what it adds up to is you're against contingencies and really if you were in my position, you'd do nothing." "I guess, Mr. President," McNamara replied, "what I mean to say is that I'd go down fighting, and I'm damn sure I'd go down. [He laughs.] A lot easier for me to say." The President interjected, "Do you think that's wiser for us to do?" McNamara responded, "Well, I don't know, I don't know;" and he added that if the decision was to do nothing, the administration would have to wage "a tremendous publicity campaign" with editors, scientists, and opinion leaders to win public support.

President Johnson then turned to the budget. He said that Senator Russell wanted to see him before he closed it. McNamara urged him to see Russell before the opening of the next session of Congress. Russell, he warned, "is just going to tear us apart this year. He will probably want to tell you that we ought to go all the way on nuclear power for service ships and increase the bombing of North Vietnam and just a lot of other things. We ought to push ahead on a manned bomber and push ahead on the ABM and push ahead on new air defense and so on."

When the President asked whether the Joint Chiefs of Staff were "reconciled" to the budget, McNamara responded affirmatively, adding that "there's no great emotional feeling that they ought to have more." The Chiefs had had "a good hearing" and the decisions "were not bad." But the problem was that these were "emotional issues," and when the Chiefs testified before Congress, they would be told, "surely, you're a man and not a mouse," and they would like to add these programs to the defense budget. Put in these terms, the Chiefs would say "yes." (Johnson Library, Recordings and Transcripts, Recording of Telephone Conversation Between President Johnson and Secretary McNamara, January 4, 1967, 6:40 p.m., Tape F67.01, Side A; transcript prepared in the Office of the Historian specifically for this *Foreign Relations* volume)

168. Memorandum From the Assistant Secretary of Defense for Administration (Horwitz) to the Deputy Secretary of Defense (Vance)[1]

Washington, January 5, 1967.

SUBJECT

Planning for Improving Survivability of the National Command Authorities (NCA)

The Joint Chiefs of Staff have recommended that the President be asked to approve development of a plan to improve survivability of the National Command Authorities (Tab "B")[2] based on a concept of pre-designation of the composition of Alternate NCA Groups, to include legal successors to the Presidency in each Group. The concept envisions three Alternate NCA Groups displacing to the three NMCC Alternates upon direction of the President under conditions of crises escalation. The purpose of the displacement is to insure that, in the event of general war, at least one Alternate NCA Group might survive to carry on the affairs of the nation. The JCS have suggested the following composition of the Alternate NCA Group, based on established lines of succession to the individual offices comprising the NCA:

[3 lists (5 lines of source text in each list) not declassified]

As you may recall, we studied the problem of DoD command and control support to the President in some depth in 1964,[3] and, in doing so, we examined possible courses of action the President might take in respect to Alternate Decision Groups during intense crises or general war.

Although our study pointed out there might be some advantages to pre-designation and pre-location of Alternate Decision Groups that included legal successors to the Presidency, the nature of the problem would undoubtedly prevent such an arrangement. That is, many of those in the line of succession are the ones that the President will need most to assist him in coping with the situation. Further, those of the legal successors most suited to assume the Presidential role of the Commander-in-Chief are the very men the President will want most with him, and those of the legal successors most available for relocation are the men who would be least qualified to face the immediate responsibilities to which they succeeded.[4]

---

[1] Source: Washington National Records Center, OSD Files: FRC 330 72 A 2468, 381 Cont of Govt Ops 1967. Secret.

[2] JCSM–812–66, Document 164.

[3] The conclusions of this study are printed as Document 86.

[4] In the margin next to this sentence, Vance wrote: "I agree."

Our study stated that " . . . the major decisions relating to utilization of an Alternate Decision Group that does not include the President
will be made by the President at the time of crisis. The decisions will
name the leader of the group, determine its composition, and select a
time or condition for relocation. These are problems that are particularly sensitive to the desires of a particular President, to the relationships
he has established with his Cabinet and with other personal advisors,
and to the estimate of the situation he develops at the time the groups
might be employed."

In our opinion this is a sound and realistic appraisal of the problem
of pre-designation of Alternate Decision Groups that include
Presidential successors, since the selection of an Alternate Decision
Group is essentially a political matter resting solely with the President
and based on conditions existing at the time. Accordingly, we recommend that you not approach the President on this matter.

We have prepared a memo for your signature (Tab "A")[5] that
acknowledges the receipt of the JCS proposal, noting that due consideration will be given to their suggestions along with other emergency
planning actions. This type of response will satisfy administratively the
recommendations of the JCS.

Recommend you sign Tab "A."

Solis Horwitz

---

[5] The attached memorandum to the Chairman of the JCS, dated January 7, which
Vance signed, acknowledged receipt of JCSM–812–66 and indicated that the suggestions
would "be given due consideration along with other emergency planning actions."

169. Special National Intelligence Estimate[1]

SNIE 11–10–67   Washington, February 14, 1967.
TCS 6228–67

US INTELLIGENCE CAPABILITIES TO MONITOR CERTAIN LIMITATIONS ON SOVIET STRATEGIC WEAPONS PROGRAMS

The Problem

To estimate the capabilities of US intelligence to monitor unilaterally limitations on certain Soviet strategic capabilities over the next five years or so.

Note

The Intelligence Community has been asked to assess its ability to monitor unilaterally limitations on the further deployment and improvement of certain Soviet strategic offensive and defensive weapon systems, and Soviet capabilities for evading the provisions of such limitations.

For the purposes of this assessment the following limitations are assumed to be included in the agreement:

a. *ABMs and SAMs which may have a significant ABM capability.* There would be a prohibition against initiation of construction of new sites, additional launchers at present sites, mobile launchers, and new associated radars. It is also assumed that the construction of additional long-range surveillance radars (Hen House, Dog House, or other comparable types) would be prohibited. Research, development, and testing would not be precluded.

b. *Fixed, land-based strategic missiles (ICBMs, IRBMs, MRBMs).* There would be a prohibition against any additional deployment, hard or soft, beyond those sites now complete or under construction. Research, development, and testing would not be precluded.

c. *Missile-launching submarines and surface ships.* There would be a prohibition against any construction of new ballistic or cruise missile submarines. Submarines now under construction could be completed. There would be a total prohibition against the construction or modification of surface ships to launch strategic missiles. Some Soviet surface

---

[1] Source: Johnson Library, National Security File, National Intelligence Estimates, 11–67—USSR, Box 4. Top Secret; Ruff; Trine; Zarf. Prepared in the Central Intelligence Agency and concurred in by the U.S. Intelligence Board. A title page and table of contents are not printed.

ships are now equipped with surface-to-surface cruise missiles which could conceivably be used for strategic attack purposes; such missiles are not considered in this estimate, however.

d. *Land-mobile ICBMs, IRBMs, MRBMs.* A total prohibition would be imposed on the introduction of such systems.

e. *Qualitative changes.* With regard to qualitative changes, flight testing of MRVs, MIRVs, and certain other penetration aids would be prohibited. Except as specified in subparagraph (a) above, no limit would be placed on other changes in missile characteristics.

Two general supporting provisions will also be considered for inclusion in any broad agreement:

a. *A general provision against radically new types of strategic systems.* The effort here would be to rule out unusual possibilities not foreseen and discussed during the negotiations. Such possibilities would not be enumerated, but the provision would reflect the intention of both countries to avoid steps which could damage the basic agreement.

b. *Exchange of information on strategic forces.* From our own standpoint, we could not rely on such information, but it could be of some assistance. The stated purpose would be to preclude the chance that the agreement might be violated through misunderstanding.

In our assessment, we do not consider the effect which such an agreement would have on specific US collection requirements and mechanisms; nor do we estimate the likelihood that the Soviets will develop or deploy any of the weapon systems under consideration.

Conclusions

A. In the continued absence of a large-scale Soviet program of deception and concealment we believe that we would almost certainly detect any extensive new deployment in strategic forces, although the Soviets could probably effect small-scale increases without our knowledge. The timing of detection and identification would vary with the nature and size of the program. We probably would identify a land-mobile offensive system, for example, but perhaps only after it had become operational in substantial numbers.

B. We would almost certainly detect any large-scale test program, but we could not always expect to assess accurately the test objectives or even the precise nature of the system being tested. Our capabilities are generally better in the case of offensive than of defensive weapons. We believe, for example, that we could detect and identify Soviet testing of multiple, independently-targeted reentry vehicles (MIRVs); we could probably also detect test activity associated with an ABM system, but are not confident that we could identify it as such before it became operational.

C. Our capabilities for detecting qualitative improvements in the deployed forces are better in the case of defensive weapons than offensive ones. Our chances of determining whether a SAM system had been provided with significant ABM capabilities are at present about even, but we think that they will improve. On the other hand, we see no prospect of determining whether MIRVs (if developed) or other significant improvements had been incorporated in deployed offensive missiles.

D. Soviet employment of deception and concealment on a large-scale would, of course, degrade our capabilities. The principal effect would be that of delay. Thus, while we still believe that substantial new deployment would almost certainly be detected, detection would come later in the program, perhaps not until after significant deployment had occurred. Some of the deception and concealment measures which the Soviets could employ would probably be recognizable as such, but their purpose might not be readily apparent. Additionally, we assume that the Soviets will not interfere actively with US collection systems.

E. Factors affecting intelligence collection will vary over the period of this estimate but intelligence is not expected to be able to guarantee that the Soviets have not violated one or more provisions of the agreement under consideration.

F. Finally, we wish to note that the demonstration of violations of the arms control agreement under consideration would almost certainly involve the use and possibly the compromise of very costly and highly sophisticated intelligence collection methods.

Discussion

I. US Monitoring Capabilities

1. The basic problems for intelligence, as it relates to verification of a weapons limitation agreement, are to collect information to interpret it correctly, and to satisfy US decision-makers of the validity of those interpretations in time for them to take appropriate action. No single source of information can be exclusively relied upon for these purposes, although the unique capabilities of overhead photography and signal intelligence will inevitably make them essential sources. Regardless of sources, however, intelligence cannot be expected to guarantee that the Soviets have not violated one or more provisions of the agreement under consideration. In general, our confidence in detecting and identifying violations will increase in proportion to the extent of deployment or testing involved.

2. We have generally been successful in identifying new programs during the test phase and, except for defensive systems, test data has

been an important source of information on characteristics. It should be remembered, however, that new strategic weapon systems will have been under development for several years before they are detected in the test phase. Our collection capabilities are lower with respect to production; we have identified many plants involved in weapons production, but have acquired little evidence on production rates. In regard to deployment, however, we have a high degree of confidence in our estimates of current order-of-battle for Soviet strategic forces; the physical magnitude of most of these programs and of their supporting elements has made them readily identifiable.

3. Over the period of this estimate, we believe that our capabilities to collect detailed information about Soviet strategic programs will increase, but at the same time, qualitative improvements in some Soviet weapon systems will probably be difficult to detect and evaluate. During the period of this estimate, we believe that the Soviets could probably effect minor increases in various elements of their strategic forces without our knowledge, but that any large-scale net deployment in any of these elements almost certainly would be detected—in some cases early in the program, in others not until later.

4. In the following discussion, we will attempt to quantify the degree of confidence which we have in our ability to detect further deployment or improvements to certain specific Soviet strategic weapon systems under most normal circumstances. We reserve to a later section our consideration of Soviet capabilities to evade detection through deception, concealment, or interference.

[Here follow Part II: "Strategic Weapons Deployment" (pages 8–15); Part III: "Qualitative Improvements to Strategic Weapon Systems" (pages 16–19); Part IV: "Soviet Capabilities for Concealment and Deception" (pages 20–25); Part V: "Problems of Demonstrating a Violation" (pages 25 ff.); and a 7-page Annex.]

170. Memorandum From the President's Special Assistant for Science and Technology (Hornig) to President Johnson[1]

Washington, February 14, 1967, 3:30 p.m.

SUBJECT

Scientists' Petition on Chemical and Biological Weapons

This morning (11:00 a.m.) Mr. Adrian Fisher, Deputy Director of ACDA, and I received on your behalf the attached petition and transmittal letter,[2] opposing any actions weakening the present prohibitions and restraints on the use of chemical and biological weapons and specifically criticizing the U.S. for the use in Vietnam of "non-lethal" anti-personnel chemical weapons and anti-crop herbicides.

The petition has been signed by over 5,000 scientists and physicians, including 127 members of the National Academy of Sciences. I was informed that the group would discuss the petition with the press at 2:00 p.m. today.[3]

Specifically, the petition urges you to:

—Institute a White House study of government policy regarding CB weapons.
—Order an end to the employment of anti-personnel and anti-crop chemical weapons in Vietnam.
—Declare the intention of the United States to refrain from initiating the use of chemical and biological weapons.

The covering letter commends the United States for its recent support of the UN General Assembly Resolution calling on all States to observe the principles and objectives of the Geneva Protocol[4] and recommends that the United States should now accede to the Geneva Protocol of 1925.

Mr. Fisher and I had a very good discussion with the scientists who delivered the petition. The group has clearly given this problem a great deal of responsible thought. They are seriously concerned about the broader implications of the problem, and this is not simply a disguised criticism of the Administration's policy in Vietnam.

---

[1] Source: Johnson Library, National Security File, Subject File, Warfare, Chemical and Biological, Box 51. Secret. A copy was sent to Rostow.

[2] Neither the petition nor the transmittal letter has been found, but the petition is extensively summarized in *The New York Times*, February 15, 1967, pp. 1, 16.

[3] The scientists' press conference was reported ibid.

[4] See footnote 2, Document 154.

In our initial reaction, I recommend that we simply state we are studying the petition and that I acknowledge the letter on your behalf along these same lines.

As a follow up, I would recommend that at an early press conference in response to a question on the petition, you make a statement clearly stating that we have a "no first use" policy with regard to chemical and biological warfare, with the exception of riot gases and herbicides. Although this would not directly respond to all the points in the petition or transmittal letter, it would deal directly with the most important general question. As you recall, I suggested such a statement in a memo to you (copy attached)[5] setting forth the concern of your Science Advisory Committee on the general problem of biological warfare. Although Secretaries McNamara and Katzenbach both agreed with the proposed statement, McNamara preferred not to push the matter at that time in the face of JCS objections unless there were a clear and urgent reason for doing so. If you are interested, I believe it would be possible to clear such a statement within the government, particularly if the statement were a low-key reiteration and clarification of the position we have already taken in supporting the UN resolution.

Donald Hornig

1. Hornig to acknowledge petition, stating the matter under study.

2. Hornig to clear statement on "no first use" of chemical and biological weapons with McNamara and Katzenbach.[6]

---

[5] Document 154.

[6] Neither of these options was approved or disapproved or marked to "Discuss."

171.   Memorandum From the President's Special Assistant (Rostow) to President Johnson[1]

Washington, February 18, 1967, 9 a.m.

Mr. President:

Herewith the records in our minutes of meetings of the 303 Committee (and its predecessor group, 5412 Committee) which refer to CIA connection with support for youth and student groups. The first such reference is 25 February 1959; the last is 3 December 1964.[2]

Those present at the meetings are noted.

You should know that the basic work of the 303 Committee is to examine new programs; although, in the period I have been here, I have asked for reexamination of certain programs when current issues arose.

Clark Clifford's committee may be more deeply engaged in studying the whole of the CIA program; although I am not sure about this.

W.W. Rostow[3]

Attachment

Washington, February 14, 1967.

Chronology of Briefings of 303 Committee on
Youth and Student Activities

a. 25 February 1959 Minutes

"The DCI pointed out to the Group that there are a number of Agency programs under way which began before the approval of NSC 5412/2 and thus the establishment of the Special Group.

---

[1] Source: Johnson Library, National Security File, Intelligence File, 303 Committee, Box 2. Secret; Eyes Only.

[2] An attached February 23 memorandum from Bromley Smith to Secretary of Defense McNamara notes that the enclosed chronology "was referred to by the President at the luncheon meeting yesterday." Smith was apparently referring to the weekly White House luncheon attended on February 22 by the President, Secretaries Rusk and McNamara, General Taylor, General Wheeler, Bromley Smith, and George Christian. (Ibid., President's Daily Diary) In his memorandum Smith asked McNamara to return the chronology, which McNamara did along with Smith's memorandum on which he wrote: "2/24 to Mr. Bromley Smith. Thanks, RMcN."

[3] Printed from a copy that bears this typed signature.

Members present were: Christian Herter, Gordon Gray, Mr. Irwin, Allen Dulles, Richard Bissell

b. 4 March 1959 Minutes

"The DCI showed the Group the summary of actions approved by it since its inception. Mr. Dulles repeated what he had said at last week's meeting to the effect that this summary represents only the individual actions taken by the Special Group and that some of them have since been incorporated in continuing CIA programs." (We do have the summary referred to here; it does not include [*less than 1 line of source text not declassified*].)

Members present were: Christian Herter, Gordon Gray, Mr. Irwin, Allen Dulles

c. 14 February 1961 Minutes

"Mr. Dulles, assisted by Mr. Bissell, then summarized for the benefit of the new members of the Special Group the specific actions taken by the predecessor group during the past year, and also a list of significant projects which antedate the beginning of 1960 and which it is planned to continue. (We do have the list mentioned; [*less than 1 line of source text not declassified*].)

Members present were: Messrs. McNamara, Gilpatric, Bowles, Bundy, Dulles, Gen. Cabell, Bissell

d. 24 August 1961 Paper read by the Special Group reviewing CA Operations

"*Youth and Student Organizations.* A program designed to oppose the international communist fronts in the youth and student field, the World Federation of Democratic Youth (WFDY) and the International Union of Students (IUS). To this end, CIA supports and works through the International Student Conference, Coordinating Secretariat of National Unions of Students, U.S. National Student Association, World Assembly of Youth, Young Adult Council, World University Service and the International Union of Socialist Youth, to preserve youth movements from communist leadership and to gain support of youth organizations from communist leadership and to gain support of youth organizations and potential political leaders for Western causes."

Members present at 31 August 1961 meeting were: General Taylor, Mr. Johnson, Mr. Dulles, General Lansdale

e. 12 December 1963 Minutes

"Mr. McCone stated that he agreed, and in addition to the continuing reviews made inside CIA and with the State Department, he had reviewed all of the covert action programs twice with higher authority. Mr. Alexis Johnson also affirmed that constant reviewing was being done in the Department of State and that he was satisfied with the importance and necessity of the covert action activities currently undertaken by CIA." (We have the briefing outline used by the DDP on covert political action and PM projects. Mr. Meyer covered "all other covert action" but no outline is available. It is likely that he covered Youth and Student activities.)

Members present were: Mr. Bundy, Mr. Johnson, Mr. Gilpatric, and Mr. McCone. Present from Bureau of the Budget were Mr. Gordon, Mr. Staats, Mr. Hansen and Mr. Amory. Present from CIA were Mr. Helms, Mr. Meyer, [*2 names not declassified*]

f. 30 October 1964 Minutes[4]

[*1 paragraph (15 lines of source text) not declassified*]

Members present were: Mr. Bundy, Ambassador Thompson, Mr. Vance, Mr. McCone and Mr. Meyer

g. 3 December 1964 Minutes

"*World Youth Festival*—The CIA paper entitled, 'Program of Covert Counteraction against the 9th World Youth Festival, Algiers, August 1965,'[5] was approved promptly. Mr. McCone noted that the site of this event would produce more difficulties than those encountered in the relatively friendlier areas of Helsinki and Vienna. Mr. Bundy observed that he was personally acquainted with the considerable educative impact on young Americans participating in this type of confrontation with a Communist organization, a useful by-product to an important effort." (The paper referred to does not detail the instruments available to CIA to carry out the covert action. It implies the use of democratic youth and student organizations.)

Members present were: Mr. Bundy, Ambassador Thompson, Mr. McNaughton, and Mr. McCone

[Here follow paragraphs d. and e. of Document 134.]

---

[4] See Document 58.
[5] Dated November 20, 1964; filed with December 3, 1964, minutes of 303 Committee. (Department of State, INR/IL Historical Files)

172. Memorandum to Holders of SNIE 11–10–67[1]

TCS 6232–67   Washington, March 2, 1967.

US INTELLIGENCE CAPABILITIES TO MONITOR CERTAIN
LIMITATIONS ON SOVIET STRATEGIC WEAPONS PROGRAMS

1. This Memorandum to Holders is prompted by a difference between the judgment made in SNIE 11–10–67, "US Intelligence Capabilities to Monitor Certain Limitations on Soviet Strategic Weapons Programs," dated 14 February 1967, (Top Secret Ruff Trine Zarf Limited Distribution), and previous estimates on our capability to detect Soviet testing of multiple orbit bombardment system (MOBS). Paragraph 27 of SNIE 11–10–67 states, "the similarity between flight testing of a MOBS and the orbiting of certain types of satellites would make identification of such testing virtually impossible, [1 line of source text not declassified]."

2. A review of that judgment indicates that paragraph 27 of SNIE 11–10–67 should be changed to read as follows:

27. Fractional orbit and depressed trajectory delivery systems (FOBS and DICBMs) can be identified as such during testing. [4 lines of source text not declassified] we believe that multiple orbit testing of a MOBS would be identifiable. [2 lines of source text not declassified] Determining the extent of retrofit of MIRVs, FOBS, DICBMs, and MOBS into existing, deployed missile sites would be virtually impossible.

3. In addition, column II, item 7 of paragraph B.2. of the Annex to SNIE 11–10–67 should be changed to read as follows:

Probably during full system testing, [1-1/2 lines of source text not declassified].

---

[1] Source: Johnson Library, National Security File, National Intelligence Estimates, 11–67—USSR, Box 4. Top Secret; Ruff; Trine; Zarf. SNIE 11–10–67 is Document 169.

173.   Editorial Note

In response to the recommendation of Donald Hornig for a Presidential statement affirming a "no first use" policy with regard to chemical and biological warfare (see Document 154), President Johnson requested that Walt Rostow investigate the possibility of such a statement. Spurgeon Keeny drafted a specific statement for Rostow to forward for clearance or comment by Secretaries Rusk and McNamara and ACDA Director Foster. The draft statement reads as follows:

"There should be no misunderstanding about our policy with regard to biological and chemical warfare. We have never used biological weapons, and we do not intend to initiate the use of biological weapons in the future. We have not engaged in gas warfare since World War I when such weapons were widely used, and we do not intend to initiate the use of gas warfare in the future. Riot control agents and herbicides, both of which are widely used by responsible governments, clearly do not fall in this category, and we have explained our position on them many times." (Johnson Library, National Security File, Subject File, Warfare, Chemical and Biological, Box 51)

In a March 10, 1967, note to Rostow, Keeny explained that he had kept Rostow's memoranda to the three principals "very short since the principals and their staff know the background of this problem. Moreover, I did not want to appear to prejudice the questions one way or the other except to the extent of indicating Presidential interest in making a statement if it is acceptable to the principals." (Ibid.) A copy of Rostow's brief March 10 memorandum to the three principals, which transmitted the statement for clearance or comment, is ibid.

In a March 17 memorandum to Rostow, Katzenbach responded that he concurred in the proposed public statement but suggested that the last sentence be changed, as follows:

"Riot control agents that are widely used by police forces throughout the world, and herbicides that are commonly employed in many countries, clearly do not fall in this category, and we have explained our position on them many times."

Katzenbach believed that his proposed change "would be more in line with our past statements and make it clear that these agents are widely used domestically and not solely by governments against people of other countries." (Ibid.)

No reply from Foster has been found. For McNamara's response, see Document 178.

174.   Memorandum to Holders of NIE 11–8–66[1]

Washington, March 13, 1967.

SOVIET CAPABILITIES FOR STRATEGIC ATTACK

Note

This Memorandum to Holders is prompted by a recent review of Soviet submarine order-of-battle which requires us to change the judgments made in NIE 11–8–66, "Soviet Capabilities for Strategic Attack," dated 20 October 1966, Top Secret, Restricted Data, Limited Distribution, on the size and composition of the Soviet missile submarine force.

Discussion

1. In NIE 11–8–66, we estimated that as of 1 October 1966 the Soviet missile submarine force had some 45 ballistic missile submarines (8–10 nuclear-powered) with a total of about 130 launchers, and an equal number of cruise missile units (21–23 nuclear-powered) with about 250 launchers.

2. A recent review of Soviet submarine order-of-battle indicates that as of 1 October 1966 there were 36 ballistic missile submarines in the Soviet Navy (7 of them nuclear-powered) with a total of about 100 launchers. The cruise missile submarine force—whose primary mission is to counter naval task forces—was found to have a slightly greater number of units than previously estimated, and a greater proportion of nuclear-powered units. Since the latter are equipped with more missile launchers than the diesel-powered boats, approximately 265 launchers (rather than 250) were found to be in the cruise missile submarine force.

3. We continue to believe that a new type of ballistic missile submarine will enter service by mid-1968. Since fewer ballistic missile submarines are now operational than previously estimated, however, our projection of the number of such units which will be operational in 1976 has been reduced from some 60–70 to about 55–65. There is no change in our estimate of the total number of cruise missile submarines for 1976 (i.e., 55–65 units) but we believe the proportion of nuclear submarines in the cruise missile force will be somewhat higher at that time (i.e., about 45 out of 60, rather than 40 or so out of 60).

---

[1]   Source: National Archives and Records Administration, RG 263. Top Secret; Controlled Dissem. According to a prefatory note on the inside of the cover sheet, this memorandum was distributed to the White House, National Security Council, Department of State, Department of Defense, the Atomic Energy Commission, and the Federal Bureau of Investigation. The summary and conclusions of NIE 11–8–66 are printed as Document 143.

4. A new table listing the estimated Soviet missile submarine strength for 1966 through 1968 follows. The new table supersedes that in Section IV of NIE 11–8–66.

Estimated Soviet Missile Submarine Strength, 1966–1968

	1 Oct 1966	Mid-1967	Mid-1968
Ballistic Missile Submarines			
Nuclear			
H-I (3 tubes)	3	2-1	1-0
H-II (3 tubes)	4	5-6	6-7
New class (8 or more tubes) ..	0	0	1
Subtotal	7	7	8
Diesel			
Z-Conversion (2 tubes)	6	6	6
G-I (3 tubes)	22	22	22-20
G-II (2 tubes)	1	1	1-3
Subtotal	29	29	29
Total Ballistic Missile Submarines	36	36	37
Cruise Missile Submarines			
Nuclear			
E-I (6 tubes)	5	5	5
E-II (8 tubes)	20-21	24-25	28-29
Subtotal	25-26	29-30	33-34
Diesel			
W-Conversion (1 to 4 tubes) ..	13	13	13
J-Class (4 tubes)	7-10	9-12	11-15
Subtotal	20-23	22-25	24-28
Total Cruise Missile Submarines	45-49	51-55	57-62

5. In addition, the final sentence of the last paragraph of Section VII A of NIE 11–8–66 should be deleted and replaced by the following:

In any case, we believe we could identify a MOBS sometime during its test program which would probably extend over a year or two. If the Soviets follow established test procedures, identification is likely to occur about a year prior to attainment of an accurate, reliable system.

(*Note:* paragraphs 1–4 approved by USIB—13 March 1967; Paragraph 5 approved by USIB—2 March 1967)

175.   Letter From Director of Central Intelligence Helms to the
        President's Special Assistant (Rostow)[1]

TCS–6236–67   Washington, March 18, 1967.

Dear Walt:

    In SNIE 11–10–67[2] we used, as usual, some verbal expressions to
describe our estimated capability to detect land mobile ICBM's, IRBM's,
and MRBM's, and new missile-launching submarines in the USSR. You
asked that we give you a translation into number.

    First with regard to Land Mobile ICBM's, IRBM's, and MRBM's:

    We can quote no discrete odds for detection in the early stages of
deployment. Our word "possible" in this context simply means that we
are not *certain* of being able to detect nor do we feel it is *impossible* that
we will detect. Your mathematical friends define this use of "possible"
as "non-zero probability."

    As to extensive deployment of these weapons systems we feel our
chances of detecting are *greater than even and less than overwhelming*—say
in the general bracket 65% to 85%

    Second, with regard to Missile-launching Submarines:

    As to detecting units of an entirely new class before IOC, we have
put the odds in the 65% to 85% bracket.

    As to detecting new units of an existing class before delivery to the
fleet, we put the odds about even; 50–50.

    The enclosed article which Sherman wrote some time back may fur-
ther enlighten.[3]

    Sincerely,

                                                              Dick

---

[1] Source: Johnson Library, National Security File, National Intelligence Estimates,
11–67—USSR, Box 4. Top Secret; Trine; Ruff; Zarf; Handle Via Talent-Keyhole-COMINT
Channels Jointly.

[2] Document 169.

[3] Not found.

176. Memorandum From the Central Intelligence Agency to the 303 Committee[1]

Washington, April 12, 1967.

SUBJECT

Termination of Covert Funding Relationship with The Asia Foundation

1. Summary

Pursuant to the recommendations of the Katzenbach Committee, as approved by the President of the United States,[2] the Director of Central Intelligence has ordered that covert funding of The Asia Foundation (TAF) shall be terminated at the earliest practicable opportunity. In anticipation of TAF's disassociation from the Agency the Board of Trustees on March 21, 1967, released to the American and foreign press a carefully limited statement of admission of past CIA support.[3] In so doing the Trustees sought to delimit the effects of an anticipated exposure of Agency support by the American press and, if their statement or some future exposé does not seriously impair TAF's acceptability in Asia, to continue operating in Asia with overt private and official support. To date, the March 21 statement has produced no serious threat to TAF operations in Asia, and the Trustees are now prepared to attempt to acquire the necessary support for TAF to go on as a private institution, partially supported by overt U.S. Government grants. This will take time and TAF meanwhile faces the immediate problem of the need for funds during FY 1968.

---

[1] Source: Department of State, INR/IL Historical Files, 303 Committee, May 27, 1967. Secret; Eyes Only. No drafting information appears on the memorandum, which forms Tab A–1 to the proposed agenda for the May 27 meeting of the 303 Committee.

[2] On February 15 President Johnson appointed a committee composed of Under Secretary of State Katzenbach (Chairman), Secretary of Health, Education and Welfare John W. Gardner, and Director of Central Intelligence Helms to inquire into the relationships between government agencies and private organizations operating abroad. The panel was established in response to press reports, particularly Sol Stern's article, "A Short Account of International Student Politics & the Cold War with Particular Reference to the NSA, CIA, etc.," *Ramparts* magazine, 5 (March 1967), pp. 29–39, of CIA secret funding over the years of private organizations, which became involved in confrontations with Communist-influenced groups at international gatherings. (*The New York Times*, February 16, 1967, pp. 1, 26) Text of an interim report, February 22, as well as the final report of the Katzenbach Committee, March 29, are in *American Foreign Policy: Current Documents, 1967,* pp. 1214–1217. For text of the President's statement accepting the committee's proposed statement of policy and directing all agencies of the U.S. Government to implement it fully, see *Public Papers of the Presidents of the United States: Lyndon B. Johnson, 1967,* pp. 403–404.

[3] This statement is summarized and quoted in part in *The New York Times*, March 22, 1967, p. 15.

TAF's present resources are sufficient to sustain operations through July 31, 1967, the end of the Foundation's fiscal year. [*4-1/2 lines of source text not declassified*] To meet these obligations, and to allow TAF management to plan rationally for FY 1968, immediate firm commitments must be acquired on future levels and sources of support. This Agency is prepared to provide whatever assistance remains within its authority and competence to offer. To undertake further necessary action, however, the Agency requests that the Committee now designate the Agency or official to whom TAF management should look for future guidance and direction with respect to United States Government interests.

2. Problem

  Immediate Requirements

  a. With the encouragement and support of CIA, and the guidance of other elements of the United States Government, the Trustees of The Asia Foundation on March 21, 1967, publicly declared that TAF is a private organization; that its Trustees have accepted funds from CIA intermediaries in the past and, by inference, can no longer do so; and that they fully intend to continue programming in Asia with support from both private and overt official sources. It is imperative that this declaration be supported by normal or near-normal TAF operations in Asia over the months ahead. [*4 lines of source text not declassified*] It has further authorized the Trustees to seek pledges of support from heads of private foundations and other prospective private donors; but, as a practical matter, no immediate results can be anticipated.

  [*4 paragraphs (22 lines of source text) not declassified*]

  Long-range Requirements

  c. The above immediate arrangements would insure the continuance of TAF programs at near-normal levels during the critical year ahead, during which time TAF Trustees and appropriate agencies of the U.S. Government can endeavor to arrange adequate permanent sources of support from private and official sources for FY 1969 and beyond. If by December 31, 1967, it becomes apparent that adequate support is not forthcoming, the Agency recommends that serious consideration be given to phasing down or terminating the Foundation.

  [Here follow paragraphs 3. "Factors Bearing on the Problem," and 4. "Coordination."]

5. Recommendation

  The Agency recommends that actions proposed in paragraphs one and two above be approved.

177.   **Editorial Note**

In early Spring 1967, the White House Office of Emergency Planning (OEP) completed a revised edition of its study, "Resource Mobilization Plan for Limited War." Regarding the planning and drafting of this study in 1966, see Document 138. The 31-page revised study, dated April 1967, covered the means whereby the U.S. Government could effectively mobilize the central management of resources in emergency circumstances short of a nuclear attack. It included the basic measures, policy and legal documents, and the organization structure required in the event of an emergency requiring the mobilization of the nation's resources during a limited war. Emergency action documents providing the basic authorities required for the mobilization of the nation's economic resources were included in a classified Annex A of the plan. Annex B comprised resource sections developed by the federal agencies. A copy of the entire plan was distributed to the Department of Defense under cover of a May 1 letter from OEP Director Farris Bryant to Secretary of Defense McNamara. (Washington National Records Center, OSD Files: FRC 330 72 A 2468, 381 National Resources (S–2667) 1967)

178.   Letter From Secretary of Defense McNamara to the
        President's Special Assistant (Rostow)[1]

Washington, May 3, 1967.

Dear Walt:

I have reviewed the proposed public statement on chemical and biological warfare policy which you forwarded with your memorandum of 10 March.[2] I am attaching the views of the Joint Chiefs of Staff for the President's information.[3]

The Joint Chiefs of Staff believe that the President should not be advised to make a public statement on this subject at this time. I agree that it would be preferable that the President not make a public statement now. However, if the President should decide a statement is desirable, I recommend he use the statement provided to Dr. Hornig in January. I am attaching a copy of that statement for your information.[4]

Sincerely,

Bob[5]

---

[1] Source: Johnson Library, National Security File, Subject File, Warfare, Chemical and Biological, Box 51. Secret. Copies were sent to Secretary Rusk and ACDA Director Foster.

[2] See Document 173.

[3] Not attached, but it is identified in a list of enclosures at the end of the letter as JCSM–171–67, "Proposed Presidential Policy Statement Concerning Chemical and Biological Warfare," March 29, 1967. In this paper the Joint Chiefs opposed a Presidential policy statement and as rationale referred to the draft NSAM attached to Secretary McNamara's November 17, 1966, letter to Secretary Rusk. "The proposed draft NSAM," they continued, "provides the President with options which should not be preempted by a public statement but which should be retained as the prerogative of the President. Increased efforts should be made to finalize the proposed draft NSAM for consideration by the President." They also advanced a proposed public statement if a public statement was clearly required. (National Archives and Records Administration, RG 218, JCS Files, 313 (10 Mar 67) 1967 IR #580) For McNamara's November 17 letter, see Document 145.

[4] Not found.

[5] Printed from a copy that indicates McNamara signed the original.

179. Intelligence Memorandum[1]

RR IM 67–24   Washington, May 1967.
TCS–7036/67

NEW TREND IN SOVIET ICBM DEPLOYMENT PROGRAM[2]

Summary

There is mounting evidence that a significant slowdown occurred in the rate of silo construction starts in the Soviet SS-11 ICBM deployment program after mid-1966. Although new construction is continuing, it appears likely that the rate of construction starts for this relatively light payload ICBM has been cut back by more than 50 percent from the high rate attained in the first half of 1966. Curtailment of the rate of construction starts appears to have affected at least half of the ten SS-11 complexes—specifically, the earliest five complexes, where some 300 SS-11 silos have already been started or completed—and suggests that the entire program is tapering off even though it may continue for some time. It is believed that there are currently more than 500 SS-11 silos in the USSR, of which about 150 have been completed and are now operational. Virtually all of those now under construction are likely to become operational by mid-1968.

On the other hand, new silo construction for the USSR's other current ICBM system, the heavy-payload SS-9, has continued into 1967 at a steady pace and there are clear indications that further construction starts are planned. There are an estimated 180 SS-9 silos in the USSR, including about 70 already operational; most of those that are now under construction will be operational by mid-1968.

The curtailment of the SS-11 program may indicate that the USSR is approaching its force goal for this ICBM system which, because of its limited accuracy and relatively small payload, is suitable primarily for attacking cities and other soft targets. However, the leveling off of the rate of silo starts for this system does not necessarily indicate that the

---

[1] Source: Johnson Library, National Security File, Intelligence File, TKH, August 66–July 67, Box 1. Top Secret; Ruff; Handle Via Talent-Keyhole Control System Only; No Foreign Dissem. An attached memorandum from R.J. Smith, Deputy Director of Intelligence, to Rostow, May 18, offers a one-paragraph summary of the intelligence memorandum.

[2] This memorandum was produced solely by CIA. It was prepared by the Office of Research and Reports and coordinated with the Office of National Estimates, the Foreign Missile and Space Analysis Center, and the Office of Current Intelligence; the estimates and conclusions represent the best judgment of the Directorate of Intelligence as of 1 May 1967. [Footnote in the source text.]

USSR is approaching a programmed limit in deployment of ground-launched ICBM systems. Coinciding with the change in the SS-11 program, construction activity at new missile launch areas at the Tyuratam Test Range indicates that one and possibly two new systems are under development. As yet, there is no evidence to indicate whether the next round of deployment will replace or supplement the existing ICBM force, but the new systems may foreshadow the end of additional construction for one or both of the current deployment programs in the near term, perhaps during 1967.

On the basis of current evidence, the Soviet ICBM force will attain a level of some 900 operational launchers by mid-1968 and 1,000 or more by mid-1969, if there is no phase-out of earlier generation systems. While this number could be increased still further by the introduction of new systems, any substantial increment effected by these newer systems would be expected to occur in the 1970–75 period.

---

180.   Memorandum for the Record[1]

Washington, May 27, 1967.

SUBJECT

Minutes of the Meeting of the 303 Committee, 27 May 1967

PRESENT

Mr. Rostow, Ambassador Kohler, Mr. Vance, and Mr. Helms

Admiral Taylor was present for all items.
Mr. Cord Meyer was present for Item 1.
Mr. Charles Schultze was present for Items 1 and 2.
Mr. Donald Jamison was present for Item 3.

1. The Asia Foundation

a. In the discussion of the future of The Asia Foundation,[2] the following points were made: The principals and the Director of the Bureau of the Budget felt that it was wiser to transfer [*less than 1 line of source*

---

[1] Source: Department of State, INR/IL Historical Files, 303 Committee, May 27, 1967. Secret; Eyes Only. Drafted on May 31.

[2] For the CIA paper that was the basis of discussion of this issue, see Document 176.

text not declassified] in its entirety in a secure manner to the Foundation's account rather than filter portions through AID or State at this time.

b. Ambassador Kohler agreed that the State Department would nominate a senior official to undertake the responsibility of liaison to tide the Foundation through its difficult realignment period and set it on its path to self-sufficiency in 1969. Mr Rostow suggested the name of Ambassador Winthrop Brown (if his new responsibilities would permit an added chore). Mr. Meyer indicated that such a person would have the full cooperation of a CIA officer thoroughly conversant with the project.

c. It was fully agreed that the Foundation was definitely in the national interest and should be protected and nurtured.

d. Mr. Schultze pointed out that in the future TAF would have to count on multifarious sources and, regardless of the results of the Rusk Committee findings, there never would be a single solution. He also indicated that, [*less than 1 line of source text not declassified*] a proper husbanding of resources should leave the Foundation with sufficient assets to face the future in 1969. He also wanted it emphasized that the Foundation would be competing for federal funds with other worthy causes.

[Here follow agenda items 2–5.]

Peter Jessup

181.   Memorandum From President Johnson to Secretary of Defense McNamara[1]

Washington, June 10, 1967.

SUBJECT

FY 1969 Nuclear Weapons Stockpile

I approve the proposed Nuclear Weapons Stockpile for the end of FY 1969 and the proposed adjusted stockpile composition for the end of

---

[1] Source: Washington National Records Center, OSD Files: FRC 330 72 A 2467, A–400.23 1967. Top Secret; Restricted Data. A stamped notation on the memorandum, dated June 16, indicates that Secretary McNamara saw it.

FY 1968, submitted to me by the Department of Defense and the Atomic Energy Commission on April 3, 1967.[2]

Accordingly, I approve a total of [*number not declassified*] nuclear warheads as the stockpile composition for the end of FY 1969. I also approve a total of [*number not declassified*] nuclear warheads as the adjusted stockpile composition for the end of FY 1968. This will mean a planned production by the Atomic Energy Commission of [*number not declassified*] nuclear warheads and a planned retirement of [*number not declassified*] nuclear warheads during FY 1969, resulting in a net reduction of [*number not declassified*] nuclear warheads during FY 1969 under the adjusted FY 1968 stockpile.

I have directed the production and retirement of those quantities of atomic weapons and atomic weapons parts necessary to achieve and maintain the approved FY 1969 stockpile, as well as the production of the additional nuclear warhead parts necessary for transfer to the United Kingdom pursuant to the agreement for cooperation. I have also directed the production of the additional weapons required for quality assurance and reliability testing.

I have authorized the Atomic Energy Commission in coordination with the Department of Defense to initiate production of such long lead time nuclear warhead parts as may be necessary to prepare for FY 1970 production of warheads required by the approved Five Year Defense Program.

I authorize you, in coordination with the Atomic Energy Commission, to make such changes in the total stockpile not to exceed [*number not declassified*] of the specifically stated numbers of nuclear warheads to be produced and retired in FY 1968 and FY 1969 as may be necessary to adjust production schedules to meet AEC material availabilities or production capability.

I further authorize you to make minor changes [*number not declassified*] in strategic, tactical, and fleet anti-submarine/anti-air warfare warhead totals that may be required because of adjusted delivery assets or changes in military requirements. Any changes indicative of a major shift in defense policy or AEC production capability will be submitted for my approval.

Lyndon B. Johnson

---

[2] Not printed. (Johnson Library, National Security File, Subject File, Nuclear Weapons—Stockpile, Vol. I, Box 32)

182.   Memorandum From Director of Central Intelligence Helms to the President's Special Assistant (Rostow)

Washington, June 26, 1967.

[Source: Johnson Library, National Security File, Agency File, CIA, Filed by LBJ Library, Box 10. Secret. 2 pages of source text not declassified.]

---

183.   National Intelligence Estimate[1]

NIE 11–4–67   Washington, July 20, 1967.

MAIN TRENDS IN SOVIET MILITARY POLICY

The Problem

To review significant developments in Soviet military policy and programs, and to estimate main trends in Soviet military policies over the next 5 to 10 years.

Scope

This estimate assesses broad trends in Soviet military policy and doctrine. It does not attempt to recapitulate existing NIEs on Soviet strategic attack, strategic air and missile defense, and general purpose forces. Our most recent detailed estimates on the size, composition, and capabilities of these principal components and the supporting elements of the Soviet military forces are as follows:

NIE 11–8–66, "Soviet Capabilities for Strategic Attack," dated 20 October 1966, Top Secret, Restricted Data (Limited Distribution).[2]

---

[1] Source: Johnson Library, National Security File, National Intelligence Estimates, 11–67, USSR, Box 4. Secret; Controlled Dissem. A cover sheet, prefatory note, title page, and table of contents are not printed. According to the prefatory note, the CIA and the intelligence organizations of the Departments of State and Defense and the NSA participated in the preparation of this estimate. Representatives of the CIA, State Department, DIA, NSA, and AEC concurred; the FBI representative abstained, the subject being out his jurisdiction.

[2] Document 143.

NIE 11–14–66, "Capabilities of Soviet General Purpose Forces," dated 3 November 1966, Secret.[3]
NIE 11–3–66, "Soviet Strategic Air and Missile Defenses," dated 17 November 1966, Top Secret.[4]

Conclusions

A. In the past year, there has been no major change in the broad Soviet military policy, which continues to place primary emphasis on strategic weapons. Outlays for defense have accelerated with the continuation of large-scale deployment of strategic missiles, both offensive and defensive, and continued research and development (R&D) on new strategic weapon systems. The Soviets are building forces which we believe will give them, in the next year or two, greatly increased confidence that they have a retaliatory capability sufficient to assure the destruction of a significant portion of US industrial resources and population. They will probably also seek, through both strategic attack and defense programs, to improve their ability to reduce the damage the US can inflict on the USSR should deterrence fail and war in fact occur. We believe that the Soviets would not consider it feasible to achieve by the mid-1970's strategic capabilities which would permit them to launch a first strike against the US without receiving unacceptable damage in return.[5]

B. The most important issues of military policy at present center upon the strategic relationship with the US. Certain major deployment programs are either slowing or nearing completion. The Soviet leaders are probably now considering further development and deployment of strategic systems for the 1970's. For the present, we rate the chances as less than even that they would agree to any extensive program of arms control or disarmament.

C. The Soviets almost certainly believe that their strategic position relative to that of the US has improved markedly. In the next year or so

---

[3] A copy is in the Johnson Library, National Security File, National Intelligence Estimates, 11–66, USSR, Box 3.

[4] Document 146.

[5] Major Gen. Jack E. Thomas, the Assistant Chief of Staff, Intelligence, USAF, would substitute for the last sentence of Conclusion A the following:

"The Soviets may not consider it feasible to achieve by the mid-1970's strategic capabilities which would permit them to launch a first strike attack against the US without receiving unacceptable damage in return. On the other hand, the sustained intensity with which the USSR is pursuing its massive military R&D efforts and the pace of its strategic systems deployment suggest the Soviets could be seeking, over the long term, a combination of capabilities which could yield a credible first strike capability against the US. Even if the Soviets considered that this still would not make rational deliberate initiation of nuclear attack against the US, they might well believe that achievement of a credible first strike capability would be worth the cost in view of the strong backup this would provide for aggressive pursuit of objectives in other areas of world." [Footnote in the source text.]

they will approach numerical parity in ICBM launchers, which we believe to be their present goal. They are aware, however, of planned improvements in US strategic offensive missile forces which in their view would threaten to erode their strategic position. Possible Soviet responses could take the form of a considerable increase in the numbers of ICBM launchers, development of mobile ICBMs, a greater emphasis on ballistic missile submarines, or qualitative improvements such as the development of very accurate ICBMs, possibly equipped with multiple independent reentry vehicles (MIRVs).

D. The Soviets have probably concluded that if no arms control agreement is reached a US decision to deploy ABMs will soon be forthcoming, and are probably concerned lest a US ABM deployment seriously degrade their retaliatory capabilities. A US decision to deploy either heavy or light ABM defenses would probably lead the Soviets to develop and deploy penetration aids and possibly MIRVs for their ICBM force, or they might increase the size of that force. Systems designed to elude US ABM defenses, such as aerodynamic vehicles or space weapons, might be given greater emphasis. Whatever their specific responses to developments on the US side, we believe that the Soviets will hold it essential to maintain what they would consider to be an assured destruction capability.

E. We continue to believe that the Soviets will deploy ABMs in defense of areas other than Moscow, but their decision may await the availability of an improved system. In any case, given the lead-times involved, ABM defenses will probably not become operational outside the Moscow area before the early 1970's. We would expect to detect construction of such additional defenses two to three years before they became operational.[6]

F. Developments in the general purpose forces indicate a greater concern with meeting contingencies short of general war and a recognition of the possibility of postponing, limiting, or avoiding the use of nuclear weapons. In part this represents a reaction to the US and NATO

---

[6] Lt. Gen. Joseph F. Carroll, Director, Defense Intelligence Agency; Brig. Gen. James L. Collins, Jr., Acting Deputy Chief of Staff for Intelligence, Department of the Army; and Maj. Gen. Jack E. Thomas, the Assistant Chief of Staff, Intelligence, USAF, note that this paragraph considers the Moscow ABM system is the only ABM system currently being deployed and does not ascribe an ABM capability for the Tallinn system. They believe that the information available at present is still insufficient to estimate with confidence the full capabilities and mission of the Tallinn system. They agree that the available evidence does support a conclusion that the Tallinn sites have a defensive mission against the aerodynamic threat except against low altitude threats. However, they also believe that the system, where augmented by the Hen House type radar, has a capability against ballistic missiles over a substantial portion of the deployment area; and that the system has considerable growth potential. They therefore would evaluate its continuing development and deployment with this capability in mind. [Footnote in the source text.]

strategy of flexible response, but it also represents a more general interest in broadening the range of Soviet military capabilities. Sealift and airlift have been considerably expanded. We do not believe, however, that the Soviets are developing the sea and air combat capabilities required for distant limited military action against opposition. They evidently see advantages in wars fought by proxy with indigenous forces rather than by their own forces, a practice which reduces both military risks and adverse political reactions. In extending their influence abroad they will continue to give economic and military aid on a large-scale, and to use political and diplomatic means.

G. The Soviets now describe China as a power with a policy "clearly hostile" to the USSR. They have increased their military strength in areas close to the Chinese and Mongolian borders, and are moving to strengthen the defenses of Mongolia. At present they appear to regard the Chinese as posing more of a border security problem than a major military threat, but they almost certainly see the potential threat of China as increasing over the longer term. So long as the Sino-Soviet conflict persists, Soviet military planners will have to take account of the possibility of large-scale war with China and China's emerging strategic nuclear capabilities.

H. The internal situation appears generally favorable to the continuation of a strong military effort. The present leaders seem more responsive than was Khrushchev to the opinions of the military hierarchy. Estimated military and space expenditures for 1967 represent an increase of 16 percent over 1965, a marked change from the more stable level of spending during 1962–1965. The adverse effects on the economy of large military and space programs will exert some restraining influence on military spending. We believe that military expenditures will continue to rise, but at a rate generally consonant with the growth of the Soviet economy.

I. A strong effort in military R&D will be continued despite resource allocation problems. The Soviets probably regard such an effort as imperative in order to prevent the US from gaining a technological advantage and also to gain, if possible, some advantage for themselves. But in deciding to deploy any new weapon system they would have to weigh the prospective gain against the economic costs and the capabilities of the US to counter it.

J. Soviet foreign policy will continue to be based primarily upon political and economic factors, but the military capabilities that the Soviets are developing and the military relationships that are evolving will affect their attitudes and approaches to policy. They will probably seek to gain some political or propaganda advantage from their improving military position, and may take a harder line with the US in various crises than they have in the past. We do not believe, however, that their improved military capabilities will lead them to such aggressive courses of action as would, in their view, provoke direct military confrontation with the US. The Soviet leaders recognize that the USSR as well as the US is deterred from initiating general war, and will continue to avoid serious risk of such a war.[7]

[Here follows the Discussion section (Parts I–V, pages 6–23).]

[7] For the longer term, Major Gen. Jack E. Thomas, the Assistant Chief of Staff, Intelligence, USAF, believes his footnote to Conclusion A is pertinent. [Footnote in the source text.]

---

184. Memorandum From the Joint Chiefs of Staff to Secretary of Defense McNamara[1]

JCSM–425–67   Washington, July 27, 1967.

SUBJECT

    Initiation of Nike-X Production and Deployment (C)

1. (S) Reference is made to your draft Presidential memorandum, dated 17 January 1967, subject: "Production and Deployment of the Nike-X (C),"[2] which recommended that negotiations be initiated with the Soviet Union "designed, through formal or informal agreement, to limit the deployment of antiballistic missile systems." It was further recommended that the decision not to deploy Nike-X be reconsidered "in the event these discussions prove unsuccessful."

2. (S) Subsequent attempts to negotiate such an agreement with the Soviet Union have indicated little promise of success. Ambassador Thompson, in his recent discussion with the Joint Chiefs of Staff, made the assessment that the Soviet Union would not be ready for talks on this subject until completion of the Nonproliferation Treaty talks.

3. (S) The Joint Chiefs of Staff are agreed that the timing of a Nike-X deployment decision is critical to an effective defense of the United States. Among the actions recommended to maintain a reasonable strategic posture in JSOP 69–76,[3] no other single action is considered

[1] Source: Washington National Records Center, OSD Files: FRC 330 72 A 2467, 471.94 ABM (Jul–Aug) 1967. Secret. A stamped notation on the memorandum reads: "Sec Def has seen Brief."
[2] See footnote 1, Document 160.
[3] Not found.

more necessary than the deployment of Nike-X. Delay of Nike-X deployment provides the Soviet Union with the combined advantages of continuing their own ballistic missile buildup without complicating their attack strategy and, concurrently, continuing their antiballistic missile deployment, which already poses significant problems to the US strategic offensive forces.

4. (S) Since the United States first proposed negotiations to limit both strategic offensive and defensive forces in 1964, the Soviet Union has shown no evidence of slowing down the deployment of such forces nor have they stated any intent to do so. Indeed, USSR representatives have indicated no interest in this subject at the Eighteen Nation Disarmament Conference and intelligence information indicates that the Soviets have accelerated their deployment of such forces. At the same time, the communist Chinese are advancing toward a strategic capability at a faster rate than had been anticipated as evidenced by their recent detonation of an air-dropped thermonuclear device. The apparent progress they are making toward developing an intercontinental ballistic missile with an initial operational capability as early as 1970 adds to the urgency of initiating a Nike-X deployment.

5. (S) In JCSM–804–66, dated 29 December 1966, subject: "Production and Deployment of Nike-X (C),"[4] the Joint Chiefs of Staff advised against delay in deploying Nike-X, pending initiation or conclusion of arms control negotiations. They stated that, in addition to the military advantages to be gained, initiation of Nike-X deployment would provide the United States useful negotiating leverage. The Soviet Union is now benefiting from a US limitation on ballistic missile defenses, whereas the United States is without compensating benefits. While there is considerable incentive for the Soviets to engage in protracted and indecisive negotiations, there is no apparent advantage now for their agreeing to a limitation on ballistic missile defense. A Nike-X deployment decision would either stimulate Soviet participation in meaningful negotiations or disclose their lack of serious interest in this matter. In view of recent events, Ambassador Thompson's assessment, and the negative Soviet attitude evident following the President Johnson–Premier Kosygin talks,[5] the Joint Chiefs of Staff consider that a decision now to deploy Nike-X is even more advisable.

6. (S) For these reasons, the Joint Chiefs of Staff conclude that further delay in the deployment of Nike-X is detrimental to the interests of

---

[4] Document 162.

[5] Documentation on the meetings between President Johnson and Chairman Kosygin at Glassboro, New Jersey, June 23 and 25, 1967, is in *Foreign Relations, 1964–1968*, vol. XIV Documents 217 ff.

the United States. They again recommend that production and deployment of Nike-X be initiated now to provide an initial operating capability in FY 1972 and that the funds appropriated by Congress for FY 1967 and those funds included in the FY 1968 budget be released for this purpose.

For the Joint Chiefs of Staff:
Earle G. Wheeler
Chairman
Joint Chiefs of Staff

---

185.   Memorandum From the President's Special Assistant
(Rostow) to President Johnson[1]

Washington, August 2, 1967, 11:15 a.m.

Mr. President:

I have just had a long and useful telephone conversation with Bob McNamara on both the ABM issue and the question of Senators worried about stalemate.

1. With respect to ABM's, he has completed a first draft—and plans to circulate on next Monday[2] a second draft—of a speech which would announce that we were going to proceed with a Chinese-oriented thin ABM system. The speech is scheduled for delivery September 17 at San Francisco before the UPI editors. As you know, the system would also have a capacity to protect to a significant degree our Minuteman against Soviet attack. Although he has some reservation about the dates given for a ChiCom ICBM delivery capability against the U.S., the speech would, essentially, accept those dates.

2. He would prefer to hold to the mid-September date of delivery—assuming you approve his recommended decision incorporated in the speech—because there are two or three loose ends he would like to clear up on the technical side.

---

[1] Source: Johnson Library, National Security File, Country File, USSR, ABM Negotiations (II), Box 231. Secret; Sensitive. A handwritten notation reads: "Rec'd 11:50 a."

[2] August 7. McNamara circulated a draft on Wednesday, August 9; see Document 192.

3. As for the press handling of this matter, he suggests that we use the unclassified version of his Congressional testimony published January 23, 1967.[3] Starting on page 38 there is an extended passage describing the difference in our approach to the Soviet and the ChiCom capabilities. We should emphasize that we are working at highest priority to develop the technology of an ABM system and that deployment has in no way been delayed by decisions we have taken because the system is now in a development stage (in fact, Bob believes that the first production orders related to deployment could only rationally be given in December of this year, given the unresolved development problems).

4. I would add that in backgrounding on this matter tomorrow and in the days ahead, we should try to deflate the notion that we are in a hysterical race between a ChiCom development of an ICBM system and our development of an ABM system. The simple fact is that the ChiComs have shown themselves systematically extremely cautious in military operations and extremely respectful of U.S. military power, including our nuclear power. They have talked an aggressive doctrine but behaved cautiously at the time of Quemoy Matsu; the Tibet engagement against India; the India/Pak war; and in Viet Nam. They obviously have some nuclear devices now which could be dropped from aircraft. They have not proceeded to do so. There is every reason to believe on the record that they will be deterred by our overwhelming retaliatory power. This does not mean that we shall not deploy, necessarily, a thin ABM system against them. It does mean that there is no reason for panic.

5. In any case, I believe you will wish personally to design the press handling of this matter in the government.

[Here follow Rostow's account of McNamara's thoughts on dealing with U.S. Senators concerned about a possible stalemate in the Vietnam war; and notice that McNamara would be away from Washington for 3–4 days.]

Walt

---

[3] Text of McNamara's unclassified statement on January 23 before a joint session of the Senate Armed Services Committee and the Senate Subcommittee on Department of Defense Appropriations on the fiscal year 1968–1972 defense program and 1968 budget, which was released on January 26, is in the National Archives and Records Administration, RG 200, Defense Programs and Operations, Unclassified Statement FY 1968, Box 69.

186.   Memorandum for the Record[1]

Washington, August 7, 1967.

SUBJECT

Minutes of the Meeting of the 303 Committee, 7 August 1967

PRESENT

Mr. Rostow, Mr. Thomas L. Hughes, Mr. Nitze, and Mr. Helms

Admiral R.L. Taylor was present for all items
Mr. William Broe was present for Items 4, 8, and 9
Mr. John Marsh was present for Item 5
Mr. Cord Meyer was present for Items 6 and 7

[Here follow agenda items 1 and 2.]

3. Termination of NSA Occupancy of CIA-Owned Buildings[2]

Mr. Helms indicated that he had been visited by Joseph Rauh, Jr., an attorney representing the NSA on behalf of the UAW. Rauh's tentative proposal was that the title and mortgage be handed over (approximate cost $64,360). On its part, the Agency felt the unspent accrued funds be allocated to the NSA, thus constituting a write-off. Mr. Helms indicated, however, that in view of general student leader intransigence on negotiations, this was a propitious solution. The principals went along with this as an efficacious egress from an awkward situation.

[Here follows discussion of item 4.]

[*Agenda items 5–9 (1 page of source text) not declassified*]

[Here follow agenda items 10–14.]

Peter Jessup

---

[1] Source: Department of State, INR/IL Historical Files, 303 Committee, August 7, 1967. Secret; Eyes Only. Drafted by Jessup on August 7. Copies were sent to Kohler, Nitze, and Helms.

[2] In an August 4 memorandum to Thomas L. Hughes (INR), William C. Trueheart (INR/DDC) provided background on this issue, as follows: The Central Intelligence Agency owned buildings at 2115–2117 S Street, N.W., Washington, D.C., which the National Student Association (NSA) leased from the Independence Foundation, publicly identified as a CIA conduit. The leaders of the NSA, which held "a virtually irrevocable occupancy agreement with the Foundation, at the cost only of maintenance and repair," had refused to give up the buildings gracefully. (Ibid.)

187.   Memorandum From the President's Special Assistant
(Rostow) to President Johnson[1]

Washington, August 9, 1967, 10:30 a.m.

Mr. President:

I believe you will wish to read at least the summary at the beginning of this estimate.[2]

The situation it describes is not alarming; but I suspect it will be
exploited as a political issue in 1968.

The Soviets are increasing the number of their hardened ICBM's
while we are increasing the number of our warheads.

Therefore, it will be argued, they are "closing our nuclear superiority gap."

The argument will be buttressed by evidence, from the statistical
war games that are played each year, that:

—the number of Soviet targets is increasing faster than our megatonnage on targets;
—a nuclear exchange would result in increasing U.S. fatalities and
industrial damage, decreasing Soviet fatalities and Soviet damage;
—we now have to take the Chinese Communist threat more seriously.

Again, no one thinks we are moving to a position where a Soviet
first strike is likely to become rational in the foreseeable future. But the
numbers will be moving unfavorably over the coming year; and you
may wish to begin to work out with Bob McNamara[3] how we deal with
the political problem which may arise.

Walt

---

[1] Source: Johnson Library, National Security File, National Intelligence Estimates
11–67, Box 4. Secret.
[2] The attached NIE 11–4–67 is printed as Document 183.
[3] The words "begin to work out with Bob McNamara" are circled with a line to the
bottom of the page where the President wrote: "Ask him to do this." At the end of the
memorandum is Rostow's handwritten notation: "8/10/67 done by WWR."

188.   Paper Prepared by the Joint Chiefs of Staff[1]

Washington, undated.

MILITARY STRATEGY FOR FY 1970 THROUGH FY 1977 (U)

Part I

Introduction

Purpose

1. (U) This Volume of the Joint Strategic Objectives Plan develops the military strategy for the period FY 1970–FY 1977. It emphasizes those elements of the strategic concept which influence major issues that should be addressed in the FY 1970 Department of Defense budget. It also considers the implications of the current conflict in Southeast Asia relative to the strategic concept for the mid-range period.

Objectives

2. (U) *General.* As one of the elements of national power, military force is justified on the basis of its contribution to the support of national policy. US national security policy is not contained in any single, nationally-approved document. It is constantly and dynamically evolving through informal and formal processes. It emerges from this process that US national security interests will be served best by fostering a peaceful international community which is not inimical to the US Government and is based upon consent of the governed, dignity of the individual, and respect for the rule of law. Attainment of this world of peace with justice through peaceful means is a US national goal in the most fundamental sense. Nevertheless, throughout the mid-range period the presence and exercise of US military power will continue to be essential to protect the interests of the United States and its allies, while conditions favorable to peaceful attainment of this goal are being pursued.

---

[1] Source: National Archives and Records Administration, RG 218, JCS Files, 511 (27 Jul 67) Sec 1 IR 1870. Top Secret. A title page, foreword, and table of contents are not printed. This paper forms Enclosure A to a report by the J–5 to the Joint Chiefs of Staff (JCS 2143/312) entitled "The Joint Strategic Objectives Plan for Fiscal Year 1970 Through Fiscal Year 1977 (JSOP 70–77)," which is not printed. Although the report bears the date July 27, 1967, it was actually written later, for it notes that the Joint Chiefs of Staff, after making amendments, approved Enclosure A at their August 11 meeting and forwarded it to the military services and the commanders of the unified and specified commands on August 18. The foreword to the paper printed here identifies it as Volume I of a 3-volume paper comprising JSOP 70–77 and also lists proposed Annexes A–L to supplement Volumes II and III. Neither Volumes II and III nor the Annexes has been found.

3. (U) *National Security Objective.* The basic national security objective is to preserve the United States as a free and independent nation, safeguard its fundamental institutions and values, and preserve its freedom to pursue its national objectives as the leading world power. The development of a world community which lends itself to this objective is implicit in its meaning.

4. (S) *Basic Military Objectives.* The basic US military objectives derived from the national security objective are:

a. Deter any military attacks against the United States; if deterrence fails, deal effectively with such attacks by conducting the operations required to terminate hostilities under conditions of relative advantage to the United States, while limiting damage to the United States.

b. Deter, in conjunction with available friendly forces, any military attacks against other areas the security of which is essential to US objectives; if deterrence fails, deal effectively with such attacks by conducting the operations required to terminate hostilities under advantageous conditions which facilitate achievement of US and compatible allied objectives, while minimizing damage to US and allied interests.

c. Assist in the self-defense efforts of selected governments to prevent or defeat subversion, insurgency, and encroachments, when the stability and survival of these governments are important to US objectives.

d. Ensure freedom of the sea, air, and space regions for the United States and friendly powers, maintain surveillance over the use of those portions of these regions important to US security, and deny their use for purposes adverse to US interests.

e. Employ military forces and resources to accomplish such other missions as may be directed by US national political authority, to include:

(1) Support of US foreign policy and diplomatic undertakings.

(2) Protection, in areas outside the United States, of US nationals, their properties, and lawful interests; US property; and selected foreign nationals and property.

(3) Assistance in the maintenance of order under constituted authority within the United States.

Part II

Global Appraisal

World Situation

5. (C) The increasing economic gap between the developed and developing areas of the world is a principal factor contributing to international tensions. Progress is hindered by deficiencies in their technological and educational base, primitive production means, inefficient

land distribution, overpopulation, archaic customs, religious, racial, or caste rigidity, the inability or unwillingness of governments to cope with these conditions, and in some cases, a lack of resources. The progressive withdrawal of colonial powers will create power vacuums. These developing areas will be characterized by social and political turbulence, which the communist states will try to aggravate and exploit. Both the USSR and the Chinese Peoples Republic (CPR), each desirous of improving its relative position in the world power structure, have reoriented their strategies; i.e., the Soviets' espousal both of peaceful coexistence and of "wars of national liberation," and the Chinese communists' doctrine of "peoples war." Whether the problems will be settled through armed conflict or through peaceful means will depend primarily on whether the Free World will retain a willingness and capability to execute successfully effective political, economic, psychological, and military programs for the prevention or defeat of subversion and insurgency.

6. (S) The Sino-Soviet rift is likely to persist and may widen. As it continues, the rift lessens the likelihood of a coordinated military threat to the United States. At the same time, competition between the USSR and Communist China for leadership in the communist movement probably will increase. These individual activities probably will conflict with interests of the United States. Accordingly, the planning that precedes major decisions should, where appropriate, include consideration of what effect these decisions might have on USSR-CPR relations.

7. (S) A significant element in the world environment is the potential proliferation of nuclear weapons. Canada, India, Israel, and Sweden have the capability to develop nuclear weapons. The Federal Republic of Germany (FRG) and Japan could also attain such a capability. The emergence of new nuclear powers during the period of this appraisal, while not necessarily leading toward nuclear conflict, would produce more pressures for arms control, and nuclear guarantees or sharing, and would complicate the risk assessment in crises. The greatest continuing threats to the United States and its allies will be posed by the Soviet Union and Communist China.

8. (C) Another factor is a trend toward weakening of alliances. As western-oriented nations grow stronger economically, and the threat of war appears to diminish, their common interests will recede, their national interests will attain new prominence, and they will be less willing to meet common military needs. On the other hand, the resurgence of nationalism in East European nations and the pressures to broaden relations between Eastern and Western Europe will militate against the success of Soviet efforts to maintain the current level of military, economic, and political integration of Eastern Europe.

9. (TS) Space competence is important to national security just as it is to national technological progress and prestige. The Soviets have the capability to orbit a nuclear-armed satellite and frequently have alluded to "orbital rockets." Recent Soviet feasibility tests could lead to orbital bombardment systems. The United Nations resolution against offensive weapons in orbit and the celestial bodies/outer space treaty are steps in the direction of agreements defining rules for space use. There would be political liabilities for any nation which repudiated or violated their provisions. Nevertheless, hostile offensive orbital systems, even in limited numbers, would seriously augment the principal threat of ballistic missile attack against the United States. Accordingly, the US strategic posture should provide capabilities for surveillance of and active defense against potential orbital threats, as protection against possible covert or precipitous overt violation of agreements and against possible threats by nations not parties to agreements.

10. (U) The maritime capabilities of most of the major nations are essential elements of their economic and strategic power. This factor alone will account for a continued interest in the oceans and in the traditional principle of freedom of the seas. The strategic importance of the ocean areas will continue to increase as science and technology provide better ways of exploiting their military and economic value. The exploitation of the oceans for food and marketable products will assume increasing importance, as will rights to oil and minerals from the ocean bed. Increasing international interest in the ocean gives rise to problems of territorial sovereignty over the contiguous sea areas extending in many cases beyond traditional limits of territorial waters. Conflicting concepts of the extent of territorial waters, with particular regard to territorial seas that do or may comprise international straits, will be a continuing source of serious international friction. US interests require that the principle of freedom of the seas, in the sense of free passage, be preserved. Increasing pressures for extended rights to commercial exploitation should be recognized in US strategy. The United States should seek legal solutions to those pressures, but should recognize that it may have to enforce such solutions once they are reached.

11. (C) The aviation potential of most of the major nations is a significant element of their national power. In addition to the important capabilities provided by military aircraft, civil air carriers complement merchant shipping and show the flag throughout the world. The use of air transportation to provide US assistance to some of the less developed nations provides an incentive for those nations to develop aircraft support facilities which may be of use to the United States in future contingencies.

12. (S) US forces could be hampered or delayed in responding to certain contingencies by lack of overflight rights and adequate bases. In

anticipation of this problem, the United States should seek to obtain and maintain overflight and foreign base rights in strategic areas throughout the world.

13. (S) Additional limited arms control measures, such as nonproliferation treaties, additional nuclear test bans, nuclear free zones, agreements on peaceful use of outer space, and mutual force reductions may be negotiated during the mid-range period. The achievement of general and complete disarmament is highly unlikely, although the United States and the USSR, as the two leading nuclear powers, will continue to consider such measures. There is ample evidence to indicate that the USSR and other communist states will not agree to a complete verification system such as required by the United States.

Balance of Military Power

14. (S) The most dangerous threat to the United States is posed by the rapidly growing strategic nuclear forces of the Soviet Union. This threat is so serious in its potential consequences, regardless of the estimated intentions of the Soviet Union, that it must receive primary cognizance in the formulation of military strategy and in the development of force levels. Although Soviet strategic offensive forces can inflict enormous damage upon the United States in a first strike, they cannot, at the present time, destroy enough of the US nuclear offensive and defensive forces to preclude retaliatory destruction of Soviet Union urban-industrial resources. However, the Soviets are continuing to build forces, which it is believed will increase their confidence in a retaliatory capability sufficient to assure the destruction of a significant portion of US industrial resources and population. They are also active in efforts, through both strategic offensive and defensive programs, to improve their ability to reduce the damage the United States can inflict on the USSR should deterrence fail and strategic nuclear war occur. In addition, the USSR has the capability to conduct a massive nuclear attack against Eurasia. In the absence of continued US improvements in strategic capabilities, Soviet offensive and defensive systems could attain in the course of their development significant counterforce and defensive damage-limiting capability against the United States. It is necessary, therefore, for the United States to make timely improvements in its strategic offensive and defensive capabilities, to preserve a credible deterrent to convince the Soviets that they cannot achieve a viable first strike option.

15. (S) Irrespective of the unlikelihood of deliberate Soviet initiation of a strategic nuclear attack, the possibility of strategic nuclear war through escalation or miscalculation cannot be dismissed. Further, the United States cannot safely discount the possibility that Soviet leaders might launch a preemptive strike if they considered themselves inextri-

cably involved in a major confrontation over critical objectives. Finally, they might launch a preemptive strike if they believed nuclear attack upon the USSR were imminent.

16. (S) The US and USSR strategic nuclear capabilities are expected to remain superior to those of all other nations for the period of this appraisal. However, by 1970, the CPR probably will have sufficient missiles and warheads to attempt nuclear blackmail in the Western Pacific-Asian area. In the early 1970s, the CPR is expected to be able to pose a limited nuclear threat to the United States and to the USSR.

17. (S) Strategic power relationships could be upset by: unmatched technological advances in weapon systems, particularly in strategic nuclear systems; violations of major arms control agreements; unbalanced arms reductions; and major shifts in alliances and alignments. For example, if the Soviets were to achieve warheads having significantly improved nuclear effects for their ballistic missile defense systems, prior to compensating accomplishments by the United States, the military power relationship would be upset, perhaps critically, in favor of the USSR. For these and other reasons, a vigorous US nuclear test program is necessary within the restrictions of the present Limited Test Ban Treaty.

18. (S) The Warsaw Pact and the CPR have significant general purpose forces which pose major threats to Western Europe, the Middle East, and Asia, and a limited threat outside these areas. The USSR will gradually modernize its general purpose forces to improve their capabilities to engage in sustained nonnuclear as well as nuclear warfare. The emphasis probably will be on improving active combat support and service support units. It is believed that the resulting augmentation will be accompanied by a corresponding reduction in the number of divisions, so that toward the end of the mid-range period there will be a reduced number of larger divisions with better support, with no significant change in the total number of men in the ground forces. Soviet capabilities for airborne and amphibious assault remain tied to support of Eurasian operations. These contiguous capabilities are being expanded markedly as the capacity and efficiency of air and sealift forces are increased. The expansion of the Soviet merchant fleet and the development of very large transport aircraft will also improve Soviet capabilities to move unopposed military forces to distant areas. However, developments thus far do not signify any urgent Soviet program to acquire capabilities for opposed distant operations.

19. (C) The increasing maritime strength and capability of the Soviet Union derive from three elements of seapower: a combatant navy, a merchant marine, and a fleet of oceanographic, survey, and fishing vessels. The Soviet merchant marine and oceanographic fleet can be classed with those of the leading nations of the world. The Soviet navy,

although not a balanced force by Western standards, is quantitatively the second largest in the world, and is undergoing qualitative improvement in both the strategic and general purpose categories. As Soviet maritime capabilities continue to grow, the USSR will increase its capability to meet its own shipping requirements and to expand its political influence throughout the world through economic and military assistance.

20. (S) Evidence indicates that the Soviets have stockages to support substantial chemical warfare operations and that training of personnel in their use has been extensive. Research to improve toxic nerve agents and efforts to develop nonlethal incapacitating agents are continuing. The Soviets have a variety of chemical munitions and delivery vehicles for dissemination of chemical agents and a wide range of defensive chemical warfare equipment.

21. (C) The likelihood of conflicts involving US interests during the mid-range period, as well as their form and outcome, will depend upon the degree to which the United States and its allies maintain a military capability that provides a credible deterrence and effective flexible response throughout the spectrum of potential conflicts. However, even if the US posture is improved to counter the growing and increasingly complex threat, deterrence will not be infallible, and conflicts will occur. Some judgments on the likelihood of conflict are possible in the context of such continuing US posture improvements.

a. Strategic nuclear war, although the most dangerous threat, is the least likely of all levels of warfare.

b. A conventional war of the dimensions of World War II is the least likely of all forms of nonnuclear warfare, primarily because of the probability of escalation to or beyond the use of tactical nuclear weapons.

c. Nonnuclear conflicts, limited in scope and/or objectives, are more likely.

d. Continued low-intensity conflicts, particularly in underdeveloped areas of the world, are certain and these conflicts may increase in frequency.

Part III

Regional Appraisals

General

22. (U) This Part expands the global appraisal in Part II into more specific appraisals for each of the major regions of US security interest. These regional appraisals, and the preceding world appraisal, provide the background for the strategic concept which follows in Part IV. Together, the appraisals and concept serve as a basis for subsequent presentation in Part V of force planning guidance for over-all objective force level analysis and derivation in succeeding Volumes and Annexes

of JSOP 70–77. The sequential treatment of regions and areas does not imply a fractionalization of the threat or a priority among mutually exclusive area concepts, since the threats to all areas are in some respects identical and in most respects overlapping. The regional and area concepts and the US global concept for strategic nuclear offensive and defensive operations are interrelated.

Europe, The Mediterranean, and North Africa

23. (S) NATO Europe, with its industrial, economic, technological, and military strength and potential, is second only to the United States in strategic importance as a Free World power center. Loss of this area to communism would be intolerable. The principal strategic significance of the Mediterranean and North African areas results from their geographical location with respect to the southern flank of NATO Europe. The Mediterranean is one of the primary trade routes for Western Europe and, with its airspace, is the principal avenue for deployment of US forces into the southern flank of NATO and into the Middle East and North Africa. The United States continues to maintain bases in some countries bordering the Mediterranean for the support of NATO, communications, training, storage of pre-positioned war reserve stocks and weapons, custody of part of the NATO nuclear stockpile, and potential staging facilities.

24. (C) The US objectives for NATO and the Mediterranean area, including North Africa, seek to insure the security of those areas against communist aggression and influence and to further their economic growth and political stability. The United States should support North Atlantic Alliance efforts to keep the peace and maintain the independence of its members in a way which would provide a basis for détente, further Atlantic ties, foster European unity, and promote arms control. In addition, the United States encourages a prominent role for the other members of the Alliance in worldwide peacekeeping.

25. (C) The pressures of national sovereignty and regional rivalries will continue to be major obstacles to the achievement of a more closely integrated European defense community than that now represented by NATO. However, during the mid-range period, the United States should pursue the goal of an economically, militarily, and politically integrated Western Europe as the principal way in which Western Europe can realize its full potential. The United States believes that Europe should be "outward-looking" and accept its share of world responsibilities. The United States supports the movement of other eligible European nations such as the United Kingdom toward full-fledged membership in the European Economic Community (EEC). Admission of the United Kingdom to the EEC could stimulate the creation of new European defense arrangements. These developments

could provide the added military capability required to cope with most nonnuclear contingencies which will threaten Europe, and contribute to worldwide peacekeeping, while the United States provides the preponderance of the nuclear deterrent, and the additive forces to cope with major aggression.

26. (S) The uncertain character of French cooperation in the event of war in Europe, and the denial of the use of French territory and facilities in peacetime, adversely affect the readiness and capabilities of NATO to respond to Warsaw Pact aggressions. Current efforts by NATO and French military authorities to identify a workable formula for wartime cooperation between the two forces indicate that, though French forces have been withdrawn from NATO, France is still willing to consider under what conditions it would resist various Warsaw Pact aggressions in concert with its allies. The denial of French territory and airspace divides NATO territory and military defense into two principal regions making mutual support far more difficult than in the past. The weakening of the center emphasizes the importance of the problems of the flanks. Unless overflight of France is granted, the support and reinforcement of the southern flank will be provided principally by NATO forces in the Mediterranean area and deployments from the CONUS. Support or reinforcement of the northern flank without further weakening the center will necessitate increased reliance on NATO's Atlantic naval forces and deployments from the CONUS.

27. (S) The United States now relies upon a line of communication (LOC) through the UK-Benelux countries to support forces in Central Europe. This restricted LOC must be shared with other NATO Allies and the demands of the civilian populace. It is more vulnerable to attack than was the LOC through France. To exploit fully all LOC capabilities within this area, much greater reliance must be placed upon capabilities to protect channel convoys and the use of inland waterways. In addition, highways and railroads must be improved in the region of the FRG-Benelux frontier.

28. (S) The NATO nations are militarily dependent upon the United States. The US strategic deterrent and general purpose forces are essential to Western European security. Continued US efforts to maintain the credibility of this deterrent to both the Warsaw Pact and US NATO Allies are necessary.

29. (S) The Soviet leaders apparently desire to avoid involvement of their own forces in war with the West, but have not renounced as an ultimate goal the extension of Soviet influence throughout the world. Even though the policies and strategy by which the Soviets seek to realize their ends show signs of evolving in response both to political changes in the world and to the continuing existence of a credible Western deterrent, the fundamental issues underlying the tension

between East and West have not been resolved. Soviet policy, which is supported in varying degrees by the Eastern European countries, will continue to be based on economic and political means, propaganda, subversion, and military power.

30. (S) The Soviet leaders actively exploit opportunities outside Europe to achieve positions from which to threaten or harass NATO wherever they can do so without military risk to the Soviet Union. This is especially true in Africa, Latin America, and the Middle East. Within Europe, the Soviet leaders appear to have followed a more cautious line in recent years, influenced significantly by the continued maintenance of strong NATO forces.

31. (S) The military capabilities of the Warsaw Pact constitute a formidible element of the threat. While the Warsaw Pact leaders probably believe that they now possess sufficient military power to deter NATO from resorting to all-out nuclear war, except under extreme threat to its critical interests, they are, nevertheless, expected to continue to spend large sums on improving their capabilities. In particular, the Soviets probably will continue to:

a. Seek by every possible means, including research, development, and production, to acquire a clear military advantage over NATO. They can be expected to exploit any significant increase in their military capability.
b. Pursue their objectives from a position of impressive military strength based on nuclear, massive conventional, chemical, and biological capabilities.
c. Improve and expand their nuclear and antiballistic missile capabilities.
d. Deploy naval forces and merchant fleets worldwide on an increasing scale and in increasing competition with NATO countries.
e. Increase the Warsaw Pact forces' capabilities for a wide range of military operations.

32. (S) In the Mediterranean and North Africa, the USSR and CPR can be expected to continue attempts to exploit instability and local sources of friction in order to neutralize or eliminate other influence. The USSR may attempt to increase its presence in this area by providing equipment and advisors, and by attempting to exercise some measure of indirect control over local military operations, thereby improving the foundation for further Soviet penetration of the Middle East. The Arab nations' compelling desire for, and attempts to acquire, relatively large and modern military forces will continue. Also, precipitous military actions can be expected to recur periodically, with or without foreign encouragement, as a result of traditional animosities or the ambitions of individual leaders.

33. (S) While the continuing Arab-Israeli confrontation will be the most dangerous threat to peace throughout the Arab world, other local

quarrels will persist in North Africa. Libya feels threatened by potential United Arab Republic (UAR) political expansion and military aggression, although the greatest threat to Libyan stability stems from internal friction between those who support the monarchy, and those who, like Nasser, espouse a radical socialist form of government. The moderate positions of the Tunisian, Moroccan, and Libyan Governments with respect to Israel have evoked the distrust of the radical Arab States. Border disputes between Algeria and Tunisia, Morocco, and Libya could develop into open hostilities, particularly in view of the buildup of USSR-provided military equipment in Algeria.

34. (S) Notwithstanding the divisive factors described above, the North African nations have shown some willingness to act in concert with or support the remainder of the Arab nations whenever Israel is involved. The Arab nations have the capability to deny their oil to the West, close the Suez Canal, sabotage Western-owned oil installations, and nationalize the oil industry. However, for economic reasons, such actions would probably not be of long duration. Should they provide bases for Soviet military deployments/operations in the Mediterranean, the adverse consequences would include a diminution of US prestige and influence in the area in peacetime, and a heightened threat to US and NATO operations in wartime.

35. (S) Continued unrestricted use of the Strait of Gibraltar is essential to the United States and its allies. It is also in the interest of both NATO and the United States that the continuing discussions between Spain and the United Kingdom be concluded in a manner which preserves over-flight rights and access to Gibraltar.

36. (S) The UK force drawdowns in Malta have had an unsettling effect on the Maltese political and economic situation. A failure of the Maltese economy could lead to a takeover by leftist groups. The United States should monitor the situation in Malta closely, and, if necessary, take steps to deny its use as a base for military operations by the Soviet Union.

Middle East, Sub-Saharan Africa, and South Asia

37. (S) The Middle East's strategic significance stems from its geographic location, the Suez Canal, its vast oil resources, its ports, the potential for use of its important forward staging and base areas, and its potential as a foundation for increased Soviet influence. Most of the forces and factors that have given this region a high potential for conflict in the past will continue into the mid-range period. The June 1967 Arab-Israeli conflict points up the unpredictability of specific alignments in the area and the miscalculations which deep-seated enmities can stimulate; reinforces the improbability of a near-term accommodation between the two sides; and emphasizes the need for an enduring

solution. Other divisive intraregional quarrels will persist, such as the Yemen dispute and the maneuvering for control of South Arabia subsequent to UK withdrawal from Aden. Despite the adverse reflection on the USSR aid investment which the outcome of the Arab-Israeli conflict caused, the USSR objective to reduce further US and UK influence in the Arab world was advanced. For the longer term, while direct combat involvement of Soviet forces in the area during the coming decade is unlikely, force deployments cannot be ruled out in all circumstances, due to USSR proximity and the likelihood of its continued alignment with the Arab cause.

a. Israel will seek to maintain the military superiority over the Arab nations which it demonstrated in the recent short but intensive war. The USSR, by recent resupply actions following the establishment of the cease-fire, has clearly demonstrated an intent to continue the provision of war matériel to the Arab nations. However, the Soviets are likely to reappraise the worth of their military assistance to the Arabs, and military aid is likely to be on a more selective basis. There is a better than even chance that Israel will decide to develop a nuclear capability during the mid-range period. The probability would be heightened by [illegible—any?] of several factors, e.g.: sizeable rearming of the Arabs; a settlement of the current situation which does not provide for Israel's security, right of innocent passage through the Strait of Tiran and the Suez Canal, and bilateral negotiations between Israel and Arab nations; and increased membership by other nations in the nuclear weapons community with consequent lowering of the onus against entry.

b. Iran, the pivotal CENTO state, has hoped to use this defense organization to counter what it considers the Arab threat. The Shah, concentrating on the solution of economic problems, brought about in part by excessive expenditures on military hardware, has recently demonstrated a desire for greater Iranian independence in political, military, and economic matters. Nevertheless, the Shah and any probable successor will likely continue to look to the West, particularly the United States, as a major source of protection against Soviet expansionist actions, as well as against any threat by Arab radicals, particularly from Iraq.

c. CENTO is a link, albeit a weak one, in the containment chain around the communist world. UK participation probably will continue. Barring a political upheaval, it is expected that Turkey, Iran, and probably Pakistan will continue CENTO membership. However, unless unforeseen circumstances necessitate a US decision to commit major military strengths directly to CENTO on a continuing basis, which is unlikely, CENTO's military importance will continue to be minor. Hence, the security of this region will rest primarily on US bilateral arrangements.

d. Although existing bases in Turkey can facilitate execution of US contingency plans, their use for actions unrelated to NATO or not in Turkish interests may be denied. Pakistan, Iran, Turkey, and Ethiopia provide critical communications, surveillance, detection, and other support facilities, which will continue to be important.

38. (S) Sub-Saharan Africa is certain to experience political and social turmoil during the next decade. The greatest threat to peace stems from the instability occasioned by changes in leadership and the coupling of the modernization process with racial and tribal tensions. This instability and receding Western influence leave an environment susceptible to communist exploitation. Communist influence probably will increase if Western Europe continues to reduce its levels of assistance. Sub-Saharan Africa is of significance largely because of its potential were it to fall within the sphere of communist influence. In addition, base, transit, and overflight rights, and other such requirements are significant in the event operations develop which involve US participation. Both sea and air base facilities assume greater significance in use of alternate routes during any closure of the Suez Canal. South Africa presents special problems to the United States. It has the most significant armed forces in Africa south of the Sahara and its facilities would be of increased value in the event of Suez Canal closure. However, South Africa's apartheid policy runs counter to US national policies. This cause of friction between the two governments makes less likely, as time progresses, any arrangements for mutual military support and cooperation.

39. (S) South Asia, with its vast land mass and large population, is strategically significant because of its long-range potential. Its loss to communism would be seriously disadvantageous to US interests and long-range objectives in Asia.

a. India is wary of Pakistan's cooperation with the CPR, and appears determined to check further Chinese expansion in the northern border area. If the CPR maintains its bellicose attitude, India probably will seek additional US, British, and Soviet assistance, but is not likely to invite direct foreign military presence unless there is a renewal of large-scale hostilities in the Sino-Indian border region. India will face many political difficulties aggravated by inflation, religious strife, student unrest, internal communist agitation, and slow progress in overcoming governmental inertia in dealing with food supply and population growth problems. Military self-sufficiency may be substantially realized toward the end of the mid-range period, but India will require foreign assistance in the interim if it is to achieve its planned military capability. India could be the next nation to develop a nuclear weapon capability, which, while tending to offset the CPR strength, would constitute a major stimulus to Pakistan to move closer to the CPR and/or to seek, through a combination of external assistance and its own effort, to attain some military nuclear capability.

b. Pakistan, through its membership in CENTO and SEATO, had hoped to counterbalance India, which it has viewed as the more immediate threat to its security. Prospects for permanent settlement of the Kashmir dispute and improvement of relations with India are dim. The conflicting difficulties of seeking security against India, the USSR, and the CPR could cause Pakistan to continue its drift toward nonalignment or toward the CPR in contrast to its previous pro-Western stance. Hence, only minimal participation in regional defense treaty organizations is to be expected.

The Pacific Area

40. (C) Asia has become the arena for open military conflict arising from three interrelated confrontations: US-CPR, USSR-CPR, and US-USSR. US policy in Asia since 1949 has emphasized containment of the multiple threats posed by the USSR and the CPR. SEATO was created for this purpose and has proven to be a useful instrument. A policy emphasizing containment will continue during the mid-range period, dealing with the threats generated by subversion, insurgency, and armed intrusion in Asian mainland areas and in the adjacent Western Pacific. The threat of such aggressions stems directly or indirectly from the CPR. US political, economic, psychological, and military measures taken in the peripheral areas should be oriented to an over-all strategy centered on Communist China.

41. (C) The end results of US efforts in Vietnam will influence strongly the future of Asia and will bear critically on the prospects for US influence on the developing nations of the world. Additionally, long-term Asian issues which will impact on the US security interests are: the extent to which India, Japan, and Australia develop their military capabilities and display a willingness to play a positive role in the affairs of Asia; the willingness and ability of the United Kingdom to continue to play a power role in Southeast Asia; the ability of the Philippines to resist a growing threat to its political stability; the ability of Indonesia to achieve stability and become a constructive factor in Southeast Asia / Southwest Pacific affairs; the ability of South Korea to maintain a stable, noncommunist government and deter aggression; and the extent to which the free countries of Asia will seek increased mutual accommodation to create a counterweight to Chinese power.

42. (S) CPR military capabilities will improve over the next decade, with continued emphasis on the attainment of significant nuclear weapons capabilities. Long-term CPR goals include achievement of major power status, dominance in Asia, ideological leadership of international communism, and the expulsion of US power and influence

from Asia. Corollary objectives include: control over territory now held by the Government of the Republic of China (GRC), detachment of Japan from its alliance with the United States, neutralization of India as a competitor for regional power, and the restoration of Chinese suzerainty over Korea and mainland Southeast Asia. The CPR is not likely to resort to overt military intervention or aggression so long as it considers the probable losses greater than the likely gain and can anticipate success through other means. Nevertheless, the use of CPR military force must be anticipated if Chinese border areas are threatened, if the CPR leaders wrongly assess US intentions, or if a neighboring communist state, such as North Vietnam, is near collapse or requests Chinese assistance. The CPR military capability to attack the Republic of Korea, Southeast Asia, and India is significant. The major weaknesses of CPR armed forces are in sea power, logistic support, and lack of modernization of their substantial air forces, which would limit the scope of their military operations. The CPR now has a limited capability for nuclear strikes against peripheral Asian targets which it can be expected to exploit politically. This capability is expected to increase significantly during the mid-range period.

43. (S) The USSR also poses a serious threat in the Pacific area because of its ability to provide material assistance to insurgent movements and modern arms to governments susceptible to Soviet influence, and because USSR forces have a capability to strike, harass, or neutralize a large portion of the US military forces in the Pacific-Asian area. Moreover, the expansion of the Soviet merchant marine and the development of very large transport aircraft will improve Soviet capabilities to move unopposed military forces and equipment to distant areas.

44. (S) Japan is by far the strongest nation in Asia in economic terms. At its own pace, it probably will increase its military strength and may slowly and cautiously assume larger security responsibilities in Northeast Asia. The possibility that Japan will eventually assert a position of leadership in Pacific-Asia warrants specific consideration in US planning. As Japan enlarges its role in Asia, preservation of close US-Japanese ties is important to US interests worldwide. US base rights in the Japanese homeland and on Okinawa and available skilled Japanese manpower and industrial support are major elements in support of US military posture throughout the Western Pacific. Pressure for the restoration of the Ryukyus to Japanese sovereignty and control in some form can be expected, but continued US use of the Ryukyuan bases will remain fundamental to US strategic concepts for the area.

45. (C) South Korea, with its growing economy and industrial base, is an anchor point of US forward strategy in Northeast Asia. The presence of US combat forces on South Korean territory provides evidence

of a firm commitment, adding to the credibility of the US deterrent in Northeast Asia. So long as the United States continues its firm commitment to assist in the defense of South Korea and provides appropriate military and economic assistance, South Korea probably will continue as a cooperative ally in Asia, will be able to provide forces for its own defense, and may contribute forces to other operations in Asia. Overt aggression from the north remains a possibility in the mid-range period but the more immediate danger probably will be the growing incidence of communist infiltration, propaganda, and subversive activity from North Korea. A North Korean intensification of this activity would add to the difficulties of the ROK Government in providing combat forces outside of Korea and would increase pressure on the United States for additional MAP assistance and a continued US presence in Korea.

46. (S) The GRC has a capability for continued and improved economic viability on Taiwan, but does not have sufficient military power to reestablish itself on the mainland or to defend Taiwan unaided against a large-scale sustained CPR assault. The military importance of the GRC in terms of US security interests stems from US access to bases and facilities on Taiwan, the denial of these facilities to the CPR, and from the substantial threat GRC armed forces pose to the mainland tying down CPR forces in the coastal provinces. While military limitations and concern over US response will deter the CPR from attempting military conquest of Taiwan, the CPR may periodically undertake military action in the Taiwan Straits area to test GRC defenses and probe US determination. The present US objective of preventing a CPR military seizure of Taiwan will continue; however, it is also in the US interest to avoid involvement in, and to discourage GRC initiation of, a war with the CPR in an attempt to restore its control over the mainland.

47. (S) The Philippines provide major US base facilities essential to the forward strategy in the Pacific-Asian area. The Philippine Government is expected to continue its alliance with the United States but will require strong US support. For the mid-range period, the threat of external attack, other than the potential Chinese intermediate range ballistic missile (IRBM) threat, is not great; however, the potential for subversion and insurgency is significant and rising. This threat stems from a variety of dissident minority groups, including the illegal Communist Party and remnants of its military arm—the Huk. In addition, a strong Muslim group, which does not fully support the government, exists in the southern islands, and Indonesian claims to the southern island, though now dormant, can become an issue during the mid-range period. These factors, together with signs of a breakdown in law and order and extensive unemployment, are causing a progressive deterioration of governmental control. Additionally, an element of extremism is emerging that includes considerable anti-US sentiment

and opposition to the Philippine Government for sending forces to Vietnam. These conditions are inimical to the longstanding US interests in the Philippines.

48. (S) The United Kingdom has stated its intention to reduce further its military forces in the Far East during the next few years. It is in the US interest to encourage the United Kingdom to delay its final departure from the Singapore base as long as possible and particularly until the situation in Southeast Asia is resolved. The United States, because of its heavy commitments elsewhere, is not in a position to assume the added responsibility for the security of the Singapore-Malaysia area.

49. (S) Australia and New Zealand have close defense ties with the United States and basically adhere to a forward defense strategy in Asia. As the military presence of the United Kingdom recedes and CPR bellicosity continues—both likely eventualities—Australia and New Zealand will rely increasingly on the United States rather than the United Kingdom. Australia is increasing its military potential and, over the long run, could become the only non-Asian nation, other than the United States, with significant power in the Pacific.

50. (S) In Indonesia, in view of the anticommunist violence which accompanied the 1965 change of regime, the present government has a large stake in preventing a return of communist power. Indonesia's membership in the United Nations has been renewed, Indonesian relations with the West have improved, and there has been a distinct withdrawal from the formerly strong associations with the CPR, North Vietnam, and North Korea. The CPR can be expected to attempt to regain its former influence in Indonesia. The USSR will seek to restrict or eliminate Western influence in Indonesia, as well as to thwart any CPR move to regain ascendancy. While continuing to seek military assistance and aid from both the United States and the USSR, Indonesia probably will strive to maintain a nonaligned position in its relation with the USSR and the West.

51. (S) Southeast Asia currently presents the most serious and complex problems facing the United States in sustaining its containment policy. The United States has chosen to take a stand in Vietnam against communist use of "peoples war" and "wars of national liberation." Involved in the outcome of this conflict are such long-term issues as: (a) the confidence of other nations in the US collective security policy and, consequently, their will to resist aggression and insurgency; (b) the future of US influence in the affairs of Asia; (c) the prospect of more or fewer communist-inspired and supported insurgencies throughout the underdeveloped world; (d) leadership of the world communist movement; and (e) the extent of progress by the CPR toward its basic goal of dominating Asia and excluding Free World interests and influence. The

US purpose in Vietnam will continue to be to assist the Government of Vietnam in defeating communist subversion and aggression, in winning the allegiance of the people, and in attaining an independent, noncommunist society functioning in a secure environment.

52. (S) In Thailand, deployments of US forces are largely to meet the needs of the Southeast Asia conflict, including operations in Laos. The facilities developed during this conflict could be used to provide a base for future US/SEATO deployments, should this become necessary. Thailand is faced with a growing problem of insurgency primarily in the northeast sector, supported by the Pathet Lao and North Vietnam. The Thais, with aid provided through the US Military Assistance Programs, will probably be able to hold this insurgency in check as long as US/allied effort continues to contain the primary threat in South Vietnam. The United States looks to Thailand to play a role in strengthening regional resistance to aggression and has declared that full support of the SEATO Treaty would be provided in the event of direct communist attack. The other nations of the Southeast Asian peninsula—Burma, Laos, Cambodia, Malaysia, and Singapore—will be unable to provide, without outside assistance, for their own defense against either external communist aggression or major internal subversion. The neutral status of Laos and Cambodia has been undermined by their use as sanctuaries by North Vietnam/Viet Cong combat forces. Accordingly, although the United States respects the neutral status of these countries, operations by US forces are required to negate such use by the North Vietnam/Viet Cong forces.

The Americas

53. (S) The primary threat to North America will be from Soviet strategic nuclear forces. The ballistic missile threat is expected to increase. That threat may be supplemented by weapons deliverable from orbit or with depressed trajectories, if such systems are developed. The CPR will represent a growing threat in the 1971–1980 time frame. Since the most likely air or intercontinental ballistic missile (ICBM) attack approach is via the polar regions, Canada's aerospace and participation in NORAD continue to be of great significance. Inasmuch as submarine-launched missiles pose a threat off both coasts of North America, it is important that US-Canadian antisubmarine warfare arrangements be continued. It is expected that military relations between Canada and the United States will continue to reflect the fundamental identity of common defense interests, but may be affected by Canada's growing nationalism and by its increasing sensitivity to any form of US pressure.

54. (S) In most of Latin America, political, sociological, and economic instability, frequently exploited by communist subversion and

insurgency, will continue. The principal threat to US interests will continue to be such communist subversion and insurgency. Although now remote, the possibility of insurgencies of serious proportions occurring simultaneously in several Latin American countries, must be taken into account. The communists seek to: (a) erode US influence, exploiting the anti-US character of Latin American ultranationalism; (b) undermine the Organization of American States (OAS) and the Alliance for Progress; (c) neutralize Latin American armed forces; and (d) subvert legitimate reform and nationalist movements. Cuba will continue to be the main base in Latin America for communist subversion as long as the Castro regime retains control but, in the near-term, Cuban-instigated movements are not expected to reach sufficient proportions to overthrow Latin American governments. However, other sources of violence and discontent may well overthrow weak governments because of lack of public support or military disenchantment.

55. (S) A prime communist objective will be to weaken the OAS and prevent the establishment of regional peacekeeping forces which could thwart a communist takeover of any nation in the area. It is not likely that the USSR, Communist China, or Cuba would participate in direct military operations and risk a confrontation with the United States. However, communist countries can be expected to provide material, economic, psychological, and political support of communist-inspired activities in Latin America, together with training of local communist leaders.

56. (S) Most Latin American governments and their armed forces will probably remain pro-United States and anticommunist, although nationalist tendencies will become more pronounced. If the military leaders cannot obtain what they believe to be sufficient US military equipment, their US-orientation will diminish and they will continue to seek and obtain military assistance from other sources.

57. (S) Close cooperation in countering communist insurgents can be expected between certain countries; e.g., Guatemala and Honduras, Bolivia and Argentina, and Colombia and Venezuela. Nevertheless, most Latin American security forces would be unable to cope with widespread insurgency without external assistance.

58. (S) Latin American desire to stay clear of a nuclear power struggle has resulted in a Nuclear Free Zone (NFZ) Treaty having been agreed to by most Latin American countries. The NFZ will undoubtedly come into existence but the Treaty is worded so that there should be no adverse effect on US transit and overflight rights. However, there are other important factors associated with this Treaty, such as extravagant territorial sea claims, which are potentially inimical to US interests.

Part IV

Strategic Concept

General Considerations

59. (S) *General.* The principal objective of US military strategy is the deterrence of aggression at any level, with emphasis on deterrence of strategic nuclear attack on the United States since national survival would be clearly in jeopardy. Should deterrence fail, the principal objective of US military strategy is the termination of hostilities under conditions of relative advantage while limiting damage to the United States and minimizing damage to US and allied interests. Accordingly, the three basic elements of the US strategic concept are collective security, credible deterrence, and flexible response.

60. (S) *Collective Security.* The first goal of collective security is to acquire and assist allies who will contribute to US security interests worldwide, particularly through mutual efforts to counter threats posed by the Soviet Union and Communist China and their respective allies. The second goal is to obtain the cooperation and assistance of other nations in programs to eliminate internal weaknesses and instability which attract and facilitate subversion, insurgency, and armed aggression.

a. The United States should enter alliances and other collective security arrangements selectively, stressing maximum reliance upon indigenous forces to protect their national and regional interests. US participation should be based upon the degree to which US interests are involved; the threat; and the willingness, desires, and capabilities of the peoples concerned to support mutual goals.

b. Inherent in collective security is forward defense. This comprises a combination of elements, including strong indigenous military forces; forward-deployed US forces; pre-positioned equipment and supplies; forces fully capable of rapid deployment, quick entry into combat, and sustained operations, as necessary; and US strategic mobility capabilities; all complemented by US strategic nuclear power. Collective security embodies cooperative efforts toward common goals, which include combined action to counter aggression and to assist other nations. There must be increased emphasis on regional efforts toward self-help and economic and military assistance by third nations.

61. (S) *Credible Deterrence.* Deterrence is a state of mind brought about by a credible threat of unacceptable counteraction. Credible deterrence is a function of obvious capability and known determination to employ it when necessary. Deterrence could fail for a number of reasons, important among which are miscalculation of intent or resolve, underestimation of military capabilities, or commission of an irrational

act. Forces structured solely to deter may be insufficient to achieve US objectives if deterrence fails. It is important that deterrent credibility be established for all levels of conflict. There is an essential relationship among all the levels of deterrence.

a. The United States must be known to possess a level and mix of strategic offensive and defensive weapon systems, which have sufficient survivability and assured capability to penetrate under all conditions of war outbreak, to guarantee unacceptable damage to any state, or combination of states, and which have, concomitantly, the capability to limit damage to the United States and its allies.

b. Deterrence of an enemy's use of nuclear weapons within a theater requires survivable, controlled, and versatile strategic offensive and defensive forces and dual-capable (nuclear and nonnuclear) general purpose forces, capable of rapid and discriminate response at levels of intensity appropriate to the circumstances.

c. Deterrence of nonnuclear aggression is based on both US and allied dual-capable general purpose forces and US strategic forces. Requirements include continued efforts by Free World nations to strengthen their military capabilities; US forces capable of arriving in potential conflict areas quickly, in strength, and prepared for peacekeeping and such combat operations as may be necessary; strategic mobility capabilities; and US forces deployed to selected forward locations as evidence of US determination and unequivocal involvement.

d. Deterrence of subversion and insurgency is best accomplished through preventive efforts aimed at establishing effective political, economic, technological, psychological, sociological, and military programs. The key military requirements are to deter outside military support to insurgency, to assist in the creation and employment of indigenous military and paramilitary forces capable of contributing effectively to internal security and stability, and to participate in support of other government agencies in nonmilitary programs.

62. (S) *Flexible Response.* A capability for flexible response requires the United States to have an array of options to cope with all the levels and scopes of conflict. This will provide a capability for controlled increases or decreases in the application of military power to US advantage throughout the spectrum of warfare. US initial engagement, and subsequent increases in commitment if necessary, should be on a scale and intensity such that the enemy will have neither the time nor the capability to accommodate to our efforts, thereby insuring his timely defeat, minimum costs in US and allied lives and resources, and achievement of US objectives. Additionally, US forces must be capable of executing national options of response that are not limited to the location and manner of conflict selected by the enemy.

a. To defeat subversion and insurgency, US strategy must encompass and integrate diplomacy, military and economic aid, technical assistance, cultural exchange, economic sanctions, psychological operations, and unconventional warfare. Preventive programs must be continued and strengthened. Maximum possible use must be made of indigenous forces to deal with local insurgents; in addition, US forces may be necessary to support local forces, to engage and defeat the insurgents, and to interdict or defeat external support.

b. The United States must have the capability of committing general purpose forces in accordance with terms of alliances, in support of UN resolutions, and on the basis of US unilateral decisions. This objective necessitates a high degree of flexibility, a strategic deployment capability to all points of the globe, a versatile capability to engage enemies whose capabilities range from primitive to sophisticated, and the ability to deploy to and fight in all environments.

(1) Against the background of the relative total military capabilities of the United States and the USSR, the strategic implications of conflict at sea become significant as a means for bringing military pressure to bear in support of limited objectives.

(a) In the case of the United States and its allies, it provides options to deter and coerce the Soviet Union and its allies to the advantage of Free World interests.

(b) In the case of the Soviet Union and its allies it provides options to bring military pressure to bear in selected instances against vulnerable US and allied sea lines of communications to gain limited objectives.

(2) US employment of coercive options at sea should take into consideration joint employment of over-all US military strength if major interests are at stake.

c. General purpose forces must include a strong tactical nuclear capability for the option of effective quick response in raising the threshold of conflict against enemy superiority, when necessary to defeat the enemy, and to respond to possible enemy use of tactical nuclear weapons. For such quick response, tactical nuclear weapons must be collocated with dual-capable forward-deployed forces.

d. At the level of strategic nuclear war, US strategy must provide multiple options to national authorities, to include a selection of execution choices as to countries and tasks under varying conditions of war outbreak. Under all conditions, US strategic offensive and defensive forces must comprise a capability to inflict unacceptable damage upon the war-supporting and urban-industrial resources of the enemy. Concomitantly they must be capable of: destroying or neutralizing (with or without collateral damage constraints) a comprehensive military target system; limiting damage to the United States and its allies;

maintaining continued strategic superiority; conducting selective attacks; and terminating hostilities under conditions of relative advantage to the United States. These capabilities would also provide options to deter and coerce the enemy. General purpose forces also figure importantly in US options for flexible response at the level of strategic nuclear war. They contribute both during and subsequent to strategic nuclear operations and exploit the advantage achieved in these operations, thus furthering progress toward achievement of US objectives in the post-termination period.

Regional Considerations

63. (S) *Europe, the Mediterranean, and North Africa*

a. NATO Strategy[2]

(1) The over-all US military objective for NATO, essentially the same as that of the other member nations, is to prevent war by creating an effective deterrent to all forms of aggression. For this purpose the Alliance needs a full spectrum of military capabilities ranging from conventional forces through tactical nuclear weapons to strategic nuclear forces.

(2) To provide the minimum requirements for the deterrent strategy the Alliance must act jointly and maintain at least:

(a) A credible capability for direct defense (i.e., either defeats aggression on the level at which the enemy chooses to fight or places upon the aggressor the burden of escalation) to deter the lesser aggressions such as covert actions, incursions, infiltrations, hostile local actions, and limited aggression (i.e., any nuclear or nonnuclear military action in which it appears that an armed attack imperils neither the survival of nation(s) nor the integrity of military forces).

(b) A credible capability for deliberate escalation (i.e., scope and intensity of combat deliberately raised but, where possible, controlled) to deter more ambitious aggressions.

(c) A credible capability to conduct a general nuclear response [2-1/2 *lines of source text not declassified*] as the ultimate deterrent.

(3) Should aggression occur the military objective must be to preserve or restore the integrity and security of the North Atlantic Treaty area by employing such force as may be necessary. In the fulfillment of this objective, the area of Allied Command Europe is to be defended as far forward as possible. In this event the Alliance should:

---

[2] Draft MC 14/3 is now under consideration by the NATO Military Committee as a Strategic Concept for NATO to replace MC 14/2. The present draft represents major progress in accommodating the various strategic views of the member nations. The Joint Chiefs of Staff have concurred in this strategic concept for the Alliance. [Footnote in the source text.]

(a) Meet initially any aggression short of a major nuclear attack with the available direct defense.

(b) Conduct a deliberate escalation of the conflict if the aggression could not be held and the situation restored by direct defense.

(c) *[1-1/2 lines of source text not declassified]*

(4) The political and military control arrangements of the Alliance should permit timely political consultation required by indicators of attack, and consultation required for the use of nuclear weapons. The use of nuclear weapons should be consistent with the following guidelines:

(a) *[4-1/2 lines of source text not declassified]*
(b) *[5 lines of source text not declassified]*
(c) *[5-1/2 lines of source text not declassified]*

(5) A capability for rapid augmentation of the forward posture is necessary so that maximum use may be made of any period of political tension which may precede a possible aggression or to take advantage of any forewarning provided by any other indications. This capability must provide:

(a) For the timely deployment of any active forces not located near their emergency defense positions.

(b) For supplementing effective local forces in-being on the flanks through an improved NATO capability for rapid reinforcement without impairment of M-Day defensive capabilities elsewhere.

(c) For the provision of trained, equipped, and readily mobilizable reserve forces which might be committed to NATO.

(6) Plans for rapid augmentation capability should take full account of the mobilization and force expansion capabilities of NATO countries, provide a base for longer-term increases in a prolonged test of political determination, and take account of the possibility that neither French forces nor French territory, air space, or facilities would be available to NATO in a crisis or war.

b. *Additional US Aspects of Strategy for Western Europe*

(1) Provisions for the defense of Western Europe should include the option for US and allied forces, appropriately reinforced, to defend, without the use of nuclear weapons, against aggression by Warsaw Pact forces against NATO forces, with the objective of demonstrating to the Soviet leaders the escalatory risk involved in pursuing further military aggression.

(2) The United States must prepare unilateral plans for Europe which provide, among other things, for the participation of French forces and the use of French territory and facilities in the event of war, and for the control and use of nuclear weapons should the NATO system not function properly. In addition, the United States should plan for

alternatives in those situations in which, due to the multinational character of NATO decision-making, combined action critical to US objectives may be infeasible or subject to unacceptable delay.

(3) Defense of the European area, undertaken by the United States
in conjunction with participating allies, will be conducted as far forward as possible along the general line of [7 *lines of source text not declassified*]. In all cases this will require securing and controlling essential
bases and LOCs, including control of the sea and air approaches thereto.

(4) Although sea forces of the Atlantic Command must be prepared
primarily to respond to overt aggression at any level, in conjunction
with land, air, and amphibious operations, mid-range strategy should
give greater emphasis than heretofore to the protection of US/allied
maritime interests under conditions short of a major war in continental
Europe. In this context, the strategy should provide for a naval posture
with a recognizable capability to deter or respond to any hostile act or
threat of aggression at sea with a degree of force sufficient to oblige the
aggressor to choose between intensifying the confrontation, with a clear
prospect for defeat at any higher level of engagement, or withdrawing.
One measure that is expected to be adopted in furtherance of this objective is establishment of a permanent nucleus of a NATO standing naval
force (STANAVFOR).

c. *US Strategy for the Mediterranean and North Africa.* US strategy
must be one which maintains continued freedom of access and operations in the Mediterranean and stresses noninvolvement of US military
forces in Africa. Primary reliance should be placed on peacekeeping
forces of the United Nations when military action in North Africa is
required. If the United Nations does not respond, the United States
should next seek solutions using NATO institutions and forces or ad
hoc multilateral arrangements. Only when all other means have been
exhausted and US national interests are involved should a unilateral
commitment of US forces be made. This general policy should not preclude timely action by the United States, including deployment of land,
sea, and air forces, when other means threaten delay which jeopardizes
US objectives. Essential to this strategy are actions which will:

(1) Ensure maintenance of LOCs into and through the
Mediterranean.
(2) Encourage maximum use of indigenous forces for internal security and defense of those countries important to the defense of Western
Europe.
(3) Maintain base rights, port facilities, transit, and overflight rights
to support LOCs to Europe's southern flank.
(4) Provide LOCs and entry rights and facilities to ensure introduction of US forces into the area and into the Middle East and Africa South
of the Sahara.

(5) Continue contact and influence with both military and civilian elements of countries in the area to foster US orientation.

64. (S) *Middle East, Sub-Saharan Africa, and South Asia.* US military strategy supports the following major US objectives for these areas: to limit communist influence; to prevent the establishment of Soviet bases; to promote a sufficient degree of internal security to allow orderly national development and stability; to discourage arms races; to encourage peaceful settlements of disputes between nations; to preserve uninterrupted access to strategic resources and facilities; to ensure retention of and/or access to essential bases and facilities; and other strategic capabilities such as use of the Suez Canal, overflight and transit rights, and staging services.

a. In the Middle East, US policy seeks to maintain the independence and territorial integrity of the nations in the area. In furtherance of this policy, US military strategy is:

(1) Use of peacekeeping forces of the United Nations, or of ad hoc multilateral arrangements to maintain stability. Participation by US forces should not be sought unless the multilateral arrangement includes Soviet participation and/or the participation of US forces appears to be a prerequisite to a multilateral agreement to act.

(2) Unilateral commitment of US forces only when other means do not materialize and US objectives are threatened.

(3) Assistance, including logistic support, of indigenous forces in the forward defense of CENTO in the event of Soviet aggression. Should the forward defense fail, lodgments should be retained, to the extent practicable, in the Karachi, Persian Gulf, Aden Gulf, and Suez areas.

b. In Sub-Saharan Africa, US military strategy is:

(1) Take full advantage of existing and potential indigenous military and paramilitary resources to prevent and/or defeat subversion, infiltration, and insurrection.

(2) Encourage initial response by allied and regional forces in event outside assistance is required.

c. In South Asia, US military strategy is:

(1) Rely on defense primarily by allied and indigenous forces against communist aggression.

(2) Plan for US support, to include tactical air, air defense, naval, and logistic support forces.

(3) Manage arms support and sales in such a manner as to hold the India-Pakistan arms race in check.

(4) Seek to establish facilities, such as on Aldabra and Diego Garcia, in strategic areas.

65. (S) *The Pacific Area*

a. Problems in Asia cannot be met by the same formula the United States has applied to Europe. In particular, broad-based, collective security is more difficult to achieve, subversion and indirect aggression are more prevalent, and deployments to and operations in areas along the mainland periphery are more difficult to maintain in Asia than in Europe.

b. The basic tenet of US military strategy in Asia is containment. A strategy of containing Asian communism has three interrelated elements: (1) deterring or defeating direct or indirect aggression; (2) strengthening the areas threatened by aggression or subversion; and (3) influencing the leaders of the CPR and other Asian communist nations to abandon their expansionist policies and seek a constructive relationship with the outside world.

c. The US strategy for containment of Asian communism for the duration of the Vietnam conflict will be close-in containment of Communist China, North Vietnam, and North Korea while assisting in the defense of free nations of the area against communist aggression. The post-hostilities strategy will be dependent upon the military and political conditions under which hostilities are terminated. Either a close-in or offshore strategy, or a combination of both, would: (1) lend credibility to military alliances; (2) keep open land, sea, and air routes between the Pacific and Indian Oceans; (3) give Free World access to strategic exports from the area; and (4) help independent countries achieve political stability within a framework of economic development and progressive social change.

d. An example of the types of conflict for which US forces must be provided in the mid-range period is the current war in Southeast Asia, the successful prosecution of which requires the maintenance of simultaneous pressure against all elements of the enemy's war-making capability. In South Vietnam, this involves extensive ground, air, and naval operations against the Viet Cong/North Vietnamese main forces and major base areas, while continuing political, social, and economic development and vigorous offensive operations against Viet Cong provincial forces and guerrillas. Against North Vietnam this involves a comprehensive and coordinated air/naval campaign which will: (1) bring military pressure on its internal war-supporting resources; (2) effectively impede the importation of external resources; and (3) increase interdiction of infiltration routes in North Vietnam, Laos, Cambodia, and along the coast. This strategy envisions a degree of pressure which is beyond the enemy's capability to accommodate and seeks the following military objectives: (1) to make it as difficult and costly as possible for North Vietnam to continue effective support of the Viet Cong and to cause North Vietnam to cease direction of the Viet Cong insurgency; (2) to defeat the Viet Cong and North Vietnam forces in South Vietnam and force the withdrawal of North Vietnam forces; (3) to extend Government of South Vietnam domination, direction, and control over

South Vietnam; and (4) to deter the CPR from direct intervention in Southeast Asia and elsewhere in the Western Pacific and to be prepared to defeat such intervention if it occurs. Until these objectives are realized, the United States must retain the initiative and maintain momentum in the conflict using such forces as are required.

e. In the event that cessation of Southeast Asia hostilities is brought about by a military truce or a de facto "fading away" of the enemy, planning should provide for retention in South Vietnam of a balanced combat and logistic capability sufficient to assure the security of the United States/Free World military assistance forces (US/FWMAF) from major attacks or intensive harassment by Viet Cong/North Vietnamese forces. The size of retained forces can be reduced gradually as evidence of Viet Cong/North Vietnamese compliance with any agreements and desire for peace accumulates.

f. In the event that cessation of Southeast Asia hostilities is brought about by a political settlement that entails major withdrawal of US military forces from Vietnam, the alternative containment posture for the United States should provide for forces and activities in the Pacific-Asian area in the range between the pre-Vietnam levels (1 August 1964) and the current levels, including: (1) a Military Assistance Advisory Group in South Vietnam; (2) advisory, logistical, security, and tactical forces and facilities in Thailand; (3) balanced forces in the offshore areas and Korea; (4) back-up ready forces elsewhere in the Far East and Pacific, and in the CONUS; (5) major US naval forces in the South China Sea/Gulf of Siam area or elsewhere in the Western Pacific for rapid response in troubled areas; and (6) facilities and matériel in forward areas to permit rapid deployment of combat forces.

g. In the event of a war with the CPR or the CPR and the USSR, the US military strategy for the defense of the Far East is for the United States and allied nations to defend as far forward as possible while conducting offensive naval and air operations against the enemy, including the CPR proper. This requires a military capability for an active defense of the continental areas of South Korea, South Vietnam, and Thailand, as well as a capability for offensive operations. Within this strategy, the United States must hold, as a minimum, the strategic area encompassed by the general line of [2 *lines of source text not declassified*]. In addition, control of the seas must include the Strait of Malacca, South China Sea, Formosa Strait, East China Sea, Japan Sea, Bering Sea, and the Bering Strait. [4-1/2 *lines of source text not declassified*]

h. Some reduction in US forces in Korea may become possible in the future, depending upon the outcome of the conflict in Southeast Asia and based upon: assurances of continuing AID and MAP support; an agreed ROK-US strategic concept for defense, [*less than 1 line of source text not declassified*] and a residual US presence as part of a credible deterrent and defense posture. Proposals for withdrawal of US forces from Korea must also be considered in context with the evolving patterns of ROK-Japanese and US-Japanese relations, and the capabilities of the ROK Government to deal with the existing and projected threat from the north.

i. The United States should strongly resist pressure for any change in the existing arrangements for US control of the Ryukyus in view of their strategic importance. US strategy and base planning, while holding firm on the requirements for continued unrestricted use of the bases in the Ryukyus, should include planning for alternative arrangements should these become necessary.

j. [12-1/2 lines of source text not declassified]

k. The post-hostilities posture in the Pacific-Asian area should include those military assets, bases, and facilities needed to continue the forward deployment of US forces in order to strengthen the resolve of friendly countries, to deter aggression by communist countries, and to assist in the defeat of such aggression if it occurs.

66. (S) *The Americas*

a. Canada should be encouraged to continue its close and traditional cooperation with the United States, and broaden its military, economic, and political activities in intrahemisphere affairs. An important step would be for Canada to become a member of the OAS. It is essential to the defense of North America that good US-Canadian relations be maintained in order to support expansion of NORAD capability to make it effective in meeting the threat.

b. Instability in Latin America will require that the United States act to prevent or defeat aggression or insurgency inimical to US interests and assist in maintaining the security and integrity of selected nations. Of particular interest are those nations in which subversion would threaten the use of the Panama Canal and those most susceptible to the establishment of communist regimes. The presence of the US Military Assistance Advisory Groups and US Military Groups in the countries of Latin America must be maintained as a fundamental element of US influence in the Hemisphere. It will continue to be necessary to provide US military matériel to Latin American countries on a selective basis in order to modernize Latin American security forces, participate in the choice and composition of such forces, minimize third country incursions, and maintain close rapport with the Latin American countries.

c. US military forces must be prepared for deployment into the Latin American area preferably as part of a regional force, but unilaterally if necessary. Overflight rights, airfield facilities, ports, storage-withdrawal rights, and staging areas will be required on a case-by-case basis.

d. In addition to the maintenance of stability, emphasis in the event of war will be placed on: (1) defending the Panama Canal; (2) preventing the establishment of enemy bases in Latin America or the use by enemy forces of any Latin American facilities; and (3) retaining access to strategic materials and existing industrial capacity of the area. The United States must retain bases in Panama in order to ensure that US security interests are protected relative to the present lock canal, and any future sea-level canal, and to provide for hemispheric security activities. The United States must also control the sea approaches thereto and be capable of secure rerouting of shipping around South America. Close US-Chile relations are critical to the achievement of the latter objective. The retention of Guantanamo to support US operations in the area and to maintain US presence in Cuba is required both for operational reasons and for its contribution to US prestige in the Caribbean. The United States also has a requirement for maintaining sound surveillance stations, missile tracking stations, and military air routes in the area.

e. In the event of strategic nuclear war between the United States and the USSR, initial US support to the area will be limited to that accruing from US defense of the Panama Canal and control of associated sea and air lines of communication.

Part V

Force Planning Guidance

General

67. (U) This Part of the strategy presents broad guidance to serve as a bridge between the strategic concept and the analyses and judgments essential in the planning process continued in the succeeding Volumes and Annexes.

Strategic Offensive and Defensive Forces

68. (C) The US strategic offensive and defensive forces should have an assured predominance over the collective capability of the USSR, the CPR, or any other state or group of states. These forces must be sufficient to ensure that following a strategic nuclear war the United States will retain a position of strategic advantage relative to other nations of the world.

69. (C) A clearly superior US strategic nuclear military posture requires offensive and defensive forces which are capable, under all conditions of war outbreak, of assuring destruction of the enemy's urban-industrial areas (i.e., assured destruction) while limiting damage to the United States (i.e., damage limiting) and, to the extent practicable to its allies.

70. (S) [6 *lines of source text not declassified*] Forces assigned the damage-limiting task provide the capability through offensive and defensive means to reduce the effect of the enemy's attack. Damage-limiting forces should be in balance with assured destruction elements. An effective damage-limiting capability requires a combination of offensive forces, ballistic missile defense, air defense, space defense, antisubmarine warfare (ASW) forces, and civil defense. A force of survivable strategic offensive forces, intelligence and early warning systems, strategic defensive forces, command and control systems, and effective passive defense measures will strengthen the credibility of the US deterrent against attacks on the United States and its allies. This in turn will strengthen the assurance that the fear of escalating nonnuclear conflicts works to the advantage of the United States. A proper mix of US strategic offensive and defensive capabilities would tend to make increased defensive efforts and expenditures the enemy's preferred response option, and would exact greater direct and indirect attrition of the enemy's attack, so as to reduce the potential for damage to the United States and its allies if deterrence fails.

71. (S) A mix of strategic offensive forces is necessary to permit a range of options at varying levels of intensity of attack against alternative target systems. A combination of land and sea-launched missiles and manned aircraft carrying bombs and missiles, equipped with active and passive defense systems, will be required through the mid-range period. Such a mix provides options ranging from a show of force to the assured destruction task. These forces must be survivable, continue to be maintained in a high degree of alert, and must be capable of discriminate and controlled use.

a. [2-1/2 *lines of source text not declassified*] To the extent feasible, US deployment of forces for this option should emphasize their commitment to the Communist Chinese threat in order to reinforce the deterrent effect upon Communist China, reassure US allies in Asia, and derive the potential benefits of [3 *lines of source text not declassified*].

b. Residual strategic offensive and general purpose forces must provide an effective capability, [4 *lines of source text not declassified*].

c. Command and control facilities and arrangements must be secure, reliable, and survivable to ensure that strategic forces are immediately responsive to political and military decisions on the initiation, conduct, and termination of hostilities.

72. (S) The United States should have active and passive defenses in depth for protection against attack from land, sea, air, and space, by all types of weapon systems, whether employed selectively or simultaneously. A foremost requirement for the defense of the United States is the deployment of a ballistic missile defense system. Such a system should provide a significant limitation of damage to US population, military capabilities, industrial and other resources. This defense must

be integrated with an improved defense against aerodynamic vehicles, improved ASW capabilities, a comprehensive civil defense program, and a program for protection of military forces against attack effects, to assure the necessary damage-limiting capability.

73. (S) The United States requires reliable and near real-time surveillance of enemy and friendly forces. Enemy forces must be kept under surveillance prior to the outbreak of hostilities in order to obtain technical intelligence, to perform mission identification, to monitor arms control agreements and treaties, and to provide strategic warning. During hostilities, surveillance must provide tactical warning. In the exercise of command and control, surveillance is required to insure that US forces and resources are employed with maximum effectiveness. This surveillance should provide indications of enemy strategy, and knowledge of enemy tactics, order of battle, and the effectiveness of enemy and US weapons. Timely and precise analysis of the relative success of an exchange is required so that the best interests of the United States can be served in controlling the progress of hostilities and achieving advantageous war termination. These missions will require aircraft, satellite systems, ocean surveillance systems, and other systems and sensors.

General Purpose Forces

74. (S) General purpose forces, supported by appropriate strategic mobility capability, are an integral part of the over-all US deterrent posture. They constitute the principal means to meet threats at levels less than strategic nuclear war. Their capabilities also provide options to deter and coerce the enemy. General purpose forces will usually operate in association with allies, under the collective security and forward defense aspects of the strategic concept. This requires consideration of allied or other friendly in-being and potential force capabilities. Whenever feasible, these capabilities should be developed as the first line of defense against aggression. US military assistance should be considered in that context.

75. (C) Active and Reserve general purpose forces should be balanced in combat capability and sufficient in quantity, quality, mobility, and logistic support to provide forward deployed forces and a strategic reserve of US-based forces which, in conjunction with allied forces, can assure the defense of key strategic areas and essential LOCs, and respond to contingency situations. They should be supported by appropriately structured strategic lift forces and pre-positioned matériel, and include a training, replacement, and rotation base in the United States for deployed forces.

76. (S) General purpose forces must be capable of operating in a nuclear or nonnuclear environment. They should be equipped with

both single-purpose and dual-capable weapons systems for air, land, and sea operations. These should include air and missile elements on quick reaction alert. Tactical nuclear capabilities should provide a variety of options for responding to, initiating, and waging nuclear warfare at all levels below strategic nuclear war. They must be capable of selective application for military advantage in circumstances where significant military gain without further expansion of conflict is likely. In addition, they should be capable of conducting military operations in strategic nuclear war in conjunction with strategic offensive and defensive forces.

77. (S) During the mid-range period, there will be a continuing requirement for a substantial US military presence in and around Europe facing the Warsaw Pact. Even after the Vietnam conflict has ended, substantial deployed forces, including forces afloat, and land and sea-based prepositioned equipment and supplies will be required in the Pacific-Asian area to face the Soviet and CPR threats and to contribute to area stability.

78. (S) US military forces must be capable of employing chemical and biological weapons, of conducting operations in a toxic environment, and of defending against their use by an enemy.

79. (TS) Unconventional warfare forces should be prepared to exploit the resistance potential in areas which are denied to the United States, overrun, or likely to be overrun by enemy forces. US personnel should have the capability to assist indigenous elements in the creation, support, and direction of capabilities to conduct guerrilla warfare and other unconventional operations to reduce the enemy's combat effectiveness, industrial capacity, LOCs, and will to resist, and to assist in establishing friendly political controls in hostile areas. Means should also be provided to assist in evasion and escape of US and allied military personnel and other selected individuals from enemy-held territories.

80. (S) In all types of conflict, military psychological operations to support national and military objectives should be planned and conducted in coordination or integrated with like operations of governmental and nongovernmental agencies and/or friendly indigenous assets.

81. (TS) [7-1/2 lines of source text not declassified]

82. (S) Although a fully developed forward base structure is desirable, it is not possible to establish or maintain such a structure in all parts of the world where US general purpose forces may be employed. Therefore, US general purpose forces must be capable of deployment into and operation in areas in which bases are lacking, relatively austere, or hastily prepared, and be capable of conducting amphibious and airborne assault operations.

83. (C) A survivable and readily expandable reserve and mobilization base for augmentation of Active Forces is essential. Strategic airlift and sealift forces, both military and civil, are a critical requirement for this element of the force as well as for the Active element of the force. The balance between Active and Reserve component forces should be determined based upon two considerations:

a. The size and composition of Active general purpose forces must be sufficient to meet continuing military requirements, as well as those in contingency situations, considering the availability and readiness of Reserve component forces. These Active Forces should be sufficient to meet the requirements of contingency situations for a period of time sufficient to permit timely and orderly mobilization of Reserve component forces and industrial mobilization in those situations where successful termination of the conflict cannot be accomplished without such mobilization.

b. Reserve component forces must be of sufficient strength and appropriate type to augment Active Forces in the event of a direct confrontation with the USSR or the CPR and in contingencies when operations are of either an unexpected scope or prolonged duration. Such forces must be sufficient in size to meet the requirements of these situations until additional forces can be mobilized.

84. (C) The combination of Active and Reserve forces, augmented by further mobilization of military and industrial resources, must provide the capability to carry out US strategy throughout the full range of potential conflict situations that confront the United States. As substantial uncommitted Active land, sea (including amphibious), or air forces are deployed in response to contingency situations, additional forces must be readied so that the United States continuously has sufficient forces to be capable of initiating or responding to, on a timely basis, an expansion of conflict in area, type, intensity, or duration, or of responding to an unforeseen contingency. Such forces should be maintained for the duration of the contingency/conflict.

85. (S) General purpose force level objectives should be determined in consideration of the foregoing capabilities and should be keyed to military contingencies which have a reasonably high probability of occurrence, singly or simultaneously. Accordingly, based upon the basic military objectives, threat appraisal, strategic concept, and risk assessment, such contingencies govern the design of general purpose forces. Therefore, while maintaining essential deployments in areas not directly involved in the contingency situation, a US support, training, and rotation base, and the capability to conduct successful operations in other contingencies where force commitments are of a minor nature but where their timeliness may be crucial, general purpose forces are required to meet the following contingency situations:

a. *Situation I*—Without Mobilization: Conduct successful combat operations, either nuclear or nonnuclear, in any one major contingency outside the NATO area not involving direct engagement with the military forces of the USSR or the CPR (e.g., North Vietnam/Viet Cong aggression in Southeast Asia), while maintaining the capability for initial defense of NATO.[3]

b. *Situation II*—With Mobilization: Meet the requirements of either of the following two situations:

(1) Situation II–A—Major Aggression Against NATO: Successfully conduct and terminate combat operations, in concert with allies, against a major attack by the Warsaw Pact nations, while maintaining a holding action[4] against major CPR aggression in Asia.
(2) Situation II–B—Major Aggression in Asia: Successfully conduct and terminate combat operations, in concert with allies, against major aggression, not necessarily limited to one location, by the CPR in Asia, and provide forces for the initial defense of NATO.

Airlift and Sealift Forces

86. (C) Airlift and sealift force level and pre-positioning objectives should be directed to a capability which will:

a. Provide mobility to meet a wide variety of contingencies through employment of forward-deployed forces together with rapid deployment of forces from the United States.
b. Meet the time-phased deployment requirements of the contingency situation and provide the required capability to support employment of combat forces.

87. (C) Analyses of strategic lift requirements and other factors affecting strategic mobility to derive airlift and sealift force level objectives should include consideration of the readiness of deployable units (Active and Reserve) and their location and posture relative to aerial and surface ports of embarkation; air and sea LOCs, including overflight, transit and access rights; the availability, likely condition, and capacity of air and sea ports in the objective area; operation of overseas terminals and provisions for reception, matériel handling and equipment processing; buildup of overseas logistical bases and their matériel inventories, including pre-positioned equipment and supplies; and the intratheater transportation systems. Intratheater transportation systems

---

[3] Reinforcement for the purpose of improved posture in NATO during periods of heightened tension up to a posture which would also provide initial defense, in conjunction with allied forces, against a Warsaw Pact attack for a period of time sufficient to permit further reinforcement by Reserve component forces or redeployment of certain Active Forces from other areas. [Footnote in the source text.]

[4] To include possible offensive operations, primarily naval and air. [Footnote in the source text.]

include all elements from theater mainland and offshore air and sea ports of entry to the using units during the deployment and employment phases of combat operations in a theater.

88. (C) In developing airlift and sealift force level objectives, the possible effects of hostile political or military action and sabotage on: lift vehicles; LOCs; overflight, transit, and staging rights; pre-positioned equipment and supplies; and facilities must be considered. Additional factors include the probable warning of hostile action, the nature of the attack, and the enemy and friendly forces already on the scene.

89. (C) Force level objectives for airlift and sealift forces will be derived from time-phased deployment lists developed from the framework of the strategy herein, with emphasis on the general purpose forces contingency situations outlined in paragraph 85, above.

Local Forces and Military Assistance

90. (S) It is in the US interest to provide selected countries with military assistance, while recognizing that local forces are not always a substitute for US forces. National needs should be considered carefully in providing assistance and the level and type of aid set accordingly, recognizing that there are limits on the US ability to control its use. Most important, local forces should be assessed realistically and considered in conjunction with US resources in determining US strategy, preparing US military plans, and analyzing US force level objectives. Likewise, when determining the level and type of assistance to be provided in country and regional military aid programs, it is important to examine the role of local forces in US strategy and plans, together with political and economic factors affecting their use. In the underdeveloped countries, the military assistance program should also be designed to complement the civic and economic development of the country and to improve receiving, staging, and operating facilities that contribute to US strategic mobility requirements.

189.   National Security Action Memorandum No. 364[1]

Washington, August 14, 1967.

TO

  The Secretary of State
  The Secretary of Defense
  The Chairman, Atomic Energy Commission

SUBJECT

  Nuclear Weapons Dispersal Authorization for FY 1967–FY 1968

The President has noted the request for nuclear weapons dispersal authorization for FY 1967 and FY 1968 as contained in the Department of Defense memorandum dated May 26, 1967,[2] and as corrected by the DOD memorandum dated July 5, 1967 to the holders of the May 26 memorandum,[3] and has taken the following actions in connection therewith:

1. The Department of Defense is authorized to:

a. Disperse nuclear weapons in the United States without limit.

b. Disperse nuclear weapons to areas outside the United States in the numbers indicated in the last column of Appendix A to the May 26 memorandum, as amended, with the provisos that: (1) the total in each area may be exceeded by 10% in the event of unforeseen contingencies, (2) weapons, for which dispersal in support of non-U.S. NATO forces is authorized for planning purposes only, may be dispersed in support of U.S. forces pending additional and specific dispersal authorizations on a case-by-case basis, and (3) the grand total of weapons outside the U.S. (areas under foreign sovereignty and areas under U.S. control other than U.S.) shall not exceed [*number not declassified*] nuclear weapons. Such dispersals will be subject to the yield restrictions specified in NSAM 143 and policy regarding permissive action link devices contained in NSAM 160.[4]

c. Continue to disperse nuclear weapons and to provide nuclear weapon support to non-U.S. forces in accordance with the current dispersal authorizations which have been approved under NSAM 143 and which are tabulated in the column "Non-U.S. Forces—Authorized FY

---

[1] Source: Washington National Records Center, OSD Files: FRC 330 72 A 2467, A–471.61 Dispersal 1967. Top Secret; Formerly Restricted Data.

[2] From Vance to President Johnson. (Ibid., OASD/ISA Files: FRC 330 71 A 4919, 471.6 1967 May–Aug)

[3] Not found.

[4] See footnote 4, Document 90.

1966" (Column C) of Appendix B to the May 26, 1967 Department of Defense memorandum.

2. The President has noted that the Department of Defense has concurred in a recommendation of the Joint Chiefs of Staff that the dispersal authorization for the Pacific Theater be increased over the current dispersal authorization by approximately 5%. The President has accepted the recommendation of the Department of Defense in this matter. The President understands that the Pacific Theater requirements will be given further review during consideration of the next dispersal authorization request.

3. In connection with his action of the FY 1967–FY 1968 dispersals, the President has directed that in the future dispersal authorizations should be handled as follows:

a. A deployment plan will be submitted annually by the Secretary of Defense approximately in mid-November of each year concurrent with the nuclear weapon stockpile approval request.

b. Presidential authorization will establish levels in terms of (1) total overseas, (2) total by area, and (3) total by type of weapons (e.g., strategic offensive, tactical air, ASW) within each region. The Secretary of Defense will have authority to exceed control levels (2) and (3) by 10% to meet unforeseen contingencies.

c. The plan will contain actual deployment figures for the end of the previous fiscal year, deployments previously authorized, and proposed deployments for the same two fiscal year period as covered by the stockpile request.

d. Authorized deployments will be those planned as of the end of each fiscal year. The Secretary of Defense will have reasonable flexibility to manage and alter quantities during the course of the year to cover unavoidable peaks in deployment due to logistical factors. Plans for contingency deployments included in the Presidential authorization will be shown separately with adequate explanations.

e. The plan will include, on a highlight basis, the rationale for and major changes in the deployment plans.

4. The initial plan on the revised basis should be submitted by November 15, 1967 and should have the concurrence of the Department of State and the Atomic Energy Commission.

W.W. Rostow

Attachment

NUCLEAR WEAPONS DISPERSAL—BY COUNTRY/COMMAND

[*table (11 columns and 29 rows) not declassified*]

---

190. Memorandum of Conversation[1]

Washington, September 12, 1967, 10 a.m.

SUBJECT

  ABM Deployment

PARTICIPANTS

  Canada
  Minister of National Defense Paul Hellyer
  Elgin B. Armstrong, Deputy Minister of Defense
  H. Basil Robinson, Deputy Under Secretary, External Affairs
  Ambassador A. Edgar Ritchie
  Air Marshal F.R. Sharp, Vice Chief of the Defence Staff

  United States
  Secretary of Defense McNamara
  Gen. J.P. McConnell, Acting Chairman, Joint Chiefs of Staff
  Deputy Secretary of Defense Paul H. Nitze
  John S. Foster, Director, Defense Research and Engineering
  Alain C. Enthoven, Asst. Secy. Defense, Systems Analysis
  Lt. Gen. A.W. Betts, Chief of Army, R and D and Nike-X
  George S. Springsteen, Deputy Asst. Secy., EUR

Secretary McNamara welcomed Minister Hellyer and referred to their previous conversations on the question of ABM's.[2] He wanted to continue those consultations because we are now on the point of announcing publicly the deployment of a light ABM system.

---

[1] Source: National Archives and Records Administration, RG 59, Central Files 1967–69, DEF 12. Secret; Exdis. Drafted by Springsteen. The meeting was held in the Secretary of Defense's dining room at the Pentagon.

[2] Secretary McNamara discussed the question of ABMs with Hellyer and other NATO Defense Ministers at the Nuclear Planning Group meeting April 6–7. See *Foreign Relations, 1964–1968*, vol. XIII, Document 246.

He noted that for some time the research and development on such a system had been going forward and had now developed to the point where decisions were possible. He said that we had continued to press the Soviets for discussions which might lead to some kind of agreement on limiting such deployment but that the Soviets were defensive about it. In response to Mr. Hellyer's question, Secretary McNamara said that he was certain such discussions would be taken at some time in the future. However, at the moment, he said, Viet-Nam stands in the way. He noted that Kosygin had been pressed very hard on this at the time of the Glassboro Summit and had given a more or less propagandistic reply. We shall, however, continue to press the Soviets and will press it again this week with them.

Secretary McNamara noted that our current budget had several hundred million dollars for the development of an ABM system. We have stated publicly that, depending on the outcome of talks with the Soviets, we might or might not use such funds to protect offensive weapons.[3]

Secretary McNamara noted that the engineering development of an American ABM system had only recently progressed to the point where a production decision was possible.

He said, however, that today we have reached that point and expressed his satisfaction at the high quality of people and contractors working on the system. He said that the difference between today and the past is that we now have the Chinese threat and an engineering design which permits those in authority to make the decision to proceed with production.

He stressed that we had not yet made a final decision on this but believes we will announce such a deployment next week.[4]

He said that the purpose of the system is to protect the American population against a Chinese attack in the mid-1970's and to provide some protection for our offensive weapons against Soviet attack.

Secretary McNamara then asked Mr. Foster to describe the system.

Mr. Foster said that two elements were involved—radars and missiles. [6 lines of source text not declassified] This radar is used to guide the intercepter to the impact point.

The intercepter is the Spartan which has a yield of [3 lines of source text not declassified].

---

[3] See, for example, Secretary McNamara's statement before a subcommittee of the Senate Appropriations Committee on January 25 and President Johnson's statement and replies to questions at his press conference on March 2. Texts are in American Foreign Policy: Current Documents, 1967, pp. 441–449 and 450–451.

[4] Reference is to McNamara's upcoming speech to the United Press International Editors and Publishers in San Francisco on September 18. See Document 192.

Mr. Foster noted that the system we proposed to deploy would [1-1/2 lines of source text not declassified].

He said that the eye of the system is the radar. To deny the enemy an opportunity to attack them, [3 lines of source text not declassified].

Mr. Foster stressed that the system is an area defense. There are only a few sites covering the whole country. He said, however, that the system does not provide coverage in depth for our strategic offensive weapons. Therefore, we have considered this problem and have decided to put Sprints in to protect a goodly number of our Minutemen.

The cost of the entire system, he said, is about five billion dollars.

Mr. McNamara said that we were proceeding to undertake consultations with our other allies.[5] He said that we would also be talking to the [less than 1 line of source text not declassified] here and that our Embassy would be talking with the [less than 1 line of source text not declassified]. He noted also that we would be talking in the North Atlantic Council tomorrow. He then asked if the Canadians had any questions.

[4-1/2 lines of source text not declassified] Mr. McNamara said that all equipment would be in the United States.

Secretary McNamara stressed that this is a United States financed and oriented system and that we felt it provided an optimum degree of protection for the United States. One by-product, however, is some protection for Canada.

Secretary McNamara then read off the cities in Canada which would be protected—[2 lines of source text not declassified].

He reiterated that all of these would be protected and that this is a by-product of the U.S. system. He said that we could modify the U.S. system at extra cost to provide greater coverage for Canada. If Canada wants greater benefits, however, she must share in the cost and make an early decision. Mr. McNamara stressed that a Canadian decision by the end of this year would be necessary.

Dr. Armstrong asked Secretary McNamara what the cost might be. Secretary McNamara, before responding to the query, noted that Rand, on a recent study of the differences between cost estimates and actual costs on military contracts, found that the actual costs generally exceeded the estimates by 300 to 1,000 per cent. Hence the Canadians should be aware that the costs will be high. Current estimates for the American system are $4 to $5 billion. To increase the Canadian coverage would cost an additional $1 billion. This would give [less than 1 line of source

---

[5] Regarding these consultations, of which the present meeting was a part, see Document 192.

text not declassified] coverage in Canada. It was stressed, however, that these are unescalated figures.

[*1 paragraph (2-1/2 lines of source text) not declassified*]

Secretary McNamara, again speaking of costs, said that we could reduce costs by reducing the coverage of the entire system. He said that we could achieve a 20 per cent reduction in costs by reducing coverage by 5 per cent. But this, of course, would raise political problems as part of the population would be left out of the coverage.

Mr. Hellyer said that there was no political problem in Canada now with regard to an ABM, because at the moment Canada is violently anti-ABM. But he noted this might change.

Minister Hellyer's comment led Secretary McNamara to talk about this attitude in the context of the development of neo-isolationism. He noted that this was caused by our view that our allies are standing back from what we regard to be joint responsibilities. He felt that an ABM deployment system could determine a country's inclusion or exclusion from world affairs. In the case of Canada, he cited particularly Asian affairs.

Minister Hellyer said that he agreed with Mr. McNamara on neo-isolationism but felt that the current attitude on such things in Canada at the moment was determined by Viet-Nam.

Secretary McNamara cited the reaction of our allies in connection with the Middle East. He said that they had just walked away from the situation. He cited all this to indicate that the ABM would have an influence, albeit minor, on all this.

Dr. Armstrong asked how coverage is determined.

Mr. Foster said that it was related to population density and that to cover Canada would not expose U.S. cities.

Secretary McNamara said that we need to know soon if the Canadians want to join because plants must be built from the ground up in order to supply the components of the system.

In response to a question by Minister Hellyer, Secretary McNamara said that the deployment of this system will not lead to the deployment of a Soviet-oriented system. He said that it is not intended to move toward a heavy system and stressed that deployment of this system is *not* the first step in the deployment of a larger system.

In support of this, Mr. Foster said the proposed system protects all of the United States but it does have some technical limitations. [*2-1/2 lines of source text not declassified*]

Ambassador Ritchie asked if [*less than 1 line of source text not declassified*] were included.

Secretary McNamara said that [*1 line of source text not declassified*].

Basil Robinson asked what difficulties would ensue if Canada waited two or three years before joining.

Secretary McNamara said that there would be greater cost.

Dr. Armstrong asked, if Canada participated in the system, could some of the equipment be produced in Canada. Mr. McNamara said that we hadn't looked into this but he doubted it.

Minister Hellyer asked if there was an altitude limitation on explosions.

Mr. Foster replied in the affirmative.

Mr. McNamara said, [4 lines of source text not declassified].

Asked what the relationship of the system was to NORAD, Secretary McNamara said that it does not influence the NORAD agreement. Regarding command and control, it will be assigned to NORAD if the agreement were modified to have NORAD embrace the ABM's, or it could be assigned elsewhere.

Minister Hellyer noted that to put it in NORAD, or even to suggest putting it in NORAD at this time, would complicate consideration by the Canadians of renewal of the agreement.

When asked whether or not there was a strong possibility of the ABM's being related to NORAD, Secretary McNamara said that depended upon Canada.

He also noted, in response to Minister Hellyer's inquiry, that there was no overlap between the Air Defense System and the ABM's because they were independent systems.

When asked if there would be any savings from having the two systems thrown together, Mr. Foster said that he did not know of any such savings.

In response to Mr. Armstrong's query, Mr. Foster said that the ABM systems would operate against submarine missiles.

Mr. Hellyer asked why we had to protect missile farms. He said that he thought he remembered Mr. McNamara saying at the last consultations that these farms did not need protection.

Secretary McNamara said that there were two options available here. We could either expand the offensive system or defend the present offensive system. The U.S.S.R. is expanding their offensive system, so we must insure ourselves. We are buying insurance by the protection of the missile farms. Essentially, we are looking toward the time in the future when Soviets expand both their offensive and defensive systems beyond the present NIE threat limits.

Mr. Hellyer asked about the influence of the ABM system on the Air Defense System and the relationship envisaged. Secretary McNamara said that at this level they were unrelated. China has no air threat. He noted that other factors threatened the Air Defense System and not this one. We have problems in the Air Defense field which we want to discuss soon with the Canadians.

Mr. Hellyer asked how we prevent atomic bombs from being brought into American ports in boats.

Secretary McNamara said that we just have to depend primarily upon intelligence. He also noted, however, the degree of intimidation in such a situation would be limited in view of our ability to retaliate.

Minister Hellyer said that he wished to speak for a moment on the situation in Canada.

He said that he believed that Canada would be able to renew the NORAD agreement without inclusion of any reference to ABM's. If ABM's are introduced into the agreement, however, it would jeopardize approval of the agreement.

He said that the feeling against ABM's is so strong in Canada at the present time that there is an inclination, on the part of some members of the government, that when Canada renews the NORAD agreement, the government should issue a statement saying that it will not involve itself in a system at the present time.

Concluding, he said that at the moment there is "absolutely no chance" of Canadian involvement in the U.S. ABM system. His conclusion was that there was no more than one chance in a hundred of getting a decision for such participation.

Ambassador Ritchie asked Secretary McNamara when the announcement would be made. The Secretary replied on Monday.[6]

Minister Hellyer noted that this announcement, plus having all the hardware in the United States, plus reassuring statements on fallout effects, would serve to clear the air in Canada and make for a much more rational discussion. Then the Canadians could talk of real plans and not hypothetical situations. He noted that the Canadians themselves had been doing some studies on the effect on Canada of the deployment of an American system. He had been discussing these with some Parliamentarians. He felt that the U.S. announcement would facilitate better understanding of the problem.

Secretary McNamara said that Minister Hellyer could publicly state that he had been consulted by the Americans about this deployment.

Mr. Hellyer also noted that, with regard to NORAD, the Canadian position will be officially given at the Permanent Joint Defense Board (PJDB) meeting next week. (Basil Robinson revealed after the meeting that the Cabinet was convening to discuss this issue this afternoon.)

---

[6] September 18.

At this point there was a brief discussion on the possibility of expanding the coverage of the U.S. deployed system by lowering the detonation ceiling from [*less than 1 line of source text not declassified*]. The point made here was that while the ceiling is now at the higher level it could be lowered and increased coverage obtained, but other problems would ensue.

Dr. Armstrong asked if Defense Research Board experts could come down and talk to Mr. Foster about the ABM system.

Secretary McNamara said that he was delighted but that the classification on the system was exceedingly important and this must be given every consideration.

Dr. Armstrong asked what the system did in terms of preventing casualties.

Secretary McNamara reviewed the probable outlook for a Chinese ICBM deployment and said that our estimates were that without an ABM system, and in the event of a Chinese attack, we might suffer a [*less than 1 line of source text not declassified*]. With the ABM system he said this loss would be practically zero.

He did note, however, that if the Chinese force expands—its missiles rising from 75 to 100—we would have to expand our own system in order to keep the casualty figure down low.

Concerning the Soviets, Secretary McNamara said that we must be wary of regarding the system as giving much help against the Soviets except from the standpoint of defending our missile farms. He said that the Soviets, if they attack, would launch sufficient weapons to do considerable damage.

Dr. Armstrong asked if Secretary McNamara still would adhere to his philosophy that we could offset any Soviet ABM deployment.

Secretary McNamara replied in the affirmative. He said that we must exercise the offensive and take advantage of every technological development to be able to penetrate the Soviet system.

Mr. Hellyer asked if he could do anything further for Secretary McNamara. The Secretary replied in the negative and said that he was very glad to meet with the Canadians and that their officials would be welcome when they wished to come down here.

Mr. Hellyer said that he thought the announcement would come as no surprise and will definitely facilitate rational discussion.

191.   Memorandum From the Secretary of the Air Force (Brown)
        to Secretary of Defense McNamara[1]

Washington, September 14, 1967.

SUBJECT

    Deterrence of Strategic Nuclear War, and Damage Limiting

I am concerned about our general approach to the problem of deterring strategic nuclear war, and I am also concerned about the relation of our damage limiting capability to deterrence and to planning for actual war fighting should deterrence fail.

In my view, deterrence will depend on a Soviet judgment not only of their own losses but also of relative US losses and surviving military capability. The political stakes and the nature of the Soviet leadership will also be important. In some future equivalent of the "Cuban missile crisis" 20% Soviet fatalities might not be enough, if US losses would be 80%. Soviet leaders might believe that the US would cease to exist while the USSR could successfully recover, using surviving nuclear forces to dominate the European industrial complex.

Our evaluation should consider possible surprise Soviet tactics as well as force capabilities: pin-down, FOBs, cruise missile submarines, medium bombers, and coordinated offensive/defensive operations. My feeling is that we have become too theoretical—that our calculations are too removed from the most likely patterns of admitted unlikely wars, and hence from the probable Soviet judgments which determine deterrence.

I believe we should consider a new criterion for deterrence. We should try to insure that Soviet losses would be at least as severe as US losses in any strategic war, and that the resultant surviving military balance would not be in favor of the Soviets. With regard to this latter point, I recognize that there are arguments both pro and con, but feel that it deserves our serious consideration.

Further, we should examine our forces in the light of how they would perform if a strategic exchange began, using various scenarios for its beginning. I suggest that under such circumstances the execution of the option to destroy Soviet population and industry would be our poorest choice. Rather, we would probably act to maintain the threat of such assured destruction while operating our forces to minimize Soviet potential for destruction on the US urban/industrial complex. A force

---

[1] Source: Johnson Library, National Security File, Agency File, Department of Defense, Vol. V, August 1967 [2 of 2], Box 12. Secret. The date is handwritten. A copy of the memorandum was sent to Deputy Secretary of Defense Nitze.

planned for that purpose could well look very different from one aimed at preserving assured destruction in the face of a "Greater Than Expected" Threat.

Harold Brown

192. Editorial Note

Secretary of Defense McNamara proposed to include an announce-ment of the Johnson administration's decision to deploy an ABM sys-tem in an upcoming address before the United Press International Editors and Publishers in San Francisco on September 18, 1967. For McNamara's early thoughts on the purposes of this speech, see Document 185.

In an August 8 memorandum to McNamara, Assistant Secretary of Defense for International Security Affairs Paul Warnke advised that McNamara's speech should say only that he was leaning toward a THIN-X and a China-oriented ABM deployment, "but avoid making a firm commitment to proceed with a deployment," which, he felt, should wait until the President's budget message in January. He added that such a postponement would allow time for consultation with U.S. allies, "who are undoubtedly still relatively unfamiliar with the arguments favoring deployment of a THIN-X system, as opposed to a Soviet-ori-ented deployment." He went on to remind McNamara that he had promised Canadian Defense Minister Paul T. Hellyer that he would consult with him before any U.S. decision was made, and he outlined how the NATO allies as well as Japan and other Pacific allies could be consulted. At the least, he believed that if McNamara announced the ABM deployment in his September speech, the administration should first undertake urgent consultations with Canada and other U.S allies. On Warnke's memorandum, McNamara initialed the option recom-mending to the President that he make a firm commitment to deploy in his September address, and he added a note: "If a 'commitment' is to be made in the S.F. speech, remind me to 'consult' with Hellyer ahead of time." (Washington National Records Center, OSD Files: FRC 330 72 A 2468, 471.94 ABM (Jul–Aug) 1967)

In an August 16 memorandum to McNamara, Warnke quoted as reclama a memorandum of conversation at the April 6 NATO Nuclear

Planning Group meeting in which McNamara promised that the United States would not act unilaterally on ABMs without consulting its allies. In case McNamara still pressed for a full announcement in his San Francisco speech, Warnke offered four initiatives to prepare U.S. allies in advance for this eventuality. None of the "Approve" or "Disapprove" options following each initiative is checked. (Ibid.)

Meanwhile, on August 9 McNamara circulated a draft of his speech to key principals in the Johnson administration. In an August 16 memorandum to McNamara, Under Secretary of State Katzenbach commented that the draft was "a masterful job." He wondered, however, if McNamara had to be so specific regarding ABM deployment in the speech when "we are committed to consult further with our allies and in particular with the Nuclear Planning Group," which would not meet until September 28–29. He suggested that McNamara intimate in his address only that the administration was "moving in the direction of a thin deployment, stopping just short of announcing a final decision." Among a few other suggestions, he also warned against emphasizing the Chinese nuclear threat as a reason for the decision. "It might be better," Katzenbach cautioned, "to balance the protection of our offensive missiles with the protection against the Chinese threat." (Ibid.)

Under cover of an August 19 memorandum to President Johnson, McNamara forwarded the August 9 draft of his speech to the White House. In this memorandum McNamara quoted Katzenbach's suggestion to delay final announcement of the decision, but added, "I disagree. We are prepared now to make the decision and I believe we must make it. If we decide to go forward with the 'thin deployment' but fail to announce the decision, we are placing ammunition in the hands of our critics who will use it for partisan purposes." The President initialed the draft, presumably indicating his approval, but he also asked for comments on the draft from Joseph Califano. (Johnson Library, National Security File, Agency File, Department of Defense, Vol. V, Aug. 1967 [2 of 2], Box 12) Califano generally endorsed its contents, but thought that there should be a statement in the speech or in an accompanying announcement of the budgetary impact of the ABM decision. He wanted to consult with Rostow before the speech was given on how to handle its impact domestically, "since all hell is likely to break loose from the liberals and the urbanists." (Memorandum from Califano to Rostow, August 27; ibid.)

When Adrian S. Fisher, Acting Director of the Arms Control and Disarmament Agency, learned of McNamara's proposed San Francisco speech, he urged Secretaries Rusk and McNamara to delay the announcement of the ABM deployment, which would adversely affect the ongoing negotiations on the Nuclear Non-Proliferation Treaty. His September 1 letter to Foster is printed in *Foreign Relations, 1964–1968,*

volume XI, Document 204. He also submitted an ACDA paper, dated
August 25, on the arms control considerations of a U.S. ABM deployment decision, attached to an August 28 memorandum to Secretaries
Rusk and McNamara and Walt Rostow. For text, see ibid., Document
202. In an August 31 memorandum, McNamara thanked Fisher for the
paper and added that "my staff has been giving active consideration to
the problems it discusses, and they will be in touch with your staff
regarding them." (Washington National Records Center, OSD Files:
FRC 330 72 A 2468, 471.94 ABM (July–Aug) 1967)

In an August 28 handwritten letter to Rostow, Spurgeon Keeny
agreed that the proposed light anti-Chinese solution was "probably the
best solution" and that the draft speech effectively provided the strategic background and rationale for the ABM decision. Like Warnke,
Katzenbach, and Fisher, however, he opposed an early announcement:

"I still think that the decision is premature, politically as well as
technically, and that, if it is made this year, it should be as part of the
regular budget cycle. A decision in mid-September will focus all attention on this issue in isolation from other military hardware decisions;
and in its present form I am afraid it will meet strong objections from all
sides. The anti-ABM forces will consider it a foot in the door, and the
pro-ABM forces will consider it a grossly inadequate system which fails
to protect the U.S. population against the Soviet threat. Technically, I
think there are some unanswered questions as to how well and how
long this system would actually deal with the early Chinese threat."

Realizing that McNamara was determined to make the full
announcement, Keeny offered specific comments on parts of the draft
speech. (Johnson Library, National Security File, Agency File,
Department of Defense, August 1967, Vol. V [2 of 2], Box 12)

Also on August 28, Keeny sent Rostow a memorandum warning
against the "categorical statements" in the speech on the U.S.-Soviet
strategic balance. He worried that if the administration later "had to
back off from any of them, it will seriously undercut confidence in the
Administration and our present strategic posture. Moreover, I am afraid
these statements will antagonize rather than convince Congressional
critics, and I am sure that they will complicate any possible discussion
of the issue with the Soviets." He argued that McNamara should
instead "emphasize not our strategic superiority but our very high level
of confidence in the reliability of our deterrent under any circumstances." (Ibid., Country File, USSR, ABM Negotiations (II), Box 231)
For text of an August 29 memorandum to Rostow, in which Keeny reiterated his arguments for postponing an announcement of the ABM
decision until January, see Foreign Relations, 1964–1968, volume XI,
Document 203.

Two days later, Keeny sent a memorandum to Rostow elaborating on the technical questions relating to the effectiveness of the proposed ABM deployment against even an early Chinese ICBM threat. To his memorandum he attached NIE 11–4–67 (Document 183), and the Montgomery Report Summary, an internal OSD study, dated August 10, 1967. The latter has not been found, but it warned among other things, according to Keeny's summary of it, "that the Chinese could include first-generation penetration aids on the same time-scale as our ABM deployment and a more sophisticated family of penetration aids a few years later at relatively small cost (10% of their ICBM program)." In conclusion, Keeny advised that "it would be wise to spend a few more months understanding this problem before we announce deployment of a specific system." (Johnson Library, National Security File, Country File, China, Vol. 10) For Rostow's summary and assessment of NIE 11–4–67, see Document 187.

To a September 6 memorandum to McNamara, Warnke attached a suggested added paragraph to the speech, which indicated that despite the ABM decision the U.S. Government was still anxious to reach agreement with the Soviets on limiting offensive and defensive strategic arms. (Washington National Records Center, OSD Files: FRC 330 72 A 2468, 471.94 ABM (Sep) 1967)

Meanwhile, the Johnson administration developed plans to notify U.S. allies in advance of the contents of McNamara's speech. Attached to a September 8 memorandum from Keeny to Rostow is a schedule, approved by an interdepartmental working group, for briefing European and Asian allies, the Soviet Union, other key Asian and Middle East countries, and U.S. posts abroad. (Johnson Library, National Security File, Country File, USSR, ABM Negotiations (II), Box 231) For a memorandum of McNamara's conversation with Hellyer on September 12, see Document 190. For text of the statement to be delivered to the North Atlantic Council on September 14, see *Foreign Relations, 1964–1968*, volume XI, Document 210.

Internal memoranda and telegraphic instructions relating to the briefing of U.S. allies are in the National Archives and Records Administration, RG 59, Central Files 1967–69, DEF 12. Llewellyn Thompson, Ambassador to the Soviet Union, expressed his concerns about the deployment decision and the announcement in telegram 896 from Moscow, September 2; text in *Foreign Relations, 1964–1968*, volume XI, Document 207. Instructions to inform the Soviet Representative to the Eighteen-Nation Disarmament Committee of the September 18 speech were sent in telegram 37260 to Geneva, September 14. (National Archives and Records Administration, RG 59, Central Files 1967–69, DEF 18–6) The text of a letter from John A. Gronouski, Ambassador to Poland, to the Chinese Embassy in Poland, notifying the People's

Republic of China of McNamara's impending announcement, was transmitted in telegram 38805 to Warsaw, September 16. (Ibid., DEF 12)

McNamara apparently incorporated into the final text of his speech several of the suggestions advanced by administration principals and his Department of Defense advisers. He included verbatim, for instance, the first sentence of Warnke's suggested draft paragraph attached to his August 16 memorandum. Text of McNamara's September 18 speech is in *American Foreign Policy: Current Documents, 1967*, pages 16–25.

---

193. Memorandum From the Joint Chiefs of Staff to Secretary of Defense McNamara[1]

JCSM–520–67   Washington, September 23, 1967.

SUBJECT

Assurance Against the Unauthorized Use of US Nuclear Weapons (U)

1. (TS) The Joint Chiefs of Staff and the Services have made repeated studies in depth in regard to devices, techniques, and procedures designed to assure positive control of nuclear weapons. In aggregate, the studies point to the conclusion that the principle of [*3-1/2 lines of source text not declassified*].

2. (S) In response to a request by the Deputy Secretary of Defense, dated 26 December 1963,[2] the Joint Chiefs of Staff completed in 1964 a comprehensive review of all US nuclear weapon systems with the view of providing recommendations concerning any changes in procedures, controls, or weapon components that should be incorporated to provide a higher degree of assurance against their unauthorized use. This review included the views of the Services and the commanders of the unified and specified commands.

---

[1] Source: Johnson Library, National Security File, Agency File, JCS, Filed by the LBJ Library, Box 29. Top Secret. Attached is a September 26 transmittal memorandum from Robert N. Ginsburgh of the NSC Staff to Keeny and Rostow. At the bottom of this memorandum, Keeny wrote: "Walt—I have a number of questions about this and plan to follow up on the details of the JCS proposal and the current OSD position on the subject. I have been very interested in the possibilities of PALs, which I consider very important, ever since I put together the original NSAM on PALs for NATO forces. Despite the JCS reservations, I am glad that we have the PALs we have."

[2] Not further identified.

3. (TS) As a result of this review, the Joint Chiefs of Staff recommended, in JCSM–941–64, dated 9 November 1964,[3] that:

[1 paragraph (8-1/2 lines of source text) not declassified]

4. (TS) In response to a proposed draft memorandum for the President on unauthorized use of nuclear weapons, the Joint Chiefs of Staff, in JCSM–17–65, dated 9 January 1965,[3] advised you that:

"In summary, the Joint Chiefs of Staff recognize and support fully the requirement to assure the security of nuclear weapons against unauthorized use. [8 lines of source text not declassified]"

5. (TS) [2-1/2 lines of source text not declassified]

6. (TS) [6 lines of source text not declassified]

7. (TS) In order better to determine future Air Force policy relative to PAL devices in general, the Chief of Staff, US Air Force, directed that a comprehensive study be accomplished. The completed study represents the position of the Air Force on PAL philosophy and PAL systems and was forwarded to the Joint Chiefs of Staff for review. The study reaffirms the position of the Joint Chiefs of Staff and concludes that present controls against the unauthorized use of nuclear weapons are sufficient and that additional restrictive devices are not required. [8-1/2 lines of source text not declassified]

[4 paragraphs (21-1/2 lines of source text) not declassified]

8. (TS) [5 lines of source text not declassified] If, however, the national authority directs additional mechanical constraints, the PAL concept described by the Air Force could provide an improved, technically reliable system with significantly less operational degradation and lower costs than other proposed PAL devices and would eliminate costly retrofit of additional nuclear weapons. [4 lines of source text not declassified]

9. (TS) The Joint Chiefs of Staff recommend that:

[5 paragraphs (16-1/2 lines of source text) not declassified]

For the Joint Chiefs of Staff:
Harold K. Johnson
Acting Chairman
Joint Chiefs of Staff

---

[3] Not found.

194.   Letter From Secretary of State Rusk to Secretary of Defense McNamara[1]

Washington, November 24, 1967.

Dear Bob:

Thank you for sending me the first installment of your memoranda to the President on the FY 69–73 Defense program under cover of your letter of October 28.[2]

I note that the Strategic Forces memorandum is to be revised this month and understand it will include a new program for North American air defense and some other revisions of the October 4 draft.[3] I would like to defer comment until I receive the newer version. I would, however, like to make a few comments on some of the other memoranda.

In your ASW memorandum[2] the analysis supporting the retirement of the ASW carriers and the transfer of their mission to aircraft operating from land bases abroad argues that insurance against the loss of a few bases, such as the Azores, is not a sufficient case for maintaining and modernizing the carrier forces since there will be other bases available. I am less sanguine than you are about the prospects five years hence of being able to use all of the primary or secondary ASW bases you cite, and I think we may have to face more than the loss of just a few bases over the next five years. Thus I think it could be a mistake to plan any long term increase in our dependence on foreign bases for a major function such as ASW.

As you know a joint State–Defense base study is to get underway in January. It should throw some light on the likely availability of ASW bases. A final decision on the carriers might if possible be deferred until the study's findings are available and can be assessed by our staffs.

The theatre nuclear forces memorandum argues that our stockpile of nuclear warheads in [*less than 1 line of source text not declassified*] is

---

[1] Source: Washington National Records Center, OASD/ISA Files: FRC 330 71 A 4919, 381 1967 Nov–Dec. Top Secret. The word "Personal" is handwritten on letter. Copies were sent to Walt Rostow and Charles Schultze (BOB), and a stamped notation indicates that Warnke saw the letter.

[2] Not found.

[3] A copy of this 21-page draft memorandum to the President on strategic offensive and defensive forces is in the Johnson Library, National Security File, Agency File, Department of Defense, Draft Memorandums to the President for the FY 69 Defense Programs.

more than adequate, particularly in [*less than 1 line of source text not declassified*].[4] It is not clear, however, what specific reductions are planned and on what sort of schedule. I would like to be kept informed of the major changes you have in mind since our allies are often extremely sensitive to adjustments in levels of nuclear weapons support.

I am in full agreement with your air and sea lift objectives,[5] but I can foresee that your renewed request for FDL funding may well run into the same difficulties in Congress that it did last year. To the extent that the objections of Senator Russell and others to the FDL rest on its foreign policy implications, the State Department would be prepared to lend a hand in defense of the ship program, if this would be useful to you. It is my feeling that the argument for the program will be most effective if it emphasizes our need for these ships to support our normal overseas deployments and long standing commitments, rather than the great advantages they offer for meeting a broader range of contingencies.

There are two memoranda, NATO Strategy and Research and Development, that were not in the group you sent. I will defer comment, therefore on your recommendations on European forces issues until I receive them.

With warm regards,

Sincerely,

Dean

---

[4] A draft memorandum to the President (for comment) on theater nuclear forces, June 28, is in the National Archives and Records Administration, RG 200, Defense Programs and Operations, Draft Memoranda to the President, Annotated, FY 1968–73, Box 73. A Record of Decision copy on the same subject, January 11, 1968, is ibid., Draft Memoranda to the President, 1969–1973 Budget, Vol. I, Tab 2, Box 77.

[5] A draft memorandum to the President (for comment) on airlift and sealift forces, July 12, which contains many handwritten revisions, is ibid., Draft Memoranda to the President, Annotated, FY 1968–73, Box 73. A Record of Decision copy on the same subject, January 3, 1968, is ibid., Draft Memoranda to the President, 1969–1973 Budget, Vol. I, Tabs H–J, Box 77.

195. Draft Memorandum From Secretary of Defense McNamara to President Johnson[1]

Washington, December 1, 1967.

SUBJECT

Defense Department Budget for FY 69 (U)

My review of the Department of Defense military program and financial budget for the next fiscal year has proceeded to the point where I can present certain conclusions to you. Preliminary estimates indicate that the military forces (Tab A)[2] and procurement programs which I recommend for your approval will require new obligational authority for Military Functions, Military Assistance, and Civil Defense of $79–82 billion for FY 69. These amounts and previous budgets and appropriations are summarized in the following table:

	New Obligational Authority ($ Billions)[c]		
	FY 1967	FY 1968	FY 1969[a]
DOD Normal Budget	$50.3	$50.1	$54-57
Southeast Asia	22.4	23.3	25
Total NOA Required	$72.7	$73.4	$79-82

This will result in the following estimated expenditures and share of Gross National Product:

	Expenditures	% GNP[b]
FY 1967	$68.5	9.0%
FY 1968	73.9	9.1%
FY 1969	77-78	8.9-9.0%

---

[a] Based on December 1, 1967, estimates. Subject to further revision.
[b] Based on a GNP of $862 billion in FY 69.
[c] Includes $.8 billion in FY 68 and $1.2 billion in FY 69 for the FY 68 pay raises.

The FY 69 Budget was prepared on the basis of two key assumptions:
1. Provision was made for deployments to Southeast Asia, comprising 525,000 men in South Vietnam and 46,700 in Thailand, 3,608

---

[1] Source: Washington National Records Center, OSD Files: FRC 330 71 A 3470, Final Memo to the President 1 Dec 1967, Notes of Meeting with JCS 11/17 & 11/24, Folder 157. Top Secret.
[2] Not printed.

helicopters, 1,572 fixed-wing non-attack aircraft, 1,074 attack aircraft, and 707 ships and boats by June 30, 1969.

2. Provision was made for combat consumption for all items through FY 69 reorder lead time, enabling continuation of the war indefinitely at the currently planned activity levels, barring unforeseen contingencies, without an FY 69 Supplemental.

The Military Forces supported by this budget are summarized in the tables available for your review. Although I have reduced the budgets proposed by the Services for FY 69 by approximately $16–19 billion, my recommended force structure is based on requirements for national security and has not been limited by arbitrary or predetermined budget ceilings. In my review of the Service proposals, I attempted, as last year, to eliminate all non-essential, marginal, and postponable programs with the objective of minimizing the costs of supporting the required forces.

In developing the program and reviewing the budget proposals, I have had the continuing counsel and assistance of the Joint Chiefs of Staff.[3] The points of difference between my recommendations and those of the Joint Chiefs of Staff are set forth in the attachment at Tab B.[4] It should not be necessary for you to study the attachment in detail—of the differences with the Chiefs, I believe they will wish to discuss with you only three issues affecting the FY 69 budget.

1. *Advanced Strategic Bomber (AMSA):* The Joint Chiefs of Staff recommend Contract Definition and, subject to favorable review, beginning full-scale development of a new strategic bomber in FY 69, at an FY 69 cost of $40 million. Their plan would aim at an Initial Operational Capability in FY 76. Mr. Nitze and I recommend continuing development of advanced aircraft technology and bomber penetration aids, at an FY 69 cost of $25 million. We recommend against beginning full-scale development of a new bomber in FY 69 because we do not believe an Initial Operational Capability in FY 76 is needed. Development, deployment, and five years of operation of a force of 150 AMSAs would cost about $7.3 billion.

2. *Modernization of the Fourth (Reserve) Marine Air Wing:* The Joint Chiefs of Staff recommend buying 15 A-6As and 8 RF-4Js at a cost of about $92 million in FY 69 to provide more modern aircraft for Marine Air Wings. This would free A-6As and RF-4Bs for assignment to the

---

[3] Secretary McNamara met with the Joint Chiefs of Staff on November 17 and 24 to discuss this draft memorandum to the President. Although no formal record of these meetings has been found, McNamara's detailed (and often illegible) handwritten notes on both meetings are in the Washington National Records Center, McNamara Files: FRC 330 71 A 3470, Final Memo to the President 1 Dec 1967, Notes of Meeting with JCS 11/17 & 11/24, Folder 157.

[4] Not printed.

reserves. This is in addition to the 358 Navy/Marine Corps Fighter, Attack, and Reconnaissance aircraft I recommend buying in FY 69 at a cost of $1,485 million. For FY 69, they also recommend procurement of 25 CH-46 helicopters for the reserves at a cost of about $50 million, in addition to 130 helicopters I recommend buying for the Marines in FY 69 at a cost of about $180 million. (Procurement of all new aircraft for the Fourth Marine Air Wing would add about $1 billion to my recommended plan over the next five years.) Mr. Nitze and I recommend against this procurement because, without it, we are greatly increasing the total tactical airpower and helicopter lift capability of all of our forces, including the Marine Corps, and because we believe the total inventory of Marine aircraft is adequate. Moreover, our general policy is not to buy new aircraft for reserve air forces. Under our recommended plan, from 1961 to 1971, the destruction capability of the Marine fighter and attack forces will increase more than fourfold and the helicopter troop lift capability will increase more than tenfold.

3. *Development of New Tactical Fighter (F-X/VFAX):* Both the Air Force and the Navy want to develop a new fighter to replace the F-4. They believe it is needed to counter the latest Soviet fighters. They recommend that we plan to proceed with "Contract Definition" in FY 69 leading to an Initial Operational Capability in 1975. The FY 69 cost of their latest proposal is estimated at about $104 million. Mr. Nitze and I agree that a new fighter ought to be developed for the mid to late 1970's, and we recommend including $60 million in the FY 69 R&D budget for this purpose. This will permit an IOC in 1976.

Dr. Foster, the Director of Research and Engineering, has informed me that a properly defined and substantiated joint-Service plan for F-X/VFAX has not yet been developed. Several important issues have not yet been resolved including the extent to which the two Service versions can be common, the size of the crew, and the extent to which all-weather air-to-ground electronics should be included. The recommended $60 million will support an extensive experimental effort in avionics and propulsion to help resolve these issues and to reduce program risks, permitting start of full-scale development in FY 70.

In addition although the JCS do not recommend FY 69 budget action on a Soviet-oriented ABM system, they want to repeat their view that ultimately the U.S. should deploy such an ABM system to protect U.S. population centers against heavy Soviet attacks.[5]

---

[5] In a November 27 memorandum to Secretary McNamara, General Wheeler wrote in part: "The issue of the level of Nike-X deployment does not bear directly on the FY 1969 budget; however, it is of sufficient significance to the Joint Chiefs of Staff to warrant discussion with the President." (Washington National Records Center, McNamara Files: FRC 330 71 A 3470, Final Memo to the President 1 Dec 1967, Notes of Meeting with JCS 11/17 & 11/24, Folder 157)

The recommended program has been discussed with the Director of the Bureau of the Budget, and the President's Special Assistant for Science and Technology. They are in agreement with my recommendations with two exceptions. Dr. Hornig is concerned about the apparent decrease in the level of R&D on tactical weapons, and what he considers an inadequate rate of application of new technology to Vietnam. However, he will not be in a position to make specific counterproposals until our R&D budget estimates are more firm. Mr. Schultze believes the FY 69 RDT&E total obligational authority should not exceed $7.45 billion. Our tentative proposal for FY 69 is $7.4–7.7 billion.

Robert S. McNamara

Tab B

SUMMARY OF RECOMMENDATIONS BY THE SECRETARY OF DEFENSE AND RELATED RECOMMENDATIONS BY THE JOINT CHIEFS OF STAFF WITH FY 69 BUDGET IMPLICATIONS[6]

A. Strategic Retaliatory Forces

1. The Secretary of Defense recommended maintaining a Minuteman force of [3 *lines of source text not declassified*] for each Minuteman II. The JCS concurred in the Minuteman force level, but recommended that MK-17s be deployed for Minuteman II and later for Minuteman III. The Secretary of Defense reaffirmed his recommendations. Subsequently, the Secretary of the Air Force recommended slipping the Initial Operating Capability (IOC) of the MK-17 one year to January, 1970, and retaining MK-11s for Minuteman II in the interim. The Secretary of Defense later recommended canceling MK-17 development and slipping Minuteman III an additional six months.

2. The Secretary of Defense recommended continuing the previously approved program of buying area penetration aids for all Minuteman missiles and terminal penetration aids for Minuteman III. He also approved deploying an improved version of Minuteman II penetration aids at a cost of $35 million in FY 69. The JCS concurred.

3. The Secretary of Defense recommended that no additional Titan II missiles be bought and the Titan force be phased down as missiles were fired in Follow-on-Tests. The Secretary of the Air Force recommended procuring 11 additional Titan II missiles to maintain the force at 54 missiles with a test rate of 6 per year. The JCS recommended

---

[6] McNamara initialed at the bottom of the first page.

retaining the Titan force at 54 UE missiles until a new large throw-weight ICBM is available as a replacement. The Secretary of Defense then recommended maintaining the Titan force at 54 UE missiles by buying 5 missiles in FY 69 (for $11.3 million) and 4 missiles in FY 70 and reducing the test rate to 4 per year.

4. The Secretary of Defense recommended developing a stellar-inertial guidance system for the Poseidon force and deploying an average of [less than 1 line of source text not declassified]. He recommended against developing an option [less than 1 line of source text not declassified] by end FY 72. The JCS and the Secretary of the Navy concurred in the development of a stellar-inertial guidance system, but recommended retaining the option [less than 1 line of source text not declassified]. The JCS recommended planning on [less than 1 line of source text not declassified] missile. The Secretary of the Navy proposed to initially procure [1 line of source text not declassified] by 1975 if a review in 1969 does not indicate that higher loading is necessary. The Secretary of Defense then reaffirmed his recommendation to deploy [less than 1 line of source text not declassified] throughout the entire period.

5. The Secretary of Defense recommended against deploying area and terminal penetration aids for Polaris A-3 at a cost of $200 million in FY 69. The JCS and the Secretary of the Navy agreed to defer the deployment, but recommended retaining the option to deploy these penetration aids at a cost of $9 million in FY 69. The Secretary of Defense agreed to retain this option.

6. The Secretary of Defense recommended continuing Advanced Development of an Advanced ICBM, but recommended against starting Contract Definition in FY 69. The JCS recommended completion of Contract Definition in FY 69, and dependent upon favorable review, full-scale development of the missile element of the Advanced ICBM (WS-120A), with the objective of an IOC in FY 73. They also recommended delaying a decision on expenditures unique to a specific deployment mode until study results are available. The Secretary of the Air Force recommended beginning Contract Definition in FY 69 at a cost of $79 million. Subsequently the Secretary of Defense and the Secretary of the Air Force agreed to develop [less than 1 line of source text not declassified] that are capable of accepting either Minuteman III or the WS-120A missile; the program would support a deployment date of Minuteman in such silos in FY 72 and an Advanced ICBM IOC in FY 74. Of the $207 million total hard silos R&D program, the Secretary of Defense will authorize $40 million in FY 69. This includes $38 million R&D money for the dual-capable silo and $2 million for site surveys. An additional $10 million was authorized for advanced ICBM technology.

7. The Secretary of Defense recommended against procuring a prototype Ballistic Missile Ship (BMS) in FY 69. The JCS recommended Concept Formulation and, dependent upon favorable review, construction of one prototype BMS to be available for tests and training in FY 71. This would require $120 million in FY 69 funds. The Secretary of Defense reaffirmed his recommendation.

8. The Secretary of Defense recommended retaining the current basing program for the bomber force and deferring a decision on equipping B-52 G/H bombers with SRAMs until there is evidence that the Soviets have a good low-altitude terminal defense. He also decided not to reduce further the number of Hound Dog missiles in FY 69. The JCS and the Secretary of the Air Force concurred in the bomber force basing program. The JCS recommended equipping the B-52 G/Hs with SRAMs, beginning in FY 70. The Secretary of the Air Force recommended modification of B-52 G/Hs beginning in FY 69 at a cost of $68 million and additional SRAM procurement beginning in FY 70. The Secretary of Defense subsequently decided to modify 30 UE B-52s for SRAM in FY 69, at a cost of approximately $45 million, with no increase in the total number of SRAMs to be procured, but retaining an option to buy more in FY 70.

9. The Secretary of Defense recommended continuing development of advanced aircraft technology and bomber penetration aids, but recommended against beginning Contract Definition for the Advanced Manned Strategic Bomber (AMSA) in FY 69. The JCS recommended completion of AMSA Contract Definition in FY 69, and subject to favorable review, full-scale development to preserve an IOC of FY 76. The Secretary of the Air Force recommended Contract Definition in FY 69. The Secretary of Defense reaffirmed his recommendations.

B. Continental Air and Missile Defense

1. The Secretary of Defense recommended a Chinese-oriented, system (tentatively with the option of providing for the defense of Minuteman with Sprint missiles following the initial Spartan installation) at an investment cost (including AEC costs) of $4.1 billion in FY 69–73. The Secretary of the Army concurred, but also recommended deploying Nike-X to protect U.S. cities against a Soviet attack. The JCS accepted the proposed light Nike-X deployment as a first step, and concurred in the FY 69 part of the plan, but also recommended deploying Nike-X at the "Posture A" level (at about $10 billion) to protect U.S. cities against a Soviet attack. The Secretary of Defense reaffirmed his recommendation. (The investment cost of his recommended plan is now estimated at about $5 billion, including AEC costs.)

2. The JCS recommended production now for deployment of 12 UE F-12 interceptors in FY 72, and initiating Contract Definition now for an

Airborne Warning and Control System (AWACS) for an IOC in FY 73. The JCS recommended against phasing down of our air defense without modernizing the force. The Secretary of the Air Force and the Secretary of Defense later agreed on a new continental air defense plan including deployment of Over-the-Horizon radars; full-scale development of prototype AWACS with a procurement decision based on flight tests; and development and deployment of an improved F-106X aircraft. The plan also includes provisions for augmenting the defense with Tactical Air Command, Navy, and Marine Corps forces in time of emergency, and selective phase-downs of current Century interceptors and portions of the SAGE/BUIC system. An F-12 development program is under review.

3. The Secretary of Defense recommended continuing feasibility studies on the sea-based ABM system. The JCS recommended speeding up feasibility and Concept Formulation studies on both the sea-based and airborne missile intercept systems. The Secretary of the Navy recommended acceleration of the sea-based missile intercept system. The Secretary of Defense reaffirmed his recommendation.

4. The Secretary of Defense recommended continuing the approved program for military survival measures (fallout protection for military personnel) at a cost of $47 million in FY 68–73. The JCS recommended a larger program at a cost of $191 million. The Secretary of Defense reaffirmed his recommendation.

C. Theater Nuclear Forces

1. The Secretary of Defense recommended phasing out 18 Mace in Europe and 36 Mace [*less than 1 line of source text not declassified*] in FY 69. The JCS and the Secretary of the Air Force recommended against the phaseout. The Secretary of Defense affirmed the Mace phase-out in Europe, but deferred the Mace phase-out in [*less than 1 line of source text not declassified*] until FY 70.

2. The Secretary of Defense recommended phasing out one Pershing battalion now in CONUS in FY 69. The JCS and the Secretary of the Army recommended against the phase-out. The Secretary of Defense then recommended deferring phase-out until FY 70.

3. The Secretary of Defense recommended against developing a MIRV missile for Pershing. The JCS (less the Air Force Chief of Staff) and the Secretary of the Army recommended development and deployment of Pershing MIRV at a cost of $43 million in FY 69. The Secretary of Defense reaffirmed his recommendation.

4. The Secretary of Defense recommended reducing the tactical nuclear bomb stockpile [*number not declassified*]. The JCS and the Secretary of the Air Force recommended increasing the tactical nuclear

bomb stockpile to [*number not declassified*]. The Secretary of the Navy contended that [*number not declassified*] tactical nuclear bombs would be insufficient. The Secretary of Defense then recommended a stockpile of [*number not declassified*] tactical nuclear bombs in FY 69 and [*number not declassified*] bombs in FY 70 and thereafter.

5. The Secretary of Defense recommended phasing down the tactical Nike Hercules nuclear warhead stockpile to [*number not declassified*] warheads per U.S. and allied battery. The JCS recommended retaining [*number not declassified*] warheads per U.S. battery and [*number not declassified*] warheads per allied battery. The Secretary of the Amy recommended deferring decision pending further study. The Secretary of Defense then agreed to defer decision.

6. The JCS recommended the following tactical nuclear warhead stockpiles, compared to the program recommended by the Secretary of Defense:

[*list (4 lines of source text) not declassified*]

These recommendations are now under review.

D. Army and Marine Corps Land Forces

1. The JCS recommended the following total FY 69 Army force structure compared to that recommended by the Secretary of Defense:

	JCS	SecDef
Active Division Equivalents	21-2/3	19-2/3
Active ISIs	21-2/3	19-2/3
Active SSIs	17-1/3	12
Reserve Division Equivalents	9	8
Reserve ISIs	9	8
Reserve SSIs	13-1/3	15-2/3
Division Force Equipment Sets	30-2/3	27-2/3 (less 2/3 of an SSI set)

The Secretary of Defense reaffirmed his recommendations.

2. The Secretary of Defense recommended a total FY 69 Marine Corps force structure of 5 division forces (4 active, 1 reserve) with an active manpower strength of 298,000. The JCS concurred with the number of division forces, but recommended an active manpower strength of 330,000. The Secretary of the Navy concurred with the number of division forces, but recommended an active manpower strength of 322,000. The Secretary of Defense will review total manpower strength in connection with specific requirements.

3. The Secretary of Defense recommended procuring 540 UH-1D helicopters in FY 69. The Secretary of the Army recommended procur-

ing 744 UH-1Ds. Total UH-1D procurement requirements are now under review.

4. The Secretary of Defense recommended reducing the previously approved FY 69 CH-47 procurement from 60 to 26. The Secretary of the Army recommended retaining the currently approved program to procure 60 CH-47s in FY 69. The Secretary of Defense then recommended procuring 48 CH-47s in FY 69 and long lead-time components for 36 CH-47s in FY 70. The Secretary of the Army then concurred.

5. The Secretary of Defense recommended procuring the new TOW and Dragon anti-tank missiles only for active Army armored and mechanized divisions. The JCS, the Secretary of the Army, and the Secretary of the Navy recommended procuring these missiles for all active and reserve Army and Marine Corps division forces. The Secretary of Defense reaffirmed his recommendation.

6. The Secretary of Defense recommended reducing the previously approved procurement program for M60 Shillelagh tanks because of technical difficulties in Shillelagh. The JCS recommended procurement not be reduced. This recommendation is now under review.

7. The Secretary of Defense recommended changing the mix of Vulcan and Chaparral units and reducing the number of fire units per battalion from 64 to 48. The JCS and the Secretary of the Army recommended no decision be made until completion of a new Army study. The Secretary of Defense then agreed to consider the change in mix to be tentative, pending the results of Army tests and studies next year. (The FY 69 procurement of Vulcan and Chaparral may not be sensitive to the mix decision.)

8. The Secretary of Defense recommended deactivating 8 Hercules batteries in Europe in FY 69. The JCS and the Secretary of the Army recommended deferring deactivation because of slippage in the Vulcan/Chaparral force. The Secretary of Defense agreed to defer deactivation until FY 70.

9. The Secretary of Defense recommended reducing the number of Hawk batteries from 83 to 79. The Secretary of the Army concurred. The JCS recommended retaining the previously approved program of 83 batteries. The Secretary of Defense reaffirmed his recommendation.

10. The Secretary of Defense recommended gradually eliminating all 40mm automatic weapons units from the Army reserve components as Vulcan phases into the active Army. The JCS recommended all 56 40mm reserve units be maintained and modernized with 20mm Vulcan. The Secretary of the Army recommended phasing down the number of reserve units to 40 batteries for which equipment is available, and then phasing down to 16 batteries as Vulcan is deployed in the active Army. The Secretary of Defense agreed to the Secretary of the Army's alternative.

11. The Secretary of Defense recommended changing the mix of Marine Corps assault transport helicopters in the three active wings from 360 CH-46s and 72 CH-53s to 252 CH-46s and 144 CH-53s. The JCS and the Secretary of the Navy concurred in this change provided three new light transport helicopter squadrons were approved. The Secretary of Defense then reaffirmed the change in the CH-46/CH-53 mix and recommended creating three temporary light transport helicopter squadrons using existing UH-1E assets in FY 68 and FY 69.

12. The Secretary of Defense deferred decision on procuring the AH-1G as a replacement for the UH-1E in Marine Corps light observation squadrons (VMOs). The JCS and the Secretary of the Navy recommended procuring 55 AH-1Gs to provide 12 of these aircraft for each of the three active VMOs. The Secretary of Defense then recommended procuring 38 AH-1Gs to provide 12 aircraft for each of the two VMOs deployed to Southeast Asia.

13. The Secretary of Defense recommended that no new CH-46 helicopters be procured to complete the modernization of the 4th (Reserve) Marine Air Wing. The JCS and the Secretary of the Navy recommended that new CH-46s be procured to replace UH-34s in the Reserve Wing. The Secretary of Defense reaffirmed his recommendation.

14. The Secretary of Defense made no recommendation on any type of crane helicopter for the Marine Corps. The JCS recommended developing and procuring 15 CH-54B crane helicopters for the active Marine Air Wings at a cost of $48 million in FY 69. The Secretary of the Navy recommended procuring 5 for $15 million. The Secretary of Defense then decided not to budget in FY 69 for development or procurement of CH-54Bs.

E. Navy Anti-Submarine Warfare Forces

1. The Secretary of Defense recommended continuing the previously approved undersea surveillance system (SOSUS) program in FY 69 at a cost of $73 million. The JCS supported a Navy proposal to expand the SOSUS system to include four rather than two mid-Pacific arrays, to install a new long-range cable in the Philippine Sea System, and to approve an installation in the eastern Atlantic area. The FY 69 cost of this proposal is $120 million. The Navy proposal is now under review.

2. The Secretary of Defense recommended disapproving development of a new carrier-based ASW aircraft (VSX). The JCS and the Secretary of the Navy recommended continuing VSX development. The Secretary of Defense deferred final decision pending further review. Subsequently, the Secretary of Defense approved development of the VSX as part of a plan for 5 CVS carriers and 4 air groups after the war in Southeast Asia, an Authorized Active Inventory (AAI) of 135 VSX

aircraft, and a land-based patrol aircraft force of 24 P-3 squadrons when the VSX is phased in. The Secretary of Defense also recommended reducing the end FY 69 force by 2 CVS air groups to bring the number of air groups into balance with the available carriers.

3. The Secretary of Defense recommended continuing Contract Definition of a new class of ASW escort, the DX, but deferring construction of the first of these ships to FY 70. The JCS supported the Navy proposal for constructing 9 DXs in FY 69. The Secretary of the Navy later recommended constructing 5 DXs in FY 69 at a cost of $252 million. The Secretary of Defense then agreed to the Secretary of the Navy's recommendation.

4. The Secretary of Defense recommended procuring 3 nuclear attack submarines (SSN) in FY 69 at a cost of $254 million. The JCS and the Secretary of the Navy recommended procuring 5 SSNs at an estimated cost of $423 million in FY 69. The Secretary of the Navy later recommended procuring 3 SSNs in FY 69 and procuring long lead-time items for FY 70 SSNs at a cost of $284 million in FY 69. The Secretary of Defense then recommended procuring 2 SSNs in FY 69 and procuring long lead-time items for 2 FY 70 SSNs, at a FY 69 cost of $178 million.

5. The Secretary of Defense recommended procuring 40 P-3C land-based patrol aircraft in FY 69. The JCS and the Secretary of the Navy concurred in the number to be procured. Subsequently, the Secretary of Defense recommended a reduced P-3C buy in FY 69 as part of the new airborne ASW plan. The exact number of P-3Cs to be procured is under review.

F. Navy Amphibious Assault, Fire Support, and Mine Countermeasures Forces

1. The Secretary of Defense recommended a FY 69 amphibious assault shipbuilding program of 2 amphibious assault ships (LHA) and 7 tank landing ships (LST). The JCS and the Secretary of the Navy concurred. The Secretary of the Navy later withdrew his recommendation on LST construction. The Secretary of the Navy's recommendation is now under review.

2. The Secretary of Defense recommended deferring the construction of one amphibious flagship (AGC) from FY 69 to FY 70. The Secretary of the Navy concurred, but the JCS recommended the AGC not be deferred. The Secretary of Defense reaffirmed his recommendation.

3. The Secretary of Defense recommended deferring Contract Definition of the landing force support ship (LFS) from FY 69 to FY 70 and not constructing an LFS in FY 69. The JCS and the Secretary of the Navy recommended Contract Definition not be deferred. The JCS also

recommended FY 69 procurement of one LFS. The Secretary of Defense then approved the JCS/Navy recommendation regarding Contract Definition, but reaffirmed his recommendation against constructing an LFS in FY 69.

4. The JCS and the Secretary of the Navy recommended a force level of 6 CA/CAGs plus 2 battleships for Southeast Asia. The Secretary of Defense then recommended a force of 4 CA/CAGs plus one battleship for Southeast Asia.

5. The Secretary of Defense recommended rehabilitating 10 minesweepers (MSO) in FY 69, but recommended against constructing any new MSOs in FY 69. The JCS and the Secretary of the Navy concurred with the recommendation to rehabilitate 10 MSOs, but recommended constructing 5 new MSOs in FY 69. The Secretary of Defense reaffirmed his recommendations.

6. The Secretary of Defense recommended deferring one mine countermeasures support ship (MCS) and one special minesweeper (MSS) from FY 69 to FY 70. The JCS and the Secretary of the Navy concurred.

G. Naval Replenishment and Support Forces

1. The Secretary of Defense recommended an underway replenishment force of 81 ships (including a 10 ship Southeast Asia augmentation) in FY 69. The JCS and the Secretary of the Navy recommended a force of 87 ships (including a 12 ship Southeast Asia augmentation) in FY 69. The Secretary of Defense then recommended an underway replenishment force of 83 ships (including a 12 ship Southeast Asia augmentation) in FY 69.

2. The Secretary of Defense recommended deferring FY 69 procurement of replenishment helicopters. The JCS and the Secretary of the Navy recommended procuring 18 UH-46s at a cost of $28 million in FY 69. The Secretary of Defense reaffirmed his recommendation.

3. The Secretary of Defense recommended deferring the FY 69 procurement of 8 patrol craft (PC) to FY 70. The JCS and the Secretary of the Navy concurred.

4. The Secretary of Defense recommended constructing 3 replenishment fleet oilers (AOR), 5 salvage tugs (ATS), and one destroyer tender (AD) in FY 69. The JCS and the Secretary of the Navy concurred.

H. Navy and Marine Corps Tactical Air Forces[7]

1. The Secretary of Defense recommended a 15 CVA force (augmented by *Intrepid* during the war in Southeast Asia). The JCS (less the

---

[7] All aircraft force level recommendations in items 3 through 8 are on a Unit Equipment (UE) basis. [Footnote in the source text.]

Chairman and the Chief of Staff of the Air Force) and the Secretary of the Navy recommended 17 CVAs (including *Intrepid* until replaced by a new CVA) for the duration of the war in Southeast Asia. The Chairman recommended 16 CVAs but did not address the *Intrepid* issue, and the Chief of Staff of the Air Force recommended 16 CVAs (including *Intrepid* until replaced by a new CVA). The Secretary of Defense reaffirmed his recommendation.

2. The Secretary of Defense recommended constructing one new CVAN in FY 69. The JCS and the Secretary of the Navy concurred.

3. The Secretary of Defense recommended a force of 1,004 Navy fighter/attack aircraft in FY 69. The JCS recommended a force of 1,192 Navy fighter/attack aircraft in FY 69. The Secretary of the Navy recommended a force of 1,060 Navy fighter/attack aircraft. The Secretary of Defense reaffirmed his recommendation.

4. The Secretary of Defense recommended a force of 70 Navy reconnaissance aircraft in FY 69. The JCS recommended a force of 71 aircraft. The Secretary of the Navy recommended a force of 87 aircraft. The Secretary of Defense then recommended a force of 82 Navy reconnaissance aircraft.

5. The Secretary of Defense recommended a total of 203 aircraft of other types (airborne early warning, utility, electronic countermeasures, tankers, and helicopters) in Navy combat units in FY 69. The JCS recommended a total of 226 aircraft. The Secretary of the Navy recommended a total of 194 aircraft The Secretary of Defense then recommended a total of 190 of these aircraft.

6. The Secretary of Defense recommended a force of 417 Marine Corps fighter/attack aircraft and 27 Marine Corps reconnaissance aircraft for FY 69. The JCS and the Secretary of the Navy concurred.

7. The Secretary of Defense recommended a total of 55 aircraft of other types (electronic countermeasures and tactical air control) in Marine Corps combat units in FY 69. The JCS and the Secretary of the Navy recommended a total of 63 of these aircraft. The Secretary of Defense reaffirmed his recommendation. Subsequently, the Secretary of Defense concurred with the JCS/Navy recommendation.

8. The Secretary of Defense recommended a total of 315 aircraft (fighter/attack, reconnaissance, electronic countermeasures, and tactical air control) in Navy and Marine Corps reserve combat units in FY 69. The JCS and the Secretary of the Navy recommended a total of 353 of these aircraft. The Secretary of Defense reaffirmed his recommendation.

9. The JCS and the Secretary of the Navy recommended procuring the following tactical aircraft in FY 69 compared to that recommended by the Secretary of Defense:

	JCS	SecNavy	SecDef
A-6A	113	124	36
A-6D	48	24	
A-7A/B	375		
A-7E		240	214
F-4J	112	150	36
F-111B	42	42	30
RA-5C	57	24	24
RF-4B/J	30	24	10
EA-6B	31	19	8
E-2A/B	9	9	
TC-4Cs	18		
TOTAL	835	656	358

The Secretary of Defense's recommendations may be revised to reflect the latest Southeast Asia attrition estimates.

I. Air Force Tactical Air Forces[8]

1. The Secretary of Defense recommended a total of 1,777 fighter/attack aircraft for FY 69. The Secretary of the Air Force concurred. The JCS recommended a total of 1,807 aircraft. The Secretary of Defense reaffirmed his recommendation. The Secretary of the Air Force later recommended reducing the FY 69 force to 1,771 aircraft.

2. The Secretary of Defense recommended a tactical reconnaissance force of 360 aircraft for FY 69. The JCS and the Secretary of the Air Force concurred.

3. The Secretary of Defense recommended a Special Air Warfare force of 354 aircraft for FY 69. The JCS recommended a total of 420 aircraft. The Secretary of the Air Force recommended a total of 390 aircraft to include 36 UH-1 helicopters. The Secretary of Defense then recommended a FY 69 force level of 396 aircraft and a FY 69 buy of 37 UH-1s.

4. The Secretary of Defense recommended a total of 391 other aircraft (night warfare, electronic warfare, and tactical air control) in Air Force combat units for FY 69. The JCS recommended a total of 427 aircraft. The Secretary of the Air Force recommended a total of 505 aircraft. The Secretary of Defense then recommended a total of 455 aircraft and the Secretary of the Air Force concurred.

---

[8] All aircraft force level recommendations in items 1 through 4 are on a Unit Equipment (UE) basis. [Footnote in the source text.]

5. The JCS and the Secretary of the Air Force recommended procuring the following tactical aircraft in 69 compared to that recommended by the Secretary of Defense:

	JCS	SecAF	SecDef
A-7D	135	220	220
AX	22		
F-4E	150	113	113
F-5A/B	49		
F-111A	181	181	181
RF-4C	59	51	51
RF-111	45		
A-37	81	50	50
UH-1F	60	37	37
OV-10	30		
Utility Transports	52		
TOTAL	864	652	652

The Secretary of Defense's recommendations may be revised to reflect the latest Southeast Asia attrition estimates.

J. Airlift and Sealift Forces

1. The Secretary of Defense recommended procuring 27 C-5As in FY 69 at a cost of $548 million. The JCS concurred.

2. The Secretary of Defense recommended procuring 4 Fast Deployment Logistics (FDL) ships in FY 69 at a cost of $187 million. The JCS concurred.

3. The Secretary of Defense recommended that the Forward Floating Depot (FFD) program be cancelled. The JCS and the Secretary of the Army recommended that the FFD program be continued. The Secretary of Defense then concurred.

4. The Secretary of Defense recommended procuring 2 small tanker ships in FY 69 at a cost of $21 million. The JCS concurred.

5. The Secretary of Defense recommended no additional C-130 procurement in FY 69. The JCS did not comment on C-130 procurement in FY 69. However, the JCS supported force level of C-130 aircraft would require procuring about 27 C-130s in FY 68–69. The Secretary of the Air Force recommended procuring 25 C-130s in FY 68 at $60 million, and 28 in FY 69 at $70 million. The Secretary of Defense reaffirmed his recommendation. The Secretary of the Air Force later recommended buying 27 C-130Es at $10 million in FY 68, $40 million in FY 69, and $30 million in FY 70. The Secretary of Defense again reaffirmed his recommendation.

6. The Secretary of Defense recommended no additional procurement of C-2A (COD) aircraft in FY 69. The JCS did not comment on C-2A procurement. The Secretary of the Navy recommended procuring 18 C-2As at a cost of $56.8 million in FY 69. The Secretary of Defense reaffirmed his recommendation.

7. The Secretary of Defense recommended no additional procurement of KC-130 aircraft for the Marine Air Wings. The JCS did not comment on KC-130 procurement in FY 69. However, the JCS-supported KC-130 force structure would require procuring about 24 KC-130s in FY 69. The Secretary of the Navy recommended procuring 24 KC-130Hs at a cost of $83 million in FY 69. The Secretary of Defense reaffirmed his recommendation.

8. The Secretary of Defense recommended against procuring Tactical Support Transport aircraft for the Marine Air Wings and that 26 C-47/54/117s be deleted from the force structure in FY 69. The JCS did not comment on procurement, but recommended that the 26 C-47/54/117s be retained through FY 69. The Secretary of the Navy recommended $31.2 million in FY 69 for the procurement of 12 Tactical Support Transport aircraft. The Secretary of Defense then recommended retaining the 26 aircraft through end FY 69 and then phasing them out without replacement.

9. The Secretary of Defense recommended phasing out all 336 C-119s from the reserves in FY 69. The JCS did not comment on this recommendation. The Secretary of the Air Force recommended retaining 160 C-119s in the reserves through FY 69. The Secretary of Defense then concurred with the Secretary of the Air Force's recommendation.

10. The Secretary of Defense recommended that 20 Navy C-118s be deleted from the airlift force structure in FY 69. The JCS concurred, but recognized a need for some Navy Tactical Support Airlift. The Secretary of the Navy recommended a plan (the FY 69 part of) which would phase 10 Navy C-118s into the reserves to replace 13 C-54s. The Secretary of Defense then recommended phasing 14 Navy C-118s into the reserves in FY 69 to replace 20 C-54s.

K. Logistics Guidance

1. The Secretary of Defense recommended a procurement objective of 90 days of combat support for U.S. forces committed to NATO. The Secretary of the Air Force concurred. The JCS recommended 180 days of combat support for these forces. The Secretary of Defense reaffirmed his recommendation.

2. The Secretary of Defense recommended a 135 day pipeline for forces in the Indefinite Combat category. The JCS and the Secretary

of the Navy recommended a 180 day pipeline. The Secretary of Defense reaffirmed his recommendation.

3. The Secretary of Defense recommended the ASW forces be supported at 90 days plus shipfill for the full force (equivalent to 135 days of combat for deployed forces plus shipfill for the full force). The JCS and the Secretary of the Navy recommended support at 180 days for the deployed forces plus shipfill for the full force. The Secretary of Defense reaffirmed his recommendation.

4. The Secretary of Defense recommended equipment stocks for forces in the Indefinite Combat category through the first 180 days after war starts. The Secretary of the Navy recommended D to P plus a 180 day pipeline. The JCS recognized that provision must be made for replacement of attrition of equipment (including aircraft) beyond 180 days; however, a specific recommendation was withheld pending further analysis by the JCS. The Secretary of Defense reaffirmed his recommendation that more equipment would be bought only when it can be shown that its lack would keep these forces from being able to fight indefinitely.

5. The Secretary of Defense recommended 90 days of logistics support for two armored Army Reserve division force equivalents. The JCS recommended that these forces be given logistics support to enable them to fight indefinitely (D to P). The Secretary of Defense reaffirmed his recommendation.

L. Major Fleet Escorts

The JCS recommended procuring one nuclear frigate (DLGN) and two guided missile destroyers (DDGs) in FY 69. The Secretary of the Navy recommended procuring two nuclear frigates and modernizing two conventional frigates (DLGs). The Secretary of Defense recommended constructing three nuclear guided missile destroyers (DXGNs) in FY 69, one using FY 68 funds. The Secretary of the Navy tentatively concurred with the recommendation pending further review.

REMAINING SIGNIFICANT FY 69 BUDGET DISAGREEMENTS
BETWEEN THE JOINT CHIEFS OF STAFF AND THE SECRETARY
OF DEFENSE

A. Strategic Retaliatory Forces	JCS	SecDef
1. Procurement of MK-17s for Minuteman II	Yes	No
2. Deploy MK-17s on Minuteman III	Yes	No
3. Procurement of Titan II missiles		5
4. Option to deploy MK-17s on Poseidon by end FY 72	Yes	No

REMAINING SIGNIFICANT FY 69 BUDGET DISAGREEMENTS
BETWEEN THE JOINT CHIEFS OF STAFF AND THE SECRETARY
OF DEFENSE—Continued

	JCS	SecDef
5. Average number of MK-3s per Poseidon missile	[*]	[*]
6. R&D on Advanced ICBM	$75 million	$11 million
A. Strategic Retaliatory Forces	JCS	SecDef
7. Prototype Ballistic Missile Ship	$120 million	$0
8. R&D on AMSA	$65 million	$25 million

B. Continental Air and Missile Defense

1. Anti-Soviet Nike-X deployment	Yes	No
2. Introduce AWACS; phase down SAGE/BUIC; modernize F-106 and reduce total number of interceptors; continue R&D on F-12	Yes, but use F-12 in lieu of F-106X, and delay phasedown	Yes
3. R&D on sea-based and airborne ABM systems	$20 million	$1 million
4. Military survival measures program	$30 million	$10 million

C. Theater Nuclear Forces

1. Phase out of 18 Mace in Europe	No	Yes
2. Pershing MIRV	$43 million	$0
3. Tactical nuclear bomb stockpile	[*]	[*]
4. Tactical Nike Hercules nuclear warhead inventory	[*]	Under Review
5. FY 69 tactical nuclear warhead inventory	[*]	Under Review

D. Army and Marine Corps Land Forces

1. Army active division equivalents	21-2/3	19-2/3
2. Army reserve division equivalents	9	8
3. Army division force sets of equipment	30-2/3	27-2/3
4. Marine Corps FY 69 active end strength	330,000	Under Review
5. UH-ID helicopter procurement	744	Under Review
6. CH-47 helicopter procurement	60	48

[*entry in table not declassified]

REMAINING SIGNIFICANT FY 69 BUDGET DISAGREEMENTS
BETWEEN THE JOINT CHIEFS OF STAFF AND THE SECRETARY
OF DEFENSE—Continued

7. TOW and Dragon procurement	All active and reserve Army and Marine divisions	Active Army armored and mechanized divisions
	JCS	SecDef
8. Reduction in M60 Shillelegh procurement	No	Under Review
9. Force objective for Hawk batteries	83	79
10. Army reserve 40mm automatic weapons units	56	40
11. Complete modernization of 4th (Reserve) Marine Air Wing	Yes	No
12. CH-54B crane helicopters for active Marine Air Wings	15	0

E. Navy Anti-Submarine Warfare Forces

1. SOSUS program	$120 million	Under Review
2. DX procurement	9	5
3. SSN procurement	5	2

F. Navy Amphibious Assault, Fire Support, and Mine Countermeasures Forces

1. AGC procurement	1	0
2. LFS procurement	1	0
3. CA/CAG force level	6	4
4. Battleship force level (Southeast Asia)	2	1
5. MSO procurement	5	0

G. Naval Replenishment and Support Forces

1. Underway replenishment ship force level	87	83
2. UH-46 replenishment helicopter procurement	18	0

H. Navy and Marine Corps Tactical Air Forces

1. Attack carrier force	16	15
2. Navy fighter/attack aircraft force level	1,192	1,004
3. Recommended aircraft procurement	835	358
4. VFAX and E-2B development	Accerate Development	Under Review

REMAINING SIGNIFICANT FY 69 BUDGET DISAGREEMENTS BETWEEN THE JOINT CHIEFS OF STAFF AND THE SECRETARY OF DEFENSE—Continued

I. Air Force Tactical Air Forces	JCS	SecDef
1. Fighter/attack aircraft force level	1,807	1,777
2. Special Air Warfare force level	420	354
3. Electronic Warfare force level	137	75
4. Recommended aircraft procurement	864	615
5. F-X and A-X development	$128 million	$60 million
J. Airlift and Sealift Forces		
1. C-130 procurement	Yes	No
2. KC-130 procurement	Yes	No
K. Logistics Guidance		
1. Support of U.S. NATO-oriented forces	180 days	90 days
2. Pipeline for forces in Indefinite Combat category	180 days	135 days
3. ASW support	180 days plus shipfill	90 days plus shipfill
4. Logistics support for two Army reserve armored division force equivalents	D to P	90 days
L. Major Fleet Escorts		
1. DLGN procurement	1	0
2. DXGN procurement	0	2
3. DDG procurement	2	0

196.   Notes of Meeting[1]

Washington, December 4, 1967, 12:23–1:35 p.m.

NOTES OF THE PRESIDENT'S MEETING
WITH
Secretary McNamara
Undersecretary Nitze
General Wheeler
General McConnell
General Johnson
General Greene
Admiral Moorer

Secretary McNamara said this is the annual meeting with the President to review budgetary issues which the JCS feels are important enough to discuss with the President.

General Wheeler said the Joint Chiefs of Staff had two very long and productive sessions with Secretary McNamara concerning U.S. strategic forces and general purpose forces.[2] He said there are only four issues which will be brought to the President's attention, and one has no impact on the FY'69 budget.

General Wheeler said this has been the most far-reaching and most extensive exchange of views the JCS has had in the four years he has participated. He said that budget decisions are still being considered, so it does not necessarily mean that additional questions will not be brought to the President's attention in the future. He said the questions before them today concern force modification and force structure. This does not affect Southeast Asia operations.

General McConnell said there is disagreement on whether we should have a new advanced strategic bomber in 1976. He says the JCS believe we should have one and Secretary McNamara does not believe we should have one.

Secretary McNamara said he believed General McConnell presented the issue well. He said by 1976 we would have 465 bombers including B-52s and FB-111s. In 1976 there will be 1542 missile launches "on line," and 8,190 separately targetable bombs or warheads.

---

[1] Source: Johnson Library, Tom Johnson's Notes of Meetings, December 4, 1967—12:23 p.m., Joint Chiefs of Staff. No classification marking. The meeting was held in the Cabinet Room of the White House.

[2] See footnote 3, Document 195.

The National Intelligence Estimates (NIE) are that our forces could adequately destroy Soviet capabilities as currently programmed.[3] If the Soviets go beyond NIE estimates, we go to what is called "greater than expected" threats. Even in the event that the "greater than expected" threat develops, we still have means of coping with this situation. These include adding the Spring Defense to the Minuteman system; the addition of hardened silos for the Minuteman missile; adding 150 more Minuteman missiles; and the addition of newer missiles to the B-52 bomber.

General McConnell did say that it is better to have these new bombers than to have to modify the system were the "greater than expected" threat to develop.

The President asked how much this would cost. General McConnell said it would range up to 7-1/2 billion dollars for 150 aircraft, but the amount asked for in FY'69 was only $40 million for contract definition.

Secretary McNamara said he would recommend only about $25 million and that this would delay the bomber program about a year. Under his plan, the current force would be modified and the $7-1/2 billion investment would not be necessary.

General McConnell said it was his judgment that the bomber is superior in "sure destruction" of cities than is the missile. He recommended going to the contract definition on the bomber immediately.

Secretary McNamara said he felt that the threat is not realistic. If it does not develop we will not need the bomber. "I say we stand a good chance of not having to spend the $7 billion. We are talking about 1976. We do not know what the Soviets will do between then and now."

General Johnson said there is some difference of opinion about the assumptions built into this which leads to the figures given in the NIE estimate.

General McConnell said the newest B-52 will be fourteen years old in 1976. "I believe we will need a new bomber by then."

Secretary McNamara said he did not think a new bomber would be necessary.

General Wheeler said the next issue was the modernization of the Fourth Military Air Wing. He said this is a reserve wing.

General Greene said that a later type aircraft is needed in this wing. He said, for example, they have no planes in this wing which can fly in storms or at night and there are no photo reconnaissance aircraft. He also said there is a shortage of helicopters in this wing and that more were needed.

---

[3] A reference presumably to Document 183.

General Greene said that about 23 fixed wing aircraft and 25 choppers would be required to bring this wing up to par with the other wings. The budget request for FY'69 would be $130.1 million and the projected cost for the total project would be $631 million. Secretary McNamara said he did not believe that it was necessary. Secretary Nitze agreed with Secretary McNamara.

General Greene said it was a matter of what the President wanted this wing to be capable of doing in the event it were to be needed in actions independent of Vietnam. "If they are going to operate independently they are not able to do the job with the current equipment."

Secretary McNamara said the wing was ready to go if necessary.

General Greene said the wing has only thirty choppers.

Secretary McNamara asked how many choppers did it have three years ago?

General Greene said there were none three years ago.

Secretary McNamara said that was just the point—there has been significant modernization in the wing during the last three years and that choppers could be reallocated in the event this wing were to be activated for duty.

The President asked if the Defense Department was doing all it could to get choppers to Vietnam.

Secretary McNamara said that indeed there was every priority given to putting more choppers into Vietnam. He said there now was a problem of parts, and there may be a need to shift the tension from choppers to parts. He said, in fact, that there were more choppers than could be used well.

General Johnson said there are 140 choppers per month coming into Vietnam.

Secretary McNamara said there was chopper pilot problems now. He said the need is for more roads in Vietnam so that much of the travel which is now by chopper can be handled on roads. In fact, he said that much of the movement could be handled more efficiently on roads rather than by chopper.

Secretary McNamara said Ambassador Komer and Ambassador Bunker asked for $65 million in road money but that he could only give $40 million.

General Greene said that if we have another crisis somewhere else in the world we would not have this Marine wing equipment well enough to sustain itself.

Secretary McNamara asked for more time to study this problem. He said it was his impression that the wing was not able to sustain itself.

Admiral Moorer said there is a need for a new tactical fighter. He said the F-4 is being used as a first line fighter. There is a need for a general purpose fighter for both services. He said that the services were asking for $100 million for contract definition and that there is no dispute for a need for a fighter. The dispute is over the amount.

Secretary McNamara said Admiral Moorer stated the case well. There is a need for a modern fighter. He said the difference between the JCS and the Secretary is over $60 million versus $100 million.

Secretary McNamara said we will go as fast with money as decisions can be made, but that he would be inclined to leave the budget figure at $60 million.

General McConnell said that the $100 million figure would permit them to overcome any differences in design or contract definition.

Admiral Moorer said that the Secretary had agreed to make up any difference out of funds, were more than $60 million required, so that was satisfactory to him.

General Johnson said that the JCS expected questioning on the differences between their position and that of the Secretary of Defense on the need for ABM defenses. He said the JCS still favors a heavy defense while the Secretary favors a thin defense.

Secretary McNamara said the arguments are well known. The Joint Chiefs are saying they haven't seen anything to change their views and I certainly have not seen anything to change mine.

The President urged that the JCS and the Secretary try to reconcile their differences before testifying. He pointed out the bad results which came out of the Stennis hearings this past session.[4] "These differences permit them to propagandize that we have deep divisions between the civilian and military leadership. I certainly have seen no evidence of that while I have been here. I think you all are superior and stable and dependable.

"However, you must take into account not only what you say but the effects of what you say. You must keep in mind the relation between the military committees of Congress and the Chief Executive. Some committee chairmen think they should run the strategy of the war rather than the President. I base this on all my years in the Congress. We do want the understanding of the committees, but it does not strengthen our system to air our differences.

"I am pleased and proud of your performance, your competence, and your dedication.

"All of you know that you are welcome to visit me anytime you want. You do not have to go through Marvin Watson. You can call my

---

[4] Not further identified.

secretary and slip in through the side door if you have some personal problem or some complaint. There is nobody that stands between you and me if the issue is serious enough to bring it up.

"All of you should know that at any meeting where you are not represented Secretary McNamara has presented your view often better than his own. I remember several situations in which the Secretary presented his position and then presented the position of the Joint Chiefs and I went with your recommendation.

"We are going into a very difficult period ahead. We are going to have a new Secretary of Defense.[5] Most people do not realize how much our wife means to us until she leaves us. Then you learn how difficult it is to do your own cooking. It is the same way with the Secretary. We are going to have to learn to work these things out. It will require all you can—particularly since this is going to be an election year and we are facing some serious financial problems.

"It appears we are not getting a tax bill. Interest rates are rising. We have a potential deficit of $25–$35 billion depending on which assumptions you consider. Our revenues are down. Our expenditures are up.

"I am going to cut $4 billion. $2 billion of that will come from Defense. Even after that $4 billion cut we will still have $1-1/2 billion more than what we went in with on the budget in January.

"So I ask you to return to your departments and sharpen up your lead pencils. Take your lowest priority items and see what you can do to forgo everything except the pay increases and the men and matériel necessary."

---

[5] On November 29 President Johnson announced that he had accepted Secretary McNamara's resignation as Secretary of Defense to become President of the World Bank. For text, see *Public Papers of the Presidents of the United States: Lyndon B. Johnson, 1967*, Book II, pp. 1077–1078.

197.   Action Memorandum From the President's Special Assistant
        (Rostow) to President Johnson[1]

Washington, December 16, 1967, 9:15 a.m.

Mr. President:

As the attached minutes of yesterday's 303 meeting indicate, we now have firm agreement, including Secretaries Rusk and McNamara, on how to proceed with respect to Radio Free Europe and Radio Liberty.

Your decision is required over the weekend because the deadline for informing the organizations in New York is, apparently, December 18.

Under the proposal we would:[2]

—Provide [*number not declassified*] million in a lump sum payment ("surge funding") to cover the two radios at present levels of activity down to the end of fiscal 1969.

Under existing New York law the two organizations would not have to file with the New York Attorney General their revenues until December 1968.

—Inform the two radios that it is the intent of the U.S. Government to find in the year ahead an alternative way to keep them in business. For your information, the two major options are: the overt creation by the Congress of a special public corporation for this purpose, or an arrangement via USIA.

With respect to questions at the end of the year about the implementation of the Katzenbach report,[3] we agreed that, if asked, we would say that no exceptions were made to the recommendation of the Katzenbach committee; and, in certain cases, funds were provided to permit organizations to adjust to a new status; but we would make no breakdown as to what organizations were supported or what amounts had been given in surge funding.

—Inform the Radio organizations in New York that they were to maintain tight security about the method of financing through fiscal 1969; and we would request them to end the solicitation of small private donations via radio and television—a method which is in the

---

[1] Source: Johnson Library, National Security File, Intelligence File, 303 Committee, Box 2. Secret; Eyes Only.

[2] The President wrote "Whose?" with an arrow pointing to the word "proposal."

[3] See footnote 2, Document 176.

process of ending in any case. Solicitation of funds from large corporations which are aware of government financing would continue.

Walt

Proposal approved[4]

Disapproved

See me

Attachment

Memorandum for the Record[5]

SUBJECT

Minutes of the Meeting of the 303 Committee, 15 December 1967

PRESENT

Mr. Rostow, Mr. Katzenbach, Mr. Nitze, and Mr. Helms.

Admiral R.L. Taylor and Mr. William Trueheart were present for all items.

Mr. Charles Schultze, Mr. Hugh Tovar, and Mr. John Richards were present for Items 1 and 2.

1. Radio Free Europe/Radio Liberty

a. The meeting began with a résumé of the meetings and steps which began on 5 May 1967,[6] resulting in today's confrontation.

b. Mr. Rostow began by asking where State stood. Mr. Katzenbach replied promptly, "Behind Mr. Schultze's recommendation for surge funding."[7] [This may be summarized as follows: surge funding both Radio Free Europe and Radio Liberty before December 31, 1967, at the FY-68 funding levels (no modernization) so that both can continue operation until July 30, 1969. This would give us another year to decide what to do with both RFE and RL. [*less than 1 line of source text not declassified*]][8]

---

[4] This option is checked.

[5] Copies were sent to Katzenbach, Nitze, and Helms.

[6] Covert funding of private organizations first came before the 303 Committee at its May 5 meeting, but discussion of the subject was deferred until May 27. See Document 180.

[7] Schultze outlined his plan for surge funding in a memorandum to Secretary Rusk, dated early December 1967. (Johnson Library, National Security File, Intelligence File, 303 Committee, Box 2) In a December 13 memorandum to Rostow, Jessup wrote: "As it now stands, Mr. Rusk, at first reluctant, has bought the Schultze formula." (Ibid.)

[8] Outside brackets in the source text.

c. But what happens afterwards? Mr. Katzenbach alluded to special legislation towards a public communications authority or other overt or even possibly covert funding. The point was made that it would be less difficult to reconstitute covert funding after the election than it would be now.

d. Mr. Nitze interposed that the Secretary of Defense thought an announced exception to the Katzenbach formula would be the least difficult solution.

e. Mr. Helms said, o.k., if we accept surge funding, was the thrust toward continuation?

f. Mr. Rostow said yes and at least the staff work on the options had been performed (an allusion to the exhaustive Trueheart report),[9] and one of the rejected paths, that of the public broadcasting authority or British Council approach, could be reopened in view of the new time available, i.e. one year, to resolve the problem.

g. Mr. Katzenbach agreed, but said we are face to face with the public relations aspect. He was in favor of a simple statement to the effect that with the terminations, certain funds had been provided, but there should certainly be no specific breakdown as to what organizations were supported or what amounts had been given.

h. Mr. Schultze provided an outline along the following: While it is not our policy to identify organizations, specific contributions had been made to various valuable institutions until such time as adequate legislation or new ways of funding from the private sector have been discovered.

i. Mr. Katzenbach elaborated that the Department had the choice, as the deadline neared, of waiting for questions or planting the question in advance.

j. The question was raised as to the timing of the two radios filing appropriate statements with the Internal Revenue Service. Mr. Schultze observed that the surge-funding figure would only appear in the 1968 declaration in early 1969. The inference here was that the main objective was to smoothly sail past the election date in the fall of 1968.

k. The point was made that the directors of the radios should be informed that their statements, preferably brief (left to their proven judgment in the past), should indicate they intend to continue.

l. [7 *lines of source text not declassified*]

m. [3-1/2 *lines of source text not declassified*]

n. On the question of fund raising, Mr. Katzenbach felt that witting corporate contributors presented no problems but that radio solicitation

---

[9] Not further identified.

for individual donors should be stopped at once. It was agreed that the radios would be so instructed.

o. It was agreed that the statement for Mr. McCloskey should be drafted by Mr. Trueheart for submission to Mr. Katzenbach and general agreement by the principals.

2. Project Review

Mr. Rostow noted that we had ridden right into the middle of December and had a legal obligation to have covered all covert efforts which might possibly be construed to come under the aegis of the Katzenbach Committee rulings. He asked where we now stand. Mr. Tovar noted that every effort had been made to cover the field; he could assure the chairman that every major project and expenditure in this field had been examined, that there might be bits and pieces and marginal efforts which had not yet been prepared for screening. Mr. Rostow implied that in the marginal field there might be some potential cliff hangers, and Mr. Helms directed that a list of these be prepared promptly for Mr. Rostow so that he would know what could be expected on forthcoming agendas in the grey area. Mr. Tovar noted that the review of the marginal projects was a continuous year-round process and was not limited to a specific search scheduled to end 31 December.

[Here follows Item 3.]

Peter Jessup

198.   Letter From Secretary of State Rusk to Secretary of Defense
McNamara[1]

Washington, December 18, 1967.

Dear Bob:

Your prompt and responsive reply of December 1[2] to my letter of November 24[3] concerning the DPMs on General Purpose Forces was greatly appreciated. In my earlier letter I said I would defer until later comment on the DPMs dealing with Strategic Forces and NATO. I have now completed my review of these latter memoranda.

I have no specific suggestions for changes in this year's force decisions. I do have some thoughts on the effect of our foreign relations of projected future trends in our strategic force posture and what we say about this posture. I believe it would be more useful, however, to comment on these in terms of a study which my staff recently completed rather than on the DPMs themselves.

Several months ago I requested an assessment of the foreign policy implications of recent and projected changes in US and Soviet military forces, with particular emphasis on the strategic forces. I enclose a copy of that study.[4] I would very much appreciate your comments on it.

It is clear that many of the issues raised in this study require further examination. However, I do think the study highlights the importance of what we say about our strategic posture because of the way in which these statements may be interpreted both by the Soviets and our allies. In particular I think we should try to lead discussions away from such oversimplified concepts as "superiority" or "parity."

I am sure you agree that it is important that we carefully coordinate the statements which we make to Congress on this score as we have done in past years. To this end I have asked Phil Farley to be in touch

---

[1] Source: Washington National Records Center, OASD/ISA Files: FRC 330 72 A 1499, 320.9 1968 I–36267/67. Top Secret. The letter forms Tab B to a December 29 memorandum from Warnke to McNamara. A Department of State study is Tab C and a summary of the study prepared for Secretary McNamara forms Tab D (see footnote 4 below). Tab A is a proposed letter from Secretary McNamara to Secretary Rusk, dated January 3, 1968, replying to the latter's December 18 letter.

[2] Not found.

[3] Document 194.

[4] The Department of State staff paper, entitled "A Study of US-Soviet Military Relationships 1957–1976: Foreign Policy Implications," December 18, included three attachments: "Comparisons and Trends," "Soviet Appreciation of the Emerging Military Balance," and "US Strategic Views." The study and attachments are not printed, but a Defense Department summary of the paper is printed below.

with your staff on the posture statement and to focus particularly this year on the strategic forces portion of that statement as well as the review of the international situation.

With warm regards,

Sincerely,

Dean Rusk[5]

Attachment

SUMMARY OF STATE PAPERS ON CHANGING US-SOVIET MILITARY RELATIONSHIPS

The central theme of the studies is that the US Government should take a fresh look at the political and military implications of the growing strategic parity and changing US-Soviet strategic relationships. The State papers suggest that this can be done through: 1) SIG arrangement for contingency planning on where and how the Soviets would be most likely to intervene in local conflicts, and 2) joint State–Defense development of rationale for US strategic forces, focusing on the rhetoric of deterrence and the major asymmetry in US-Soviet strategies and postures between offense and defensive oriented systems.

The substantive points of the studies fall into three categories: 1) strategic nuclear relations, 2) problems created by increased Soviet strategic mobility and 3) NATO.

On strategic nuclear relations, intelligence estimates point to increased Soviet capability to damage the US in a nuclear exchange, and, over the next decade, the expectation that continued Soviet expansion of their strategic forces may lead to their surpassing the US in some categories of strategic strength. While perceptions of these matters are probably more significant than the "actual" balance, these trends, State tentatively concludes, do not now or in the next five years seem to jeopardize the US deterrent. The problems will not likely be deterrence, but a) increased US domestic controversy, b) uncertainties and pressures leading to "worst case" assumptions in budget planning, c) complications on non-proliferation given obvious vulnerability of US to nuclear attack, and d) greater Soviet inclination to intervene in third areas.

It is this last problem coupled with gradually increasing Soviet strategic mobility that may be of more immediate concern. Evidence of extensive worldwide naval activity, expansion and modernization of

---

[5] Printed from a copy that bears this typed signature.

airlift-sealift capabilities, allowing for distant but limited operations may tempt the USSR to be more responsive to requests from governments and factions for military support.

On the NATO part, the Soviets have maintained superiority in Central Europe and have modernized their forces (including tactical nuclear weapons). But with US realization that we were not far behind conventionally, the consensus is that a Soviet attack on Western Europe is unlikely. The problem, however, is that the over-all US-Soviet strategic relationship may cause our allies to be more deferential to Soviet political pressures, leading to a further European questioning of the reliability of US commitments.

---

199.   Memorandum From the Joint Chiefs of Staff to Secretary of Defense McNamara[1]

JCSM–3–68   Washington, January 2, 1968.

SUBJECT

    Clandestine Introduction of Nuclear Weapons to the United States (C)

    1. (S) Reference is made to a memorandum by the Deputy Secretary of Defense, dated 13 November 1967, subject as above,[2] which identifies certain security problems for the United States arising from the proliferation of nuclear weapons capabilities, particularly those of Communist China, and the possible clandestine introduction of such weapons into the United States.

    2. (TS) The Joint Chiefs of Staff, in considering the reference, note that in a statement of national policy contained in National Security Council 6022/1, dated 18 January 1961, entitled "U.S. Policy on Continental Defense,"[3] the primary responsibility for implementing policy guidance concerning the internal security of the United States is assigned to the Interdepartmental Intelligence Conference (IIC) and the

---

    [1] Source: Washington National Records Center, OASD/ISA Files: FRC 330 72 A 1498, 471.6 1968 Jan–Feb. Top Secret.

    [2] Not found.

    [3] Text of NSC 6022, December 13, 1960, is included in *Foreign Relations*, 1958–1960, vol. III, Microfiche Supplement. Copies of NSC 6022/1 are in the National Archives and Records Administration, RG 59, S/P–NSC Files: Lot 62 D 1, NSC 6022 Series, and Eisenhower Library, NSC Staff Papers, Disaster File.

Interdepartmental Committee on Internal Security (ICIS). The Internal Security Section of NSC 6022/1 stipulates, in paragraph 28, that the ICIS, in coordination with the IIC, shall "provide adequate deterrents to the clandestine introduction of nuclear weapons."

3. (C) National Security Action Memorandum (NSAM) Nr. 161, dated 9 June 1962, subject: "U.S. Internal Security Programs,"[4] transferred the supervision of the IIC and the ICIS from the National Security Council to the Attorney General of the United States and directed that the ICIS effect coordination in all phases of the internal security field except in those certain functions assigned to the IIC. The ICIS is composed of representatives of the Departments of State, Treasury, Defense, and Justice. Other Government agencies participate as ad hoc members of the ICIS when matters involving the responsibilities of such agencies are under consideration.

4. (TS) Within the structure of the ICIS and the IIC, a Joint ICIS–IIC Committee on Countermeasures, referred to as Committee "B", has been responsible, since its inception in 1953, for considering ways and means of safeguarding against the clandestine introduction of nuclear weapons. This committee, composed of representatives of the Bureau of Customs, Federal Bureau of Investigation, Departments of Defense and the Army, and the Atomic Energy Commission, periodically submits studies concerning this subject to the Chairmen of the ICIS and the IIC. The most recent study prepared by Committee "B" on this subject is a "Reappraisal of the Threat of Clandestine Introduction of Nuclear Weapons," dated 27 June 1963.[5] In conjunction with the preparation of this reappraisal, the committee first generated a requirement for a National Intelligence Estimate (NIE) on this subject. This resulted in the publication by the Director of Central Intelligence, in coordination with the United States Intelligence Board (USIB), of NIE 11–7–63, dated 13 March 1963, subject: "The Clandestine Introduction of Weapons of Mass Destruction into the US."[6]

5. (TS) The Joint Chiefs of Staff believe that a comprehensive review of this matter is required at this time, since neither NIE 11–7–63 nor the 1963 ICIS study deals with the Chinese communist nuclear threat or many of the other cited problems. In view of the authority and responsibilities vested in the ICIS and the IIC by the NSC policy statement and White House memorandum previously cited, a reassessment of the complete threat should be initiated and conducted at the ICIS and the

---

[4] A copy is in the Johnson Library, National Security File, National Security Action Memoranda, NSAM 161—U.S. Internal Security Programs, Box 1.

[5] Not found.

[6] A copy is in the National Archives and Records Administration, RG 263.

IIC level. The DOD representative to the ICIS (Director for Security Policy, Office of the Assistant Secretary of Defense (Administration)) could most logically introduce these issues and request a reassessment. The USIB should consider the other relevant problems raised in the reference and submit an up-to-date estimate. In this respect, the Joint Chiefs of Staff are requesting that the USIB update NIE 11–7–63.[7]

6. (U) Since the Joint Chiefs of Staff share your concern over this matter and as nuclear proliferation becomes an increasing problem, they propose that, as a second phase of the study effort, the Joint Chiefs of Staff would review the findings of the ICIS and the IIC in the context of the issues cited in the reference. This review, to be conducted in coordination with your staff, would provide the basis for a report to you on the military aspects of the problem and possible further action by the Department of Defense to contribute to a concerted national effort to contain the threat.

For the Joint Chiefs of Staff:
Earle G. Wheeler
Chairman
Joint Chiefs of Staff

---

[7] This request was conveyed in a January 2 memorandum from the Joint Chiefs of Staff to the Chairman of the U.S. Intelligence Board (JCSM–4–68). (Washington National Records Center, OASD/ISA Files: FRC 330 72 A 1498, 471.6 1968 Jan–Feb)

---

200. Draft Memorandum From Secretary of Defense McNamara to President Johnson[1]

Washington, January 15, 1968.

SUBJECT

Strategic Offensive and Defensive Forces (U)

I have reviewed our Strategic Offensive and Defensive Forces for FY 69–73. The tables on pages 3 and 4 summarize our force goals.[2] For the FY 69 budget, I recommend that we:

---

[1] Source: Washington National Records Center, OASD/ISA Files: FRC 330 72 A 1499, 320.2 1968 I–35149/68 8 Feb 1968. Top Secret. "Record of Decision" and "Revised" are typed at the top of each page.
[2] Not printed.

1. Maintain a force of 1,000 Minuteman missiles. Plan on a Minuteman II force of 500 missiles in FY 69, but replace Minuteman Is and IIs used in follow-on-tests (FOTs) with Minuteman IIIs/MK-12s, leading to a force of 520 Minuteman IIIs by end-FY 73. Delay the Initial Operational Capability (IOC) of Minuteman III from December, 1969 to July, 1970. Cancel the MK-17 re-entry vehicle program for a saving of $309 million in FY 69–73. Develop an option to deploy Minuteman III in very hard silos or supplement the present Minuteman deployment at a cost of $40 million in FY 69 and a total cost of $212 million in FY 69–73. Continue the previously approved programs for buying area penetration aids for all Minuteman missiles, and terminal penetration aids for Minuteman III. Minuteman II penetration aids may not be effective against certain types of anti-ballistic missiles (ABMs). Therefore, deploy an improved version of the Minuteman II penetration aids at a cost of $22 million in FY 69 and a total cost of $44 million in FY 69–73. With all the above changes, the Minuteman force will cost $147 million less in FY 69–73 than the previously programmed Minuteman force.

2. Maintain the JCS-recommended Titan force structure by buying four missiles in FY 69 for $12.6 million and five in FY 70 for $13.6 million and reducing the FOT rate to four per year.[3]

3. Continue development of Poseidon, and procure 47 missiles in FY 69 at a total FY 69 investment cost of $329 million. Plan on an IOC of November, 1970, based on a sixteen month re-order lead time (the same as Polaris re-order lead time). Build up to a force of 384 on-line Poseidon by FY 75, for a total FY 69–73 investment cost of $4,998 million. [1 line of source text not declassified] and plan on a force of 31 Poseidon submarines carrying an average of [number not declassified] MK-3s per deployed missile. Procure 167 MK-3s in FY 69, 1,387 in FY 70, and a total of 3,781 in FY 69–73. Against expected threats, this Poseidon force will have the same effectiveness as the previously programmed force with [number not declassified] MK-3s per missile, but will cost $84 million less in FY 69 and $394 million less in FY 69–73.

4. Defer indefinitely the JCS recommendation to deploy area and terminal penetration aids for Polaris A-3 at a cost of $200 million in FY 69 and a total cost of $220 million in FY 69–73.

5. Disapprove the JCS recommendation to start Contract Definition of an Advanced ICBM at a cost of $79 million in FY 69. Instead, continue Advanced Development at a cost of $10 million in FY 69. Development, deployment, and operation of the JCS-recommended

---

[3] The often different positions of Secretary McNamara and the Joint Chiefs of Staff on specific programs for the FY 1969 Defense budget were summarized in Tab B to Document 195.

force of 350 Advanced ICBMs would cost from $7 to $10 billion in FY 69–75, depending on the basing.

6. Disapprove the JCS recommendation to procure a prototype Ballistic Missile Ship for $120 million in FY 69. Ten-year costs of ten Ballistic Missile Ships would be about $1.6 billion.

7. Approve the Air Force recommendation not to reduce the current base program for the bomber force. Defer, until we have evidence of a good Soviet low-altitude terminal defense, the JCS recommendation to equip the B-52 G/H bomber force with 1,020 Unit Equipment (UE) Short-Range Attack Missiles (SRAM) beginning in FY 70. Additional SRAMs for B-52s would cost $68 million in FY 69 and a total of $251 million in FY 69–73. As a special force for suppressing anti-bomber defenses, modify thirty UE B-52s to carry some of the previously approved SRAMs at a FY 69 cost of $54 million and a total cost of $56 million in FY 69–73.

8. Disapprove the JCS recommendation for Contract Definition and full-scale development of the Advanced Manned Strategic Aircraft (AMSA) in FY 69. Development, deployment, and five-year operating costs for 150 AMSA would be $7.3 billion. Approve instead further development of aircraft technology, as well as a program to develop bomber penetration aids.

9. Approve procurement of Sentinel, a [less than 1 line of source text not declassified] area ABM system which also provides an option for the defense of Minuteman. The total Sentinel system investment cost will be $4.9 billion in FY 69–73.

10. Continue feasibility studies on the sea-based ABM system (SAB-MIS).

11. Disapprove the JCS recommendation to deploy a Nike-X defense of U.S. cities against attack by the USSR. (Not a FY 69 issue; the JCS consider the FY 69 budget for Sentinel an adequate first step toward the defense they recommend.)

12. Disapprove the JCS recommendation to produce and deploy twelve UE F-12 interceptors for continental air defense at a FY 69–73 cost of $800 million. Approve instead the Air Force recommended plan for a modernized continental air defense force that includes: (a) development and deployment of 198 improved F-106X aircraft; (b) if the Overland Radar Technology program is successful, engineering development of the Airborne Warning and Control System (AWACS) on a schedule that permits a system demonstration before substantial production funds must be committed; (c) development of the Over-the-Horizon (OTH) radar, addressing production release in September, 1970; (d) examining the possibility of augmenting our air defense force during periods of high tension with at least 300 fighters from Tactical

Air Command (TAC), Navy, and Marine Corps training units plus carrier-based aircraft as available; and (e) selective phase-down of the current Century interceptor force and portions of the SAGE/BUIC system, the National Air Space Surveillance System, and Nike-Hercules radars.

13. Extend the civil defense program at a FY 69 cost of $77.6 million.

14. Disapprove the JCS recommendation for $191 million for military survival measures. Continue instead the approved program at a cost of $47 million for FY 68–73.

15. Approve a JCS recommendation to accelerate Program 440L OTH warning system against Fractional Orbit Bombardment Systems (FOBS) at a FY 69 cost of $39.3 million. Disapprove a JCS recommendation to accelerate Program 949, a satellite warning system for the same purpose.

I. The General Nuclear War Problem

The main objective of our nuclear forces is to deter nuclear attacks on the U.S. Our ability to strike back and destroy Soviet society makes a Soviet decision to strike the U.S. highly unlikely. By choosing to develop and deploy harder-to-attack forces, we can reduce even more the likelihood of such an attack. Unable to destroy most of our nuclear striking power, the Soviets would gain little by striking first.

Although the U.S. and the USSR are strongly deterred from nuclear attacks on each other, a nuclear war anywhere in the world could lead to a war—and most likely a nuclear war—between the two countries. Thus to avoid a nuclear war with the USSR, we try to make all nuclear wars unlikely. This objective includes:

1. Reducing any possible loss of control of forces in a crisis.
2. Deterring nuclear attacks or intimidation of allied or neutral countries.
3. Discouraging additional countries from acquiring nuclear weapons.
4. Emphasizing and maintaining the firebreak between conventional and nuclear weapons.

Like us, to deter a first-strike nuclear attack, the Soviets maintain the ability to strike back and destroy our society. When they take steps to reduce the damage that we can inflict (e.g., by deploying ABMs), we react to offset these steps. I believe that the Soviets would react in the same way to similar U.S. steps to limit damage to ourselves.

Our analysis shows that the Soviets can protect their second strike capability against any threat we might pose. Since a second strike capability is vital to the USSR, I believe they will insure the survival of this capability. Convinced that the Soviets would counter a major U.S. attempt to take away their second strike capability, we have chosen not to start a major Damage Limiting program against the USSR.

These considerations lead us to depend upon deterrence to keep the USSR from attacking us. [less than 1 line of source text not declassified] conversely, we can buy an effective defense of CONUS as insurance against a failure of deterrence. [less than 1 line of source text not declassified] allow us to develop an effective defense against her nuclear attack capability into the 1980s.

What if deterrence fails and a nuclear war with the USSR occurs? If the war began with an all-out Soviet attack, including our cities, we would reply in kind. If the war started with less than an all-out attack, we would want to carry out plans for the controlled and deliberate use of our nuclear power to get the best possible outcome. The lack of such nuclear war plans is one of the main weaknesses in our posture today.

II. Soviet and Chinese Strategic Forces

The following table compares U.S. and Soviet intercontinental forces in terms of total megatons, launchers, and bombers.

U.S. vs. Soviet Strategic Nuclear Forces[a]

	1968		1970		1972	
	U.S.	USSR	U.S.	USSR	U.S.	USSR
Ballistic Missile Launchers						
Soft ICBMs	—	128-142	—	90-128	—	—
Hard ICBMs	1054	720-782	1054	859-1026	1054	1020-1251
FOBS	—	0-10	—	20-50	—	20-75
Mobile ICBMs (non-add)	—	—	—	(0-25)	—	(0-100)
SLBMs	656	43-46	656	123-158	656	267-318
Total Launchers	1710	891-980	1710	1092-1362	1710	1307-1644
Intercontinental Bombers	646	150-155	558	130-150	534	105-130
Total Force Loadings						
Weapons	[*]	1115-1199	[*]	1276-1566	[*]	1409-1760
[text not declassified]	[*]	[*]	[*]	[*]	[*]	[*]
[text not declassified]	[*]	[*]	[*]	[*]	[*]	[*]
Alert Force Loadings						
Weapons	[*]	610-672	[*]	765-949	[*]	954-1211
[text not declassified]	[*]	[*]	[*]	[*]	[*]	[*]
[text not declassified]	[*]	[*]	[*]	[*]	[*]	[*]

[*entry in table not declassified]

[a] U.S. programmed vs. National Intelligence Estimates (NIE) for USSR.

Numbers of missile launchers and bombers are a poor measure of the relative capabilities of U.S. and Soviet strategic forces; total megatons are worse. Yet these measures are frequently used in drawing comparisons between U.S. and Soviet nuclear capabilities. The important question is not total megatons or numbers of delivery systems, but whether our forces can effectively carry out their missions—Assured Destruction and attacks on Soviet forces to limit damage. Factors such as accuracy, reliability, survivability, and control are decisive in evaluating the effectiveness of our forces. Our missiles appear to be more reliable than Soviet missiles; they are more than twice as accurate. In 1972, programmed U.S. missile forces could destroy some 700 hardened targets. The expected Soviet ICBM force could destroy only some 300 such targets.

We are buying large numbers of smaller, accurate weapons because they better meet our strategic objectives—even while reducing total U.S. megatons. The following table compares the number of targets destroyed by [*number not declassified*] of the MK-3 warheads programmed for Poseidon, with a [*3 lines of source text declassified*] as many targets.

Effectiveness of Alternative, Equal-Weight Payloads[a]

	[*text not declassified*] Weapons	[*text not declassified*] Weapon
Number of airfields	8.3	0.83
Number of hard silos[b]	1.7	0.83
Number of small cities (100,000)	2.9	0.83
Number of medium cities (500,000)	0.6	0.83
Number of large cities (2,000,000)	0.5	0.5
Number of defensive interceptors needed to counter[c]	11.0	1.1
Total megatons	0.5	10.0

[a] Reliability equals [*number not declassified*] Circular Probable Error (CEP) equals [*number not declassified*].

[b] [*less than 1 line of source text not declassified*] per square inch (psi) at [*number not declassified*]; three [*less than 1 line of source text not declassified*] weapons target per silo.

[c] ABM interceptor reliability equals [*number not declassified*].

Such calculations have convinced me and the Services of the superiority of Multiple Independently-targetable Re-entry Vehicles (MIRVs) over single, large megaton weapons for attacking cities or military targets, defended or otherwise. Therefore, the best way to increase the effectiveness of our forces is by putting MIRVs on Minuteman and Poseidon.

During 1964–65, the USSR maintained small silo (SS-11) ICBM construction starts at the rate of about 150 launchers per year. It doubled this rate during the first half of 1966, then returned to the original rate. The SS-9 ICBM deployment appears to have stopped except for filling out groups already under construction.

A new solid-fueled Soviet missile has been identified. Present intelligence estimates assume it is an ICBM, which will come into the Soviet inventory as a supplement to (rather than a replacement for) the SS-11.

The Soviets have continued to test Fractional Orbit Ballistic Systems (FOBS), which would be useful in an attempt to deny warning to our strategic bombers, if we took no counter actions.

A recent re-evaluation of the present Soviet submarine force indicates about 20% fewer operational Soviet ballistic missile submarines than previous intelligence estimates. The USSR is, however, now making operational a new class of large, nuclear-powered, ballistic missile submarines to carry sixteen 1,000 to 2,000 nautical mile (NM) missiles. Intelligence estimates project ten to thirteen of these ships in service by mid-1971 and 35 to 42 by 1976. Diesel-powered Sea-Launched Ballistic Missile (SLBM) submarines no longer are estimated to be part of the Soviet threat to the U.S.

The Soviets also appear to be pursuing two advanced defensive programs: (1) a long-range anti-ICBM system around Moscow with about 100 launchers, and (2) a system across European USSR (the Tallinn system or SA-5) with about 3,000 reloadable launchers, [*1 line of source text not declassified*]. We expect both systems to become partially operational this year. There are conflicting intelligence evaluations of the Tallinn system. While it appears to be designed for air defense, the system could have some capabilities against ballistic missiles. The NIE estimates the system is designed entirely for air defense, while a dissenting view emphasizes a dual air defense/ABM role. Since last year, the dissenting view has lost ground as we discovered that the defensive missile is much too slow to intercept missiles successfully, and the engagement radars have little capability when operating independently against ballistic missiles.

We still have seen no evidence of Soviet development of a good low-altitude Surface-to-Air Missile (SAM). However, the Foxbat Interceptor is now estimated to have a limited "look-down, shoot-down" capability.

The Chinese were expected to begin operational deployment of a Medium Range Ballistic Missile (MRBM) with a fission warhead in 1967, but did not do so. China also has under development a much larger and more complex missile system, possibly an ICBM. They were expected to complete a large facility for large launchers late in 1967, but did not do this either. It appears that they are about six months behind the ICBM schedule that we had previously estimated, which would still allow an initial operational ICBM deployment in the early 1970s.

III. Assured Destruction

We deter a rational enemy from launching a first strike against us by maintaining a strong and secure ability to retaliate under any circumstances. We measure our second strike ability in terms of Assured Destruction—the capability to inflict unacceptable damage, calculated under extremely conservative assumptions, on the USSR, even after sustaining a surprise Soviet first strike. I believe that our ability to kill from [less than 1 line of source text not declassified] of the Soviet people, including at least [less than 1 line of source text not declassified] of the people and industry in their large cities, is enough to deter the USSR from launching a first strike against the U.S., even in extreme situations.

However, our Assured Destruction capability does not indicate how we would use our forces in a nuclear war. We must design our forces to cope with many situations, including a war which neither side intended. We reduce the likelihood of such a war by keeping tight control over U.S. forces under all circumstances; by maintaining communications at all times with our forces, the governments of our Allies, and, as appropriate, our enemies; and by retaining options in selecting appropriate responses. If we failed to deter nuclear war, we would want to be able to follow a policy of limiting our retaliatory strikes to the enemy's military targets and not attacking his cities if he refrained from attacking ours. In most situations we would have many missiles surviving to attack Soviet military targets, while withholding enough for [1 line of source text not declassified].

A. Against the Expected Soviet Threat

Against the expected Soviet threat, our strategic forces can survive a well-executed Soviet surprise attack and carry out an effective second strike. Even after a surprise Soviet first strike with the strongest Soviet forces in our NIE, we could launch more than 4,300 weapons, with a yield of more than 1,800 megatons, against the USSR in 1976.

How much damage the surviving weapons could cause depends on the effectiveness of Soviet defenses. The next table shows that even against high NIE-estimated threat, the U.S. Assured Destruction capability is much greater than [less than 1 line of source text not declassified] which I believe is needed for deterrence against a Soviet first strike.

Capabilities of U.S. Programmed Force for Assured Destruction
(Percent of Soviet Population Killed)

	FY 69	FY 72	FY 72
Against High NIE Threat	[*]	[*]	[*]
Against Low NIE Threat	[*]	[*]	[*]

[*entry in table not declassified]

If we could be sure that Soviet forces would stay within the range of the NIE—both in quality and numbers—we could consider smaller strategic forces.

B. Against China

While China may be able to threaten her neighbors and U.S. bases in Asia by 1972, she will not pose a threat to the U.S. second strike capability. [*6 lines of source text not declassified*]

[*1 line of source text not declassified*] The recommended strategic forces are sufficient to inflict this destruction on [*less than 1 line of source text not declassified*] while still maintaining our Assured Destruction capability against the Soviet Union.

C. Against Greater-Than-Expected Soviet Threats

The vital importance of our Assured Destruction capability to our national security requires us to be prepared to cope with Soviet strategic threats greater than those which the NIE projects. While unlikely, the Soviets might add a very extensive ABM defense or much improved anti-bomber defenses. They might improve their IBM force by putting accurate MIRVs on the SS-9, and by replacing or improving the SS-11 with a new, accurate ICBM. Conceivably, they might take all these actions.

The following table compares the 1976 balanced greater-than-expected threat, used in the following analyses, with the high NIE threat.

	High NIE	Greater-Than-Expected
Independently-targetable missile warheads on-line	2100	5500
Air Defenses		
Look-down fighters[a]	200	400
Low-altitude SAM Launchers	2700	4200
ABM Launchers		
Area	1700	1700
Terminal[b]	1025	7125

[a] With F-12/AWACS capability.
[b] Includes 125 launchers in the Moscow System.

Programs required to support such an effort should prove technically difficult, expensive, and, since we have clearly indicated we would respond, hold little hope of providing the Soviets with a net gain in effective first strike capability. Nevertheless, to ensure that these threats remain unlikely, and to maintain our deterrent should they appear, we make sure that we have available the options needed to counter them.

If the USSR replaces or improves the accuracy of its SS-11s and adds accurate MIRVs to its SS-9s, it could destroy Minuteman missiles in their silos. Even if the Soviets could destroy all Minuteman missiles, they would not eliminate our Assured Destruction capability. Our remaining SLBMs and alert bomber force can penetrate the NIE-estimated Soviet defenses and kill at least [less than 1 line of source text not declassified]. Similarly, at least through 1976, a very extensive Soviet ABM system and air defense, without greater-than-expected ICBMs, would still let the U.S. programmed force maintain an Assured Destruction capability [less than 1 line of source text not declassified]. Our programmed force can cope with a greater-than-exexpected ABM because we already have programmed ABM hedges—Poseidon plus MIRVs and penetration aids for Minuteman.

The next table shows that the U.S. programmed force can keep its Assured Destruction capability through FY 75 by putting [number not declassified] MK-3s on each Poseidon missile, even if the Soviets deploy greater-than-expected balanced missile and bomber defenses. Short-Range Attack Missiles (SRAMs), SRAM decoys, and an air-to-air missile to protect the bombers against advanced interceptors would keep our Assured Destruction capability against this threat [less than 1 line of source text not declassified].

U.S. Assured Destruction Against Greater-Than-
Expected Balanced Defenses
(Percent of Soviet Population Killed)

	FY 69	FY 70	FY 71	FY 72	FY 73	FY 74	FY 75	FY 76
U.S. Programmed Force	[*]	[*]	[*]	[*]	[*]	[*]	[*]	[*]a
U.S. Programmed Force plus [number not declassified] MK-3s on Poseidon	[*]	[*]	[*]	[*]	[*]	[*]	[*]	[*]a

[*entry in table not declassified]

a The first percentage shows fatalities if we are required to kill at least [less than 1 line of source text not declassified]. The second percentage shows fatalities without this restriction.

Only against a combined greater-than-expected Soviet ABM, air defense, and accurate ICBM force, costing the Soviets $20 to $30 billion above the high NIE, would our retaliatory forces need major new additions. Because of high cost and little return, the Soviets probably will not attempt to attain such a posture. Moreover, because of uncertainties about performance and cost, we should not deploy new systems as replacements for existing systems until a threat appears which cannot be economically met by improving the existing systems. We should develop new systems only as options which would restore our Assured Destruction capability should the greater-than-expected threat occur, realizing that it is not likely to occur. Thus, we should select options with small initial costs. If the threat actually materializes, we can, by later investment, develop these options fully. (No augmentation is needed for FY 69–72. Hence, I am recommending against the deployment of the JCS-proposed Antelope penetration aids for Polaris A-3s, which improve their capability against ABM only in that time period.)

The following table shows the effect of the combined greater-than-expected Soviet offensive and defensive threat on our Assured Destruction capability. It indicates the U.S. programmed force capability and the effects of buying SRAMs, SRAM decoys, an advanced bomber decoy, and an air-to-air missile to protect bombers against an advanced interceptor.

U.S. Assured Destruction Against Greater-Than-Expected
Soviet Balanced Offenses and Defenses
(Percent of Soviet Population Killed)

	FY 69	FY 70	FY 71	FY 72	FY 73	FY 74	FY 75	FY 76
Programmed Forces	[*]	[*]	[*]	[*]	[*]a	[*]a	[*]a	[*]a
+ bomber options	[*]	[*]	[*]	[*]	[*]	[*]	[*]a	[*]a
+ bomber options, [text not declassified] and either [text not declassified]	[*]	[*]	[*]	[*]	[*]	[*]	[*]	[*]

[*entry in table not declassified]
a The first percentage shows fatalities if we are required to kill at least [less than 1 line of source text not declassified] of the people in defended cities. The second percentage shows fatalities without this restriction.

This table shows that even if the bomber defense missile works, the greater-than-expected threat would call for a more effective U.S. Assured Destruction capability by FY 76. In addition, for Assured Destruction we do not want to rely primarily upon bombers which depend upon tactical warning for survival. Therefore, our alternative is to provide our missile forces with added protection. The degree of this protection depends upon how much and for how long we are willing to rely on bombers in the interim. ([number not declassified] MK-3s on Poseidon and [number not declassified] Minuteman defended or in [num-

ber not declassified] psi silos, when added to the above bomber options, result in [*number not declassified*] Soviet fatalities in 1976.) In any event, we should not take steps—such as reducing the number of bomber bases—that lessen our confidence in the bombers' survival.

D. *Options to Protect Our Assured Destruction Capability*

1. *Increased Warheads on Poseidon*

We are providing the production base so that by FY 74 we could put up to [*number not declassified*] MK-3s on each Poseidon missile as a hedge against a heavy Soviet ABM or an increased threat to Minuteman.

2. *Improve Our Bomber Force*

Against improved terminal bomber defenses we can put SRAMs on B-52s in addition to the SRAMs on FB-111s. By initiating procurement in FY 70, the B-52s could be equipped with SRAMs by FY 72.

If Soviet air defenses improved, but their ABM did not, no increase in the size or expense of our strategic forces would be called for. However, for the cost of the present B-52 program we could improve our effectiveness by putting SRAMs on 195 B-52s and phasing out the other sixty.

If Soviet air defenses improved as part of a balanced Damage Limiting program, SRAMs plus penetration aids for the whole bomber force would prove worthwhile and would total about $2.7 billion in ten-year systems costs above the present program.

3. *Improvements to Minuteman Missiles*

As a hedge against a heavy Soviet ABM system we could replace all the Minuteman II by Minuteman III/MIRV at a cost of $1.9 billion over the present program. As a hedge against the failure of our penetration aids, at a cost of $6.2 billion we could convert to 1,000 Minuteman III missiles and buy [*number not declassified*] MK-18 MIRVs for each missile. We could have an all MK-18 Minuteman III force by FY 76. We could develop super-hard [*numbers not declassified*] psi silos for Minuteman as possible replacements for the present [*less than 1 line of source text not declassified*] or provide for additional Minuteman IIIs as an alternative to a new ICBM (item #6 below) if we should want more payload. This would cost about $200 million in research and development ($40 million in FY 69) for an IOC in FY 73. Procurement costs would be $5 million per silo, 150 of which could be built per year.

4. *Defense of Minuteman*

Deployment of the light defense of Minuteman, shown below, might dissuade the Soviets from developing and deploying systems which otherwise could destroy Minuteman. In any event, it would provide a useful defense of Minuteman against the expected Soviet ICBM force without accurate MIRVs and furnish a base for developing a stronger defense against a Soviet force equipped with MIRVs. The median defense of Minuteman would protect against less sophisticated MIRVs on the SS-9s (about six per SS-9). Finally, the heavy defense of Minuteman would guard against the very sophisticated counterforce threat (eighteen accurate MIRVs per SS-9) assumed in the greater-than-expected threat for 1975 and 1976. The following table summarizes these three defenses.

Levels of Minuteman Defense

	Sprints	Spartans	Investment Cost[a] ($ Millions)	Annual Costs ($ Millions)
Light Defense of Minuteman	264	120	$400	$10
Median Defense of Minuteman	1050	200	1400	40
Heavy Defense of Minuteman	1700	200	3600	160

[a] Defense of Minuteman is considered an add-on to the Sentinel [*less than 1 line of source text not declassified*] defense.

5. *More Poseidon Submarines*

We could order more Poseidon submarines, which require a $280 million investment per ship and a four-year lead time. By initiating procurement in FY 70 we could have ten new Poseidon submarines by the end of FY 75 and twenty by the end of FY 76. The more Poseidon missiles we have the less we would have to rely upon Minuteman.

If we chose to deploy additional Poseidon instead of defending or hardening Minuteman, and if Soviet ICBM accuracy improved markedly (to about [*1-1/2 lines of source text not declassified*]). In this case, we should phase it out. Thus, choosing Poseidon might result in upsetting the balance of our forces. It would be undesirable to be without a land-based missile force as part of our offensive posture because we would become potentially more sensitive to unexpected Soviet advances in anti-submarine warfare.

6. *New ICBM*

Contract Definition begun in January 1968 would permit an IOC by FY 75. We could deploy this new missile in new silos as part of a defended or undefended fixed land-based system. Conversely, we could deploy it as a land-mobile or ship-based system or base it in a new class of submarines. In order to develop a new ICBM, we would require a $2 to $3 billion research and development program. The ten-year cost of buying a new ICBM totals some $11 to $20 billion.

The following table compares the costs of these alternatives against the greater-than-expected Soviet threat. The costs shown are over and above the cost of presently programmed forces. All options provide an Assured Destruction capability of [*less than 1 line of source text not declassified*] against the greater-than-expected Soviet threat in 1976.

Costs of Various Missile Options To Protect Assured Destruction
Against Greater-Than-Expected Threat
($ Billions)

	R&D	Program Costs (FY 68–76)
Defense of Minuteman		
Median—Against large-MIRV		
threat[a]	$0.5	$2.0
Heavy—Against small-MIRV		
threat[b]	0.5	4.3
16 Additional Poseidon		
Submarines and [*less than 1 line of source text not declassified*]		
on all Poseidon	0.0	6.6
[*number not declassified*]		
Additional Minuteman		
in super-hard silos	0.2	6.1
New ICBM		
Land-based	2.5	8
Sea-based	2.5	8

---

[a] The large-MIRV threat assumes the Soviets will deploy six [*less than 1 line of source text not declassified*] MIRVs on their improved SS-9.

[b] The small-MIRV threat assumes the Soviets will deploy eighteen [*less than 1 line of source text not declassified*] MIRVs on one-half of their improved SS-9 force.

If the Soviets do not react by developing and deploying these MIRVs, we can defend Minuteman at less cost than we could procure Poseidons. If they develop a small MIRV threat, the cost of Minuteman defense would about equal the cost of acquiring Poseidons. Super-hard silos for Minuteman are not competitive with a light Minuteman defense, but they offer an alternative to heavier Minuteman defenses against the small-MIRV threat. A posture combining defense (calling for small-MIRVs) and super-hard silos (calling for very high yield warheads) would be very difficult to attack. None of the new ICBMs enjoys a clear cost advantage over defending Minuteman, putting Minuteman in super-hard silos, or acquiring Poseidons until the Soviet ABM becomes much stronger than the greater-than-expected threat.[4]

If we choose to buy more Poseidon, we would have to order them in FY 70 and FY 71, before we could see the extent of the Soviet threat. If we develop super-hard silos, we would not have to decide to deploy them until FY 73.

A defense of Minuteman can be bought in stages and is likely to hold down the total cost of hedging our Assured Destruction capability. To deploy the heavy defense of Minuteman by FY 76, we would have to decide on the light defense by FY 70, the median defense by FY 71, and the heavy defense by FY 73. Other hedges, such as more Poseidon submarines or the Ballistic Missile Surface Ship, are unnecessary. Super-hard silos can be built in response to the threat and they are competitive with the defense of Minuteman. The choice between super-hard silos and defense of Minuteman depends on the direction the Soviet threat takes. To preserve the option to go either way, we should develop them both.

E. Advanced Manned Strategic Aircraft (AMSA)

Recent studies have reviewed the value of a mixed ballistic missile/bomber force against reasonable projections of Soviet defenses into the 1970s. They show the bombers add some measure of assurance against greater-than-expected Soviet threats and induce the USSR to divert resources to their anti-bomber defenses. A mixed offensive force enjoys certain advantages against terminal defenses. By attacking some cities with missiles only, and others with bombers only, we force the Soviets to use more resources to protect all defended cities with both bomber and missile defenses. In order to accomplish this objective, however, we do not need large bomber forces.

The previous section discussed the hedges to our programmed strategic offensive forces, especially to their missile components. Since we intend to keep the missile force well-hedged, the issue is whether we *also* want to hedge our bomber force with an AMSA.

Is an AMSA a good hedge? It is not. Against the NIE range of threats our programmed forces are adequate. Since the strategic forces are already well-hedged, we can keep an Assured Destruction capability against greater-than-expected threats without the AMSA.

To counter a Soviet greater-than-expected threat, under most circumstances, including the most probable ones, U.S. offensive forces

---

[4] This might happen sometime after 1976. Thus, in order to provide a basis for more total missile payload against a possible heavy ABM sometime after this date, continuing Advanced Development of a new ICBM is still desirable. Furthermore, the submarine-carried Advanced ICBM has some promise of eventually replacing Poseidon, in the 1980s, on an equal-cost basis. [Footnote in the source text.]

equipped with AMSA cost more than forces with equivalent effectiveness but without the advanced bomber.

What does AMSA cost as a hedge? To answer this question we must compare the cost of bomber forces needed to cope with various levels of Soviet threat. The following two tables make this comparison.

Costs of Alternative FB-111/B-52 Forces
($ Billions)

Bomber Force	Program Costs (FY 68–82)[a]
A. 210 FB-111s	$ 7.2
B. 210 FB-111s and 255 B-52s without SRAMs	12.4
C. 210 FB-111s and 255 B-52s with 18 SRAMs per B-52	15.3

[a] AMSA IOC in FY 76.

Force B represents the programmed force and would cope with the higher range of the NIE-projected Soviet strategic forces. It would also let us expand to meet a greater-than-expected Soviet threat. Force A, costing $5.2 billion less, would be appropriate for the lower range of NIE threats. Force C adds SRAMs to the B-52s, providing the expansion needed to meet the greater-than-expected threat. This option would cost $2.9 billion more than Force B.

The next table compares the cost of hedging against the greater-than-expected threat.

Costs of Alternative Strong Bomber Forces of Equal Effectiveness
($ Billions)

Bomber Force	Program Costs (FY 68–82)
C. 210 FB-111s and 255 B-52s with 18 SRAMs per B-52	$15.3
D. 210 FB-111s and 68 AMSAs	15.3
E. 138 AMSAs	16.6

Both Force D and E are about equal in effectiveness to the programmed force plus SRAMs against the greater-than-expected threat, provided B-52 penetration aids work. Force D represents the smallest AMSA force which we can use as a hedge. It costs $2.9 billion more than the programmed forces. The all-AMSA Force E costs considerably more than either Force A or C, $9.4 and $1.3 billion respectively.

Considerations other than costs make the Force D option less attractive than Force C. First, developing AMSA requires a longer lead time than deploying SRAMs on B-52s, and imposes a substantial initial investment before we could determine that an increased Soviet threat has occurred. Conversely, since the SRAM option has a shorter lead time, we can delay the decision to deploy this missile until the increased threat begins to appear. Secondly, if we decide to proceed with AMSA now and the greater-than-expected threat does not appear, we will have wasted $3 to $10 billion.

In sum, to achieve equal effectiveness, AMSA contributes only marginally at great cost. Thus, Engineering Development is not called for now. However, we should proceed with Advanced Development to provide aircraft technology and to keep open the option of replacing the B-52s.

IV. Strategic Defense

A. Damage Limiting Against the Soviet Threat

Our Assured Destruction capability makes any kind of nuclear war with the Soviets unlikely. Therefore, we first buy enough forces to give us high confidence in our deterrent. As insurance in the unlikely event deterrence fails, we then consider adding forces that might reduce damage to our population and industry. Damage Limiting forces, unlike those for Assured Destruction, cannot and need not work perfectly under all conditions. They should insure against the more probable risks, such as wars growing out of a deep crisis, or threats posed by the growth of Chinese nuclear forces. The basic Damage Limiting question is whether we should deploy Nike-X in defense of our cities.

A defensive system to save U.S. cities from a Soviet nuclear attack must attempt to keep ahead of the Soviet threat, including their reactions to our deployment. In this analysis we use two stages in such a deployment. The first, "Posture A", represents a light defense of cities. It has an area defense of the entire CONUS, providing overlapping coverage of key targets. It has a relatively low-density Sprint defense of 25 cities. It is estimated that initially it would cost about $9 billion in investment and $600 million a year to operate. The second, "Posture B", is a heavier defense with a higher density Sprint defense of 52 cities. It is estimated that initially it would cost $18 billion and $1.1 billion a year to operate. Because of probable Soviet reaction, with Posture B we would also need improved air and civil defense and ASW forces at a cost of $4 to $5 billion in investment. Moreover, experience convinces me that the pursuit of effective defenses would eventually lead us to spend about $40 billion.

[1 paragraph (7 lines of source text) not declassified]

U.S. Killed In All-Out Strategic Exchange in 1976
Assumes No Soviet Reaction to U.S. ABM
(In Millions)

U.S. Programs	Soviets Strike First		U.S. Strikes First Soviets Retaliate	
	U.S. Fatalities	Soviet Fat.	U.S. Fatalities	Soviet Fat.[b]
Approved Program (Sentinel)	100	[*]	90	[*]
Posture A[a]	40	[*]	10	[*]
Posture B	20	[*]	Less than 10	[*]

[*entry in table not declassified]
[a] The JCS currently recommend this deployment.
[b] [2 lines of source text not declassified]

This table shows that if the Soviets do not respond, they lose their deterrent. They would be forced to react to increase the ability of their forces to survive and strike back. They could do so in several different ways: (1) by stepping up deployment of SS-9s and SS-11s now in production; (2) by defending their present missile force; (3) by adding MIRVs, chaff, or other penetration aids to their missiles; (4) by deploying a new, large ICBM (either mobile or defended); or (5) by deploying a new submarine-launched missile like our Poseidon. They have the technical capability to do any of these things by the mid-1970s.

If the Soviets choose to respond to our ABM with MIRVs, penetration aids, and missiles which would survive a U.S. attack (MIRVs and penetration aids against Sentinel plus 100 missiles against Posture A and 550 against Posture B), they would regain their Assured Destruction (second strike) capability. A larger Soviet response could raise probable U.S. fatalities still higher.

U.S. Killed In All-Out Strategic Exchange In 1976
Assuming Soviets Respond To U.S. ABM
(In Millions)

U.S. Programs	Soviets Strike First		U.S. Strikes First Soviets Retaliate	
	U.S. Fatalities	Soviet Fat.	U.S. Fatalities	Soviet Fat.
Approved (Sentinel)	120	[*]	110	[*]
Posture A	110	[*]	90	[*]
Posture B	100	[*]	90	[*]

[*entry in table not declassified]

As part of their response, the Soviets could add large numbers of offensive missiles that would threaten our Assured Destruction capability. We, in turn, would have to react. Viewing each other's buildup in forces as an increased threat, each side would undertake counteracting steps, thereby increasing the costs to both with no gain in security. Therefore, I believe deploying the Nike-X system to protect American cities would be neither wise nor effective.

B. Protection Against Small Urban Attacks

A light U.S. ABM system would protect against a [*less than 1 line of source text not declassified*] ICBM attack. By protecting the U.S. against such a threat, it probably would enhance our ability to deter [*less than 1 line of source text not declassified*] nuclear intimidation of other [*less than 1 line of source text not declassified*] countries. [*2-1/2 lines of source text not declassified*] The area defense of CONUS would give us a realistic Damage Limiting capability against [*less than 1 line of source text not declassified*] for the mid-1970s, as shown in the next table.

U.S. Fatalities In a Small-Scale Attack[a]
(In Millions)

	[heading not declassified]			*[heading not declassified]*		
Number of ICBMs	[*]	[*]	[*]	[*]	[*]	[*]
No Defense	[*]	[*]	[*]	[*]	[*]	[*]
Light ABM	[*]	[*][b]	[*][b]	[*]	[*]	[*]

[*entry in table not declassified]
[2 footnotes (2 lines of source text) not declassified]

C. Civil Defense

Civil Defense provides low cost insurance for our people in the unlikely event of a nuclear attack. As a by-product it has also proven to be a significant aid in natural disasters. This program should be pursued. More effort is needed to identify useful shelters in home basements. This can fill a large part of the current shelter deficit at a very low cost—about $0.45 per space added.

D. Continental Air Defense

The number of lives which would be saved by air defense if the Soviets were to attack the U.S. depends on our ballistic missile defense. With only a light missile defense, even a very strong air defense could not save many lives. The Soviets could simply target cities with their missiles. A Soviet first strike, with missiles only, could kill 120 million people; their bombers could then add less than ten million fatalities even if we had no air defense at all. A force of either 200 improved F-106 interceptors with AWACS (ten-year cost $9.9 billion) or 54 F-12s with AWACS (ten-year cost $11.6 billion) would reduce these fatalities by less than five to eight million.

However, there are other objectives of continental air defense which must also be considered. These include defense against countries other than the Soviet Union, defense against bomber attacks on those strategic forces that we withhold in a controlled nuclear war, peacetime patrolling of our air space, discouraging Soviet bomber aspirations, and the use of continental air defense forces in missions outside the U.S. We can achieve these objectives with a modern, more effective air defense force that costs less over the next twelve years than our present force. This modern force will consist of 200 improved F-106 fighters (the F-106X), 42 AWACS, two OTH radars, and the Federal Aviation Agency National Air Space system for back-up command and control. The cost through 1979 for the modern force is $13.7 billion compared with $13.9 billion for the current force. However, the lower operating costs of the modern force will result in substantial savings over the present force after FY 79.

Surveillance is presently the weakest part of our air defense system. Therefore, we should proceed with engineering development of AWACS (if the Overland Radar Technology program is successful) and with development of back-scatter OTH radars. We should also develop, and deploy on the F-106, advanced air-to-air missiles and an advanced fire control system. With these improvements to the F-106, there is little to be gained from the high performance characteristics of the F-12. Thus, we can avoid the additional $1.7 billion cost of an F-12 force and still meet our air defense objectives.

201. Memorandum From the Deputy Secretary of Defense (Nitze) and the Chairman of the Atomic Energy Commission (Seaborg) to President Johnson[1]

Washington, March 11, 1968.

SUBJECT

FY 1969–70 Nuclear Weapons Stockpile

Submitted herewith for your approval is the proposed Nuclear Weapons Stockpile for the end of FY 1970 and certain related adjustments to the FY 1969 Nuclear Weapons Stockpile approved on 10 June 1967.[2] The Requirements stated herein are based on the forces detailed in the Five Year Defense Program submitted to you separately.[3]

The stockpile which you approved on 10 June 1967 authorized a total of [*number not declassified*] nuclear warheads[4] for FY 1969. Reappraisal, in the light of the proposed force levels and the continuing review of nuclear weapons requirements, indicates that the FY 1969 stockpile should now be adjusted to a total of [*less than 1 line of source text not declassified*] warheads. The detailed composition of the initially approved FY 1969 stockpile is shown in Column 1 of Inclosure 1;[5] the proposed adjusted FY 1969 stockpile is shown in Column 2. The proposed adjustments result principally from the impact of adjustments in force modernization programs for Minuteman, Polaris–Poseidon and tactical missiles, reappraisal of requirements for air-to-air missiles and from reprogramming [*less than 1 line of source text not declassified*] bomb production during FY 1968, FY 1969 and FY 1970 due to technical difficulties. The reprogramming has caused a reduction of [*number not declassified*] in the number of [*less than 1 line of source text not declassified*] bombs approved by you on 10 June 1967, for inclusion in the FY 1968 stockpile. This reduction has been offset by the retention of [*less than 1 line of source text not declassified*] tactical bombs previously scheduled for retirement during FY 1968, pending delivery to stockpile of those bombs which are now programmed for FY 1969.

The proposed FY 1970 operational stockpile, submitted for your consideration, consists of [*number not declassified*] nuclear warheads.

---

[1] Source: Washington National Records Center, OSD Files: FRC 330 72 A 2467, A–400.23 1967. Top Secret; Restricted Data. The date is handwritten.

[2] Document 181.

[3] Document 200.

[4] "Nuclear Warhead" as used herein is an atomic weapon as defined in the Atomic Energy Act of 1954, as amended. [Footnote in the source text.]

[5] None of the enclosures is printed.

This objective is to be achieved during FY 1970 by the production of [*less than 1 line of source text not declassified*]. This is a net reduction of [*number not declassified*] warheads from the adjusted stockpile recommended for end FY 1969.

The production proposed for FY 1970 represents the continuing program to improve our nuclear weapons posture by modernizing existing weapons (Minuteman II), and by providing new warheads in support of new capabilities (Poseidon, Minuteman III, FB-111) to be introduced concurrently with the phase-out of older systems. The proposed reductions include some obsolescent weapons in excess of present requirements (Davy Crockett tactical missiles and Lulu depth charges); those warheads being replaced during modernization actions (Minuteman and Polaris); and other weapons whose programmed inventory can no longer be operationally justified (strategic bombs and surface-to-air missiles). The detailed composition of the FY 1970 stockpile is shown in Column 4 of Inclosure 1. The incremental changes in warhead quantities required during FY 1970 to achieve the proposed stockpile are shown in Column 3 of Inclosure 1, with appropriate footnotes where necessary to identify the nature of the change. Associated with the proposed operational stockpile, and shown as Inclosure 2, are non-nuclear components which provide different operational capabilities for the same warhead and/or are required in excess of a one-for-one ratio with basic assemblies.

The Joint Chiefs of Staff have reviewed the nuclear weapons stockpile through FY 1970. While it does not fully reflect all of their earlier recommendations, they accept the adjusted FY 1969 and proposed FY 1970 stockpile figures as reflected herein.[6]

In addition to the operational stockpile (Inclosure 1), warheads required for the quality assurance and reliability testing programs are shown in Inclosure 3. These additional warheads are needed to offset reductions in operational capability during stockpile sampling programs, joint firing test programs, and foreseeable major retrofit actions requiring temporary and permanent withdrawals from the operational stockpile. For strategic missiles we provide warheads to offset temporary and permanent withdrawals. For other systems we allow a decrease in the operational stockpile for permanent withdrawals for testing, unless this can be offset by delayed retirements or, in the case of warheads still in production, by additional production. Withdrawals for non-destructive testing, limited to a small percentage of the warheads concerned, are permitted to temporarily decrease the operational stockpile. Additionally, warheads for systems being phased down are also

---

[6] The views of the Joint Chiefs of Staff were attached to a December 23, 1967, memorandum from General Wheeler to Secretary McNamara (CM–2869–67). (Washington National Records Center, OSD Files: FRC 330 72 A 2467, A–400.23 1967)

retained where economies may be realized thereby, mainly by reducing the requirements for rebuild of warheads subsequent to future planned quality assurance tests. Finally, warheads are provided in this category when dictated by unusual circumstances such as foreseeable major retrofit programs or in cases involving severe logistics problems.

The Atomic Energy Commission will also be required to produce those nuclear warhead parts intended for transfer to the [*less than 1 line of source text not declassified*] pursuant to the terms of the agreement for cooperation. These parts are considered annually in a separate action by the Atomic Energy Commission and the Department of Defense.

The proposed FY 1970 stockpile is within the presently projected availability of special nuclear and by-product materials, and the number of weapons recommended to be produced in FY 1970 is within the planned capability of the Atomic Energy Commission weapons fabrication system. An Atomic Energy Commission summary of special nuclear and by-product materials required by the nuclear weapons program for FY 1969 and FY 1970 is shown in Inclosure 4.

The preliminary Atomic Energy Commission estimate of the weapons production and surveillance operations costs proposed for FY 1970 is approximately, $332 million which excludes the cost of special nuclear materials, equipment and plant amortization. The FY 1970 $332 million estimate may need to be revised when the FY 1971 stockpile composition is firm. The above data for production and surveillance costs exclude costs of Weapon Tests (including development of supplemental test sites) and Research and Development, which are estimated to be approximately $575 million for FY 1970. The above figures are Atomic Energy Commission estimates and do not include additional expenses incurred by the Department of Defense.

In accordance with your directions, as conveyed by Mr. Rostow in his memorandum of 10 February 1967,[7] the Atomic Energy Commission has been transferring to the Department of Defense finished nuclear warheads and components as they are produced and certified by the Atomic Energy Commission, subject to the production and retirement provisions of the currently applicable stockpile composition directive of the President. Such transfers for FY 1969 and 1970 will, therefore, be made in accordance with the stockpile composition recommendations of this memorandum if approved.

The Department of Defense and the Atomic Energy Commission accordingly recommend that you:

1. Approve the stockpile of [*number not declassified*] nuclear warheads for end FY 1970 tabulated in Column 4 of Inclosure 1.

---

[7] Not found.

2. Approve the revised stockpile of [*number not declassified*] nuclear warheads for end FY 1969 tabulated in Column 2 of Inclosure 1.

3. Approve the quantities of warheads required for quality assurance and reliability testing tabulated in Columns 2 and 4 of Inclosure 3.

4. Direct the production and retirement of those quantities of nuclear warheads and nuclear warhead parts necessary to achieve and maintain the above stockpiles; as well as the production of the additional nuclear warhead parts necessary for transfer to the United Kingdom pursuant to the agreement for cooperation.

5. Authorize the Atomic Energy Commission in coordination with the Department of Defense to initiate production of such long-lead time nuclear warhead parts as may be necessary to prepare for FY 1971 production of warheads required by the approved Five Year Defense Program.

6. Authorize the Atomic Energy Commission, in coordination with the Department of Defense, to make such changes in the FY 1969 and FY 1970 stockpiles as may be necessary because of changes in Atomic Energy Commission production/retirement capability, material availabilities or quality assurance requirements.

7. Authorize the Department of Defense, in coordination with the Atomic Energy Commission, to make such changes in the FY 1969 and FY 1970 stockpiles as may be required because of adjusted delivery assets or changes in military requirements.

Any changes indicative of a major shift in defense policy or Atomic Energy Commission production capability will be submitted for your specific approval. A draft implementing directive is submitted herewith for your consideration (Inclosure 5).[8]

Paul H. Nitze

Glenn T. Seaborg[9]

---

[8] An undated draft memorandum from McNamara and Seaborg to President Johnson; not printed.

[9] Signed for Seaborg in OATSD/AE on March 11. The stamped date of December 29, 1967, appears below Nitze's signature.

202. **Memorandum From the Joint Chiefs of Staff to Secretary of Defense Clifford[1]**

JCSM–221–68   Washington, April 10, 1968.

SUBJECT

   Worldwide US Military Posture (U)

   1. (TS) The Joint Chiefs of Staff are increasingly concerned about the state of US worldwide military posture when measured against existing commitments and likely contingencies. This memorandum is intended to provide you with a current appraisal of the worldwide US military posture and to express concern about the limited capability of our military forces to respond rapidly to crisis situations.

   2. (TS) Prior to the commitment of major forces to Southeast Asia in 1965, the major deployable general purpose forces based in CONUS, Hawaii, and Okinawa included 9-1/3 Army divisions, 2-8/9 Marine Corps division/wing teams, nonforward-deployed Navy forces, and approximately 48 Air Force tactical fighter squadrons. Meeting the requirements of the extended contingency in Southeast Asia has resulted in a reduction in the number of forces available to reinforce forces now deployed and for other contingencies as well as reduced combat readiness. At the present time, none of the CONUS-based land forces are deployable within existing tour/rotation policies and without extension of terms of service. After the approved deployments under Program 5 and Program 6 have been made, the only Air Force tactical fighter and reconnaissance units which will be available for immediate deployment are two F-100 tactical fighter squadrons and two reconnaissance squadrons ordered to active duty from the Air National Guard. Further, the deployment to Southeast Asia of the equivalent of 10-2/3 Army and Marine Corps division forces, one-half of the Marine aircraft squadrons, major surface and air forces of the Navy, and major tactical and strategic elements of the Air Force exceeds the force level which can be sustained by the existing active force structure under current tour/rotational policies. The Air Force must also sustain the forces deployed, for a yet-undetermined period of temporary duty, to northeast Asia in response to the USS *Pueblo* incident.[2]

   3. (TS) Shortages in personnel with the required skills, shortages in critical items of equipment, and the inability of units to attain the nec-

---

   [1] Source: Washington National Records Center, OASD/ISA Files: FRC 330 72 A 1499, 320.2 1968. Top Secret.
   [2] Documentation on the *Pueblo* crisis is printed in *Foreign Relations*, 1964–1968, volume XXIX, Part 1.

essary training level are the primary reasons for the limited deployability of the forces remaining within the strategic reserve. In addition, the combat readiness of forces deployed in other forward areas has been lowered substantially since they have been required to contribute heavily in both personnel and equipment to support and sustain Southeast Asia deployments.

4. (TS) It is the decreased readiness of US military forces worldwide and the limited capability of the strategic reserve that most concern the Joint Chiefs of Staff. Further, the risks associated with the current military posture and the possibility of communist-inspired diversionary contingencies erupting elsewhere increase as the commitment in Southeast Asia is prolonged and the active US military resources are further extended. Accordingly, the following assessment is provided:

a. *Strategic.* Though this appraisal is primarily concerned with general purpose forces, the principal threat to the United States is the large and rapidly improving strategic offensive forces of the USSR. Soviet policy is clearly aimed at improving the strategic position of the USSR relative, to the United States. It is noted that the current level of fighter/attack and B-52 sortie rates in the western Pacific and the additional deployments of aircraft to Korea have resulted in a SIOP degradation of about 250 alert weapons programmed against more than 200 targets.

b. *Europe/Middle East/North Africa.* The most likely pressure points for Soviet diversionary efforts are Europe, the Mediterranean, north Africa, and the Middle East. The NATO military posture, already weakened by France's nonparticipation, is being jeopardized further by proposed US, British, and Belgian troop reductions and redeployments. In addition to the Soviet capability to strike in Western Europe, particularly against the vulnerable Benelux line of communication (LOC), the Soviet naval presence in the Mediterranean, together with Soviet aid to certain Arab States, provides added opportunity for the USSR to promote incidents in these areas. The United States must be able to respond to direct or indirect aggression in the Middle East and north Africa without significant drawdown on US forces in central Europe. The significance of the threat in these areas is increased by our limited capability to provide the forces required for the initial defense of the NATO area.

(1) Of the eight Army divisions committed to NATO, five are M-day divisions stationed in Europe. One of these, the 24th Infantry Division (Mech), is in the initial stages of redeploying from Germany (Reforger), wherein the division, less one brigade, will return to CONUS but remain under the operational command of USCINCEUR. Two of the three CONUS divisions normally committed to NATO by M+30 days, the 1st and 2d Armored Divisions, will require at least 12 weeks after mobilization to achieve a deployable status. The 5th Infantry Division (Mech), the third CONUS division normally commit-

ted to NATO by M+30 days, is currently preparing one brigade for deployment to Southeast Asia, and the division(–) will require a minimum of 12 weeks after mobilization to achieve a deployable status. Due to the reduced readiness of these three divisions, the United States has agreed to make two airborne divisions, the 82d and 101st, available to NATO by M+30 days. However, during the past 6 months, the 101st Airborne Division and one brigade of the 82d Airborne Division were deployed to Southeast Asia. The readiness of the 82d Airborne Division(–) was reduced in preparing this brigade for deployment, and the division(–) will require 8 weeks' training after receipt of replacements to achieve a deployable status. Provision of these replacements will not be completed until October 1968, unless there is a Reserve callup. Thus, there are no major Army combat forces ready to reinforce NATO on a timely basis without redeployment from Southeast Asia.

(2) Two Marine division/wing teams are committed to NATO to arrive in Europe by M+30 and M+60 days. However, only 1-3/9 currently are available without redeployment from Southeast Asia. These forces also provide a defense force for Guantanamo and amphibious ready forces in the Mediterranean and Caribbean and constitute the sustaining base for Marine Corps deployments to Southeast Asia.

(3) Navy commitments to NATO include 10 CVAs and seven CVSs by M+30 days. This represents two-thirds of the Navy's CVAs and seven of eight available CVSs. Navy ships are committed fully in sustaining worldwide deployments, and, thus, the reinforcement of NATO would require substantial redeployment from Southeast Asia. It is noted that 26 ships of the Atlantic Command have been placed in caretaker status or are operating with reduced manning because of personnel drawdowns to support Southeast Asia commitments.

(4) Twenty-one Air Force tactical fighter squadrons are now based in Europe and committed to NATO on M-day. Of those, four squadrons (Crested Cap) are programmed to become dual based in CY 1968 but will remain under the operational command of USCINCEUR. USCINCEUR plans call for an augmentation force of 37 tactical fighter squadrons by M+30 days. However, only six active squadrons (Air National Guard) are currently available in CONUS for deployment, of which two are approved for deployment to Southeast Asia under Program 5 and two are approved under Program 6. Therefore, the balance of USCINCEUR's air support requirements can be provided only by redeployment of forces from Southeast Asia or Korea and from the remaining 15 Air National Guard tactical fighter squadrons.

c. *Southeast Asia*

(1) In South Vietnam, the enemy has become increasingly aggressive throughout the country, with attacks against population centers

and military installations. Elements of four North Vietnamese infantry divisions have been deployed in the vicinity of the demilitarized zone and Khe Sanh. The North Vietnamese Army has the capability of reinforcing the demilitarized zone/Khe Sanh area with between one and two additional division equivalents in possibly 30 days time. The North Vietnamese, with the aid of the USSR and Communist China, are rebuilding their Air Force and improving their air defense capability. Military and economic resources continue to reach the enemy through North Vietnamese ports, the Mekong–Bassac River system, and over the land routes from southern China.

(2) The North Vietnamese and Pathet Lao have achieved recent successes in Laos. It is possible that North Vietnam may seek to extend its control in order to protect its LOC into South Vietnam.

(3) In Thailand, the northeast region continues to be a center of insurgency, and the incident rate continues to rise. In recent months, a serious outbreak of insurgent incidents has been initiated by dissident tribesmen in north Thailand.

(4) In Burma, there is evidence of increased external communist assistance to the Karen and Shan dissidents and to the White Flag Communist Party. This, coupled with a deteriorating economic situation, indicates that the Burmese insurgency problem could assume serious proportions.

(5) Cambodia continues to be used as a sanctuary for North Vietnamese/Viet Cong forces and as a source of supplies, despite recent official US attempts to reach an agreement with Prince Sihanouk on denying the enemy this refuge.

(6) Communist China has the capability to launch and sustain a major invasion of Southeast Asia. In addition, the Chinese Peoples Republic could support an attack with a small number of nuclear weapons delivered by aircraft and could have a limited MRBM capability later this year. Chinese naval units have the capability to conduct limited submarine, torpedo boat, and surface-to-surface missile attacks.

d. *Northeast Asia.* It is still uncertain whether the marked increase over the past year in North Korean provocations, culminating in the attempted assault on the Blue House and the seizure of the USS *Pueblo*, was intended to divert US attention from Southeast Asia or to constitute the early phase of renewed communist aggression on the Korean Peninsula. It is prudent to recognize the first possibility and prepare for the second. For the past several years, US forces in Korea have been assigned a low priority in personnel and equipment modernization. Until a week after the seizure of the USS *Pueblo*, the Air Force had no tactical air support forces in Korea. There are now deployed in Korea, on a temporary basis, five tactical fighter squadrons and one augmented fighter interceptor squadron. Army forces deployed in Korea continue to be under recommended strength and, as a result, are at a reduced level of combat readiness.

e. *Atlantic.* The strategic significance of the Atlantic stems from NATO's reliance upon sea and air LOCs through that area for its economic survival and mutual support. The Soviet submarine fleet represents the principal threat to Free World shipping and to NATO naval forces. The Atlantic serves as a launch area from which the Soviets can conduct offensive nuclear warfare against the countries of the Western Hemisphere and Europe.

f. *Latin America.* The USSR, the Chinese Peoples Republic, and Cuba will continue to view Latin America as a prime target for subversion. This threat, as well as internal instabilities, should be met by development of an appropriate indigenous security capability and the encouragement of selected Latin American nations to provide trained and equipped units for use in OAS/UN peacekeeping missions. However, there is currently little assurance that Latin American countries would furnish units for peacekeeping purposes under circumstances considered essential principally to US national interest. Therefore, a capability still must be maintained for direct intervention—through the OAS, if possible, but unilaterally if necessary—to prevent establishment of another Castro-style communist government in the Western Hemisphere. Cuba continues to pose a threat to US security interests, and the US base at Guantanamo presents an opportunity for diversionary action by the communists.

5. (C) In addition to the external threats, there are domestic considerations that must be recognized. Many major cities in the United States are threatened with civil disturbances stemming from radial disorders and antidraft/anti-Vietnam movements. Forces from the Ready Reserve and CONUS-based Active Forces will be capable of coping with these threats. However, the simultaneous employment of Reserve forces, under State or Federal control, in a number of different cities, or the prolonged use of Active Forces in this role would reduce the capability to reinforce forces now deployed and to respond to other contingencies.

6. (S) The current steps to establish a workable basis for negotiation with North Vietnam are acknowledged. However, it is considered prudent that there be no relaxation of efforts to attain an improved military posture while awaiting results from those steps. Past experience provides ample evidence that negotiation with the communists is conducted best when backed by visible and credible force.

7. (TS) The Joint Chiefs of Staff conclude that the strategic military options now available to the United States are seriously limited by the reduced combat readiness of military forces worldwide, other than those deployed to Southeast Asia, and by the limited size and reduced

combat readiness of our present strategic reserve. Measures should be taken to improve the US military posture in order to:

a. Sustain and permit more effective use of forces already in Southeast Asia.
b. Provide and sustain the additional forces approved for deployment to Southeast Asia.
c. Restore and maintain NATO-deployed and -augmentation forces.
d. Restore and maintain other deployed forces.
e. Respond effectively to other contingencies.
f. Establish and maintain a high state of readiness in the Reserve component forces in order to augment Active Forces rapidly, when required.

8. (S) The level of forces necessary to achieve the required posture is set forth in JSOP 70–77.[3] The urgency in attaining these levels is emphasized, and the need to move ahead quickly on reequipping and modernizing our forces is of the utmost importance.

For the Joint Chiefs of Staff:
Earle G. Wheeler
Chairman
Joint Chiefs of Staff

---

[3] Document 188.

---

203.   **Letter From the Chairman of the President's Foreign Intelligence Advisory Board (Taylor) to the President's Special Assistant (Rostow)[1]**

Washington, April 18, 1968.

Walt:

At the recent meeting of the Foreign Intelligence Advisory Board, several matters occurred to which I wish to call your attention.

The first is the attached memorandum to the President suggesting that he issue a statement with regard to the importance of the foreign intelligence effort.[2] The Board is taking inventory of its own resources

---

[1] Source: Johnson Library, National Security File, Intelligence File, Foreign Intelligence Advisory Board, Vol. 2 [1 of 4], Box 6. Top Secret; COMINT.
[2] Dated April 15 on a list of attachments at the end of the letter; not found.

and methods in the hope of providing better service to the President in the intelligence field and would appreciate the reinforcement afforded of such a statement by the President. Would you please forward it to the President?

As a result of the inventory mentioned above, the Board has reorganized its panels as indicated in an enclosure hereto.[3] The regional panels now coincide territorially with the interests of the IRG's and the regional Assistant Secretaries of State.

In considering how best to keep an eye on the covert activities of the CIA, the Board felt that it would be timely at our next meeting in June to review activities of the 303 Committee in keeping tabs on the Agency. We hope that you will be willing to attend and give us your impression of the effectiveness of the 303 controls. The meeting will be held on June 6–7 and I hope that you will be able to spend a little time with us on one of these days. I shall confirm this invitation later in writing.

You are well aware of the excellent work being done by NSA in intercepting and deciphering the low level infiltration and logistics traffic of the North Vietnamese. Unfortunately, a great deal of this traffic is not intercepted because of a lack of SIGINT aircraft with this primary mission. Pat Carter has been trying in vain to obtain a total of 15 aircraft for this purpose but, thus far, he has been frustrated, largely by the issue of operational control of aircraft on this kind of collection mission—shall that control be military or NSA? The issue is set forth in the attached letter which I hope you will be willing to dispatch to Clark Clifford.[4] In the past, the latter has always been sympathetic to the needs of NSA and I would expect him to react quickly to such a letter and cut the red tape which has thus far held back this much needed reinforcement in the SIGINT field.

I am sending these matters over in writing which normally I would have taken up with you in person because of your absence in Honolulu and my departure on a short trip which will last until April 25. I shall be back in my office on the following Friday.[5]

M.D.T.

---

[3] Dated April 17 on a list of attachments at the end of the letter; not found.

[4] Not found.

[5] April 26.

204. Paper Approved by the Senior Interdepartmental Group[1]

Washington, undated.

UNITED STATES POLICY ON INTERNAL DEFENSE IN
SELECTED FOREIGN COUNTRIES

I. Purpose and Authorities

This policy (short title "Foreign Internal Defense Policy") supersedes "United States Overseas Internal Defense Policy (USOIDP)"
issued under cover of National Security Action Memorandum (NSAM)
No. 182 of August 24, 1962. It is consistent with NSAMs 182, 119, 124,
162, 173, 177, 283, and 341.[2] Its provisions govern the foreign internal
defense policies, plans, programs, and operations of all U.S. government Departments and Agencies concerned. The appropriate
Departments and Agencies should update statements of their roles and
missions in support of this policy to replace those set forth in the superseded 1962 policy paper. The new statements should be submitted to
the Senior Interdepartmental Group for approval. Departments and
Agencies should also issue implementing directives as necessary.

II. Policy Considerations

A. The Problem

Internal security situations in certain developing countries are a
matter of concern for the United States. Because of location or economic resources, the need for U.S. military or other facilities and operating
rights (such as transit rights), political alignments, or for other reasons,
the United States must pay special attention to these countries and to
the ability of their governments to maintain internal order. In certain
circumstances, the United States may have to provide governments
with assistance for internal defense purposes in order to help protect

---

[1] Source: Washington National Records Center, OASD/ISA Files: FRC 330 72 A 1498,
381 1968 June. Secret. The Senior Interdepartmental Group approved the paper on May
23. It forms Tab A to a June 27 memorandum from Deputy Secretary of Defense Nitze to
the Secretaries of the Military Departments and the Joint Chiefs of Staff, among others,
which instructed recipients "to review all relevant existing policy statements and activities under your responsibility to insure that they are consistent with the FIDP." Tab B to
the June 27 memorandum is printed as Document 205.

[2] NSAM Nos. 182, 119, 124, and 162 are printed in *Foreign Relations, 1961–1963*, vol.
VIII, Documents 105, 65, 68, and 91, respectively. A copy of NSAM No. 173 is in the
National Archives and Records Administration, RG 59, S/S–NSC Files: Lot 72 D 361,
NSAM 173. NSAM No. 177 is printed in *Foreign Relations, 1961–1963*, vol. IX, Document
150. NSAM Nos. 283 and 341 are printed ibid., 1964–1968, vol. XXXIII, Documents 191 and
56, respectively.

United States local and strategic interests which might be threatened by internal disorder or subversion. Subversion involves systematic efforts from internal or external sources to undermine or overthrow the established political and social order. Internal defense consists of the full range of action programs to maintain internal security, including, in addition to political and diplomatic activity and economic and military assistance, such specialized programs as civil police, psychological, paramilitary, and counterinsurgency operations; counterguerrilla activity, unconventional warfare, military civic actions, and public works.

In some developing countries, independence from significant influence or control by a foreign power may be a major U.S. security objective for political, military, or economic reasons. Such control or influence could result from communist subversion or from communist exploitation of local failure to maintain adequate internal security.

The United States must, therefore, be constantly alert to conditions of internal security in developing countries in order to identify situations where subversion, insurgency, or disorder endanger significant U.S. interests. In these cases, the United States must be prepared to assist governments in appropriate internal defense programs.

B. The U.S. Position

It is a part of our overall foreign policy that ultimately nations be able to develop according to their own traditions and that each be governed in accordance with the will of the majority of its citizens. We believe that governments should respond adequately to the aspirations of the people for political, economic, and social conditions appropriate to their environment, and should move toward the establishment of institutions which will provide some guarantees for the continuation of these conditions as governments change. The development of institutions responsive to local national patterns of behavior is more important, however, than progress toward an objective goal of representative democratic institutions as the United States has traditionally viewed them. In many cases, it is primarily the economic and technical aspects of modernization which are attractive goals in developing countries, and there is often great resistance to changes in political and social systems, no matter how important or appropriate these changes may seem to us.

The process of modernization in developing countries is often destabilizing in itself, and changes in political and social systems often are accomplished by revolutionary activity. While the United States would usually prefer basic changes in a society to be evolutionary rather than revolutionary, the growth process is generally accompanied by unrest, upheaval, and violence. In U.S. policies toward foreign internal security situations, it is important to make a distinction between disorder and insurgency which may be a function of national growth and that which is a result of subversion.

Thus, the position which the United States should take with respect to the internal security situation in a foreign country is an integral, inseparable part of the overall U.S. policy toward the country and the region in which it is located. It cannot be formulated in isolation from other aspects of U.S. policy nor implemented as a separate program. The policy problem is to make judgments about the nature and speed of the process of national development and, where U.S. interests require it, to find ways to influence the process constructively.

The United States does not regard every situation of political instability or social disorder and violence as a foreign internal security problem threatening U.S. interests and requiring U.S. assistance for internal defense programs. In some cases, the forces making for instability and political upheaval may contribute, in the long run, to the achievement of objectives deserving of encouragement and support from the United States. In any case, it does not seem possible entirely to deprive people of the use of force for purposes of social change, and action which is too repressive may worsen the problem by forcing the pressures for alterations in institutions outside legal or acceptable channels and into subversive forms.

In countries where significant U.S. interests are not threatened by internal disorder or subversion, the United States should seek to avoid becoming involved in internal defense policies, plans, and operations of local governments. Even in these cases, however, it may be in the U.S. interest to provide internal defense equipment or training assistance appropriate to the situation and to U.S. objectives in the countries concerned.

Internal defense policy and programs for countries the United States may be prepared to assist will need to be determined on a case-by-case basis and carefully tailored to the specific and unique aspects of each situation. Important considerations which will affect the determination of the kind and nature of U.S. internal defense policy and programs for particular countries are: first, U.S. interests in the area; then the sources, kinds, and degree of threat to internal security; dangers from external exploitation; the possibility of local conflict broadening into larger-scale wars; the consequences of the internal security problem for overall development within the country; the will and ability of the local government to handle the situation with indigenous resources; the effect of U.S. programs on other programs within the country; the consequences of U.S. policies and programs on the U.S. position in other countries; the availability of external assistance from other nations or international organizations.

One of our primary concerns is to anticipate situations requiring U.S. foreign internal defense action far enough in advance, and to devise in cooperation with local governments, effective programs which will make unnecessary the engagement of U.S. combat troops. The long-term implications of use of U.S. military forces should be carefully studied in any consideration of such a step.

C. *The Importance of Local Efforts*

The process of change within a country is largely stimulated by local initiative, guided by national leaders, reliant on indigenous resources, and ultimately bears a national trademark. The role of internal defense is to permit the changes to take place in as orderly a manner as possible and without outside interference. The kind and amount of police and military action required to maintain internal security for each country are most likely also to be determined according to the character of the government and the people and the requirements for such force as seen by them. It is clear that the United States should persuade the countries concerned to do as much as they can for their own internal defense. We should realize, however, that many resource-poor countries are unable to attain their goals for political and economic modernization or their objectives of improved conditions of law and order without external help. Where U.S. interests warrant it and U.S. resources can be made available, the United States can provide such assistance or, in combination with other nations which share our common goals, see that it is provided.

D. *U.S. Actions*

The nature of the U.S. response toward foreign internal security situations may be a selection from or mix of the following policy options:

—non-involvement
—diplomatic persuasion, either bilateral or through regional groupings, and advice (including efforts to influence opposition groups or leaders where appropriate)
—special technical, economic, public information, civil security, police or military assistance to include operational assistance for internal defense programs and psychological operations
—assistance as a means of inducing policies designed to counter underlying causes of internal security problems
—boycott of a government through denial of normal diplomatic or economic relations
—use of military force to assist in restoring or maintaining internal order.

It will always be necessary for responsible U.S. officials both in Washington and in the field to make judgments, in individual country situations, concerning the character of U.S. action and the degree of U.S.

assistance which may be desirable (from the U.S. point of view or the country's own standpoint) or tolerable or effective or available. Judgments of the appropriateness of political, military, economic, and psychological activities must be applied on a continuing basis as the situation in a country changes or develops.

Political development programs to provide for improved communication between the population at large and the central government can strengthen nations vulnerable to subversion and unrest. Encouragement of increasing popular involvement and wider participation in indigenous private and government institutions can induce people to seek desired social and economic opportunities and reforms through overt legal means rather than through subversion and violence. Such institutions as local development committees, regional councils, and rural production and marketing cooperatives may act as effective vehicles for participation in local and national development programs leading to the evolution of self-reliant societies resistant to subversion and insurgency. Legal development and public administration programs also may contribute to the achievement of this goal.

Effective police and public safety activities can play an important part in the prevention and handling of internal security problems. A capable and humane police force can be invaluable in coping with and controlling internal security situations at minimum cost with limited use of force and within the framework of civil law. It can be a factor in preventing dissension and dissatisfaction from growing outside the bounds of legitimate opposition and becoming subversion. In developing countries, U.S. police assistance programs can play an important role, not only in the preservation of public order, but in the building of indigenous civil security institutions which can keep pace with and assist in the nation's growth process. The effectiveness of public safety forces can be greatly enhanced if programs for their development are instituted in advance of potential crises. Such programs may be justified also to keep developing countries from obtaining police assistance from Communist or other countries hostile to the United States. Among the responsibilities which the indigenous security agencies can be brought to assume are the protection of broadening freedoms and the prevention of crime and terror which jeopardize the freedoms and interfere with national development. Public information programs can facilitate public acceptance of this role for the police.

The armed forces of a developing country can constitute the means for protection against internal insurrection beyond the capability of civilian police to control. The existence of loyal, appropriately trained, and effective military forces can represent an important deterrent against terrorism or guerrilla warfare and is an important element in internal defense planning. In addition, in many countries, the military establishment possesses equipment and skills representing a major national investment and resource. Frequently the United States can influence governments to use this resource in the nation building process without detracting from the capability of the military to perform its primary defense function.

Students, other youth groups, and labor are often prime target groups for local programs. The United States may be of assistance through these groups in promoting social progress in the developing society. Opportunities may also exist for influencing opposition leaders where Communist or other adverse influences seem likely to prove too disruptive.

Information activities, both person-to-person contact and mass media can play a significant part in the communication process by creating a favorable climate for change and self-help and providing facts and focus for political dialogue.

There may occasionally be opportunities for the resources of U.S. business firms and philanthropic foundations to be applied in support of U.S. objectives. Many private U.S. firms and foundations engage in programs to improve social and economic conditions in countries abroad and can usefully be encouraged to provide assistance and to adopt employment practices which will identify them with popular improvements and aspirations in support of U.S. goals.

Considerations affecting the level of U.S. assistance when provided, include the availability of U.S. and indigenous official and private resources, the financial and manpower impact of U.S. assistance on local governments, and opportunities to obtain assistance from third countries or international organizations.

The choice of U.S. programs and the determination of levels will also be influenced by the degree of identification with the local government we are willing to accept. In most cases, we will want to do everything possible to see that critical sectors of the local society understand the role that the United States is seeking to play. Psychological operations and information programs can assist in achieving this goal.

E. Implementation of the Policy

For the United States to act promptly and effectively when required by U.S. interests in connection with foreign internal defense problems, the responsible Departments and Agencies must be well informed about countries and regions where internal security problems exist or may arise. Intelligence and other information must be constantly available to allow policy makers and operators to anticipate contingencies. Planning, development, and coordination of programs and operations must take place in advance to ensure that necessary internal defense activities are provided for and will be supported from U.S. resources. The Senior Interdepartmental Group and the Interdepartmental Regional Groups, established by NSAM 341, March 2, 1966, are the mechanisms by which interdepartmental activities overseas are directed, coordinated, and supervised by the Secretary of State. Foreign internal defense activities explicitly fall within the scope of this NSAM. In the field, the Chief of the U.S. Diplomatic Mission, assisted by representatives of other agencies, has responsibility for plans and programs concerning foreign internal defense.

III. Courses of Action

To support this policy, the United States should, through the SIG–IRG mechanism established by NSAM 341 of March 2, 1966,

A. identify and establish priorities for countries in which an internal security situation represents a threat to significant U.S. interests and where U.S. internal defense assistance would be desirable and feasible; keep the list of such countries and their priorities under constant review;

B. develop a comprehensive plan to provide U.S. internal defense assistance to each country identified under A. above; the plan may be a separate internal defense plan or part of a more comprehensive country plan; in either case it should

1. be prepared, according to format, timing, and other guidelines established by the Senior Interdepartmental Group and the relevant Regional Interdepartmental Group,
2. be, under normal circumstances, the responsibility of the Chief of the U.S. Diplomatic Mission in the country concerned,
3. integrate internal defense with other U.S. foreign affairs programs and activities,
4. take into account the capabilities of political advice, diplomatic persuasion, public information programs, public safety operations, civic action programs, other economic and military assistance, and psychological, counterinsurgency, countersubversive, unconventional warfare, and other appropriate operations to contribute to internal defense,
5. focus on improving the capabilities of the country itself—its leaders, its government, and its people—to strengthen its own internal security, using U.S. programs and resources in supporting roles,
6. discuss in detail the funds required for implementation and those available from existing resources, along with a recommendation as to sources of additional funds required, U.S. or local,
7. be coordinated interdepartmentally,
8. be subject to critical review, along with operations under it, and periodic updating.

C. provide for, in the plans referred to in B. above maximum possible emphasis on the development by each country concerned of its own capability to anticipate, prevent, and defeat subversion or insurgency; when external assistance is necessary, the United States should urge other resource-abundant nations to provide help and should, insofar as feasible, work through international and multilateral institutions;

D. prepare and coordinate interagency contingency studies for the possible use of U.S. military forces in situations where the U.S. national security interest is threatened by subversion, insurgency, or disorder in foreign countries;

E. maintain and strengthen intelligence and other reporting procedures where necessary to enable responsible U.S. officials to anticipate and to follow closely foreign internal defense situations of interest to the United States;

F. maintain and strengthen training programs where necessary to ensure that selected personnel may be able to carry out effectively all of the functions referred to above, both in the field and in Washington.

---

205. Memorandum by the Chairman of the Senior Interdepartmental Group (Katzenbach)[1]

Washington, June 10, 1968.

TO

Executive Chairman, IRG/AF
Executive Chairman, IRG/ARA
Executive Chairman, IRG/EA
Executive Chairman, IRG/EUR
Executive Chairman, IRG/NEA
Chairman, Political-Military Group

SUBJECT

Implementation of U.S. Policy on Internal Defense in Selected Foreign Countries

In implementation of the "U.S. Policy on Internal Defense in Selected Foreign Countries", approved by the SIG on May 23, 1968, the following responsibilities are assigned to you:

---

[1] Source: Washington National Records Center, OASD/ISA Files: FRC 330 72 A 1498, 381 1968 June. Secret. The memorandum forms Tab B to a June 27 memorandum from Deputy Secretary of Defense Nitze to the Secretaries of the Military Departments and the Joint Chiefs of Staff; see footnote 1, Document 204.

1. Each IRG will provide the SIG by July 1 with names of countries within its area of responsibility where the internal security situation represents a threat to significant United States interests and where United States foreign internal defense assistance would be desirable and feasible under the criteria of the revised policy. The list should be supported by a brief explicit statement of the reasons for including each country.

Strict application of the revised criteria necessarily will reduce the number of countries worldwide that qualify for United States assistance in the field of internal defense. However, it is recognized that in some countries current programs will have to be continued (although phased down over time) even if not completely justifiable on the grounds of an internal security threat to significant United States interests. Valid reasons for such exceptions may be preservation of a special political or military relationship, supplementing economic development assistance, repayment for United States overseas base rights, or protection of other United States interests. Each IRG will be expected to distinguish clearly between those countries which fully qualify for foreign internal defense assistance under the revised policy, and those which the IRG believes should continue to receive such assistance for other reasons, submitting to the SIG only the names of those countries in the former category.

2. Upon approval by the SIG of a country's inclusion and its priority in the foreign internal defense action list, a comprehensive analysis of the internal defense situation in that country will be prepared under the supervision of the Chief of Diplomatic Mission for review and approval by the IRG. This analysis will include a detailed summary of host country, United States, third country, and international agency programs proposed to meet the internal threat.

This may take the form of a separate plan or be included in an overall foreign affairs planning document for the country concerned. In either case, internal defense considerations should be carefully related to and integrated with other political, economic, military, psychological, and informational aspects of United States policies and programs, and should focus on improving the capability of the country itself to strengthen its own internal security, using United States programs and resources in supporting roles. The country internal defense plan will be the basis for departmental and interdepartmental decisions on United States policies and programs concerning internal defense. Except as a new crisis may require, the plan should be submitted early enough in the budget cycle so that Washington guidance may be available to the field for use in the development of agency program documents. An outline showing the desired scope and a possible format for the internal defense section of a country plan or for a separate country internal defense plan is attached.[2]

To avoid duplication of effort, each IRG should make maximum use of reports already submitted in the preparation of internal defense plans. For example, the internal security section of the Country Analysis and Strategy Papers (CASPs) submitted by Latin American posts in almost every case, following IRG review, will satisfy the requirement established by this directive.

3. Countries should be nominated for addition to or removal from the foreign internal defense action list by each IRG as individual circumstances warrant. The proposal by the IRG to place a country on the list should contain an explicit statement of the reasons therefor and for the priority recommended. The proposal to remove a country should indicate what change in circumstances has occurred. Each country on the list, and countries which the IRG feels are potential candidates for the list, should be re-examined no less often than annually as a basis for evaluating on-going programs and determining whether the status of the country has changed. Additions to, or deletions from, the foreign internal defense action list must have SIG concurrence.

4. The Political-Military Group, acting on behalf of the SIG, will be responsible for:

a. Recommending priorities among countries selected for United States action in the foreign internal defense field;

b. Exploring inter-regional and overall foreign policy implications of internal defense strategies and resource allocations recommended by the IRGs;

c. Reviewing interagency contingency studies involving the possible use of United States military forces in situations where the United States national security interest requires it;

d. Ensuring interdepartmental coordination of foreign internal defense research and development activities to make sure that United States resources are used most effectively to provide information, hardware, and techniques for application in the foreign internal defense field;

e. Reviewing, on the basis of the above, all internal defense country plans and related reporting; assisting the IRGs; bringing to the attention of the SIG additional options or alternative approaches in the light of overall United States resources, strategies, and commitments, and other matters requiring decision or consideration at that level; reporting at regular intervals to the SIG on foreign internal defense matters.

5. When carrying out its responsibilities under this directive, the Political-Military Group should include representatives from all Departments and Agencies holding membership in the SIG and IRGs.

---

[2] Not printed.

206.   Intelligence Memorandum[1]

SR IM 68–16   Washington, June 10, 1968.
TCS–1939/68

RECENT DEVELOPMENTS IN THE MOSCOW ABM SYSTEM

Summary

Within the past year the Soviets appear to have made further reductions in the construction of ballistic missile defenses at Moscow. The early evidence suggested that the Moscow ABM system would have a force level of 128 launchers at 16 launch sites—four sites in each quadrant. In early 1964, construction in the southeast quadrant was abandoned, and the number of launch sites dropped to 12. Work has now apparently ceased on two more sites in the northeastern and two in the southwestern environs of Moscow. If construction is not resumed at these sites, the final force level for the completed system will be eight sites and a total complement of 64 launchers.

Partial system operational capability is probably near. All elements of the system are expected to be operational by mid-1970.

The cutbacks will not materially change the strategic role of the system, since even at originally indicated levels it could not have coped with a determined US attack. The Soviets may now feel a greater need for improved capabilities—for example, against penetration aids and multiple warheads—before filling in the Moscow system or extending ABM coverage into other parts of the Soviet Union. The cutbacks thus could represent a pause while improvements are being sought.

If so, the Soviets may now view arms limitations discussions with the US as a way of probing—at no penalty to themselves—the firmness of the United States' intent to carry out improvements presently programed for its strategic forces. Although the Soviets have not formally

---

[1] Source: Johnson Library, National Security File, Intelligence File, Miscellaneous CIA Intelligence Memoranda, [2 of 4], Box 13. Top Secret; Ruff; [*codewords not declassified*]; Handle via Talent-Keyhole-COMINT Systems Jointly; No Foreign Dissem. According to a note on the first page, this memorandum was produced solely by the CIA, prepared jointly by the Office of Scientific Intelligence and the Office of Strategic Research, and coordinated with the Offices of Current Intelligence and National Estimates. An attached June 13 note from R.J. Smith, Deputy Director of Intelligence, to Rostow, calls this memorandum to his attention because it "is of such significance." A handwritten note, which has been crossed out, reads, "For the President from Walt Rostow: Herewith summary of CIA Study on Recent Developments in the Moscow ABM System." Another handwritten note reads, "sent Ranch via wire 6/15/68 CAP 81313."

responded to US initiatives for arms limiting talks, they have carefully kept alive the possibility that they will eventually do so.

Meanwhile, work on elements of the Moscow ABM system is progressing:

The forward early warning and tracking radars at Olenegorsk and Skrunda are now believed to be operational.

At Moscow, three of the present eight launch sites and the northwestern faces of the Dog House target acquisition and tracking radar are probably undergoing checkout for operational readiness later this year.

Recent ground clearing and associated activities at Skrunda and Moscow raise the possibility that deployment of new ABM-related radars is under way.

Completion of the launch sites still under construction will probably mark the end of deployment of the system in its current form. However, activity at the Sary Shagan missile test center indicates a continuing effort to improve ballistic missile defense systems. A better system, based on present technology and work currently under way at Sary Shagan, could be ready for deployment within a year or two but probably would not be widely deployed and operational much before 1973 or 1974.

---

207.   National Security Action Memorandum No. 370[1]

Washington, June 11, 1968.

TO

The Secretary of State
The Secretary of Defense
The Chairman, Atomic Energy Commission

SUBJECT

Nuclear Weapons Deployment Authorization for FY 1969 and FY 1970

The President has noted the proposed Nuclear Weapons Deployment Ceiling Plan for FY 1969, along with projected deployment ceilings for FY 1970, contained in the Department of Defense memorandum dated March

---

[1] Source: Washington National Records Center, OASD/ISA Files: FRC 330 72 A 1499, 471.6 1968 Jan–June. Top Secret.

19, 1968.[2] The President understands that the number of weapons shown reflect end-year ceilings with specific contingencies treated on a separate basis. The President also understands that actual deployments against these ceilings will be controlled by the Secretary of Defense, and he wishes to be advised as a matter of information of any significant changes in contemplated actual overseas deployments within these ceilings. In addition, the President will consider FY 1970 in next year's plan, which will deal with both FY 1970 and FY 1971. The President continues to be interested in Pacific Threatre requirements and will expect additional consideration of such requirements to be reflected in the next plan. The President has authorized the Department of Defense in FY 1969 to:

1. Deploy nuclear weapons to areas outside the United States as indicated in Appendices A and B, hereto, with the provisos that: (a) the FY 1969 end-year total authorized in each separate country/command area within each region (Appendix A) or the total by category of weapons within each region (Appendix B) may be exceeded by [*number not declassified*] in the event of unforeseen contingencies; however, the ceiling of [*number not declassified*] weapons in NATO Europe may not be exceeded; (b) the grand total of weapons outside the United States (areas under foreign sovereignty and areas under full U.S. control other than the U.S.) shall not exceed [*number not declassified*] weapons at end FY 1969; and (c) weapons to be deployed under the specific contingencies cited in Appendix C may be deployed under the noted conditions as additive to (a) and (b).

2. All weapons deployed to NATO Europe must have permissive action link devices installed. In addition, the President has noted that permissive action devices will be installed as soon as possible on weapons now at forward deployment sites [*1-1/2 lines of source text not declassified*] and further, that as a second priority, permissive action devices will be installed prior to deployment on weapons to be deployed to forward resupply positions at [*less than 1 line of source text not declassified*].

3. Support non-U.S. forces in accordance with the units and numbers of warheads indicated in Appendix D hereto and the provisions below. The provisions of NSAM 197[3] continue to apply; however, the procedure of case-by-case requests for authority to provide additional support of non-U.S. units pursuant to NSAM 143[4] is hereby amended.

---

[2] Not found. A March 9 memorandum from Deputy Secretary of Defense Nitze to President Johnson, requesting approval for nuclear weapons deployment for FY 1969 and enclosing a draft NSAM for the President's approval, is ibid.

[3] Dated October 23, 1962, and entitled "Improved Procedure—Communication to Other Countries of RD on Nuclear Weapons." A copy is in the Kennedy Library, National Security Files.

[4] Entitled "Nuclear Weapons for NATO Forces"; see footnote 4, Document 90.

Future requests for changes in support of non-U.S. forces will be reflected in the annual Nuclear Weapons Deployment Ceiling Plan and separate case-by-case requests will be submitted only to meet requirements which are not identified in annual deployment plans. The support authorized in Appendix D is subject to the following conditions:

(a) The Department of Defense memorandum requests authority to disperse weapons in support of non-U.S. NATO 155mm Howitzer units should this action prove desirable as a result of pertinent studies now underway. Prior to making firm commitments to NATO allies for specific support of 155mm Howitzer units, the Department of Defense should submit the proposed action for Presidential approval together with a current evaluation of the utility of such support.

(b) The yield restrictions of NSAM 143, as amended by NSAM 199,[5] apply.

(c) The Programs of Cooperation remain essentially the same as those pertaining when each NSAM 197 action was approved.

(d) Custodial arrangements will be completed and units and facilities will be operational, to include U.S. unilateral communications to the U.S. custodial detachment, prior to deployment in support of non-U.S. units.

(e) Weapons may be deployed in support of U.S. forces pending compliance with (d) above.

The yield provisions of NSAM 199 are hereby amended to exempt the Mk 61 in support of U.S. forces from the [*less than 1 line of source text not declassified*] limitation on land-based alert strike aircraft on station in NATO.

The next deployment ceiling plan should be submitted in mid-November 1968 in conjunction with the stockpile approval request.

W.W. Rostow

Appendix A

Authorized Ceilings on Nuclear Weapon Deployments
(Region and Country / Command Totals)
FY 1969

[*table (4 columns and 32 rows of source text) not declassified*]

---

[5] Entitled "Loading of SACEUR Land-Based Alert Strike Aircraft." A copy is in the National Archives and Records Administration, RG 59, S/S–NSC Files: Lot 72 D 316, NSAM 199.

Appendix B

Authorized Ceilings on Nuclear Weapon Deployments
by Category of Weapon—FY 1969

	Western Europe	Atlantic	Pacific
Strategic Offensive[1]	[*]	[*]	[*]
Strategic Defensive[2]	[*]	[*]	[*]
Tactical Offensive[3]	[*]	[*]	[*]
Tactical Defensive[4]	[*]	[*]	[*]
Fleet ASW and AAW	[*]	[*]	[*]
TOTAL	[*]	[*]	[*]

[*entry in table not declassified]

[1] Includes Strategic Offensive Surface-to-Surface Missiles, Bombs, and Air-to-Surface Missiles

[2] Includes Strategic Defensive Air-to-Air Missiles and Surface-to-Air Missiles

[3] Includes Tactical Bombs, Surface-to-Surface Missiles, and Artillery

[4] Includes Atomic Demolition Munitions, Tactical Air-to-Air Missiles, and Surface-to-Air Missiles

Appendix C

Contingency Deployments

Country/Command	Weapons	Quantity FY 1968	Quantity FY 1969	Conditions
[text not declassified]	Strategic Bombs	[*]	[*]	For support of US FB-111 forces if deployed
[text not declassified]	Strategic Missiles	[*]	[*]	For temporary off loading of [text not declassified] for maintenance purposes
	Strategic Bombs and ASMs	[*]	[*]	For advance readiness or during brief periods for operational reasons
[text not declassified]	Fleet ASW & AAW	[*]	[*]	For wartime ASW operations
[text not declassified]	Fleet ASW & AAW	[*]	[*]	For wartime ASW operations
[text not declassified]	Fleet ASW & AAW	[*]	[*]	For wartime ASW operations
[text not declassified]	Artillery	[*]	[*]	For advanced readiness of Fleet Marines
	ADMs	[*]	[*]	For advanced readiness of Fleet Marines
[text not declassified]	Strategic Bombs and ASMs	[*]	[*]	[text not declassified]
[text not declassified]	Tactical Bombs	[*]	[*]	For temporary off loading of Navy Ships
	Fleet ASW & AAW	[*]	[*]	For temporary off loading off Navy Ships

[*entry in table not declassified]

Appendix D

Authorized Ceilings on Nuclear Weapons In Support
of Non-US Forces

[table (5 columns and 46 rows of source text) not declassified]

---

208.   National Intelligence Estimate[1]

NIE 4–68   Washington, June 13, 1968.

THE CLANDESTINE INTRODUCTION OF WEAPONS OF MASS DESTRUCTION INTO THE US

The Problem

To assess the capabilities of foreign nations to introduce biological, chemical, or nuclear weapons clandestinely into the US, and to estimate the likelihood of such introduction over the next few years.

Conclusions

A. Virtually any industrial nation could produce biological warfare (BW) and chemical warfare (CW) agents and introduce them clandestinely into the US in relatively small quantities. We do not believe, however, that any potential enemy would plan the clandestine use of BW or CW on a scale sufficient to achieve strategic military objectives. We do not rule out the use of BW or CW for sabotage and other special purposes for which they could be very effective. The relatively small quantities required for these purposes could be covertly produced in the US without great difficulty or risk of detection. Therefore we consider that their clandestine introduction would be unnecessary, and unlikely in view of the risks involved.

---

[1] Source: Johnson Library, National Security File, Intelligence File, Miscellaneous CIA Memoranda [4 of 4], Box 14. Top Secret; Restricted Data. A title page and prefatory note are not printed. According to the prefatory note, the CIA and the intelligence organizations of the Departments of State and Defense, the Atomic Energy Commission, and the National Security Agency participated in the preparation of this estimate. Representatives of the CIA, Department of State, DIA, NSA, and AEC concurred; the FBI representative abstained, the subject being outside his jurisdiction.

B. The Soviets could introduce nuclear weapons clandestinely into the US, and might consider doing so if they planned a deliberate surprise attack on the US. Considering the large numbers of strategic weapons now in their arsenal, however, the Soviets would see the contribution of a clandestine emplacement effort as marginal and would consider any advantages it offered as outweighed by the risks of jeopardizing surprise and of precipitating a US preemptive attack.

C. Because the Chinese have no other means of attacking the US with nuclear weapons, they might consider a clandestine emplacement effort with the object of deterring the US from attack on Communist China. Their capabilities to carry out such an effort, however, are much less than those of the USSR. Moreover, they could not be sure that the US would be deterred and they would have to consider that detection might result in, rather than stave off, a devastating US strike. For these reasons, we think it unlikely that Communist China will attempt to introduce nuclear weapons clandestinely into the US.

D. We have considered the possibility that a third country (e.g., Cuba) might assist the USSR or China in the clandestine introduction of nuclear weapons into the US. We consider this unlikely. We doubt that either the Soviets or the Chinese would seek to enlist the aid of another nation in such a sensitive undertaking. If they should, that nation's leaders would almost certainly react unfavorably to a proposal that could jeopardize their national survival merely to support Soviet or Chinese policy.

Discussion

I. Introduction

1. In considering the clandestine introduction of weapons of mass destruction into the US, enemy leaders would have to weigh any possible advantages against the grave consequences which would follow from discovery. Despite all precautions there would always be risk of detection arising not only from specific US security measures, but also from the chance of US penetration of the clandestine apparatus, the defection of an agent, or sheer accident. The enemy leaders would almost certainly judge that use of this tactic would be regarded by the US as a warlike act, if not as a cause for war, and that it would precipitate an international political crisis of the first magnitude.

2. We believe, therefore, that the range of circumstances in which weapons of mass destruction might be clandestinely introduced into the US is quite narrow—that an enemy nation would consider this course only in the context of planning an attack on the US or of deterring the US from an attack on itself. Smaller stakes would not be worth the risk. Such weapons could not be brought in secretly in sufficient

quantities to have a decisive effect on the outcome of a war. Any plans for their use, we believe, would envision the use of limited quantities to achieve results unattainable by other means.

3. Virtually any industrial nation could produce biological warfare (BW) and chemical warfare (CW) agents and introduce them clandestinely into the US in relatively small quantities. Although small quantities of BW agents could be effective against large targets, the delayed action of such agents makes them unsuitable for use in situations requiring an immediate or precisely timed effect. Relatively large quantities of CW agents are required to obtain effective concentrations over extensive target areas, and it would be difficult to introduce them clandestinely in such quantities. Moreover, the effects of BW and CW agents cannot always be predicted accurately; adverse weather can limit or even prevent the effective use of BW and CW agents against some targets.

4. We do not rule out the use of BW and CW for sabotage and other special purposes for which they could be very effective. But because the relatively small quantities required for these purposes could be covertly produced in the US without great difficulty or risk of detection, we consider that their clandestine introduction would be unnecessary, and therefore unlikely in view of the risks involved. The following discussion, therefore, is limited to a consideration of the clandestine introduction of nuclear weapons.

5. Only four foreign nations—the USSR, the UK, France, and Communist China—have developed and tested nuclear weapons. Beyond these, only India is likely to undertake a nuclear weapons program in the next several years; Israel and Sweden might do so. We can foresee no changes in the world situation so radical as to motivate the UK, France, or any of the potential nuclear powers to attempt to clandestinely introduce nuclear weapons into the US. For this reason, the balance of this discussion will be concerned only with the remaining nuclear powers, the Soviet Union and Communist China.

II. *Soviet and Chinese Capabilities*

6. Both the USSR and Communist China can produce nuclear weapons which could be adapted for clandestine introduction into the US. [11 lines of source text not declassified]

7. Nuclear weapons with weights of up to 1,500–2,000 pounds could be brought across US borders by common means of transport without great difficulty. [1-1/2 lines of source text not declassified] a Chinese weapon could yield [less than 1 line of source text not declassified]. The difficulties and risks of introducing higher yield or heavier weapons into the US, even in a disassembled state, are probably suffi-

ciently great to seriously discourage such attempts. But higher yield weapons could be brought into US waters in merchant ships and detonated without removal from the ship. Such devices could also be carried in by fishing boats or similar small craft to which transfer had been made at sea.

8. Both the USSR and Communist China could make the physical arrangements necessary to bring nuclear weapons secretly into the US, but Soviet capabilities in this respect are much greater than Chinese. We believe that if either country undertook such a program, they would rely on their own agent organizations rather than on political sympathizers in the US. Soviet intelligence services have assigned a high priority to the development of espionage and sabotage capabilities in the US and presumably have formed an organization for the latter purpose. Should the Soviets undertake the clandestine introduction of nuclear weapons, they almost certainly would employ the highly trained and reliable agents of these services. They could also employ diplomatic personnel and could bring in weapons or weapon components under diplomatic cover. The large diplomatic establishments in Canada and Mexico could serve as bases for the operation.

9. There are no Chinese Communist diplomatic establishments in the US, Canada, or Mexico. The absence of such bases precludes the use of diplomatic pouches for the clandestine introduction of nuclear weapons or their components and the use of secure diplomatic communications for planning and control of such an operation; it also makes more difficult the introduction and control of agents. Nevertheless, the Chinese could introduce agents under the guise of bona fide immigrants.

10. In considering Soviet and Chinese capabilities, we have also considered the possibility that a third country (e.g., Cuba) might assist the USSR or China in the clandestine introduction of nuclear weapons into the US. We consider this unlikely on two counts. We doubt that either the Soviets or the Chinese would seek to enlist the aid of another nation in such a sensitive undertaking. And if they should, that nation's leaders would almost certainly react unfavorably to a proposal that could jeopardize their national survival merely to support Soviet or Chinese policy.

III. Strategic Considerations

11. If the Soviets or Communist Chinese have considered the clandestine introduction of nuclear weapons into the US, they have almost certainly been influenced by the same general considerations: the element of risk, the opportunities for clandestine introduction, and the results that could be achieved. The two countries, however, occupy

vastly different strategic positions vis-à-vis the US. Thus, while we believe that neither would consider the use of this tactic except in the context of a possible general war, differing strategic considerations might lead the Soviets and the Chinese to see the clandestine introduction of nuclear weapons in a somewhat different light.

12. *The USSR.* The Soviet leaders, like those of the US, must take account of the possibility of general war in their military planning. In such planning, the Soviets would consider the clandestine introduction of nuclear weapons into the US, if at all, only as a supplement to the main attack by their large strategic attack forces. Because they have already achieved an assured retaliatory capability, they would probably consider a clandestine emplacement effort as potentially useful only in support of a deliberate or preemptive Soviet attack and directed toward delaying or reducing a US retaliatory attack. Possible targets might include important government headquarters, key military command and control facilities, missile detection and tracking radars, and possibly some manned alert forces. The Soviets would recognize, however, that even if such an effort were successful, it could not prevent US retaliation or reduce it to an acceptable level.

13. In considering clandestine attack as a supplement to other weapons, the Soviets would have to weigh their ability to initiate such attack rapidly, with little preparation, and in close coordination with the main weight of attack. Thus, clandestinely introduced weapons would have to be in position at the time the attacks were launched. In the case of a preemptive attack, the circumstances would not allow sufficient time for the introduction and delivery of such weapons after a decision to preempt. To prepare for this contingency beforehand, the Soviets would have to accept the risk of maintaining weapons in the US for an indefinite period of time. These difficulties would not obtain if the USSR decided deliberately to initiate general war in a period of low tension; weapons could be introduced into the US a relatively short time before use. But the Soviets would have to consider the risk of jeopardizing the element of surprise on which this course of action relies, and that discovery might precipitate a US preemptive attack which would be disastrous for the USSR. For these reasons, we think it unlikely that the USSR will attempt to introduce nuclear weapons clandestinely into the US.

14. *Communist China.* The Chinese have no capability at present to attack the US with nuclear weapons. They probably have an ICBM system in the early stages of development, which could become operational several years from now. But they may fear that when it does the US antiballistic missile deployment will have rendered it largely ineffective. In these circumstances, they might see some advantages in clandestinely introducing and emplacing nuclear weapons in the US.

Inasmuch as they could not deliver such an attack on a scale sufficient to achieve a decisive military objective, their object would presumably be to deter the US from a course of action that gravely threatened their national security. Consequently, the most likely targets would be population centers.

15. Clearly, the Chinese would also see grave disadvantages in such a move. So long as the US was unaware of their existence, the concealed weapons would have no effect upon its actions. Indeed, the risk of their discovery would be an ever-present, continuing danger to the Chinese themselves. Once the Chinese announced that nuclear weapons were emplaced in the US, the announcement would touch off an intensive search and extraordinary security measures. Moreover, the Chinese could not be sure that the US would in fact be deterred. On the one hand, the US might consider such an unverified announcement as a mere bluff. On the other it might take the clandestine introduction of such weapons as a casus belli and, having taken such action as it could to safeguard its population, launch a devastating nuclear attack on China. [3 *lines of source text not declassified*] It is conceivable that some Chinese regime might be willing to accept such risks of national destruction, but we think it unlikely.

---

209.   Memorandum From the Deputy Director of Coordination, Bureau of Intelligence and Research (Trueheart) to the Assistant Secretary of State for East Asian and Pacific Affairs (Bundy)[1]

Washington, June 27, 1968.

SUBJECT

Minutes of the Meeting of the 303 Committee, 21 June 1968

The Minutes of the Meeting of the 303 Committee, 21 June 1968, contained the following item:

---

[1] Source: Department of State, INR/IL Historical Files, 303 Committee, January–June 1968. Secret; Eyes Only.

708 Foreign Relations, 1964–1968, Volume X

"7. The Asia Foundation

a. Mr. Meyer called to the committee's attention the financial predicament of The Asia Foundation, [*1 line of source text not declassified*]. Mr. Rostow felt that the Board of Directors contained some movers and shakers and wondered if they had done all they could to raise money in the private sector. He also felt that both State and AID should be told of the relative high priority of this project and should not be allowed to treat it as a routine item.

b. Mr. Bohlen indicated that he would discuss the matter with William Bundy and a meeting at State had been scheduled on The Asia Foundation for Thursday, 27 June 1968.[2]

c. [*3-1/2 lines of source text not declassified*] Since State and/or AID support may or may not constitute line items in their respective budgets, this is susceptible to congressional cuts. Thus, no one can accurately predict what, if any, federal monies will be allocated; this completes the vicious circle with potential Foundation support remaining in the wings until the picture is clearer.

d. If there were deep sighs for the good old days of straight covert funding, they were not audible due to the hum of the air conditioner in the White House Situation Room."

---

[2] No record of this meeting has been found.

210.   Draft Memorandum From Secretary of Defense Clifford to President Johnson[1]

Washington, July 29, 1968.

SUBJECT

Strategic Offensive and Defensive Forces (U)

We have reviewed our Strategic Offensive and Defensive Forces for FY 70–74 and reached the following major conclusions:

1. Against the expected Soviet threat, our present strategic offensive forces provide a more than adequate Assured Destruction capability.

2. The program that we are recommending not only assures that we maintain our Assured Destruction capability, but provides timely and efficient options to meet the designed Greater-Than-Expected (GTE) Soviet threat to our deterrent throughout the FY 70–77 planning period.

3. Achieving a strategically significant Damage Limiting capability against the Soviet Union does not appear to be feasible with current technology and in relation to its cost and the other demands on our resources.

4. The Soviet program appears to reflect a similar conclusion about the feasibility of taking away our deterrent.

5. We will continue to maintain strategic "nuclear superiority" over the Soviets in terms of nuclear warheads. Based on our own experience, however, we doubt that this superiority can be converted into meaningful political power, particularly now that the Soviet Union also has a large and well-protected Assured Destruction capability.

6. We cannot depend on our nuclear forces alone to fulfill our nation's commitments and insure our national security; we must also maintain very strong nonnuclear forces.

7. Based on our view of U.S. security needs, and without considering the implications of possible arms control agreements that might result from discussions with the Soviets, we recommend:

---

[1] Source: Washington National Records Center, OASD/ISA Files: FRC 330 72 A 1499, 320.2 1968 June–July. Top Secret. The memorandum is marked "For Comment Draft" within the Department of Defense. It is attached to a July 29 memorandum from Acting Secretary of Defense Nitze to the Director of Defense Research and Engineering and four Assistant Secretaries of Defense, among others, informing them that he was also sending copies to the Chairman of the JCS and the Secretaries of the Military Departments for comments. For the response of the Joint Chiefs of Staff, see Document 213.

a. Maintaining a land-based ICBM force of 1,000 Minuteman and a slowly decreasing number of Titan IIs.

b. Continuing development of Poseidon and maintaining the previous schedule for converting 31 Polaris submarines to the Poseidon configuration.

c. Maintaining the effectiveness of the programmed strategic bomber force—reaching 281 B-52s and 253 FB-111s in FY 72—by developing and, when needed, procuring advanced weapons and penetration devices as protection against possible advanced Soviet bomber defenses.

d. Continuing the previously approved Continental Air Defense Plan to introduce the Airborne Warning and Control System (AWACS), give the F-106 interceptor the most modern fire control and missile system available, add Over-The-Horizon (OTH) radars for complete peacetime surveillance, and phase down the remaining interceptors and most of the ground-based radar and control systems.

e. Continuing the deployment of the Sentinel system but reorienting the program so that procurement funds for only one site need be obligated in FY 69.

Specific recommendations are discussed in Section V. Financial and force summaries follow.

Total Obligational Authority[a]
($ Millions)

	FY 69	FY 70	FY 71	FY 72	FY 73	FY 74[b]	Total FY 70–74
Strategic Offense							
Previously Approved	8,340	8,598	6,607	5,817	4,867	4,533	30,422
SecDef Recommended		8,541	6,578	5,827	4,904	4,634	30,484
JCS Proposed		10,182	10,040	10,798	10,277	9,679	50,976
Strategic Defense							
Previously Approved	3,609	4,528	4,684	3,713	3,770	2,861	19,556
SecDef Recommended		3,906	4,374	3,581	3,611	3,349	18,821
JCS Proposed		5,706	7,981	7,579	7,831	6,683	35,780
Totals							
Previously Approved	11,949	13,126	11,291	9,530	8,637	7,394	49,978
SecDef Recommended		12,447	10,952	9,408	8,515	7,983	49,305
JCS Proposed		15,888	18,021	18,377	18,108	16,362	86,756

---

[a] Includes all primary program costs and allocated support costs, excluding programs 3, 6, and 9.

[b] Previously Approved FY 74 figures are projections included to make the totals comparable.

[Here follow 3 pages of additional tables.]

I. The General Nuclear War Problem

The main objective of our nuclear forces is to deter nuclear attacks on the United States. Our ability to strike back and destroy Soviet society makes a Soviet decision to strike the United States highly unlikely. By developing and deploying forces that are difficult to attack we can reduce even more the likelihood of such an attack. Unable to destroy most of our nuclear striking power, the Soviets would gain little by striking first.

Although the United States and the Soviet Union are strongly deterred from nuclear attacks on each other, a nuclear war anywhere in the world could lead to a war—and most likely a nuclear war—between the two countries. To avoid a nuclear war with the Soviet Union, we try to make all nuclear wars unlikely. This objective includes:

1. Maintaining control of our forces in a crisis.
2. Deterring nuclear attacks on or intimidation of allied or neutral countries.
3. Discouraging additional countries from acquiring nuclear weapons.
4. Emphasizing and maintaining the firebreak between conventional and nuclear weapons.

To deter a first-strike nuclear attack, both we and the Soviets maintain the ability to strike back and destroy the other's society. When they take steps to reduce the damage that we can inflict—for example, by deploying Anti-Ballistic Missiles (ABMs)—we react to offset these steps. The Soviets would undoubtedly react in the same way to similar U.S. steps to limit significantly damage to ourselves.

Our analysis shows that the Soviets can protect their second strike capability against any threat we might pose. Since a second strike capability is vital to the Soviets, they will insure the survival of this capability. Convinced that the Soviets would counter a major U.S. attempt to take away their second strike capability, we see no effective way to implement, with present technology and within available resources, a major Damage Limiting program against them, although we are continuing development work that might eventually support such a program.

These considerations lead us to put primary reliance upon deterrence to keep the Soviet Union from attacking us. [*less than 1 line of source text not declassified*] on the other hand, we can buy an effective defense of CONUS as insurance against a failure of deterrence. [*less than 1 line of source text not declassified*] allow us to develop an effective defense against her nuclear attack capability into the 1980s.

What if deterrence fails and a nuclear war with the Soviet Union occurs? If the war began with an all-out Soviet attack, including our cities, we would reply in kind. If the war started with less than an all-out attack, we would want to carry out plans for the controlled and deliberate use of our nuclear power to achieve the best possible outcome. The lack of such nuclear war plans is still a continuing weakness in our present posture.

II. Soviet and Chinese Strategic Forces

The following table shows the National Intelligence Estimate (NIE) of Soviet intercontinental forces.

Soviet Intercontinental Nuclear Forces

	1968	1970	1972
Ballistic Missile Launchers			
Soft ICBMs	128-142	90- 128	—
Hard ICBMs	720-782	859-1,026	1,020-1,251
FOBS	0- 10	20- 50	20- 75
Mobile ICBMs (Non-add)	—	(0- 25)	(0- 100)
SLBMs	43- 46	123- 158	267- 318
Total Launchers	891-980	1,092-1,362	1,307-1,644
Intercontinental Bombers	150-155	130- 150	105- 130

A new solid-fueled Soviet missile has been identified. Present intelligence estimates assume it is an ICBM, which will come into the Soviet inventory as a supplement to (rather than as a replacement for) the SS-11.

The Soviets have continued to test Fractional Orbit Ballistic Systems (FOBS). If we took no counter actions, these systems would be useful in an attempt to deny timely warning to our strategic bombers.

The Soviet Union is now making operational a new class of large, nuclear-powered, ballistic missile submarines which carry 16 missiles with a range of about 1,000 nautical miles (nm). Intelligence estimates project that 10 to 13 of these boats will be in service by mid-1971, and 35 to 42 by 1976.

The Soviets are also engaged in a continuing effort to improve their strategic defenses. They have modified and improved the capabilities of the SA-2 air defense missile system; they are developing and producing a series of new interceptor aircraft; they are deploying the SA-5 air defense missile system; and they are in the advanced stages of constructing a ballistic missile defense system around Moscow. The intelligence community estimates that the Soviets have a formidable capability against medium to high-altitude air threats, a limited capability against low-altitude air threats, and probably little or no capability against ballistic missiles.

The SA-5 system is being deployed in all important areas of the Soviet Union. It has two to five firing sites per complex. Each site has six launchers [2 *lines of source text not declassified*]. In addition, the system may have some capability against ballistic missiles, although this now appears unlikely.

The ballistic missile defense system around Moscow with about 100 launchers may be fully operational by 1971. It is believed to be a long range, exoatmospheric system using large yield warheads.

We still have seen no evidence of Soviet development of a good low-altitude Surface-to-Air Missile (SAM). However, the new Foxbat interceptor is now estimated to have a "look-down, shoot-down" capability.

The Chinese were expected to begin operational deployment of a Medium Range Ballistic Missile (MRBM) with a fission warhead in 1967, but they did not do so. China also has under development a much larger and more complex missile system, possibly an ICBM. They were expected to complete a facility for large launchers late in 1967, but they did not. It appears that they are at least nine months behind the ICBM schedule that we previously estimated. However, this delay would still allow an initial operational ICBM deployment as early as 1972.

III. Assured Destruction

We deter a rational enemy from launching a first strike against us by maintaining a strong and secure ability to retaliate under any circumstances. We measure our second strike capability in terms of Assured Destruction—the ability to inflict unacceptable damage, calculated under extremely conservative assumptions, on the attacker, even after a surprise attack. Our ability to [3-1/2 *lines of source text not declassified*].

However, our Assured Destruction capability does not indicate how we would use our forces in a nuclear war. We must design our forces to cope with many situations, including a war which neither side intended. We reduce the likelihood of such a war by keeping tight control over U.S. forces under all circumstances; by maintaining communications at all times with our forces, the governments of our allies, and, as appropriate, our enemies; and by having the options to choose an appropriate response. If we failed to deter nuclear war, we would want to be able to follow a policy of limiting our retaliatory strikes to the enemy's military targets and not attacking his cities if he refrained from attacking ours. In most situations we would have many missiles surviving to attack Soviet military targets, while withholding enough for [*less than 1 line of source text not declassified*]. For this task, missile accuracy is very worthwhile.

In measuring the capability of our forces, we cannot simply count total megatons or delivery systems, we must measure the amount of damage each side could do to the cities, population, industry, and military forces of the other. Factors such as accuracy, reliability, survivability, defense penetrability, and control are often much more important than warhead size in determining damage levels. The relative importance of these factors depends heavily on the attack objectives and the characteristics of the target system attacked. And, of course, the relative costs of additional weapons, yield (megatonnage), accuracy, survivability, reliability, and penetrability also affect how much of each of these factors should be bought to achieve any particular level of destructive capacity.

The next table illustrates the relative effectiveness of equal payloads of alternate warheads used against Soviet targets. It compares [3-1/2 lines of source text not declassified].

[table (3 columns and 13 rows of source text) not declassified]

As the table shows, comparisons of missile launchers or megatons are not very meaningful. If a single imput must be used as a measure, however, the best indicator of the relative capabilities of our forces is the number of weapons they can deliver. While the Soviet forces may exceed ours in megatons by 1972, the Soviets still cannot take away our Assured Destruction capability, largely because we will maintain a commanding lead in the number of weapons available and because our forces are relatively invulnerable to a Soviet first strike.

The following table compares the weapons, megatons, and megaton equivalents of the U.S. and Soviet forces.

U.S. and Soviet Intercontinental Nuclear Forces[a]

	1968 U.S.	1968 Soviet	1970 U.S.	1970 Soviet	1972 U.S.	1972 Soviet
Total Force Loadings						
Weapons	[*]	1,200	[*]	1,300-1,600	[*]	1,500-1,800
Megatons	[*]	6,000-6,400	[*]	6,400-8,300	[*]	6,000-8,900
1 MT Equivalents	[*]	2,300-2,400	[*]	2,500-3,100	[*]	2,500-3,300
Alert Force Loadings						
Weapons	[*]	600-700	[*]	800-1,000	[*]	1,000-1,200
Megatons	[*]	3,700-4,000	[*]	4,200-5,700	[*]	4,400-6,600
1 MT Equivalents	[*]	1,300-1,400	[*]	1,500-1,900	[*]	1,700-2,300

[*entry in table not declassified]

[a] Shows the U.S. programmed force and the NIE for the Soviet force. (The table will be updated when NIE 11–8–68 is available.) [NIE 11–8–68 is Docuement 217.]

A. *Against the Expected Soviet Threat*

Against the expected Soviet threat, our strategic forces can survive a well-executed Soviet surprise attack and carry out an effective second strike. [*2-1/2 lines of source text not declassified*]

How much damage these surviving weapons could cause depends on the effectiveness of Soviet defenses. Against the high NIE-estimated threat, the U.S. Assured Destruction capability would kill more than [*less than 1 line of source text not declassified*] of the Soviet people in every year through 1977. This is far above the [*less than 1 line of source text not declassified*] we believe is needed to deter a Soviet first strike.

B. *Against China*

While China may be able to threaten her neighbors and U.S. bases in Asia by 1970, she will not pose a threat to the U.S. second strike capability. [*6 lines of source text not declassified*]

[*1 paragraph (4-1/2 lines of source text) not declassified*]

C. *Against the Greater-Than-Expected Soviet Threat*

The vital importance of our Assured Destruction capability to our national security requires us to be prepared to cope with Soviet strategic threats greater than those which the NIE projects. While unlikely, the Soviets might add a very extensive ABM defense or much improved anti-bomber defenses. They might improve their ICBM force by putting accurate Multiple Independently-targetable Re-entry Vehicles (MIRVs) on the SS-9, or by replacing or improving the SS-11 with a new, more accurate ICBM. Conceivably, they might take all these actions. In order to test the adequacy of our forces under the worst conceivable conditions, we have designed what we call a "Greater-Than-Expected" threat. This threat includes all of the above offensive and defensive actions plus others which the Soviets might undertake in an effort to take away our Assured Destruction capability. The following table compares the 1977 balanced GTE threat, used in the following analyses, with the NIE threat.

	NIE Threat	GTE Threat
Offensive Missiles		
Independently-targetable		
Missile Warheads On Line	1,500-2,200	7,000-9,100
Exoatmospheric Aim Points[a]	1,500-2,200	31,000
Air Defenses		
Look-Down Fighters	300- 400	600
Low-Altitude SAM Launchers	0-2,700	6,100
ABM Launchers		
Area	400-2,000	2,400
Terminal[b]	100-1,300	6,100

[a] Targets for long-range ABMs.
[b] Includes launchers in the Moscow system.

Soviet programs required to support such an effort would be technically difficult, expensive, and, since we have clearly indicated we would respond, hold little hope of providing the Soviets with a net gain in effective first strike capability. Nevertheless, to insure that these threats remain unlikely, and to maintain our deterrent should they appear, we make sure that we have the options needed to counter them.

The Soviet Union, by replacing or improving the accuracy of its SS-11s and adding accurate MIRVs to its SS-9s, could destroy Minuteman missiles in their silos. Even if the Soviets could destroy all Minuteman missiles, however, they would not eliminate our Assured Destruction capability. Our remaining Sea-Launched Ballistic Missiles (SLBMs) and alert bomber force can penetrate the NIE-estimated Soviet defenses and kill at [less than 1 line of source text not declassified]. Putting [number not declassified] Mk-3s on each Poseidon and increasing the bomber alert to [less than 1 line of source text not declassified] against the greater-than-expected offensive threat through 1977.

Similarly, at least through 1976, a very extensive Soviet ABM system and air defense, without greater-than-expected ICBMs, would still let the U.S. programmed force maintain an Assured Destruction capability of [less than 1 line of source text not declassified]. Our programmed force can cope with a greater-than-expected Soviet ABM system because we already have programmed ABM hedges— Poseidon plus MIRVs and penetration aids for Minuteman.

By putting [number not declassified] Mk-3s on each Poseidon missile and increasing the bomber alert rate, the U.S. programmed force can keep its Assured Destruction capability through FY 77, even if the

Soviets deploy greater-than-expected, balanced missile and bomber defenses (without improving their offensive forces). We do not have to exercise these options now to meet this threat.

Only against a combined greater-than-expected Soviet ABM, air defense, and accurate ICBM force, costing the Soviets $20 to $30 billion above the high NIE, would we need major new additions to our retaliatory forces. The following table shows the effect of the combined greater-than-expected Soviet offensive and defensive threat on our Assured Destruction capability. It indicates the U.S. programmed force capability and the effects of developing and deploying Poseidon decoys, increasing the bomber alert rate to 60%, and buying advanced bomber penetration aids. The JCS-recommended inventories of [*number not declassified*] Unit Equipment (UE) Short Range Attack Missiles (SRAMs) and [*number not declassified*] UE Subsonic Cruise Armed Decoys (SCADs) are used.

[*table (9 columns and 3 rows of source text) not declassified*]

As the table shows, while the combined GTE threat would call for a more effective U.S. Assured Destruction capability for FY 74, we can maintain our Assured Destruction against this threat without buying any new missiles or bombers. We can do this by using technological advances that greatly increase the penetration capability of our Poseidon and bomber payloads.

We have, however, three main reasons for wanting additional options to maintain our Assured Destruction capability against the GTE threat. First, we do not want to rely primarily on alert bombers which depend on tactical warning for survival. Second, depending on how far ABM technology advances, we may not want to depend on decoys for missile penetration. Third, unless we protect our land-based missile force, the greater-than-expected Soviet offense could destroy it in its silos. In such a case, we should either protect Minuteman or phase it out, since a vulnerable missile force encourages—rather than deters—a first strike. We do not need to buy protection for our land-based missiles until we see the threat, since we can rely on bombers and Poseidon in the interim.

As discussed below, we propose to develop and maintain a number of options to allow us to keep our Assured Destruction capability against the GTE threat, even though this threat is not likely to appear. Since the threat is unlikely, we should select options with small initial costs. If later evidence does not rule out the threat, we can then develop these options fully. Because of uncertainties about the performance and cost of new systems, it is usually unwise to deploy them as replacements for proven, existing systems until a threat appears which cannot be economically met by improving the existing systems.

Once an option has been developed, however, we examine it to see if it would be an economical replacement for part of the programmed force. In some cases, advances in technology permit us to save money by replacing an existing system with a new one, even though the new system does not provide more total effectiveness than the one it replaces.

D. *Options to Protect Our Assured Destruction Capability*

Discussed below are the principal options which we have available to protect our Assured Destruction capability against the GTE threat.

1. *Increase Warheads on Poseidon*

[1 paragraph (4 lines of source text) not declassified]

2. *Add Terminal Penetration Aids for Poseidon*

We could develop terminal decoys for Poseidon. These decoys would aid in penetrating large ABM defenses if the threat to our land-based missile forces became severe. By initiating development in FY 70, we could equip all Poseidon with decoys by FY 75. The development costs would be $200 million in FY 70–73 and the procurement costs would be $250 million in FY 73–74.

3. *Improve our Bomber Force*

If Soviet air defenses improved, but their ABM capability did not, no increase in the size or expense of our strategic forces would be necessary. However, if the Soviet ABM threat became greater than the highest NIE, we might wish to respond by increasing the capability of our bomber force. Increasing the alert rate to 60% would cost about $190 million per year. By doing this, buying the JCS-recommended inventories of SRAM and SCAD, and putting penetration aids on Poseidon, we could maintain our Assured Destruction capability, as shown above.

Although we would not want to rely only on the bomber force, the next table shows the Assured Destruction capability of an improved bomber force used alone against the GTE threat. Against balanced terminal and area defenses, we could add a mixture of SRAMs, which are better against terminal defenses, and SCADs, which are better against area defenses. The SCADs could act as bomber decoys, carry nuclear warheads, or both. Contract Definition in FY 70 would lead to an Initial Operational Capability (IOC) in FY 74. The 10-year systems cost of the improved bomber force considered below would be $2.1 to $2.6 billion more than that of the presently programmed force, excluding the cost of increasing the alert rate.

U.S. Assured Destruction Capability of Improved Bomber Force
Against the GTE Soviet Threat[a]

	FY 70	FY 71	FY 72	FY 73	FY 74	FY 75	FY 76	FY 77
SRAM (UE)	150	450	1,000	1,545	1,545	1,545	1,545	1,545
Cruise Missiles (UE)[b]	—	—	—	—	700	1,400	2,100	2,700
Bombers Alone in an Assured Destruction Scenario (Percent of Soviet Deaths)[c]	25%	25%	21%	15%	24%	24%	23%	22%

[a] Adding SRAMs and cruise missiles plus increasing the alert rate to 60%.

[b] All cruise missiles are assumed to have warheads, and [*number not declassified*] of them are effective as bomber decoys.

[c] [*1-1/2 lines of source text not declassified*]

As the table shows, by buying and arming more SCADs than recommended by the JCS, we could maintain a substantial bombers-only Assured Destruction capability against the GTE threat through FY 77 simply by improving the programmed force. Thus, an Advanced Manned Strategic Aircraft (AMSA) is not needed. We would deploy AMSA only if an AMSA force of equal effectiveness costs less than the improved programmed force. Such a force would require about 138 AMSAs and would cost $4.9 billion more than the improved programmed force in FY 69–78. Thus, we do not need to maintain an option to deploy AMSA by FY 77.

Considerations other than cost also make an AMSA force less attractive than improving the programmed force. First, developing AMSA requires a longer lead-time than deploying SRAMs and cruise missiles on the programmed force and thus imposes a substantial initial investment before we could determine that an increased Soviet threat has developed. Second, if we decide to proceed with AMSA now and the GTE threat does not appear, we will have spent $3 to $10 billion unnecessarily. Third, we do not yet know whether AMSA should be designed primarily as a penetrating aircraft or primarily to carry stand-off cruise missiles, nor do we know the value of supersonic speed and advanced avionics. Starting AMSA now, before we have resolved these issues, could force us to make costly changes later.

4. *Improving Minuteman*

We have a development program designed to test [*less than 1 line of source text not declassified*] which could provide replacements for the present [*less than 1 line of source text not declassified*] or accommodate additional Minuteman or a new ICBM. The complete development of each silo would cost $260 million and provide an IOC in FY 74. Procurement costs would be $4.5 million per silo and the deployment rate would be 200 missiles per year.

As a hedge against a heavy Soviet ABM system, we could replace all the Minuteman II by Minuteman III/MIRV at a cost of $2.2 billion over the present program. In addition, we could add penetration aids to all Minuteman III.

5. *Defend Minuteman*

A defense of the programmed Minuteman force could use the same components being developed for the Sentinel system: Sprint, Spartan, Perimeter Acquisition Radar (PAR), and Missile Site Radar (MSR). An option for a light defense of Minuteman is being maintained in the current Sentinel deployment plan. This light defense, although not increasing the number of Minuteman surviving a heavy Soviet attack, might show our determination to protect Minuteman and indicate that we would expand the defense if the threat grew larger. In a less than all-out attack on Minuteman (about 1,200 reliable, accurate re-entry vehicles), the light defense could save about 300 Minuteman missiles. The median defense would be an expansion of the light defense to defend more Minuteman and could be supplemented with additional Minuteman III in hard rock silos. The ABM defense and hard rock silos would insure enough Minuteman surviving against large MIRVs on the SS-9 to maintain, together with our other forces, our Assured Destruction capability. The heavy defense of Minuteman would maintain our Assured Destruction capability even against a Soviet small-MIRV threat. The table on the next page summarizes the three levels of defense.

Levels of Minuteman Defense

Defense	Sprints	Spartans	MSRs	Defense Investment Cost[a] ($ Billions)	Level-Off Annual Operations Cost[a] ($ Millions)
Light	320	120	4	$0.4	$ 30
Median (With Hard Rock Silos)	1,480	120	15	3.9[b]	310
Heavy	2,220	120	15	4.4	380

[a] Assumes the deployment of Sentinel. Fifty-six Sprints, 120 Spartans, and four MSRs are deployed as part of Sentinel.

[b] Does not include the cost of hard rock silos.

6. *Add Poseidon Submarines*

We could order more Poseidon submarines with missiles which requires a $290 million investment per ship and a four-year lead-time. By initiating procurement in FY 70 we could have 10 new Poseidon submarines by the end of FY 76 and 20 by the end of FY 77. With terminal penetration aids added to the whole Poseidon force, fewer new submarines would be needed.

7. *New ICBM*

Beginning Contract Definition in FY 70 would permit an IOC for a new ICBM in FY 76. We could deploy this new missile in new silos as part of a defended or undefended fixed land-based system. Conversely, we could deploy it as a land-mobile or ship-based system or base it in a new class of submarines called the Undersea Long-range Missile System (ULMS). Developing a new ICBM would require a $2 to $3 billion research and development program. The 10-year cost of buying 280 new ICBMs totals about $9 billion.

The next table compares the costs of these alternatives to the costs of other missile options designed to maintain our Assured Destruction capability against the GTE Soviet threat in 1977.

Costs of Various Missile Options To Protect the U.S. Assured Destruction Capability Against the GTE Soviet Threat[a]

	$ Billions	
	R&D	10-Year System Cost[b]
Defense of Minuteman		
Threat A[c]	$0	$ 7
Threat B[d]	0	8
Additional Minuteman in Hard Rock Silos		
Threat A	.3	12
Threat B	.3	10
New ICBM		
Threat A	2.6	14
Threat B	2.6	12
20 Additional Poseidon Submarines	0	14
5 Additional Poseidon Submarines		
With Decoys on All Poseidon	.2	3
12 ULMS Submarines	2.0	13
3 ULMS Submarines With Decoys on All		
ULMS and Poseidon	2.2	5

[a] Costs are over and above the cost of programmed forces with [*number not declassified*] Mk-3s on programmed Poseidon and an increased bomber alert rate.

[b] Includes Research and Development (R&D) costs.

[c] Threat A is the basic GTE threat. It has six [*less than 1 line of source text not declassified*] MIRVs on an improved SS-9.

[d] Threat B is a response to our deployment of ABM defenses. It has 11 [*less than 1 line of source text not declassified*] MIRVs on an improved SS-9.

We have many options to meet the GTE threat that do not require a major effort now. Adding five Poseidon boats and terminal decoys on all Poseidon is clearly the least expensive option. If we start a decoy development program now, the development time for the decoys would be about two and one-half years, and it would take another one and one-half years to deploy them on the programmed Poseidon force. We could then make a decision next year on adding more submarines and still meet the GTE threat.

The Soviets might deploy an improved ICBM force, alone or as part of a combined GTE threat, capable of destroying Minuteman. In some situations, a vulnerable Minuteman force might invite rather than deter an attack. In this case we could phase out Minuteman and rely on Poseidon for our Assured Destruction capability. However, it is desirable to maintain some land-based missiles as a hedge against unexpected threats to the Poseidon force, such as Soviet advances in Anti-Submarine Warfare (ASW) capability.

To protect the land-based missile force, we can defend Minuteman with an ABM system at less cost than we can add hard rock silos for Minuteman. None of the new ICBMs has a clear cost advantage over defending Minuteman with an ABM system or putting Minuteman in hard rock silos until we need a much larger surviving payload to penetrate a Soviet ABM system that is much stronger than the one we envision as part of the GTE threat.

Not only is it cheaper to protect our land-based missile force with an ABM system alone (compared to a mix of ABM defense and hard rock silos), but it is much cheaper in the early years. However, we would not want to rely only on an ABM system. We are uncertain about the effectiveness of a heavy ABM defense against a heavy attack and the sensitivity of an ABM defense to larger numbers of smaller yield MIRVs and penetration aids. We would need lower levels of ABM defense and smaller numbers of hard rock silos if we deployed a combination of these two to hedge against a greater variation in threat. This suggests the following decision strategy: (1) maintain an option to proceed with an ABM defense of Minuteman (decision in CY 69, initial funding in FY 71) which could be expanded as the threat increased; (2) if the threat becomes more severe, stop expanding the ABM defense and plan on deploying 100 Minuteman IIIs in hard rock silos in FY 77; and (3) reduce near term costs for hard rock silo development to fit this schedule and to allow more time to find out how hard the silos actually prove to be.

IV. Strategic Defense

A. Damage Limiting Against the Soviet Threat

Our ability to strike back and destroy Soviet society, even under conditions and assumptions favorable to the Soviets, makes any kind of nuclear war with the Soviets unlikely. Thus, we first buy forces to give us high confidence in our deterrent. As insurance in the unlikely event deterrence fails, we then consider adding forces that might reduce damage to our population and industry. Since we have offensive forces available for attacking military targets, the basic Damage Limiting issue is whether we should deploy Nike-X in defense of our cities.

A defensive system to save U.S. cities from a Soviet nuclear attack must attempt to keep ahead of the Soviet threat, including their reactions to our deployment. Such attempts are costly. In our analyses we use two stages in such a deployment.[2] The first, "Posture A," is an initial step recommended by the JCS. It represents an area defense of CONUS and a light defense of 25 cities. It would cost about $12 billion in investment and $900 million a year to operate. The second, "Posture B," is an attempt to keep ahead of the threat. It includes a higher density local defense of 52 cities. It would cost about $20 billion in investment and over $1.2 billion a year to operate. For Posture B we would also need improved air and civil defenses and ASW forces at an additional cost of $4 to $5 billion in investment. We believe the pursuit of effective defenses would eventually cost much more. Our commitment would be open-ended.

The United States can justify these costs only if they could limit significantly the ability of the Soviets to kill Americans. Our attempt to limit damage if our deterrent fails also operates to take away the Soviet deterrent. The following table shows what happens if the defense works and the Soviets do not react.

---

[2] Because the language in the rest of this section is very similar to that presented in Enthoven and Smith, *How Much Is Enough?*, pp. 188–190, it is likely that these paragraphs and tables (not to mention much of the rest of the document) were drafted in the Systems Analysis Office headed by Assistant Secretary of Defense Enthoven. The two tables in the book (pp. 189–190) and the authors' account provide additional information on a U.S. first strike (ibid., passim). Secretary McNamara's statement to the Senate Armed Services Committee on February 2, 1968, also includes a table of U.S. and Soviet fatalities for both a Soviet first strike and a U.S. first strike in the mid-1970s. See *Authorization for Military Procurement, Research and Development, Fiscal Year 1969, and Reserve Strength: Hearings Before the Committee on Armed Services, United States Senate, Ninetieth Congress, Second Session* (Washington: Government Printing Office, 1968), pp. 122 ff.

Deaths In an All-Out Strategic Nuclear Exchange in 1977,
Assuming No Soviet Reaction to a U.S. ABM System
(In Millions)

U.S. Program	Soviets Strike First, U.S. Retaliates		U.S. Strikes First, Soviets Retaliate		Soviet Assured Destruction Calculation
	U.S. Killed	Soviet Killed	U.S. Killed	Soviet Killed	
No ABM	120	[*]	120	[*]	[*]
Sentinel	90	[*]	100	[*]	[*]
Posture A	40	[*]	40	[*]	[*]
Posture B	10	[*]	10	[*]	[*]

[*entry in table not declassified]

As the table shows, the Soviets lose their deterrent if they do not respond. They would be forced to react to increase their ability to strike back. The Soviets have the technological and economic capability to respond in many ways by: (1) adding MIRVs and penetration aids to their projected missile inventories; (2) adding a mobile ICBM, the SS-Z-2; (3) adding a new, higher payload, mobile missile; (4) deploying additional SLBMs; (5) defending all or a portion of their ICBM force; (6) launching all or a portion of their ICBM force on warning; (7) adding more bombers; or (8) some combinations of these responses. Against Posture A, the Soviets must respond with at least 100 new mobile ICBMs or an equivalent force in order to maintain their Assured Destruction capability; against Posture B, they must respond with at least 500 new mobile ICBMs or an equivalent force. These responses, while restoring their Assured Destruction capability, also restore their ability to kill Americans in a first strike. The table below shows what happens if the Soviets do respond.

Deaths In an All-Out Strategic Nuclear Exchange in 1977,
Assuming a Soviet Reaction to a U.S. ABM System
(In Millions)

U.S. Program	Soviets Strike First, U.S. Retaliates		U.S. Strikes First, Soviets Retaliate		Soviet Assured Destruction Calculation
	U.S. Killed	Soviet Killed	U.S. Killed	Soviet Killed	
No ABM	120	[*]	120	[*]	[*]
Sentinel	100	[*]	110	[*]	[*]
Posture A	90	[*]	100	[*]	[*]
Posture B	90	[*]	90	[*]	[*]

[*entry in table not declassified]

As part of their response, the Soviets could add large numbers of offensive missiles, which would threaten our Assured Destruction capability. We, in turn, would have to react. Viewing each other's buildup in forces as an increased threat, each side would take counteracting steps, generating a costly arms race with no net gain in security for either side.

The above tables also show an important and paradoxical result regarding first strikes. The number of U.S. killed when the Soviet Union strikes first is less than or equal to the number of U.S. killed when the United States strikes first. The main reason for this is that there are two opposing effects in a strategic nuclear exchange. On the one hand, the country that strikes first can destroy a large number of the other's bombers and missiles on the ground, thereby limiting retaliatory damage to itself. On the other hand, the country that strikes second, facing an enemy that has partially disarmed himself, is likely to concentrate on attacking cities with its surviving force because there is little to be gained by firing back at empty missile silos and air bases. In the past, when neither side had a significant second strike force, the country that struck first could expect to achieve some strategic advantage. Now, however, the United States and the Soviet Union have reached a point where both have a large, hard-to-attack second strike force. Therefore, the country that now strikes first may destroy some of the other's weapons, but by freeing all of the enemy's remaining weapons to strike its own cities, it more than compensates for the enemy weapons it destroys and loses more than it gains. This result strengthens our belief that neither the United States nor the Soviet Union stands to benefit by striking first.

B. Damage Limiting Against the Chinese Threat

There has been evidence that the Chinese are devoting very substantial resources to the development of both nuclear warheads and missile delivery systems. Within a period of less than three years, they successfully detonated six nuclear devices. Last December, they detonated a seventh device, but this test was apparently a partial failure. These seven nuclear tests, together with their continuing work on surface-to-surface missiles, lead us to believe that they are moving ahead with the development of an ICBM. Indeed, if their program proceeds at its present pace (although there is some evidence it has been delayed) they could have a modest force of ICBMs by the mid-1970s.

The reasons for deploying an ABM system against the Chinese are: (1) it would prevent damage to the United States in a Chinese first strike; (2) it could increase the credibility of our commitments to defend Asian countries against Chinese nuclear intimidation or nuclear attack; and (3) it could lessen China's ability to drag the United States and the Soviet Union into a nuclear war. In addition, a defense against a light and unsophisticated Chinese threat would not deprive the Soviet Union of its Assured Destruction capability.

On the other hand, we already have a massive deterrent against a Chinese attack. A Chinese-oriented ABM system might enhance the prestige of the Chinese nuclear program and reduce confidence in the ability of our offensive forces to deter attacks on our allies. Further, it might suggest that we think the Chinese would act irrationally when many believe they would not. Leaving Asia and our Asian bases exposed, this system might suggest that the United States is retreating from Asia to a "Fortress America." Finally, it might keep Asian countries from adhering to a nonproliferation treaty by drawing attention to the threat and causing them to raise demands for their own defense, possibly as a step toward developing their own offensive nuclear capability.

On balance, however, we believe the advantages of a Chinese-oriented ABM system outweigh the disadvantages. Thus, deployment of the Sentinel system was initiated in September 1967.

We do not have to depend on deterrence alone to keep the Chinese from attacking us. The Sentinel system can be deployed at an investment cost of about $5 to $6 billion and should be highly effective against the kind of threat the Chinese may pose in the 1970s. The effectiveness of this deployment in reducing U.S. deaths from a Chinese attack in the 1970s is shown below.

[table (5 columns and 3 rows of source text) not declassified]

[1 paragraph (4 lines of source text) not declassified]

C. Conclusions

Our analysis of the ABM system and its relationship to our strategic offensive forces leads us to conclude that:

1. The Soviets can substantially offset any Damage Limiting measures we might undertake, provided they are determined to maintain their deterrent against us. Thus, we should not deploy Nike-X to defend our cities against Soviet attacks.

2. We should deploy Sentinel, an effective defense of our cities against an unsophisticated Chinese ICBM attack. The nature of this decision makes the program sensitive to threat and cost. Since the Chinese appear to be behind in the ICBM development schedule by as much as one year over what we predicted last year, we can somewhat delay the Sentinel deployment schedule and thereby reduce FY 69–70 expenditures.

The estimated investment cost for the Sentinel program has increased by about $1 billion since the deployment decision was made. This has occurred while Sentinel is still in the planning stage and has not yet experienced the design changes and cost increases that normally result from testing a new system. By delaying the development schedule oriented to deployment of a prototype battery, we can provide time to analyze the reasons for rising costs and attempt to find ways to reduce costs.

3. An ABM defense of Minuteman is the cheapest option to insure the survivability of the Minuteman force. We should maintain the option for the defense of Minuteman using Sentinel components, while continuing the hard rock silo research and development program at a reduced level. A Sentinel delay now would still allow an ABM defense of Minuteman by FY 74.

D. Continental Air Defense

Our current air defenses are costly to operate and relatively ineffective. Without a strong and effective missile defense, even a very effective air defense cannot save many lives. The Soviets could simply target cities with their missiles. In the 1970s the Soviets could kill 110 million Americans if we had no air defense system and 100 million if we had a perfect one.

However, there are other objectives of Continental Air Defense which must also be considered. These include: (1) defense against countries other than the Soviet Union, (2) defense against bomber attacks on those strategic forces that we withhold in a controlled nuclear war, (3) peacetime patrolling of our air space, (4) discouraging Soviet bomber aspirations, and (5) the use of continental air defense forces in missions outside the United States. We can achieve these objectives with a modern, more effective air defense force that costs less over the next 14 years than our present force. This modern force will consist of 200 improved F-106 fighters (the F-106X), 42 UE AWACS aircraft, and two OTH radars. It will use the Federal Aviation Agency National Air Space system for back-up command and control. The cost through FY 78 for the modern force is $12.3 billion compared with $11.7 billion for the current force. However, the lower operating costs of the modern force will result in substantial savings over the present force after FY 79.

The following table compares the relative performance of the current force, the modernized force, and an alternative force of 54 F-12s.

Number of Bombers Surviving an Area Bomber Defense

	Current Force	AWACS/F-106X	AWACS/F-12
10-Year Program Cost, FY 69-78 ($ Billions)	$ 11.7	$ 12.3	$ 13.7
Threat			
Current Soviet Heavy Bombers (100 Aircraft)	84	26	37
Potential Threats			
Current Soviet Heavy Bombers Plus Medium Bombers (100 Aircraft)	150	74	127
New ASM—600 nm Range (100 Aircraft)	100	62	53
New Supersonic Bomber (100 Aircraft)	90	70	60

Against the expected threat, the F-106X force is much more effective than the current force and somewhat more effective than the F-12 alternative. It is also more effective than the F-12 force against the medium bomber force or a heavy bomber force with advanced decoys or SRAMs, where numbers of interceptors are important.

The following table compares mixes of F-106Xs and F-12s:

Mixed Forces	10-Year System Cost ($ Billions)	Enemy Bombers Surviving	
		100 Subsonic	100 AMSA
Force with AWACS			
198 F-106Xs	$ 9.9	26	70
198 F-106Xs/12 F-12s	11.0	8	53
108 F-106Xs/54 F-12s	13.6	5	30

Adding a small number of F-12s kills more bombers, but at an additional cost of $1 to $4 billion over 10 years. Furthermore, the total number of lives lost in a nuclear war is nearly the same with any of these alternatives.

Surveillance is presently the weakest part of our air defense system. Therefore, we should proceed with Engineering Development of AWACS (if the Overland Radar Technology program is successful) and with development of back-scatter OTH radars. We should also develop, and deploy on the F-106, advanced air-to-air missiles and an advanced fire control system. With these improvements to the F-106, there is little to be gained from the high performance characteristics of the F-12. Thus, we can avoid the additional $1.1 to $1.4 billion cost of an F-12 force and still meet our air defense objectives.

The same arguments about Damage Limiting also apply to our SAM programs. The Soviets could target SAM-defended cities with missiles and use their penetrating bombers on undefended cities, producing very nearly the same number of deaths. Costly systems such as SAM-D are not justified for CONUS defenses. Our other air defense objectives can be met with area air defense. In line with the perimeter defense concept in the F-106X/AWACS modernization plan, we can phase out 12 existing Nike-Hercules batteries in the interior of CONUS.

V. Specific Recommendations

The JCS have recommended strategic offensive and defensive forces that would cost $15.9 billion in FY 70 and $86.8 billion in the period FY 70–74. The program we are recommending will cost $12.4 billion in FY 70 and a total of $49.3 billion in FY 70–74. Specifically, we recommend:[3]

1. Deferring, until we have evidence of a good Soviet low-altitude SAM defense, the JCS recommendation to equip the B-52 and FB-111 force with 1,545 UE SRAM. This program would cost $137 million in FY 70 and $824 million in FY 70–77.

2. Disapproving the JCS recommendation for Contract Definition and full-scale development of the AMSA in FY 70. The 10-year cost of developing, procuring, and operating a force of 138 AMSAs would be $8.5 billion, including the costs of weapons and tankers.

3. Approving the JCS recommendation for Contract Definition of an advanced subsonic cruise missile, subject to favorable review of Concept Formulation. This program will require $30 million in FY 70 and $145 million in FY 70–74 for development. Deploying a force of 780 missiles would require a total of $361 million in FY 70–77.

4. Disapproving the JCS recommendation for Contract Definition of a new tanker based on the C-5. The present KC-135 fleet is satisfactory. The 10-year cost of developing, procuring, and operating a force of 210 C-5 tankers would be $5.5 billion.

5. Disapproving the JCS recommendation for full-scale development of an advanced airborne command post. The 10-year cost of developing, procuring, and operating a force of 14 command posts would be $1.2 billion.

6. Maintaining a force of 1,000 Minuteman missiles. Maintaining the IOC for Minuteman III at July 1970, resulting in 430 Minuteman II and 570 Minuteman III missiles by end-FY 74. Deferring procurement of

---

[3] All cost data used in the recommendations include Atomic Energy Commission (AEC) costs, but not the direct support and training costs of Programs 7 and 8. [Footnote in the source text.]

terminal penetration aids for Minuteman III until we have evidence of Soviet low-altitude ballistic missile defenses.

7. Disapproving the JCS recommendation for full-scale development of the Mk-18 Re-entry Vehicle (RV). To complete this program would require $17 million in FY 70 and a total of $380 million in FY 70–74.

8. Disapproving the JCS recommendation for Contract Definition of the advanced ICBM system (WS-120A). This missile provides little improvement over Minuteman. The 10-year cost of developing, procuring, and operating a force of 280 missiles would be $9.1 billion.

9. Continuing Advanced Development of the ULMS, but deferring a decision on Contract Definition in FY 70 until completion of the ULMS Development Concept Paper.

10. Disapproving the JCS recommendation for Contract Definition on a Surface-ship-based Long-range Missile System (SLMS) in FY 70. This ship could not replace Poseidon and offers little advantage and many disadvantages, when compared to ULMS. The 10-year investment and operating costs for 10 ships would be $4.6 billion.

11. Disapproving the JCS recommendation for a prototype surface-ship-based intermediate range missile system (called the Ballistic Missile Ship). We do not need additional payload on the crash schedule that would justify this program. Construction of a prototype would cost $250 million, plus $75 million for five years of operation.

12. Continuing to plan for an average of [number not declassified] Mk-3 RVs per Poseidon missile. (The JCS recommend an initial load of [number not declassified] Mk-3s per missile, at an additional cost of $217 million in FY 70.) Procuring [less than 1 line of source text not declassified] in FY 70, and a total of [number not declassified] in FY 70–74. Continuing development of Poseidon and, in FY 70, procuring 181 missiles and converting six Polaris submarines to the Poseidon configuration for a total investment of $1.3 billion in FY 70. Planning to build to a force of 31 Poseidon submarines by FY 76 for a total FY 70–74 investment of $3.9 billion.

13. Disapproving the JCS recommendation to provide a large-yield warhead for Poseidon. Development of such a warhead plus the modifications required for the Poseidon missile would cost $210 million.

14. Approving the JCS proposal to continue converting to Polaris A-3 missiles those remaining submarines not included in the Poseidon conversion program. This program requires no funds in FY 70.

15. Deferring decision on the JCS recommendation to deploy 12 additional communication relay (TACAMO) aircraft for command and control of the Polaris fleet. The JCS program would cost $48 million in FY 70 and $216 million in 10-year system costs. As an alternative for decision in October, we should consider adding new modulation tech-

niques and satellite communications to the current force to greatly extend its capabilities.

16. Disapproving the JCS recommendation to deploy a ballistic missile defense of the United States against the Soviet threat. The JCS program would require $270 million in FY 70 in addition to the Sentinel program. The JCS-recommended objective for a Nike-X defense would cost $10 billion in 10 years above the cost of the Sentinel system.

17. Continuing the deployment of the Sentinel system, but reorienting the program so that procurement funds for only one site need be obligated in FY 69. This results in an FY 69 cost of $739 million and an FY 70 cost of $1.3 billion. The estimated total system investment cost is $5.5 billion, plus $986 million transferred from the Nike-X development program and $250 million in AEC costs.

18. Approving the JCS recommendation to preserve the option for a light defense of Minuteman using Sentinel radars plus additional Sprint missiles. For an IOC in FY 74, no additional funds are needed in FY 70.

19. Disapproving the JCS recommendation for Contract Definition on a ballistic missile defense ship (SABMIS) in FY 70. The research and development and 10-year investment and operating costs for eight ships would be $5.9 billion.

20. Disapproving Contract Definition for the Airborne Missile Intercept System (ABMIS), a concept for which there is no advanced development program.

21. Continuing implementation of the Continental Air Defense Plan, as recommended by the JCS. In FY 70, this action involves $37 million for development of the F-106X interceptor, $229 million for a full-scale development of AWACS, and $8.5 million for developing the back-scatter OTH radar. This air defense plan will cost $11.6 billion in FY 69–77 compared to $10.7 billion for the previously approved program.

22. Disapproving the JCS proposal to resume development of the F-12 interceptor. The 10-year cost of 10 F-12s, as recommended by the Air Force, would be $0.8 to $1.0 billion. The 54 UE F-12s in the JCS objective force would cost $3.4 billion.

23. Approving selected parts of the JCS recommendation to expedite a comprehensive improvement program (MOHEC) for Nike-Hercules, at a cost of $11.2 million in FY 76. The entire JCS plan would cost $35 million in FY 70 and a total of $375 million to complete.

24. Deferring decision on the JCS recommendation to deploy a surveillance satellite system (Program 949) in FY 70, and deferring until October a decision on continued development. This program would cost $114 million in FY 70 and $1.2 billion in 10-year system costs.

25. Disapproving the JCS recommendation to extend the approved military survival measures program from $38 million to $190 million over five years. In view of the present financial situation and our needs in Southeast Asia, deferring initiation of the approved program until FY 71.

26. Disapproving the JCS recommendation for a $150 to $200 million annual Civil Defense program. Approving instead an austere holding program at an FY 70 cost of $84 million.

27. Phasing out the B-58 force in the first quarter of FY 70, instead of at the end of FY 71 as previously planned, in order to save $55 million in FY 70 and $39 million in FY 71.

---

211.   Memorandum From the Chairman of the President's Foreign Intelligence Advisory Board (Taylor) to President Johnson[1]

Washington, August 9, 1968.

In the course of the Board's continuing appraisal of the adequacy of our Government's intelligence coverage of Soviet plans and actions affecting U.S. national security, we have had discussions of the desirability of reinstituting a periodic examination of the relative strategic strength of the United States and the USSR. We have noted that the Net Evaluation Subcommittee of the National Security Council which had been charged with this work was inactivated in 1963 and that no other agency in the government has been given the responsibility for continuing an interdepartmental analysis of this matter.[2] Meanwhile, from the intelligence point of view, we see the increasing need for reliable information on the status of Soviet advanced strategic military capabilities, and on related Soviet research and development efforts.

---

[1] Source: Johnson Library, National Security File, Memos to the President, Walt Rostow, Vol. 92, Box 39. Top Secret. Attached to an August 26 memorandum from Rostow to President Johnson briefly summarizing Taylor's proposal and noting that he had informed Secretary of Defense Clifford about it. Rostow added that he was generally sympathetic to Taylor's proposal, given "the relative evening up of U.S.-Soviet nuclear capabilities" and "the possibility that we may enter strategic nuclear weapons talks. The critical issue will be the best form of organization, I suspect."

[2] Regarding the termination of the Net Evaluation Subcommittee, see Documents 72 and 82.

Based on discussions with former members of the Net Evaluation Subcommittee, our conclusion is that the former evaluation procedure would hardly be adequate to cope with the current problem which is now far more complex than the one which confronted us in the past. These complexities arise from the growing sophistication of strategic offensive and defensive weapons systems, the many unknown factors with regard to the performance of these new weapons and the sensitivity of the kind of study which we have in mind.

The kind of analysis we envision would call for an evaluation of the composition, reliability, effectiveness and vulnerability of the strategic offensive and defensive forces of both sides, to include their command and control systems. It would also call for a close study of the urban-industrial structure of both nations in order to assess the probable effects of strategic attacks on urban-industrial targets. These analyses should be based upon the best available information and foreign intelligence. A by-product of the kind of new study we are discussing would be to focus attention on the gaps in the intelligence data and to accelerate measures to collect the missing pieces.

After the development of the best possible understanding of the likely performance of the opposing strategic forces, it should then be possible to construct one or more scenarios for war game purposes in order to measure the interactions of these forces in nuclear war. The results would then permit our best military and scientific minds to draw pertinent conclusions as to the relative strength of our forces and the considerations which should influence future decisions and actions in the strategic field.

The agencies interested in such a study and with a contribution to make to it include the White House, State, Defense, JCS, CIA, Justice and AEC. Since the study would draw heavily upon the scientific community, the President's Science Advisory Committee should be included as a participant.

Taking into account this breadth of governmental interest, the question arises as to the best way of organizing it. The old Net Evaluation Group did not have adequate scientific support to carry on a study of the scope which we are proposing. Furthermore, it reported through a committee chaired by the Chairman, Joint Chiefs of Staff to the National Security Council. Under present conditions, the Board believes that the proposed study could best be done under the Secretary of Defense acting as executive agent for the President.

Recommendation

It is the recommendation of your Board that the Secretary of Defense be directed to prepare proposed terms of reference whereby he would undertake the net evaluation studies in collaboration with the appropriate other government agencies, along the lines suggested above.

Maxwell D. Taylor

---

212.   **Paper Prepared by the U.S. Intelligence Community**

Washington, August 16, 1968.

[Source: Washington National Records Center, Central Policy File: FRC 383 86 A 5, Folder 3015. Top Secret; Noforn. 5 pages of source text not declassified.]

---

213.   **Memorandum From the Joint Chiefs of Staff to Secretary of Defense Clifford**[1]

JCSM–520–68   Washington, August 26, 1968.

SUBJECT

Draft Presidential Memorandum on Strategic Offensive and Defensive Forces (U)

1. (TS) The Joint Chiefs of Staff have reviewed the "for comment" draft Presidential memorandum (DPM) on strategic offensive and defensive forces.[2] The tentative recommendations in the DPM could lead to the conclusion that, rather than improving our military capabilities, we are compromising US strategy to accommodate to the Soviet improved posture. The Soviet technical ability and national purpose are demonstrated by their capability to develop and deploy a ballistic missile defense, a new nuclear submarine with ballistic missiles, and the new Foxbat interceptor, while continuing to expand their hardened

---

[1] Source: Washington National Records Center, OASD/ISA Files: FRC 330 72 A 1499, 320.2 1968 August. Top Secret.

[2] Document 210.

ICBM force and developing a new ICBM and the fractional orbit bombardment system. The development of these Soviet capabilities without corresponding improvements in US strategic force capabilities continues the shift of the strategic balance away from the United States.

2. (TS) The implications of the rationale and the tentative recommendations in the DPM are that the United States has neither the capacity nor intent to acquire the strategic force capabilities, to include damage limiting, required to pursue effectively a complete military strategy. While the principal military objective of the United States with regard to strategic nuclear warfare is to deter an attack upon the United States, our deterrent could fail for a number of reasons. Important among these are miscalculation of intent or resolve, underestimation of military capabilities, or commission of an irrational act. Should deterrence fail, the principal objective is to terminate hostilities under conditions of relative advantage while limiting damage to the United States and minimizing damage to US and allied interests. This latter objective is considered to be as important as deterring nuclear war since, if deterrence fails, we must ensure the continued existence of the nation by safeguarding the survival of our essential political, military, and economic structure.

3. (TS) The Joint Chiefs of Staff are concerned about the views in the DPM relative to the general approach to deterring strategic nuclear war and the relationship of damage-limiting capability to deterrence. While they concur that deterrence of a rational enemy is dependent on our maintaining a strong and secure ability to retaliate under any circumstances, they also believe that a Soviet decision to initiate hostilities will be influenced not only by their own expected losses but also by US losses and the relative surviving military capabilities. It is difficult to quantify the level of fatalities that will deter the Soviets. The Soviets may not consider their fatalities as the only influencing factor or think of them in terms of a quantitative threshold. If they sustain 20 percent fatalities as compared to 80 percent for the United States, for example, they might not be deterred from initiating an attack against the United States. Our judgments of what may deter the Soviets must not be based on calculations limited to a narrow set of hypotheses or which are too far removed from the most likely pattern of admittedly unlikely wars. Further, such judgments should include evaluations of possible Soviet attacks utilizing improved tactics and force capabilities, including pindown, the fractional orbit bombardment system, cruise missile submarines, and medium bombers.

4. (TS) The Joint Chiefs of Staff do not concur with the allegation that nuclear war plans for the controlled and deliberate use of nuclear weapons do not exist. Planning for strategic nuclear war

must consider a range of options dependent upon the circumstances of war initiation and the objectives of the attack. [*13 lines of source text not declassified*] The Joint Chiefs of Staff believe that further improvements in command and control capabilities will provide additional flexibility for the controlled and deliberate use of nuclear weapons.

5. (TS) The Joint Chiefs of Staff are cognizant of the fiscal and political restraints related to certain of their recommendations. However, they conclude that the choice is not one of degree within an acceptable level of risk but rather whether or not the United States will possess the strategic capability necessary to support its national policies effectively. Based on the DPM's specific recommendations and the rationale as related to strategies, objectives, and force employment concepts, the Joint Chiefs of Staff conclude that the United States may not, if the present trend continues, possess the strategic capability to support effectively its national policy in the mid-range period.

6. (TS) The existence of US strategic superiority for the past two decades has deterred a global war and permitted flexibility in international affairs. As the relative strategic position of the United States is challenged—and the increasing Soviet capabilities most certainly reflect a challenge—two principal dangers are identifiable: first, that an increasing confidence in their strength will lead the Soviets to high-risk courses, and, second, the possibility that such courses will escalate into strategic nuclear war. Unless the presently programmed strategic force levels of the United States are improved, erosion of our relative strategic position will continue. Concomitantly, flexibility in pursuit of national goals will be constrained by our inability to deal from a position of strength. As this erosion continues, the margin for error in the conduct of international affairs will be reduced, and the risks attendant to each decision will increase at an accelerated rate. The alternative to acceptance of the risks associated with the erosion of our strategic position is to insure that the Soviets have no doubt of the US determination and capability to deter a deliberate enemy decision to attack and, should such deterrence fail, to insure that the United States and its allies emerge with relative advantage irrespective of the circumstances of initiation, response, and termination. To accomplish this, we must continue a vigorous program of research and development; increase survivable missile throw weight; deploy an effective ballistic missile defense against the Soviet threat; continue modernization of forces, including development of a replacement strategic bomber aircraft; and continue to improve strategic command, communications, and warning systems.

7. (TS) In summary, the Joint Chiefs of Staff reaffirm that the force level objectives stated in JSOP 70–77[3] constitute strengths essential for the maintenance of an effective strategic nuclear posture during the mid-range time period. Accordingly, they believe that, despite the financial constraints anticipated in FY 1970, we should proceed with strategic offensive and defensive programs necessary to maintain and improve our strategic posture in pace with the threat and within an acceptable margin of risk. Therefore, they recommend that the foregoing rationale and the comments and recommendations contained in the Appendix hereto[4] be used as a basis for your decision on strategic offensive and defensive forces.

For the Joint Chiefs of Staff:
Earle G. Wheeler
Chairman
Joint Chiefs of Staff

[3] Document 188.
[4] Not printed.

214. **Telegram From the President's Special Assistant (Rostow) to President Johnson in Texas[1]**

Washington, September 3, 1968, 1911Z.

CAP 82362. Herewith Clark Clifford's letter to me[2] commenting on General Taylor's suggestion that we reestablish something like the former Net Evaluation Subcommittee of the NSC.[3] As you see, Sec. Clifford and Gen. Wheeler believe that present staff work within the Department of Defense fully covers the work formerly done by the Net Evaluation Subcommittee and, therefore, they do not believe a new study is required.

[1] Source: Johnson Library, National Security File, Memos to the President, Walt Rostow, Vol. 93, Box 39. Secret. The President was at the LBJ Ranch in Texas August 23–September 4. (Ibid., President's Daily Diary)
[2] A copy of Clifford's August 30 letter to Rostow, which is quoted below, is ibid., National Security File, Intelligence File, Foreign Intelligence Advisory Board, Volume 2 [1 of 4], Box 6. Another copy and supporting documentation on the drafting of the Department of Defense response on this issue are in Washington National Records Center, OASD/ISA Files: FRC 330 72 A 1499, 381 1968 June– .
[3] See Document 211.

I will make Sec. Clifford's letter available to Gen. Taylor.

"In response to your request that we look into Max Taylor's suggestion for a resumption of the sort of study last conducted by the Net Evaluation Subcommittee of the NSC in 1963, I have had my staff review existing studies to determine whether a new NES-type effort would be worthwhile.

Needless to say, the NES studies were initiated in the 1950's at a time when our strategic capabilities were far less than they are today and more significantly for purposes of a new study, we lacked the analytical capability to assess relative U.S. and Soviet performance in various scenarios. General Wheeler and I find that existing current material fully covers the ground of the Net Evaluation studies.

Our intelligence in regard to Soviet capabilities has vastly improved, as reflected in periodical NIEs on Soviet strategic offensive and defensive systems, updated versions of both of which will be forthcoming shortly (NIEs 11–8 and 11–3).[4] Each year the Joint War Games Agency writes a Soviet objectives plan (RISOP) which they game against our SIOP. These results give us a very detailed evaluation of our near-term capabilities against the Soviets and their capabilities against us. When dealing with capabilities over the next ten years, the DOD strategic force and effectiveness tables, last revised on August 7, 1968,[5] consider relative strengths in a number of different strategic situations, and we have the capability of readily preparing additional tables for any particular scenario not covered. The forthcoming DPM on U.S. strategic and defensive systems also covers much of the same ground.[6]

In the light of the availability of this material General Wheeler and I are convinced that it would not be desirable to proceed with a new net evaluation study."

---

[4] Documents 217 and 221.

[5] According to the preface to the tables, 17 in all, they "list the programmed forces and options considered in the Draft Memorandum for the President on Strategic Offensive and Defensive Forces, along with the expected Soviet threat and the Greater-Than-Expected (GTE) Soviet threat." The preface and tables are attached to an August 7 memorandum from Nitze to the Secretaries of the Military Departments and the Chairman of the Joint Chiefs of Staff, among others. (Washington National Records Center, OASD/ISA Files: FRC 330 72 A 1499, 320.2 1968 I–35737/68 7 August 1968)

[6] No later draft memorandum to the President during 1968 has been found.

215. **Letter From Secretary of Defense Clifford to the Chairman of the President's Foreign Intelligence Advisory Board (Taylor)[1]**

Washington, September 20, 1968.

Dear Max:

Thank you for sending me a copy of the memorandum you propose to send to the President in regard to the FIAB proposal for a new Net Evaluation Study.[2] In general you have done justice in presenting my views, although there are many more evaluations going on than I mentioned in my letter to Walt Rostow[3] or than you mention in your memorandum to the President.

I would like to emphasize, however, that while I believe a new administration might wish to have a hand in initiating as far-reaching a study as you propose, my main point is that existing studies and existing coordinating mechanisms for bringing information to bear on the problem are adequate to do the job.

This is not to say that there are no intelligence gaps, or that we intend to rest on the merits of studies we have already completed. I am convinced, however, that our current efforts are able to identify—and take steps to fill—any gaps in our intelligence, our research and development, and our analysis.

I believe that our current efforts have the interdepartmental inputs that you feel would be the main benefit of your proposed study. What is lacking most in our current efforts is the relaxed, long-range view that could best be supplied by studies at IDA, Rand, etc. I have been promoting such studies and would appreciate your help in focusing such studies on the pertinent issues.

I have enclosed brief descriptions of a few of the more important continuing efforts that we are making to evaluate the relative strategic strength of the United States and the USSR. I would be glad to provide briefings on any of these efforts to you personally or to the FIAB.

Sincerely,

Clark

---

[1] Source: Johnson Library, National Security File, Foreign Intelligence Advisory Board, Vol. 2 [1 of 4], Box 6. Top Secret. Attached to a September 24 note from Taylor to Rostow; see footnote 1, Document 216.

[2] Document 211.

[3] Quoted in Document 214.

Enclosure

Major DoD Efforts to Evaluate the Relative Strategic
Strength of the United States and USSR

1. Political-Military War Games

Political-military war games are conducted and analyzed by the Joint War Games Agency (JWGA). These (non-computer) games explore major international issues, problems, and questions bearing upon our national security. The White House, the Departments of State, Treasury, and Defense, the USIA, the AID, the ACDA, and the Military Services provide participants for these war games. These games address broad political, economic, psychological, and technological considerations as well as military strategy. The JWGA usually conducts at least four of these games each year. They provide an excellent vehicle for obtaining inter-departmental inputs for an examination for the relative strategic strength of the U.S. and USSR. Two games, played in 1967, studied the effect that anti-ballistic missile defenses might have on a strategic exchange between the U.S. and the USSR.

2. RISOP–SIOP War Games

The Red Integrated Strategic Operational Plan (RISOP) is developed by the JCS and the Services. It is our Soviet equivalent of the U.S. Strategic Integrated Operational Plan (SIOP). In developing this plan the Red Planning Board tries to maximize the effectiveness of the Red forces and exploit known or expected weaknesses of the U.S. strategic posture or forces. The RISOP is approved by the Joint Chiefs of Staff and then war gamed against the SIOP. The war gaming effort involves computer facilities in Omaha, the National Military Command System Support Center in Washington, and the Navy computer facility at NAVCOSSAC. Two independent war games are conducted, one in Omaha by the Joint Strategic Target Planning Staff and the other in Washington by the JWGA. The results are briefed to the JCS and to appropriate CINCs. Applicable portions of the plans are provided to the Office of Civil Defense.

3. Post-Nuclear Attack Study

The Post-Nuclear Attack Study (PONAST) is being conducted in the JCS Special Studies Group. It was initiated about two and one half years ago and is now nearing completion. PONAST considers two general war scenarios, which include strategic and theater nuclear forces, in order to examine possible follow-on military and non-military operations in the post-SIOP period of the war. The Office of Emergency Planning (OEP) and the Office of Civil Defense (OCD) have been active participants. Some twenty-seven other agencies were called upon for various contributions, through the auspices of OEP. The Department of State and the Defense Intelligence Agency have played major roles. The study will identify problems that probably will confront national civilian and military leaders during the successive stages of a general war, and will assess capabilities to cope with such problems.

A feeling for the depth and scope of the study can be gained from the fact that it took more than 4,000 hours of computing time on our most modern computers. Except that it does not specifically focus attention on gaps in intelligence data, it is exactly the kind of analysis that appears to be envisioned by the FIAB in that it evaluates the composition, reliability, effectiveness, and vulnerability of the strategic offensive and defensive forces of both sides, including their command and control systems. It also closely studies the urban-industrial structures of both nations in order to assess the probable effects of strategic attack on urban-industrial targets, as well as the capability of the nations to recover from these attacks. This study was based on the best available intelligence information since the RISOP–SIOP war games, appropriately expanded, were used as the basis for the study.

4. Strategic Forces Draft Presidential Memorandum

The Strategic Forces DPM presents the recommendations of the Secretary of Defense on the strategic offensive and defensive force structures for the next five years, as well as the rationale behind these recommendations. An essential part of this rationale is calculations of the ability of our strategic forces to accomplish their major objective— deterrence of nuclear war.

To do this the DPM first calculates the capability of our programmed forces against a combination of the upper-range of the National Intelligence Projections for Planning (NIPP) projections for *each* element of the Soviet strategic forces. Excursions then are made to study cases where we lose major components of our forces, to make sure that our capability is not vulnerable to an unforeseen technological breakthrough. If these calculations show that our capability is not sufficient, the DPM recommends developing and deploying enough forces to make it sufficient.

Next, the DPM tests our programmed forces against a threat specifically designed to take away our deterrent capability. It then examines force options which will restore our capability to an acceptable level against this threat. It also examines the lead-times necessary for development of these options and recommends actions which will insure that we can maintain our capability even against this greater-than-expected threat.

Finally, the DPM next examines our capability to limit damage to the United States in the event that a nuclear war occurs. In this situation the DPM examines likely scenarios instead of the limiting ones used to examine our deterrent capability. It also takes into account possible Soviet reaction to the deployment of a U.S. damage limiting force.

The DPM is sent out for comment to the Services and the JCS. In addition, comments on appropriate parts of the DPM are usually solicited from the State Department and the Central Intelligence Agency. The Secretary of Defense considers these comments in writing the Record of Decision version of the DPM. The recommendations in the Record of Decision DPM then form the basis for the budget submitted to Congress.

5. DoD Strategic Force and Effectiveness Tables

The DoD Strategic Force and Effectiveness Tables (SF&ET) contain calculations, for each of the next ten years, of the capability of the U.S. to sustain a first strike by the high NIPP threat and retaliate. Fourteen different scenarios are considered, most of which test the effect of unforeseen vulnerability of a major portion of our forces. The tables also contain calculations, for each of the next ten years, of the retaliatory capability of 14 combinations of strategic force options against a greater-than-expected threat. In addition, they contain calculations of our damage limiting capability with different levels of U.S. ABM defenses in five different scenarios against six different Soviet reactions to our deployment of ABM systems. [3 *lines of source text not declassified*]

The SF&ET also contain a detailed listing of the U.S. forces and options, the Soviet threat (from the NIPP), and greater-than-expected Soviet threats designed to take away our deterrent capability or our damage limiting capability. The characteristics of these forces are listed in detail.

These tables form a point of departure for all calculations within DoD of the capabilities of our strategic forces. They are coordinated with the Services and the JCS and comments on the greater-than-expected threat have been obtained from the Central Intelligence Agency.

6. Study of Sub-SIOP Options

The Secretary of Defense requested the Secretary of the Air Force to study sub-SIOP nuclear options (NU-OPTS) involving limited nuclear exchanges between the U.S. and the USSR. A pilot study has been completed which indicates that the U.S. and USSR can conduct coercive warfare with strategic weapons, at relative high levels, with each side retaining its capability throughout the exchange to deter an all-out city attack. The Air Staff, SAC, ADC, USAFE, and the Rand Corporation are now investigating the strategic and operational considerations associated with limited nuclear operations, with emphasis on target selection criteria, required damage expectancies, attack levels, types of delivery systems, and the command and control, reconnaissance, intelligence, and communications elements which will be necessary to conduct strategic operations at lower levels of controlled response. These elements are being analyzed both for the U.S. and the USSR. The purpose of this study is to develop a logic for the conduct of strategic war, at levels less than SIOP, in order to provide the President with additional options for the limited use of our strategic forces.

7. National Intelligence Estimates and Projections

The composite views of the intelligence community on Soviet military posture and capability are found in four major National Intelligence Estimates (NIEs): NIE 11–3, Soviet Strategic Air and Missile Defense Forces; NIE 11–4, Main Issues of Soviet Military Policy; NIE 11–8, Soviet Strategic Attack Forces; and NIE 11–14, Soviet and East European General Purpose Forces.[4] These estimates are produced yearly and, when necessary, updated during the year. Special NIEs are produced when urgent situations require them. Such a special estimate was issued recently to assess our capability to unilaterally detect changes in Soviet strategic offensive and defensive force structures.[5] The U.S. Intelligence Board (USIB) produces these estimates. This Board consists of representatives from the Departments of State, Defense, and Justice, the AEC, and the NSA. (Normally the Department of Justice abstains from the above NIEs since the subject is outside their jurisdiction.)

The National Intelligence Projections for Planning (NIPP) is prepared annually by the USIB to serve as a supplement to the NIEs on Soviet programs and capabilities. It is much more detailed than the NIEs. The added detail is principally a quantification and projection over a ten-year period of the broad trends and capabilities indicated in the NIEs. Its purpose is to: (a) include in a single document the quantitative data on all major aspects of Soviet military forces, (b) to present the quantitative data by mid-years for a ten-year period, (c) to organize the data into mission-oriented categories, and (d) to indicate ranges of uncertainty associated with each projection.

---

[4] Four versions of NIE 11–3 are printed as Documents 69, 106, 146, and 221; for NIE 11–4, see Documents 84, 131, and 183; for NIE 11–8, see Documents 97, 143, and 217; for NIE 11–14, see Document 98.

[5] An apparent reference to SNIE 11–10–67, Document 169.

216.   Letter From the Chairman of the President's Foreign
        Intelligence Advisory Board (Taylor) to Secretary of Defense
        Clifford[1]

Washington, September 24, 1968.

Dear Clark:

Your letter of 20 September[2] will be most helpful to your old colleagues of the FIAB in dealing with the intelligence aspects of its central
theme. Although aware of some of them, I found the tabulation of DOD
efforts in the field most impressive and would like to take advantage of
your offer of a briefing on some of them.

With regard to the use of IDA, Rand, etc. for studies in this field,
speaking under my IDA hat I can assure you of IDA's readiness to work
on any aspect of these problems which are within its competence.

Sincerely,

Maxwell D. Taylor[3]

---

[1] Source: Johnson Library, National Security File, Foreign Intelligence Advisory
Board, Vol. 2 [1 of 4], Box 6. Top Secret. Attached to a September 24 note from Taylor to
Rostow indicating that "Unless you have other thoughts on the subject, I would like to
suspend further consideration of our recommendation until I have had time to discuss the
matter further with the Board at its next meeting on October 3."

[2] Document 215.

[3] Printed from a copy that bears this typed signature.

217.   National Intelligence Estimate[1]

NIE 11–8–68   Washington, October 3, 1968.
TCS 582–68

SOVIET STRATEGIC ATTACK FORCES

The Problem

To estimate the strength and capabilities of Soviet strategic attack forces through mid-1970 and to estimate general trends in those forces over the next 10 years.

Conclusions

A. The primary objectives of Soviet strategic policy have been to achieve a more formidable deterrent and to narrow and eventually to overcome the US lead in capabilities for intercontinental attack. Toward this end the Soviets have built strategic forces, both offensive and defensive, which provide a large assured destruction capability and important damage-limiting capabilities as well. While they have only begun to narrow the gap in submarine-launched ballistic missiles and remain inferior in heavy bombers, the Soviets will shortly overcome the US lead in numbers of ICBM launchers. Current programs will bring further improvements in the USSR's strategic position, already the most favorable of the postwar period. But the Soviets face in the future a strategic situation changed and complicated by projected improvements in US forces—Poseidon, Minuteman III, and the antiballistic missile system—that threaten to erode their relative position.

B. In deciding upon the future size and composition of their strategic forces the Soviets are almost certainly exploring a number of alternatives. They are evidently interested in strategic arms control as an option that could conserve economic resources and protect their improved strategic position. In the absence of an arms control agreement, we believe that they will continue the arms competition with the

---

[1] Source: Johnson Library, National Security File, Intelligence File, Miscellaneous CIA Intelligence Memoranda [4 of 4], Box 14. Top Secret; Ruff; [*codeword not declassified*]; [*classification marking not declassified*]. A title page, prefatory note, an October 3 letter from Helms to recipients of NIE 11–8–68 indicating that the extreme sensitivity of this NIE required that it not be reproduced or its existence revealed to unauthorized persons, and a table of contents are not printed. According to the prefatory note, the CIA and the intelligence organizations of the Departments of State and Defense, the Atomic Energy Commission, and the National Security Agency participated in the preparation of this estimate. Representatives of the CIA, State Department, DIA, NSA, and AEC concurred; the FBI representative abstained, the subject being outside his jurisdiction.

US, seeking to maintain and if possible improve their relative strategic position. In any case, they will probably give increased attention to qualitative improvements, particularly those designed to enhance survivability and capacity to penetrate defenses.

C. *Intercontinental Ballistic Missiles (ICBMs).* The great improvement in the USSR's strategic position results primarily from the rapid and extensive ICBM deployment of the past few years. The Soviet ICBM force now has about 900 operational launchers and our evidence on construction activity indicates that it will surpass the US force in numbers by 1970. The Soviets have begun deployment of a small solid-propellant ICBM, they probably are developing a new large liquid-propellant system, and they probably will develop a mobile ICBM system. In addition, they are flight-testing multiple reentry vehicles (MRVs).

D. We believe that for the period of this estimate the Soviet force goal will lie somewhere between 1,100 and 1,500 ICBM launchers.[2] If it lies near the low side, the Soviet ICBM force would probably peak at a higher level until older launchers were phased out. Such a force would probably embody considerable qualitative improvements including better accuracy, more sophisticated reentry vehicles such as MRVs and multiple independently-targeted reentry vehicles (MIRVs), and possibly penetration aids. A force toward the higher side of our estimate would also include qualitative improvements, and it would rely in part upon larger numbers to attain improved capabilities.

E. *Space Weapons.* At the time of our last estimate the Soviets were conducting extensive flight tests which we believed related to development of a fractional orbit bombardment system (FOBS). Developments since that time have lowered our confidence that we understand the intended purpose of the system under test; the Soviets may be trying to develop a FOBS, a depressed trajectory intercontinental ballistic missile, or perhaps a dual system which could perform both missions. Until our evidence is more conclusive, we are unable to make a confident estimate as to the type of system being developed, when it could reach initial operational capability (IOC), or how it may be deployed. We continue to believe it unlikely that the Soviets will develop a multiple orbit bombardment system.

F. *Medium-Range Ballistic Missile/Intermediate-Range Ballistic Missile (MRBM/IRBM).* There has been little change in the size of the MRBM/IRBM force, which still stands at about 700 launchers. We estimate that new MRBMs and IRBMs will supersede present systems

---

[2] For the position of Maj. Gen. Jammie M. Philpott, the Acting Assistant Chief of Staff, Intelligence, USAF, and Maj. Gen. Wesley C. Franklin, for the Assistant Chief of Staff for Intelligence, Department of the Army, see their footnote to paragraph 33. [Footnote in the source text.]

within the next 10 years. The Soviets will continue to maintain massive strategic forces against Eurasia, but the introduction of improved missiles may result in some decrease in numbers. We believe that the Soviets are developing and will deploy, in both a fixed and a mobile configuration, a new solid-propellant MRBM (designated SS-14) of about 1,500 n.m. range which could reach IOC in a year or two. We estimate that they will also develop a solid-propellant IRBM with a range of about 3,000–3,500 n.m., and that it will reach IOC in 1970–1971. It will probably be deployed in both fixed and mobile launchers and with its extended range will provide more flexible coverage of Eurasian targets.

G. *Submarine-Launched Missiles.* The Soviets have clearly embarked upon a high priority program to improve and expand their ballistic missile submarine force. Six, possibly 7, of the 16-tube Y-class submarines have now come down the ways and there is evidence suggesting that the production of this class will be stepped up soon. We believe that the Soviets are building toward a ballistic missile submarine force that will confront the US with a threat roughly comparable to that which the Polaris force presents the USSR. They could reach that position by the mid-1970's, when they will probably have some 65–80 ballistic missile submarines, of which 35–50 will be Y-class types.

H. *Long-Range Aviation.* Attrition and retirement of older models will gradually reduce the Soviet heavy bomber force. The medium-bomber force will probably also decline as Badgers are phased out, but at a slower rate than we estimated last year. The introduction of a new air-to-surface missile into the Badger force suggests that the Soviets intend to extend the useful life of some of those aircraft for a few more years. We still believe that the Soviets are unlikely to introduce a follow-on heavy bomber; they may introduce a follow-on medium if the Blinder does not satisfy their future requirements.[3]

Discussion

I. Trends in Policy and Doctrine

1. The most important issues of Soviet military policy concern the strategic balance between the US and the USSR. The goals of Soviet strategic weapons programs were set at a time when the US enjoyed such a superiority in intercontinental delivery systems as to put the USSR at a political and psychological disadvantage. The aim of Soviet strategic policy, therefore, has been to achieve a more formidable deterrent and to narrow and eventually to overcome the US lead. Toward this end, the Soviets have built strategic forces, both offensive and defen-

---

[3] For the position of Maj. Gen. Jammie M. Philpott, the Acting Assistant Chief of Staff, Intelligence, USAF, see his footnotes to Section VI. [Footnote in the source text.]

sive, which provide a large assured destruction capability and important damage-limiting capabilities as well, and they have substantially reduced the US lead in numbers of intercontinental delivery vehicles.

2. The great improvement in the USSR's strategic position results from the buildup of Soviet strategic forces begun by Khrushchev several years ago. The new leaders have made some decisions as to the size and composition of their strategic forces, but they have generally followed the strategic policies and programs that they inherited. In the future, however, they face a strategic situation significantly changed from that which led to present Soviet policies. Projected improvements in US strategic forces—Poseidon, Minuteman III, and the antiballistic missile (ABM) system—threaten to erode their relative position. Now the Soviet leaders are confronted with the necessity for new decisions on the future size and composition of their strategic forces. Other military requirements and the growing needs of the general economy are among the factors which the leaders must consider in making these decisions.

3. Under the collective leadership, military expenditures have continued to rise, primarily as the result of the continuing development and large-scale deployment of strategic weapons, which account for about half of the total military expenditures. The requirements of these programs for scarce high-quality resources of the sort needed to sustain economic growth have aggravated the impact of defense spending on the economy. Now, events in the Far East and in Europe have posed new military requirements which probably will result in a substantial increase in the strength of Soviet theater forces. Thus the perennial problem of resource allocation promises to sharpen. Economic considerations almost certainly were among the principal reasons for the Soviet decision to discuss arms control with the US.

4. Nevertheless, the economic considerations contributing to the Soviet decision are probably no more compelling than the strategic considerations. Considering US plans for improvements in its strategic forces, the Soviets probably recognize that a considerable sustained effort would be necessary to maintain the relative position they have now achieved. They may also be concerned lest the end of the Vietnam War enable the US to divert additional resources to its strategic forces. Finally, they may reason that further increments to their strategic forces would have little effect on the relationship between the US and the USSR so long as the US maintained its large, second-strike assured destruction capability. If these arguments were to prevail in the USSR, the Soviets would probably seek an agreement that preserved their present strategic relationship with the US.

5. It is too early to assess the full implications of the Czech crisis for Soviet policy toward arms control. The Soviets still have the same basic

economic and military incentives; indeed, it is possible that the new military requirements generated by the Czech crisis have added to those incentives. Moreover, the present Soviet line seems to be that the Czech crisis is an internal Communist Bloc affair that should have no effect on the USSR's relations with the US. It is possible, therefore, that the Soviets will seek to proceed with arms control talks. At a minimum, however, the Czech crisis has delayed the opening of talks with the US and has dampened the prospects of any real progress toward strategic arms control in the near term.

6. In any case, the Soviet leaders cannot base their strategic planning on the possibility of strategic arms control and will almost certainly explore other alternatives. At a minimum, they might consider a policy of deterrence aimed only at maintaining a large assured destruction capability. Or they might consider a try for strategic superiority of such an order that it could be translated into significant political gain. We consider it highly unlikely that the Soviets will select either of these courses of action. The first, that of unilateral deescalation, would involve a decision to sacrifice the hard-won gains of recent years. The second would involve economic sacrifices that are probably unacceptable to the present leadership and would almost certainly provoke a strong US reaction. We believe, therefore, that in the absence of a strategic arms control agreement, the USSR will continue the arms competition with the US with the object of maintaining and if possible improving its relative strategic position.

7. For several years, the Soviets have given the highest priority to the effort to overcome the US lead in numbers of intercontinental delivery vehicles, particularly in intercontinental ballistic missiles (ICBMs). By 1970, the Soviets will probably surpass the US force in numbers of ICBM launchers but they will remain inferior in submarine-launched ballistic missiles and heavy bombers. To maintain an assured destruction capability in the strategic situation that is emerging, qualitative improvements, particularly those related to survivability and capacity to penetrate defenses, become more important. There will undoubtedly be pressures for a continuing enlargement of the ICBM force, and it may continue to grow. But having attained rough numerical parity with the US in ICBMs, the Soviets will probably give increased attention to other options designed to enhance the survivability and effectiveness of their strategic attack forces.

[Here follow Parts II–VII, an annex, and seven tables (pages 6–41).]

218.   Letter From the Chairman of the President's Foreign
        Intelligence Advisory Board (Taylor) to Secretary of Defense
        Clifford[1]

Washington, October 8, 1968.

Dear Clark,

I thought that you would like to know that during our Board meeting of October 3–4,[2] we reconsidered our recent recommendation to the
President[3] that there be established within the Executive Branch an
interagency mechanism for the preparation of comparative evaluations
of the strategic military offensive and defensive capabilities of the
United States and the USSR.

In the course of our discussions, we had the benefit of your views
and comments as set forth in recent communications to Walt Rostow
and me.[4] Your frank expression of views on the subject was appreciated
by all members of the Board.

Upon further consideration of the matter it was the Board's conclusion that, rather than pursue this subject in the form of a further recommendation to the President at this time, the matter should be included
in a final Board report to the President toward the close of this year, in
a section devoted to the identification of intelligence problems of continuing concern.

On behalf of the Board I express thanks for the help which you provided to us in our deliberations on this question.

Sincerely,

Maxwell D. Taylor[5]

---

[1]   Source: Johnson Library, National Security File, Foreign Intelligence Advisory
Board, Vol. 2 [1 of 4], Box 6. Top Secret. A copy was sent to Rostow.

[2]   No other record of this meeting was available.

[3]   Document 211.

[4]   See Documents 214 and 215.

[5]   Printed from a copy that indicates Taylor signed the original.

219.   Notes of Meeting[1]

Washington, October 14, 1968, 1:40 p.m.

NOTES OF THE PRESIDENT'S MEETING WITH

Secretary of Defense Clark Clifford	Walt Rostow
Secretary of State Dean Rusk	George Christian
General Earle Wheeler	Tom Johnson
Admiral Thomas Moorer	
General Leonard Chapman	Joining the Meeting:
General John McConnell	
General Bruce Palmer	Senator Richard Russell
Bromley Smith	General William Westmoreland

Secretary Clifford: There have been instructions issued on authority to release nuclear weapons [*1-1/2 lines of source text not declassified*].

The project's code-name is "Furtherance."

We recommend three major changes:

[*3 paragraphs (8 lines of source text) not declassified*]

We all recommend this.

Walt Rostow: We think it is an essential change. This was dangerous. We recommend going forward.

General Wheeler: All the Joint Chiefs of Staff and commanders have been consulted. We recommend approval.

General McConnell: I concur, Sir.

General Chapman: I concur.

Admiral Moorer: I concur.

---

[1] Source: Johnson Library, Tom Johnson's Notes of Meetings, October 14, 1968—1:40 p.m., Foreign Policy Advisory Group Meeting, Box 4. Eyes Only for the President. The meeting was held in the Cabinet Room. The President asked Senator Russell, Secretary Rusk, and General Westmoreland to join the meeting as soon as they arrived at the White House, but they did not get there until 2:22 p.m., 2:45 p.m., and 3:15 p.m., respectively, and probably were not present for this discussion. (Ibid., President's Daily Diary) A record of Part II of this meeting is ibid., Tom Johnson's Notes of Meetings, October 14, 1968—1:40 p.m., Foreign Policy Advisory Group Meeting, Box 4.

220. Memorandum From the Deputy Secretary of Defense (Nitze) to the Chairman of the Joint Chiefs of Staff (Wheeler)[1]

I–25100/68   Washington, October 23, 1968.

SUBJECT

    Chemical and Biological Warfare Policy (CM–3676–68)

Reference is made to your memorandum on the above subject, dated 25 September 1968,[2] requesting that the Department of State be queried on when their position on the DOD draft NSAM[3] would be available and to a memorandum of 1 October 1968, from the Deputy Assistant Secretary for Policy Planning and Arms Control, ISA, to the Director, Joint Staff, in which the Director was informed that DOD had requested that the State Department convene the Political-Military Group to discuss State's position on the subject.[4]

A meeting of the Political-Military Group was held at the Department of State on 16 October 1968.[5] Each principal designated a representative to participate in a Working Group to resolve differences now existing between State and the DOD draft NSAM. The Working Group has representatives from State, ACDA, ISA, and J-5 of the Joint Staff. Mr. Keeny of the Executive Office of the President has been invited to attend. The first meeting of the Working Group was held Tuesday, 22 October 1968 at the State Department.[5]

Paul H. Nitze

---

[1] Source: Washington National Records Center, OASD/ISA Files: FRC 330 72 A 1498, 384 1968 Jan– . Secret.

[2] This memorandum to the Secretary of Defense noted among other things that the Department of State had not yet replied to Secretary McNamara's November 17, 1966, letter to Secretary Rusk (Document 145) and requested asking the Department of State for a statement of its position "preferably prior to the beginning of CY 1969." (Washington National Records Center, OASD/ISA Files: FRC 330 72 A 1498, 384 1968 Jan–)

[3] Not printed; see Document 145.

[4] The memorandum from Morton H. Halperin is in the Washington National Records Center, OASD/ISA Files: FRC 330 72 A 1498, 384 1968 Jan– .

[5] No record of this meeting has been found.

221.   National Intelligence Estimate[1]

NIE 11–3–68   Washington, October 31, 1968.

SOVIET STRATEGIC AIR AND MISSILE DEFENSES

The Problem

To estimate the strength and capabilities of Soviet strategic air and missile defense forces through mid-1970, and general trends in these forces through 1978.[2]

Conclusions

A. Throughout the postwar period the USSR has devoted a major effort to strategic defense. This effort can be attributed primarily to the size and diversity of US strategic attack forces, although for the future the Soviets must consider the threat posed by third countries, particularly China.

B. We believe that the competition for resources in the USSR is likely to intensify, not only between civilian and military programs, but also within the military establishment. These pressures may exercise a restraining influence on the strategic defense effort, but are unlikely to reduce it below present levels. The trend for the longer term will depend heavily upon Soviet decisions concerning antiballistic missile (ABM) deployment and the related question of strategic arms control.

C. The Soviets have built a formidable system of air defenses, deployed in depth, which would be very effective against subsonic and low-supersonic aircraft attempting to penetrate at medium and high altitudes. The system is less effective against higher performance aircraft and standoff weapons; it has virtually no capability

[1] Source: Johnson Library, National Security File, Intelligence File, Miscellaneous CIA Intelligence Memoranda [4 of 4], Box 14. Top Secret; [*classification marking not declassified*]; Controlled Dissem. A cover sheet, title page, prefatory note, and a table of contents are not printed. According to the prefatory note, the CIA and the intelligence organizations of the Departments of State and Defense, the Atomic Energy Commission, and the National Security Agency participated in the preparation of this estimate. The representatives of the CIA, State Department, DIA, NSA, and AEC concurred; the FBI representative abstained, the subject being outside his jurisdiction.
[2] This estimate considers only those Soviet strategic defensive forces located in the USSR and Eastern Europe. The Soviet antisubmarine warfare effort, with its implications for Polaris, will be discussed in the forthcoming NIE 11–14–68, "Soviet and East European General Purpose Forces." [Footnote in the source text. NIE 11–14–68 is in the National Archives and Records Adminstration, RG 263.]

against low-altitude penetration below about 1,000 feet except in a few, limited areas. The Soviets recognize these shortcomings and are deploying new interceptors, surface-to-air missiles (SAMs), and radars in an effort to overcome them.

D. At present, the major effort is directed to counter the threat posed by high-performance aircraft and standoff weapons. Deployment of the SA-5 long-range SAM system is the largest single defensive weapon program now underway. This system represents a considerable improvement over older systems in terms of range, velocity, and firepower. It is being deployed as a barrier defense around the European USSR and for point defense of selected targets. We estimate that there are some 60 SA-5 complexes, and that nearly half are operational; we believe that some 100 complexes will be operational by 1973. The Soviets have also been testing an airborne warning and control system (AWACS) that will probably enter service soon. This system, deployed in coastal areas and used with long-range interceptors, could greatly extend the area in which incoming aircraft could be engaged.

E. The Soviets are also attempting to strengthen their air defenses against low-altitude attack, but their efforts of the past year have resulted in minor improvements rather than in any fundamental solution to the problem. They have deployed all-weather interceptors with improved capabilities for low-altitude attack, and they will probably introduce more advanced SAMs and interceptors better suited for low-altitude defense. The primary limitation on low-altitude defense, however, is surveillance and control. Deployment of new radars has improved tracking capabilities in limited areas down to altitudes of 500 feet and even below, but we expect little advance in ground-based continuous tracking capability at low altitudes during the period of this estimate.

F. The Moscow ABM system (ABM-1), under deployment since 1962, has probably achieved some operational capability. Its deployment has apparently been cut back substantially from the originally planned level; the elements still under construction will probably be operational in 1970. We believe that the Soviets plan additional deployment of an improved ABM system at Moscow. ABM development continues, but we cannot determine whether it involves an improved version of the Moscow system or a substantially improved, second-generation ABM system, although we consider the latter more likely. We still do not believe that there is any deployment of ABM defenses outside the Moscow area. We believe that the SA-5 long-range SAM system is unlikely to have a present ABM capability, although the state of available evidence does not permit us to exclude this possibility, and we consider it unlikely that it will be modified for an ABM role.[3]

G. Deployment of ABM defenses beyond Moscow will probably await the availability of a second-generation system. If such a system is now under development, it could reach an initial operational capability in the 1973–1975 period; like the Moscow system, it will probably be designed for long range, exoatmospheric intercept. The extent of future deployment will depend heavily upon economic as well as technical considerations. Deployment of a national defense system on a scale sufficient to cope with the full US missile threat does not appear to be a feasible course of action for the USSR within the period of this estimate. We believe that the Soviets will decide upon a program that would provide some defense for the most important target areas in the USSR. Some part of this defense would probably be deployed against Communist China and other third country threats.

H. We have no evidence of a Soviet antisatellite weapons program nor of Soviet development of hardware specifically for this purpose. It would be technically possible, however, for the Soviets now to have a limited antisatellite capability. With existing radars and missiles armed with nuclear warheads, they could almost certainly destroy or neutralize current US satellites up to about 2,000 n.m. during an early phase of their mission. With terminal homing in the interceptor missile, they may even be able to neutralize satellites using a nonnuclear warhead. Soviet technical capabilities are such that they could develop and deploy during the next 10 years any of several types of antisatellite systems if they chose to do so. We believe, however, that the Soviets would realize that any use of antisatellite systems in peacetime would expose their own satellites to attack, and consider it unlikely that they would do so except in retaliation.

Discussion

I. Soviet Strategic Defense Policy

1. Soviet strategic defense forces have gone through several stages of development since World War II. Through the mid-1950's the Soviets attempted to counter the large US strategic bomber force in being with large numbers of air surveillance radars and interceptor aircraft, reinforced at Moscow with large numbers of surface-to-air missiles (SAMs). As the US force obtained higher performance intercontinental bombers,

---

[3] For the views of Maj. Gen. Jack E. Thomas, the Assistant Chief of Staff, Intelligence, USAF, and Maj. Gen. Joseph A. McChristian, the Assistant Chief of Staff for Intelligence, Department of the Army, on the mission and capabilities of the SA-5 (Tallinn) system, see their footnote on page 17. [Footnote in the source text.]

the Soviets in the late 1950's developed and deployed Mach 2 interceptors and extended SAM defenses throughout the country. When the US,
in the face of this extensive defense, began practicing low-altitude penetration tactics, the Soviets began in the early 1960's deploying the
Firebar interceptor and the SA-3, both possessing better capabilities for
low-altitude intercept than earlier systems. The US deployment of a
standoff capability with air-to-surface missiles (ASMs), was followed by
Soviet development and the current deployment of the Fiddler interceptor and the SA-5 system, which have greater ranges than earlier systems.

2. In their efforts to have a defense in being against an immediate
threat, the Soviets have generally deployed a system quite early in the
development cycle, using available technology, rather than wait for the
development of more advanced but unproven techniques. These systems have then generally been modified and improved during the period of deployment. In some cases, however, deployment has been can-
celed early in the program either because the system proved relatively
ineffective or because a better one was in the offing. When an improved
system has been deployed, older ones are not rapidly retired or
replaced. The Soviets tend to have extensive defenses deployed in
depth, usually with considerable redundancy. This redundancy may
give the defenses as a whole a greater capability than analysis of each
weapon system alone would indicate. On the other hand, some elements of the defenses are always somewhat out of date, and do not represent the most effective Soviet counter to new US systems or concepts
of operation.

3. Soviet military planners probably see the US strategic threat in
the mid-1970's as consisting of three major forces: bombers and ASMs,
intercontinental ballistic missiles (ICBMs), and submarine-launched
ballistic missiles (SLBMs). They are aware that the threat will become
more sophisticated and formidable with the incorporation of improvements—new aircraft, ASMs, aerodynamic and ballistic penetration aids,
and multiple independently-targeted reentry vehicles (MIRVs). The
weight of a US attack could be increased by the strategic forces of
Britain and France; the Soviets probably view the British forces as simply adding to the Polaris threat, but French intermediate-range ballistic
missile (IRBM) deployment will pose a threat from a new quarter.

4. The Soviets probably believe that the massive air defense forces
they have built and are building will provide an effective counter to the
medium and high-altitude bomber threat, although they realize the
problem of low-altitude defense is not yet satisfactorily solved. The
most critical requirement of Soviet strategic defense, and the one most
difficult to meet despite more than a decade of effort, however, is
defense against ballistic missiles. The nature and extent of antiballistic

missile (ABM) deployment is almost certainly one of the major questions of Soviet military policy.

5. For the period of this estimate, the US and its allies will continue to pose the principal strategic threat to the USSR, but Soviet military planners must also be concerned with the emerging strategic capabilities of a hostile China. The substantial military buildup along the Chinese border over the past few years has consisted primarily of theater forces. The strengthening of air defenses has been modest in comparison, and at a deliberate pace that in the Soviet view probably matches Chinese offensive capabilities. The Soviets almost certainly believe that their great superiority in offensive strategic weapons will enable them to cope with any threat that might materialize in the foreseeable future, and they hope for a political change in China that would remove this possibility. For the longer term, however, Moscow must consider the problem of ABM defenses against a new threat from the south.

6. Soviet decisions as to how best to meet the strategic threat of the mid-1970's will be affected not only by the Soviet view of the threat and the pace of technological development, but also by the constraints of economics. The present Soviet leadership has shown a general disposition to accommodate military programs, and military expenditures have continued to rise. Moreover, within the military establishment strategic defense has long enjoyed a favored position. We estimate that the Soviet strategic defense effort is larger, both in absolute terms and as a share of the total military budget, than that of the US. Developments of the past year, however, have strengthened the demands of competing claimants, both civilian and military. The Soviet leaders have shown rising concern over the adverse effects of military spending upon economic growth; we believe that this was a major consideration in their decision to discuss strategic arms control with the US. Now the Czech crisis has raised new requirements for theater forces in Europe which, together with the continuing buildup on the Chinese border, will probably bring a significant increase in Soviet theater forces. Thus, we believe that competition is likely to intensify, not only between civilian and military programs, but also within the military establishment.

7. Current pressures may exercise a restraining influence on the strategic defense effort, but are unlikely to reduce it. For the near term, at least, expenditures for strategic defense will probably be maintained at their present high level, while military expenditures as a whole continue to rise. The trend for the longer term will depend heavily upon Soviet decisions concerning ABM deployment—potentially the most costly single military program on the horizon—and the related question of strategic arms control. If the Soviets embark upon any sizable new

program of ABM deployment within the next few years, expenditures for strategic defense will increase and by the middle 1970's are likely to exceed those for strategic attack by a substantial margin.

[Here follow Parts II–V and three tables (pages 6–29).]

---

222.   Report Submitted by the Chairman of the President's Foreign Intelligence Advisory Board (Taylor) to President Johnson[1]

Washington, November 25, 1968.

SUBJECT

Review of U.S. Foreign Intelligence and Related Activities

This report supplements previous submissions which have been made to the President on the subject by the President's Foreign Intelligence Advisory Board.

Because this is the Board's final report to you, it undertakes to account for the highlights of the Board's operations since its establishment on May 4, 1961. It also includes our current views respecting selected, long-term, intelligence-related problems which we deem worthy of continuing attention.

Origin and Function of the Board

The Board was established by Executive Order 10938, dated May 4, 1961 (Attachment A)[2] immediately following the Bay of Pigs episode and the Order was reconfirmed by you at the beginning of your Administration.[3]

---

[1] Source: Johnson Library, National Security File, Intelligence File, Foreign Intelligence Advisory Board, Vol. 2 [1 of 4], Box 6. Top Secret; [*codeword not declassified*]. Attached to a November 25 transmittal letter from Taylor to President Johnson, which reviews the origins and mission of the President's Foreign Intelligence Advisory Board, the Board's belief in "these continuing reviews of the intelligence activities of these [several military and civilian] agencies," and its opposition to the creation of a "Congressional 'Watchdog' Committee" to oversee the U.S. foreign intelligence effort. Also attached is a note from Jim Jones to Rostow, January 6, 1969, informing Rostow that Taylor presented the report to President Johnson that afternoon.

[2] Not printed.

[3] President Eisenhower was served by a similar foreign intelligence board which functioned from February 1956 to January 1961. [Footnote in the source text.]

The charter of the Board directed that it (a) conduct a continuing, independent review and assessment of all functions of the Central Intelligence Agency and of other departments and agencies having responsibilities in the fields of foreign intelligence and covert activities, and (b) advise the President periodically with respect to the objectives and conduct of those activities required in the interest of foreign policy, national defense and security.

When you became President you reaffirmed the need for the Board, continued its terms of reference, reappointed the personnel who then comprised the Board, and thereafter made additional appointments to the Board. On occasion you have reemphasized the role and mission of the Board in directives to your principal advisors (Attachment B, dated October 19, 1965, and Attachment C, dated May 1, 1968).[4]

Membership of the Board

In accordance with the provisions of the Executive Order, the membership of the Board has been drawn from qualified individuals outside of Government. The individuals appointed to serve successively as Chairmen of the Board have been Dr. James R. Killian, from May 1961 to April 1963; Mr. Clark M. Clifford, from April 1963 to February 1968; and General Maxwell D. Taylor, USA, (Ret.), from February 1968 to the present. Present membership of the Board is listed in Attachment D.[5] The Executive Secretary of the Board, Mr. J. Patrick Coyne, by reason of consecutive Presidential Appointments has been associated continuously with this and earlier Presidential Boards since 1956. The Board has found his services to be invaluable.

Increasing Magnitude of Intelligence Activities

The heightening of world tensions and the spread of Communist aggression in recent years has resulted in a substantial increase in the size, cost, complexity and importance of the national intelligence effort. [4 lines of source text not delcassified] About [number not declassified] personnel, civilian and military, are engaged in some aspect of intelligence activities in which many departments and agencies take part. Most of the money and manpower resources devoted to foreign intelligence activities are allocated to intelligence-related elements of the Department of Defense, including the Departments of the Army, Navy and Air Force; the Joint Chiefs of Staff; the Unified and Specified Commands; the Defense Intelligence Agency; the National

---

[4] Both are printed in *Foreign Relations, 1964–1968*, vol. XXXIII, Documents 239 and 277.

[5] Not found.

Reconnaissance Office; the Cryptologic Agencies of the Military Services; and the National Security Agency. [7 lines of source text not declassified] The remaining costs, [less than 1 line of source text not declassified] are allocated to other units of the Department of Defense and to the intelligence components of the Department of State and the Atomic Energy Commission.

The magnitude of this effort is a reflection of the steadily increasing volume of intelligence collection requirements levied upon the system. A substantial portion of our intelligence resources is allocated to the top-priority acquisition of data concerning the strategic military capabilities (offensive and defensive) of the Soviet Union and Communist China. The war in Vietnam has added greatly to the burden of our intelligence agencies. The need to know more about economic, political and military developments in newly-emerging nations has added further to the intelligence workload. If, in the aftermath of the Vietnam war, there should be a trend to review and possibly to revise U.S. commitments abroad, there will be a corresponding requirement for intelligence to serve as a basis for such judgments.

In the course of meeting national intelligence needs, it has become necessary to develop advanced and elaborate facilities for the collection and analysis of information in great volume. These facilities include photographic reconnaissance aircraft and satellite systems [3-1/2 lines of source text not declassified]. A portion of the U.S. intelligence effort is concerned with espionage and counterespionage activities, including penetrations abroad of foreign governmental regimes, military organizations, political groups, and the development of intelligence resources among the diplomatic corps abroad. There are also overt collection sources such as the observations of hundreds of U.S. diplomats and Military Attachés; voluminous information is acquired daily from foreign broadcasts, [less than 1 line of source text not declassified] and other sources, adding to the heavy burdens of analysis placed upon the U.S. intelligence system.

All of these activities produce information essential for the preparation of estimates of enemy capabilities and intentions, and provide the intelligence base required for the formulation of U.S. foreign policy and for defense and budgetary planning. For the indefinite future, we foresee the continuing demand for an ever-improving intelligence system to meet critical needs of the decision-makers in the fields of foreign policy and national security.

Working Procedures of the Board

The Board is the only organization of the Executive Branch having the responsibility for maintaining a continuing scrutiny of the complex but indispensable U.S. foreign intelligence effort, an effort which is large, expensive and widely-dispersed. The complexity of the effort and magnitude of the resources involved are such that the Board's concerns include proper utilization of the powers and authorities of the departments and agencies engaged in intelligence and associated activities. In the discharge of its functions the Board has conducted intermittent reviews of all significant intelligence activities of the several agencies engaged therein, including those of the Central Intelligence Agency; the Departments of State, Defense, Army, Navy, and Air Force; the Defense Intelligence Agency; the National Security Agency; the Service Cryptologic Agencies; the Joint Chiefs of Staff; the Unified and Specified Commands; the AEC; and the foreign intelligence aspects of the operations of the Federal Bureau of Investigation (particularly counterintelligence). The Board has received the generous cooperation of the senior officials and subordinates of these departments and agencies.

The review function of the Board has not only served to keep it fully informed, but has also had the beneficial effect of causing the component agencies of the intelligence community to test and examine on a continuing basis the performance of their respective roles and responsibilities.

The Board has carried out its review responsibilities through the following means:

1. *Meetings of the Full Board.* The Board has held two-day meetings on alternate months. During your Administration the full Board held meetings totaling 52 days and during President Kennedy's tenure meetings of the full Board totaled 39 days. At these meetings the Board has: (a) received extensive briefings from representatives of the intelligence community on significant current intelligence developments and problems; (b) reviewed and acted upon reports of the Board's Panels and reports of on-the-scene reviews made by representatives of the Board; (c) held discussions on matters of mutual interest with the Director of Central Intelligence and the heads of the member agencies of the community; (d) met with high-level consumers of the intelligence community's products to obtain their views on problem areas requiring remedial attention; (e) reviewed implementation by the intelligence community of earlier Board recommendations; and (f) prepared reports to the President.

2. *Board Panels.* Designated Panels of the Board (composed of selected members and the Executive Secretary) have been responsible for keeping the full Board informed with respect to significant actions, problems, gaps, overlaps and deficiencies in specified areas of the overall foreign intelligence effort. Certain of the Panels have investigated the conduct and interrelationships of intelligence operations in various geographic areas of the world. Others have examined the scientific and technological aspects of intelligence operations. Still others have dealt

with the organizational and management aspects of the intelligence community as a whole and of the component elements of the community such as the National Reconnaissance Office, the National Security Agency, the Central Intelligence Agency and the Defense Intelligence Agency. One of the Panels has been concerned exclusively with counterintelligence problems and with the improvement of means to counter the attempts of foreign espionage services to penetrate our Government.

3. *On-the-Scene Reviews.* The Board has attached great importance to its on-the-scene reviews in the U.S. and abroad. It has been a long standing practice for individual Board members, together with the Executive Secretary, to make first-hand examinations of our intelligence operations in various regions of the world. Overseas these reviews have included consultations with U.S. Ambassadors, Chiefs of the Political and Economic Sections of our Embassies, our CIA Station Chiefs, our Defense Attachés and others as appropriate. Through personal observations, briefings and discussions Board representatives have been able to obtain a vivid picture of our intelligence activities, of the operational environment in which they are conducted, and of the special problems faced by our intelligence personnel in the field. At the same time we believe that these on-the-scene reviews, known to have been made on behalf of the President, have served to stimulate morale and job performance among the representatives of the intelligence agencies.

Recent overseas reviews conducted by the Board have included surveys of U.S. intelligence activities in Southeast Asia, the Far East, Western Europe, the Middle East and Latin America. In some of these areas, where critical U.S. intelligence interests were involved, repeated on-the-scene surveys were made by representatives of the Board. [2 *lines of source text not declassified*]

4. *Review of Reports.* The Board has required the submission of periodic and special reports by the various military and civilian intelligence agencies. These reports include annual submissions by each agency of the intelligence community, accounting to the Board in great detail with regard to all major aspects of their respective operations. This reporting procedure keeps the Board informed concerning significant intelligence programs, successes, problems, gaps and deficiencies, and at the same time compels the agencies periodically to take stock of the progress made in meeting their responsibilities.

5. *Review of Major Intelligence Publications.* The Board has maintained a continuing review of major intelligence publications which are produced on a daily, weekly, monthly, or "spot" basis by the Central Intelligence Agency, the Defense Intelligence Agency, the Department of State and by the U.S. intelligence community collectively. These publications include current intelligence reports and appraisals of signifi-

cant day-to-day developments, National Intelligence Estimates, Special National Intelligence Estimates, and the intelligence results of satellite and aircraft reconnaissance missions.

6. *Discussions with the Principal Intelligence Consumers.* In the course of its reviews and studies the Board has found it essential to consult from time to time with high-level users of intelligence including the President, the Secretaries of State and Defense, the Chairman, JCS, the President's Special Assistant for National Security Affairs, the Director of Central Intelligence, and the heads of the various intelligence agencies, as a means of determining whether their critical intelligence requirements are being met adequately.

7. *Special Studies.* From time to time the Board has conducted special studies, at the request of the President, in regard to intelligence-related matters of particular national security interests. The subjects covered in these studies have included such matters as the following.

a. The performance of U.S. intelligence agencies in providing advance information on the erection of the Berlin Wall in August 1961.

b. The intelligence community's performance respecting the introduction of Soviet strategic missiles into Cuba in 1962.

c. The Soviet penetration in the 1961–1963 period of highly sensitive elements of the National Security Agency, prompting improved counterintelligence measures relating to personnel security investigations, clearances and to the safeguarding of sensitive intelligence data.

d. The intelligence coverage of the Gulf of Tonkin incident involving U.S. Naval forces in September 1964.

e. The quality, timeliness and handling of intelligence bearing on the enemy military offensive in South Vietnam during the Tet holidays in January 1968.

f. The intelligence aspects of the Israeli attack on the USS *Liberty* in June 1967, and the North Korean capture of the U.S. Signals Intelligence vessel, *Pueblo*, in January 1968.

g. The system for the control of military intelligence/combat aircraft operating over North Vietnam and the Tonkin Gulf, with a view to minimizing navigational errors and unintentional intrusions over the Chicom border.

h. The intelligence community's coverage of the Soviet invasion of Czechoslovakia in August 1968.

i. Measures to strengthen the intelligence community's capability for providing the President and other top officials with timely, interagency evaluations on developing crisis situations.

j. The scope and effectiveness of the intelligence community's special programs to keep abreast of Soviet and Chinese Communist scientific and technological developments, particularly in the strategic weapons field.

Meetings with the President

Throughout its tenure the Board has found it most helpful to have had meetings with the President to discuss major aspects of the foreign intelligence, counterintelligence, and covert operations of our Government. Since its establishment in 1961, the full Board was privileged to have had 12 such meetings.

Reports and Recommendations of the Board

In keeping with its charter, the Board has reported its findings and recommendations directly to the President at frequent intervals. Following the submission of its reports, and after notification of actions directed thereon by the President, the Board has made a point to follow up on the implementation of its recommendations by the departments and agencies concerned.

From May 1961 to the present time, the Board has submitted a total of 41 reports to the President containing over 200 specific recommendations.

Areas of Improvement in the Intelligence Effort

We believe that Presidential actions on Board recommendations, and the continuing support given by the Board to innovations and improvements in the agencies' intelligence programs, have made an important contribution to the noteworthy progress which has been made in various areas of the total intelligence effort. Some of the significant areas of progress to which we refer are listed below:

1. *Reorganization of the United States Intelligence Board (USIB).* The USIB, established by National Security Council Directive, is the principal vehicle employed by the Director of Central Intelligence in the coordination of the total intelligence effort. Consistent with various Board recommendations, actions taken with a view to improving that coordination have included a reduction in the number of military agencies represented on the USIB, and realignment of the USIB's basic structure and methods of operation.

2. *Internal Reorganization of the Central Intelligence Agency (CIA).* The establishment within the CIA of a Deputy Directorate for Science and Technology (on a coordinate level with the Deputy Directorates of Intelligence and Clandestine Operations) was undertaken in 1963, consistent with recommendations which the Board had made with a view to assuring maximum exploitation of science and technology in the furtherance of major intelligence programs and projects. As a result, progress has already been noted in special research and developmental areas concerned with intelligence applications of the natural sciences, behavioral research, and advanced photographic and other sensors.

3. *Establishment of the Defense Intelligence Agency (DIA).* Since the establishment of the DIA in 1961 with the endorsement of the Board, that Agency has undertaken improvements in several segments of the

Defense Department's intelligence activities, including a reduction in the dispersion of effort in intelligence areas of interest to the Joint Chiefs of Staff.

4. *Establishment of the Defense Attaché System.* The dissolution of the three separate Service Attaché Systems and the authorization in 1964 of a single Defense Attaché System under DIA's centralized management and control have resulted in more efficient use of attaché resources, better handling of [*less than 1 line of source text not declassified*] requirements levied by the Department of Defense and the Military Services, and improved [*less than 1 line of source text not declassified*].

5. [*17-1/2 lines of source text not declassified*]

6. *Strengthening of the National Signals Intelligence Program.* Close and continuing attention by the Board, and its close collaboration with the Director of the National Security Agency, have led to substantial improvement in the management and conduct by the National Security Agency of the intercept and analysis of foreign communications and electronic intelligence. This large, complex and costly activity is targeted against the [*1-1/2 lines of source text not declassified*] of selected foreign nations. The program continues to provide unique data of major interest to U.S. policy officials, both civilian and military, including insights into the [*less than 1 line of source text not declassified*] capabilities of a number of target countries. [*5 lines of source text not declassified*]

7. [*12 lines of source text not declassified*]

8. *Attacking the Information-Handling Problem.* In response to a series of reports and recommendations by the Board, combined action has been initiated by the member agencies of the intelligence community toward the planning, development and ultimate establishment of a computer-assisted, community-wide system for the management, storage and retrieval of the vast quantity of intelligence information which is collected, processed, analyzed and reported by these agencies on a continuing basis.

9. *Improved Intelligence Collection Effort in the Vietnam War.* Based on repeated on-the-scene reviews made by the Board in the Vietnam theater and on resulting recommendations to the President, there has been over the past three years an expanded and improved effort on the part of the entire intelligence community with respect to intelligence collection efforts in the Vietnam theater, with increased emphasis upon Signals Intelligence capabilities, clandestine agent operations, interrogation of prisoners of war and returnees, and processing and analysis of captured enemy documents.

10. *Measures to Improve Personnel Security Screening Procedures and the Handling of Particularly Sensitive Information.* As an outgrowth of Board recommendations, the intelligence community has put into effect

uniform personnel security standards governing the screening of personnel for access to sensitive compartmented information. These uniform standards have resulted in stringent personnel security clearance criteria and enlarged requirements for background investigations leading to the issuance of security clearances.

11. [9-1/2 lines of source text not declassified]

Problem Areas of Long-Term Significance

Although gratifying advances have been made in our national intelligence effort (a few important examples of which are cited above) there remain a number of problem areas which we suggest should receive continuing attention. For the purpose of this report, we give only a bare summary to identify them as matters deserving priority attention for the future, noting that they are documented in greater detail in the files of the Board.

1. *Current Intelligence Support to the President.* As the Board's recent review of the performance of the intelligence community at the time of the Tet offensive has again emphasized, there is still an unresolved problem of meeting the President's day-to-day—sometimes hour-to-hour—requirements for intelligence without excessive resort to spot reports by-passing the responsible evaluation process of the intelligence apparatus. The problem consists of two parts—first, how to keep the Director of Central Intelligence continuously aware of the changing intelligence interests and needs of the President, and second, how to respond thereto with minimum delay. Whatever procedure is developed to meet this need, it is essential that the Director of Central Intelligence should continue to have a close rapport with the President and be, in every sense, his principal intelligence officer.

A possible means of meeting the need of the President for timely, evaluated spot intelligence would be for the DCI to assign a senior intelligence officer to the White House to work alongside the Special Assistant to the President for NSC Affairs for the purpose of anticipating Presidential intelligence needs and expediting the process by which the intelligence community satisfies them. This process could include a small group of analysts working directly under the DCI for the specific purpose of satisfying White House requirements with quick access to all the resources of the intelligence community.

2. *Early Warning Capabilities.* We shall probably never be satisfied with our early warning capabilities for crisis situations in spite of the continued efforts of the Director of Central Intelligence and the United States Intelligence Board to improve early warning procedures. In view of the transcendent requirement for timely warning of foreign actions related to our national defense and security, this subject is deserving of priority attention on a continuing basis.

3. *Comparative Evaluations of Military Capabilities.* The Board believes that national security interests would benefit from the establishment of an interagency mechanism (representing civilian and military departments and agencies) for making periodic, comparative evaluations of the military offensive and defensive capabilities of the U.S. and the USSR. It is important that this be an interdepartmental effort involving as participants all appropriate elements of the Executive Branch. We envisage that from time to time this body would evaluate the composition, reliability, effectiveness and vulnerability of the offensive and defensive forces of both sides, thus providing an informed basis for national policy decisions. An anticipated by-product of such studies would be the identification of significant gaps in the intelligence community's coverage of the USSR.

4. *Science and Technology.* In spite of progress made in linking scientific and technological resources with intelligence activities, the Board believes that an even greater effort should be made to ensure that the substantial and innovative resources of the nation's scientific and technologic community are brought to bear upon critical intelligence problems, including the development and application of concepts for long-term, sophisticated systems for the collection and timely communication of critically-needed intelligence. This coupling of the intelligence community with key elements of the scientific and technological community has proved to be extremely rewarding in the case of the National Signals Intelligence Program and of the National Reconnaissance Program.

5. *Signals Intelligence.* Continued efforts by the Secretary of Defense are needed to assure the most effective possible management, organization and conduct of the U.S. Signals Intelligence effort as an essentially national resource, having as its primary mission the satisfaction of critical national (as distinguished from departmental) intelligence needs.

6. *Communication of Signals Intelligence.* In order that the National Security Agency may carry out its mission, it is imperative that it manage and control all [*less than 1 line of source text not declassified*] Signals Intelligence material [*2 lines of source text not declassified*]. This requires continued administration by the National Security Agency of facilities for the communication of such material and messages.

7. *National Security Agency Direction.* In the past, the National Security Agency has been handicapped by the too frequent rotation of its directorship. The Board is convinced that in order to achieve increased management effectiveness of this highly important intelligence activity, longer tours of duty should be established for the directorship. Consideration should also be given to the alternative of a military or civilian appointee to this position.

8. *Information-Handling.* Although a beginning has been made toward improved management and handling of the great volume of intelligence information, there is need for continued stimulus, at highest Governmental levels, to energize and integrate the efforts being made by elements of our intelligence community to exploit automated procedures, machine aids and computers for the collection, processing, analysis, communication and reporting of intelligence information.

9. *Espionage.* In general, the Board regards the results of U.S. espionage efforts as inadequate and urges an intensification of efforts to obtain significant intelligence on priority targets through clandestine agent collection operations. [5 *lines of source text not declassified*]

10. *Counterespionage.* Because of the unrelenting efforts of foreign intelligence services to subvert military and civilian personnel of our Government and to acquire access to our classified information, the intelligence community must be on the alert constantly to detect and defend against such operations on the part of foreign powers. It is essential that this effort include the positive clandestine collection of intelligence both at home and abroad with respect to these hostile operations. The Board considers that there is a most critical gap in this counterespionage coverage resulting from the absence of policy authorization for the use of audiosurveillance devices against the espionage activities of foreign agents operating within the U.S.

11. [6 *lines of source text not declassified*]

12. *Validation of Intelligence Requirements.* There is an unsatisfied need for more effective methods for the screening of intelligence collection requirements with the objective of assuring that assignments of collection tasks take into account national intelligence needs, objectives and priorities; the collection resources which would have to be utilized; and the expected value of the intelligence information which would be obtained. Improved methods could result in a substantial reduction in the vast workload and great costs entailed in trying to meet the countless requirements which are continually levied and which tend to bog down our foreign intelligence apparatus.

13. *Covert Operations.* We believe that the 303 Committee should lend greater emphasis to periodic review of all approved covert programs in order to evaluate progress being made, and in appropriate instances, cancel unproductive projects.

14. *Defense Intelligence Agency.* This Board endorsed the concept of Defense Intelligence Agency as announced by the Secretary of Defense just prior to his establishment of the DIA in a directive issued in August 1961. As indicated previously in this report we believe that the DIA shows promise of achieving the principal objectives for which it was created. To insure that the full realization of this promise is not unduly

delayed, it is of first importance that the DIA receive the real and continuing cooperation of each of the military departments, and be provided as soon as possible with all necessary means in the way of proper space, advanced equipment and qualified personnel needed for the accomplishment of its critical mission.

15. *Increased Policy Guidance by the National Security Council*. It is the opinion of the Board that a number of the major problems confronting the intelligence community stem from inadequacies in the policy guidance and coordination which is provided to the intelligence community. We believe that the prosecution of the national intelligence effort would be materially enhanced if stronger policy direction and guidance were made available by the National Security Council. As a first step in that direction we suggest an early review, and up-dating where appropriate, of the National Security Council Intelligence Directives and related directives which govern the responsibilities and activities of the Central Intelligence Agency and the conduct of the total U.S. foreign intelligence and covert action effort. These directives have not been reviewed for several years, and we consider it essential that they be reexamined by the NSC at an early date, with a view to effecting such revisions as are necessary to assist the intelligence agencies in the improved performance of their respective missions, and to lend increased support of the President and the NSC to the Director of Central Intelligence in discharging more effectively his responsibility for coordination of the U.S. intelligence effort as a whole.

16. *Retention of Overseas Intelligence Facilities*. The Board is aware of the review that is being conducted of the future need for the overseas bases and installations which are presently maintained in support of our foreign policy. Among those which may be considered for elimination there undoubtedly will be some having important intelligence functions which, in the interest of the national security, must continue to be performed. The Board urges that intelligence requirements receive careful consideration before making decisions to eliminate bases having important intelligence missions which cannot otherwise be performed.

Conclusion

We have directed attention in this report to selected topics which we believe should continue to receive priority attention by Government officials having responsibility for the management and implementation of the national intelligence program. There are other aspects of the intelligence effort which have been the subject of Board studies, reports and specific recommendations, and are in our opinion appropriate for periodic reexamination and follow-up action.

In closing, we would like to reiterate our feeling of the increasing importance of the national intelligence effort to our security. It is a field of great complexity requiring the services of thousands of dedicated professionals of ability, training and experience who should receive the firm and continuing support of senior officials of Government. It is of the utmost importance to attract and retain these valuable specialists and instill in them an esprit de corps based on a feeling of the importance of their work and the esteem in which it is held by the nation. The Board has noted in recent times an unhappy tendency in Congress, the press and elsewhere to denigrate intelligence in the public eye and to undermine public confidence in our intelligence agencies, particularly the CIA. This dangerous trend is in part fomented by foreign and domestic enemies of our national security. The Board expresses the hope that in the future the senior spokesmen of Government will continue to give serious thought to the need, in the national interest, to reverse this trend and to give voice to the importance and quality of the work being done by the intelligence community.

For the Board,
Maxwell D. Taylor

---

223.   Editorial Note

During 1968 the Joint Chiefs of Staff proceeded to develop a Joint Strategic Objectives Plan for FY 1971–1978 (JSOP FY 71–78). The Joint Chiefs of Staff forwarded Volume I, Strategy (65 pages), under cover of a July 6, 1968, memorandum (SM–456–68) to the Secretaries of the Military Departments, the regional Commanders in Chief, and the Commander in Chief of the Strategic Air Command. This memorandum noted that Volume I was to be used in the development of military recommendations for the preparation of Volume II, Analyses and Force Tabulations; Volume III, Free World Forces; and appropriate Annexes. (Washington National Records Center, OASD/ISA Files: FRC 330 72 A 1499, 381 JSOP 71–78 1968 Volume I–Strategy) Volumes II and III and the annexes have not been found. Under cover of a December 5 memorandum to Secretary of Defense Clifford (JCSM–713–68), the Joint Chiefs of Staff transmitted Volume I with the recommendation that the military strategy in Volume I "be used as the basis for the development of DOD policy on major strategic issues and in analyses leading to development of the Five-Year Defense Program." (Ibid.)

224. Memorandum From the Chairman of the Joint Chiefs of Staff (Wheeler) to Secretary of Defense Clifford[1]

CM–3811–68   Washington, December 19, 1968.

SUBJECT

    FY 1970 Defense Budget Discussion with the President (U)

    1. (U) Reference is made to my memorandum, dated 26 November 1968,[2] which contained information on the forthcoming FY 1970 defense budget discussion with the President.[3]

    2. (U) A copy of the statement that I plan to give and the illustrative examples to be discussed by each Service Chief are attached for your information.

    3. (C) Since information concerning many budgetary and force level decisions is not available at this time, it may be necessary to revise the illustrative examples prior to meeting with the President. I shall appreciate an opportunity to discuss with you the time and place for our meeting with the President.

    4. (U) Without enclosures, this memorandum is Confidential.

Earle G. Wheeler

Enclosure A

STATEMENT BY THE CHAIRMAN, JCS ON
FY 1970 DEFENSE BUDGET

Introduction

    Mr. President, recognizing the financial constraints under which the FY 70 budget is being developed, the JCS decided against addressing individual issues as has been the custom in the past. Instead, we

---

    [1] Source: Johnson Library, National Security File, Agency File, JCS, Filed by the LBJ Library, Box 29. Top Secret.

    [2] Not found. A 21-page "Summary of Recommendations by the Secretary of Defense and Related Recommendations by the Joint Chiefs of Staff with FY 70 Budget Implications," November 19, 1968, and a 4-page list, entitled "Remaining Significant FY 70 Budget Disagreements between the Joint Chiefs of Staff and the Secretary of Defense," also dated November 19, are in the Library of Congress, Manuscript Division, Nitze Papers, Top Secret File, Box 1.

    [3] The Joint Chiefs of Staff, along with Secretary of Defense Clifford, Walt Rostow, and others, met with the President in the Cabinet Room of the White House on December 26, 11:17 a.m.–12:25 p.m. (Johnson Library, President's Daily Diary) No summary record of this meeting has been found.

propose to discuss the general posture of our armed forces with emphasis on the impact of FY 70 budget decisions on present and future military capabilities. I will provide a brief assessment and each Service Chief will provide illustrative examples highlighting his key areas of concerns.

The JCS are fully aware of the wide variety of demands on our nation's resources and the hard decisions which must be taken in allocating these resources. The war in Southeast Asia, coupled with the dangerous situation in Northeast Asia, and the unstable and uncertain environments in the Middle East and Europe, challenge our capability for adequate and timely response to other contingencies which might arise.

First, The Threat—

The Soviet threat continues to expand in size and improve in quality. There is no indication that it is leveling off nor is there any sign of self-imposed limitations based upon achievement of a particular force capability. We expect an increase in Soviet land and sea-based missiles, an increased deployment of anti-ballistic missiles, an improvement in air defense, and an overall improvement of their general purpose forces.

Regarding Strategic Forces—

Despite US progress in certain areas, rapid increases in USSR capabilities have eroded our once clearly superior strategic position.

The Soviet missile force is growing in size. Our strategic force is undergoing qualitative improvements, such as Poseidon and Minuteman III, which will increase our force effectiveness; however, it is programmed to remain static in numbers. While our bomber force is being reduced, the loss in numbers is partially offset by the introduction of a short-range attack missile and a new decoy missile. Our capability to defend the continental US against the bomber threat will be reduced by force reductions programmed for FY 70. The lack of an effective ballistic missile defense is also cause for concern, although the planned Sentinel deployment represents a significant first step in this direction.

In the General Purpose Forces Area—

The JCS are concerned with the decreased readiness of our general purpose forces and their capability to respond to possible worldwide contingencies. Our fighting forces in Vietnam are the best equipped and supported in history; however, the higher priorities given Southeast Asia, together with manpower and funding limitations, have resulted in constraints on personnel and matériel in other areas of the world. The resulting personnel turbulence, curtailment of training, and diversions of logistic assets to meet unprogrammed requirements magnify the deficiencies in our current military posture.

In this regard, the plan for the improvement and modernization of the Republic of Vietnam Armed Forces is receiving priority attention and support. The JCS note, however, that it will require diversions of service equipment programmed and procured for US forces. An uncompensated diversion of matériel from US forces will have an adverse effect upon the readiness of general purpose forces not directly committed to the conflict in Southeast Asia.

In Summary—

The JCS consider that US strategic force levels, when compared with the growing Soviet strategic capabilities, represent a declining trend in the US strategic position vis-à-vis the USSR. Additionally, we believe that the existing conventional capability of our general purpose forces provides only a limited choice of options at the present time outside Southeast Asia. It does not provide the capability to reinforce NATO adequately in a timely manner, nor of simultaneously providing a response to other than minor contingencies elsewhere.

Risks associated with the capabilities of our programmed forces can be reduced by short-term actions such as: (1) improving the readiness of deployed forces, (2) modernizing current forces, (3) retaining forces scheduled for phase down, and (4) providing adequate logistic support.

Deferral of such actions is generating an accumulation of unfunded requirements which reduce current force capabilities and will have an adverse impact on force capabilities in the future.

In amplification of these judgments, and to provide further insight into these matters, each Service Chief is prepared to discuss his areas of concern, with illustrative examples.

Enclosure B

ILLUSTRATIVE EXAMPLES

Army—Low manning levels in Korea and Europe, and STRAF structure and manning level problems.

Navy—Shortages of personnel, and budget constraints related to capability and staying power of naval forces.

Air Force—Reductions in Strategic Bomber and Air Defense Forces.

Marine Corps—Degradation of amphibious assault capability.

225. Record of Meeting of the Senior Interdepartmental Group[1]

Washington, December 19, 1968.

CHAIRMAN'S SUMMARY OF DISCUSSIONS AND DECISIONS
AT THE 48th SIG MEETING ON DECEMBER 19, 1968

PRESENT

> The Under Secretary of State, Chairman
> The Deputy Secretary of Defense
> The Chairman, Joint Chiefs of Staff
> Admiral Taylor, for the Director, Central Intelligence Agency
> Mr. Poats for the Administrator, Agency for International Development
> Mr. Akers for the Director, United States Information Agency
> The Under Secretary of Treasury
> The Under Secretary of State for Political Affairs
> The Deputy Under Secretary of State for Political Affairs
> SIG Staff Director
>
> SSDSG—Ambassador McClintock
> SSDSG—General McDonald
> DOD—Dr. Halperin
> DOD—General Orwat
> DOD—General Ginsburgh
> BOB—Mr. Clark
> NASA—Mr. Morris
> NASA—Mr. Radius
> State—Ambassador Leonhart
> State—Mr. Farley
> State—Dr. Ruser

A. Chairman's Opening Remarks

Mr. Katzenbach regretted that General Wood, Director of the Study,[2] was unable to attend. He would try to meet with General Wood later on to obtain his personal views and conclusions.

Mr. Katzenbach said he recognized that SIG members had not had a great deal of time to review the study. But, inasmuch as the SIG had commissioned this work, he felt the SIG should discuss next steps. Also, any preliminary comments SIG members might have would be helpful in the follow-on.

---

[1] Source: National Archives and Records Administration, RG 59, S/S Files: Lot 70 D 263, SIG/DOC: #49—12/17/68—U.S. Overseas Base Requirements in the 1970s. Secret; Restricted Distribution. Prepared by Hartman on December 24. Attached to a January 2, 1969, covering memorandum from Hartman to the SIG members requesting members to "hold the attached minutes very closely."

[2] This study, a review of U.S. overseas base requirements, has not been found.

He personally found the report a very valuable, interesting document. He had no doubt that it would have a significant influence on policy making. It was encyclopedic in its survey of our overseas installations and facilities. Even if this were all, it would have considerable value to the new Administration.

Mr. Katzenbach noted the separate treatment on overseas intelligence facilities. He would like to discuss this volume with General Wood in a more restricted forum.

B. Ambassador McClintock's Presentation

The Ambassador said he would like to pay tribute to General Wood's role in the project. General Wood had provided intellectual leadership and teamwork. The Study clearly had his personal imprint.

The Study was the first effort in some 10 years to review all of our overseas installations and facilities. It differed in several respects from the earlier Nash report:[3]

First, it examined our overseas base requirements on the basis of alternative strategies and options, whereas the earlier study has simply projected current doctrine;

Secondly, it covered intelligence facilities, as well as other functional and regional requirements;

Thirdly, it considered in some depth a series of special technical problems associated with our installations, including their balance of payments and budgetary cost, the relationship with military and economic assistance programs, the implications of disarmament and arms control, and the impact of the accelerated advance of science and technology.

In preparing the Study, Ambassador McClintock said, the Group had examined United States security interests and commitments, and prospective trends in the world environment during the 1970s. In addition, it had prepared a comprehensive tabulation of all our installations and facilities country-by-country.

The United States now had overseas about the same number of people as it had ten years ago. These numbers, however, included troops deployed in Viet-Nam. Excluding Viet-Nam, personnel had been cut by half. These reductions were not concentrated in any one place but ranged from Korea and North Africa and Western Europe.

The Study fell into two parts—our overseas facilities as related to global requirements and the facilities needed essentially for the support of regional policies.

---

[3] Frank C. Nash, former Assistant Secretary of Defense for International Security Affairs, headed a task force during the Eisenhower administration to study the problem of preserving U.S. overseas bases. The study was completed in December 1957, adopted with some revisions at a meeting of the National Security Council on March 13, 1958, and approved by President Eisenhower 2 days later. See Foreign Relations, 1955–1957, vol. XIX, pp. 334n, 709–710; and ibid., 1958–1960, vol. III, pp. 44–49.

In the first category, the Group had considered the requirements for strategic offensive and defensive weapons systems, ASW, intelligence, early warning systems, and for research and scientific activities such as NASA tracking stations and the atomic energy detecting system.

As regards the treatment of regional policies and strategies, the Ambassador noted the alternative approaches discussed in the summary of the report, namely, the choice, for purposes of analysis, of assuming alternative base structures and examining their strategic implications, or of specifying alternative strategies and developing base systems to support them. The Group had chosen the latter course.

This was a basic point of methodology. It involved eight essential steps.

—First, specify the military deployment requirements to support a particular regional strategy.
—Second, determine which of these deployment patterns would require changes in the base structure.
—Third, lay out the available base structure.
—Fourth, assess the probability that the existing base facilities would not be retainable for political reasons.
—Fifth, evaluate the vulnerability of the facilities to enemy attack.
—Sixth, assess the extent to which available bases would support various regional strategies.
—Seventh, highlight the specific changes from the present base structure required to support various regional strategies.
—Eighth, estimate the cost of these changes.

Ambassador McClintock said the key chapter in the Study was Chapter 5, entitled "Policy-Strategy Alternatives and Base Structures for the 1970s", which reviewed in some detail the base structures required for support of each regional strategy. Each base and base complex had been costed out in terms of its initial investment cost and the annual balance of payments drain or savings.

Generally speaking, these cost estimates were fairly rough. In the case of the Pacific region, however, the various regional strategies had been subjected to a much more detailed costing by a special sub-group (Vol. VII).

The Study Group had been much encouraged because the results of this detailed costing were about the same as the rough estimates made by the Study Group itself.

This was the first time that major strategies for a world region had been subjected to this kind of systematic analysis.

Ambassador McClintock stressed that the Study Group had set forth certain broad alternatives only. They evidently had not been able to consider all the variations. One of the first tasks was to pinpoint which of these strategies should be analyzed in greater depth—a task for the new Administration.

Ambassador McClintock then proceeded to review the results of the regional analyses.

As regards *Europe,* the Study outlined five alternative strategies. The major constraint was that of geography. Unlike Asia, there was no realistic off-shore, over the horizon, deployment possibility. United States forces must be deployed in an area allowing only limited defense in depth—or they must be deployed 3,000 miles away in the United States.

The two key strategies were those of the NATO DPM—alternative 2A—and of forward defense with early selective use of nuclear weapons—alternative 3. The latter would result in an annual $250 million balance of payments saving. The other strategies—alternatives 4 and 5—which assumed a thinning out—or removal—of the United States presence—envisaged a European (conventional and tactical nuclear) build-up to compensate for the withdrawal of the United States forces. They would permit an annual balance of payments saving of up to $1.25 billion (alternative 5).

Turning to the *Pacific,* Ambassador McClintock noted that the problem here had been to formulate alternative policies in a post Viet-Nam environment. One important conclusion was that withdrawal of forces from the mainland of Asia must not be equated with a budgetary saving because of the cost of moving United States forces to alternate locations and the cost of new installations in these locations. In fact, some of the withdrawal strategies were extremely expensive, e.g., redeployment of United States forces to Hawaii and the Pacific Trust Territories.

For each alternative, it was assumed that United States forces available for various contingencies were those of existing DPMs.

Another important point was the trade-off between military assistance and United States forces deployments. For example, alternative 4 assumed forward defense on the mainland by indigenous forces only. This strategy involved an annual balance of payments saving of about $600 million. But, to be fully implemented, it would entail an estimated investment cost of $5–$10 billion over, say, a ten year period to modernize indigenous forces.

A third conclusion was the critical importance of the Pacific Trust Territories. The United States did not now possess clear title to these territories. There was some danger that the Japanese would become so popular with the islanders that a plebiscite would return the islands to the Japanese.

Mr. Katzenbach noted that the problem was one of Congressional attitudes. There was unanimity within the Executive Branch on the need to do more in these Territories. He felt some progress had been made this past year in increasing Congressional awareness of the importance of this problem.

As regards the *Western Hemisphere,* Ambassador McClintock said the Study had considered three, progressively more interventionist, strategies. The conclusion was that we were able to handle virtually any contingency from our facilities in Puerto Rico and the Canal Zone. This pointed up a general lesson, viz. that the United States has a great deal of valuable territory suitable for support of various overseas strategies (e.g., Alaska and the Aleutian Islands, Hawaii and Guam, and our possessions in the Caribbean).

The other point to make was related to the importance of control over the Atlantic Narrows in the event of conventional war. In this connection, our access and overflight rights in Brazil were of considerable value.

Turning to the *Near East,* the main contingency, although it was not used as the basic situation, was that of an Arab-Israeli confrontation leading to United States involvement.

The main conclusion for this region was this: the DPM envisaged a maximal United States deployment of three divisions and 19 tactical air squadrons in support of Iran. The analysis has shown that such a deployment would not be feasible without additional access rights in Liberia, Morocco, Tunisia, Saudi Arabia and Ethiopia.

In the *Indian Ocean* area, all the alternatives pointed to the importance of Diego Garcia as a supply base and staging area. Even the Indian leadership, as it became more alarmed at Soviet activities, seemed to find such a facility less and less objectionable. For example, the possible deployment of Poseidon-armed nuclear subs would be much easier to handle from this island base.

Ambassador McClintock then summarized some general conclusions.

General Wood had objected to firm policy/strategy recommendations but had concurred in setting forth a series of findings. Some of these were:

—First, the value of our security talks with Japan and Australia. In this connection, the question arose whether similar security talks at an appropriate level might perhaps be desirable with the Philippines.

—Second, the desirability that Ambassadors and unified commanders be asked for periodic assessment of the capabilities of their facilities, so that the Executive Branch has a better, more up-to-date understanding of what these facilities are capable of and how they can support functional or regional requirements.

—Third, the importance of economic and military assistance as a way to preserve access and staging rights and build up local forces in lieu of United States deployments.

—Fourth, the fact that research and development can be useful in reducing requirements in host countries. This had to be qualified in the sense that scientists and engineers were not sensitive to the need to avoid proliferation of our overseas bases and facilities.

—Fifth, the fact that withdrawal of United States forces from forward positions may increase, rather than decrease, budget costs because of the expense of relocating troops and facilities.

—Sixth, the point that certain base systems, such as those in the Western Hemisphere, can support multiple strategies and are not tied to any specific regional strategy.

—Seventh, the continued importance of certain naval base facilities in Western Europe and the Mediterranean.

—Eighth, the fact that reversion of Okinawa is inevitable. We would be better off trying to make the best possible deal rather than waiting until reversion is forced upon us. On the other hand, there was no reason to give up more than administrative responsibility [1 *line of source text not declassified*].

—Ninth, the desirability of taking another close look at the possible uses of Sattahip and Singapore in support of United States deployments, the latter through commercial arrangements using the facilities left behind by the British.

—Tenth, the fact that staging and overflight rights in Africa and Latin America cannot be secured except on an ad hoc basis. We would have to be reconciled to this situation over the foreseeable future.

In conclusion, Ambassador McClintock said he would like to emphasize that preparation of this Study was a massive worldwide effort. The Group had enjoyed excellent cooperation from the Unified Commands, notably General Lemnitzer and CINCPAC, as well as the various Ambassadors.

C. Discussion

Mr. Barr[4] wondered about the costs of strategies that envisaged withdrawal of our forces from forward positions. He felt that a distinction should be made between budgetary and foreign exchange costs. Ambassador McClintock agreed that redeployment of our forces to the dollar area, while costly in budgetary terms, would yield sizable foreign exchange savings. Budgetary costs and IBOP savings for each alternative are contained in the Study.

Mr. Eugene Rostow said that he found our staging rights in the Indian Ocean/Persian Gulf area quite unsatisfactory. As of now, our forces would be severely handicapped if they had to enter the Gulf. A United States presence in this area was important in view of the rivalry between the Shah and the Arabs and the importance of the oil supplies.

Mr. Bohlen asked about the status of Diego Garcia. Mr. Nitze said that he had authorized a construction survey and that construction funds had been included in the FY 70 Defense budget. The cost of the planned installation was estimated at $26 million. The diplomatic side of this problem had been solved.

[4] Joseph W. Barr, Under Secretary of the Treasury.

General McDonald said he wanted to elaborate on the Study's cost estimates. These all assumed constant force levels. The costs and savings shown resulted from different deployment patterns exclusively. In this respect, the Study differed from others which usually included savings resulting from changes in force structure.

Mr. Poats suggested that the funding of base rentals be examined on a world-wide basis. In the case of Spanish facilities, this was a problem in FY 70. If it was decided to put the Spanish MAP into the Defense budget, the question arose whether this principle should not also be followed for other military assistance programs, which in effect represent a rental payment.

D. *Disposition of the Study*

The SIG then discussed next steps for review and disposition of the Study.

Mr. Katzenbach observed that, in his view, this was a matter for the next Administration. The SIG should, however, make interim arrangements to permit some follow-on work to go forward until the new Administration could decide on its own arrangements.

In addition, he felt it was very important not to foreclose any of the new Administration's options by premature disclosures. The Study contained extremely sensitive information. He saw some danger that bits and pieces would leak out, conveying a totally erroneous impression.

Accordingly, he would like to propose:

—First, recipients personally take responsibility to restrict distribution of the document in their own departments. As regards the State Department, those with a need to know, essentially the Assistant Secretaries, had copies. No further distribution was contemplated.

—Second, there would be no distribution beyond that already made between now and January 20. In particular, he did not believe there should be an overseas distribution until the new Administration has an opportunity to review the document and the arrangements.

—Third, as and when field comment is required, he questioned whether the whole report should be distributed. It might be preferable to limit distribution to pertinent portions of the report, i.e. a "sanitized" version containing all those sections pertinent to the addressee.

General Wheeler said he would like the JCS to study the various strategies contained in the paper. He would like the Chief to begin thinking about alternative regional strategies in these terms. He felt the Study contained important material for the next Administration's policy making.

Mr. Katzenbach said he had no particular difficulty with an internal JCS distribution on a need-to-know basis. In some respect, the JCS staff was perhaps more familiar with handling this kind of document. This also applied to the intelligence community.

Mr. Barr said he would like Treasury to review the foreign exchange cost estimates. What was important about these estimates was not only the overall balance of payments cost of the various strategies, but also where the balance of payments drain was occurring—whether it involved, e.g., Japan, Germany or the franc area.

Mr. Barr agreed that it was unlikely Treasury would be able to do much work on this problem before January 20 and that only part of the information was actually needed for review purposes.

Mr. Katzenbach emphasized that he did not advocate a rewriting of the Study. The Study was there to use. Rather, he was proposing that pertinent portions be excerpted from the complete report for further follow-on work on a need-to-know basis.

The SIG then discussed the Study Group's proposal to cost and additional strategies in greater detail—similar to the costing in Volume VII on West Pac. Mr. Katzenbach observed that the Study Group would require policy guidance on which of the various alternatives were worthy of further analysis. This guidance would have to come from the new Administration.

Another problem, Mr. Katzenbach said, was that the SIG did not know how the new Administration wanted to organize the national security process and, therefore, how to dispose of a study of this kind. (A similar problem existed with respect to a number of other SIG projects.) He would like to entrust to the Political-Military Group responsibility for further work, including:

1. Coordination of the interdepartmental review; and,
2. The preparation of appropriate recommendations.

He thought it better that the SIG assign responsibilities which the new Administration then could approve or modify as it saw fit. He did not feel that these arrangements would preempt the new Administration's options. The Political-Military Group would not be able to do more than begin the review of this massive study between now and January 20.

Mr. Katzenbach said the proposal was to include intelligence facilities under these arrangements, with the understanding that the Political-Military Group would redelegate the intelligence part to a more restricted sub-group.

The intelligence facilities were of course a separate system. But, as the report recognized, there was a relationship between these facilities and other installations. There was need for a central point where conclusions about these various systems could be put together.

Admiral Taylor agreed that further work was needed on the intelligence parts of the Study. He found composition of the Political-Military Group somewhat amorphous. The membership appeared to vary from problem to problem. He would designate Major Gen. John M. Reynolds as the Agency's representative for this purpose. Also, the intelligence chapter should be taken up in a special sub-group of the PMG.

As regards the IRGs, Mr. Katzenbach suggested that the PMG try to identify specific issues on which it would like to have the IRGs' views and recommendations. (The IRGs would, of course, be free to comment on other pertinent aspects of the Study.)

The suggestion was made that the PMG might want to use a few of the more experienced cost analysts of the Study Group for its follow-on work.

Before adjourning, the SIG briefly took up three additional matters:

—Mr. Katzenbach said he would like to include in the SIG directive[5] some substantive guidance on the focus of the follow-on work in the Political-Military Group;

—Mr. Katzenbach proposed a revision in the stand-by press guidance;

—The Group agreed that there was no need for Congressional briefings at this time inasmuch as the Study was a technical report rather than a decision document.

Arthur A. Hartman
Staff Director

---

[5] See Document 226.

226.   Directive Issued by the Senior Interdepartmental Group[1]

Washington, undated.

SIG DIRECTIVE

At its 48th meeting on December 19, 1968, the Senior Interdepartmental Group received a report on the results of the overseas base study undertaken by the joint State/Defense Study Group.[2]

The SIG agreed that the Political-Military Group should be charged with responsibility for:

a) coordination of the interdepartmental review of the Study;
b) the preparation of appropriate recommendations to the SIG.

To this end, the five IRGs are requested to review appropriate sections of the Study and submit their conclusions and recommendations to the Political-Military Group. Taking these views and recommendations into account, the Political-Military Group is requested to submit its recommendations on further action to the SIG by March 1, 1969.

These should, to the extent feasible, include recommendations regarding (1) working assumptions on the strategies which should guide future base planning; (2) bases in which significant changes could be made in the near future (two years); (3) bases in which significant changes could be foreseen in the 1970s; (4) bases in which no significant changes can be foreseen; and (5) any steps that should be taken to improve the examination of future base problems in the United States Government.

A special sub-group with appropriate membership shall be established to review the intelligence chapter and submit appropriate recommendations.

Additionally, it is understood that the PMG may ask the State/Defense Study Group to reconstitute the special sub-group that prepared Annex J to cost out additional alternative base structures for strategies in various regions.

To ensure a systematic unified review of the Study's findings, the SIG noted the desirability that the Political-Military Group be free to

---

[1] Source: National Archives and Records Administration, RG 59, S/S Files: Lot 70 D 263, SIG/DOC: #49—12/17/68—U.S. Overseas Base Requirements in the 1970s. Confidential; Restricted Distribution. Attached to a January 2, 1969, covering memorandum from Hartman to the SIG members indicating that Chairman Katzenbach had approved the directive.

[2] See Document 225 and footnote 2 thereto.

pose specific issues for the IRGs to consider. Review of the Study by the IRGs would not, however, be restricted to these specific issues; rather the IRGs should be free to comment on any other points pertinent to their jurisdiction. The Political-Military Group's final report should discuss remaining differences on conclusions and recommendations between the IRGs and the Political-Military Group.

The SIG also agreed that the Study not be distributed further at this time pending:

a) a review of the arrangements for disposition of the Study by the new Administration; and,
b) some progress by the Political-Military Group in defining facts and issues requiring review by the IRGs, the constituent agencies, and the field.

In this connection, SIG members are requested to take responsibility for the handling of this sensitive document within their respective agencies. No field distribution is contemplated pending additional guidance from the new Administration. The SIG Staff Director should be consulted on such limited additional distributions as may be necessary in the several agencies to commence review of the report.

The SIG also agreed that, as a general principle, access to the document in the agencies should be restricted to a need-to-know basis. Furthermore, access by staffs should be limited to those portions of the Study actually required for review purposes.

The SIG also considered the question of Congressional briefings and consultations. It noted that the existence of the Study had received considerable attention in the press, and that Congressional inquiries might be expected from time to time. The SIG agreed that it would be premature to brief members of the Congress on the contents of the report inasmuch as:

a) evaluation of the Study is still under way; and,
b) the Study is a technical document, setting forth basic data for policy options, rather than a document advocating specific lines of action.

Approved guidance for handling press inquiries is attached.

Attachment

PRESS GUIDANCE

In the event recipients are queried by the press or others about the base study, the following guidance is provided. (Recipients may also draw upon earlier guidance provided in State 211289 (African posts only), 211290, and 261970.)[3]

The long-range study on the overseas bases has been completed. It is one of a number of classified studies undertaken by the joint State/Defense Study Group. The results have been submitted to the SIG on 19 December and contain no specific recommendations, but are simply designed to aid those who will face future policy decisions. It would not be appropriate to discuss the content of the report or to release it.

---

[3] Circular telegram 211289, July 30, was sent to ten African posts; circular telegram 211290, July 30, was sent to all posts except those in Africa; and circular telegram 261970, October 25, was sent to ten African posts and all non-African posts. All three telegrams reproduced newspaper articles about the Special State–Defense Study Group Base Study. (National Archives and Records Administration, RG 59, Central Files 1967–69, DEF 15 US)

---

227.   Memorandum From the Chairman of the Joint Chiefs of Staff (Wheeler) to the President's Special Assistant (Rostow)[1]

CM–3943–68   Washington, December 26, 1968.

SUBJECT

FY '70 Budget Discussion

1. This memorandum responds to our telecon on the evening of 24 December.[2]

2. The JCS decided that, in view of the complexity of the FY '70 budget problem and the numerous hard decisions which had to be made, it would be profitable to focus our discussion with the President[3] on the impact of FY '70 budget decisions on our present and future military capabilities. As you will recognize, this is a departure from the past practice of having each Chief in effect reclama the decisions made in certain specific programs.

3. Accordingly, I will lead off for the JCS by discussing the Soviet threat, our capabilities in the strategic area relative to the Soviets, the capabilities of our general purpose forces, and the trends seen by us.

---

[1] Source: Johnson Library, National Security File, Agency File, JCS, Filed by the LBJ Library, Box 29. Secret. A copy was sent to Secretary Clifford.

[2] No record of this telephone conversation has been found.

[3] See footnote 3, Document 224.

Thereafter, the other Chiefs in turn will illustrate our concerns by addressing one or two specific items in their particular areas of professional interest. We propose the following sequence and subjects:

a. Gen Palmer—Low manning levels in Europe and Korea, and Strategic Army Force structure and manning level problems;
b. Adm Moorer—Shortages of personnel, and budget constraints related to capability and staying power of naval forces;
c. Gen McConnell—Reductions in strategic bomber and air defense forces;
d. Gen Chapman—Degradation of amphibious assault capability.

4. We will, of course, be prepared to discuss other subjects as desired by the President; for example, questions raised by him at luncheon on Tuesday[4] regarding Sentinel, ammunition procurement, the F-14, etc.

Earle G. Wheeler

---

[4] December 31; no record of this luncheon meeting has been found.

Index

References are to document numbers

ABM (anti-ballistic missiles). *See under*
  Missiles.
Advanced Manned Strategic Aircraft
  (AMSA), 1, 10, 31, 61, 103, 139, 150,
  158, 195, 200, 210
Africa, 12, 43, 80, 118, 188, 225
African Development Bank, 79
Agency for International Development
  (AID), 19
Air National Guard, 202
Airborne Warning and Control System
  (AWACS), 103, 139, 195, 200, 210,
  221
Aircraft (*see also* Advanced Manned
  Strategic Aircraft):
  A-6A, 195
  A-*11*, 15
  Anti-bomber defense program, 61
  B-*52*:
    Age and diminishing capability, 1,
    10, 31
    Airborne alert, 108
    Budget for Defense Department,
    195, 196, 200
    JCS view of worldwide U.S. mili-
    tary posture, 202
    McNamara's recommendations for
    strategic forces for FY *1967-71*,
    103
    McNamara's recommendations for
    strategic forces for FY *1968-72*,
    139
    Nuclear weapons delivery, 28
  B-*58*, 10, 31, 103
  B-*70*, 15
  Budget for Defense Department, 65,
  195, 196, 200
  C-2A, 195
  C-*47/54/117*s, 195
  C-*118*, 195
  C-*130*, 195
  Clifford's recommendations for strate-
  gic forces for FY *1970-74*, 210
  CX-(HLS), 65
  F-4, 195
  F-*12*, 139, 195, 200
  F-*106*, 200
  F-*106*X, 200
  F-*111*, 139
  F-*111*A, 139
  F-*111* (TFX), 65, 67

Aircraft —*Continued*
  FB-*111*A, 103
  FB-*111*M-3, 103
  FB-*111*/SRAM, 103
  Force structure changes, Defense
    Department summary of, 67
  Hound-Dog A, 139
  JCS and McNamara/Vance, disagree-
    ment between, 158
  JSOP-*68-75*, 119
  JSOP-*69*, 21
  JSOP-*70-77*, 188
  KC-*130*, 195
  Manned Orbital Laboratory, 65
  McNamara's recommendations for
    strategic forces for FY *1967-71*,
    103
  McNamara's recommendations for
    strategic forces for FY *1968-72*,
    139
  National Guard, release of nuclear
    weapons to, 38
  NIE *11-3-65*, 106
  NIE *11-3-68*, 221
  NIE *11-8-64*, 55
  NIE *11-8-65*, 97
  NIE *11-8-68*, 217
  NIE *11-14-65*, 98
  Overseas bases, survey of, 26
  Oxcart, 11, 13, 15
  RF-4B, 195
  RF-4J, 195
  U-2, 32
Air Force, U.S., 38, 53, 55, 59, 103, 191,
  193, 195, 202, 215
Airlift capabilities, 21, 67, 120, 148, 188,
  194, 195
Alaska, 103
Algeria, 43, 188
Alternate Joint Communications Center
  (AJCC), 77
Alternate National Military Command
  Center (ANMCC), 77, 86, 92
Amory, Robert, 171
Anthony, Robert N., 110
Anti-ballistic missile (ABM). *See under*
  Missiles.
Anti-Submarine Warfare Panel (ASW),
  99, 101, 103, 124, 125, 194
Arab-Israeli dispute, 188
Argentina, 188

787

McNamara, Robert S.—*Continued*
Nuclear weapons/issues—*Continued*
Stockpile of nuclear weapons, U.S.
production and, 35, 46, 133, 136
Oxcart, 15
Resignation, 196
Rostow's reflections on U.S. national
security policy, 80
Satellite reconnaissance and photogra-
phy, 5, 45, 53
Shipbuilding, 150
Strategic retaliatory forces, 31, 80
Strategy Discussion Group, 115
Strategic forces for FY *1967-71*, pro-
posed, 103, 105
Strategic forces for FY *1968-72*, recom-
mended, 139, 148
Strategic forces for FY *1969-73*, recom-
mended, 194
Submarines, 150
303 Committee, 115
Wheeler, communications with, 61, 112
McNaughton, John T., 60, 80, 113, 115,
123, 148, 163, 171
McPherson, Harry, 134
Mediterranean area, 188
Mexico, 23
Meyer, Cord, 134, 171, 180, 186, 209
Meyer, Gen. John C., 125
Meyers, Howard, 26
Middle East, 12, 43, 80, 188, 202, 225
Minuteman. *See under* Missiles.
Missiles (*see also under* China, People's
Republic of *and* Soviet Union),
102
ABM (*see also* Nike-X *below*):
Budget for Defense Department for
FY *1969*, 195
Canada-U.S. relations and, 190
CIA assessment of recent develop-
ments in the Moscow system,
107, 130, 179, 206
Clifford's recommendations for
strategic forces for FY *1970-74*,
210
Hornig's assessments/recommen-
dations, 156
JCS and McNamara/Vance, dis-
agreement between, 158
Johnson and science advisers,
meeting between, 166
Johnson/JCS/McNamara meeting,
150

Missiles—*Continued*
ABM—*Continued*
Johnson-McNamara communica-
tions, 167
Johnson-Rostow communications,
185
Keeny's assessments/recommenda-
tions, 102, 141, 165
McNamara's assessments/recom-
mendations, 103, 148, 160, 192
NIE *11-3-66*, 146
NIE *11-3-68*, 221
Owen's assessments/recommenda-
tions, 140
Rostow's assessments/recommen-
dations, 157
Tallinn system, debate on, 161
U.K.-U.S. relations and, 95
U.S. guidance, 163
Vance's assessments/recommenda-
tions, 155
Advanced Manned Strategic Aircraft
proposal by LeMay, 1
Air Force dissents to NIE, 59
Anti-satellite systems, 53
Army-BTL ballistic missile defense
system, proposed U.S. deploy-
ment, 101
Assured destruction, 128
Atlas, 31, 61, 71
Ballistic missile ships, 139, 195
Budget for Defense Department, 65,
66, 71, 195, 200
Clifford's recommendations for strate-
gic forces for FY *1970-74*, 210
Computers, 160
Damage limitation, 128
Force structure planning/changes,
Defense Department and, 63, 67
Future strategic ballistic force capabil-
ities, programmed, 117
Galosh, 160
JCS and McNamara/Vance, disagree-
ment between, 158
JSOP-*68-75*, 118
JSOP-*69*, 12, 21
JSOP-*70*, 43
Johnson-McCone meeting, 2
Johnson-McNamara communications,
200
McNamara's recommendations for
strategic forces for FY *1967-71*,
103, 105

ISBN 0-16-051033-3

90000

9 780160 510335